The Representational and the Presentational

An Essay on Cognition and the Study of Mind

Benny Shanon

HARVESTER
WHEATSHEAF

New York   London   Toronto   Sydney   Tokyo   Singapore

First published 1993 by
Harvester Wheatsheaf
Campus 400, Maylands Avenue
Hemel Hempstead
Hertfordshire, HP2 7EZ
A division of
Simon & Schuster International Group

Typeset in 10/12pt Ehrhardt
by Hands Fotoset, Leicester

Printed and bound in Great Britain by
Hartnolls, Bodmin, Cornwall

British Library Cataloguing in Publication Data

A catalogue record for this book is available from the British Library.

ISBN 0-7450-1094-6 (hbk)
ISBN 0-7450-1095-4 (pbk)

1 2 3 4 5

Contents

Prologue

It is only shallow people who do not judge by appearance. The mystery of the world is in the visible, not the invisible.

Oscar Wilde

Let me start with a question drawn from a domain quite different from the one I shall study in this book – the domain of figurative art. How should one go about drawing a human figure? Consider two answers actually given to this question in the artistic tradition of the West. The first is taken from the first modern theoretical essay on the art of painting, Leon Battista Alberti's *Della Pittura* (1435/1966):

> He [the painter] has good memory. Before dressing a man we first draw him nude, then we enfold him in draperies. So in painting the nude we place first his bones and muscles which we then cover with flesh so that it is not difficult to understand where each muscle is beneath. (p. 73)

A different answer is given by Federico Zuccaro (1607/1961), the chief spokesman of seventeenth-century mannerism:

> But I do say – and I know I speak the truth – that the art of painting does not derive its principles from the mathematical sciences, indeed it need not even refer to them. . . . The painter . . . becomes a skillful man through mere natural judgement. With proper care and observation . . . without any aid from or need for mathematics . . . the [artist's] intellect must be not only clear but also free, and his spirit unfettered, and not thus restrained in mechanical servitude to such rules. . . . We, professors of Design, have no need of other rules than those which Nature herself gives for imitating her. (p. 133)

The two answers present two fundamental ways to achieve the task defined by my opening question. The way advocated by mathematically minded Alberti regards the process of painting as one of model construction. The painter adopting this method would start with the skeleton, continue with the muscles, and eventually stretch the skin and cover it with garments. This step-by-step construction grounds the final, overt product in hidden, underlying structures; it is based on factual knowledge and is guided by the canons of reason. By contrast, Zuccaro directs the painter to focus his gaze on what there is on the surface and can be seen, on that which will eventually appear on the canvas – the skin and the garments. For this, the painter should put his faith in his eye and let it guide his hand. If the gaze is careful, the faith solid and the hand secure, he is certain to end up with the desired depiction.

Here, then, are two ways: one based on the mediation of structured knowledge, the other assuming the unmediated attuning of the observer to the objects of his or her inspection. Which is the better way? It seems to me that this is not the right question. Some painters would opt for the first way, others for the second, and surely one could not characterize the painters of either persuasion as being in any sense better or more accomplished than those of the other. But in fact, the two ways are not merely two ways of painting. They epitomize two ways of knowing, two ways by which the human mind may achieve understanding of the world.

Artists differ in their choice of the method of painting. Over the centuries, there have been recurrent debates between the followers of the two persuasions, and both ways have gained honourable places in the annals of artistic creation. The cognitive sciences have not been as tolerant. The contemporary study of both the human mind and the so-called artificial intelligence of computers is heavily biased towards one perspective, that based on the mediation of represented knowledge. Specifically, the conceptual dogma that in the past two decades has dominated cognitive science – cognitive psychology with its affiliated disciplines of cognitive social psychology, neuropsychology and anthropology as well as the discipline of artificial intelligence – is one defined by the following three tenets:

(*) 1. People behave by virtue of their possessing knowledge.
     2. Knowledge is constituted by mental *representations*.
     3. Cognitive activity consists in the manipulation of these representations, i.e., the application of *computational* operations to them.

The theoretical framework of which (*) is the basis will be referred to here as the *representational-computational view of mind*, henceforth *RCVM* or *representationalism*. This framework is presented most clearly in Fodor (1968a, 1975), Newell (1980) and Pylyshyn (1984); paradigmatic works embracing it include Newell and Simon (1972), Schank (1972), Anderson and Bower (1973), Kintsch (1974) and Norman and Rumelhart (1975).

This book attempts to mark the limitations of RCVM and to propose a more balanced psychological picture. The discussion will try to show that the representational-computational framework is inadequate in several fundamental respects and that it cannot offer the basis for a general theory of human behaviour. While the development of a full-fledged alternative psychological theory is beyond the scope of this book, general characteristics of non-representational, non-computational models of mind will be suggested. With these, the status and role of mental representations will be reappraised, new questions for psychological investigation will be formulated, and outlines for further research will be drawn.

These, in turn, will lead to a new conceptualization of psychological theory and a redefinition of psychological explanation.

Until several years ago the dominance of RCVM was questioned only by dissenting minority voices. Perhaps the only such voice in North America was that of James Gibson's (1966a, 1979) ecological psychology, a framework largely ignored by the professional establishment. In Europe, the situation was different. Indeed, alternative, non-representational views of mind were developed in the continent even before the representational-computational paradigm of contemporary cognitive science was conceived. Such views were originated by Bergson (1929), were extensively developed by Heidegger (1962) and Merleau-Ponty (1962) and are at the heart of the Piagetian enterprise (Piaget, 1983). Alternative frameworks have also been entertained in the Soviet Union by Vygotsky (1986) and his followers in the school of activity theory, as well as in Latin America in the theory of autopoiesis of Maturana and his students (Maturana, 1978; Maturana and Varela, 1980; see also Winograd and Flores, 1986). With few exceptions, mainline academic psychology has paid no attention to these works. Recently, however, a major shift has taken place. With the new school of connectionism (Hinton and Anderson, 1981b; McClelland and Rumelhart, 1986a; Rumelhart and McClelland, 1986a) there is a veritable change in the *Zeitgeist*, and for the first time a non-representational perspective is entertained at the core of cognitive research, both psychological and computational.

While sympathetic to these recent developments, my critique is independent of them, in terms of both its course of development and the conceptual framework in which it is embedded. The critique summarizes an investigation that began when the reign of the representational-computational paradigm was virtually unchallenged (cf. Shanon, 1982a, 1983a, 1984a). Substantively, the argumentation on which it is based is different from that employed in connectionism. It is founded on a comprehensive consideration of psychological phenomenology rather than on computational, mathematical and biological considerations. Given this twofold independence, and since RCVM is still the most important general conceptual framework in psychology, the discussion takes dogma (*) to define cognitive orthodoxy. The conceptual framework thus defined is so fundamental that it calls for serious consideration even if the dogma has already lost its absolute hegemony. Furthermore, just as the lines of argumentation marshalled against the representational-computational view of mind may differ, so the alternatives to this view may vary. Towards the end of the book the differences between the present perspective and other non-representational frameworks will be spelled out and the possible relations between them will be examined.

The ideas to be presented here evolved in the course of seminars on conceptual issues in cognition that I have conducted at the Hebrew University since 1979. I cannot recall the first time when alternative views of cognition entered my mind (in retrospect, first signs are to be found in my doctoral dissertation – Shanon, 1974 – most of which seems, now, so distant). The first focal stimulants, however, were the philosophical works of Noam Chomsky and Jerry Fodor. The first of my seminars was devoted to the Chomsky–Piaget debate (Piatelli-Palmerini, 1980) and to *The Language of Thought* (Fodor, 1975). New works by Fodor came to the fore at an amazing speed, and they have been topics of study and discussion in the seminars practically every year. While much of the following discussion is directed against the conceptual framework propounded by Fodor, it is clear to me that this is precisely because of the great influence Fodor's writings have had on the evolution of my own thinking. It is to a great extent due to (rather than despite) my disagreement with the Fodorian theses (coupled with a great admiration for the rationalistic coherence and consistency of their presentation) that this book developed. After all, had the Fodorian position in cognition not existed, it would have had to be invented (see Dennett, 1979a). My actual work on this critique started in 1980, when a first oral presentation of it was given (at Cerisy-La Salle, France; subsequently published as Shanon, 1983a). As my reflections evolved, a number of articles were written and submitted for publication. Many of them were rejected and never published (in particular, Shanon, 1982a); others appeared only a long time after their inception (my study of Plato's *Meno* – Shanon, 1984a – is based on my first undergraduate course at the Hebrew University, conducted in 1976). As I worked, the above-mentioned changes in the cognitive *Zeitgeist* started. The most prominent was the emergence of connectionism, to which I was first exposed in the annual meeting of the Cognitive Science Society at the University of Rochester in 1981. Later developments included Johnson-Laird's *Mental Models* (1983) as well as the constant bombardments originating from Jerry Fodor's desk. For personal and professional reasons, the new developments in both the orthodoxy and the heterodoxy halted my writing. They forced me to reappraise my position and to define in which ways it differed from the new ideas in the field. With time, I came to appreciate the force of the emerging *Zeitgeist* and the fact that many flowers may bloom at the same time. In many respects this work is appearing much too late – it is no longer a lone, radical cry. At the same time, repeated inspection has taught me to clarify the respects in which this work is different from other non-representational frameworks. Inasmuch as they pertain to cognitive content, these differences are noted in the last part of this book. The greatest difference is, however, not necessarily in the final station, but in the path. The path, after all, is the meaning, and the ideas presented in this book are the presentation of one particular path.

While the atmosphere at the Hebrew University has been over these years much more tranquil than the hectic scene across the Atlantic (a state of affairs which was extremely conducive to the development of independent, out-of-the-line thinking), I have not worked in complete isolation. Most significantly, let me mention students, notably those who participated in the seminars mentioned above. Of these, those who stand out in my memory are (in largely chronological order) Kariel Pardo, Helen Baron, Meir Grad, Naomi Goldblum, Gabi Trainin, Annie Cerasi, Amnon Levav, Dani Lassri. As the Talmud says: 'From all my teachers have I learnt, and more so from my friends, and even more so from my students' (*Tractate Ta'anit*, p. 7a). While many of these students are now friends, there is one who has always been precisely that, a friend: the conversations with Georges Amar were ever refreshing and illuminating. The one person with whom I constantly discussed the ideas presented here, and who always offered wise comments and warm encouragement, is Henri Atlan – to him I am deeply grateful.

Throughout the extended period in which I was working on this project I was helped by many diligent student-assistants – Shlomo Beinhart, Ofer Bergman, Annie Cerasi, Zvi Cohen, Gil Diesendruck, Eda Flaxer, Naomi Goldblum, Dani Kaplan, Amnon Levav, Dan Mingelgrin, Jonathan Shimoni, Gabi Trainin and Daniel Weiser. My deep thanks to them all as well as to Ran Lahav and Anat Ninio, who (in addition to Jonathan Shimoni) have read the manuscript and commented on it. And then there are those of whom I can literally say that without their help this entire enterprise might never have reached completion. Annie Cerasi and Amnon Levav not only read the text over and over again and came back with invaluable comments and suggestions, they also made sure that I myself re-read the chapters and rewrote them lest there still remain a sentence that could be rephrased, an argument that could be better presented. For their vigilance, continuous encouragement and moral support at times of ups and of downs, this book is presented to the two A's as a token of gratitude and friendship.

This book was written at the Department of Psychology of the Hebrew University. Conditions of work in Israel are not easy, and I appreciate the constant and friendly support of the entire staff of the Department, and in particular Miriam Bajayo, who, as all who have worked with her know, is just incomparable. Some chapters were edited during a stay at the Rockefeller Study and Research Center in Bellagio, Italy. The generosity of the Rockefeller Foundation and the amiability of the staff of the Villa Serbelloni are warmly acknowledged. Lastly, thanks are extended to Farrell Burnett, Jill Birch and the staff of Harvester Wheatsheaf for their help in turning a manuscript into a book.

This work is consecrated to the memory of my grandfather, Akiva Schneior, who first pointed out to me the intricacies of natural language and taught me to appreciate what a big mystery it all is.

Preliminaries

I *Why representations?*

For only where there seems to be a duality, there one sees another, one feels another's perfume, one tastes another, one speaks to another, one listens to another, one touches another and one knows another.

The Upanishads

Before we engage in the critique of RCVM let us examine why representations are postulated in the first place. This examination will be helpful by way not only of obtaining a more balanced appraisal of their role and status in cognitive theory, but also of clarifying the meaning of this fundamental psychological concept.

The following discussion is guided by the appraisal that the various reasons for the postulation of representations are associated with different senses of that key term 'representation'. Furthermore, it seems that the different reasons and senses do not always converge. In particular, reasons that support the postulation of representations in one sense may not support such a postulation in another. Sorting the various rationales for the postulation of representations and the various senses associated with them will be helpful, then, not only in clarifying the case for the postulation of representations, but also in laying the first ground for the case against it.

Representations: senses and rationales

Concrete, external representations

In the most general, unqualified manner, a representation is something that stands for something else (see, for instance, Bobrow, 1975; Palmer, 1978; Rumelhart and Norman, 1988). In this minimal sense, the term's field of denotation need not be confined to the internal, mental domain, and it can include entities in the external, physical world. Examples of *concrete, external* representations abound – photographs, street signs, knots in handkerchiefs and many, many more (for further discussion on this subject, see Shanon, 1990a).

The first, general sense of 'representation' is not associated here with any special rationale, and this for two reasons. First, being so basic, it is practically definitional, hence there is not much that can be said about it. Second, it does not specifically pertain to the internal, psychological domain. It is only in this domain that representations *qua* entities other than those observed in the real world are postulated, and it is only with such a postulation that special rationales have to be invoked. Admittedly, in a psychological context like the present one, one might dismiss the concrete, external sense of 'representation' as irrelevant. Indeed, throughout most of our discussion no reference whatsoever will be made to representations in this first sense. Towards the end of the book, however, we shall return to this sense and, somewhat unexpectedly, find that it is of psychological relevance none the less.

Representations as phenomenological entities: The experiential rationale

Moving from the external world to the internal one, I turn to the examination of rationales for the postulation of *mental* representations. The simplest such rationale is the *experiential* one. The existence of mental representations is postulated because such entities are part and parcel of the phenomenology of human experience. After all, we have all observed the appearance in our head of verbal-like phrases, of visual-like images, and perhaps of entities associated with other modalities as well. These entities are not in the physical world, yet direct acquaintance attests to their existence. It is only natural to refer to such entities as mental representations. The experientially based postulation of representations, note, is pre-theoretical and it neither specifies any particular characteristics of representations nor imposes any constraints on them.

Representations as the locus of mental activity: The naive rationale

Also pre-theoretical is the *naive* rationale. I refer to it thus both because it pertains to naive reasoning about psychology and because it is analogous to rationales characterized as naive in the context concerning the reality of the physical world – naive realism. The rationale is founded on common observations like the following: I meet a person I have not seen for some time, I recognize him and even remember his name; I am presented with a problem and after a while I come up with a solution to it; I am troubled by a conflict and eventually I make a decision and resolve it. While in all these cases I may not be aware of the processes involved (Nisbett and Wilson, 1977), I conclude that something has happened in my head. In other words, mental activity has taken place. Mental representations are postulated by way of accounting for such activity. The sense attributed to mental representations by the naive rationale, then, is that of locus of mental activity. No further specifications of the characteristics of mental representations are made.

The substrate of meaning: The epistemic rationale

The next, *epistemic* rationale is theoretical, and recurs in various versions in the philosophical literature. It is grounded in the observation that human behaviour exhibits meaningfulness, attests to knowledge of the world, and is orderly and rule-like. For manifestations of behaviour – such as the words and sentences of natural language – to be meaningful, they have to be the expressions of a substrate that carries meaning (for classic presentations of this position, see Wittgenstein, 1922; Tarski, 1944). Thus, for the word 'table' to mean what it usually means, it has to express a concept specifying this meaning, and for the utterance 'The table is in the room' to be meaningful, it has to express an idea that is being entertained by the person who utters it. Similarly, if human behaviour manifests a repertory of knowledge, this knowledge has to be stored, or represented, in the mind. As for representations of rules, the argument for their postulation runs through the epistemological writings of Chomsky (1972, 1975b, 1980). Human language, Chomsky points out, is defined by a system of rules; the verbal behaviour of speakers, in turn, is in accordance with these rules; speakers' behaviour, in other words, attests to the fact that although they cannot state them explicitly, they know the rules of language; the rules, therefore, have to be represented in people's minds.

Be they of content or of rules, representations in the epistemic sense are postulated as an *underlying* substrate for knowledge that is manifested by people's behaviour. It is by virtue of this substrate that expressions of behaviour are said to gain their meaningfulness and rule-like characteristics.

It should be pointed out that while similar, the naive and the epistemic rationales are distinct. The epistemic rationale is theoretical: it is grounded in a specific philosophical position, namely, that for expressions of behaviour – notably, linguistic expressions – to be meaningful and rule-like there must exist covert structures that make this possible. Representations are postulated in order to satisfy this theoretical requirement. By contrast, the naive rationale is pre-theoretical. It only reflects the appraisal that 'something must be happening in the head'.

Although the sense associated with the epistemic rationale (like that associated with the naive rationale) does not attribute any particular properties to representations, it is none the less the more constrained. As pointed out by Fodor (1975), mental representations must have an expressive power at least as strong as that of the languages – usually, natural language – to which they bestow meaning. Further, because they are postulated so as to satisfy a correspondence with other expressions – paradigmatically, the expressions of natural language – mental representations may be attributed with the properties of those expressions. Thus, the epistemic characterization of mental representations can be said to be *parasitic*: it is made not on the basis of a direct investigation of mental activity itself, but rather by means of an inference from the analytic (as contrasted with the empirical, psychological) study of another, corresponding theoretical domain – in this case, language.

Representations as mediating functions:
The functionalist rationale

The *functionalist* rationale lies, in a fashion, half-way between the philosophical and the psychological. It is based on the consideration of the relationship between the behaving organism and its environment. Since it is not possible to characterize the behaviour of the organism solely in terms of the constituents of the environment, mediating functions have – according to this rationale – to be invoked. The structures in which these are instantiated are the postulated internal representations. Schematically, this line of argumentation may be characterized as follows: ideally, one would have liked (for reasons of parsimony) to define behaviour as in the simple functional relationship presented in (1); in this formula B stands for behaviour and E for factors pertaining to the enviroment:

$$1. \quad B = f(E)$$

Given that a characterization of behaviour in the manner of (1) is not possible, the more complex functional relationship presented in (2) is introduced; in it, R stands for representation:

$$2. \quad B = f(E, R)$$

The functionalist rationale comes in two forms depending on the reading given to the term 'environment'. According to the first, the environment is the totality of external stimuli to which the organism is exposed. The rationales for the postulation of internal representations that correspond to this reading are the arguments marshalled against behaviourism. The arguments are numerous and varied and this is not the place for a comprehensive review of them. (The classical critique of behaviourism is presented in Chomsky 1959 – one of the most important heralds of the cognitive revolution.) Basically, it is noted that, on different occasions, the same stimulus may trigger different responses or, at times, no response at all; conversely, the same response may be produced following different stimuli; further, responses that are functionally equivalent may be articulated in different physical instantiations (e.g., different modalities; cf. Pylyshyn, 1980). Given these patterns, representations are postulated to specify the mediation between the manifest input to the organism and the output of its behaviour.

By the second reading, the environment is the biological substrate in which behaviour is couched. The corresponding arguments for the postulation of mental representations are those marshalled against the reduction of psychology to biology. Again, this is not the place for a comprehensive review; suffice it to say that it is based on the appraisal that an explanation of psychological phenomenology cannot be achieved by means of a physiological account. The impossibility of reduction may be a matter of principle or only a contingent limitation reflecting the present state of scientific knowledge. Either way, the conclusion is the same: between the level of psychological phenomenology and the physiological level, an intermediate cognitive level has to be postulated. Representations, by this reading, are the constituents of this intermediate level. (For paradigmatic discussions see Fodor, 1968b, 1975; Putnam, 1973.)

The two readings are distinct, but both attest to the same pattern: the impossibility of explaining behaviour directly in terms of given, external factors. This impossibility is attributed to the behaving agent having an intrinsic contribution, one that gives it autonomy with respect to the environment. The higher the degree of this autonomy, the more ground there is for the postulation of representations.

The functionalist sense of 'representation' may be interpreted in three ways that differ in strength. The strongest is to regard representations as real entities, actual constituents of the psychological machinery. A weaker stance is to avoid existential claims and to regard representations as theoretical constructs invoked by the analyzing observer in order to formulate lawful explanations of behaviours studied. While these two interpretations are found in the literature (see Haugeland, 1978; Palmer, 1978; Dennett, 1979b; Pylyshyn, 1984; Palmer and Kimchi, 1986) the following, third interpretation is not standard; it is presented here as a suggestion for further consideration.

According to the functionalist rationale, the postulation of representations is a function of the inability to characterize behaviour in terms of environmental factors. This inability, however, may depend on the identity of the observer attempting the characterization. Specifically, the inability may reflect this observer's ignorance: the less the observer knows, the more likely he or she is to postulate representations. Such representations exhibit two characteristics not associated with the previous senses. First, the postulation of representations is relative to the observer making it: some observers but not others may attribute representations to the same behaving agent. Second, the attribution of representations need not be an all-or-none characterization: it may take any value on the continuum between these two extremes; the higher the level of available knowledge, the smaller this value will be.

While the relative, context-dependent characterization of representations may, at first sight, seem strange, the consideration of different contexts of investigation lends credence to it. Thus, consider Aristotelian physics. According to Aristotle (1963), the stone falls because its natural place is down whereas the balloon rises because its natural place is up. The natural places are, in other words, parameters which define the intrinsic qualities of the various physical bodies. Functionally, they are mediators between the behaviour of the physical body under consideration and the environment that surrounds it; throughout the foregoing discussion such mediators have been referred to as internal representations.[1] But then, different observers of the same physical bodies, with different information or world-views, will characterize these physical bodies differently. The Newtonian observer, for instance, does not attribute representations to the stone or the balloon because he or she can define the movement of these bodies solely in terms of their environment. Newtonian physics allows one to characterize the movement of physical bodies as the integration of all the external influences that act upon them; as this provides a complete kinematic account, no postulation of internal parameters (or representations) is needed.

Before continuing, let me note a possible variant of the functionalist rationale, one which is also related to the epistemic – the *intentional* rationale. This is couched in the appraisal that cognitive agents behave by virtue of their having beliefs, desires and goals. Representations are postulated as the entities that specify these beliefs, desires and goals (see Dennett, 1979b). The intentional rationale is related to the epistemic one because representations are defined in both as entities that specify some content. It may be regarded as a variant of the functionalist rationale because these entities mark further respects in which the behaving agent exhibits autonomy *vis-à-vis* the environment. Either way, the rationale does not present a distinct sense of 'representation', one not already presented by the other rationales in this survey.

Technical-psychological representations

To return to the main line of the discussion: the last and most important sense of 'representation' is that usually employed in cognitive psychology; I will refer to it as the *technical-psychological* sense of 'representation'. While differing in some details, representations as they are usually employed in the cognitive literature exhibit the following core of basic characteristics:

1. Representations are *symbolic*. In other words, they consist of entities defined by the coupling of two facets – the *medium* of expression or articulation and the *information* or *content* being expressed or conveyed.
2. Representations are *canonical*. They are phrased in terms of one given, predefined code which defines a particular, uniform resolution. This code is *complete* and *exhaustive*: all that is known is represented in full. Further, the canonical representations are *determinate*: each expression is defined by one canonical representation and each representation specifies a particular, single-valued interpretation.
3. The canonical code is *structured*. On the one hand, the atomic constituents of representations are *well defined*: they comprise a vocabulary that is factorized into a small set of categories. While the categorization may be ambiguous or fuzzy, for any given representation it is specific. For instance, the principal categories may be subject and predicate, acts and variables, or semantic roles. On the other hand, the molar compositions of the atomic entities are *well formed*: they are composed in accordance with a system of rules; in other words, they are governed by a syntax.
4. Representations are *static*. Unless it changes, knowledge is specified by one, *permanent* representational structure. The underlying assumption is that, basically, the mind consists of the totality of the representations stored in it. At times – as in learning and in forgetting – the representations do change. Such changes, however, are viewed as the occasional modifications of given

structures. Furthermore, it is assumed that the distinction between structures and processes is well demarcated. Thus, the representations are both defined and assumed to exist independently of the processes that are applied to them.

5. Finally, the representations are *abstract* in two distinct and independent respects. First, the particular *medium* of their articulation is totally immaterial. Mentalese, the language of thought (Fodor, 1975), is neither a natural language nor articulated in any sensory modality. Second, the particular *material realization* in which the representations are instantiated is of no relevance. Specifically, it is assumed that mental representations may be defined and studied with a total disregard of the body in which mental activity takes place. This appraisal is fundamental, as it is the basis for a central tenet of contemporary cognitive science, namely, that cognitive psychology and artificial intelligence are both aspects of the same field of inquiry – that of the study of cognition and intelligence.

These characteristics render mental representations *semantic* representations. Together, these characteristics present a precise definition of the term 'representation' that appeared undefined in the tripartite characterization of RCVM in (*) in the Prologue; henceforth, they are referred to as (**). For paradigmatic works employing 'representation' in this technical-psychological sense, see Newell and Simon, (1972), Anderson and Bower (1973), Kintsch (1974), Norman and Rumelhart (1975), Schank (1972, 1975), Newell (1980); for further theoretical discussion, see Chomsky (1959), Fodor (1968a, 1975) and Pylyshyn (1984). By way of summary, the profile generated by (**) may be described as follows:

> (**) Semantic representations (representations in the technical-psychological sense) are well-formed structures of well-defined abstract symbolic entities constituting a complete and exhaustive canonical code which is determinate and static.

While the different characteristics of (**) are distinct and independent, there is a common denominator by which most of them are related fixedness. Fixedness manifests itself in three respects. First, being canonical, the representational code is given and defined prior to and independently of any cognitive activity associated with the representations specified by it. Second, being determinate, for each epistemic or cognitive state the code specifies one and only one representational characterization. Third, being static and of relative permanence, semantic representations manifest fixedness in time. It will be noted that these three respects pertain to different levels. In the first, fixedness is a structural characteristic of the entire representational code as a system; in the second, it is a structural characteristic of each representational token; and in the third, it is a temporal quality pertaining to both the system and its particular instantiations.

The psychological sense of 'representation' differs significantly from the others we have surveyed: it is the only one that specifies what representations actually are. The first, experiential sense points to representations directly but does not offer a definition; all the others define mental representations indirectly – by their status (the epistemic sense), function (the functionalist sense) or accomplishments (the naive sense). The psychological sense, by contrast, specifies the structure of representations and provides clear, operational criteria for their identification. In this respect, it is regarded as stronger than all the others.

While the psychological sense is the most specifically defined of those surveyed, it is the most problematic in terms of the rationale it offers for the postulation of representations. Apparently, for a good number of years, cognitive research was guided by the belief expressed by Fodor (1975) when defining the conceptual foundations of RCVM: 'The only psychological models of cognitive processes that seem even remotely plausible represent such processes as computational . . . Computation presupposes a medium of computation: a representational system'. (p. 27). It is only recently – notably, due to the challenge posed by connectionism – that explicit reasons for the postulation of representations in the technical-psychological sense have been argued for in the literature. The clearest statements to this effect are those presented by Fodor and Pylyshyn (in particular, see Pylyshyn, 1984; Fodor, 1987; Fodor and Pylyshyn, 1988a; see also Pinker and Prince, 1988). Basically, they argue that representations in the strong sense have to be postulated when a cognitive system can be demonstrated to be sensitive to its structural properties and to make use of them. The regularity of human behaviour and its systematic productiveness indicate that this is, indeed, the case. The prime manifestations of this are the unbounded generative power of cognitive expressions, the ability to compose constituents into larger structures, and the ability to extrapolate, draw inferences and learn.

Although the proponents of representationalism regard these cognitive accomplishments as definite demonstrations that semantic representations have to be postulated, the argument is not conclusive. In fact, much of the debate between orthodox representationalism and the alternative school of connectionism hinges precisely on the issue of whether the regularities exhibited in behaviour require the postulation of representations in the technical sense. A main contention of connectionism is that systematic regularity can be generated even without the explicit specification of generative rules in underlying representations. (For representative works see McClelland and Rumelhart, 1986a; Rumelhart and McClelland, 1986b; Smolensky, 1988.)

Senses and distinctions

Six senses of the term 'representation' have been noted: as concrete, external entities, as phenomenological entities, as the locus of mental activity, as the substrate of meaning and of knowledge, as mediating functions, and as specific theoretical constructs employed for the modelling of mind. Together, these different senses reveal a number of contrastive distinctions which are, I think, crucial for any analysis of mental representations and representational theories in cognitive science. To my knowledge, they have not been made – at least not explicitly – in the literature.

The first distinction is that between *underlying* representations and representations in general. In the cognitive literature the term 'representation' is usually regarded as synonymous with 'underlying representation'. In the representational view of mind, representations are covert mental structures which serve as the substrate for any overt behaviour. But, as pointed out above, there are representations that are neither covert nor mental. In general, these are entities that serve for referring to objects and states of affairs other than themselves.

The second, and perhaps most important, distinction is that between two perspectives, to which I will refer as the *vertical* and the *horizontal*. The vertical perspective has to do with the relationship between two levels of reality or of scientific discourse. Viewed from this perspective, representations are postulated in order to characterize the relationship between two such levels. We have met this perspective in conjunction with the epistemic and functionalist senses of 'representation'. Epistemically, representations serve to mark the relationship between the overt behaviour of cognitive agents and the underlying, covert reservoir of knowledge that makes this behaviour possible. Functionally, representations account for the relationship between the behaving organism and either the world outside or the biological substrate of the body. By contrast, the horizontal perspective has to do with patterns and relations pertaining to one, single level. Two senses of 'representation' may be distinguished within this horizontal perspective, one *strong* and one *weak*. The weak refers to the locus that serves as the substrate for mental activity and that enables psychological activity; the strong refers to a particular model in cognitive science postulated in order to model such activity. This model is defined by a profile of specific structural characteristics, which we outlined in (**).

The difference between the vertical and the horizontal perspectives reflects a more basic difference between two professional perspectives – the *philosophical* and the *cognitive*. By and large, philosophers study representations from the vertical perspective whereas cognitive scientists of all persuasions – linguists, cognitive psychologists and students of artificial intelligence – study them from the horizontal one. (For a similar observation, see Winograd, 1978.)[2] It should be noted that although conceptually orthogonal, historically the philosophical and cognitive perspectives are not on a par. It was philosophers who first established the discipline of semantics and defined its key terms. Hence, pedantically, the vertical sense of 'representation' may be regarded as the more accurate. The current situation in the cognitive sciences, however, is not – and need not be – bounded by historical precedence.

The distinction between the two perspectives is not confined to the study of representations; it involves the interpretation of what semantics is, and the consequent definition of what semantic research should consist of. For the philosopher, semantics pertains to the relationship between linguistic and other entities (for the classical definitions see Morris, 1938). In this perspective, meaning is regarded as constituted by the relationship between linguistic or cognitive expressions and states of affairs, be they in the actual world or in other possible (or non-possible) worlds. The central topic of philosophical semantics, then, is the relationship between word and object, between language and the world (cf. Wittgenstein, 1922; Quinne, 1960; Kripke, 1980). Cognitive scientists other than philosophers – linguists, psychologists and artificial intelligence researchers – who claim to study semantics are not at all concerned with this question (cf. Winograd, 1978, Fodor, 1980). Thus, consider the definition of semantics given by Katz (1972) in a book sketching a linguistic semantic theory:

> We shall attempt to answer the question 'What is meaning?' by constructing a theory that explicates the concept of meaning within the framework of a full systematization of the empirical facts about semantic structure in natural language. The goal is a theory of the underlying principles that will interrelate and thus organize the empirical facts within the domain of semantics . . . To model our attempt to construct a semantic theory on this example, we should first seek to break down the general question 'What is meaning?' into a number of narrower, more specific questions that are inherently part of the larger one . . . [For example] 'What is sameness of meaning?' 'What are similarity and difference of meaning?' . . . 'What is multiplicity or ambiguity of meaning?'. (p. 4)

By this definition, semantics is not concerned with the relationship between two levels of reality or two domains of discourse. Rather, it focuses on relations such as sameness and difference of meaning, entailment and presupposition – that is, relations between entities on the same level or in the same domain. Correspondingly, the cognitive psychologist investigates the structures in which representations are instantiated in the mind and the processes that relate representational to other such structures. In all cognitive investigations it is assumed that the entities under study are semantic, or representational, in the philosophical sense, but this property is taken for granted and not examined. Furthermore, it is assumed that this property is kept invariant under the application of the semantic operations in the linguistic sense.[3] In point of fact, not only is it the case that cognitive semantics is not concerned with the relationship between mind and the world, it cannot in principle address this relationship at all. This was first appreciated by Wittgenstein (1922), who closed his *Tractatus* with the desperate conclusion that a horizontally (in the present sense) defined representational system can never account for its being representational in the vertical sense. A modern variant of this was put forth by Fodor (1980), who pointed out that representational cognitive psychology assumes a principled methodological solipsism. Unlike classical solipsism, methodological solipsism does not question the existence of the external world. Rather, it marks the impossibility of representational psychology accounting for how the mind succeeds in relating to the world and in establishing contact with it. In professing such methodological solipsism Fodor accepts this state of affairs. In so doing, however, some of the most fundamental issues of psychology are placed outside the realm of cognitive science. As will be argued throughout this book, this cannot be accepted.

The critique of representationalism

Just as there are different senses of 'representation' and different reasons for their postulation, so there are different types of critique that can be marshalled against them. Specifically, analogous to the philosophical and cognitive orientations of research there are distinct philosophical and cognitive critiques of representationalism. The main line of the philosophical critique pertains to *reification*. It appears that, with the exception of the experiential rationale, all the arguments surveyed make an inference which is not logically required, namely, that mental representations are entities. The naive rationale points to products and accomplishments of cognitive agents, which attest to the fact that mental activity takes place, but is it necessary to assume that this employs the medium of representation? The epistemic rationale marks the meaningfulness and rule-like order of human behaviour, and concludes that there must exist an underlying substrate of which these are overt manifestations; that this conclusion involves a conceptual jump is the fundamental observation of Wittgenstein's *Philosophical Investigations* (1953). The functionalist rationale notes that there is no direct mapping between the environmental inputs and the behavioural outputs of the organism, and therefore defines mediating functions to relate the two; but is there a need to ground these in any mental entities, real or theoretical? The reifications noted here are of prime philosophical significance and as such are worthy of in-depth investigation. Indeed, a substantial part of the philosophical research of the second half of this century has been devoted to such an investigation (cf. Wittgenstein, 1953; Rorty, 1980; Putnam, 1981; for other philosophical critiques of representations see Barwise and Perry, 1983; Stich, 1983; Putnam, 1988).

The cognitive critique of representationalism is different. It focuses not on the analysis of fundamental philosophical concepts, but rather on the evaluation of a particular paradigm of scientific research. This evaluation involves conceptual considerations only inasmuch as they bear on the appropriateness and usefulness of the given paradigm in accounting for the phenomenological domain.

The critique presented in this book is cognitive. It consists of arguments indicating that semantic representations as usually defined in the cognitive literature do not satisfy the desiderata of the rationales for the postulation of such representations. Specifically, semantic representations cannot fulfil the functions associated with the two most important rationales presented above – the epistemic and the functionalist: they can neither capture the knowledge that people manifest nor account for the relationships between cognition and the world.

This critique is guided by the appraisal that there is a discrepancy between the different senses of 'representation' on the one hand, and the rationales for their postulation on the other. It may be that representations are postulated in one sense but the support for this postulation corresponds to representations in another sense. These considerations are especially pertinent to representations in the technical-psychological sense, because this is the strongest and most specific of them all. Even if some of the most important functions that representations are supposed to fulfil might constitute reasons for the postulation of representations in some of the weaker senses, they need not necessarily require this postulation in this stronger sense. Specifically, the requirement that there should be a locus in which mental activity takes place justifies the postulation of representations in the naive sense only; the requirement that there be internal structures in which knowledge is coded justifies the postulation in the epistemic sense only; the need for mediating functions to account for the relationship between mind and world justifies the postulation in the functionalist sense only. These requirements or needs may justify the postulation of some internal underlying mental entities; they do not necessarily call for the postulation of representations exhibiting the specific characteristics associated with the technical-psychological sense.

Bearing in mind all the distinctions introduced above is crucial. Confronted with arguments marshalled against the postulation of representations, many are likely to shrug in surprise and retort: how can it be? Things have to be represented. Given that the mind relates to the world, and since it does so by means of some mental structures, how could there not be representations? This retort involves, however, the very confusion between perspectives against which I have cautioned. It is tantamount to a rephrasing of the naive argument, and, as such, it pertains to the vertical perspective. That representations in the naive (or even the stronger epistemic) sense have to be postulated does not imply that representations as defined from the horizontal perspective of psychology should be postulated as well.

Similarly, arguments against representations in the strong technical-psychological sense need not necessarily hold against representations in any weaker sense (as the naive or the epistemic ones). The failure to appreciate the difference between the various senses of 'representation' gives rise to a confused state of affairs where students of mind who are clearly anti-representationalists (i.e., who oppose the representational view of mind that bases psychological modelling on structures of the type defined by (**)) talk about psychological representations none the less. A notable case is that of opponents of connectionism, as well as some of its prominent proponents, who have characterized connectionist networks as representational (e.g. Rumelhart and McClelland, 1986b; McClelland, 1988; Smolensky, 1988). Manifestly, this involves a confusion of senses. Connectionist networks are representational only in the weak, naive sense: they serve as a locus for cognitive activity. The standard cognitive models, by contrast, are representational in the much stronger sense referred to here as technical-psychological. Clearly, maintaining the distinction between the two senses is crucial in order to keep things clear and not blur differences which are very real.[4]

From the present perspective, the critique against representations is concerned with the strong sense of that term. In arguing against the representational view of mind I am not denying the existence of cognitive structures and patterns of activity that exhibit a representational profile. Rather, I am arguing that representations cannot serve as the basis of cognitive modelling. They are not conceptually primary, they do not characterize what is generally the case, and they have neither procedural nor developmental primacy. Such a non-representational position does not imply that representational structures do not play a role in cognition and in cognitive modelling. What is argued, rather, is that representational structures, if and when they exist, are the products of cognitive activity, not the basis for it.

Lastly, one possible objection to the present characterization of representationalism is that it is strictly Fodorian, and need not be shared by all cognitive psychologists of the representational school. Given that most practising cognitive scientists are not explicit about their theoretical assumptions and philosophical stance, verification of this statement is not straightforward. Yet I do not think that the characterization is improper. First, Fodor – along with Pylyshyn, who has the same view of representationalism – are undoubtedly the most explicit and articulate of all representationalist psychologists. Theirs is the clearest statement of the theoretical position in the literature. Second, this characterization of representationalism defines the essence of the framework in question. Specific representational models may differ in details and application, but the basic perspective is definitely not specifically Fodorian. Indeed, all the specific models cited above abide by all the characterizations made here. Third, given that the theoretical position is usually left unstated, I would not be surprised if, when pressed to be explicit and pushed to draw their position to its ultimate logical conclusions, most representational psychologists found themselves agreeing with Fodor and Pylyshyn. This might be the case even if, on first sight, the investigators may balk at the Fodorian position as being too extreme. After all, Fodor is the first to have admitted that his position is, indeed, such; he just does not see any possible alternative (see Fodor, 1975; Fodor and Pylyshyn, 1988a).

Notes

1. One could, of course, object to the attribution of representations to non-human or inanimate objects on the grounds that they do not know or behave. Important as such an objection is, it bears on philosophical considerations which belong to a context very different from the one here. The present functionalist arguments can be taken independently, disregarding such considerations.
2. Of course, the distinction pertains to an intellectual perspective, not to individual investigators. Thus, one of the most important figures in the study of representations, Jerry Fodor, has adopted both these perspectives. As a cognitive psychologist he has focused on the horizontal perspective (see, for instance, Fodor, 1975), and he has even marked the impossibility for representational psychology of addressing the vertical question (see Fodor,

1980). In addition, as a philosopher, he has also addressed the vertical question (Fodor, 1987, 1990).

3. This assumption is far from being trivial. To my knowledge, it is generally taken for granted without any explicit justification. It is worthy of independent, serious philosophical discussion.

4. This characterization of connectionist models as not representational in the technical-psychological sense is somewhat idealistic. Close examination reveals that in practice these models may not be as pure as one might have expected. In other words, a discrepancy is noted between the connectionist meta-psychology on the one hand, and specific connectionist modelling of cognitive performances on the other hand. Specifically, connectionist models often include some structures that are, in fact, analogous to semantic representations. I shall return to this issue in Chapter 21, where alternative theoretical frameworks in psychology are discussed.

Part I

The representational-computational view of mind: a critique

Introduction

Part I presents a critique of RCVM. The critique proceeds along three main lines. The first and second lines are based on the contrast between representations in the technical-psychological sense and the desiderata imposed by the two main rationales for the postulation of representations – the *epistemic* and the *functionalist*. The first line will show that representations as usually defined in orthodox cognitive science cannot serve the epistemic function. Specifically, fixed, abstract, semantic representations cannot fully characterize the knowledge people have of the world and the totality of meanings they invest it with. The second line will show that representations in the technical-psychological sense cannot meet the requirements of the functionalist rationale. Specifically, such representations cannot account for the relationship between the cognizing organism and the external world. The third line focuses on the last characteristics specified in (**), those having to do with the temporal aspects of representations, and tries to show that fixed, static representations cannot account for the origin of knowledge, its development and its progression in time.

Following the three main lines of the critique a fourth, secondary line is presented. Whereas the former are concerned with the particular characteristics of representations in the technical-psychological sense, the latter is concerned with some more basic problems pertaining to the notion of representation itself. Some of these are akin to ones raised in philosophical critiques of representation. Here, however, they are discussed in the light of cognitive-psychological considerations.

Each of the four lines of criticism marshalled here presents a number of arguments marking the limitations of RCVM and the inappropriateness of semantic representations as the basis for the modelling of mind. The various arguments are presented in terms of basic conceptual problems that pertain to several structural determinants of representations. This contrasts with another possible scheme, one based on domains of mental function and psychological activity. This choice of scheme is not a mere matter of exposition or style. Rather, it bears on the very nature of the critique to be presented. First, the structural scheme emphasizes the generality and comprehensiveness of this critique of RCVM. As RCVM purports to be a comprehensive theoretical framework for the study of mind, one serving as the basis for the modelling of all psychological performance, any critique of RCVM should be comprehensive as well, and not confined to any particular domain of psychology. Second, this scheme mirrors what is fundamentally problematic about RCVM. The many different phenomena in the various domains of psychology for which RCVM fails to account are not unrelated to one another. Rather, they are the symptoms that reflect more basic inadequacies and shortcomings of RCVM. These are associated with a series of structural factors that are not specific to any particular subject domain. Consequently, the ensuing problems manifest themselves in different domains. The scheme adopted here directs attention to what there is in common between these problems. Third, this scheme highlights an internal logic that characterizes the space of problems associated with the representational framework. The problems associated with the different structural factors are themselves interrelated; there are affinities and analogies between them, and together they compose one coherent structure. Not only does this structure turn the present critique into one compact, unified whole, it also lays the grounds for an integrated alternative view of mind. The internal structure of both the critique and the alternatives it presents will become more and more apparent as our discussion proceeds; they will be spelled out fully in Part II.

The fact that the following arguments draw on considerations from many diverse domains of human psychology imposes a limitation on how extensive and detailed the discussion in each particular domain can be. By necessity, the treatment of none of these can be complete: doing justice to each problem in each domain is simply impossible within one book. Thus, this discussion by no means purports to be exhaustive. I hope, however, that this book presents a comprehensive, integrated overall picture of what might be called the *problematics* (in the continental sense of *problematique*) of RCVM and the theoretical issues associated with it.

It may very well be that in itself, none of the arguments to be presented here is conclusive. For each, the reader (or rather, different readers for different arguments) may find counter-arguments that might salvage RCVM. Again, however, it is the overall picture that is important. RCVM may be salvaged locally, but the more basic questions remain: what kind of picture of mind does representationalism present? What basic premises regarding human cognition does it imply? What type of cognitive theory does it entail? What questions does it define and where does it direct the focus of study and investigation? The aim of this book is to solicit the reader to view human cognition from a different perspective. It will suggest on the one hand that the principles underlying the workings of mind are different from those assumed by RCVM, and on the other hand that cognitive investigation should be directed to domains and issues with which RCVM has not been concerned. With this, new questions for cognitive research may be defined and new avenues for investigation opened.

The first line of the critique

In the first line of the critique I will argue that semantic representations cannot satisfy the desiderata stipulated by the epistemic rationale. In other words, I will try to show that representations in the strong technical-psychological sense cannot account for the knowledge manifested by human behaviour and the meaning exhibited by cognitive expressions or associated with them. In a nutshell, the following discussion attempts to show that this knowledge cannot be captured by a fixed canonical code exhibiting the structural characteristics outlined in (**). In particular, the discussion focuses on three facets of such a code. The first is its determinateness. It will be argued that the knowledge people have and the meanings of their cognitive expressions cannot be characterized in terms of a code that exhibits fixedness in the first two of the three aspects specified in Chapter 1. The second facet is its abstractness in the first sense specified in point (5) of (**). It will be argued that a code that imposes a principled distinction between medium and message cannot adequately characterize the knowledge and meanings in question. The third facet is fixedness in the sense of predetermination. It will be argued that human behaviour defies any universal code fixed prior to cognitive activity and independently of it.

To these three facets of the first line of the critique, three arguments correspond: the argument from *context*, the argument from the *medium*, and the argument regarding *coding and recoding*. The argument from context is presented in two steps, in Chapters 2 and 3; the two other arguments are presented in Chapters 4 and 5.

2   Context

> [Sense] is like a flow of meanings with no speech and of as many meanings as of men.
>
> *Wallace Stevens*

If knowledge is the basis of all cognitive activity, and if all knowledge is constituted in semantic representations, then it should be possible to provide characterizations of all behaviour in terms of determinate, well-defined, well-formed symbolic structures. The argument from context shows that this is not possible. The argument is couched in the observation that behaviour is context-dependent and in the appraisal that the variation of contexts is, in principle, without bounds. Indeed, since contexts pertain to the world, from the perspective of psychology they are given and psychological theory cannot impose any constraint on their range and variability. However, psychological theory – like any scientific theory – has to be constrained, and the repertory of psychological entities has to be confined to a manageable set. The contrast between the unbounded variation of contexts and the boundedness of the cognitive system implies that fixed determinate representations cannot capture all the knowledge that is in effect manifested in human behaviour. In other words, representations in the strong technical-psychological sense cannot satisfy the demands set by the epistemic rationale for the postulation of mental representations.

Examining the problems that RCVM faces due to the effect of context, the following discussion will focus primarily – but not exclusively – on the representation of meaning as it is expressed in language. This is only natural, for by and large the meaning of words in language comprises people's knowledge about the world. Indeed, by RCVM the semantics of language is the semantics of knowledge, and the basis for all cognition is a language of thought. Thus, if RCVM is correct, it should be possible to characterize the meanings of all words and of all linguistic expressions in terms of semantic representations as defined in Chapter 1. Conversely, if such representations cannot capture the semantics of language, *ipso facto* they cannot be the basis for psychology that they are purported to be.

The treatment of context as it manifests itself in the representation of meaning and in the semantics of natural language will be more extensive than that of other topics, for several reasons. The first is that noted above, namely, the pivotal role that the semantics of natural language plays in RCVM. The second is the fact that the linguistic domain is the one most studied in contemporary cognitive science, and that the theoretical accounts for it are the most developed. The third is due to the place of the argument from context in this essay. Being first in the discussion, the argument from context lays the foundation for the others. For one thing, the discussion of context starts from scratch; for another, it presents several lines of reasoning that will be referred to later.

The following argument from context will proceed in three parts. First, general problems regarding the definition of word meaning will be noted; second, specific difficulties due to context will be pointed out; third, in the light of a possible retort to the second part of the argument, a two-stage model will be evaluated and dismissed. The dismissal will complete the critique of RCVM with regard to the representation of meaning.

The definition of the meanings of words

Following Wittgenstein (1958), I shall start by asking 'What is the meaning of a word?'. According to RCVM, words gain their meaning by virtue of being the overt reflections of underlying mental representations. The simplest conceivable representational account is that defined by abstract concepts that correspond to the words of natural language. A word such as 'table' will be characterized as the reflection of the corresponding abstract term *table*, and it is by dint of this correspondence that it has the meaning it has. While models actually entertained in the cognitive literature are not that simple, some of their basic characteristics, as well as the problems associated with them, derive from this fundamental assumption of correspondence.

Disregarding the philosophical problems raised by the correspondence account of meaning (see Wittgenstein, 1953; Putnam, 1988), let me examine its viability as a psychological model. Even before considering empirical data, we note that the account suffers from two fundamental theoretical shortcomings. First, given that to each word of the language there corresponds a concept specifying its meaning, it follows that the mental lexicon should be by and large as sizeable as the lexicon of the natural language that is being accounted for. Furthermore, given that the number of words is not bounded, it follows that, in principle, the number of underlying entities in mental representation is not constrained either. This runs against the methodological principle requiring that psychological theory be constrained. In point of fact, in the psychological case the constraint is a matter not only of methodology but also of substance. After all, mental representations are instantiated in a mind whose performance is constrained in scope, capacity and time, and in a brain which is limited in both size and resources.

Second, the simple concept-word correspondence model does not have much explanatory force. Underlying representations are postulated not only by way of defining the source or carrier of meaning, but also in order to account for the phenomenology of meaning relations and of the patterns of behaviour associated with them. The correspondence model does not capture anything that is not already revealed by the words of the language themselves. Specifically, the model fails to capture possible relations between words and regularities that cut across different classes and categories thereof. For these to be captured, the underlying vocabulary of mental representations should be smaller than that of the natural language one wishes to explain. This quest for explanation is the basic *raison d'être* of the postulation of representational models that define the meaning of words in terms of smaller semantic units. Such units – be they semantic features (Katz and Fodor, 1963) or any variant of semantic primitives (Schank, 1972) will be of use only if they are small in number and if they allow a unified, exhaustive characterization of all the words in the language (for a general discussion of semantic primitives, see Winograd, 1978). What is proposed, in other words, is a semantic reduction, a reduction which is analogous – both in structure and in explanatory utility – to that practised in natural sciences such as chemistry. The evaluation of this reduction will be the starting point of this critique of semantic representations.

Seminal to all modern critiques of semantic reduction is the later work of Wittgenstein (1953, 1958). His critique is couched in the observation that the meanings of words cannot be defined by any set of necessary and sufficient semantic features. The example he brings by way of marking this limitation – the meaning of the word 'game' – is by now a classic, and even though most readers are no doubt familiar with it, I think it still deserves to be quoted in full:

> Consider for example the proceedings that we call 'games'. I mean board-games, card-games, ball-games, Olympic games, and so on. What is common to them all? – Don't say: 'There *must* be something common, or they would not be called "games"' – but *look and see* whether there is anything common to all. – For if you look at them you will not see something that is common to *all*, but similarities, relationships, and a whole series of them at that. To repeat: don't think, but look! – Look for example at board-games, with their multifarious relationships. Now pass to card-games; here you find many correspondences with the first group, but many common features drop out, and others appear. When we pass next to ball-games, much that is common is retained, but much is lost. – Are they all 'amusing'? Compare chess with naughts and crosses. Or is there always winning and losing, or competition between players? Think of patience. In ball-games there is winning and losing; but when a child throws his ball at the wall and catches it again, this feature has disappeared. Look at the parts played by skill and luck; and at the difference between skill in chess and skill in tennis. Think now of games like ring-a-ring-a-roses; here is the element of amusement, but how many other characteristic features have disappeared! And we can go through the many, many other groups of games in the same way; can see how similarities crop up and disappear.
>
> And the result of this examination is: we see a complicated network of

similarities overlapping and criss-crossing: sometimes overall similarities, sometimes similarities of detail. (Wittgenstein, 1953, para. 66)

This semantic observation is just one facet of Wittgenstein's more general argument against the involvement of mental representations and rules in verbal expression, communication and reasoning. For semantic representations to underlie any of these cognitive tasks they have to capture the specific meaning intended in the given context of their use. The unconstrained variation of contexts defies any such characterization.

Moreover, even if for the individual speaker in any given context meaning could be so specified, there would be no way of objectively determining what this meaning is or of verifying its constancy over time. In this regard, Wittgenstein's analysis of the use of colour terms is famous. How does one know that the same colour term always refers to the same hue? Any reference to an internal colour chart would require reference to still another, higher-order mental representation so as to determine the matching between it and the internal pattern serving for its evaluation. This, however, leads to the insurmountable problems of both infinite regress and solipsism. The problems loom with respect to the meanings of expressions as they are employed both by different speakers and by the same individual on different occasions. Furthermore, these problems are encountered both in conjunction with verbal expressions and with respect to the tokens of terms one might use in one's mentation. After all, the problems associated with the reference to independent semantic criteria are just the same when the expression is a word one utters or an idea one entertains. On the basis of such observations, Wittgenstein rejected the notion of meaning as being 'in the head' and the psychological reality of rules and underlying mental states in general.

Wittgenstein's critique is radical in that it holds against both the philosophical and the psychological notions of representation. Its philosophical aspect will not concern us here (I shall return to some philosophical problems in Chapter 15). I shall now proceed with the consideration of the psychological aspect.

The simplest and most straightforward definitional analysis is by means of semantic features. Such analysis has been prominent in linguistic, psychological and computer models alike (see, for instance, Fodor and Katz, 1963; Schank, 1972; Anderson and Bower, 1973). Yet, remarkably, investigators from various quarters, whose views on cognitive matters are otherwise in conflict, have come to the same conclusion, namely, that well-defined semantic features cannot offer an adequate characterization of the meaning of words. Among such investigators are Putnam (1975b, 1981, 1988), Fodor *et al.* (1980), Kripke (1980), and Winograd (1980).

The purest line of psychological argumentation is, I find, that presented by Winograd; since the points he raises are basic to all the ensuing discussion, I will present them in some detail. Winograd (1976) attacks the featural definition of words by examining the word 'bachelor', a word whose analysis has been seminal in the semantic literature in general and in representational accounts in particular. By this analysis, 'bachelor' is defined by the following concatenation of features:

'1. human, adult, unmarried, male'. But – argues Winograd (1980: 276–7) – consider the following cast of characters:

A. Arthur has been living happily with Alice for the last five years. They have a two year old daughter, and have never officially married.
B. Bruce was going to be drafted, so he arranged with his friend Barbara to have a justice of the peace marry them so he would be exempt. They have never lived together. He dates a number of women, and plans to have the marriage annulled as soon as he finds someone he wants to marry.
C. Charlie is 17 years old. He lives at home with his parents and is in high school.
D. David is 17 years old. He left home at 13, started a small business, and is now a successful young entrepreneur leading a playboy's life style in his penthouse apartment.
E. Eli and Edgar are homosexual lovers who have been living together for many years.
F. Faisal is allowed by the law of his native Abu Dhabi to have three wives. He currently has two and is interested in meeting another potential fiancée.
G. Father Gregory is the bishop of the Catholic cathedral at Groton upon Thames.

Following Winograd (1980), one may add to this list:

H. Helen is a successful independent career business woman who in her local Californian jargon is commonly referred to as 'bachelor'.

The cases exemplified by these characters indicate that the features specified in (1) are neither necessary nor sufficient. There are cases (e.g. E and G) in which the conditions of the definition are met and the label 'bachelor' is not appropriate, and there are cases (e.g. F and H) in which the conditions are violated but the label is employed none the less.

The natural response to such inadequacies is to accommodate (1) by modifying and/or adding features to it. Such features, Winograd notes, may be ones like the following: '2. Not currently officially married, not in a marriage-like living situation, potentially marriageable'. The strategy of amending the featural definition is, however, doubly problematic. First, as fine-grained as the definition may be, one can never be certain that it is foolproof. For any featural characterization offered, additional features may still be needed. With this, the featural characterization may cease to be constrained, and it may thus lose the very basis for its postulation. After all, featural characterizations are theoretical constructs postulated by scientists in order to offer an explanatory account of the phenomenology in their domain of investigation. For the account to be useful the set of constructs it introduces has to be not only bounded but also significantly smaller than the set of phenomena under consideration. If this is not the case, then one might as well phrase the explanation in terms of the observable level of overt phenomenology and not postulate a non-observable level at all. Clearly, the postulation of such a covert level involves a theoretical cost, one that is justified only if it affords a significant reduction in the complexity of the explanation. Second, as pointed out by Winograd (1976), the finer the definitions, the more they are prone to introduce features which are semantically not simple, perhaps even some that are more complex than the notions they are supposed to explain. But, if the explication of such a simple term as 'bachelor' requires sophisticated appraisals of social interaction, the utility of the definition becomes questionable indeed.

In passing, let me note that this state of affairs is analogous to that encountered in Ptolemaic astronomy. In its original form, the Ptolemaic model places the earth at the centre of the universe and characterizes the trajectories of the sun and the planets as circles drawn around the earth. In the light of discrepancies between the theory and the astronomical data, and in order to maintain the basic geocentric picture, epicycles were introduced. As more and more discrepancies were detected, more and more epicycles were added. There came a point, however, when these corrections became just too cumbersome. Even if any given problematic instance could be salvaged, the model as a whole became less and less appealing. Eventually, parsimony dictated that the model be rejected.[1]

A telling example of the perennial incompleteness of the featural characterizations of meaning is presented by Fodor (1981a) in his analysis of the verb 'to paint'. A reasonable characterization of its meaning is 'to cover a surface with paint'. Some reflection reveals, however, that this characterization is not complete. The case of an explosion in a paint factory indicates that the postulation of an agent is needed. Further, Michaelangelo's not having painted the ceiling of the Sistine Chapel, but having painted a fresco on it, indicates that the painting has to be executed with the intention of its being the primary result of the agent's act. Yet – continues Fodor – there are still cases where 'X paints Y' is not coextensive with 'X is an agent and X covers the surface of Y with paint, and X's primary intention in covering the surface of Y with paint [is] that the surface of Y should be covered with paint in consequence of X's having so acted upon it'. A painter dips her brush in a particular paint in preparation for work; it goes without saying that the painter does not paint the brush. One could go on, but the moral is clear: the quest for definition leads to an unconstrained host of specifications. Indeed, as pointed out by Fodor (1981a), the open-ended specification will, in the limit, bring about a state of affairs whereby the definition of even seemingly simple terms is affected by everything one knows. In sum, the strategy of amending definitions is unboundedly cumbersome, never foolproof, and ultimately self-defeating.

Contextual variations

Contextual variations exacerbate the problematic nature of the featural characterization. Not only can a definition not account for all possible cases, but the definition of each case may itself be subject to contextual variations. As noted by Winograd

(1976), a given characterization may hold in one context but not in another: for instance, Faisal – see the list of characters in the previous section – will be grouped with the bachelors in the context of a bachelor party but not in the contexts of a religious ceremony or of inheritance laws.

One may persist and attempt to respond to the contextual problems with further featural modifications. Specifically, one may subcategorize the contexts and associate with each one a subcase of the definition. With this, one will define two types of feature: pragmatic features for the characterization of contexts and semantic features for the definitions of meaning. To determine the meaning of a given expression one would first define the context of its occurrence in terms of the pragmatic features; these would then refer one to the particular semantic definition associated with the context at hand. This proposal presents, however, two serious problems. First, there is no reason why the pragmatic features should not face the problems already noted in conjunction with the semantic ones. In fact, since contexts are not cognitively constrained, it is certain that such problems will arise. Second, even if contexts could be classified in some fashion, the mapping between a context and the semantic case corresponding to it could itself be subject to unconstrained contextual variation.

This second problem has not been much discussed in the literature, so I will present it in more detail. The following exposition is based on an example presented by Searle (1980b, 1983), although the general context of Searle's discussion as well as the theoretical conclusion he draws are different from mine. The example pertains to the verb 'cut'. The cutting of a cake, Searle observes, is different – in its physical characteristics – from the cutting of grass: the former consists of slicing, the latter of trimming. Therefore, one could be tempted to subdivide the definition of 'cut' according to the different contexts of its employment, of which those of cake and grass are two. The problem is that one could always find instances pertaining to one case in which the cutting is executed in the manner generally associated with the other. For example, in industrial settings grass may be heaped and sliced the way pieces of cake are usually cut. Thus, not only do the meanings of words vary with context, but the mappings that relate the different meanings of words and the contexts with which they are associated are themselves context-sensitive. This second-order variation with context implies that the proposal suggested above will not do. Specifically, one cannot amend the featural characterization of meaning by supplementing it with a featural characterization of contexts. To salvage a featural-based semantics by adding a featural-based pragmatics to it is hopeless; the latter can only exacerbate the problems that the former presents.

Polysemy

Not only is the meaning of words not exhausted by specific semantic definition, but words generally have more than one meaning. The systematic polysemy in natural language suggests that underlying representations cannot capture the meanings of words as they are employed there.

Following Nunberg (1979), consider the following pairs of sentences:

1a. The newspaper is bulky.
1b. The newspaper is worth reading.

2a. The book is green.
2b. The book is interesting.

The nominals in the sentences marked (a) refer to physical objects whereas those in the sentences marked (b) refer to bodies of information. If meanings correspond to well-defined semantic representations then one would be inclined to account for polysemies like these by postulating distinct lexical entries, each specifying one of the different meanings at hand. Specifically, to account for the difference between (1a) and (1b) and that between (2a) and (2b), a distinction is to be made between the entries 'newspaper$_1$' and 'newspaper$_2$', and 'book$_1$' and 'book$_2$', respectively. This account, however, is not viable, for it fails to capture the fact that the polysemy is systematic, as manifested by several patterns. First, there is a full parallelism between the two cases. Second, the same pattern of polysemy is encountered with other items, e.g. journal and document. Third, unlike homophonic lexical ambiguities, polysemies of this kind are invariant under translation. Furthermore, similar systematic ambiguities are also noted in other unrelated words; this is shown in (3) and (4):

3a. The window was broken.
3b. The window was boarded up.

4a. The game is hard to learn.
4b. The game lasted one hour.

In (3a) 'window' is used in the sense of a piece of glass, whereas in (3b) it is used in the sense of an opening. In (4a) 'game' is used in the sense of a system of rules, whereas in (4b) it is used to refer to a specific activity.

And yet, while they are distinct, the different meanings comprising the polysemous pattern are all associated with the same, single lexical item. This is demonstrated by the possibility of conjoining different such meanings by an anaphoric relationship, as in the following example:

5. Although the newspaper is bulky it is devoid of interest.

A similar example is presented in Fauconnier (1985):[2]

6. Plato and Aristotle are on the top shelf. They are bound in leather. You'll find that they are very interesting.

Such anaphoric conjunctions of polysemous words stand in marked contrast to similar conjunctions of homophones. Two homophones cannot be anaphorically related; thus, the pronominalization of (7a) into (7b) is not possible:

7a. The bank [financial institution] is just by the [river] bank.
7b. The bank is just by it.

Taken together, the plurality of meanings and the singleness of the word indicate that the polysemy cannot be specified by underlying semantic representations. Such specification would either not exhaust the meaning of the expressions at hand or not be single-valued. To specify fully the distinct meanings comprising the polysemous pattern, multiple representations could be postulated, but these would fail to capture the fact that all of these meanings are non-accidentally associated with a single lexical item.

Polysemy further suffers from the contextual unboundedness noted in the previous section. New readings of the same word can always be thought of. Thus, in addition to the senses noted in (1a) and (1b), the word newspaper can have the sense of company, as in (8a), and that of a category of stocks, as in (8b):

8a. The newspaper is bankrupt.
8b. Newspapers went up yesterday.

The systematic patterns exhibited by word polysemy, their prevalence within and across languages, and their interaction with the rules of grammar all indicate that this phenomenon is not accidental.

In an attempt to salvage the representational account, one could suggest that distinct semantic representations be ascribed only to meanings associated with markedly different contexts. Such a qualification would not make much difference. Markedly different contexts are no more constrained than contexts in general, and eventually their number is bound to be so large that the problems indicated above would present themselves just the same. Moreover, the very distinction between contexts which are markedly different and contexts which are not is itself context-dependent.

Contextual expressions

There is thus no sharp line of demarcation between the different senses in which words are used. The following discussion will show that there is no such demarcation between standard and novel usages of words either. Thus, all the arguments marshalled with respect to polysemy are expected to apply to novel usages of language as well. If anything, with such usages the force of the arguments should be even greater.

Novel usages of words have been specifically investigated by Clark and his associates (Clark and Clark, 1979; Clark, 1983; Clark and Gerrig, 1983); these usages are referred to as *contextual expressions*. An example is expression (9a) as uttered by an employee of the phone service in response to a person who has dialled 411:

9a. You have to ask a zero.

In the given context the meaning of (9a) is (9b):

> 9b. You have to ask that employee of the phone service who is reached by dialling 0.

While (9) exemplifies the novel use of an existing expression, examples (10)–(12) present novel derivations of verbs and nouns. (The expressions and their interpretations are again marked (a) and (b)):

> 10a. He porched the newspaper.
> 10b. He threw the newspaper onto the porch.
>
> 11a. He Houdinied his way out of the trunk.
> 11b. He managed to escape in the manner classically attributed to Houdini.
>
> 12a. Last night they played a Beethoven.
> 12b. Last night they played a piece by Beethoven.

Remarkably, the novelty of these expressions poses no problem in the actual course of comprehension. The interpretation is clear even though the particular linguistic form at hand was not previously known to the hearer; in fact, in many cases it is not known beforehand even to the speaker who uttered it.[3]

Misusages

The novel usages of language border on what might be considered deviant verbal behaviour. Specifically, speakers may utter words but refer to things totally different from those usually associated with them. The words may actually refer to things that even the speaker does not normally associate with them; moreover, even in the particular context the speaker's intention may not have been to use the words in the manner that he or she does. Such misusages of language are of interest because they indicate that the contribution of context can be so great as to override all other semantic considerations. Even though wrong words are uttered, the hearer none the less achieves correct comprehension. Consider the following three scenarios:

> 13. A is tapping B on the shoulder, addressing her as C; B turns and responds.
>
> 14. A presents B with a tray of candies and says 'Have a cookie'; B helps himself to a candy.
>
> 15. A asks B: 'Do you have a pencil and paper?'; B responds by giving A a pen and a scratch-pad.[4]

What is remarkable about such misusages of language is how unobtrusive they are in actual discourse. Hearers seldom react to them, and often neither the speaker nor the hearer is at all aware that a misusage has taken place.

Phrasal composition

So far the discussion has focused on the meaning of single words. However, just as they may be related to concepts and objects, words may also be related to words. The consideration of the semantics of phrasal composition reveals still another manifestation of the problems surveyed. In particular, let me examine the meaning of noun–noun compounds as a function of the meanings of their constituents. As noted by Downing (1977), the semantic relationships between such constituents cannot be characterized in terms of finite lists. Rather, the meaning of the compound depends on the particular terms, the particular interaction between them, and the context of their use. Thus, a 'coffee can' is a container in which powder is stored, but a 'coffee cup' is a container in which liquid is served. A 'coffee bush' is a plant which grows coffee, 'coffee powder' is (supposedly) 100 per cent pure coffee whereas a 'coffee cake' is a comestible one of whose ingredients (probably not the largest) is coffee. A 'coffee man' is not a man wholly or partially made of coffee nor one who tastes like coffee but rather one whose occupation is dealing with coffee. Finally (but, of course, the list does not exhaust all possible variations), a 'coffee break' is a time set to drink coffee, but also tea, fruit juice and on occasion even alchohol.

The problem of compositionality is, of course, not specific to nominal compounds. Analogous patterns are noted in adjectival phrases. The following exposition of the problem is taken from Lahav (1989):

> Consider the adjective 'red'. What it is for a bird to count as red is not the same as what it is for other kinds of objects to count as red. For a bird to be red (in the normal case), it should have most of the surface of its body red, though not its beak, legs, eyes, and of course its inner organs. Furthermore, the color should be the bird's natural color, since we normally regard a bird as being 'really' red even if it is painted white all over. A kitchen table, on the other hand, is red even if it is only painted red, but not necessarily its legs and bottom surface. Similarly, a red apple . . . needs to be red only on the outside, but a red hat needs to be red only in its external upper surface, a red crystal is red both inside and outside, and a red watermelon is red only inside. For a book to be red is for its cover but not necessarily for its inner pages to be mostly red, while for a newspaper to be red is for all of its pages to be red. For a house to be red is for its outside walls, but not necessarily its roof (and windows and door) to be mostly red, while a red car must be red in its external surface including its roof (but not its windows, wheels, bumper, etc.). A red star only needs to appear red from earth, a red glaze needs to be red only after it is fired, and a red mist or a red powder are not red simply inside or outside. A red pen need not have any red part (the ink may turn red only when in contact with paper). In short, what counts for one type of thing to be red is not what counts for another. (p. 264)

In the same manner, consider prepositional phrases. The following examples are due to Schank (1973):

> 16. The man went to the park with the girl.
>
> 17. The man went to the park with the stick.
>
> 18. The man went to the park with the statue.

While structurally similar, these sentences are interpreted differently. The girl in sentence (16) is an accompanying agent, the stick in (17) is an instrument, and the statue in (18) is a descriptor of a location. Similar patterns may be noted in possessive phrases. The house of the old man is the house that belongs to the old man, or the house in which the old man resides; a bouquet of flowers is a concatenation of flowers, and liqueur de menthe is a concoction of which mint is a major ingredient. The variety of possible cases is, of course, endless.

All cases noted are telling. They show that the semantic interpretation of coupled words is not a simple linear function of the composition between them. To understand the meaning of a phrasal composition one has to know what relationships may obtain between the entities denoted by the words of which the phrase is composed. Thus, in order to understand the meaning of the composition one already has to know the manner in which its constituents may be composed. In other words, the meaning of the phrasal composition is not determined through a well-defined function of the meanings of its lexical constituents. Rather, each composition presents a wholistic *Gestalt* whose interpretation is determined by the particular constituents. It might be said that the words with which a word is being conjoined serve as a context for that word. Just as they vary with context, the meanings of words vary with the words with which they are conjoined. And in both cases, the variation is unbounded and meaning cannot be specified beforehand in any determinate manner.

Translation

That the meaning of words is context-dependent and that it cannot be fully characterized by determinate, well-structured semantic representations is also indicated by cross-language phenomena. If meaning could be fixed in such a fashion then translation should be rather simple – it would involve the mere change of one overt expression of the underlying semantic representation for another. That translation is far from being a simple matter is, of course, well known. Two examples, drawn from literature, emphasize the contribution of context in this regard.

The first is taken from Borges' story 'Pierre Menard, author of the Quixote' (Borges, 1970). Pierre Menard, Borges' fictional hero, lived in the first part of our century and set himself to write Don Quixote. Borges recounts:

Cervantes's text and Menard's are verbally identical, but the second is almost infinitely richer. (More ambiguous, his detractors will say, but ambiguity is richness.)

It is a revelation to compare Menard's *Don Quixote* with Cervantes's. The latter, for example, wrote (part one, chapter nine):

... *Truth, whose mother is history, rival of time, depository of deeds, witness of the past, exemplar and adviser to the present, and the future's counsellor.*

Written in the seventeenth century, written by the 'lay genius' Cervantes, this enumeration is a mere rhetorical praise of history. Menard, on the other hand, writes:

... *Truth, whose mother is history, rival of time, depository of deeds, witness of the past, exemplar and adviser to the present, and the future's counsellor.*

History, the *mother* of truth: the idea is astounding. Menard, a contemporary of William James, does not define history as an inquiry into reality but as its origin. Historical truth, for him, is not what has happened; it is what we judge to have happened. The final phrases – *exemplar and adviser to the present, and the future's counsellor* – are brazenly pragmatic.

The contrast in style is also vivid. The archaic style of Menard – quite foreign, after all – suffers from a certain affectation. Not so that of his forerunner, who handles with ease the current Spanish of his time. (pp. 66–9)

The second excerpt is taken from Hofstadter's *Gödel, Escher, Bach* (1979):

Take a look at the first sentence of Dostoevsky's novel *Crime and Punishment* in Russian and then in a few different English translations. . . . The first sentence employs the street name 'S. Pereulok' . . . What is the meaning of this? A careful reader of Dostoevsky's work who knows Leningrad (which used to be called 'St. Petersburg' – or should I say 'Petrograd'?) can discover by doing some careful checking of the rest of the geography in the book . . . that the street must be 'Stoliarny Pereulok'. Dostoevsky probably wished to tell his story in a realistic way, yet not so realistically that people would take literally the addresses at which crimes and other events were supposed to have occurred. . . . First of all, should we keep the initial so as to reproduce the aura of semi-mystery which appears already in this first sentence of the book? (p. 379)

These excerpts present two opposing scenarios that complement each other to give one unified picture that underlines the paramount significance of context in translation. The excerpt from Borges indicates that given sufficient variation in context, meaning may be different even if the words employed in two texts are identical. That from Hofstadter shows that given sufficient variation in context, capturing the meaning expressed in two different contexts may require the use of words that are by no means the translation of each other. Here, again, the contribution of context overrides all standard semantic factors. On the one hand, the words may be identical and, given the context, the meanings totally different; on the other hand, the words may be totally different, yet given the difference in context, the meanings (in some sense) the same.

These problems are of course not confined to literature and to high forms of translation. Problems of this nature confront every person who speaks more than one language and are most often handled without the speaker being aware that a problem exists. The basic phenomenon is that the semantic fields of words in different languages are not fully overlapping. The dictionary tells us that the English 'chair' is the French 'chaise' and the Hebrew 'kisseh'. However, there are items that the English speaker would call 'chair' but the French speaker 'fauteuil' and the Hebrew speaker 'kursa' (for other examples, see de Saussure, 1916/1966; in particular pp. 115–17). Not only is the mapping of words across languages not one-to-one, it is not even many-to-one or one-to-many. Consider the patterns revealed by verbs in English and in Hebrew. The verb 'direct' would be translated as 'le-nahel' (as in direct an enterprise), 'le-khaven' (as in direct the course of events) and 'le-bayem' (as in direct a play). Moving in the opposite direction, the first of these Hebrew verbs would be rendered 'direct', 'guide', 'coordinate' and 'conduct', the second 'direct', 'guide' and 'tune', and the third 'direct', 'create a scenario' and 'fabricate'. Going back to English, 'guide' corresponds to 'le-khaven' and 'le-nahel', as noted, but 'coordinate' will introduce 'le-argen' and 'conduct' introduces 'le-natzeach'. The last item corresponds to 'conduct' when predicated of a musical conductor (in French and German, the cognate of 'direct' would be used); more often it translates as 'win' or 'gain' as well as 'defeat'. The moral of the story is that words in different languages do not map onto each other in a simple manner. Languages code and dissect the world differently, and each word usually has a distinct semantic profile, one which need not be associated with one single word in any other language. When translating one word it is necessary to consider many other words, and the more words enter into the picture still more words must be introduced. (In other words, when translating the words from one language to another one cannot confine oneself to a well-circumscribed, small lexical set, one that mathematicians would characterize as a class.) Eventually, the entire lexicons of the two languages should be consulted.[5] In sum, accounting for translation while maintaining the view that words are the expressions of underlying concepts would lead one to postulate as many distinct conceptual systems as the number of languages the polyglot knows. Since the number of languages people can master can be very large, this is far from appealing[6].

But in fact, the problem is encountered even within the realm of one language. No one has ever been presented with definitions that distinguish between words such as those noted. Yet, people do have definite preferences for the use of one word rather than another. The feat of choosing between different words that more or less 'mean the same thing' is nothing less than stunning. How does one actually make the choice? It is not that people who are better writers have at their disposal more refined definitions of words. Rather, good writers often juggle with different words: they try one and then another. It is as if different words bring along different rhythms, a different music. When the sentence is composed in one way, it sings or dances differently from when it is composed in another, and one verbal melody sounds better than another, it feels right, it is more in tune. Furthermore, just as different words may be likened to different notes, so different languages may be likened to different musical instruments.[7] All instruments play the same tune, yet how different they are! The difference is due not to the tones themselves, but to the overtones. Likewise, words and their meanings: technically exact translation, as dictated by dictionary definitions, and in a manner not affected by the context that the entire text defines, would be like having music without overtones. The words would be there, but the meaning – like the music – would be totally gone. I shall return to these issues in Chapter 4, when I discuss the medium of expression. (For further discussion see Steiner, 1975.)

Labelling

The variety of semantic relations between words and the meanings associated with them need not be confined to the relationship between words and covert mental entities such as concepts and intentions. Patterns (and problems) analogous to those above are also met in the relationship between words and things, for both appear overtly as concrete entities in the real world.

Consider the domain of labelling (see Shanon, 1980), i.e., the association of a written tag with a physical object. In examples (19)–(24), those marked (a) describe labelling situations and those marked (b) specify the manner in which they are usually interpreted.

> 19a. In a scientific conference, the label 'Prof. Cohen' is attached with a pin to a shirt worn by a man.
> 19b. The man wearing the shirt is Prof. Cohen.

> 20a. A plate with the words 'Prof. Cohen' is attached to a door.
> 20b. Prof. Cohen is the name of the person usually occupying the office to which one enters by that door. It is not the name of the door itself, nor is it clear that Prof. Cohen is presently in the office.

> 21a. An envelope is inscribed in its centre with the words 'Prof. Cohen'.
> 21b. Prof. Cohen is the addressee of the letter placed in the envelope.

> 22a. An envelope is inscribed in its upper left–hand corner with the words 'Prof. Cohen'.
> 22b. Prof. Cohen is the sender of the letter placed in the envelope.

> 23a. In a warehouse, a mattress is marked in ink 'Prof. Cohen'.
> 23b. Prof. Cohen is the person who purchased the mattress.

> 24a. In a warehouse, a mattress is marked in blue paint 'Prof. Cohen'.
> 24b. Prof. Cohen is the brand name of the mattress.

The variety of labelling is enormous, and these exemplify only some of its manifestations. They indicate that interpretation of the label is determined by the interaction of various factors. The content of the label is one of these but definitely not the only one; others include physical attributes of the label (e.g. its size, style, shape, colour), the manner in which it is attached to the object (e.g. the permanence of the attachment, its degree of fixation), and the context in which the labelling occurs (e.g. location, time, social and cultural environment). The multitude and open-endedness of these factors and their interactions suggest that the relation between labels and associated entities cannot be characterized by any list of independently defined features computed in an algorithmic fashion. Rather, interpretation of the label calls for consideration of the entire context.

Labels need not be confined to nominals or referring expressions; at times labels consist of verb phrases specifying procedures or calling for action. The following contrasting pair exemplifies the role of labels as determinants of human action; it also shows how crucial the interaction is between the different features of the labelling as instantiated in a particular context:

25. Someone is driving. He passes a huge painted sign reading 'Coca Cola'. He does not slow down and look for a bottle of coke.

26. Someone is driving. She passes a small sign inscribed 'fresh mushrooms'. She slows down and looks for a person selling mushrooms.

This also shows that one does not first determine that an object is a label and then compute an interpretation for it. Rather, determination and interpretation are intertwined, and both require the overall evaluation of the situation.

The great affinity between the patterns of labelling and those encountered in more standard semantic phenomena suggests that these substantive cognitive issues are not confined to the domain of covert psychology.

Prototypes

Given that the discussion so far has centred on featural characterization of meaning, the generality of the critique of semantic representations may be questioned. A prime example of a representation which is not defined by features is the prototype (cf. Wittgenstein, 1953; Rosch, 1978), which raises issues worthy of separate discussion (for insightful critiques see Osherson and Smith, 1981; Armstrong *et al.*, 1983; Lakoff, 1987a, b). I confine myself to pointing out why the case of prototypes does not detract from the generality of this critique of semantic representation.

First, while featural representations are not the only possible kind of representation of meaning, they define perhaps the most important kind of semantic representation in the literature.

Second, as far as the present issues of definition and context are concerned prototypes just push the problem one level down. In essence, prototypes are fuzzy areas in a multi-dimensional semantic space. This area may be ill-defined but the dimensions that generate the space are not. In fact, the definition of the space is very much like the definition of features. The prototypical definition of words and concepts discards the commitment to features for each particular item, but not the precise definitions of the dimensions that span the entire family of items in the semantic domain in question. The contextual problems noted here apply to any set of fixed, well-defined specifications of underlying stored representations. In this respect, the distinction between features of words or concepts and dimensions of semantic domains is immaterial. Indeed, not all the arguments marshalled above are dependent on the postulation of features as such. The context-dependence of meaning and its consequent openness hold against any fixed specification of meaning. In particular, the phenomena associated with contextual expressions and misusages indicate that meaning is generated in context, not retrieved from any underlying representation, whatever its particular form.

Third, the effects commonly associated with prototypes may not be due to representational structures at all. As argued by Lakoff (1987b), these effects may be due either to processes applied to structures which are themselves not prototypes, or to the confluence of other factors. Thus, it appears that patterns which normally serve as the basis for the postulation of prototypes can be accounted for without recourse to this postulation. As pointed out by Medin and Schaffer (1978) and by McClelland and Rumelhart (1986b), a sensitive enough system may reflect all patterns usually associated with prototypes by recording all the relevant exemplars only. Obviously, such an exemplar-based account is more parsimonious than that based on prototypes.

An interim summary

The foregoing discussion indicated that the meanings of words cannot be defined by means of a given set of terms or distinctions. This was taken to imply that semantic representations of words must be either incomplete, hopelessly cumbersome, or ultimately uninformative. Contextual variations subsequently indicated that the recourse to series of subdefinitions will not be of any help, for the application of these subdefinitions may itself be context-dependent. Polysemy presents further problems of subcategorization, and indicates that this strategy obscures some basic patterns of language. With contextual expressions the contribution of context is accentuated: meaning in context is not only varied, it is novel. For both substantive and methodological considerations such novelty implies that no fixed mental entities – even undefined ones – can represent word meaning. Misusages of language indicate that the contribution of context may be so great that it can counter, and override, any semantic consideration. Throughout the discussion it was noted that the determinants of meaning are confined neither to language nor to the internal domain, but also pertain to the external world. I now turn to the consideration of people's knowledge of the world.

Knowledge of the world

Since representational models are defined in a manner very similar to language, and since they assume that by and large the semantics of natural language captures people's knowledge of the world, it follows that the foregoing critique of RCVM with respect to semantic-linguistic issues is *ipso facto* a critique of its viability as an account of people's knowledge of the world in general. Indeed, all the problems noted above pertain to meaning both as it is employed in the public domain, as in verbal discourse, and in the private one, as in mentation and reasoning. As I draw towards the end of this critical discussion of context, let me turn to a focal consideration of contextual problems as they are encountered in people's knowledge of the world. Given the linguistic bias of RCVM, even here language will not be totally outside the picture.

One of the most influential representational models for the characterization of people's general knowledge of the world is Schank's script (Schank, 1972). This has had much influence not only in the domain of artificial intelligence (where it originated) and in cognitive psychology, but also in social psychology (see Schank and Abelson, 1977). A much quoted example of the script model pertains to people's knowledge about how to behave in restaurants. It is a paradigmatic manifestation of the spirit of RCVM. One facet of people's behaviour – namely, going to restaurants and doing whatever is necessary and proper in them – is noted. It is taken for granted that this is achieved by virtue of people's having knowledge about restaurants stored in their minds. Here is how Schank (1972: 424) described it:

> Script: restaurant
> Roles: customer; waitress; chef; cashier
> Scene 1 – entering
> PTRANS–go into restaurant
> MBUILD–find table
> PTRANS–go to table
> MOVE–sit down
> Scene 2 – ordering
> ATRANS–receive menu
> MTRANS–read menu
> MBUILD–decide what self wants
> MTRANS–order to waitress
> Scene 3 – eating
> ATRANS–receive food
> INGEST–food
> Scene 4 – exiting
> MTRANS–ask for check
> ATRANS–receive check
> ATRANS–give tip to waitress
> PTRANS–go to cashier

> ATRANS–give money to cashier
> PTRANS–go out of restaurant

Things, however, are not so simple. How does one know how to match the roles in the script to people in the world? Are there different scripts for each of the role players? And what if the waitress is actually a waiter? (Thus, the script has to be appended with heuristics on what to do in case the situation in the world does not match the conditions specified in the script.) And what if there is neither waitress nor waiter (as in a cafeteria)? And if one does not receive a menu, or if there is actually no menu at all? Or if one has to pay before one starts eating? (Thus, the sequence of scenes and acts in the script cannot be fixed.) And what if just as you sit down the waiter comes and asks you if you would care for some drinks? (The script is not complete then.) And what if the waiter was the worst possible – would you tip him? And besides: what is a tip? How much tip should one leave? (Recall, in different countries and in different types of restaurants the rules of tipping vary.)

In response to some such objections Schank proposed the addition of general rules for dealing with the unexpected (Schank and Abelson, 1977). But, as pointed out by Dreyfus (1981), appreciating what is unexpected or non-standard already requires knowledge and understanding of the situation. The list of *ad hoc* solutions will never be complete, nor does it capture what is essential and interesting about human behaviour.

The whole point about scripts was that they specified all the information needed for the generation of behaviour. This, it appears, cannot be done. On the one hand, they can never be complete. On the other hand, to use the script-based knowledge in real situations one has to be able to accommodate the specifications in the script to the unbounded variations in the world – to add to and subtract from them, to change and modify them. Since the ability to make these accommodations cannot be specified, one has to leave room for knowledge which is not script-based. Given, however, that the domain of application of this knowledge is not fundamentally different from that of the original domain that scripts are supposed to account for, it follows that one might as well dispense with scripts altogether. In other words, if the accommodation can be achieved without scripts, then so can all behaviour.

Not only the application of the script, but also its very definition is problematic. As pointed out by Dreyfus (1981), neither the whole script nor even the basic, so-called primitives of which it is composed can be defined outside the context. The problems are, in effect, exactly those encountered with semantic primitives in the definition of word meaning and in conjunction with polysemy and contextual expressions, so I will not repeat them here.

A related problem has to do with the notion of fact. The specification of knowledge in the manner of scripts presupposes that knowledge is constituted of well-defined, isolated facts that combine into large data-structures. But, apparently, such atomic, context-free pieces of knowledge do not exist. Consider Dreyfus' (1981) comments on people's knowledge of chairs:

This ability presupposes a repertoire of bodily skills which may well be indefinitely large, since there seems to be an indefinitely large variety of chairs and of successful (graceful, comfortable, secure, poised, etc.) ways to sit on them. Moreover, understanding chairs also includes social skills such as being able to sit appropriately (sedately, demurely, naturally, casually, sloppily, provocatively, etc.) at dinners, interviews, desk jobs, lectures, auditions, concerts (intimate enough for there to be chairs rather than seats), and in waiting rooms, living rooms, bedrooms, courts, libraries, and bars (of the sort sporting chairs, not stools). (p. 184)

As Dreyfus points out, the situation is even more complex, hence even more problematic as far as the representational account is concerned. Not only does each 'fact' relate to many others, but the determination of which facts are related to which is itself context-dependent. Indeed, part and parcel of knowing how to deal with a situation is to know which 'facts' are relevant and which are not.

A similar analysis is given by Searle (1983) with regard to the simple act of opening a refrigerator:

Think of what is necessary to go to the refrigerator and get a bottle of cold beer to drink. The biological and cultural resources that I must bring to bear on this task, even to form the intention to perform the task, are (considered in a certain light) truly staggering. But without these resources I could not form the intention at all: standing, walking, opening and closing doors, manipulating bottles, glass, refrigerators, opening, pouring and drinking. (p. 143)

On the basis of observations like these Searle arrives at the notion of the background,[8] the set of non-representational mental capacities that enable all representing to take place. While Searle introduced this notion in conjunction with knowledge of the world, his observations are pertinent to language as well. As he noted, just as the background is needed for action in the world, so it is needed for the understanding of language; indeed, for context-dependent expressions of the very kind considered in this chapter. As he further notes, the representationalist confronted with the information associated with the background may respond by phrasing it in semantic-representational terms and incorporating it within the putative representational data-base. But, for any information to be phrased in this manner, still more background will have to be postulated. I shall return to a further examination of knowledge in Chapter 22, where an even more radical criticism of the representational account of knowledge will be marshalled.

Personal knowledge

Throughout the foregoing discussion I talked of cognitive agents in general: the semantics and pragmatics of natural language, the behaviour of speakers and of hearers, people's knowledge of the world. But, of course, in reality only individual agents exist, only individual persons speak, think, know. The generalization of knowledge across individuals presents a further problem for RCVM.

The problem is a direct extension of those problems discussed above. I noted that both the semantics of language and knowledge of the world are sensitive to context and dependent on it. Each of us, however, lives in a different context, one which is determined by the repertory of his or her beliefs, previous knowledge, interests and past history. Therefore, for each person, the meanings associated with each word or any other item of information may be different. The same word may receive different meanings not only in different contexts, but when used by different cognitive agents, which implies that there cannot be mental semantic structures specifying meaning in a universal manner. Hence, semantic entities cannot be invested with meaning through universal mappings from representational structures to semantic interpretations. It seems to me that while they might not always be explicit about it, all representational models assume the existence of such mappings.

The first to appreciate this problem was Wittgenstein (1953). He pointed out that just as different utterances of a word have different meanings that cannot be fixed by a given semantic representation, so the different occurrences of thoughts exhibit contextual variation and novelty that defy their characterization by the same cross–situational concept. A similar assessment is at the heart of Putnam's theory of meaning (Putnam, 1975b, 1988). Showing that the meaning of terms depends on the entire matrix of beliefs, both personal and communal, in which they are embedded, Putnam concludes that identity of terms is not necessarily a criterion for identity of senses.

In psychology, pertinent observations were made by Kolers and Smythe (1984) who differentiate between two types of symbol: consensual and personal. Consensual symbols (e.g. marks on paper, photographs) are encountered in the public domain whereas personal ones are confined to the individual's private domain. Mental representations are, by this terminology, personal symbols and as such 'exist only for the person experiencing them, and cannot be subjected to scrutiny in the way that a piece of paper, a magnetic tape, or other inscription in a physical medium can' (p. 299). The person in question has privileged access to these symbols and unique authority with regard to their interpretation. There is no sense in talking about these symbols outside the context of the cognitive agent's belief system, and any characterization of them in terms of public representations is totally misleading. Furthermore, since no two situations are identical, the personal symbols have to be open to unbounded use and interpretation; in other words, they cannot be characterized by means of any fixed, well-defined coding system. Observations along this line were also made by Schlesinger (1986).

Positive considerations

So far context has been regarded primarily as a 'negative' factor, one that introduces complications and so makes the modelling of mind more difficult. However, context may be seen positively – as a factor that facilitates the workings of mind and as far as the cognitive system is concerned, is highly beneficial.

Clearly, this is true for language. If all pertinent semantic information had to be mentally specified, language would not be possible at all. Language is salvaged by being incomplete. Polysemy is a clear attestation to this: it allows the use of the same word in different contexts and thus endows language with indispensable flexibility. In particular, existing words may be employed in a variety of contexts, including ones in which they have never been used before. If words were not inherently polysemous, language could not accommodate the unbounded and unforeseen variety of contexts. Barring polysemy, each different context would require the coinage of a new word, and eventually the number of words would become totally unmanageable (for further discussion see Schlesinger, 1986).

Being context-dependent, words may be likened to tools in that on different occasions they may be used in different manners, and the manner is not fully specified (or even known) before the actual execution of tasks. It need not be, because the speaker of language (as well as its hearer) can rely on the context. Remarkably, the reliance on context is so ingrained that one is usually not even aware of it. Note, for instance, that speakers of language are generally not aware of the metaphoricity and pervasive polysemy of words.

The same holds for knowledge in general. Given that it is impossible to specify all the information about all the possible scenarios in the world, it is crucial to make use of as much help as one can get from the world *in situ* at the time of performance. Were cognitive agents required to know all there is to know about any performance before they actually execute it, behaviour would be impossible. In other words, the knowledge that is assumably manifested by people's behaviour cannot be known. The way out of this seeming impasse is provided by context. Not all the information necessary for the execution of a task may be known by the cognitive agent, but much of it may be found there, in the context in which one acts.

The crucial reliance of knowledge of the world on context was especially noted in the works of existential and phenomenological philosophers. Specifically, it is in line with the notion of throwness advocated by Heidegger (1962) and Sartre (1957), as well as with the view of behaving agents as immersed in the world, both physical and social, propounded by Merleau-Ponty (1962) and Gadamer (1975).

Various empirical findings corroborate these theoretical claims. Consider memory and the phenomenon of *encoding specificity*. As shown by Tulving and Thompson (1973), the retrieval of information from memory is sensitive to the particular contingencies of context in which the information was first acquired. When these are changed, memory is significantly hampered. Experiments demonstrated that the more similar the context of testing is to the context in which the tested information was acquired, the higher is subjects' level of recall (see Smith, 1982; Bekerian and Bowers, 1983). What is suggested here is that not only is information sensitive to context, its very definition is dependent on it.

A personal anecdote highlights the embedding of memory in context and the crucial facilitatory contribution context makes to remembering. It concerns a trip I took to Hong Kong, but there is nothing specifically Hong-Kongian (or Chinese) about it. Having taken the Hong Kong underground trains several (not many) times, I knew that coming to the station Admirality, Tsim Sah Tsui would follow and then Jordan. In practically no time I also knew that red banknotes are of one denomination and green notes are of another. Opening my wallet, I did not have to look at the numbers on the notes; I saw the colour and I knew. And then, leaving Hong Kong all this knowledge dissipated. After a couple of hours' flight, I was in Sydney, Australia. There were new stations and new banknotes, and all the Hong Kong knowledge disappeared.

I can also recount the converse case, that of failure to remember when being out of context. I was in Australia, and I was putting my wallet in order. I went over the many pieces of paper that had accumulated there and stumbled upon what I eventually realized to be a train ticket for the Princeton–New York line. That it had taken me quite some time to identify this piece of paper was striking. One month before, this ticket was part of my routine – I was using it at least once a week.

Together, these observations indicate that like meaning, remembering is a function of the total set of experiences to which the pertinent information belongs and in which it is embedded. Like meaning, knowledge and memory cannot be specified out of context. Since knowledge and memory are the basis for all cognitive functioning, by implication, the assessment is true of all cognitive activity. For further argumentation in this vein, see Garner (1974), Bransford *et al.* and Jenkins (1977).

Notes

1. I am aware that not all contemporary historians of science will agree with this classical albeit perhaps simplistic presentation of Ptolemaic astronomy, but what is of interest to me here is the basic conceptual scheme, not history as such.
2. The example is changed somewhat due to the fact that English (unlike French, in which the example was originally phrased) has different pronouns for animate and inanimate objects.
3. It could be argued that contextual expressions reflect morphological non–specificity. As attested by these examples, in English the same word can serve for different parts of speech; this characteristic affords flexibility and might therefore be the prime contributor to novelty exhibited by contextual expressions in English. But, although all the investigations of contextual expressions in the literature are in English, this counter-argument is not warranted. An unpublished research I have conducted in Hebrew, a language with an elaborate morphological system, indicates that the semantic flexibility of words does not depend on the morphological non-specificity of English. Speakers of Hebrew also manifest novel production and comprehension of contextual expressions. Their behaviour is particularly interesting because the

novel usages involve the coinage of new words, a process that involves non-trivial morphophonemic processing.

4. I have even heard the phrase 'Do you have a pencil and a pen?' being uttered and functioning as a speech act.

5. Since different languages are embedded in different cultures, even this is bound to be problematic.

6. Incidentally, all this implies that one cannot separate the knowledge of individual words from one's knowledge of the language at large. Thus, the totality of the words of a language may be regarded as defining a context in which the words of that language are used. In other words, just as knowing the meaning of a word is knowing how to use it in a given situation or context, knowing the meaning of a word is knowing its place in the matrix of all words in that language. Problems associated with translation highlight this, but the recourse to more than one language is not logically necessary. This state of affairs holds within any single language. Monolinguals, however, are less likely to be aware of these phenomena than polyglots.

7. This analogy is based on comments made by Shulamit Har-Even, an Israeli writer and translator, in a colloquium on artistic translation in Jerusalem in 1987.

8. As pointed out by Dreyfus (1981), this notion originated in the philosophies of Husserl and Heidegger; see also Winograd and Flores (1986).

3   *The two-stage strategy*

[Metaphor] is perhaps one of man's most fruitful potentialities. Its efficacy
verges on magic, and it seems a tool for creation which God forgot inside one
of his creatures when He made him.

Ortega y Gasset

To the argument from context one can respond as follows. Admittedly, the meaning
of verbal expressions is context-dependent; therefore, well-structured, fixed
semantic representations may, indeed, be unsuitable for accounting for the variation
of meaning with context. This, however, need not imply that semantic
representations should be altogether discarded. They might still be suitable by way
of accounting for expressions whose meaning is not affected by context. These
context-free expressions presumably constitute the standard case, in which words
are employed and interpreted in their literal readings. It is only when the standard,
literal readings do not apply that semantic representations are found to be lacking
and context has to be taken into consideration. In order to compensate for this lack
and to account fully for the meaning of such non-standard expressions, additions
and modifications to the representational apparatus have to be made. With these,
the standard meanings specified in the stored semantic representations are changed
so that the contextual effects can be accommodated.

By this rationale, then, the characterization of the meaning of non-standard
expressions is achieved through two components. The first specifies the standard
meanings of linguistic expressions; it consists of stored semantic representations
and is context-free. The second is invoked only when the meanings associated with
linguistic expressions are not standard. In these cases, context has to be taken into
consideration and the given semantic representations have to be amended with
context-sensitive operations. The operations apply to the representations and
change the meaning of the expressions so that they are in line with the context.

This characterization implies that whereas standard expressions are accounted
for by one component – the standard representational one – non-standard
expressions are accounted for by two components – the representational one and
the transformational one appended to it. This is the case both in the atemporal
theoretical characterization of meaning and in the modelling of the psychological
processes employed in the production of verbal expressions and in their
comprehension. In the latter, procedural case the two-componential scheme

manifests itself in a two-stage processing model. Two-stage models have been proposed by many investigators, both linguists and philosophers studying the semantics of natural language and psychologists modelling language production and comprehension; references are given below, when the pertinent models are surveyed.

The following discussion shows that the two-stage model is not appropriate. The arguments marshalled against it will be based on four types of consideration: conceptual and methodological, procedural, developmental, and cultural. These arguments will focus on two kinds of non-standard linguistic expressions – metaphors and speech acts. The discussion will close with further supporting data pertaining to the non-verbal domain.

Conceptual and methodological considerations

At first glance, the two-stage account seems to be parsimonious. Intuitively, context-sensitive operations seem to be more complex than context-free ones. *Prima facie*, then, the account has the advantage of sparing the necessity of invoking expensive means when one can do with relatively cheap ones. It offers a simple characterization in the regular and presumably by far more frequent cases, and introduces complexity only in the special, non-regular cases. For this appraisal of parsimony to be valid, however, three conditions must be met. First, the distinction between literal and non-literal usages of language should be clear-cut. Second, the division between the context-free and the context-dependent cases should likewise be well demarcated; in fact, this division should exactly mirror the distinction between the literal and the non-literal. Third, the literal, context-free cases should be the standard and by far more frequent ones. If, however, these conditions are not met then the appraisal of parsimony reverses itself. Specifically, if recourse to context is standard and if there are no clear demarcation lines between what are supposed to be standard and non-standard cases, then it is more advantageous to have a unified characterization and to apply the more general, context-sensitive considerations or processes throughout.

Metaphor

Let me start with metaphor. By the two-stage model, the literal processing of verbal material is a first, mandatory stage. First, listeners must always attempt a literal interpretation of given expressions; only when this fails is a metaphorical interpretation invoked. Thus, whereas literal language requires one stage of processing, metaphorical language requires two. Accounts along these lines have been presented, for instance, by Kintsch (1974) and Searle (1979). Such accounts imply that metaphors are deviant usages of language, ones that violate semantic restrictions or are simply false (cf. Chomsky, 1965; Matthews, 1971; Lowenberg,

1975; Davidson, 1978). Furthermore, the two-stage model dictates that the processing of metaphorical language require more resources than that of literal language, and that developmentally metaphorical language should be a later accomplishment than non-metaphorical.

Before I start to evaluate the two-stage model, let me emphasize that the definition of what is metaphorical itself calls for consideration. Indeed, the settling of the substantive issues at hand is directly affected by the stance – implicit or explicit – taken on the definitional issue. The major distinction of relevance is between a *strong* and a *weak* definition of metaphor. The strong definition labels a usage of language metaphorical only when the speaker knows the literal sense and is deliberately deviating from it; this he or she does on the basis of the detection of a similarity between two semantic domains. In other words, the strong definition assumes that for a metaphorical expression to be either produced or comprehended, two distinct, well-defined semantic domains must already be given. Further, it assumes that the metaphorical use of language presupposes the prior appreciation of these two domains and that metaphor is established through a mapping between them. (For details of how this mapping is conceived, see Chapter 5.) Thus, such a use implies that the speaker already knows the literal meaning of the words he or she utters, and means something different from what he or she says. The weak definition does not involve such presuppositions. It makes no assumption regarding the speaker's knowledge or purported motivation. Rather, it regards a use of language as metaphorical if an external observer deems it figurative or semantically multi-determined. For an expression to be so deemed it is not necessary that there be two (or more) priorly established semantic domains, nor is any reference to an already established literal meaning needed. In sum, according to the strong definition metaphor consists of a transformation of literal meaning defined by some mapping between two given semantic domains. According to the weak definition metaphor is a mere label marking a certain quality of expression or potentialities of intepretation. An external observer may define this quality by reference to a multi-dimensional semantic space, but this does not imply that the dimensions have independent prior existence, or that the production of metaphorical expressions is based in any actual manner on distinct, given semantic domains or pre-established meanings associated with them.

Evidently, these definitional distinctions are allied to the substantive issue that concerns us here. The strong definition assumes the recourse to distinct, well-defined cognitive and linguistic entities, hence (tautologically) it implies that metaphorical language presupposes the prior existence of fixed literal meaning; the weak definition does not make these assumptions. Thus, if the strong definition is adopted, the substantive issue is settled before the discussion begins: literal language is more basic, and consequently, the processing of metaphors should follow the two-stage model. Indeed, the way in which investigators appraise empirical data depends on the definition of metaphor that they adopt. Specifically, the data will be analyzed and interpreted differently according to whether one defines metaphorical meaning as presupposing two distinct literal notions or not.

As will be seen, this is especially pertinent to developmental data (for further discussion see Verbrugge, 1979).

Let me turn to the two-stage model and the specific assumptions associated with it and make two points. First, metaphorical language is not as rare a phenomenon as some analyses might lead one to think. Second, standard usages of language are not always literal and metaphorical usages are sometimes standard. For instance, the standard reading of expression (1) is not literal:

> 1. It is a miracle!

Moreover, whether a sentence is metaphorical or not may not always be decided independently of the context of its use. Thus, following Johnson (1980), consider (2):

> 2. All men are animals.

This sentence is literal when uttered by a biology teacher but metaphorical when uttered by a professor of ethics or an angry woman. In general, the attribution of literalness is context-dependent. Given a context, the evaluation of what is literal and what is non-literal may be totally opposite to the common evaluation of what is standard and non-standard. One might do better to characterize expressions as being in accordance with one's beliefs, world-view or line of interpretation rather than as literal. Within a context, particular readings may be characterized as standard or literal, but this cannot be done *a priori* without consideration of the context of use. (For further exposition, as well as more elaborate examples, see Fish 1980; for supporting empirical data, see Keysar, 1989.)

The problematic nature of the distinction between literal and metaphorical meaning is further indicated by this pair of sentences, presented by Rumelhart (1979):

> 3a. The policeman raised his hand and stopped the car.
> 3b. Superman raised his hand and stopped the car.

While these sentences may not be characterized as metaphorical, it is not at all clear which one of them defines the regular, literal case. If it is the sentence referring to the more common state of affairs it is (3a), whereas if it is the one referring to the more concrete activity it is (3b). The particular labelling, however, is not important. What is significant is that both sentences require the general consideration of context for their interpretation. Only on the basis of one's knowledge of policemen and of Superman can one understand what happened to the car in each case (see also Bransford and Franks, 1971; Anderson and Ortony, 1975).

Examples like these (and indeed, the entire discussion of contextual effects in Chapter 2) indicate that non-metaphorical usages of language are not free from contextual considerations. Therefore, the literal/non-literal distinction does not converge with the context-free/context-sensitive one, nor is recourse to contextual considerations encountered only in rare, specialized or deviant cases of language use.

On conceptual and methodological grounds the two-stage characterization of metaphor is therefore inadequate. Indeed, given that the distinction between literal and non-literal readings is not categorical, and since both involve the evaluation of context, then, as metaphorical interpretation defines the more general case, for considerations of parsimony one might as well say (with Lakoff and Johnson, 1980a; and Lakoff, 1987b) that all language is metaphorical.

Speech acts

An analogous state of affairs is encountered with speech acts. Usually, a distinction is made between two types of speech act – direct and indirect. Direct speech acts are 'the simplest cases of meaning in which the speaker utters a sentence and means exactly and literally what he says'; indirect speech acts are ones 'in which one illocutionary act is performed indirectly by way of performing another' (Searle, 1975). Thus, consider expression (4) as it is uttered at a dinner table:

4. Can you pass the salt?

Interpreted directly, (4) is a question, and the answer to it is either 'yes' or 'no'. Usually, however, the expression is indirectly interpreted as a request and the appropriate response to it is to pass the salt. The standard analysis of this phenomenon follows the two-stage pattern: the direct reading is assumed as basic and the indirect reading is derived from it. Specifically, given that the former is found not to be appropriate, the latter is generated through operations which refer to contextual considerations. The analysis is based on Grice's (1975) theory of conversation and further developments to it introduced by Searle (1975). This is founded on the *principle of cooperation*. According to this principle, participants in conversations are maximally cooperative and say only what is pertinent. Uttered at the dinner table and interpreted as a question, (4) constitutes a violation of this principle. The speaker knows that the hearer can, in fact, pass the salt, and the hearer knows that he or she does. When the speaker utters (4), he or she seems not to be abiding by the assumed conversational contract. Rather than draw this undesirable conclusion, the hearer concludes that the utterance does not mean what it appears to, and interprets it in an indirect fashion, as a request. This is achieved by means of a context-sensitive meaning-changing operation, *conversational implicature*.

While the two-stage analysis has been the basis for both theoretical linguistic analysis (Gordon and Lakoff, 1971) and empirically based psychological modelling (Clark and Lucy, 1975), it seems to me conceptually flawed. To conclude that the cooperative principle is violated the hearer has to arrive at a global interpretation of the context. In this example, he or she would have to realize that the participants in the conversation are engaged in eating behaviour, that there is a salt shaker which is closer to the hearer than to the speaker, his or her interlocutor, and that the speaker is in need of it. If, however, the hearer appreciates all this, he or she already understands that the utterance is a request, not a question. In other words, the mechanism that is said to detect the violation of the conversational cooperativeness is the very one which allows for the immediate comprehension of the so-called indirect reading of the speech act in question. But then, the understanding of the so-called indirect speech acts does not depend on that of the so-called direct ones; the decipherment of the direct meaning and the employment of the conversational implicature are, therefore, both superfluous. Thus, not only is the indirect reading not dependent on a direct one (cf. Clark, 1979) but, in fact, the former, pragmatic reading is the one which is primary. (For a more detailed exposition, see Shanon, 1987a; see also Winograd, 1980.)

Procedural considerations

In the two-stage model, the processing of standard meaning is a first, mandatory stage in that of non-standard meaning. Therefore, the model implies that the processing of non-standard expressions should always require more time and resources than that of the standard ones. Empirical data suggest, however, that this is not the case. These data include findings obtained in experiments conducted with normal subjects, patterns drawn from the behaviour of brain-damaged patients, and observations on the workings of the unconscious. A survey of such data follows; again, the discussion begins with the consideration of metaphorical expressions and then turns to indirect speech acts.

Metaphor

A basic finding is that of Glucksberg et al. (1982) who discovered that sentences take longer to be judged as literally false when they have readily interpretable non-literal meanings. From this, they concluded that metaphoric meaning cannot be ignored and that its processing is automatic and not dependent on literal meaning. Indeed, whereas various researchers have discovered that in isolation metaphorical sentences took longer to be processed than literal ones, when context was supplied this was no longer the case (see Ortony et al., 1978; Kemper, 1981; Inhoff et al., 1984). Likewise, Harris and his associates (Harris, 1976; Harris et al., 1980) found that the time it took subjects to read poetic metaphors and paraphrase their meaning was not significantly longer than that for the comparable task with literal statements, and Pollio et al. (1984) found that metaphors required no extra time to be classified.

Also holding against the characterization of metaphoric interpretations as derivative from literal ones are microgenetic studies of the order of processing in short periods of time (Werner, 1948; Flavell and Draguns, 1957). These findings suggest that the metaphorical, multi-faceted and fuzzy aspects of meaning are appreciated before the literal, fixed and well-defined ones. Related to these (although not directly bearing on metaphorical expressions) are findings by

Kunst-Wilson and Zajonc (1980; for a general review see Zajonc, 1980) that the overall affective and evaluative characteristics of stimuli may be perceived even without recognizing what these stimuli are (see also Marcel, 1983a, 1983b).

Speech acts

Analogous findings are encountered with speech acts. Examining sentence comprehension in context, Clark (1979) found that the comprehension of indirect speech acts need not require more time than that of the corresponding direct ones. Likewise, Gibbs (1979) discovered that, in isolation, indirect readings require more time to comprehend than direct ones, but in context this was not the case. In another study, Gibbs (1983) tested people as they judged whether targets were meaningful English sentences. The sentences were presented after stories whose last sentence imposed either a direct or an indirect reading. Reaction-time measurements indicated that prior readings of the indirect requests facilitated responses to targets associated with indirect readings. but not with direct readings. This pattern of results suggests that in comprehending indirect expressions subjects do not automatically compute the corresponding literal meanings. (For a general survey of Gibbs' work as well as further theoretical arguments, see Gibbs, 1984.)

Neuropsychological considerations

There are also pathological observations of relevance. In aphasic patients, dysfunctions in the comprehension of literal linguistic material and of metaphorical material are associated with different organic impairments (for a general review, see Myers, 1986). Patients with left-hemisphere damage can recover metaphorical readings but fail in the understanding of literal ones. By contrast, patients with right-hemisphere damage tend to interpret linguistic stimuli literally and manifest significant impairment in the interpretation of metaphors and idioms (see Winner and Gardner, 1977, 1979; Gardner and Winner, 1978). Further, these patients tend to disregard context and have difficulty grasping the overall structure of texts as well as the humorous aspects of language (see Gardner *et al.*, 1975, 1983; Wapner *et al.*, 1981). The differential patterns of linguistic impairment also indicate a dissociation between the referential and affective aspects of word meaning: patients with left-hemisphere damage have difficulties with the former but not with the latter, whereas in patients with right-hemisphere damage the converse is the case (see Brownell *et al.*, 1984). Together, these neuropathological observations present further evidence that comprehension of metaphor is not dependent on the determination of literal meaning. Significantly, the hemisphere which is sensitive to metaphor is not the left, language-dominant one, but the right, which is linguistically more primitive (see also Kennedy-Hewitt, 1979; Ross, 1983; Brownell *et al.*, 1991).

Developmental observations

If metaphorical expressions and non-direct speech acts were derived from literal expressions and direct speech acts respectively, then the latter would also precede the former in ontogenetic development. The following observations suggest that this is not the case.

While, at first glance, whether young children can produce and comprehend metaphorical language seems to be a straightforward question of fact, the issue is far from simple. Indeed, the literature does not present a single, unanimous stance on it. Until recently the question of empirical fact was the basis of serious contention (see Clark, 1983), but it now appears that the disagreement involves methodological problems. When appropriate methodological care is taken, much of the disagreement subsides and it is conceded that very young children exhibit a rather remarkable use of metaphors. Given that the methodological considerations have substantive implications, it is worthwhile to specify them. Metaphorical language in young children is more likely to be detected when one studies production rather than comprehension. When producing language, children are on their own and their individual linguistic capabilities are observed. By contrast, comprehension tests may require cognitive and linguistic knowledge and skills extraneous to the issues under investigation and beyond the children's abilities. These may hinder children's performance on the test, hence their metaphorical comprehension will be artificially lowered. Difficulty with the contents of the material administered (e.g. full understanding of human emotions) and with the metalinguistic skills required for responding (e.g. paraphrasing) are such factors. By contrast, metaphorical language is more likely to be encountered when verbal behaviour is embedded in children's actual activities in the world. Indeed, the earliest instances of metaphor are predominantly associated with pretend actions in symbolic play (Winner, 1979; Winner *et al.*, 1980). Thus, when methodological precautions are taken it does, indeed, appear that very young children (of preschool age) exhibit metaphorical language (Winner *et al.*, 1979; Vosniadou *et al.*, 1984; Vosniadou, 1989). In fact, 3-year-olds tend to produce figurative language more often than children of any other age group until young adulthood (Gardner *et al.*, 1975; Pollio and Pickens, 1980).

For the two-stage model to be evaluated from a developmental point of view, however, it is not enough to show that children, even young children, produce and comprehend metaphors. The key question for my discussion is whether metaphorical language in the young child presupposes literal language or not. Only if the answer to this question is negative can the two-stage model be refuted. The literature presents conflicting positions. While all parties to the controversy agree that young children do exhibit metaphorical language, some (notably, Asch and Nerlove, 1960; Winner *et al.*, 1976, 1980; Cometa and Eson, 1978) still take the first steps of language to be literal, whereas others (Verbrugge, 1979; Vosniadou *et al.*, 1984; Vosniadou, 1989) maintain that metaphorical language does not developmentally presuppose literal language. The disagreement has to do with the very definition of metaphor. Indeed, it is here that the distinction between strong and weak definitions of metaphor is crucial. As indicated above, if the strong definition is adopted, the substantive issue is settled before the discussion begins: developmentally, literal language has to precede metaphorical. Thus, the resolution of this developmental issue involves more than the mere examination of empirical facts (for further discussion, see Verbrugge, 1979).

Given that the perspective associated with the strong definition presupposes what is in the context of this discussion the very issue of inquiry, let me consider a study conducted from the perspective of the weak definition. Vosniadou and Ortony (1983) asked children between the ages of 3 and 6 to complete sentences while giving them a choice between: (1) literal similarity between members of the same semantic category (e.g. *A river is like a lake*); (2) non-literal similarity between members of different semantic categories (e.g. *A river is like a snake*); and (3) anomaly (i.e., cases with no discernible similarity across different semantic categories; e.g. *A river is like a cat*). The 3-year-old children preferred the meaningful similes to the anomalies, but they did not exhibit preference for the literal over the non-literal ones. The investigators concluded that these results vitiate any developmental account which stipulates that metaphorical similarity requires the prior acquisition of literal similarity. They suggested that children start with an undifferentiated notion of similarity, which at about age 4 becomes differentiated into literal and non-literal. This differentiation is accompanied by an increase in children's knowledge of the world and eventually enables them to produce more abstract relational metaphors.

More recent work by Vosniadou (1989) points to a pattern noted in the framework of reaction-time studies – the facilitation of metaphorical capacity in context. Young children's reliance on context is critical: their metaphorical performance crucially involves an interaction with it. Consequently, any study conducted without the overall consideration of context is bound to present a biased picture, one which detracts from the child's metaphorical capability.

Taking a broader developmental perspective, it appears that whereas very young children tend to be very metaphorical, children in the 9–11 age group are more literal (see Pollio and Pickens, 1980), while with older children the use of metaphorical language again increases. This trend is interesting in two respects. First, it indicates that the use of literal language constitutes a particular stage of development, not a primitive state of affairs. Second, it marks a distinction between two stages of metaphorical expression. The early stage is primitive in that it is not differentiated and the distinction between the two semantic domains involved in the metaphor is neither defined nor conscious. By contrast, in the advanced stage of metaphorical expression the speaker knows that the metaphor constitutes a non-standard form of speech and relates two distinct semantic domains. These two stages correspond to the weak and strong senses of metaphor. Finally, further developmental progression marks yet another stage: the adult not only understands metaphor without context, but can artificially create a context of interpretation when being presented with a metaphorical expression. Some adult speakers – namely, poets (be they publicly acknowledged as such or not) – can even create new forms of non-standard usages of language. I shall return to this special capability later.

Speech acts

The examination of speech acts also suggests an overall developmental trend that counters the prediction of the two-stage account. Rather than pertaining to complex, non-standard patterns of behaviour that manifest themselves in the later stages of linguistic development, context-dependency appears to be primary and basic. Specifically, children's first utterances are rooted in action, and it is only with further development that they can divorce their utterances from the particular contexts of their use. Thus, it is observed that children first learn not the so-called literal meanings of utterances but rather their social or pragmatic meanings. Only gradually do the linguistic utterances gain what appears to be literal meaning, one exhibiting autonomy relative to the particular context of action.

Consistent with this view are observations regarding the development of word meaning. A good illustration was provided by Piaget (1962), who reports a child whose utterance 'dog' constituted a request to get any object that the child wanted from a particular balcony. In other words, the term indicated not particular referents but rather particular contexts of action defined by the child's perspective. Similarly, Shvachkin (cited in Bates, 1976) notes an early use of the term 'kitty' specifically associated with a particular context, in which the child would demand the return of a toy cat she had thrown from her crib; the child used the same word to demand the return of other thrown objects as well.

As for speech acts, Bates *et al.* (1979) found that directives are acquired earlier than assertives and that assertives first play the role of indirect requests. Furthermore, young children treat ambiguous directives as requests for action before they treat them as requests for information. (For empirical data supporting this general developmental picture see Bruner, 1975a; Gelman and Shatz, 1978; Shatz, 1978; Bates *et al.*, 1979; Pea, 1980). Likewise, Pea observed that the first meaning of negation is rejection; this is followed by self-prohibition, and only later is negation used to deny the truth of assertions.

In sum, the basic developmental trend is not one by which sensitivity to context is increased but rather one of *decontextualization*. This eventually enables the child to produce veritable symbolic expressions (for a comprehensive presentation of such a perspective see Werner and Kaplan, 1963; for more recent empirical evidence see Bruner, 1975b; Halliday, 1975; Bates, 1976, 1979; Greenfield and Smith, 1976; MacNamara, 1977; Snyder *et al.*, 1981).

Cultural considerations

The last line of argumentation against the two-stage characterization of so-called non-standard expressions of language is more speculative than the preceding ones. It bears not on the consideration of the verbal behaviour of the individual but rather on the linguistic expression of the culture as a whole. The cultural considerations have both synchronic aspects to do with the nature of artistic creation, and diachronic aspects to do with the historical development of culture.

Artistic creation

Metaphorical expressions as they manifest themselves in the arts are pertinent for several reasons. First, they are significant in being naturalistic; as such, they contrast with practically all usages of metaphor examined in the psychological literature, which are artificially constructed for laboratory testing. The naturalistic metaphors are likely to be richer, more complex, and not biased by prior theoretical conceptions that the scientist might have (for discussion see Lakoff and Turner, 1989; Goldblum, 1990). Second, the consideration of metaphorical expressions in the arts draws attention to the issue of production. Often, cognitive psychologists focus on the comprehension of metaphor, and ignore its other facet – production. This facet, however, is not only another major accomplishment of the human cognitive system that has to be investigated; it brings forth a question that is at the heart of our entire discussion: why are non-standard expressions employed at all?

Why does the poet employ metaphorical language? Why do people in general do so? In the cognitive-psychological literature, this fundamental question is seldom asked. Yet, if everything one knows is represented in one's mind, if knowing a language is tantamount to the expression in words of what one has in one's mind, and if the underlying representation is coded in a system of well-defined, well-formed semantic system, then *prima facie* there seems to be no reason for linguistic expressions which are not standard. Thus, the very existence of metaphors and indirect speech acts is a puzzle that RCVM cannot resolve. Indeed, if, as RCVM stipulates, metaphors involve extra cognitive resources, then the fact that they are being used must indicate that when using figurative language people can achieve what cannot be achieved with so-called standard, literal language. Or perhaps metaphors do not involve additional resources and if anything, are more basic and more simple than literal expressions. Above various indications have been noted that this is indeed the case. The historical considerations that follow further support this claim. In Chapter 5 we shall return to this topic and consider the more general ramifications of the alternative view just proposed.

Historical speculations

To draw analogies between ontogenetic development and cultural evolution is not uncommon. Such analogies can also be drawn with respect to language. A number of authors have argued that in its first historical stages human language could not have been direct and literal. While the arguments substantiating this claim are not scientific in any rigorous empirical sense, they are, I think, conceptually interesting. As will be apparent, some of them are similar to ones raised in the foregoing discussion, especially on language development.

The claim that metaphorical language historically preceded literal language appears in some of the earliest speculations in modern philosophy on the nature of language. Vico was of the opinion that 'the first language must have been formed in singing' (see Vico, 1948; and Haskell, 1987a). Similarly, Rousseau argued that 'As man's first motives for speaking were of the passions, his first expressions were tropes. Figurative language was the first to be born. Proper meaning was discovered last. At first only poetry was spoken' (see Rousseau, 1966; for further discussion, see Derrida, 1976). Similar ideas were suggested earlier, by the Gaon (genius) from Vilna, one of the prominent rabbis of the sixteenth century, when interpreting the biblical story of the Tower of Babel. In his interpretation, the one predeluvian language of the human species was akin to what we today would consider music. This view bears on the medium characteristics of language, and I shall return to it in the next chapter. (For related discussion, see Nietzsche, 1956.)

An especially insightful line of argument on the development of metaphorical language and against its reduction to literal language is presented by Barfield (1977). 'Literalness', Barfield claims, 'is a quality which some words have achieved in the course of their history; it is not a quality which the first words had.' The target of Barfield's critique is a model that, at first glance, seems to be the most straightforward possible. This model assumes that at the initial historical stage words had exclusive, literal meanings and referred to concrete, material objects. Progressively, concomitant figurative connotations emerged, the literal connotations diminished and the original, material meaning gave place to a non-material one. At the end of the process, this new meaning itself became literal. For example, the word 'spirit' (in the spiritual sense) first meant 'wind' and only by metaphorical extension coupled with a semantic shift did it end up having the literal, non-material meaning it has today.

Barfield attacks this model by examining the status of the figurative notion at the time before the appearance of the metaphorical expression. Two alternatives are considered. The first assumes that at that time, the figurative notion could be expressed literally. However, for this to be possible, people should have possessed other words with a non-material reference. How did those acquire their reference? If it was by metaphorical activity, before the appearance of metaphorical language still other words with figurative meaning would have to be assumed. Recursive argumentation, however, will drive this assumption *ad infinitum*. The second alternative assumes that the immaterial content was first conceived separately without the help of any verbal vehicle. There was the notion of the immaterial entity but no words for it. This, Barfield argues, is not tenable because understanding and symbolization are simultaneous and correlative. While it is feasible that growing awareness of that which today we mean by 'spirit' was inextricably linked with a new use of the word for wind, it is not possible that up to that moment the word for wind had been semantically aloof. If there was prior affinity between the concept 'wind' and the other immaterial concept 'spirit', the latter must have been originally framed without the aid of any symbol, and this does not seem to make sense. Taken together, the consideration of the two alternatives suggests that in its original state, primitive language must have blurred the distinction between the literal and the figurative. It was only with cultural progress that the distinction between the two crystallized.

While, admittedly, historical claims like these are speculative and not experimentally provable, there are none the less other, related considerations which lend them further plausibility. Thus, consider the relative prevalence of literary genres across cultures. Poetry is an ancient and ubiquitous mode of expression, prose is less prevalent, and seemingly banal journalistic and scientific writing is both recent and peculiar to a small minority of human cultures. If meaning is represented in the structured, well-defined manner suggested by RCVM, this fact is puzzling (see also Chapter 14).

In sum, I suggest that poetry is ancient and universal because the seemingly amorphous metaphorical language – not the presumably exact literal language – is the more direct expression of the workings of the human mind. The fact that human behaviour (and its interpretation) is multi-valued and multi-determined (Freud, 1900/1954) favours such a view. Nothing could do more injustice to the characterization of human expression than fixing it in single-valued, well-formed structures. Accounting for its multi-facetedness and ambiguity by means of several concurrent or alternating structures of this kind is artificial and can never be complete. More on this will be said in Chapter 5.

A look at other cultures

The foregoing discussion focused on non-standard expressions which are metaphorical. This is only natural given the subject domain of artistic and cultural creation. Yet, similar observations may be made with regard to speech acts. The distinction between the two types of expression is rather fuzzy, as is shown by the example of the witch-doctor or shaman engaged in the articulation of some incantation. Hearing the spell, a Western observer might scoff, dismissing this verbal expression as nonsense. More than anything, however, such an attitude attests to the limited and simplistic view of the observer, who views the incantation from a Western perspective, one which is confined to a literal reading of language. As a direct speech act which is interpreted in a literal fashion the spell may, indeed, be nonsensical. This, however, is not the way to view it. Rather than an assertion or even a dictation, the spell – like the dance which accompanies it and the various offerings which are being made – is an act. It is a constituent of a religious ritual that has to be performed in a particular fashion. As pointed out by Malinowsky (1948), the spell and the other facets of the ritual are not scientific manipulations in the Western sense. Rather, they are acts that bring together human beings and nature and give expression to their being the two participants in one integrated drama. That these acts are encountered in so-called primitive societies is not an accident. They are part and parcel of the basic human existential condition, one which maintains an organic link with the world, which Western society has unfortunately lost.

The organic link between humanity and the world permeates so-called primitive cultures and lies at the heart of both religion and myth. Consider what is perhaps the primordial form of religion – animism. Animism regards natural forces, objects and animals as agents having their own personalities. The sun is a brave, valiant warrior, the moon is a gentle, melancholic virgin, the deer in the valley are enchanted princes. Again, to view these characterizations in terms of the Western world-view would be to miss their point. When this world-view is embraced, the mythical categories lose all their force. At most, they may be regarded as original, interesting similes, but they are devoid of any power or spell. Their force is in their defining the way in which a culture views the world. The animistic figures of (again, so-called) primitive cultures are not analogies, they are the basic categories by which these cultures view the world. Unlike the categories assumed by Western science (and presupposed by RCVM), these are not couched in abstract, so-called literal concepts but rather are laden, from the start, with values and meanings. Animists are not lunatics; they do not mistake heavenly bodies and animals for people; rather, they adopt a unified world-view by which the physical world, the world of animals, and the world of human beings are all animated.

This contrast between the two world-views mirrors the conceptual contrast between the two definitions of metaphor introduced at the outset of this chapter. The Western view assumes the strong view of metaphor. It maintains that for there to be a metaphorical relationship, two distinct entities drawn from two different semantic domains must already be given; by this view, the metaphorical relationship consists of the drawing of a link between the two. The alternative view assumes the weak definition. By it, the figurative is primary, and metaphor need not presuppose distinct entities which are already given. Rather, the figurativeness of categories is intrinsic. What for the external observer seems to be the bringing together of two domains is actually, as far as human cognition is concerned, a basic state of affairs. What characterizes this state of affairs is that it is embedded in a framework that does not differentiate that which further activity – be it cultural or personal – eventually may differentiate. The analogy between this basic cultural state of affairs and the primary processes governing the workings of the individual's unconscious is, of course, not accidental. As pointed out by Freud in his later writings (Freud, 1950) and by so many scholars since, both are the manifestations of the same, basic nature of the human mind. The present critique maintains that the basic categories of cognitive-psychological theory should be in concordance with this state of affairs.

Actually, the founding of world-views on the figurative is not confined to primitive cultures. Every culture chooses some basic metaphors – root metaphors (Pepper, 1942) – by which it views the world. These categories may be quite abstract, but they are always invested with value and meaning. The Kabbalah, for instance, is a comprehensive system viewing all phenomena in terms of categories such as wisdom, justice and mercy. Again, these categories are not similes to which things are likened and to which they are being compared. Rather, they are the very fundaments of which the world – ontologically as well as epistemologically – is composed. As an epigraph by Moshe Kordovero, a sixteenth-century Jewish Kabbalist, says: 'It is not that there are ten spheres because man has ten fingers, but rather the converse, man has ten fingers because there are ten spheres.'

Western culture (and with it, modern science and also RCVM) has chosen as its root metaphors entities which are atomistic, devoid of meaning. That these entities are impoverished does not mean that they do not involve a cultural choice; they too are root metaphors. As pointed out by Atlan (1986), Western categories may be advantageous for some purposes (e.g. the development of technology), but have no intrinsic epistemic superiority.

Non-verbal phenomena

While, technically speaking, metaphorical expression pertains to the domain of language, the issues I have considered bear on phenomena not confined to this domain. Consideration of these will not only provide further support to some of the appraisals made in the foregoing discussion, but will also lay the foundations for the discussion of broader issues in Part II of this book, where alternative pictures of mind are entertained.

The non-verbal phenomenon which is akin to metaphor is synaesthesia, that is, cross-modal perception and association. Perhaps the clearest case of synaesthesia that one may encounter in everyday life is presented by people who cannot fail to see (in their mind's eye) a colour when they think of a number (see, for instance, Shanon, 1982b), a phenomenon also reported in association with letters of the alphabet, days of the week, and musical tones and keys. In the psychological literature it was first reported by Francis Galton (1883); for a comprehensive review of the literature, see Marks (1978). The systematic relationships between synaesthia and affect have also been noted by Osgood (1980), Osgood marks a parallel between synaesthetic relations in the perceptual modalities and metaphorical relations in language. Moreover, he points out that the two are defined by a multi-dimensional space couched in affective dimensions. The dimensions of this space are primitive, hence both the primacy of cross-modal and cross-domain relationships and the common root of synaesthesia and linguistic metaphor (see also Marks, 1990).

While synaesthetic perception is rather rare, synaesthetic appreciation is not. As shown in extensive research by Marks (1975), most people recognize or acknowledge similarities between sensory experiences of different modalities. A demonstrative example is presented by people's answer to the question 'Which is brighter, a sneeze or a cough?'. Practically all people say that sneezes are brighter (see Marks, 1982; see also Osgood, 1980). Of course, poets have always been aware of synaesthetic patterns of this kind, and commonly use such cross-modal metaphors. A poem entirely devoted to such metaphors and which has become a classic is 'Voyelles' by Rimbaud (1937). The poem starts with the following statement (the translation is mine):

A black, E white, I red, U green, O blue: vowels . . .

For other famous literary examples, see Baudelaire (1961) and Nabokov (1974) as well as Kandinsky (1963).

Whereas only a small minority of people experience synaesthesia as adults (incidentally, most of these are women), many more people seem to have had the experience as children (for a comprehensive study, see Marks *et al.*, 1987). Indeed, children exhibit regular cross-modal associations very early. When presented with auditory stimuli followed by visual ones, infants have been found to exhibit preferential mappings of values from one of these sensory modalities to the other. For instance, having heard a pulsing tone, infants preferred to stare at a dotted rather than a continuous line and vice versa (Wagner *et al.*, 1981). Similar findings were noted with loud sounds and bright colours (Lewkovicz and Turkewitz, 1980).

The occurrence of cross-modal associations in very young children suggests that such associations are founded in neurophysiological mechanisms and are intrinsic – in some sense innate – percepetual properties (for further discussion see Marks and Bornstein, 1987 as well as Haskell, 1987b). This in turn presents another line of argumentation against the two-stage model. Specifically, patterns of synaesthesia like those surveyed here suggest that the association between two domains which the independent observer may deem distinct is a basic feat of the human cognitive system. Thus, the association is not by virtue of the detection of similarity or resemblance between two given entities, aspects or features, but rather the manifestation of a functional equivalence which defines some basic qualities of human phenomenological experience. In other words, the cognitive system is so built as to make us experience sensory information from different modalities as similar or equivalent. Thus, the association is more basic than the entities between which it seems to be defined. Further support for this claim will be presented in Chapter 4.

Concluding remarks

These considerations all suggest that the two-stage account of non-literal language is not adequate. Conceptually, the distinction between literal and non-literal language is not well demarcated and both seem to require contextual evaluation; methodologically, the two-stage model is not as parsimonious as it may at first appear; procedurally, the comprehension of non-literal expressions need not require the previous comprehension of the corresponding literal meaning; developmentally, the use of non-literal language seems to be an early phenomenon and apparently, before it becomes symbolic, language is embedded in the context of the child's action in the world; an analogous state of affairs manifests itself in the evolution of human culture.

With the inadequacy of the two-stage model, the counter-argument to the one from context is undermined, and consequently I am led back to the conclusion that semantic representations cannot offer a full characterization of meaning. This limitation is tantamount to saying that semantic representations cannot fulfil the primary function for which they are postulated, namely, that defined by the epistemological rationale. In particular, the foregoing discussion marks a three-fold limitation of semantic representations: they cannot offer a general characterization of cognitive activity, they are not procedurally basic, and they are not developmentally primary.

I conclude with three comments. First, while a distinction between a strong and weak definition of metaphor does exist in the literature (see Winner and Gardner, 1986), that definition differs from the one presented here. In the literature, the criterion that distinguishes between metaphor in the strong and weak senses is the speaker's actual knowledge of the semantic domains and the literal meanings presumably associated with the metaphor. Conceptually, however, it is still assumed that metaphor is a transformation between two (or more) semantic domains, and consists in a deviation from the literal meaning. Thus, both the strong *and* the weak definitions of metaphor assume that the distinct semantic domains are given and the literal is more basic than the metaphorical. The view of metaphor to be presented in this book (see Chapters 5 and 22) does not make these assumptions. It rejects the postulation of given semantic domains both on the psychological, procedural level and on the theoretical, conceptual level.

Second, in arguing against the two-stage model I have argued against the principled distinction between literal and metaphorical meaning and against the primacy of the former. Yet, throughout the discussion I have made repeated reference to the notion of literal and metaphorical expressions as if these labels marked distinct, well-defined categories. My view of metaphor does not assume the existence of such categories. That expressions or usages of language cannot be classified as literal or not literal in any absolute manner, however, does not imply that they cannot be so classified in specific contexts. In general, the literal is uni-dimensional whereas the metaphorical is multi-dimensional. This distinction is, however, a context-dependent, functional one, not absolute and structural. It marks a difference in manner of use, mode of interpretation and evoked semantic effects; it by no means implies the absolute existence – either theoretically or procedurally – of distinct, pre-established cognitive or linguistic categories. Thus, an expression may be classified as literal in one context and not so in others.

Third, there is no contradiction between my claim that language (and, as will be argued in Chapter 5, cognition) is basically metaphorical and my referring to some linguistic expressions as non-metaphorical. In the view advocated here, the workings of mind defy characterization by means of notions like those associated with literal meaning. In other words, cognitive activity and expression are essentially meta-phorical. In some contexts, however, the cognitive system can adopt a literal-like mode of functioning. This implies that the question to be asked is not how metaphor is possible, but how, despite the fact that all language is basically metaphorical, literal usages of language are possible. I shall return to this question in Part II.

Lastly, at the risk of being unduly repetitive let me caution readers to keep in mind that, in this book, whenever they encounter expressions such as 'the workings of mind are intrinsically metaphorical', they should not read 'metaphorical' in the strong sense involving the presupposition of given semantic domains and already established, fixed senses and distinctions.

4   The medium

Cockadoodledoo! – In your language this means good morning, time to get up, day is breaking in Pinchev. What a lot of words you people use! For us chickens, cockadoodledoo says everything. And how much it can mean! It all depends on the melody, the accent, the tone . . . one cockadoodledoo is worth more than a hundred words.

Isaac Bashevis Singer

The second part of the first line of this critique focuses on the abstractness of semantic representations. As noted in (**) in Chapter 1, that representations are abstract is a central tenet of RCVM. Holding it is tantamount to saying that as far as semantic representations are concerned the medium is not relevant.

There are two closely related aspects to the assumption of abstractness. First, it is assumed that representations are not sensitive to the particulars of the medium. Evidently, linguistic and other cognitive expressions are articulated in specific media – the various natural languages, the different sensory modalities – yet semantic representations are oblivious to these. What they encode is only content. This aspect carries two presuppositions. The first is that the medium and the content of encoded information can be separated; the second is that, stripped from its medium, the content is unaltered. The second aspect of the assumption of abstractness pertains to the medium of the representations themselves. Since semantic representations disregard medium, they themselves are defined in a manner in which medium plays no role. For all practical purposes, then, they are abstract. In other words, in itself their medium is not informative, nor does it affect the computational processing associated with them. This is tantamount to saying that the mental code is syntactic: it is the formal structure of the code, not the particular, contingent specifications of its expression, which is relevant.[1] The following discussion will show that the specific characteristics of the medium cannot be ignored and that therefore assumptions regarding the abstractness of the representational code are not warranted. With this, the symbolic nature of mental representations is put into question and the postulation of an underlying substrate for cognition loses much of its *raison d'être*.

Conceptual considerations

Consider the following sentence:

> 1. The cat is on the mat.

What is the underlying semantic representation of this sentence? The standard representational answer would be:

> 2. THE CAT IS ON THE MAT.

(2) is an expression in an abstract propositional form that encodes the meaning of (1): it specifies the two arguments, *CAT* and *MAT*, and the relationship that holds between them. But, then, consider (3), the French translation of (1):

> 3. Le chat est sur le tapis.

Standardly, the semantic representation of (3) would, again, be said to be (2). Yet, the very fact that (1) is an English sentence whereas (3) is French makes them different. Indeed, there can always be contexts in which this difference in language may be just as relevant as the difference between (1) and (4) is:

> 4. The dog is on the mat.

An example of such a context is that of two novels written in English, the texts of which are identical except for one sentence. In one novel the sentence is (1) whereas in the second it is (3). The literary effect, hence the meaning in the particular context, of the two novels is clearly different. An actual literary case in which such a language distinction is of the utmost significance is the opening pages of Tolstoy's *War and Peace*. Even though this novel is written in Russian, the conversations in its opening pages are in both Russian and French, with the language distinction reflecting the social status and attitudes of the conversing characters.

If the language of expression contributes to the meaning of sentences, and if semantic representations should encode all relevant distinctions of meaning, then the representation should be modified to incorporate the language distinction. In the modified representation each proposition would be amended by a tag indicating what the language of expression was – English in (1), French in (3). The language of expression is, however, just one possible aspect of the medium. In verbal communication one could add to it tone of voice, intonation, rhythm, and the like. When the number of relevant aspects of the medium increases, the tagging method becomes cumbersome and non-parsimonious, and its usefulness is rendered questionable. Not only are the relevant aspects of the medium numerous, they are unconstrained. Thus, the tagging strategy presents one with problems analogous to those faced by the use of semantic features as they are employed in accounting for meaning in context. Given that the relevant aspects of the medium are not constrained, for any tagging that one may specify, another unspecified aspect of the medium may loom. Thus, for no level of tagging can there be a guarantee that it is complete: whatever its specification, the tagging may be found wanting.

A possible retort to this is to differentiate between the potential and the actual. Not all potentially relevant aspects of the medium must be specified in the modified formal representation. In each actual instance – the counter-argument would run – the number of distinctions to be specified is limited; hence, in effect, the problems noted may be dissolved. The point, however, is that the relevant distinctions are seldom marked as such, nor are they known beforehand. Specifically, medium distinctions which may not appear significant at the time at which an expression is uttered may eventually be rendered or found to be relevant. On Sunday, for example, you may be told that the person who said, 'The cat is on the mat' during the party on Friday night was Lady Chatterley's lover, whereas the person who said 'Le chat est sur le tapis' was the great-grandson of Marie Antoinette. While there may be times at which you will fail to make the identification, it is by no means an uncommon human feat. People's ability to respond to medium distinctions in such a manner indicates that the memorial representation of the verbal expressions in question has to incorporate the medium distinctions, even if these may not appear significant when they are first heard.

Given the richness of the medium one might propose still another account – a dual, two-part representation in which one part specifies the propositional content and the other specifies the medium (see, for example, Paivio, 1971). The problem with this is that the distinction between medium and contentual message is not well demarcated. Indeed, what pertains to medium and what pertains to message may itself depend on context. Thus, consider a detective novel in which every time someone enters a room, sentence (1) is uttered by some person. But then, in the last chapter of the novel, the detective enters the room and notes that the sentence is uttered by Lady Feline. It is only now that the detective – along with the reader – realizes that in all the previous instances the sentence was uttered by a man. Because of the contrast, the sex-of-utterer distinction becomes apparent and may thus be taken as significant; in the context of the novel it may even serve as a vital clue for discovering who the murderer is. The moral of this example is two-fold. First, the distinction between medium and message is not well demarcated: what appears to be a characteristic of the medium may turn out to be an aspect of the message. Second, the interplay between medium and message is itself context-dependent. Together, these two points hold against a dual representation that separates the medium and the message.

Let me take stock. I began by noting that medium distinctions may be significant and meaningful. If semantic representation encodes all meaningful distinctions of sentences, it has to incorporate the medium distinctions. Two particular proposals for such encoding have been considered and rejected. The first was to encode the medium distinctions in the standard semantic fashion and amend the propositional representations with tags that specify them. This was found to present problems analogous to those noted in the argument from context with regard to semantic features; therefore, a second proposal was considered. In it, a dual representation is employed, of which one part is propositional and encodes the message, whereas the other is non-propositional and encodes all medium distinctions in full. The problem, however, is that the distinction between message and medium is not well demarcated, and may vary with context. Discarding the two proposals considered, one is left with the conclusion that the medium has to be encoded in full and in a manner which is neither propositional nor separate from the encoding of the message. This non-separation between medium and message is tantamount to saying that the mental code is not abstract: mental representations, in other words, are not symbolic.

Empirical considerations

Medium specificity in memory

Against the foregoing conceptual considerations one may invoke experimental results indicating that, beyond a very short duration, people are not sensitive to medium distinctions. The classic study of this kind is Sachs (1967). This study purports – and is commonly taken – to show that information regarding phonological structure is rapidly lost, and that with time people retain only semantic information. Yet, there are reasons to suspect the validity of this conclusion. First, some people exhibit remarkable memory capabilities, a fact indicating the maintenance of memories in what seems to be a rather raw, sensorial form. Naturalistic data (Neisser, 1982), neurological and clinical observations (Penfield, 1959) as well as hypnosis (Chertok and Michaux, 1977) suggest that people remember much more than immediate observation and testing might suggest. Some of these studies (in particular Penfield, 1951) indicate that memories are presented in a rather raw, sensorial form; similar observations were made in the literature in conjunction with eidetikers (Haber, 1979).

More significantly, there are experimental data that counter the standard characterization of memory *à la* Sachs (1967). The Sachs study was conducted in a controlled laboratory situation in which the verbal material was contextually neutral and the subject had no real involvement with it. Several recent studies conducted in naturalistic contexts, however, present quite a different picture. Especially noteworthy are studies of conversations in which the subjects themselves participated; the conversations were recorded and the verbal material in them then served for memory testing. These studies reveal that people have remarkably good memory and detection ability of medium parameters. In particular, people can recognize semantically non-significant changes in surface structure such as variations between nouns and anaphoric pronouns (see Keenan *et al.*, 1977; Kintsch and Bates, 1977; Bates *et al.*, 1978; Hjelmquist, 1984; Masson, 1984). Significantly, it appears that people's memory performance is better for their own utterances than for those of the other participants in the conversational situation (Jarvella and Collas, 1974). Given the conceptual considerations with which this discussion of the medium opened it is particularly noteworthy to mention findings regarding language specificity. Kolers and Gonzales (1980) found that words in the original language of encoding serve as better aids to memory than their translations. Specific memory of the language of text was also found by Fisher and Cuervo (1974).

Remarkable recollection is also encountered with seemingly non-significant physical aspects of the medium, whether in the visual or the auditory model. In the latter, Geiselman and his associates discovered that subjects can remember the identities of speakers, their voices and their locations (Geiselman and Belezza, 1976, 1977; Geiselman, 1979; Geiselman and Craweley, 1983); similar findings were noted by Craik and Kirsner (1974). In the visual mode, people appear to remember non-significant details such as the particular location of items on the printed page (Rothkopf, 1971) and their typeface (Kirsner, 1973). In a series of studies, Kolers and his associates (Kolers and Ostry, 1974; Kolers, 1976) showed that subjects read a text faster when it was presented in a typography or orientation in which they had read it before. The effect was detected even a year after the original reading of the text. For a summary review of medium-specific aspects of memory, see Alba and Hasher (1983).

Content-dependence in reasoning and thinking

Patterns that cannot be captured by abstract, semantic representations are also encountered in reasoning and thinking. In this domain the specificity may be that not of the phonological or sensory modality but of the content domain at hand. The basic pattern of content-dependence is the following: logical or mathematical problems which are structurally isomorphic or formally identical yet different with respect to medium are not of the same cognitive difficulty, and this because of the differences in the contentual domains in which they are phrased. A classic example is the problem originally devised by Wason and further investigated by Johnson-Laird (for a review, see Wason and Johnson-Laird, 1972). Four cards are laid out which display characters such as *E, K, 4, 7*; if a card has a letter on one side it has a number on the other, and vice versa. The problem is to tell which card has to be turned over so as to determine whether statement (5) is true or false:

> 5. If a card has a vowel on one side then it has an even number on the other side.

It turns out that the problem is extremely difficult and very few people solve it correctly. (The correct answer is to turn over both the card marked *E* and the one marked *7*, but most subjects mention only the first card.) Yet, the particular choice of terms may be changed and the difficulty of the problem then disappears. This has been demonstrated by Wason and Shapiro (1971), who presented subjects with cards marked with the words '*Manchester*', '*Sheffield*', '*train*', and '*car*'. Again, if a card has the name of a town on one side it has the name of a vehicle of transportation on the other side and vice versa. The statement to verify is (6):

> 6. Every time I go to Manchester I travel by train.

The second task is found to be easy, and most subjects perform it correctly. In still another study, Johnson-Laird *et al.* (1972) instructed subjects to imagine themselves being postal workers sorting letters. The statement to be verified was:

> 7. If a letter is sealed, then it has a 5d stamp on it.

Again, the subjects were asked to select only those envelopes which definitely needed to be turned over to find out whether they violated this rule or not. The experimental material consisted of four envelopes: the back of a sealed envelope, the back of an unsealed envelope, the front of an envelope with a 5d stamp on it, and the front of the envelope with a 4d stamp on it. In a control condition the statement to be verified was one like (5) and the material consisted of envelopes on which – either on the front or on the back – alphanumeric characters as those employed in the original four-card studies were printed. In the postal condition almost all subjects solved the problem correctly, whereas in the control condition the usual poor performance prevailed.

Similar findings are obtained with syllogistic (Wilkins, 1928; Staudenmayer, 1975) and mathematical problems (Gonzalez and Kolers, 1982). The common pattern is that a problem may be very difficult when phrased formally, but quite easy when phrased in terms of familiar entities (see also Evans, 1982). The effect is especially marked in children (Birenbaum and Talsuoka, 1981).

Patterns of medium specificity are also encountered in the natural progression of thought. Consider *thought sequences*, i.e. trains of verbal-like phrases that spontaneously pass through one's head. Over the years I have collected a large corpus of such sequences and studied them extensively (Shanon, 1989a). One issue of interest has to do with the relationships by which consecutive expressions in thought sequences are coupled. Several bases for such couplings are noted which differ according to the information that an observer has to assume in order to render the relationship interpretable. One such basis is the particular symbolic medium of the expression at hand. For example, consider the following two sequences; the first was in English whereas the other was originally in Hebrew:

> 8. 0. reading: 'let us begin with . . .'.
> 1. begin is like Begin (the Israeli prime minister at the time).

> 9. 0. A girl calls a frisky dog 'Doni'.
> 1. He is really frisky.
> 2. She should have called him 'Shedoni'.
> 3. Or for short, 'Shed' (in Hebrew, devil).
> 4. That has a meaning in English too, 'shed'.

The medium-based couplings of relevance are related by virtue of shared graphological form in sequence (8) and that by virtue of phonological form at the end of sequence (9). In both cases, the lexical items by which the two coupled expressions are related are drawn from two different languages; thus, the coupling sheds new light on the relationship between language and thought in general, and on the role of specific languages in the mentation of polyglots in particular. A central question in the study of bilingualism is whether speakers think in one or both of the languages they know, or perhaps in an independent, abstract conceptual code. While some semantic operations may be conducted in the abstract (cf. Shanon, 1982c), these examples suggest that at least to a certain extent we do think in particular languages. This does not imply linguistic determinism of the Sapir–Whorf kind (Whorf, 1956): the suggested effect of language on thinking is cognitive-technical, not general-epistemological or metaphysical. Specifically, what is suggested is that in their mentation people can use all aspects of the linguistic expressions they entertain, not only the formal semantic content to which they refer. Hebrew and English need not channel their speakers into different *Weltanschauungen*, but given that their morphophonemic structure is different they present linguistic idiosyncrasies which may be employed in the progression of thinking. Thought sequences like (8) and (9) could not have been thought in other languages (they could not have been thought by speakers who do not know both Hebrew and English).

The significance of the medium and its being intimately entangled with the message are even more apparent in the arts. In a Van Gogh painting the consistency of the oil and the texture of the brush strokes are no less significant or meaningful than the forms (trees, meadows, moon) and their colours. It is meaningless to say that the former define the medium of the painting and the latter its message. Rendering the 'same' message in a different medium will result in an object which will lack the artistic meaning that the original painting has. In music (as well as in abstract painting) the convergence of the medium and the message is such that it makes no sense at all even to distinguish conceptually between the two. The medium is (in a non-McLuhanian sense) the message. Musical meaning is achieved not by reference to anything which is outside the realm of the musical medium; rather, the meaning is in the organization of the elements of the medium itself.

It is interesting to note here another manifestation of structures which are isomorphic and none the less perceived as different – the choice of key in musical compositions. Even though harmonic structure and melodic contours are both invariant under transposition, the particular key the composer chooses for the given piece does make a difference. Despite the fact that all the pertinent musical structure may be specified in a formal, abstract manner, the specific medium can never be factored out. (For further discussion see Shanon, 1987b.)

The moral of all this is that neither memory nor thinking can be characterized in terms of symbolic representations that do not incorporate the medium. The medium, even though it cannot be exhaustively accounted for in the abstract formalization assumed by semantic representations, is cognitively relevant. Given that whenever there is an expression there is bound to be a medium, it follows that abstract, formal representations are bound to be persistently lacking.

Cross-cultural effects

Differential patterns of cognitive performance completely analogous to those surveyed above are also encountered in cross-cultural studies. Specifically, the level and manner in which members of different cultures perform various cognitive tasks is affected by the particular contents in which problems are phrased and the semantic domains in which tasks are applied. Such differences lead to variations in the performance of otherwise identical tasks and problems: subjects succeed in performing tasks whose contents and semantic domains are familiar and meaningful to them, and may perform poorly or utterly fail otherwise. Differential performance of this kind was encountered with categorization and clustering, measurement and calculation, comprehension and problem-solving tasks, and with memorization. For instance, studying the Kpelle people in Liberia, Cole and his associates (see Cole *et al.*, 1971; Cole and Gay, 1972) found that success in categorizing objects (in the study, leaves of trees and vines) was a function of the specific names given to the conceptual categories in question. The categorization was successful only when the names were meaningful in the culture. Similar effects in problem solving are discussed by Scribner (1977) and d'Andrade (1989). One factor that should be singled out is literacy. Recently, several investigators (see, for instance, Olson, 1976; Scribner and Cole, 1981) have pointed out that literacy affects the way cognitive material is handled and, consequently, the level and kind of performance achieved with it. Recording information in writing is, in other words, not a mere technical procedure which is cognitively transparent. This brings us full circle. Just as it cannot ignore the medium which the individual employs in oral articulation, so cognition cannot ignore the medium which an entire culture (hence, each of its members as well) adopts for the transmission of information and the preservation of knowledge. For further discussion, see d'Andrade (1981) and Shweder (1991).

Apart from their cognitive significance, these observations also have methodological and even ethical ramifications. Failure to appreciate the contribution of medium and content domain is bound to lead the Western investigator to conclude erroneously that the cognitive aptitude of the members of other cultures is different from that of the members of his or her own. The fact that more often than not this difference is interpreted as a sign of lower performance, inferior ability and even limited potential makes this all the more serious. The bulk of the discussion in this chapter suggests that such a conclusion is not only ethically suspect but scientifically unwarranted as well.

Facial and bodily expressions

Let me now consider a phenomenon pertaining to a medium very different from all the others that have been considered in this chapter – the human face and its expressions. My motivation for discussing this is twofold: first, to show that the issues I have examined are specific neither to language nor to the various media of artistic creation; second, to point out that meaning is expressed even where the rationale for the postulation of underlying mental representations is manifestly not pertinent. This state of affairs indicates that cognitive expressions may, indeed, be meaningful without there being corresponding covert semantic structures by virtue of which the overt expressions are endowed with meaning. If this is the case with facial expressions, then there are good reasons to think that it may also be the case with other cognitive expressions.

By RCVM, facial expressions are regarded as the overt expression of underlying states of mind. For example, a face in which the lips turn up is happy, it expresses the underlying psychological state of happiness; by contrast, a face in which the lips turn down is unhappy, it expresses an underlying state of sadness. But, now, let us take one of the two faces and slightly change the curvature of the lips. Given that the change is slight, the expression is still that of either happiness or of sadness. Yet, it is definitely a different expression: the happy face will be happy in a different manner, and *mutatis mutandis* for the unhappy one. A schematic characterization of this state of affairs may be helpful. Let us label the original expression A and the alleged psychological state that underlies it **A**, whereas the modified expression will be labelled B and the state that corresponds to it **B**. Does the postulation of the underlying states add anything? I think not. For any slight change in the face another expression X will be defined, and with it another underlying state **X** will be postulated. Given that the distinctions stipulated on the level of representations will be as detailed as those observed externally, the recourse to representations has no explanatory value whatsoever.

These comments highlight both substantive and methodological considerations. Substantively, the patterns exhibited by facial expression accentuate those noted earlier in this chapter. Specifically, they point to the density of the medium (a term coined by Goodman in his *Languages of Art*, 1976). Given that all the variations in the medium of the face are relevant, all distinctions pertaining to the facial medium are relevant. In other words, if even slight variations in the medium of the face are significant, then all that can be said about this medium is, perforce, of relevance. Thus, what faces express is intimately tied to the particular medium of the face. Neither an abstract representation nor another medium will fully capture what this medium expresses. Methodologically, what may be referred to as an argument from *duplicity* presents itself. Since all relevant distinctions are already on the overt level of the medium, the postulation of an additional level of underlying representations adds nothing and results in unnecessary duplicity. In other words, given that the medium itself is maximally informative, nothing is to be gained by relegating the determinants of meaning to a second, distinct representational formalism.

The informative density of facial expression is, of course, significant in everybody's daily life. Both in the judgements of other people's characters and in the appraisal of their momentary moods we are all tuned to minimal facial distinctions. In this several remarkable patterns may be noted. First, people are extremely sensitive to very small changes in facial expression. Second, these changes are invested with meanings and are interpreted accordingly: whether objectively right or wrong, people's evaluations of others are based on such judgements. Third, both detection and interpretation may be conducted without the evaluating observers being aware of the particular physical variation to which they are sensitive and on which their judgement is based. All three patterns are encountered, for example, in the judgements of facial expressions of others as based on minute variations in pupil diameter. As discovered by Hess (1965), an extremely small change in this diameter may have drastic effects on how the person being observed is psychologically appreciated; observers can be sure of their judgement but will not be able to verbalize the basis for it. The remarkable sensitivity of human beings to faces also manifests itself ontogenetically. Remarkably, already in the first weeks of their lives infants can imitate the facial expressions of others (Meltzoff and Moore, 1977). For further discussion, see Ekman *et al.* (1972) and Berry and Zebrovitz McArthur (1986).

Evidently, physical expression is not confined to the face. A common such mode of expression are hand gestures. These gestures are an important channel of inter-personal communication: an open hand drawn forward and up is inviting, a hand moved closer to the body and in a swift horizontal sweep has the opposite meaning. But, indeed, one's posture, one's gait, one's motion are all meaningful in the very same manner. The fast-moving person is energetic, the person with the protruding belly is childish, and, as is attested by the psychiatric literature, the depressive and the catatonic exhibit characteristic bodily postures (see Lehman, 1980). Inert sitting with the trunk curving downward, for instance, is associated with grief; remarkably, this pattern of expression has also been found in chimpanzees (see Goodall, 1971). Are these expressions meaningful by virtue of their being the manifestations of underlying internal representations? For all the reasons indicated at the beginning of this discussion, this cannot be the case. Indeed, the consideration of the body in general presents still further support for the thesis at hand. Bodily expression is not confined to people (actually, nor is facial expression). Therefore, accounting for such expression in terms of semantic representations will result in the postulation of representations in cases where they clearly do not belong: in conjunction with any physical activity, with children at the very beginnings of their lives, and with animals.

In fact, it seems to me that the best way to appreciate the senselessness of any reduction or translation of the bodily medium to either an abstract level of representations or another medium is to observe animals as they move. A non-demonstrative example which is none the less telling is that of a cat. The cat moves in a way that embodies not only specific cat behaviour but also a definite cattish character. Surely, if a cat had the body of a dog it would move in a totally different manner and the character one would associate with it would also be different. This character is part and parcel of what the cat is. It cannot be separated from whatever is presented on the surface, from the feline medium so to speak, and there is no sense in searching for it in any covert, underlying level.

I am already touching upon the topic of the body. The phenomenology of the body and its intricate interaction with cognitive behaviour is, indeed, the basis of one of the lines of argumentation taken here against the postulation of semantic representations. It is part of the second line of the critique, and will be taken up in Chapter 7.

Medium and the self-referentiality of thought

Let me turn again to the conceptual level and consider another pattern that marks the limitations of abstract representations. The pattern is a result of the fact that the human cognitive system can reflect upon itself. Thus, consider two representations, A and A', which are formally the same and which differ only with respect to the medium in which they are phrased. In general, this difference may, in fact, not be relevant; it can always be made so. One property of the cognitive system that makes this the case is its self-referentiality. In reflecting upon itself, the mind can turn the forms in which mentation is expressed into objects of thought in their own right. With this, any formal characteristic of cognition can itself become a content that one entertains, so the medium too may become relevant. Schematically, the medium distinction that differentiates between the representations A and A' may gain relevance and become an aspect of the very content that is being entertained. Consequently, the difference between A and A' may become as substantial as the difference between, say, two representations A and B that differ in content. The two formally equivalent representations will thus be rendered cognitively distinct. From this defiance of the medium there is no escape. However extensive and detailed the representational formalism, there will always be a medium, and this medium can always be turned into still another relevant aspect of the representation. I shall return to this topic of consciousness, reflection and the self both in the second line of the critique and – more extensively – towards the end of this book.

The phenomena I have reviewed are varied, but they all point to the same basic state of affairs: the form in which information is expressed does make a difference. People are sensitive to a host of seemingly semantically irrelevant characteristics of the medium. Indeed, such characteristics have a definite effect on how people perceive information, on the meaning they associate with it, on how they are affected by things and on what they can do with them. Furthermore, variations in the medium in which information is articulated and the semantic domain in which it is couched can drastically affect people's performance.

Positive considerations

Like context, medium is indispensable. Abstract, medium-less behaviour is conceptually meaningless and empirically non-existent. For behaviour to gain its very identity and to be individuated, it has to be instantiated in a concrete realization, that is, articulated in a particular medium.

Against the above it can be argued that people can in fact perform in the abstract. Is this not what mathematicians do? Is this not what we do when we prove theorems in geometry and in formal calculi? Such performances, however, are the exception to the rule. How many of us are mathematicians? Proving theorems is undoubtedly a skill that one has to develop, and that many people find difficult or even impossible to master. The experimental data concerning problem solving and reasoning surveyed above all show this to be the case. These indicate that people can manage to perform in the abstract, but that in general this involves significant effort. Such performance is by no means a natural human activity. Students solving theorems in logic are placed in a very artificial situation, one which is, more often than not, utterly meaningless for them. They learn a performance skill, demonstrate it, and get their reward for it (another mark on their transcripts). There are, of course, people for whom such performance is actually meaningful. Evidently, this is true of mathematicians. For them, however, the mathematical world ceases to be abstract. For the mathematician, the mathematical structures are, like the physical objects in the world for all of us, invested with meaning. Here, for instance, is how Poincaré (1958) describes them:

> [W]hat are the mathematic entities to which we attribute this character of beauty and elegance, and which are capable of developing in us a sort of aesthetic emotion? They are those whose elements are harmoniously disposed so that the mind without effort can embrace their totality while realizing the details. This harmony is at once a satisfaction of our aesthetic needs and an aid to the mind, sustaining and guiding. And at the same time, in putting under our eyes a well-ordered whole, it makes us foresee a mathematical law. (p. 40)

Similarly, Gödel (1964) remarked: 'I don't see any reason why we should have less confidence in this kind of perception, i.e., in mathematical intuition, than in sense perception' (p. 271). Thus, it appears that the way to perform in the abstract is to make it meaningful and concrete; in other words, to embed it in a context and endow it with a medium.

The important contribution of medium is also manifested in everyday performance. I gather everyone has experienced the difficulty or even impossibility of retrieving a particular item of information without retrieving the entire whole of which it is a part. For instance, one may find oneself needing to reproduce an entire recitation or melody in order to recall (or verify) one of its phrases. Also familiar are problems of transfer. The transfer of skill from one mode of execution to another is not trivial, and usually it results in a decrease in one's level of performance (see, for instance, McGeoch and Iriow, 1952). Usually, this pattern is viewed in terms of the costs it entails; looked at from the converse point of view, it marks the intimate tie between the execution of a skill and the specific medium of its realization. The various content effects in problem solving surveyed above attest to the same pattern. The phenomenon of encoding specificity discussed in conjunction with context is related to these patterns as well.

Context and medium

In closing, let me consider the argument from context and the argument from medium in unison. Different as the two are, they both point to one basic problem: the human cognitive system is sensitive to variations that cannot be captured by semantic representations. Consequently, semantic representations cannot characterize all the knowledge people have and all that they find meaningful. Hence, these representations cannot meet the requirements posed by the epistemic rationale, the primary rationale on which this first line of this critique centres. Therefore, semantic representations cannot constitute the substrate of cognitive activity, nor can they serve as the basis for a general theory of mind.

The most basic pattern noted in conjunction with both factors is the extreme sensitivity of human cognition to variations that cannot be fixed by a determinate coding system. With respect to both context and medium, not only are the variations not bounded, they are not amenable to any coding which is fixed *a priori*. Furthermore, for neither factor is there a clear demarcation between those cases that may be regarded as standard and those that seem to be non-standard. This holds for both the distinction between the context-free and the context-dependent, and for the distinction between content and medium. Indeed, whatever line of demarcation is drawn, there will always be cases that breach it. Further still, it appears that in both cases the distinctions in question are themselves context-sensitive. We have seen such second-order context-sensitivity with respect to possible mappings of semantic and pragmatic categorizations, in the characterization of expressions as standard or non-standard, and in the differentiation between the content of an expression and its medium.

Note

1. The phenomenon of mental imagery does not detract from the generality of this statement. At the heart of the matter the statement holds true for both sides of the imagery debate. That this is the case for those who claim the epiphenomenal status of mental images is obvious, and the prime protagonist of this stance, Pylyshyn, is also one of the major, and most orthodox, proponents of RCVM (see Pylyshyn, 1981). The opposing stance is that mental imagery is psychologically real but in all other respects similar to RCVM. Indeed, the present consensus in the field is that images constitute a relatively shallow mode of representation and processing and that they too are generated from a still deeper, underlying semantic representational code (see Kosslyn and Schwartz, 1977; Kosslyn, 1980). This is the basic substrate of cognition and the general structure in which information is encoded and stored in the mind. Whether mental images are epiphenomenal or not does not affect this fundamental appraisal.

5 *Coding and recoding*

Suppose that orange being what it is, neither yellow nor red had yet appeared in the world. Would orange still be composed of these two colors? Obviously not.

Henri Bergson

In the three previous chapters, knowledge – primarily knowledge of language – was regarded as given and the question examined was whether semantic representations can capture it. In this chapter, a more basic issue is examined which puts into question the very possibility of representing knowledge in any given and fixed code. With this, attention is drawn from the content and form of what is being represented to some fundamental assumptions regarding the notion of representation itself. The assumptions pertain to one's characterization of both the mind and the world.

Two basic patterns will be examined and marked as problematic. The first, coding, pertains to ontological and epistemological assumptions implied by the postulation of a fixed coding system. The second, recoding, presents some limitations on psychological performance that result from such a postulation. The two will be the topics of the first two sections of this chapter. The third section will focus on a particular case in which problematic aspects of both patterns are observed, that of features as postulated in the domain of similarity judgements. The fourth section will consider some further ramifications encountered in the creation of new codes and of novelty in general. On the one hand, these ramifications will be related to the metaphorical expressions considered in Chapter 3; and on the other hand, they will lay the ground for the alternative picture of mind to be presented in Part II.

Coding

Representations code the world in terms of dimensions, aspects or features that together define a particular resolution. What is the resolution of the human representational system? The following discussion will show that such a resolution cannot be defined in any fixed, predetermined, canonical manner. First, it will be argued that, in principle, the notion of an absolute, universal resolution simply does not make sense. Second, it will be pointed out that the phenomenology of human behaviour defies any resolution by any set of pre-fixed values.

The attributes of things

The postulation of representations presupposes well-defined entities that are being represented. However, entities do not present themselves in the world as such, nor is coding a direct reflection of given entities. Indeed, since the number of distinctions that can be associated with any entity is infinite, coding is bound to involve selective interpretation. In other words, whatever is represented cannot be a simple picture of entities that reality presents; rather, it has to be an expression of the workings of the representational system itself.

The characterization of interpretation as selective should not, however, be taken to imply that dimensions are given and the cognitive system selects between them. Rather, it is the process of interpretation itself which defines the dimensions, aspects and features. Thus, the objects of cognition are not entities that can be defined prior to and independently of one's being and acting in the world. This appraisal is central to the picture of human beings and world drawn in Heidegger's monumental *Being and Time* (1962). He argues that, 'Things [are] "invested with value"' (p. 91), and that their meanings are defined by one's 'dealings' with them, i.e., by the totality of activities enabled for us by the things:

> Only in some definite mode of its own Being-in-the-world can Dasein discover entities as Nature ... The Being of those entities which we encounter as closest to us can be exhibited phenomenologically if we take as our clue our everyday Being-in-the-world, which we also call our 'dealings' in the world and with entities within-the-world. The kind of dealing which is closest to us is ... not a bare perceptual cognition, but rather that kind of concern which manipulates things and puts them to use. (p. 95)

A room, for instance, 'we encounter ... not as something "between the walls" in the geometrical sense, but as equipment for residing', a hammer as that 'uncover[ing] the specific "manipulability"' of hammering (p. 98).

The same appraisal is the basis for a theoretical framework with which I shall be concerned more and more as my discussion progresses, that of the ecological school of psychology founded by James Gibson (1966a, 1979) and further developed by his followers (for a review see Michaels and Carello, 1981). Perhaps the central tenet of this school is that perception cannot be divorced from action. Organisms perceive the world in terms of their interaction with it. Thus, the objects of one's perception are characterized not in terms of the attributes of things but in terms of the interactive coupling of perceiving agents and the constituents of their environment. Rather than features or dimensions that define things as such, the parameters of cognition are *affordances* – the patterns of action made possible by the coupling of the organism and the environment. Examples of affordances are 'passable', 'edible', 'sittable', 'flyable'. Surely, what is 'passable' ('edible', etc.) for one organism or species is not what is 'passable' ('edible', etc.) for another. By implication, the world perceived by one organism or species is not the world perceived by another (for further discussion, see Gibson, 1977; Turvey *et al.*, 1981).[1]

The postulation of affordances frees one from unnatural and even paradoxical characterizations of knowledge. Were the world defined in universal terms one would have to assume that all organisms perceiving it have the same repertory of perceptual distinctions; in all instances, this would have to comprise the maximal set of distinctions by which things in the world can be described. Such an assumption leads to unacceptable implications regarding both ontogenetic development and the behaviour of different species. As poignantly argued by Piaget (1988), it implies that both infants and lower animals possess knowledge of all the parameters by which all entities may be defined. Obviously, this is in blatant defiance of common sense; for further discussion, see Turvey *et al.* (1981) and Bickhard and Richie (1983).

This critique may be countered by reference to neurophysiological findings. One of the most famous achievements of modern neurophysiology is the discovery of a hierarchical system of feature detectors in the visual system. Employing single-cell recordings, Lettvin *et al.* (1961) and Hubel and Wiesel (1979) found that specific neurons – feature detectors – respond to specific types of stimulus or distinction. The detectors are arranged hierarchically: more complex features are detected by neurons activated by aggregates of neurons detecting simpler features. The neurons on the lowest level of the hierarchy detect the turning on and off of illumination, neurons on higher levels detect lines in particular orientations, particular angles and simple forms. Similar analyses have also been offered on the pure psychological level (Weisstein, 1969).

While the discovery of feature detectors is almost universally recognized as a solid, incontestable, empirical fact, one that earned its discoverers the Nobel prize, further inspection reveals that the situation is far from straightforward. As noted by several investigators (Rowe and Stone, 1980), one may interpret the classic neurophysiological findings in terms not of particular field properties to which particular cells respond, but of the cells' overall functional activity. Against this standard feature extraction interpretation is the finding that identical cell responses are obtained only when exactly the same test conditions are maintained. Cells cease to respond, or change their pattern of activity, not only with changes in the impinging sensorial stimuli but also with seemingly independent changes in both the external situation and the brain. It thus appears that feature detectors cannot be defined independently of the entire brain system and of the activity of the organism in the world. For further discussion of this non-standard view, see Towe (1975), Abeles (1982), Edelman (1987), Maturana and Varela (1987) and Swindale (1990); for analogous proposals on recognition by the immune system see Jerne (1974), Varela (1979) and Edelman (1991).

Things

Like the attributes of things, their very thing-hood is an assumption that cannot be taken for granted. The standard representational perspective tacitly assumes on the one hand that the world consists of things, and on the other hand that the mind consists of the representations of things. One may, however, conjecture cognitive systems whose basic objects are not things. Suggestions in this direction are, again, presented by Gibson and his followers in the school of ecological psychology. At the heart of their thinking is the appraisal that perception is not the encoding of sensory data but rather the detection of invariants. This implies that higher-order relations are psychologically more basic than things. An elegant demonstration of this is an experiment by Johansson (1973), in which lights were placed on the major joints of a person dressed in black and photographed in the dark. Viewing the lights as stationary, observers reported seeing random arrangements of dots. However, if the person to whom the lights were attached moved, the observers readily saw a person in movement. From this it was concluded that the perception of the *Gestalt* pattern of an event progressing in time is basic; it is primary with respect to atomic, static constituents and cannot be reduced to them. (For additional data supporting the perceptual primacy of global features and higher-order relations, see Pittenger and Shaw, 1975; Navon, (1977.) Developmental observations along similar lines led E. Gibson to propose a differentiation theory of development, by which new distinctions are acquired by means of contrasting relations. Higher-order contrasts, in other words, precede what the external observer might define as lower-order features (see Gibson, 1969; Gibson and Spelke, 1983). For a model of development further expanding this idea, see Melkman (1988); for further empirical evidence, see Kemler (1989) as well as the references cited in the section on features in similarity judgements below.

These observations further suggest that events extended in time are more basic than static entities or states of affairs defined without consideration of its dynamics. These and other temporal aspects of representations will be a central topic in the third line of my critique.

Other domains

Types of information students of cognition usually ignore are also directly relevant to my discussion. Consider information associated with senses other than vision and audition. Even some representationalists would concede that smell and taste do not lend themselves to a representational account (for discussion, see Skarda and Freedman, 1987). First, olfactory and gustatory data lack the arbitrariness and double-facedness that are characteristic of symbols. Second, these kinds of information seem to defy any given coding resolution because even very subtle distinctions in them count. Third, the postulation of well-defined representational parameters for the information would lead to the attribution of conceptual systems to agents for which it is dubious at best (to wit, all organisms). Fourth, the olfactory and gustatory information and its processing are intimately tied to the chemical and biological level in a way that seems to necessitate no mediating mental representations.

One may retort that the case of smell and taste is irrelevant to my discussion. That the representational account does not fit in these peripheral, not genuinely cognitive cases need not bear on the evaluation of such an account as a general framework for cognition. While smell and taste may, indeed, be characterized as peripheral, this dismissal is too off-handed. RCVM is supposed to present a general theoretical framework for psychology. *A priori*, there is no reason why symbolic representations and computations should account for processing in one modality but not in another. That the representational framework encounters problems in some domains indicates, at the very least, that this framework is not as general as its definition would lead one to expect. The problems encountered at the periphery may also hint at ones that lie in the more pertinent, paradigmatic domains the framework purports to explain. Indeed, the accomplishments of the olfactory and gustatory systems are of the types manifested by both language and the other perceptual modalities. These include detection, identification, categorization, similarity judgements and evaluation. If these accomplishments in the domains of smell and taste are not governed by symbolic representations and their computational manipulation but by some other mechanisms, then perhaps such alternative schemes should serve in the modelling of the more standard modalities as well. For a report of remarkable cognitive performance in the olfactory modality, see an interview with the creator of perfumes in the house of Chanel, in Polge (1988).

Similar problems are encountered in the perception of music. These are instructive because, unlike smell and taste, music is in many respects analogous to language, the paradigmatic case of the representational account. By RCVM, perception, like any other performance, is achieved by means of stored representations. People listen to music – they appreciate it as beautiful, their mood is affected by it, they are baffled by dissonant chords and harmonies, they recognize it as a particular piece, or categorize it as the work of a certain composer or of a certain style even if the piece itself is not familiar. The representational account would stipulate that all these performances are accomplished by virtue of the listeners' possessing semantic representations (for a proposal in this vein, see Agmon, 1990).

A moment's reflection, though, will reveal that this involves no less than the entire span of musical theory, including melody, harmony and the characterization of style. The postulation of such represented knowledge is completely analogous to that in the domain of language, but it is far more problematic. In the case of language, there is at least a *prima facie* plausibility to the postulation of innate, universal representations. One may point to the biologically determined substrate, to the non-dependence on societal and environmental factors, to the rapidity and uniformity of language acquisition, and to a host of universal features in both structure and processing. All these can be argued against, but allusion to them is, at least, reasonable as a first conjecture. In the case of music this is definitely not so. If the representational account leads one to postulate innate knowledge that all hearers have and of which practically all hearers are ignorant, then something must be wrong with the account. And if it fails with respect to music, there is at least some reason to check again whether it does not fail in the analogous case of language as well.

Another domain usually eschewed by cognitive psychologists is that of 'personality'. It appears that ambivalence and multi-valence are the rule in human traits and attitudes: one is aggressive because of one's sense of inferiority, one is daring because of one's fears, one is kind because deep down one is full of hatred, and one might even be hateful because one cannot come to terms with one's hidden kindness. In all these cases one could conjecture an account whereby two opposing attitudes are semantically represented and for dynamic reasons the activation of the one leads to the activation of the other. While logically possible, this account seems to miss the essence of the psychological patterns in question. For one thing, these patterns are too prevalent: the meeting of contradictions seems to be the rule rather than the exception. That this is the case has, indeed, been pointed out by Freud, who singled out the multi-determination of human action and the richness and variety of interpretations that may be associated with its manifestations (see Freud, 1900/1954).

Cultural considerations

Throughout this discussion, the characteristics of meaning have been considered as they pertain to individual cognition. The same considerations also apply to the socio-cultural domain. This is eloquently argued by Shweder (1991):

> No sociocultural environment exists or has identity independently of the way human beings seize meanings and resources from it, while, on the other hand, every human being's subjectivity and mental life are altered through the process of seizing meanings and resources from some sociocultural environment and using them.
>
> A sociocultural environment is [. . . a] human artifactual world, populated with products of our own design. [. . . As such, it] might contain such events as 'stealing' or 'taking communion', such processes as 'harm' or 'sin', such stations as 'in-law' or 'exorcist', such practices as 'betrothal' or 'divorce', such visible entities as 'weeds' and invisible entities as 'natural rights', and such crafted objects as 'Jersey cow', an 'abacus', a 'confessional booth', a 'card catalogue', an 'oversize tennis racquet', a 'psychoanalytic couch' or a 'living room'. (p. 74)

Recoding

Coding commits one to particular distinctions, but people, it appears, can address themselves to information they possess and view and interpret it in terms of distinctions not conceived at the original time of encoding. This cognitive feat holds against the characterization of knowledge in terms of any predetermined, fixed coding system.

Consider the following, very common pattern. One recollects an episode from one's past and realizes how naive one was, how blind, how maladroit. At the time of the original episode one had a particular stance or attitude; one was not at all aware that the situation, hence one's action, could be perceived differently and that perhaps one was quite wrong. One has never considered the situation since; time passed, and now one reminisces and sees things in a completely different light. The pattern is especially striking with respect to one's behaviour as a child. As an adult one may look at one's infantile behaviour and see it with very different eyes; surely, the distinctions by which one evaluates the behaviour now were not available to one when it originally took place. Obviously, the same phenomenon can also occur with regard to the behaviour of other persons with whom one interacted as a child. Striking manifestations of these phenomena occur in the process of psychoanalysis; for the report of a classic case see Freud (1914/1955).

Banal as they are, such episodes are not readily accountable for by the representational framework, in which information is encoded through the filter of the cognitive agent's interpretative schemes. In other words, the information that enters the cognitive system and is recorded in memory reflects the agent's knowledge and beliefs, modes of categorization, biases and points of view (see, for instance, Norman and Rumelhart, 1975). Whatever is not within the range of what the agent knows, whatever cannot be fitted into his or her conceptual framework, is bound to be lost. Yet, everyday episodes of the type just noted show that this is not the case. The child could not have appreciated (and therefore, could not have encoded) the information upon which the adult's new interpretation is based. Likewise, people engaged in an emotional interaction do not – at the time – see how their adversary sees it. The surprise, the shudder, the painful sense of shame – these would not be so strong were this otherwise. But surely, for the new viewing of the past, the relevant information has to be available. Given that at the original time of the encoding this information was outside the scope of the agent's conceptual framework, one must conclude that the information is incorporated into the cognitive system and maintained in it in a raw fashion – one which preserves details not subject to the limitations of meanings and interpretation at the time of the occurrence. Interestingly, there are suggestions along similar lines in Freud's writings (1895/1950, 1940).

Features in similarity judgements

To bring the problems of coding and recoding together, let me focus on the case of features as they appear in judgements of similarity. I choose this case both because the appraisal of similarity constitutes one of the most basic and ubiquitous cognitive operations and because in recent years it has received extensive attention in the literature. This examination will also extend the discussion beyond the semantic-linguistic domain which has been the focus so far.

Features and their role in similarity judgements will be examined here in terms of the *contrast model* proposed by Tversky (1977) and further developed in a series of studies by Tversky and Gati (see, for instance, Tversky and Gati, 1978, 1982; Gati and Tversky, 1982, 1984). The model presents patterns, and problems, very much analogous to those with which the discussion in Chapter 2 started. In this model, entities are characterized in terms of sets of features, and similarity between entities is determined by computing the ratio between their shared and non-shared features. It is thus assumed that features are defined prior to and independently of the appraisal of similarity, and that the appraisal in question is achieved by means of elementary Boolean operations. The contrast model has been substantiated by a large number of varied experiments and has received rigorous mathematical formulation. Yet, it seems to me that it is conceptually flawed (for a full exposition see Shanon, 1988a).

What are the features of an object? First, it will be noted that just as they fail to provide the definition of the meaning of words, so people fail to define the features of entities in the world. Remarkably, not even the best of writers can describe the features of a face in a manner that will enable another person genuinely to reproduce the picture of that face. If the writer is familiar with the face, and features are the basis of its mental characterization and storage, why this striking difficulty?

Second, and in line with the foregoing discussion, it is clear that features are not given and fixed in the world as such. Features, *qua* representational entities, pertain to the mind, not to the world. If there are features at all, they are determined by the cognitive agent who acts in the world and invests it with meaning. Given that features are cognitive entities, their specific definition is subject to contextual variations. The variation with context results in a threefold complex of problems. First, being cognitive entities, features cannot be defined *a priori* and independently of the particular context at hand. Second, since contexts are not constrained, features are, in principle, not constrained either. Whereas these two problems have already been encountered in my examination of word meaning in Chapter 3, the third, quite unsettling one, has not: the context-dependence of the identity of features and their definition leads to circularity, which makes the case of similarity judgements even more problematic than that of linguistic semantics. The circularity is due to the fact that context is defined, *inter alia*, by the different objects that constitute it and by the relationships between them. Given that one of the most basic of these relationships is similarity, it follows that the definition of features itself presupposes the appraisal of similarity. Thus, rather than being the basis for the psychological determination of similarity, features seem to be the products of such a determination.

That features are not constrained, that they are not independently defined, and that their very identity is dependent on similarity itself are all exemplified by people's comparative evaluation of faces. In particular, consider aunts (notably Jewish) inspecting the face of a newborn baby. Each aunt discerns similarity between the baby and one of the ancestors on her side, and both are right in the sense that the similarity is not fanciful: first similarity is postulated and only then are features defined to substantiate it.[2]

That context plays a significant role in the appraisal of similarity has, indeed, been admitted by Tversky from the onset of his research programme. To account for contextual effects, Tversky (1977) proposed a two-stage scheme similar to that encountered in the semantic, linguistic domain. In this, features are given and context affects the manner in which they are evaluated. Such an accommodation of context is, I think, not workable. In the contrast model of similarity the contribution of context is selectional: the set of features associated with an entity is given and context chooses amongst them and selects those that are relevant; it may also assign relative differential weights to the different features. Such a process, however, is not viable. If the contextual variation of features is to be accounted for by a process of selection, then given that both contexts and features are, in principle, not constrained, the process leads to the postulation of a potentially infinite set of features. A psychological model that leads to such a conclusion is clearly not tenable.

But then, in this context of coding and recoding and the conceptual assumptions associated with them, a more basic question poses itself: what is a feature? Tversky and Gati (1982) say that 'the features used to characterize a stimulus . . . may include concrete local properties such as an eyebrow or a smile as well as more global and abstract attributes as symmetry or attractiveness'. In advocating such an open, non-committal stance the two investigators emphasize that they are dealing with the general forms of thought, not with the particular contents of things known. While content is, indeed, not the subject matter of cognitive theory, the unconstrained definition of features is none the less inappropriate. Thus, consider the feature 'symmetry'. This is invoked by Tversky and Gati in order to account for the finding that the numbers '6' and '9' are judged by people as being very similar, even though the two numbers differ in most, if not all, of their local features. What, however, is the meaning of 'symmetry'? The attribution of this feature is tantamount to the assertion that one half of an item is similar (actually, identical modulo reflection along an axis) to its second half. But, then, why not have a feature 'similar to father' (for a child's face), 'similar to an elephant' (for an animal), 'similar to the USSR' (for a country), and so on? Clearly, if there is no restriction on which predicates are admissible as features, and, in particular, if these are not confined to simple, one-place predicates, then there is no reason why the predicate 'similar' should not itself be defined as a feature. For instance, one could attribute to Cuba the feature 'similar to the USSR'. The appraisal of similarity, however, requires no comparison of features. The liberal, seemingly non-committal stance *vis-à-vis* the definition of features thus results in a bankruptcy of the computational model for which the featural characterization was defined.

Bringing together this discussion of features and the analysis of meaning and knowledge in previous chapters, I conclude, first, that independently defined features cannot offer a full, exhaustive characterization of entities, be they the words of language or the objects of perception and judgement. Second, in neither case can a definition in terms of given features be salvaged by means of a two-stage model distinguishing between simple, context-free and non-simple, context-dependent cases. Such a model would account for contextual variation in either of two ways, neither of which is tenable. One would be to characterize the contribution of context as selectional; this would lead to the postulation of infinite sets of represented semantic entities, which is clearly unacceptable. Alternatively, the two-stage model may assume the existence of a well-demarcated core of context-free cases, and transformational operations that account for all other, context-dependent cases. It is not clear that such a demarcation may be defined; even if it could, it would apply only in particular, rather sheltered contexts, and hence cannot serve as a general account.

But what about the whole array of empirical results supporting the feature comparison model? As argued in detail in Shanon (1988a), these studies assume that subjects already have at their disposal sets of features associated with the items to be compared. When the features are fixed, the model can be applied. Outside the psychological laboratory, however, the features of entities are not given, and the crucial cognitive question is precisely how cognitive agents create such features. The experiments conducted by Tversky and his associates either define the features for subjects (e.g. by visual distinctness and separation) or tap their performance when the features have, in one way or another, already been defined. (Indeed, as pointed out in my critique of the contrast model cited above (Shanon, 1988a), when this is not the case, the standard patterns of results supporting this model are not obtained.) However, even if there are cognitive processes involving the manipulation of features in the manner this model suggests, these constitute only a late stage in an entire chain of processing. People may very well perform some cognitive tasks by manipulating features, but people are themselves the generators of these features. Psychologists who confine their attention to the processes that follow the definition of features and their generation are ignoring what, from a cognitive point of view, is the crux of the matter.

Lastly, there is a large body of developmental data that supports the foregoing critique of the feature comparison model of similarity. These data (ignored by Tversky and his associates) reveal that the identification and classification of objects by means of features is a relatively late cognitive accomplishment. In the course of ontogenetic development it appears after the appraisal similarity is mastered. For experimental studies, see the work of Kemler and Smith (Smith and Kemler, 1977, 1984; Kemler and Smith, 1978, 1979; for a summary review, see Kemler, 1983) as well as Shepp (1978); for pertinent general theoretical discussions see Gibson (1969), Gibson and Spelke (1983) and Melkman (1988).

New coding

Recoding naturally extends to the creation of novelty. Creation will be a focus of my discussion in the third line of the critique, when learning and development are discussed; here, however, I consider one aspect of creation that directly relates to the issues we have examined in this first line, namely, the creation of new meaning. The discussion will focus primarily on metaphor. It will be argued that metaphor is a prime mechanism for the creation of novelty in general and of new conceptual distinctions in particular.

By way of laying the ground, let me consider a basic issue not covered in Chapter 3, namely, the theoretical characterization of metaphor. Throughout practically the entire cognitive literature metaphors are characterized as consisting of two constituents associated with two different semantic domains, which the metaphor brings together. The terms most commonly used for the constituents in question are those coined by Richards (1936): the *tenor* and the *vehicle*. The tenor is the topic which is commented upon; the vehicle is whatever is used to talk about that topic. Taking these distinctions as a point of departure, the literature presents three paradigmatic views of metaphor. The first is the *substitution* view. Taking as given that any metaphorical expression is composed of tenor and vehicle, it characterizes metaphor in terms of the substitution of features, semantic aspects or connotations associated with the latter for those of the former. The second is the *comparison* view. According to it, metaphor functions by the likening of tenor to vehicle (see Henle, 1958). Richards (1936) and Black (1962, 1979), who argued against these first two views, proposed the third, *interaction* view, in which the conjunction of tenor and vehicle brings forth a particular selection and reorganization of the semantic aspects of the two. This is achieved through an asymmetric filtering or transformation of the tenor by the vehicle.

The following discussion will focus on two basic assumptions of all these models. The first is the *fixedness assumption*: all three models assume that a metaphor is a relationship between pre-existing, well-defined entities. This is at the basis of the strong definition of metaphor introduced in Chapter 3. Thus, the substitution and comparison models assume that the features of the constituents are given and that the metaphor involves a mapping or an operation on them. The interaction model allows flexibility in the choice of features, yet assumes that the initial set from which these features are selected is given. The second, *selectional assumption* goes hand in hand with the first: manifest cognitive distinctions are defined through the selection of a subset from a given set of entities or values or through the fixing of values of such entities or of their weights. This assumption has already been encountered in this discussion: it is the basis of both featural analyses of the meaning of words and the contrast model of similarity. In both contexts, however, I have argued against it, noting that meaning cannot be characterized by fixed features and that, rather than selecting among given features, context creates the features. I will argue here that if this is true of features as they are employed in the definition of word meanings and in the modelling of similarity, it is much more so in the case of metaphor. Indeed, I will argue that metaphor is a primary mechanism by which new features are generated.

What does metaphor do? It juxtaposes words in manners which are novel. The juxtaposition puts the words in new contexts. In other words, metaphor consists in the creation of contexts. Just as the placement of objects with other objects creates the features of objects, so the placement of words with other words creates new features of words. This has already been seen with phrasal conjunction in Chapter 2. Metaphor is the extreme case of this basic mode of operation of natural language.

This appraisal ties up with the characterization of metaphor as a state of non-differentiation which manifests itself in several respects. First, there is a non-differentiation between the different words and the semantic domains associated with them. Second, there is a lack of segregation between different semantic domains, readings and perspectives throughout the entire text. Third, the meanings of the single words and expressions depend on the text as a whole. Fourth, there is a non-differentiation between the purely semantic aspects of the words and other aspects such as acoustic quality, phonological form, the rhythm of the text and its musical resonance. Lastly, the text cannot be divorced from general sociolinguistic considerations, cultural connotations, and associations due to the use of the words in other contexts, notably other works of the same author and other texts that the culture deems privileged. That the primary, rudimentary cognitive state is non-differentiated does not imply that there are no cognitive states which are, indeed, differentiated. Admittedly, there are states in which well-defined entities are given, symbolic entities are well structured, and features and attributes are clearly specifiable. The point is that these do not constitute the basic cognitive stage, but rather the product of cognitive activity. As suggested by the discussion in Chapter 3, literalness is not given but produced.

With this, I am ready to consider perhaps the most basic question, that presented in Chapter 3: why do metaphors exist at all? This presents a serious challenge to RCVM. If, as this view assumes, everything that one knows is represented in one's mind, if knowing a language is tantamount to the expression in words of what one has in one's mind, and if the underlying representation is coded in a system which is formally very similar to natural language, then *prima facie* there seems to be no reason for there to be non-standard, metaphorical linguistic expressions.

Several (not mutually exclusive) answers to the question, 'Why metaphor?' may be suggested. First, metaphors can express what alternative, literal expressions cannot (see Ortony, 1975, 1980; Gerring and Gibbs, 1988). In particular, this may be the case when one does not have at one's disposal a standard vocabulary in which to express oneself, especially in the domains of sensation and affect (see Fainsilber and Ortony, 1987). Similarly, metaphorical expressions seem to be more in use in specialized domains in which specific, and rather novel, experiences are described. This is often the case in poetry, but is also true of gastronomical descriptions and advertisements for new perfumes.

Second, metaphorical expressions may have positive semantic qualities that lend them special effects and thus make them defy reduction to non-metaphorical language. Especially noteworthy are the sensory-like and imaginative qualities of such expressions, which lend them the freshness, immediacy and apparently raw form that one may associate with perception (see Wheelwright, 1962; Ricoeur, 1979).

Third, partly due to their sensory-like character, metaphors exhibit plurality and openness of meaning. Standard, so-called literal language is fixed in a particular coding system. As such, it is bound to tie one to a particular interpretation and is thus constrained and constraining. By contrast, being apparently raw, metaphorical language is – like the perceptual realm – free from the constraints of any established, well-structured codification; so metaphors present plurality of meaning and are richly open to multiple and novel interpretations. Forceful metaphors are not rigidly constrained to one sense or interpretation. The good poem (indeed, the literary text in general) is that which vibrates on more than one string and resonates on more than one level. It is freshly significative on different occasions and it gains new meanings for different people at different times and places (notoriously, great literature meaningfully reverberates throughout the ages). For an insightful survey of examples in poetry, see Empson (1947).

Fourth, even if literal sentences with equivalent information content could be composed, they would not be equivalent to the one metaphorical expression they are purported to paraphrase. What is significant about the metaphorical expression is not only the content that it conveys, but the way that it does this. The fact that this content is conveyed in one single expression is part and parcel of the force of the metaphor. The apparently raw nature of metaphorical language and the fact that it brings together different semantic domains further result in its being thick and compact. It is thick in that it says – or can say – more than is usually associated with the words in question. It is compact in that, despite the many readings that may be associated with it, the metaphorical expression is, from a lexical point of view, a single entity. Moreover, while metaphorical expressions are always open to further associations and interpretations, at the same time, these expressions are not committing: they invoke various interpretations but do not fix any one of them as *the* single and correct one. Like the world, metaphorical expressions are open to multiple viewings, but in themselves they transcend all these viewings or readings and are not exhausted by them.

All this suggests that metaphor is a prime instrument for the creation of novelty (for a comprehensive discussion see Hausman, 1984). The selectional assumption and the representational framework in which it is couched cannot account for novel creation, yet, obviously, people do create and they both produce and comprehend novel cognitive expressions. Noting that this constitutes a paradox, Hausman (1984) has argued that metaphor is the basic instrument by which human creation can none the less be achieved. Metaphor presents one with incongruence, with things that do not seem to go together. This pushes one to view things in a new light that creates conceptual distinctions not in one's repertory beforehand (for similar ideas see Wheelwright, 1962).

Taken together with Chapter 3, this appraisal suggests that what makes metaphorical language conducive to the expression of affective experiences and to the creation of novelty is its being a direct reflection of the basic nature of the human psyche. Metaphors are so useful because they mirror the workings of the mind. The various phenomena considered in Chapter 3 – synaesthesia, the nature of primary processes, developmental and cultural patterns – all point to this conclusion. Indeed, one might go even further and argue that, ultimately, there is no way to reach the world but the metaphorical one. Any fixed coding system imposes a filter in which some aspects of the world that is being described are lost. Only the compact, equivocal, impressionistic and apparently raw language of metaphor may free description from the constraints of such a filter (see Romanyshyn, 1982; Haskell, 1987a). This assessment is what brought Hausman (1984) to his insightful recommendation of how to attain cognitive openness: apprehend the world as an unbounded metaphor.

Notes

1. I appreciate that many would object to this relativistic characterization of Gibson's view, which is often regarded as a paragon of realism in contemporary psychology. I think that both appraisals are correct: Gibson is both a realist and a relativist. Since in Gibsonian terms organism and environment are defined in terms of one another, there is no contradiction in this. The world is real, but given that the world is defined by means of the encounter with the organism, different organisms live in different worlds. For further discussion of this point, see Katz (1987) and Costall and Still (1989).
2. Several first-hand witnesses have reported to me that a similar pattern is observed when the baby is adopted.

The second line of the critique

The second line of the critique examines representations from what was referred to in Chapter 1 as the *functionalist* perspective. This is concerned with relationships – between the mind and the body, between the organism and the world, between the individual mind and the social other, between cognition and other psychological systems. The following critical discussion is twofold. First, it tries to show that RCVM cannot account for relationships between cognition and other systems, domains and factors. Second, it argues that in ignoring such relationships the representational account leaves unexplained crucial facets of psychological phenomenology and leads to unnatural conclusions and unresolvable puzzles. The discussion comprises six chapters. Chapter 6 presents theoretical considerations marking the inherent closure that the representational perspective imposes on the cognitive system and the *unbridgeable gaps* that result from it. The four chapters that follow focus on actual manifestations of psychological phenomenology. They review empirical data marking the crucial involvement of so-called non-psychological factors in cognition. RCVM disregards these, hence the accounts it offers are fundamentally lacking. Specifically, Chapter 7 examines the relationship between the cognitive system and the *body*, Chapter 8 that between the cognitive system and the external physical *world*, Chapter 9 that between the cognitive system and the *social other*, and Chapter 10 those between the cognitive system and *non-cognitive systems*, primarily affect and motivation. In Chapter 11, the perspective is changed and the discussion turns from cognitive to non-cognitive behaviour. The inability of RCVM to handle activity involving the body and the world is underlined. Several more general issues are examined as well.

6 *The unbridgeable gap*

When intellectual experience and its material are taken to be primary, the cord that binds experience and nature is cut.

John Dewey

Gaps

I shall begin my discussion with an argument focusing on problems presented by a pattern I will refer to as *the unbridgeable gap*. This pattern pertains to the relationship between two domains or levels of reality. Two such domains or levels are given; manifestly, the two are linked and there is a relationship between them. Representational models, however, cannot accommodate these links and relationships, let alone offer any explanation for them. In fact, these models impose a total segregation between the domains or levels. The blatant contrast between the phenomenological state of affairs and the explanatory options offered by the representational framework is telling: it attests to a principled failure of representational models to capture what may be some of the essential aspects of psychological phenomenology. The unbridgeable gap is encountered in a variety of constellations in various areas of psychology. The following are, I think, the most important.

Reference

Remarkably, the pattern of the unbridgeable gap is encountered in the very foundation of the representational framework, namely, reference. By RCVM, symbolic entities are meaningful because they refer to objects or states of affairs in the world. Yet, this framework cannot account for how cognitive and linguistic entities are related to the world to which they refer. Reference, on which the entire representational edifice stands, lies outside the explanatory scope of the representational framework.

This limitation reflects the difference between the vertical philosophical and the horizontal, cognitive-psychological perspectives on semantics noted in Chapter 1. In the philosophical perspective, recall, semantics is that domain of investigation concerned with the relationship between linguistic and other symbolic entities on the one hand, and objects or states of affairs in the world on the other hand. Studying this relationship, the philosophical semanticist sets himself or herself to offer an account of how symbolic expressions relate to entities other than themselves. In this enterprise the problem of reference is central. By contrast, cognitive scientists – psychologists, linguists and students of artificial intelligence – study not the relationship between symbols and the world, but rather the relationships between different symbolic expressions. The linguist studies relations like analyticity, synonymity, contradiction, entailment and presupposition, whereas the psychologist and the computer scientist investigate the manipulation of symbolic expressions postulated in conjunction with the processing of information. In these investigations the meaningfulness, hence referentiality, of the symbols is taken for granted. It is assumed, not demonstrated or accounted for.

In sum, the horizontal, cognitive enterprise presupposes the success of the vertical, philosophical one. The patterns and relations which are the subject matter of the cognitive enterprise are semantic by virtue of their constituents being so from the perspective of the philosophical enterprise. Defined in representational terms, the cognitive study of semantics cannot address the problems pertaining to the vertical dimension. For the cognitive enterprise these problems define a gap that cannot be bridged. The impossibility of a representational system accounting for the relationship between its constituent symbols and the entities to which they refer was first pointed out by Wittgenstein in the concluding section of his *Tractatus* (1922). Wittgenstein's claim is as true as it is simple. Representational systems can account only for phenomena that can be expressed in terms of the symbolic repertory of which these systems are constituted. Anything not expressed in these terms is outside the scope of the system and cannot be accounted for. Thus, these systems cannot in principle account for the relationship between representations and the world, hence for the very notion of reference. Given that reference is the most elementary notion on which the entire representational framework is based, this framework loses much of its solidity: it rests on foundations the nature of which is shrouded in mystery. For Wittgenstein, facing this conclusion was a sufficient reason to stop doing philosophy for several years.

The discussion would not be complete without noting that even from the philosophical perspective the notion of reference is far from being simple. As pointed out by Putnam (1981, 1988), the relationship of reference cannot be reduced further, hence it is bound to remain unexplicated. What ensues is a curious state of affairs whereby the representational programme is grounded in a basis which is totally unaccounted for and whose adoption involves a substantial measure of good faith. This appraisal should be borne in mind in any evaluation of the seeming success of the representational programme, and in any comparison of it with alternative programmes that may be shown to be incomplete in one respect or another. This cannot be overstated. Precisely because of its primary and pervasive nature, the problematic assumption regarding reference is only too easily ignored by the practising cognitive psychologist.

Interpretation

Analogous to the gap between cognition and the world is that between symbols and the meanings attributed to them. Symbols are formal entities joined together in accordance with specifications of well-formedness so as to build larger structures, the semantic representations that are the basis for the representational modelling of mind. Thus, both the structures called semantic representations and the operations that apply to them are defined strictly in syntactic terms. But whence the meaningfulness of these representations? How, in other words, are they rendered semantic? In formal systems such as logic and linguistics, syntactic structures are invested with meaning by the imposition of semantic interpretations. This is done by an interpretative system external to the syntactic component. In and by themselves, however, the syntactic structures cannot account for meaning and interpretation (for further discussion, see Stich, 1983; Morris, 1991).

The problems of reference and interpretation are much discussed in the philosophical literature but psychologists are not too bothered by them. Yet, in the psychological context these problems are critical. The philosopher and the logician can relegate the process of interpretation to a mechanism, component or system other than the formal structures which are at the focus of their interest. Likewise, the computer scientist can dismiss these problems by reference to an external agent – the user – who lends meaning to what the computer does and the output it produces. To the cognitive psychologist none of these options is open. Unlike the computer, the mind cannot be assisted by an external, independent agent that is able to do what it cannot do by itself. Furthermore, factoring out the process of interpretation is tantamount to admitting failure in accounting for phenomena of paramount psychological significance. The attribution of meaning and the process of interpretation are no less psychological than the representational structures with which they are said to be associated. Any psychological framework that can account for the latter but not for the former (let alone one that can accomplish its account for the latter only at the price of disregarding the former) cannot be adequate. With regard to RCVM this criticism is especially pertinent. The representational framework is meant to offer a comprehensive theory of mind. Even if RCVM could fully account for the structural representation of knowledge (in other words, if the problems surveyed in the first part of this critique could be fully dealt with), even if the compartmentalization of form and interpretation could be justified, the very fact that some important facets of cognition are outside the realm that the theory can handle is a serious liability.

Mind and world

Taken together, the two gaps considered in the two previous sections entail an unbridgeable gap between the cognitive agent and the world. Specifically, models defined in representational terms cannot account for the relationship between the minds of cognitive agents and the world in which they live and act.

Curiously, this conclusion has been reached by the most important protagonist of RCVM, Jerry Fodor, whose (1980) appraisal is couched in terms of considerations analogous to those noted above. Just as it cannot handle the relationship between symbols and the world, so the representational framework cannot handle that between the mind and the world. Manifestly, the behaving agent and the external world connect and interact. Yet, for any representational model such a relationship is beyond reach. The model can, at best, explain how organisms manipulate symbols, but not how they manipulate objects, tools and the environment. How the cognizing agent relates to the real world outside, how thought processes result in actions that are concretely materialized in physical reality, are questions that no representational model can handle.

Admitting this state of affairs imposed by RCVM, Fodor concludes that cognitive psychology is couched in a principled 'methodological solipsism'. The epithet 'methodological' is employed to mark a contrast with the classical solipsism entertained in the philosophical literature; but this label is misleading. How organisms establish contact with the world is a genuine psychological question. Psychologists cannot allow themselves to say that they study knowledge people have while refraining from dealing with the question of how this is knowledge of the real world in which people live and with which they interact. The philosopher might regard such a solipsistic position as methodological; for the psychologist it is all but substantial.

Perception

Bearing on both the problem of interpretation and the gap of mind and world is the gap pertaining to perception. By RCVM, information detected by the perceptual apparatus consists of uninterpreted sense data. In this view, objects and scenes in the world give rise to sensory images on the retina which in turn produce representational structures in the mind; upon these, various operations apply which process the information, interpret it, and invest it with meaning. But how is the interpretation achieved? Just as RCVM cannot account for how the symbols of internal semantic representations are invested with meaning, so it cannot account for the interpretation of the internal images assumed to be produced by the perception of the external world.

Let us look at the representational account of perception more closely. The object table produces the image of a table, which in turn generates a representation that is compared with the permanent information stored in one's memory, thus generating the judgement that the object in front of one is, indeed, a table. But all we have here are mappings. As long as overall structural isomorphism is maintained, what prevents the object one sees being interpreted not as a table but as a chair? In fact, just as there is a gap between representations and the world, so there is a gap between sensory images and the semantic representations on the basis of which they are supposed to be interpreted (for further discussion, see Heil, 1981).

In addition to the gap of interpretation encountered at the end of the process, perception presents a gap pertaining to the relationship between the mind and the world. Perception is, after all, perception of the world. Successful perception is assumed to be veridical. By RCVM, however, this success is a mystery. How is it that we see the world as it really is? As poignantly pointed out by Descartes (1911), in themselves one's perceptions cannot tell whether what one sees is real or illusory. Usually, Descartes' question is seen as a philosophical-epistemological puzzle, one that marks a fundamental problem of dualism. As pointed out at length in Shanon (1983b), for the psychologist the classical Cartesian puzzle presents yet another: logically, there is no solution to Descartes' sceptical puzzle, yet psychologically, it appears that the puzzle has no effect. In other words, even though logically the Cartesian argument holds, people do not seem in the least bothered by it: they go about the world never doubting that their perception is veridical. The fact that RCVM predicts that people should be bothered by the Cartesian puzzle indicates that, like Descartes' epistemology, this psychological theory is wrong.

The problems of perception and the Cartesian puzzle can also be regarded from a biological point of view. Just as it cannot account for the veridicality of perception, so RCVM cannot account for the fit between organisms and the environment. If they are taken to be two independent entities, the adaptation of the former to the latter and the successful on-going interaction between the two is a mystery. The only school of psychology which has been specifically concerned with this problem is Gibson's ecological psychology (see Turvey *et al.*, 1981). An exposition of this school's critique of RCVM and of the alternative it offers will be presented in Chapters 7 and 8. As pointed out by Maturana and Varela (1987) (see also Edelman, 1987), the question of fit may also be taken from a diachronic evolutionary perspective.

Mind and body

Analogous to the gap between mind and world is that between mind and body. That mind and body are related to one another is evident. Yet, the representational framework cannot say anything about this relationship. The problem is not merely conceptual or metaphysical. It marks the failure of a psychological framework to account for basic patterns of human behaviour. Cognitive activity does not consist of the mere manipulation of symbols, but is expressed in actual work performed by our body. But how do processes of symbolic manipulation result in concrete, physically realizable actions? I shall return to this issue in Chapters 7 and 11, when the relationship of cognition with the body is discussed.

Mind and other minds

An unbridgeable gap is also encountered between mind and other minds. Just as it cannot account for the relationship between the cognitive agent and the physical world, so the representational framework cannot account for that between the cognitive agent and the social world, the world of other people. The problem of other minds is, again, a classical philosophical problem, but it also presents a challenge for modern empirical psychology. After all, interaction between people is a topic of prime psychological significance. I shall return to this in Chapter 9, which is specifically devoted to the social aspects of cognition.

Mind and will

The unbridgeable gap is encountered even within the proper realm of the psychological. Just as it cannot account for the relationships between cognition and perception or between cognition and motor performance, so the representational framework cannot account for that between cognition and other faculties of mind. Most perplexing is the relationship between cognition and volition. How is it that one's will sets the representational apparatus in motion? Representational models specify chains of operations, but what triggers these operations, what keeps them going, what brings them to an end and makes them stop? No representational model can answer any of these questions. Remarkably, even though this problem is critical, it has received very little attention in the cognitive literature; for exceptions, see Bickhard and Richie (1983), Coulter (1983) and Haugeland (1985). I shall return to this problem in Chapter 10.

The problem of the homunculus

In closing this series of unbridgeable gaps, let me note one which does not pertain to psychological phenomenology but is induced by theoretical considerations. Whereas the patterns considered so far present factual 'non-gaps' in psychological phenomenology, this one presents an artificial gap that is imposed by the cognitive theory and leads to a conceptual dead end; thus, whereas the former gaps have to be bridged, this one has to be eradicated. I refer to the problem of the homunculus. If representations and computations must be postulated to account for the production of meaningful language and its interpretation, then representations and computations (of a second order) should also be postulated for the processing and interpretation of the semantic representations in mind. This argument can be invoked recursively, thus leading to a paradoxical infinite regress. (For further discussion see, for instance, Block, 1980a.)

Trying to dismiss the paradox, one may argue (as in Fodor, 1975) that the two orders are not of the same kind: understanding natural language requires underlying semantic representations, but understanding those does not require still other representations. I do not find this claim convincing: what is it about the two modes of understanding that makes the difference? Nothing, as far as I can see.

In both cases expressions have to be read and interpreted, and if this process is accounted for by representational-computational means in the first case there is no reason that it should not be so accounted for in the second. If so, however, the argument may be taken in the converse perspective: if the underlying representations can be handled without the postulation of further, deeper representations, then so can the overt expressions of language. In other words, instead of being led to the postulation of representations of higher orders, one might as well discard representations from the start.

Since the move advocated by Fodor is often mentioned (one may also say that in the computer different modules or mechanisms are responsible for data representation and interpretation), let me add some clarifications. Here a distinction between philosophers (and computer scientists) and psychologists should be underlined. Faced with this problem of the homunculus, philosophers can, indeed, relegate the interpretation of representations to another realm, module or mechanism. (With the computer the situation is even more extreme: interpretation is pushed outside and is relegated to the person using the computer.) They can, for instance, make a distinction between first-order and second-order processes and decide that only the former (or, if they wish, only the latter) are of any concern. In philosophical analyses, such a move is quite standard; philosophers are all familiar with fundamental problems for which there is no immediate solution or no solution at all. Included in this category are problems such as that of the first cause, the origin of things, the ultimate good, and the demonstration of the existence of the external world and other people. The problem of the homunculus, or of the ultimate interpreter of representations, is very similar to at least some of these. Though philosophers may be aware of their annoying ever-presence, it is standard practice for them to put these problems in abeyance and go on conducting research. Philosophers may even settle the issue by declaring that the foundations of philosophy are couched in paradox. After all, perhaps the first comprehensive cognitive framework in modern philosophy, Kant's *Critique of Pure Reason* (1781/ 1953), is based on a series of undecidabilities, the famous antinomies. Other philosophers, of other persuasions, may, in the end, resort to religion or mysticism.

To cognitive psychologists, however, none of these options is open. They cannot resort to mysticism, or relegate the problem of the homunculus to another, defrayed compartment. The psychologist's task is to offer a comprehensive model of cognition, one that accounts for all manifestations of behaviour, and all accomplishments of the mind. The reading and interpretation of representations are, no doubt, accomplishments of this kind. Therefore, they have to be accounted for within the cognitive theory at hand. The problem of interpretation, or the ensuing problem of the homunculus, cannot be factored out and relegated to another domain or a later stage of research. Thus, the representational-computational track leads to an infinite regress: if the interpretative mechanism is itself constituted in semantic representations, and if semantic representations must be interpreted, then behind any postulated interpretative mechanism, another will always lurk.

Representationalist psychologists could, of course, say (as Fodor does) that the process of interpretation is categorially different from all other cognitive processes. The reading of representations and their interpretation, they could claim, are achieved by means other than those subsumed under the general computational machinery of the mind. Even if this process is categorially different from any other, this dismissal does not alter the basic problematics. In it, the representationalist merely declares that RCVM, so far assumed to be a general framework by which all behaviour – cognitive and otherwise – is to be accounted for, is actually limited. In sum, the representational account is not – nor can it ever be – complete. RCVM, in other words, cannot serve as a general theory of mind.

That the representational account is in principle incomplete has, indeed, been admitted in the literature (see Fodor, 1980, on its 'methodological solipsism'). This discussion reveals that the problem of the homunculus and that of reference and methodological solipsism are essentially the same. Specifically, that of the homunculus presents an internal analogue to the unbridgeable gap of reference with which I started: just as there is an unbridgeable gap between representations and the external world, so there is an unbridgeable gap between representations (of whatever order) and the master interpreter that assigns them meaning. With this, our discussion comes full circle: the problem of reference, which is at the basis of the representational account, and the problem of interpretation, which may be relegated to it, coincide.

In fact, the problem of the homunculus is related to another gap considered earlier in this chapter, namely, that between mind and will. The hurdles encountered in the reading of representations and their interpretation also present themselves in the very activation of computational operations. Who is responsible for this activation? Either some higher-order operations, and then operations of higher and higher orders, will have to be postulated, or else the prime mover is to be pushed outside the cognitive province proper and the theory is not complete.

Conclusion

The various gaps discussed, then, are highly interrelated. Indeed, they all lead to the same conclusion. Since conceptually the gaps can never be bridged, and since factually no gap is found, then perhaps rather than being real the unbridgeable gaps are the product of this theoretical framework. Hence, instead of pushing interpretation to the far end of the cognitive arena, one should perhaps bring it to the fore. In particular, if higher-order interpretative mechanisms cannot overcome the problems of reference, meaning and interpretation, then perhaps meaningful-ness is there from the very start. In other words, rather than being abstract formal structures that have to be interpreted, the basic cognitive structures (and the basic terms of cognitive theory) may be – as suggested in Chapter 5 – inherently laden with meaning. Likewise, if the manifest tie with the body, the world and the will cannot be accounted for by representational means, then perhaps this tie should be an inherent property of the building blocks of the cognitive system (and *mutatis mutandis* of the basic terms of cognitive theory). This will be a central constituent of the picture of mind presented in Part II.

Missing qualities

Related to the argument from the unbridgeable gap is that from the missing qualities. This argument marks the inability of representational accounts to capture or explain some important qualitative characteristics of human cognition. By and large, the qualities characterized as missing correspond to gaps indicated in the first half of this chapter. This is no accident. Most of the qualities to be noted are missing precisely because of the closure RCVM imposes on the cognitive system. As a whole, the problems associated with the unbridgeable gap and those presented here differ in the point of view from which they emanate. Whereas the former emanate from an external point of view focusing on entities outside the cognitive system with which the mind is supposed to interact, the latter emanate from an internal point of view that focuses on characteristics of the system itself.

Understanding

Representational systems manipulate symbols, but can such manipulation generate understanding? This problem parallels those of reference and interpretation discussed in the first part of this chapter. Whereas the problems of the unbridgeable gap focus on the interaction between the mind and the world, those of missing qualities focus on a quality of the cognitive system that is a function of this interaction.

The most famous – indeed, by now classic – presentation of the argument from missing qualities as it pertains to the issue of understanding is Searle's (1980a; see also Searle, 1990b). Searle considers the case of a person locked in a room who is being given strings of Chinese ideograms. The person knows no Chinese: he does not know how to interpret the ideograms, nor does he know the rules of the Chinese language; indeed, he may not even know how to differentiate Chinese ideograms from other, similar looking signs. He is provided, however, with rules articulated in English, a language that he does know. These specify how the characters which happen to be Chinese ideograms may be related amongst themselves. The rules are gradually elaborated and eventually allow the person to behave as if he knew Chinese. Specifically, some strings of Chinese symbols may define questions in that language, and following the (English-phrased) rules, the person responds to these questions by producing other strings of Chinese ideograms. From an external point of view, he behaves as if he knew Chinese. Yet, as far as he himself is concerned, he is merely performing computational operations on formally specified elements. What he is doing, however, is what – from the representational-computational perspective – constitutes all cognition: he is manipulating symbols. The Chinese room argument, then, demonstrates that this perspective fails to capture the very essence of semantic behaviour, namely, understanding. It triggered much discussion and disagreement; for counter-arguments and dissenting views, see the commentaries following Searle's article, as well as Churchland and Churchland (1990).

Experience

Searle's argument need not be confined to understanding. It readily applies to mental qualities in general, and in particular, to perception and the quality of one's experiencing the world in which one lives. A symbol-manipulating system encodes the shapes and colours of scenes in the world, as a TV camera would. It subsequently manipulates the pictures in various fashions; but could it be said that it sees – that it has any experience of the world?

Whereas cognitive psychologists are not greatly concerned with the problem of experience, philosophers have devoted much attention to it. In the philosophical literature it is known as the problem of qualia. It is not confined to the context of representationalism, but is presented in the larger context of the reduction of psychology, be it to brain states or to functional ones (i.e., mental states defined structurally by the input to the system, its output and the relationships with other mental states). First, the question is posed whether the special phenomenological aspects of experience can be given a reductive account. Second, if the answer is negative, the question arises as to whether this actually makes a difference. An affirmative answer to the second query is tantamount to the claim that reductive models, and in particular the functionally defined representational ones, cannot account for distinctions which, from a phenomenological point of view, are significant.

A by-now classic critique of reductive accounts with regard to the problem of experience is Nagel's 'What is it like to be a bat?' (Nagel 1974, 1986). In this paper, Nagel points out that a physicalist account of phenomenological qualities is not in place, that phenomenological experience can be apprehended only from the subjective point of view of the cognitive agent, and that one can have a full account in terms of brain states and yet not be able to grasp those experiences. Just as one cannot have knowledge of what it is like to be a bat without actually being one, so one cannot fix experience by mere functional or physiological modelling. The last prong of the critique was taken up by Jackson (1982), who pointed out that full specification of brain states cannot fix an experience such as that associated with colour perception. For further discussion, see Block (1980b) and Shoemaker (1980).

Perhaps the first to have appreciated this problem was Leibniz (1985). His voice is amazingly modern:

> It must be confessed, however, that perception and that which depends on it, are inexplicable by mechanical causes, that is to say, by figures and motions. Suppose that there were a machine whose structures produced thought,

sensation and perception. We could conceive of it as increased in size with the same proportions until one was able to enter into its interior, as he would into a hall. Now, on going into it he would find only pieces working upon one another, but never would he find anything to explain. Perception is accordingly in the simple substance, and not in the composite nor is it in a machine that perception is to be sought. (p. 228)

The philosophical discussion is complex and leads to issues that are far from the concerns of metapsychology and the specific evaluation of RCVM as realized in cognitive modelling. Amongst these are the nature of knowledge, the identity of brain and mind states, the relevance of experience and reflective knowledge in epistemic judgements, physicalism and reductionism. Being primarily philosophical, they will not be pursued here. I should say, however, that they are still open and the arguments from experience marshalled against RCVM are not conclusive. For further arguments, see, *inter alia*, Dennett (1988) and Churchland and Churchland (1990).

Whatever the status of the philosophical debate, one point most relevant to cognitive-psychological discussions can none the less be made. As pointed out by Block (1980b), even if two accounts associated with different experiential qualia are proven to be logically equivalent, it does not follow that the fact that distinct qualia are experienced makes no difference. In particular, the given experiences may play a role in further cognitive processing and constitute significant differential determinants in psychological performance. That this is the case has been the main point of the discussion of the medium in the first part of this critique.

The material aspects of cognition

The cognitive agent relates to things in the real world, not to mere representations of things, but the representational model cannot bridge the gap between symbols and things. Indeed, there is no way for the representational framework to distinguish between the two types of performance – that which involves real things and that which has to do with mental objects only. Evidently, no representational-computational characterization of milk production by the cow will ever furnish any milk (see also Dennett, 1979a).

Consciousness

Consciousness is perhaps the most significant of all the missing qualities. Yet, just as they cannot account for the qualities of experience, so representational models cannot account for the phenomenon of consciousness. Such models have been proposed: essentially they characterize consciousness as consisting in the knowers' knowledge of their own selves. The representational framework would account for this in the same way it accounts for any other knowledge. Specifically, within the repertory constituting the cognitive agent's system of knowledge and belief, a component marked 'self' would be incorporated (for actual proposals along this line, see Minsky, 1968; Wyer and Srull, 1986; Johnson-Laird, 1988; see also Jackendoff, 1987). This seemingly straightforward accommodation would miss, I think, whatever is special about the phenomenology of human consciousness.

First, this characterization does not present an accurate reflection of the phenomenological state of affairs. People rarely experience themselves as thinking selves, distinct from the objects of their thought. Consciousness involves self-awareness, but this should not be identified with an awareness of one's self. With regards to the phenomenology of consciousness proper, three patterns that the suggested representational modelling of consciousness cannot handle will be noted. These define, I think, the essential properties of human consciousness. Indeed, in one terminology or another they have been observed by both James (1890/1950) and Jaynes (1976). The three patterns are similar in that they all present the bringing together of two opposing characteristics that the representational account cannot reconcile. The first pattern is the bringing together of the aspects of *subject* and *object*. On the one hand, consciousness is always the consciousness of something, and in that sense it involves an object. On the other hand, consciousness always involves an agent who is aware, hence a subject. By contrast, anything encoded in representational terms has perforce the epistemic status of an object. That the content of knowledge is the cognitive agent itself does not alter this basic fact. The representational characterization can capture neither the aspect of consciousness as subject, nor its tie with its aspect as object. Second, consciousness brings together the *bodily* and the *mental*. On the one hand, consciousness is a mental phenomenon. On the other hand, the sense of one's being an embodied, living agent is an intrinsic ingredient of one's experience of being conscious. Just as it cannot bridge the gap between mind and body, so RCVM cannot account for this two-facetedness of the experience of consciousness. Third, consciousness is both *focalized* and *unbounded*, both *stable* and *fluid*. On the one hand, consciousness consists of an ever-present, all-framing background (see Searle, 1983), which defies fixation and is constantly in flux. On the other hand, consciousness always involves focusing on something which is, at least for a moment, bounded and well defined. By contrast, the representationalist account imposes a clear-cut, well-defined state of affairs: either one is in a conscious state or one is not. Together, these three patterns indicate that a representational account is bound to ignore precisely those characteristics which are special features of human consciousness and which make it the unique phenomenon that it is; for a more detailed presentation see Shanon (1990b).

Confronted with the difficulties RCVM faces in attempting to account for the phenomenon of consciousness, one could retort by dismissing the failure as being of no import. The dismissal may follow either of two lines: one may argue that consciousness is an epiphenomenon, or one may dismiss consciousness as not pertaining to the proper realm of cognition or of the scientific study of mind. Arguments of both these kinds have been put forward, *inter alia*, by protagonists of the cognitive establishment in response to Searle's Chinese room argument; see, for instance, Rey (1983). To my mind, neither line is admissible.

Consider first the characterization of consciousness as epiphenomenal. *Prima facie*, it is phenomenologically suspect. Consciousness is one of the prime characteristics of human mental life, and it is central in defining the world of our experience. At best, the characterization of consciousness as an epiphenomenon has to be proven. Producing such a proof, as it is the proof of a negative statement, is bound to be extremely difficult. Moreover, in order to dismiss a phenomenon as epiphenomenal one has to be sure that, indeed, it has no functional role. However, consciousness does seem to be functionally advantageous. My study of thought sequences and the phenomenology of conscious mentation (Shanon, 1989b) suggests a series of such advantages. Specifically, consciousness affords control on cognitive processes, gives momentum to the progression of thought, and, by crystallizing thoughts in particular media – such as language and mental imagery – enables thought to proceed along avenues that otherwise the thinker might not have envisaged. For a recent, most interesting, comprehensive theory of consciousness and its role, see Baars (1980). More on the topic of consciousness will be said in Chapter 19.

The other way to dismiss consciousness is to argue that it does not pertain to the proper realm of cognition. Again, I find such a move dangerous. Pre-theoretically, consciousness strikes one as being something which is distinctly human. Is it not suspect to dismiss it just because one cannot account for it within the conceptual framework one adheres to, and which one believes, for independent reasons, to be the only admissible one? This dismissal of consciousness as non-cognitive is a specific case of a more general move – the concordant readjustment of the boundaries of domains of scientific investigation and of the scopes of the theories by which one attempts to explain them. I shall return to this issue in Chapters 16 and 19.

Computers and human beings

By and large, the qualities considered above – understanding, experience, the material aspects of cognition, consciousness – distinguish human beings from computers. That this is the case is not surprising. The computer is the paragon of representationalism – a system which is nothing but representations and computational operations that apply to them. That the representational framework is especially handicapped with respect to the qualities that differentiate human beings from computers is, of course, telling.

Thus, the foregoing discussion suggests that the representational account fails precisely with respect to what is unique about human beings – to that which distinguishes them from computers. In other words, by adopting a representational-computational account the cognitive scientist imposes upon human psychology the characteristics of computers. In so doing, any potential difference between human beings and computer is eschewed before the discussion begins. The gravity of such dogmatism cannot be overestimated (for further discussion, see Dreyfus, 1979; Haugeland, 1985; Winograd and Flores, 1986; Shanon, 1991a).

Having contrasted human beings and computers, let me comment on the question of computer intelligence in general. The question of whether computers can be intelligent (or think, or engage in verbal discourse, or have emotions) is usually associated with the Turing test (see Turing, 1950). By this test (or rather, the test as it is usually conceived in the literature; see Shanon, 1989c), a computer would qualify as intelligent if it could fool a human observer communicating with it only through a teletype into believing that it was a person. (In other words, the computer would be deemed intelligent if the observer failed to discriminate between it and a person.) At first glance, the Turing test seems to be straightforward, but, as pointed out in Shanon (1989c), it actually involves a *petitio principii*. The test examines its candidates by means of teletyped communication, that is, by means of the exchange of well-defined coded symbols. Thus, the test confines itself to a particular domain – that of performances by means of computational operations executed upon semantic representations. Likewise, as far as the test is concerned, all the relevant distinctions are those that can be characterized solely in terms of representations and computations. Any difference that may be detected between computers and human beings has to be within this representational-computational domain. Representations and computations are, however, precisely those structures and processes that define computer operation. Thus, the demarcation assumed by the test is far from being innocuous. It confines human behaviour to those behaviours conducted by means of the resources available to the computer. In other words, the rationale underlying the test is the following: let us confine ourselves to behaviours that can be characterized in the terminology that might be shared by both computer and human beings, and see whether there is any difference between the two. The begging of the question is clear.

7 The body

But as soon as he began thinking what he was doing and trying to do better,
he was at once conscious how hard the task was, and would mow badly.

Tolstoy

I now turn from the consideration of basic conceptual problems to the survey of
empirical data and begin the examination of particular systems with which the
cognitive system interacts.

The first functionalist relationship I shall consider is that between the cognitive
system and the body. Let me clarify that the topic of our discussion here is not the
neurophysiological substrate in which cognition is realized. The study of this
substrate pertains to brain research and is outside the scope of cognitive psychology
proper. Of course, without the brain there can be no cognitive activity (indeed, no
biological activity whatsoever). The brain is necessary for cognition just as the bones
are necessary for locomotion, the strings inside a piano for playing, the electronics
inside my computer for typing and text editing. But just as text editing does not
involve any electronic manipulation, cognitive activity does not – in and by itself –
involve neurophysiological activity. Similarly, just as piano playing consists in the
manipulation of keys, not strings, just as walking consists in the moving of limbs,
not the activation of bones, cognition does not consist in brain activity or any other
neurophysiological activity. Rather than the brain and the neurophysiological
system, the body that is the topic of the discussion here is the phenomenological
body, that which each human being is acquainted directly with and considers his
or her own. What this body specifically consists in is the topic of independent
empirical investigation, but on which I do not wish to dwell. Whatever the details
are, the general picture is clear. Manifestly, the phenomenological body includes
as salient parts hands, arms, legs, face. This discussion tries to show that this
phenomenological body is, indeed, involved in cognitive activity and that, in
consequence, cognitive theory cannot ignore it.[1]

RCVM disregards the body. Of course, no representationalist denies that for
human cognition to be realized it has to be implemented in some biological
substrate. However, as far as the representationalist enterprise is concerned this is
outside the realm of interest. According to RCVM the objects of cognition are
abstract symbols, which – as indicated in (**) in Chapter 1 – implies that the
biological substrate in which they are materially realized is irrelevant. A major

corollary of this is the theoretical stipulation that between natural and artificial intelligence there is, in principle, no difference. Given that the underlying substrate is irrelevant, the difference between the two systems – the biological one and that made of electronic components – is immaterial (see, for example, Putnam, 1973; Newell, 1980). Indeed, representational cognitive science models both computer and human beings by means of the same conceptual machinery.

I share the representationalist's disregard of the neurophysiological substrate of cognition, but I do not draw the further conclusion that the body is not relevant. The difference between the representationalist and me is couched in the two senses of 'body'. RCVM identifies the body with the neurophysiological system, and in dismissing it it marks a division between the cognitive and the neuronal sciences. While I also maintain that the neurophysiological body is not relevant to cognitive studies, I believe that the body in its second, phenomenological sense plays a crucial role in cognitive activity and that cognitive theory cannot disregard it. It goes without saying that as far as this phenomenological body is concerned human beings and computers are categorically different.

Before I proceed let me draw a distinction which I think is fundamental. The problems that the body presents RCVM with pertain to two distinct topics. On the one hand, there is that of motor activity and its modelling in representational terms; on the other hand, there is that of the involvement of the body in cognitive activity. While the first topic is more often discussed in the literature, the prime subject matter here is the second. In the following sections, I will consider a variety of cognitive activities in whose execution the body seems to play an important, and at times crucial, role. This holds against RCVM's principled disregard of the phenomenological body. Evidently, the other, first topic also marks important limitations of RCVM. These pertain, however, not to the study of cognition proper but to the application of the representational framework to domains that are not paradigmatically cognitive. As such, to me this first topic is of secondary import. I shall return to it in Chapter 11, where its relevance to the present critique will be further clarified.

Knowing-that and knowing-how

Let me start with a simple, everyday observation on the skill of typing, which I will present from my own (far from idiosyncratic) experience. I am a good typist – I type fast without looking at the keyboard. But if I were asked to specify the position of the letters, I could not tell you. I could not take a pencil and reproduce the letters and other characters as they are placed on the keyboard – line after line, from left to right. This is curious. Surely, I know where all the characters are: if I did not, how could I place my fingers on the keyboard and type? So, while I cannot reproduce the layout of the keyboard, I can none the less specify where any given letter is. In generating such a specification I am likely to do either of two things. I may move my hand in the air, draw it to a certain position in the space in front of me, hit an imaginary key and then answer 'here'. Alternatively, I may type not a letter, but a word, one that includes the queried letter as one of its constituents. I will observe the fingers as they tap in the air, perhaps I will slow down and repeat the tapping once or twice, and then say what the position of the queried letter is. It is in executing the bodily movement that my knowledge comes into being.

One does not have to be a typist to appreciate this phenomenon. Try the following: how many syllables are there in the word 'representationalism'? How many letters? These are remarkably difficult questions if one attempts to answer them in isolation, outside the context of actual linguistic production. But, in practice, people do answer such questions well and easily. They do something analogous to what I do when asked about the placement of characters on the keyboard: they start uttering the word, 'rep-re-sen', they may accompany this by counting on their fingers, and then they say, 'Ah, seven'. The pronunciation of the entire word is not mandatory; some pronunciation, however, is.

The moral of these observations is twofold. First, one knows how to act even when one cannot articulate the knowledge that characterizes the action in question. Second, a natural strategy for eliciting such knowledge is to generate the action with one's body. One can then observe how one's body moves, record the concrete products of that movement, and read out the specifications that constitute the requisite knowledge.

The foregoing observations pertain, of course, to the classic contrast between *knowing-that* and *knowing-how*. As pointed out by Ryle (1949), the two are distinct and independent. First, people can often execute motor tasks without being able to specify the knowledge implied by their execution – most people who swim, ride bicycles and engage in verbal discourse cannot articulate the rules that govern these activities. Furthermore, people may accomplish a task perfectly but, when asked to specify details pertaining to it, furnish wrong answers. Papert (1980) of the Logo laboratory at MIT observed, for example, that verbal specifications that riders of bicycles give of the directions in which one should bend one's body in turning are opposite to the directions the same riders take in actual riding (for a general, philosophical discussion of this tacit knowledge, see Polanyi, 1962, 1966). Similar discrepancies are noted in naive physics, i.e., people's conceptions of the basic laws governing the behaviour of things in the world (see Shanon, 1976; diSessa, 1982; McCloskey, 1983). Further still, knowing the rules that generate an activity does not guarantee that one can actually do it – being able to articulate the rules that govern swimming is no evidence that one can swim. Moreover, not only is articulate knowledge not necessary for performance, it may even hinder it (see Polanyi, 1962; Dreyfus, 1979; Dreyfus and Dreyfus, 1986). A conscious reflection of how one plays the piano or performs an acrobatic act is likely to result in a disruption of the execution of the task.

All the patterns noted are simple, yet they are instructive. By RCVM, none of these should occur. According to this view, behaviour – all behaviour – is achieved by virtue of underlying cognitive activity consisting in the manipulation of symbols in mental representations. There should be no difference between talking, remembering or problem solving and any motor activity or skilled performance. From this, several corollaries follow. First, in a manner analogous to that indicated for the meaning of words, specifying the knowledge manifested by one's behaviour should always be possible. Second, since the knowledge being specified is a prerequisite of the activity, such specification should not depend on any manifest activity. Third, by RCVM one should not expect people to furnish specifications that counter the actual performance being produced. Fourth, possessing all the knowledge that characterizes a task should be sufficient for mastering that task. Thus, knowing about an activity should entail knowing how to perform this activity. And fifth, the knowledge should not interfere with task execution. The fact that all the patterns that, by RCVM, should not have occurred do, in fact, indicate that this view of mind is fundamentally flawed.

The involvement of the body in cognitive activity

Let me begin by highlighting the obvious: cognitive agents do not have any existence in the world and cannot act in it without a body. As pointed out by Merleau-Ponty (1962), the body defines the space in which cognitive agents live: it circumscribes the milieu of one's habitation in the world and constitutes one's measure of the world. Language attests to this very clearly: indexicals such as 'here' do not refer to a determinate position in an external coordinate space, but rather lay down a person-specific system of co-ordinates. The body is, to use Merleau-Ponty's words, 'the union of the subject and of the world'. Many philosophers have claimed that we know the world by means and in terms of forms of thought, categories and various conceptual structures, but, in fact, we know it by means of our body and in terms of its activities. The body is the first given, that which defines the particular identity of each of us, and by which everything else exists and has meaning.

Cognitive performance

The recourse to motor activity not only elicits tacit knowledge that is presumably there, it also plays an important role in the accomplishment of cognitive tasks that are not usually associated with physical action. Here, too, let me begin with a simple demonstration, this one of the faculty of memory. Try the following: ask a friend to tap on the table; then ask him or her to tell you how many taps there were. Of course, your subject is not supposed to count while the tapping takes place. What he or she is likely to do is analogous to what you probably did in conjunction with the words and syllables – repeat the sequence of taps. This time, your friend will slow down and count. My own experience tells me that the number of taps that can be reported in this manner exceeds by far the magical number plus or minus seven that is usually taken to mark the limit of short-term memory.

In the same vein, Zajonc and Markus (1983) observed that intellectual performance is often associated with overt motor behaviour: moving the eyes, moving the lips, scratching one's knee, knotting one's hair (Pasteur is said to have done this when struggling with scientific issues). Moving the eyes may be explicated by the activation of the cerebral hemisphere involved in the cognitive task in question (Gur *et al.* 1975), and moving the lips is surely related to subvocal verbalization, but what about the other motor activities? These seemingly insignificant movements suggest that so-called pure cognitions cannot be separated from one's body. Like typists who have to activate their fingers to indicate the location of letters on the keyboard, the solver of abstract puzzles activates hands, lips and perhaps other parts of the body as well.

Experimental findings corroborate these observations. Murray (1966) compared learning of lists of letters by subjects who just looked at the letters, whispered them, or said them aloud. The best recall was found under the last condition. Similarly, subvocalization was found to help in mental arithmetic (Fryer, 1941) and in reading comprehension (Baddeley *et al.*, 1981). Negative evidence is revealing as well: for Western Europeans, for instance, it is not easy to nod one's head vertically and at the same time say 'no'. Wells and Petty (1980) corroborated this observation experimentally: they asked subjects to execute hand movements non-compatible with what they were asked to say; the task proved extremely difficult. Zajonc and Markus (1983) further marked the common concordance between what one plays on a musical instrument and the movements one generates while playing. The playing of high notes, for example, is associated with an ascending, not a descending, movement of the brows.

The motor activity involved in cognitive performance need not be peripherally expressed. This is argued by the motor theory of thinking (for a review, see Cohen, 1986), which had been proposed by several scholars by the turn of the century, and maintains that mental activity requires motor activity, especially when no external sensation is available. A modern variant of this theory proposes that all acts of will involve activation of the motor system and that the experience of voluntariness arises only from motor activity, even if not peripherally expressed. Thus, using electromyographical measurement McGuigan and Rodier (1968) found more speech motor activity in subjects who read during auditory distraction than in ones who read in silence. Hardyck and Petrinovich (1970) found that subjects who kept their laryngeal region relaxed while reading exhibited worse comprehension than subjects who kept their forearms relaxed or who did not relax any muscle. Further, it seems that experimentally induced muscle tension can improve performance on a variety of mental tasks (for further details, see Cohen, 1986).

Lastly, let me return to memory, which is likened by RCVM to the retrieval of information from a mental store: the memory system is fully characterized in terms of symbolic structures and the computational operations associated with them. It appears, however, that – like the various thought processes surveyed above – remembrance is intimately linked to the body. Specifically, the body and associated non-symbolic factors play a crucial role in the operation of memory. Experientially, this phenomenon is, I imagine, familiar to every one, but it seems to me that no one has described it as well as Marcel Proust in his monumental *A la recherche du temps perdu*: the following lines are taken from the English edition (Proust, 1983).

> [A]s I moved sharply backwards I tripped against the uneven paving-stones in front of the coach-house. And at the moment when, recovering my balance, I put my foot on a stone which was slightly lower than its neighbour, all my discouragement vanished and in its place was that same happiness. (pp. 898–9)
>
> And almost at once I recognised the vision: it was Venice, of which my efforts to describe it and the supposed snapshots taken by my memory had never told me anything, but which the sensation which I had once experienced as I stood upon two uneven stones in the baptistery of St Mark's had, recurring a moment ago, restored to me complete with all the other sensations linked on that day to that particular sensation. (pp. 899–900)

This episode highlights several points. First, what often triggers the memory system and determines what one remembers is a non-cognitive system, namely, the body. Second, its effect on memory is unsolicited and outside the control and understanding of the cognizer. Third, in the process of recollection the experiential dimension is pivotal. As Proust beautifully describes, the rather vague and holistic recollection of mood precedes the recollection of details – both semantic and episodic – of the content. Fourth, as he explicitly points out, the whole process is based on the cognitive system's being maximally sensitive to everything that impinges upon the individual in the course of the entire history of his or her life. This sensitivity defies any fixed categorization or codification. Indeed, without such defiance the memory system could not be affected by non-semantic bodily and sensory stimulation in this way. This is in line with observations on coding in Chapter 5. Proust's observations are corroborated by modern phenomenological research; for a study that leads to a very similar characterization of the memory process, see Casey (1987).

Before turning to other manifestations of the involvement of the body in cognitive accomplishments, let me refer to the most famous of all the episodes in Proust's work, that on which the entire Proustian odyssey centres – the episode of the madeleine. It is the taste and texture of the cake soaked in tea which the old writer places in his mouth that – by dint of experiential identity – transports Proust through time, brings back the memories of his childhood and with them recaptures an entire life. The memory experience is so strong that it becomes both the driving force and the foundation for one of the longest novels ever written. In this chapter I cite another episode to emphasize the role of actual physical action in memory: as indicated by both episodes, sensory experience is involved with memory in the same way that physical action is. Indeed, bodily action and sensory experience are inextricably linked.

Gestures

The production of bodily movements in the course of cognitive performance is most salient in talking. Notoriously, people 'talk with their hands'. As pointed out by Freedman (1989), there is no such thing as motionless speech – bodily activity during spoken discourse is a universal phenomenon. In order to appreciate this, follow Gergen (1985) and try uttering a verbal expression such as, 'Hello, how are you?' without accompanying it with the usual gestures, facial expressions and body posture. Your behaviour will appear highly artificial, if not aberrant. The empirical investigations of McNeill (McNeill, 1975; McNeill and Levy, 1982) as well as of Kendon (1984) corroborate these observations and ground them in a broader theoretical framework. The investigations reveal that speech and gesture are highly intertwined and that there is an on-going synchronicity between them. From this both McNeill and Kendon conclude that speech and gesture are the two facets of one common psychological structure and computational mechanism.

What does this commonality consist of? Here, McNeill vacillates. On the one hand, he characterizes gestures as being, in a fashion, verbal. On the other hand, he argues that gestures are more basic than speech. My own sympathy is with the latter stance, which is shared by Kendon (1984). I will argue that the intimate link between words and gestures is due to the latter playing a basic role in cognition. This is because gestures present a more direct reflection of the workings of the mind than speech does. Both the structural characteristics of gestures and their ontogenetic development support this conclusion.

Structurally, the holistic and global nature of gestures is especially noteworthy. The gesturing hand depicts many characteristics of the content it conveys: the movement involved in action, its magnitude, dimensions and direction, its force and rhythm, and so forth. An example that McNeill presents is the gesture of gripping made when one talks of a knife. The gesture will depict not only the fact that a knife was gripped, but also – *inter alia* – the shape of the knife and the manner in which it was held. One gesture can, in other words, convey what discursive speech will have to express in many words. Furthermore, gestures often present details that speech does not (and cannot) convey. The global nature of gestures also has a temporal aspect: often, they convey simultaneously contents that speech expresses in succession. Indeed, gestures may anticipate speech and convey what the speaker will express verbally only later (Kendon, 1972, 1975, 1984). The remarkable speed of gestures marks their condensed informativeness, and suggests their psychological primacy and directness. Related to their comprehensiveness is their metaphoricity: remarkably, as many as half of the gestures that speakers produce are metaphorical (Duncan and Fiske, 1977). For instance, contrasting two claims, a speaker may move the right hand when introducing one claim and the left hand when introducing the other, as if to say 'on the one hand' and 'on the other hand'. At times, practically all referential gestures are metaphorical. Lastly, gestures are more immune to error than speech, which also attests to their being more basic (see Kendon, 1984).

Developmental patterns also indicate that gestures pertain to basic modes of behaviour. Early gestures especially, are very much tied to one's acting in the world. They derive from actual physical acts; thus, pointing and reaching gestures seem to be drawn from movements in which real objects are grasped and manipulated (Carter, 1975). Children's first gestures are enactments of their own actions. Indeed, early gesturing is conducted with the entire body or with those parts that are usually involved in the actions in question (e.g. speaking of running, one moves one's feet). As indicated by observations such as McNeill's, adult gesturing also exhibits such patterns, especially when adults attempt to communicate what they cannot articulate in speech. For further discussion, see Werner and Kaplan (1963), Vygotsky (1981, pp. 160–1) and Bates (1987); I shall return in Chapter 13 to some further issues in this topic.

While hand gestures are perhaps the most salient bodily expression manifested in talking, they are not the only one. As pointed out by Freedman (1989; see also Bateson, 1972), the entire body manifests the intent of what is being said. Indeed, as noted in Chapter 4, the body's posture and the way it moves reveal a person's basic stance in the world. Open legs often mark a wish for openness, rigid bodily posture goes with rigidity of personality, the movements of the arms and the hands reveal a person's mode of interaction with other people – how much he or she is in control, how receptive and responsive, how flexible. For interesting empirical observations as well as clinical applications highlighting the metaphoricity of body posture and movement, see Dascal (1991, 1992).

In sum, the intimate involvement of the body in verbal behaviour, as it manifests itself in gesture, posture and movement, seems to be due to these expressions being direct reflections of the basic dynamics of mental activity. This dynamics is not fixed in well-defined, distinct units in which message and medium are differentiated. Rather, it is holistic, does not involve a distinction between message and medium, exhibits a high degree of metaphoricity and is rooted in the agent's action in the world. The discussion of the semantics and pragmatics of language in Part I led to a similar appraisal.

Perception and action

The body seems to play a role even in cognitive accomplishments that at first glance involve no action at all, namely sensory perception. The topic of perception will feature centrally in the next chapter, where the relationship between the mind and the external world will be discussed. Here I will not elaborate on how perception is conceived by RCVM. Suffice it to say that in this view perception need not involve the body. Specifically, perception is viewed as the reception of information through special channels. The information is out there in the world, and organisms detect it by means of their various sensory organs.

Arguing against this standard view of perception has been the main thrust of the work of James Gibson, whose insights are discussed at length in Chapter 8. Here I shall consider only his arguments on the inseparability of perception and bodily movement. These are at the basis of his critique of perception (see Gibson, 1966a, 1979).

One of Gibson's most basic observations is that organisms perceive the world as they move about in it. Yet, even though organisms move, the world is perceived as stable. At the same time, the organism appreciates the fact that it itself is moving. Hence, Gibson concludes that what organisms perceive are patterns that stay invariant as they move. The perception of the external world is then intimately linked with the perception of one's own movement. For what is perceived to remain stable and coherent, the organism has constantly to take into consideration its own location, the position of its body, and its on-going movement in space. 'Vision', Gibson argues, 'is a whole perceptual system, not a channel of sense. One sees the environment not with the eyes but with the eyes-in-the-head-on-the-body-resting-on-the-ground' (Gibson, 1979, p. 205).

Experimental findings support these conclusions. Remarkably, when placed in room-like constructions in which the walls and ceiling glide over the floor, people who see only the moving walls and ceiling but not the stationary feet and floor experience the illusion of being moved forwards and backwards (Lishman and Lee, 1973). For other pertinent experimental findings, see the studies by Warren on passing through doors and climbing stairs (Warren, 1984; Warren and Whang, 1987).

The involvement of the body in perception has also been invoked in the domain of language. According to one of the most important theories of speech perception – the motor theory – speech is perceived by reference to motor patterns employed in speech production. Indeed, in a strong version of the theory, speech perception is said to involve subvocal activation of the speech organs (see, for instance, Halle and Stevens, 1964).

Finally, it will be pointed out that the intimate link between perception and bodily movement finds support in neurophysiological studies. In a classic series of experiments, Held and Hein (1963) hooked pairs of newborn kittens to an apparatus so that one could move more or less normally whereas the second was carried in a gondola, and all its gross movements (except for head turning and leg movement inside the gondola) were ones transmitted by the movements of the first kitten. The kittens were reared in darkness until the active member developed sufficient strength and coordination to move the apparatus. Pairs of kittens spent several hours a day in the experimental condition where they were exposed to identical visual stimulation; the rest of the time they were kept with their mothers and littermates in unlighted cages. After an average of about 30 hours in the apparatus the active members of all tested pairs exhibited normal behaviour in several visually guided tasks; the passive members did not. The latter did, however, develop normal behaviour within days of being allowed to run about in a normal environment. Similarly, Held and Freedman (1963) found that human subjects moving actively showed adaptation to prism goggles whereas those moving passively did not. These studies show that active body movement is essential for the normal development of the perceptual system.

Language and thinking

The body's involvement is also noted when there is neither overt bodily movement nor manifest dealing with the external world. Thus, consider the following description of the beginning of a standard day, from Johnson (1987).

> You wake *out* of a deep sleep and peer *out* from beneath the covers *into* your room. You gradually emerge *out* of your stupor, pull yourself *out* from under the covers, climb *into* your robe, stretch *out* your limbs, and walk *in* a daze *out* of the bedroom and *into* the bathroom. You look *in* the mirror and see your face staring *out* at you. You reach *into* the medicine cabinet, take *out* the toothpaste, squeeze *out* some toothpaste, put the toothbrush *into* your mouth, brush your teeth *in* a hurry, and rinse *out* your mouth. At breakfast you perform a host of further *in-out* moves – pouring *out* the coffee, setting *out* the dishes, putting the toast *in* the toaster, spreading *out* the jam on the toast, and on and on. (pp. 30–1)

As indicated by the many emphasized terms (all thus in the original), the relationship between putting things in containers and taking them out permeates ways in which we structure our experience and express it in language. Not only physical actions but also perceptual and mental ones are conceived and expressed in these terms. The patterns of relationships between objects and containers constitute one of a number of what Johnson refers to as *kinaesthetic image-schemas*. These define basic patterns by which people, as embodied agents, move about in the world and manipulate objects in it. Other image-schemas that Johnson specifies pertain to moving from sources along paths towards targets and goals, making and breaking links, and relationships between wholes and their parts. These patterns are so common and their use is so straightforward that usually people pay little attention to them. Yet, their manifestation is so pervasive that Lakoff and Johnson (1980b; see also Lakoff, 1987b) have argued that they define the very foundations of both language and cognition. In particular, Johnson and Lakoff suggest that both our encoding of the world and its expression in words are rooted in metaphors pertaining to bodily movement and action. Such terms also feature as primitives in the orthodox frameworks of semantic representation of Schank (1973) and Jackendoff (1976).

The kinaesthetic image-schemas are involved not only in the coding of experience and its expression in words but also in the associated mental processing. As pointed out by Lakoff and Johnson (1980b; see also Jackendoff, 1976), basic patterns of inference are based on the application of bodily schemas. In other words, a valid inference is one that is consistent with the patterns of action they enable. Image-schemas thus present a new basis for the modelling of human reasoning, one that contrasts with that presented by the different systems of formal logic. More on this will be said, in conjunction with Johnson-Laird's framework of mental models, in Chapter 8.

Artistic performance

The body's intimate involvement in cognitive performance is especially salient in the skilled playing of musical instruments. How are we to characterize one's playing a musical piece on the piano? The answer RCVM gives is straightforward. In the mind there is a representation that specifies how the music should be played, which, by and large, is similar to the score printed on the sheets one might actually place in front of one when playing. This seemingly straightforward characterization presents a host of problems. Many of these pertain to the representational modelling of motor performance, which is not my concern now (I shall return to it in Chapter 11). Here I point out that the representational description runs the risk of not being able to capture precisely those aspects of music playing that distinguish the accomplished artist. Rubinstein, Horowitz, Barenboim and Glenn Gould all play the same score. They all play it correctly. Yet, how very different their playing is. Rubinstein is the suave gentleman, Horowitz enthralls you with his bravura, Barenboim's restraint is metaphysical and Glenn Gould plays the classical romantics without being romantic – one listens to the music and marvels: the notes that all the performers play are the same, yet the music is so different. When one goes to a concert or buys records of this performer and not another, one makes a choice precisely in terms of these ephemeral qualities. It is not accidental that these differences are so often described in metaphors.

Whatever the characterization of artistic genius, two things are clear. The first is negative: such genius cannot be captured by any representational model. The second is positive: in commanding playing one brings to the fore one's entire being, one's personality as well as one's body. As pointed out by Clynes (1978), each player has his or her own individual touch. Using a special device for the recording of the signature of different touches, Clynes found both universal profiles associated with the different emotions and individual profiles characteristic of individual performers. The bottom line, then, is that when they are playing, players make use of their entire bodies. The more accomplished a player is the more pronounced is this effect. Experts are people who have developed extreme sensitivity coupled with keen musical understanding. Their special skill is that in expressing these they can make unconstrained use of their bodies. Pianists can express through their fingers whatever they sense, feel, believe, understand. In playing, the pianist – like any performing artist – brings together body and psyche. With the maximal use of the body in expression the two become one so that both phenomenologically and conceptually the distinction between them practically withers.

An especially tantalizing manifestation of commanding playing is improvisation. David Sudnow observed such playing and appreciated the mystery it presents. His monograph *Talk's Body* (Sudnow, 1980) emphasizes the central role of the body in piano playing. Since this study is so special, and since his poetic phrasings are not paraphrasable, I quote some of them verbatim:

There is what I call the 'improvisatory hand'. It handles the keyboard by finding itself in good positions at all times to move ahead. It knows the terrain as routes to be taken for speaking a language. Myriad scales, sequences of intervals, patterns of distances available from here to there – the improvisatory hand knows of these incredibly interlocking routes as paths with speed limits, with fingering, with configuring and balancing requirements. (p. 12)

These observations are, of course, reminiscent of those on typewriting with which this chapter began. (Indeed, the analogy between piano playing and typewriting is a central theme in Sudnow's book.) And as in the case of typewriting, in piano playing, too, higher-order structures have precedence over the elementary constituents of which they seem to be composed. Here is how Sudnow describes his 'melody-finding hand':

It is not a first note for which I aim. Rather, a phrase is being handfully taken. . . . You say: 'The Star-Spangled Banner' and, as I move toward the keyboard, the hand prepares for an opening course of movements, doing its rehearsing in the form of the most minute readjustments as it nears the terrain. It gets itself ready, as in reaching for a cup at your side, the hand rounds itself out while it approaches the target, first going a bit too straight on, perhaps, then ever so slightly shifting the axis of approach before the grasp is made. (p. 32)

The body not only guides one as one plays, it is the key determinant of the character of the entire piece:

A commitment to a particular style of music means using hands in the bebop way or ballad way or blues way or even Herbie Hancock way; a single voice emerges in and through the fingertips with no extraneous sentencing or imaging going on, no 'guidance from above' as would interfere with the maintenance of a place-by-place unfolding melody. (p. 67)

Thus:

[T]he emergence of a melody, owes not so much to the focus of one's attention or to the detection of form as it does to the body becoming present to itself in a new way . . . Rather, the theme emerges in the ways the hand now unfolds from place to place in a caretaking manner: a voice is implanted with firm intentionality into the tips of the fingers; each next place is expressly aimed at and commands a unity of bodily engrossment; a definitiveness of movement gears the fingers into a continuous self-consciousness of their pasts and futures; a focused motive is present in the commitment of wrists, arms, and shoulders. (p. 71)

The paragon of the link between music and body is the conductor. Conductors play with their entire bodies. Their instrument – the entire orchestra – is activated neither by pressing, tapping, plucking or blowing. Rather, it is through the perception of the conductor's body by other people that he or she plays:

> The conductor knows the layout of the orchestra as the pianist knows the terrain of the piano. The conductor plays that orchestra collectively somewhat like an instrument . . . The whereabouts of different orchestral voices are known to the conductor's body with a fine intimacy. He brings up a sound here, softens one there, moves from one locale to another with smooth gestural accuracy, now swinging about to wave his arm just over the second viola section in general and then pointing his look and baton right at the first oboist in particular. The sections and subsections of the orchestra are taken up as an incorporated ensemble of places for the conductor's arms, looks, swivelling torso . . . An embodied reflection of the piece as a whole, his undulating movements bear ongoing witness to the relations of the various voices to one another. (pp. 111–12)

Developmental considerations

Lastly, the link between body and cognition is also manifested developmentally. That cognitive development is rooted in the body is one of the key tenets of Piaget's developmental psychology (Piaget, 1970). Piaget characterizes human intellectual development in terms of a succession of distinct stages. The first is the sensory-motor stage, in which the child's cognitive activity is tied to perception and motor performance. Only at subsequent stages does cognitive activity gain independence from the body. In fact, the increased autonomy of cognitive behaviour relative to the body is, according to Piaget, one of the key principles underlying ontogenesis.

I shall return to developmental issues in the third line of my critique. Here, let me consider just one specific observation on music learning, which is very much in line with the various observations considered earlier in this chapter. Serafine (1988) reports that one of the traditional ways to teach American folk fiddle music to young boys is the following. The boy is made to sit next to the fiddler and their legs are tied together. As the fiddler plays and stomps the beat, the boy's leg goes up and down too. So it goes for several lessons, and only after the boy has had much practice at stomping will he be given the instrument to hold.

Note

1. For interesting discussions on the difference between the two senses of 'body' and the irrelevance of the neurophysiological one for psychological research, see Sartre (1957) and most notably Merleau-Ponty (1962), where an extensive study of the phenomenological body and its involvement in behaviour is presented.

8 The world

For the world is not atoms or molecules or radio-activity or other forces, the diamond is not carbon, and light is not vibrations of ether. You can never come to the reality of creation by contemplating from the point of view of destruction.

Rabindranath Tagore

Cognitive activity is usually said to take place in the head. This banal statement is tantamount to saying that cognition pertains to the internal, psychological domain. This characterization is twofold. First, it assumes that cognition is – or rather, can be – conducted independently of the external, physical world. Second, it assumes that cognition pertains to the domain of the individual, and is conducted independently of the social world of other people. In this chapter I will consider the first issue – the relationship of cognition with the physical world; the relationship of cognition and the social world will be the topic of the next chapter. As will be apparent throughout the discussion, the two are intimately related.

Just as the body of interest to us here is the phenomenological body, not the neurophysiological substrate that underlies behaviour, so the world with which I shall be concerned is not that investigated in the physical sciences but rather the external environment in which people live. This consists of the totality of places, objects, instruments, tools, organisms and other people that we encounter and with which we interact. The following discussion tries to show that all these are not external to cognition as RCVM suggests.

Cognition and world

Modern cognitive psychology in general and RCVM in particular ignore the world. In the extremely rare cases in which protagonists of the representational framework refer to the world they do so by way of putting it aside, not of trying to deal with it and the problems it presents. (Remember, the most articulate presentation of the problem of the unbridgeable gap comes from the pen of Jerry Fodor himself.) The one psychologist who has not ignored the world and has seriously confronted the interaction between the cognitive system and the external environment is James Gibson (for general exposition, see Gibson, 1966a, 1979). Indeed, in Gibson's framework of ecological psychology this interaction is the pivotal constituent. Ecological psychology is now a thriving school encompassing both theory and empirical research, and this is not the place for either an exegesis of Gibson's ideas or a review of the work of his followers. Here I follow the insights of Gibson and other investigators of the ecological persuasion and, on the basis of these, define the problematics of the interaction between cognition and the external world and suggest some ways in which this may be addressed. For a summary review of the ecological paradigm, see Michaels and Carello (1981); for key theoretical analyses, see Shaw and Bransford (1977), Turvey and Shaw (1979), Shaw *et al.* (1981); for interesting, sympathetic analyses of the Gibsonian position, see Ben-Ze'ev (1981, 1983) and Bickhard and Richie (1983); and for representational criticisms, see Ullman (1980) and Fodor and Pylyshyn (1988b).

Ecological psychology started as a theory of perception (notably, visual) but as it developed it evolved into a general framework for psychology. Gibson's theory of perception contrasts with the standard view in all important respects. According to the standard theory, the world is given and perception consists in the encoding of the sensory data it presents. These are translated into perceptual images to which interpretative processes are applied so as to assign meaning to what one perceives and to integrate it with one's repertory of knowledge and belief. This process is accomplished through the mediation of internal mental representations and associated computational operations. Gibson's theory denies all this. Of particular interest is an appraisal at its very heart – the rebuff of the definition of the world and the perceiver as two given, separate entities. Here is how Gibson (1979) put it: 'The words *animal* and *environment* make an inseparable pair. Each implies the other. No animal could exist without an environment surrounding it. Equally, although not so obvious, an environment implies an animal (or at least an organism) to be surrounded.' (p. 8).

Throughout his work Gibson pointed out that what is perceived is not raw, senseless sensory data, but meaningful, species-specific information. As noted in Chapter 5, this information is defined in terms of the repertory of actions that the world affords the organism and that the organism can effect in the world (see Gibson, 1977, 1979). Gibson's view of perception solves – or dissolves – practically all the problems pertaining to the unbridgeable gap. First, the relationship between the perceiving agent and the world is no longer presented as one between two protagonists on the two sides of an insurmountable divide. Given that the world which is perceived cannot be defined independently of the agent that perceives it, there is no gap to be breached. Furthermore, since the world is structured by the activities of the perceiving agent, all the information that makes for perception is in the world itself. In Gibson's terms, rather than being detected and encoded, information is picked up. Consequently, no mediation by representations is needed. Perception is, in other words, direct (for further discussion, see Ben Ze'ev, 1981, 1983).

Locomotion and place

Perhaps the most salient affordance that the world presents to higher organisms is the possibility of moving about in it. It appears that locomotion plays an integral role not only in sensory perception, but also in so-called higher cognitive processes. That this is the case should not be surprising at this point of the discussion. In Chapter 7 I surveyed various patterns marking the involvement of bodily movements in the execution of cognitive tasks. Locomotion is one such movement, which, as far as the activation of the body is concerned, is not categorically different from the various other bodily movements surveyed. It can, however, be viewed from the other, complementary perspective. Given that it consists of the body moving about in the world, locomotion can be viewed as defining an interaction not only between cognition and the body, but also between cognition and the world. It is this second interaction that will be the focus of the discussion here.

The classical example marking the cognitive import of locomotion in the world is known, after the Latin word for place, as *the method of loci*. By this remarkably reliable method, which goes back to Roman times, lists of otherwise unrelated items are memorized by associating the items with sites along a trajectory with which the cognitive agent is familiar. For instance, if one has to memorize a list starting with 'egg' and 'tomato' one can 'place' the egg on the tree at the corner of one's house, the tomato on the fence on the other side of the street, and so forth. When one wishes to retrieve the items, one goes – in the theatre of one's mind – along the trajectory, and as one passes by the tree one retrieves the egg, by the fence one retrieves the tomato, etc. Why is this method so successful? The representational framework does not provide an answer. In fact, in this framework the method makes no sense: the trajectory itself is stored in one's mind in terms of symbols in semantic representations. Structurally, these symbols are no different from those by which the items on the list are coded. If anything, the use of the method of loci should be a hindrance: instead of loading one's memory with one list, one overburdens it with two. This method could make sense only if, as far as memory is concerned, there is a qualitative difference between the list of items and the trajectory along which one travels. One possibility is that the coding in terms of the trajectory is helpful because it enables one to ground the memorization process in an activity which is akin to an activity one performs in the world outside, namely, locomotion.

I have presented locomotion because it is a movement in which the significance of the external world is salient. However, the involvement of place is equally apparent in the various other patterns of bodily movement considered in Chapter 7, as should be expected. Following the Gibsonian view, just as organism and world are complementary, so too are body and place. Whenever one engages in movement, one moves one's body or parts of it, and at the same time one goes from one place to another. Thus, when typists tap their fingers in the air, *ipso facto* they activate different positions in the space before them as if those were places on the keyboard of the computer or typewriter. In the same vein is Sudnow's (1980) suggestion that improvisation on the piano is tantamount to a promenade taken along the instrument's keyboard. Accomplished improvisors let their fingers go. The fingers, Sudnow observes, are part of a knowing body, and what the body knows is its whereabouts in the terrain which is the piano.

The following example is a personal experience from my second visit to India, a couple of years after my first. I was in a countryside railway station. I purchased my ticket and then I turned towards the lavatory. I moved to the right and headed towards the second alley to the left. I knew that the place would be there, after the turn. Just before the turn is the kiosk where they sell tea and sugared biscuits, and behind it, the big tree with the red flowers; the entrance to the toilets faces that tree. Had anyone at home, before I embarked on the trip, or even in India, that very same day, before I entered the station, asked me where the lavatory is, it is very unlikely that I could have answered; nor do I think I would even have remembered the existence of the tree with the red flowers. All this knowledge unfolded and came to the fore once I was immersed *in situ*, involved in action.

Empirical findings support these personal observations. A major conclusion of contemporary cognitive research is the context-specificity of memory. As noted in Chapter 2, the more similar the context of recollection is to the context of the original memory situation, the higher the memory performance (see Tulving and Thompson, 1971, 1973). My personal example may be regarded as the limiting case of this conditional statement. In it, the context of retrieval coincides with the original context and the memory system is maximally relieved from the burden of memorization. Rely on the world, and you will remember.

Cognitive performance

The phenomena noted in conjunction with memory extend to cognitive performance in general. As a rule, it appears that being in the world facilitates such performance and enhances it. Again, let me present a personal episode. Years ago, when conducting a seminar on conceptual issues in cognition, I used to tape-record the sessions. They involved much interaction, and often I found that as I was responding to students I was saying things I had not thought of before. As the tapes multiplied I realized that they were not much use: it took as much time to listen to them as to conduct the seminar, and I had no assistance in this. Several years later, I found them in my drawers and played them back. Doing so, I often heard a question posed by a student, and wondered: what can one say in reply to this? How can it be answered? Then I would hear myself responding and very often I would not only like my answer but actually be quite amazed by it: how did I manage to give such an answer? There are good reasons to be amazed: when I was listening to the recording I was much ahead in my thinking. By that time, I had re-read the material discussed in the seminar many times, and the ideas I had expressed were part of an overall system of thought that was part of my own being. Still, when

I listened to the tape, I simply did not know what to say. Apparently, I needed the actual being in the world, the immersion in the social interaction with the students, perhaps also the tension of being on the spot, fully observed by others and having to respond immediately. Rather than inhibit my action all these facilitated it. When I was at leisure in my own home, with much more background (some would say, stored) information, I could not act as well.

These observations suggest that accomplished performance need not be planned ahead of time. People need not behave through the execution of stored, prefabricated plans; instead they may make use of the specific state of affairs in the world in which they are situated.

Supporting these anecdotal observations are experimental findings, in particular, Scribner's studies (1984, 1986). Scribner conducted her investigations in an actual workplace – a milk processing plant – and examined various workers – product assemblers, wholesale delivery drivers, inventory personnel, and office clerks – as they assembled products, priced tickets and took inventories. The different tasks examined all revealed similar patterns. First, performance was carried out not by means of fixed, pre-established algorithms but in accordance with the particulars of the situation at hand. As a consequence, performance manifested flexibility and variation: in different situations different procedures were employed. For instance, the way workers assemble cases of milk varies according to the number of cases and their spatial distribution. Second, as a rule, the procedures of skilled workers were those requiring minimal physical effort (e.g. minimal hand movements); errors were virtually nonexistent. Third, unlike skilled workers novices tended to employ algorithmic procedures. Fourth, outside the context of the workplace, the level of performance manifested significant decrease. Thus, workers whose accuracy on the job in calculation tasks was near perfect made many errors when tested in standard arithmetic tests presenting what formally (but not contextually) could be considered the same tasks. Data presenting similar patterns were collected by Lave *et al.* (1984; see also Lave, 1988). These findings are in line with those surveyed in Chapter 4 on medium and content variation in reasoning and problem solving.

The situated nature of cognitive performance is highlighted in Suchman's *Plans and Situated Action* (1987; see also Agre, 1988). Suchman's work brings together sociological investigation and the study of man–machine interaction, and its key notion is 'situated action'. I shall return to this both towards the end of this line of the critique and in Part II. Here, let me cite the epigraph with which Suchman opens her book; the similarity between this and the comparison between the two theoreticians of painting with which my book opens (and which was written several years before the publication of Suchman's book) is, I think, striking. The passage is taken from Berreman (1966).

Thomas Gladwin (1964) has written a brilliant article contrasting the method by which the Trukese navigate the open sea, with that by which Europeans navigate. He points out that the European navigator begins with a plan – a course – which he has charted according to certain universal principles, and he carries out his voyage by relating his every move to that plan. His effort throughout his voyage is directed to remaining 'on course'. If unexpected events occur, he must first alter the plan, then respond accordingly. The Trukese navigator begins with an objective rather than a plan. He sets off toward the objective and responds to conditions as they arise in an *ad hoc* fashion. He utilizes information provided by the wind, the waves, the tide and current, the fauna, the stars, the clouds, the sound of the water on the side of the boat, and he steers accordingly. His effort is directed to doing whatever is necessary to reach the objective. If asked, he can point to his objective at any moment, but he cannot describe his course.

For further discussion, see Romanyshyn (1982, 1989).

Last but not least, reliance on the setting also plays a crucial role in language comprehension. Obviously, linguistic expressions such as 'here', 'you' or 'this' cannot be interpreted without reference to the state of affairs in the real world in which they are uttered (they are commonly referred to as 'indexical expressions'; see Bar-Hillel, 1954). Furthermore, the physical world plays an essential role in speakers' determination of what knowledge they can assume they share with their interlocutors. As shown by Clark and Marshall (1981), without relying on the world in which they are commonly situated, speakers attempting such a determination may be trapped in an infinite loop.

Developmental considerations

Analogous patterns are also observed in development. In general, it appears that immersion in the world increases children's level of cognitive performance, as Vygotsky was especially careful to note. I shall consider Vygotskian psychology in all the remaining chapters in Part I. Here, let me cite a work conducted by one of Vygotsky's disciples. Istomina (1975) gave children lists of items to memorize. There were two conditions. In the experimental condition, the children were made to engage in a shopping game. They were presented with the list, and told that it specified items they should purchase. They were then instructed to go to another room where a 'grocery' was set up. There, they had to recount the list of items so as to purchase them. In the control condition, the situation was the classical memory situation: the items were presented as lists to be memorized and the children were tested on how much they remembered. The results of the study were striking. When the memory task was immersed in action, the children's performance was significantly higher than when it was set in isolation from any real activity in the world.

The in-built reliance of cognition on the world is also manifested in the very early stages of development. Specifically, the embedding of communication in action in the world is a crucial determinant in language acquistion. As pointed out by Ochs (1979), caregivers often use the contingencies of the situation to attract children's attention and help them understand what the adult is saying.

Thought processes

The tie between cognition and the world is so strong that the latter's influence may be exercised even within the internal domain itself. In conducting mental activity the mind may operate in a manner similar to that in which it deals with objects and situations in the external world. This, I think, is what is impressive about the classical experimental results pertaining to mental rotation. As discovered by Shepard and his associates (Shepard and Metzler, 1971; Cooper and Shepard, 1973), response times obtained when people are asked to determine the identity of rotated items and their mirror images define a monotonic linear function. Specifically, the larger the angular deviation of the target from the canonical vertical position, the longer the response time. This suggests that a parameter of constant rate of rotation is to be included in cognitive modelling. The conclusion is, in a sense, revolutionary, for it implies that at least some cognitive activity is conducted in the manner of activity in the external world. What one has in one's head is not symbols that one computes, but rather object-like entities that one manipulates in the way one handles objects in the real world.

In the paradigm of mental models developed by Johnson-Laird the manipulation of objects becomes a cornerstone for thought processes in general (for a review, see Johnson-Laird, 1983; for more specific arguments, see Johnson-Laird, 1982). Johnson-Laird argues that reasoning and problem solving cannot be accounted for in terms of formal deductive processing. These activities are both facilitated and hindered by parameters which from a formal point of view should not make a difference. (Recall Wason and Johnson-Laird's four-card problem in Chapter 4.) Consequently, Johnson-Laird proposed that these activities are conducted not by means of the application of deductive operations on symbols in stored semantic representations, but rather by the examination of alternative scenarios that the cognizer constructs in the theatre of his or her mind[1]. These scenarios, Johnson-Laird argues, are like models of the real world, and thought proceeds by means of inspection of them and manipulation of the entities of which they are composed.

Parenthetically, note that Johnson-Laird does not relinquish representationalism altogether. In his view of mind, permanent knowledge is still represented in semantic representations of the classical type. It is only when the cognitive system is engaged in activity that mental models are constructed. This position is completely analogous to that which seems to define the present consensus with regards to mental images, as proposed by Kosslyn (1980; see also Kosslyn and Schwartz, 1977); its basic claim is twofold. On the one hand, it maintains that images are a non-epiphenomenal, cognitive medium, distinct from the propositional medium and affording distinct advantages in various cognitive activities. On the other hand, it maintains that the general, permanent knowledge store is representational in the classical sense, and that it is from this underlying store that mental images are generated.

Pertinent data are also encountered in my own study of thought sequences (see Chapter 4). Specifically, consider the phenomenon to which I refer as *enactment*

(Shanon, 1988b). In enactment thought expressions are not taken as ideas that one entertains but rather have conferred on them an assumed reality, thus defining an inner world that is locally endowed with a separate existence of its own. Enactment may be likened to the construction of a scenario in one's mind, a framed stage in which one performs. Sequences (1) and (2) are examples of enactment, in (1) a directed action and in (2) a conversation:

1. 1. Where is the book?
   2. In the office?
   3. Searching mentally at home (it is not there).
   4. I must look in the office.
2. 0. Imagining a conversation with Simona.
   1. They gave me a room at the Cité Universitaire.
   2. Do you know whether they supply sheets there?
   3. Oh, I can ask Simona if they supply sheets at the Cité Universitaire.

It is remarkable that in these sequences action (as it is executed in the theatre of one's mind) precedes the decision to carry out (in the world) that very same action. Indeed, it is the execution of the action in one's mind, not a detached reflection, that brings about the decision to carry it out in the world. In (1) the thinker engages (mentally) in probing around only to come to the decision that he should (actually) search for the book in the office. Similarly, in (2) it is the mental act of asking Simona whether sheets are being provided that makes the thinker realize that asking Simona is, indeed, a way to find out whether sheets are being provided. In other words, it is the simulated action already executed in the theatre of one's mind that brings about the idea to act in that manner in the world.

By RCVM, which maintains that action is the overt expression of underlying, covert symbolic processing, such a state of affairs does not make sense at all. The only way out is to reverse the picture and regard action as the primary cognitive capability. As indicated by the two examples, action is carried out through one's being immersed in a situation. Decision is the outcome of a reflection upon the action in question. The basic thing one does with one's thought is thus not to process information but to act.

Dreams and hallucinations

Throughout the foregoing discussion I have underscored the indispensable involvement of the world in cognitive activity. What would happen to the mind if the world were not there? Strictly speaking, the world is, of course, always there; yet, functionally, there is a situation in which in effect the world does not exist. We are all familiar with it – dreaming. When dreaming, our contact with the world is pretty much severed (more precisely, we dream only when our contact with the world is severed). And indeed, as we all know, the scenes we see in the dream and events that take place in it may be quite peculiar. Not only are they often things that do not or cannot happen in reality, often they even defy the basic canons of logic.

An astute account of the peculiar characteristics of the dream is presented by Henri Bergson (1911/1982) in his 'Le rêve' (The dream), a lecture delivered in 1901 and, as far as I can tell, never published in English; the following is my own free translation from the original French:

> In the state of wakefulness, visual memory which helps us to interpret visual sensations is obliged to adhere exactly to the sensation; it thus follows its progress, it occupies the same amount of time; in sum, the perception of external events lasts just as long as do the events themselves. But in the dream, the interpretative memory of the visual sensation conquers back its liberty; the fluidity of the visual sensation causes the memory not to adhere to it; thus, the rhythm of interpretative memory must no longer adopt that of reality; and the images may hence follow upon each other in a vertiginous rapidity, as would the images of a cinematographic film whose rolling is not regulated. (p. 106)

In sum, during the dream the cognitive apparatus is left to run its own free course. By way of contrast, this highlights the important role that the external world has in the conduct of normal cognitive function. By virtue of its constant presence, the world fixes the mind and holds it from running astray. I am looking through the window. The man residing in the apartment on the top floor of the opposite building is kissing his wife. I watch. Now the woman withdraws to the kitchen, and the man sits and starts reading. I continue to watch because the objects of my perception persist in the world and I go along with them in my watching. But even if for a while I turn away and stop watching what is outside, when I gaze through the window again, again I see my distant neighbours. I take it that the people I now see are the same people I saw a moment before because I know that the world is always there, and because I can rely on the fact that unless something drastic happens, this world always remains the same.

By fixing perception and the mentations associated with it, the world frees cognition from an immense load. One does not have to remember all the details of the situation in which one is and which one entertains. One can direct attention only to the focus of interest, knowing that whenever one wants to change focus and consider any of the peripheral details, the information will still be there. Or rather, the world constituted by all the details will still be there.

Hallucination demonstrates how lost the mind becomes when left on its own. In hallucinations the mind loosens the grip the world has on it and, as a consequence, runs its own associative course. In this hallucination is like the dream; yet, there is a crucial difference. Dreamers are asleep and their bodies are paralysed. The paralysis of the musculature during dreaming is apparently a measure protecting one from acting out one's dreams (see Dement, 1976). As demonstrated by Jouvet (1980), when the inhibition of the musculature is experimentally cancelled, sleeping animals start to enact their dreams in the world. Unlike the dreamers, people hallucinating are in the world, which means they have the possibility of executing concrete actions. Depending on the state of one's cognition, these can be dangerous.

Another effect of the world on hallucinating people pertains to perception. These people perceive the world; however, since fixation is lost, so is the sense of constancy. Consequently, new perceptions of things that are there may be experienced as perceptions of new things. Thus, the helping world becomes a source of extreme danger: instead of offering reliable sustenance, it mercilessly bombards the mind with new sensory input, hence with more and more sources that can lead the mind astray. Ironically, it is the same function that makes the world so helpful to the normal mind that makes its presence so dangerous to the hallucinating one (for general pertinent data, see Siegel and West, 1975).

The effects of sensory deprivation lend further support to this view. After several hours of being in complete sensory deprivation (alone in darkness and silence, immersed in water at body temperature), normal subjects start to experience hallucinations, and at times they may reach a state not unlike a psychotic one (for reviews, see Zubek, 1969). These effects are generated without any chemical or psychological triggering. The only effect is a negative one, the isolation of the mind from the sustenance of the external world.

Tools and artefacts

The world in which human beings live does not consist only of natural landscapes, physical objects and biological organisms, but also of objects that people have created. The artefacts human beings produce populate the world and alter the ecological environment in which they live. Most readers of this book (and of course, its author) would, I gather, find themselves at a loss if plunged back into the environment to which our biological bodies adapted when *Homo sapiens* evolved. The ecosystem in which we live consists, in other words, not only of the natural – physical and biological – environment of the world, but also of the manifold of human-made objects that our species has created. Consequently, the affordances presented to us by the world are those not only pertaining to the natural, physical landscape but also those pertaining to the modifications of the landscape we have made and the artefacts we have placed in the world (see Gibson, 1979; and for further extensions, Costall and Still, 1989; Heft, 1989).

Memory

The knot in the handkerchief serving as a memory aid is, of course, proverbial. A classic case of the involvement of a physical object in memory was mentioned in Chapter 7 – Proust's recollection of the past through the tasting of the madeleine. A similar episode is recounted by Cocteau in conjunction with his returning to the landscapes of his childhood. Cocteau (reported in Romanyshyn, 1982) describes how he trails his hand along the wall and as he is doing this re-experiences the past:

> Just as the needle picks up the melody from the record, I obtained the melody of the past with my hand. I found everything: my cape, the leather of my satchel, the names of my friends and of my teachers, certain expressions I had used, the sound of my grandfather's voice, the smell of his beard, the smell of my sister's dresses and of my mother's gown.

In other words, just as music may be recorded on vinyl, memory is recorded on the wall.

In fact, objects serve not only for reminding, but for recording the past, storing information about it and preserving it for future use. After all, even those of us with very good memories make occasional use of personal phone lists in order to retrieve phone numbers. And how could we remember all we do without the notes, books, photographs and computer records that we constantly use in order to store and retrieve information? On the level of society at large this reliance on physical records is even more manifest (for further discussion, see Radley, 1990).

This claim might be dismissed by saying that physical objects serve only as aids to memory. Reflection reveals that the beneficial effect of these objects is not as simple as it appears. Thus, consider the knot in the handkerchief. The person tying the knot is supposed to remember X (e.g. making a phone call, running an errand). Having made the knot, however, he has to remember two things: the original item X, and the fact that the knot indicates Y, namely, that he has to remember X. Thus, how the knot helps in reminding one of either X or Y is a real puzzle. As argued in Shanon (1990a), the puzzle dissolves when one appreciates that the knot serves not as a trigger of represented facts, but as a contextual element that, like the physical setting described in the episode of my trip to India, places the cognitive agent back in a certain context of action (see also Vygotsky, 1978). The observations towards the end of Chapter 2 corroborate this assessment.

The prevalent reliance on physical records suggests that their involvement with memory is intrinsic. Rather than being mere aids or triggers, physical objects serve as veritable memory stores and their manipulation is part and parcel of the activity of remembering. As will be argued at length in Part II, cognitive performance may be regarded not as the processing of mentally represented information, but as an activity akin to the manipulation of objects in the world. This is true of memory as well. Rather than attesting to the limitations of our memory abilities, the use of physical records demonstrates the very nature of memory and its mode of operation. Memory is primarily the re-enactment of actions that cognitive agents perform in the world; these are executed by means of the body and with the use of tools and artefacts. As argued by Vygotsky (1978; see also Asmolov, 1986; Bakhurst, 1990), remembering without manifestly acting in the world and manipulating objects in it is a derivative ability, an internalization of the more basic external memory activities, and appears only later in ontogenesis.

Cognitive performance

Various cognitive performances exhibit patterns analogous to those encountered with memory. Try this: what is 12,345 times 67,890? No reader will have any difficulty in finding the answer. I would be surprised, however, if any one came up with it without using pen and paper (assuming that one does not use instruments such as a pocket calculator or an abacus). The writing down of the two numbers and the carrying out of the computation on paper serve the same memory function as that noted in the previous section, but they do more. The skill of multiplication – at least for most of us – is intimately tied to the manner in which the numbers are written down, to their relative positions, and to the marks and notations one supplements them with (see Brown and Burton, 1978). Arithmetic calculation, in other words, consists in the manipulation of certain physical objects in a certain manner. Just as in order to talk to a friend who lives in Paris I pick up the phone, so in order to carry out long multiplication or subtraction I take up paper and a pen. And just as long-distance communication is intimately tied to the phone and the constraints imposed by it, so is arithmetic calculation with respect to the pen and paper (as well as the abacus and the calculator).

When I multiply numbers on paper I write down not only the two numbers presented to me and the final result, but also all sorts of other, intermediate numbers. What are these for? Surely, they do not represent anything of significance in its own right. The intermediate numbers, it seems, are like stepping-stones that help one cross a wide river: if the distance between adjacent stones is not too great, then the river becomes traversable. The person will step from one stone to another, from that to the next, and having made so many steps in that manner, the river will have been crossed.

The marks that one puts down on paper are not just external aids employed because of the shortcomings of one's memory. Rather, they are intimately linked to mentation in a manner that drastically blurs the distinction between the processes that go on inside the head and those that are carried out in the world. Thus, consider the process of creative writing. By RCVM, writing is the expression of ideas in words which one traces on the page. The present discussion suggests that the role which the paper (or for that matter the computer screen) plays is much more central. When I sit by the table and turn the computer on I know that I want to write a letter to a friend, or a memorandum, or a chapter. I have something in mind (no, do not take this metaphor literally!): I know that I will be informing a friend of my forthcoming trip to New York, or that the chapter will deal with the use of tools and artefacts. I know this, but I do not know exactly what I will say. I jot things down on the paper (or on the screen): some may constitute well-formed sentences that make up a running text, some may be isolated sentences and semi-sentences, some may be phrases or single words. Some of the constituents of the text may be more structured than others; some may not be structured at all. The variation will also manifest itself dynamically. At times, I will find myself engaged in the on-going writing of a smoothly flowing text; at others, I will just jot down ideas, suggestions, references for future reflection. I may start writing a paragraph, putting one sentence after another on the paper, and then find it difficult to continue. Afterwards, I may return to what I have already written, read it, and then go on writing. At times, I will find one mode of composition easier, and at others, another. At times one finds oneself bursting with ideas and engages in a veritable brainstorming on the paper, and at other times one is engaged in working out the material in front of one, in the manipulation of words and sentences and paragraphs. 'Manipulation' should be taken here in a very literal sense: what one does with the text on the paper (or screen) is move items around, clean bits and pieces, add little touches here and there. Like the far bank of the river, that which is to be written is too distant. It is simply impossible to pass, in one continuous sweep, from the state of there being nothing on the page to that in which the final, written product is there. One throws things about, enriching the world with objects of which one can make use and from which one may construct larger structures. In the case of the river these objects are stones, in the case of the act of writing they are words and phrases.

Thus, the writing of a text is not the translation of ideas one has in one's mind into words that are put down on paper. Rather, it is an interplay between jotting things down and manipulating elements in the world. These two processes are intimately linked: reading words on the page triggers more ideas, and the ideas produce more and more words on the page. There is no sense in separating the two and it is impossible to draw a clear-cut boundary between their contributions. Both are indispensable, and it is the continuous interplay between them that makes up writing (for similar observations, see Dascal, 1981).

The following report, given by Gertrude Stein in an interview, is very similar. It is of special interest for the light it sheds on the creative process:

> 'You will write', she said, 'if you will write without thinking of the result in terms of a result, but think of the writing in terms of discovery, which is to say that creation must take place between the pen and the paper, not before in a thought or afterwards in a recasting. Yes, before in a thought, but not in careful thinking. It will come if it is there and if you will let it come, and if you have anything you will get a sudden creative recognition. You won't know how it was, even what it is, but it will be creation if it comes out of the pen and out of you and not out of an architectural drawing of the thing you are doing.' (Preston, 1963, pp. 160–1)

Artistic creation

The cognitive dynamics just noted is not specific to words, but is encountered in all artistic creation. Indeed, in painting the process is much more pronounced. The painter cannot paint without paints. There is simply no sense in talking of a painting which is not there on the canvas. And as noted in Chapter 4, there is no sense in separating the medium of the painting from whatever may be regarded as its content. To provide empirical support, let me cite a yet unreported study, in which artists were observed as they engaged in the task of unplanned drawing. They were presented with meaningless doodles and were asked to develop them into drawings. What was found was a process totally analogous to that described above in conjunction with writing. At times, it appeared that the painters had in mind something they wanted to draw: a human figure, a landscape, a sequence of triangles, parallel lines, etc. At other times, however, it was clear that the painters did not know what they were about to draw until they actually drew things on the paper. They would let their hands go, perhaps even stumble and make a line that they did not originally intend to produce. But then, the very movement of the hand would lead them somewhere, they would be carried by it, and then would continue. In mid-course, they might realize what they were drawing and go on with that idea. At other times they might stop and inspect what they had painted. Not infrequently, the painters themselves would marvel at what they found they had put on the paper.

Further ramifications

We have seen that the contribution of the physical environment to cognition is not confined to performances manifestly executed in the external world. The same holds with respect to tools and artefacts. Empirical data demonstrating this were obtained by Stigler (1984), who compared Chinese and American children engaged in mental arithmetic. Both qualitative and quantitative differences were found in the two groups' patterns of performance. Remarkably, those of the Chinese reflected the operations employed in using an abacus. Indeed, users of the abacus reported that when starting mental calculations they constructed a mental image of an abacus and proceeded by moving the 'beads' in this 'mental abacus' as they would have if working with a real one.

   Let me close by noting that tools and artefacts are not the only human-created extension to the world. One should add the entities constituting what Popper (1972) referred to as World Three, the world of the creations of culture, including ideas and ideologies, theories and world-views, scientific knowledge and works of art. Thus, integrals are part and parcel of what for the mathematician is the world, and a cadence is so for the musician. Heuristics for solving integrals are tools just as the abacus is. Similarly, the totality of the beliefs, opinions and customs comprising a culture are no less real than the physical surroundings. The one and the other constitute the world in which the members of the culture live (for further discussion, see Shweder, 1991; Shanon, 1991b).

Note

1.   The phrase 'theatre of the mind' is perhaps misleading. It is not intended to

imply that cognitive material is observed by a detached internal spectator. Rather, the cognitive agent is a performer. The phrase is meant to indicate that the performance is carried out not in the external world, but in a simulated internal domain.

9 *The social other*

All phenomena with which mental sciences deal are, indeed, creations of the social community.

Wilhelm Wundt

By RCVM, cognition is essentially the study of the individual. It is a discipline concerned with how cognitive agents speak, understand language, perceive the world, memorize, think, solve problems and create. In all these cases, the domain of investigation is the mind of the single person. It is assumed that this mind can (and should) be investigated without any consideration of other minds or persons. Unlike solipsistic philosophers, cognitive psychologists do not put the existence of other persons in any doubt. Yet, they deny the relevance of these to the investigation of the cognitive system. The following discussion is guided by the appraisal that in adhering to the strict individualistic perspective the study of cognition is led astray. It will attempt to show that the social other cannot be disregarded even by those who set themselves to study the individual mind.

While most cognitive psychologists ignore the social other, social psychologists have not ignored the modern developments in cognitive psychology. In fact, a dominant paradigm in the field today is that of cognitive social psychology, which tries to analyze inter-personal phenomena using the conceptual machinery of representational cognitive psychology. (For representative investigations, see Carroll and Payne, 1976; Hastie *et al.*, 1980; Wyer and Srull, 1984, 1989; Berkowitz, 1988.) As defined by Brewer (1988, p. 1), 'Broadly speaking, social cognition is the study of the interaction between internal structures – our representations of social objects and events.' Central to the analysis is 'social knowledge', i.e., knowledge about other people. This knowledge is defined in the classical representational manner; and correspondingly, social psychological behaviour is characterized by means of computational operations applied to representational structures. The study of the social is thus incorporated within the standard representational framework. Herbert Simon (1976), when proclaiming that, 'Social cognitive psychology is cognitive psychology', epitomizes this approach.

The present discussion pertains to cognitive psychology, not social psychology, which is a discipline in its own right and outside both my field of expertise and the concerns of this book. My interest, rather, is in the nature of human cognition and the conceptual foundations of cognitive theory. Yet, in arguing against RCVM's disregard of the social other, *ipso facto* I will be making a case against the paradigm of cognitive social psychology as well. Indeed, the move recommended here is antithetical to that taken by this paradigm. Social cognitive psychology attempts to study the social in the representational-computational terms of individualistic cognitive psychology; I will argue that the individual's mind should be studied in terms drawn from the domain of the social. *Prima facie*, if the representational conceptual framework is not appropriate for the study of individualistic cognition, it is even less appropriate for the study of social behaviour. Here, however, only the social aspects of individualistic cognition will be considered. The examination of the intrinsically social aspects of inter-personal behaviour is a topic of study in its own right, pertaining not to the conceptual foundations of cognitive science but to the foundations of social science. The main question in that context is whether the various social sciences (social psychology, sociology, economics and the like) are reducible to psychology or not. This parallels questions of reduction between other sciences. The non-reductive stance on the relationship between the social and the psychological originates with Wundt (see Farr, 1982). More recently, the question has been referred to as that of methodological individuation; for non-reductive opinions see, for instance, Popper (1957) and Agassi (1973).

Definitional considerations

In proclaiming that cognition can be studied without reference to other persons, RCVM assumes that the basic terms of the cognitive domain can be defined independently of parameters pertaining to the social domain. This assumption is, however, not beyond contestation. Is the individual an independent entity whose identity can be defined without reference to the social context in which he or she is situated? Am I the same person when I am alone and when I interact with other people? Am I the same regardless of whom I interact with? These definitional questions cannot be settled by any direct empirical test. If, however, the individual's behaviour varies greatly according to whom he or she interacts with, then methodologically the postulation of independent, strictly individualistic terms is spurious. This has been argued by various investigators; amongst them are Blumer (1969) and the school of symbolic interactionism, and the advocates of social constructionism (see Berger and Luckman, 1967; Gergen, 1985). For a critique of the cognitive-individualistic orientation in contemporary social psychology, see Shotter (1975), Forgas (1983), Sampson (1988) and Gergen (1989).

The problems of independent individualistic definition and the relativistic stance proposed in response to it are largely analogous to those problems presented by the patterns of context-dependence in language and the arguments against context-free semantics in the first line of the present critique. The unbounded and pervasive context-dependence of meaning undermines the usefulness of the postulation of independent semantic terms and distinctions. In the same vein is the suggestion made in Chapter 8 that different organisms inhabit essentially different worlds.

In social psychology the same types of problem have surfaced in conjunction with the postulation of independent personality identities and traits. Like representational cognitive psychologists who attempted to characterize meaning in terms of features, social psychologists have attempted to characterize personality in terms of traits (see, for instance, Allport, 1937; Cattell, 1957; Norman, 1963). And here, too, context effects and the contribution of contingent variations render the enterprise hopeless. Apparently, in natural situations the hypothesized traits typically account for no more than 15 per cent of the diversity of individual differences; for a comprehensive critique of the trait approach to personality, see Mischel (1968, 1973).

Functionalist considerations

Like the body and the world, the social other plays a crucial role in cognitive activity. Yet, a caveat is in order. While conceptually there is full parallelism between the three, practically there is also a fundamental difference between them. We have no existence without our body and wherever we go the world is around us. By contrast, it is, of course, common for people to be alone. Thus, in asking whether human cognitive activity depends on social factors the question is not whether when left alone people can function cognitively. Nor does a stance that regards cognition as socially dependent imply that in isolation people cannot think or reason or even open their mouths and talk. Indeed, even if an empirical test were conducted and a person were placed alone on an isolated island, and his or her cognitive function deteriorated as a consequence, no clear-cut conclusions could be drawn. It is quite likely that the isolation would have a host of deleterious effects, but these might be largely due to factors which are of no concern here – affect, mood, motivation, social deprivation, and many others. With respect to the cognitive questions proper, the experiment would not tell us very much.

Thus, in saying that in studying cognition the social other cannot be ignored, and in claiming that individual cognition is functionally dependent on other people, I am not saying that for the cognitive system to operate other people have to be always present. Rather, my claim is that in the functioning of the cognitive system social factors play a crucial role, and that ignoring them leads to a distorted view of the nature of cognition and the basic principles of its operation. The claim has three facets. First, even though cognitive processes may be executed within the confines of the head, so to speak, some of the basic mechanisms of cognition involve socially defined parameters. Second, even though people can function in isolation, the presence of other people is highly instrumental for many cognitive activities – so much so that the very nature of these activities assumes that at least at times the cognitive agent will interact with other people. Third, even though the mature adult and the skilled expert may not need other people, in the development of the child and in the acquisition of knowledge by the adult the involvement of other people is crucial. In this section several patterns pertaining to the first two issues will be discussed. Developmental patterns pertaining to the third will be discussed in Chapters 14 and 17.

Meaning and the structure of language

Let me start with a topic with which I have already been much concerned – meaning and its representation. In the first part of my critique the context-dependence of the semantics of natural language was repeatedly underlined. The meanings associated with the words people utter vary with the specific settings in which people are situated and act. Typically, when one is talking one is not alone. Thus, in saying that meaning varies with context, *ipso facto* I am saying that meaning varies with the different interactions people have with others. Likewise, in saying that in natural language pragmatics plays a basic role, I am saying that verbal behaviour cannot be studied without considering the actions that people perform when speaking, and the various effects their words exert on others (see, for example, Austin, 1962). Thus, to say that the semantics of natural language is pragmatically based is to say that the meanings of words, the rules of their semantic composition, and the principles governing their use are all defined in terms which are not confined to the domain of individualistic psychology.

While most contemporary cognitive psychologists adhere to the individualistic view, two of the giants of psychological and social thought of this century, Lev Vygotsky and George Herbert Mead, were of the opposite persuasion. Vygotsky's characterization of the meaning of words gives the essence of the sociologically oriented view of language:

> A sign is always originally a means used for social purposes, a means of influencing others, and only later it becomes a means of influencing oneself . . . The mental function of the word . . . cannot be explained except through a system extended beyond individual humans. The word's first function is its social function; and if we want to trace how it functions in the behavior of an individual, we must consider how it is used to function in social behavior. (Vygotsky, 1981, pp. 157–8)

Similarly, Mead's social philosophy is guided by the appraisal that the mind cannot be defined without reference to the interaction of the cognitive agent with other people. More specifically, the very genesis of symbols is through the social process. The self and the significance of symbols arise together as individuals assume the role of the other, and stimulate themselves as the other would stimulate them (see Mead, 1934, 1938). Thus:

> All objects are originally social objects, but in the case of inanimate things we have abstracted all content except the resistance which is the stuff of perceptual things, ourselves or other things. They are all in some sense

hypothetical until we get them into the manipulatory field and complete the act which the distant experience initiates. While in a perceptual world the ultimate test is the handling of what we see, we stop far short of this in most tests of the reality of things. We depend upon the substantive meanings of what we see, that is, upon the universalized social responses, which implicate experimental data but do not demand them. (Mead, 1938, p. 151)

Likewise:

We must regard mind . . . as arising and developing within the social process, within the empirical matrix of social interactions. We must, that is, get an inner individual experience from the standpoint of social acts which include the experiences of separate individuals in a social context wherein those individuals interact. The processes of experience which the human brain makes possible are made possible only for a group of interacting individuals: only for individual organisms which are members of a society; not for the individual organism in isolation from other individual organisms. (Mead, 1934, p. 133)

Remarkably, the social other marks his or her presence not only in the semantics and pragmatics of natural language but also in its syntax. This is demonstrated in one of the most orthodox contexts of representational cognitive science, namely, generative-transformational grammar. The presence of the other is here so apparent that one is quite likely to ignore its more general cognitive ramifications. Thus, consider the pattern exhibited by the two following imperatives:

  1. Wash yourself!
  2. Wash myself!

The first sentence is grammatical whereas the second is not. The classical generative-transformational explanation is that the imperative involves the deletion of the constituent *you* which appears in the deep structure of the sentence but not in its surface structure. In the deep structure of (1) this constituent appears, and therefore the reflexive transformation can apply. Afterwards the *you* in the subject position is deleted, and the surface form with the reflexive pronoun in object position is produced. In (2) the reflexive pronoun is not coreferential with the (hidden from the surface) pronoun *you*, which makes the reflexive transformation ungrammatical.[1]

This is an old analysis; others have since been put forward. It is significant here, however, that the term *you* has been suggested as a constituent in the grammar. As a rule, grammatical theory is extremely reluctant to incorporate terms that are not the labels of structural categories. *You* is one of a very small number of terms having specific semantic value which serve as parameters in the definition of syntactical operations. Thus, the incorporation of *you* in the definition of grammatical transformations or of other linguistic operations signifies that the notion of addressee and of the subject (in the non-grammatical sense) of the speaker's verbal acts plays a role in the very definition of the formal operations of syntax. Even in what is often regarded as the pristine domain of pure cognition, the social other cannot be ignored.

In the old transformational analysis the term *you* appears only in a special class of sentences of which it is the defining marker, the imperative. In subsequent, non-orthodox generative transformational analyses a more extreme picture is drawn. In Ross (1970) it is suggested that all declarative sentences have the constituent *you* hidden in their deep structures. I will not go into details, but only emphasize that all the arguments presented to support it are formal-syntactical ones. Indeed, all are of the same kind as the old argument in support of the *you* in (1) above.

Consciousness

Usually, talking when not in the presence of other persons is not considered normal. Yet, all of us often find verbal-like expressions passing through our heads. I have already alluded to this phenomenon several times, and thought sequences of this type have occupied much of my empirical research – in particular, the pattern discussed in Chapter 8 and referred to as enactment in thought sequences. As noted there, mental enactment is also encountered in social-like interactions conducted in the province of one's own mind. For ease of reference, let me present again one of the examples introduced in Chapter 8:

    0. Imagining a conversation with Simona.
        1. They gave me a room at the Cité Universitaire.
        2. Do you know whether they supply sheets there?
        3. Oh, I can ask Simona if they supply sheets at the Cité Universitaire.

Banal as this example may seem, it is illustrative. It indicates that even in the province of our own minds we are not alone. Very often, thinking resembles simulated talking, hence, an interaction with another human being. Thus, even what might seem to be the hallmark of inner, subjective experience involves the social other.

This example – and thought sequences in general – suggest that our inner monologues consist of an internalization of activities which are primarily inter-personal. This appraisal is in line with various other, independent proposals suggesting that a central element in our mental life is there being, in our minds, a 'virtual other' (Bråten, 1987). Indeed, many thinkers – from Hegel and Marx to Mead and Vygotsky – have suggested that consciousness comes into being through the individual's interaction with other people. Mead's stance on the matter is paradigmatic. Throughout his social philosophy (see, in particular, Mead, 1922), the self gains its existence with the individual assuming the role of the other, viewing itself and responding as the other would. Just as words gain their meaning through their meeting with other words, the self comes into being through the interaction of the individual with other people. These others treat me as a person, and I respond. It is through the totality of these responses that my own being is constituted (for similar ideas, see Barlow, 1980). Thus, it may be argued that the notion of the other precedes the notion of the self. This seems to be the case not only in ontogenesis but also on the historical scale. It has been suggested (see Jaynes, 1976) that the modern conception of consciousness is a relatively recent historical phenomenon, about 2,500 years old. Before then, people attributed to voices outside them what modern people would attribute to their own inner speech.

One of the most eloquent presentations of this idea is in Vygotsky's first publication in psychology, 'Consciousness as a problem in the psychology of behaviour' (Vygotsky, 1979): 'We are aware of ourselves in that we are aware of others because in our relationship to others we are the same as others in their relationships to us. I am aware of myself only to the extent that I am as another to myself' (p. 29). Thus, consciousness is rooted in the social world. Indeed, it is by virtue of the social other in oneself that one becomes conscious. The social other, then, is a principal constituent of the individual's cognition. For further theoretical discussion, see the works of the social scientists Schutz (1967), Bateson (1972) and Shotter (1984), and the philosophers Buber (1923/1958), Dewey (1929), Sartre (1957), Heidegger (1962) and Merleau-Ponty (1973).

Cognitive performance

Let us return to enactment in thought sequences. This example indicates that to come to a decision, some interaction with another person is needed; at least, such an interaction may serve as a crucial aid. When another person is not physically available, conscious mentation serves by offering a substitute. For cognitive purposes the virtual other seems to be a fairly good substitute. That the virtual other plays such an important role in subjective mentation makes it only likely that actual others play an important role in cognitive performance.

Indeed, empirical observations indicate that the presence of other people affects the individual's cognitive performance. As shown by Zajonc and his associates (see Zajonc, 1965; Zajonc and Sales, 1966), even the mere presence of another person has such an effect. It should be noted, however, that subsequent literature does not present one consistent picture: both facilitatory and inhibitory effects are reported, a number of intervening variables are marked, and different interpretations and explanations of the effects are offered.

Interaction with other people does appear to enhance one's cognitive accomplishments. In particular, various investigators of problem-solving behaviour have pointed out that people in groups often reach solutions and achievements that they do not when acting alone (see Johnson and Johnson, 1975; Mugny et al., 1981; Glachan and Light, 1982; Rogoff, 1990). Cognitively speaking, it appears that the group is more than the sum of the people in it. One particular interaction with the other is teaching: I shall return to teaching, learning and cognitive development both in the next section and in Chapters 14 and 17.

A most intriguing case is that of memory. At first glance, memory seems to be totally explained within the province of the individual cognitive agent. Yet, as independently pointed out by Harré and his associates (Harré *et al.*, 1985; Harré, 1987) and by Casey (1987), there are some memory behaviours that are conducted only in the company of other people; a case in point is that of reminiscence. Thus, just a memory is activated by the movement of one's body and by one's presence in a given physical scene in the world, so it is activated through one's interaction with other people.

Remarkably, Bartlett, who is usually regarded as one of the forefathers of representational cognition, highlighted the social nature of memory. Apparently, later developments in psychology have distorted Bartlett's view. His famous book *Remembering* (Bartlett, 1932) is subtitled 'a study in experimental social psychology'. As recently noted by several authors (see Edwards and Middleton, 1987; Costall, 1991; Caramelli, 1993), Bartlett emphasized how remembering is intertwined with one's interactions with other people and with the cultural matrix of society. For further discussion along these lines, see Coulter (1983), Edwards and Middleton (1986), Radley (1990) and Shotter (1990).

Personality

As a last example of the social other being an integral constituent of the psychology of the individual, I refer to a domain outside the province of cognition proper – personality. Specifically, let me draw attention to the psychoanalytic theory of object-relations. This theory characterizes the individual's personality primarily in terms of significant relationships in early life that are 'taken in' and serve as templates and motives in all later interactions (see Freud, 1923; Jacobson, 1964). It has been argued that the other has a structuring effect even before it can be represented as an object distinct from the self. Pertinent to this is the concept of the 'self-object', the other who is experienced as an integral component of the self and who serves as one of its functions (Kohut 1971, 1977). A major conclusion of investigations along this line is that it is the relationship to the other that determines the personality and its development throughout life. As Winnicott (1964) states, 'There is no such thing as a baby – meaning that if you set out to describe a baby, you will find that you are describing *a baby and someone*. A baby . . . is essentially part of a relationship' (p. 88).[2]

Developmental considerations

The cognitive domain in which the involvement of the other is most salient is development: here the other plays a crucial role. It is not only that the presence of an adult is necessary as a source of information and a model for the child. Rather, the mechanisms that govern the child's cognitive development are themselves socially defined. As a consequence, any purely individualistic theory of development is bound to present a distorted view of how knowledge is acquired and accrues. Below I underline the crucial role of the social other in cognitive development; a more general discussion of learning and the evolution of knowledge will be presented in the third line of this critique, that focusing on the temporal aspects of cognition.

RCVM will, of course, not deny that adults contribute to children's cognitive development. Obviously, the newcomers to the community of humankind do not invent all they know, and are not left to discover all of it by themselves. None will dispute that much of what children come to know is taught to them by others. The point of contention is not whether teaching occurs but rather what teaching is, what are its role and contribution, and how it should be integrated within one's cognitive account. By RCVM, teaching consists of the transfer of information from one cognitive system to another, and the human teacher is no different from any other external source of information. Just as the external world presents one with information, so does the other person. In both cases RCVM assumes complete separation between the source of information and the cognitive agent who is acquiring it. In both, it is assumed that the source is essential for the information to be available, but that apart from this, the cognitive work associated with the information in question may be accounted for without reference to that source. The following discussion tries to show that this is not the case.

Let me start with language. I do so, because as far as learning is concerned language seems to present the most extreme case of individualistic cognition. Following Chomsky (1965, 1972, 1975b), the prevalent opinion is that adults determine what language the child will acquire, but that apart from superficial influence of this kind their contribution is minimal. Basically, it is claimed that adults serve as triggers for development, but that they are not involved in teaching language to their children. With this, the very existence of any language teaching is denied. This extreme denial calls for special scrutiny. The points made in conjunction with it will serve as the basis for criticizing the representational individualistic conception of learning even in cases in which RCVM does not deny the existence of teaching.

The standard representationalist stance with regard to language development is rooted in Chomsky's assertion that:

> Language is not really taught, for the most part. Rather, it is learned, by mere exposure to data. . . . No one has been taught the principle[s of grammar]. . . . But a careful study of the interactions between me and my child that result in his attaining [the state of knowing English] might give little insight into what it is that he learned. . . .
>
> Grammar [is] acquired by virtually everyone, effortlessly, rapidly, in a uniform manner, merely by living in a community under minimal conditions

of interaction, exposure, and care. There need be no explicit teaching or training, and when the latter does take place, it has only marginal effects on the final state achieved. (Chomsky, 1975b, pp. 161, 147)

These assertions are neither based on empirical research, nor corroborated by any systematic examination of population data or proper statistical measures. For a considerable period of time practically all students of language took Chomsky's position for granted. Yet, even *a priori*, there are good reasons to question the validity of his claims. Admittedly, practically all human children acquire language, and by a certain age they all attain a good mastery of it. In itself, however, this cannot be taken as evidence that social factors are not operational. First, just as all children acquire language, so practically all children are born into a social context and other people – notably, the parents – play an indispensable role in their acquistion of language. Thus, the mere fact that all children acquire language, and even the fact that the course of language development is very similar for all children, does not in itself indicate that language is not learnt and that social factors are not involved. Second, in itself the fact that all children attain linguistic command by a certain, supposedly early age does not prove anything. For how young is young? Perhaps language need not take more time to master than it actually does, and hence, the child's accomplishment, remarkable though it is, may be less extraordinary than it seems. After all, people gain perfect command of particular, highly complex fields of knowledge in periods which are no less remarkable: seven to ten years of university bring young men and women to a state of knowledge it has taken the species millennia to attain. And what if it were normal for people to take twenty years to acquire full command of language? In itself, this need neither detract from nor add to the plausibility of language being learnt (as contrasted with its knowledge being innate). Third, Chomsky's claim that there is no significant variance in the process of language acquisition is suspect. Variance is measured not in mere absolute magnitudes but in relative values. After all, in a period of two to three years children move from a state of no knowledge of language to one in which language functionally serves them pretty well; therefore, perhaps a difference in weeks or even days is significant. Such a difference can be detected only by careful empirical population surveys. Merely to declare it to be nonexistent is scientifically irresponsible. Fourth, if there are in fact inter-personal variations in the time courses of linguistic development, one should check whether there are systematic correlations between these and socio-environmental factors. Finally, inter-personal variations need not be confined to the duration and speed of acquistion. There might also be variations in the qualitative nature of the linguistic product. After all, even if Chomsky may not find it politically correct to say so, adults differ in the level and quality of their linguistic capability.

An empirical, systematic look at the details of language development reveals a picture totally different from that suggested by Chomsky. Extensive recent research indicates that there are in fact inter-children variations both in the time and course of language acquisition and in the level and quality of linguistic capabilities. In particular, the variations mark a correlation between parents' involvement and the child's linguistic proficiency. For instance, the more parents talk to the child, and the earlier they do so, the higher the child's linguistic proficiency will be. For further details, see Nelson *et al.* (1973), Newport *et al.* (1977), Cross (1978) and Furrow *et al.* (1979).

The empirical investigations also shed a new light on parents' active role in bringing the child to command language. Chomsky's stance that language is not taught is based not only on an unfounded idealization of children's accomplishments but also on his equally unfounded view of parents' contribution. According to Chomsky, parents do not teach language to their children, for they themselves do not have access to the information constituting a person's knowledge of language. This presupposes that knowledge of language consists of what the grammarian defines as the formal rules generating the set of well-formed sentences in the language. Since even grammarians do not have full knowledge of those rules, it is inconceivable that parents do; therefore, parents cannot teach language to children. This line of reasoning is doubly flawed. First, it assumes that being able to perform a task requires knowledge of the information that formally specifies the task in question; as noted in the first line of the critique, this need not be the case. Second, it assumes that teaching consists in the passing of specific information pertaining to the domain in question. Admittedly, in the case of language parents do not have such information available to them. Yet, there may be other forms of teaching. From the fact that an explicit transfer of rules does not occur, the conclusion that parents make no contribution to the child's acquisition of language is utterly unwarranted.

Let us look at some of the empirical findings. First, it will be noted that in its early stages children's verbal behaviour is part and parcel of their activity in the world, and in particular, of their joint interaction with other people. As pointed out by Charney (1979), children acquire language not as observers but as participants in discourse. Indeed, some linguistic patterns would be extremely difficult for children to learn by mere observation. The case specifically noted by Charney is that of indexicals. Theoretically, these expressions should be especially difficult: since they are not associated with any particular person, place or thing, they defy specific semantic definition. Yet, they are learned early and with few errors. This is so precisely because the child acquires their meaning as a participant in discourse, not as an observer.

Second, parents are actually very much involved in guiding their children and helping them to master language. It is not that children are merely exposed to adults talking and their use of language emerges; parents talk to children differently from the way they talk to adults (see, for instance, Kaye and Charney, 1980). Furthermore, parents adjust the way they talk to their child as a function of the linguistic level the child has already reached, and a longitudinal inspection reveals that the types of linguistic structure parents produce develop in time. Thus, Kaye (1979) found that the early interactions of mother and infant are particularly suited to preparing the way for later interactions in which language is learned. Key facets of early social interaction in infancy – joint reference to objects, turn-taking, mutual imitation, and signalling of intention – provide structures without which language (if it existed as such) could not be learned. Similarly, studying the linguistic interchanges between children of twenty to thirty-two months and their mothers, Bernstein (1981) found that the language sample children hear is suited to their developing linguistic needs. When adults address the child, they adjust the complexity of their language to suit the child's level of linguistic development. With time, as the child develops, the adults increase the complexity of their own linguistic output in an orderly manner simultaneously with the development of the child. Moreover, it is through linguistic inter-personal interaction that new syntactic structures emerge. In the course of such interaction children will employ constructions that they cannot yet employ by themselves. For further empirical data, see Morehead and Morehead (1974), Ferrier (1978), Lock (1978), Snow *et al.* (1979), Olson (1980), Wood (1980), Bruner (1983) and Adams and Bullock (1986).

These empirical observations are in line with Vygotsky's theoretical framework. The fundamental tenet underlying this framework is that all ontogenetic development exhibits a progression from the social to the mental. Specifically, all cognitive functions appear first in inter-personal interaction and only then intra-personally in the child. The mental, in other words, is an internalization of the social (see Vygotsky, 1981). According to Vygotsky, the key principle guiding cognitive development is that in joint activity with the other, children can achieve levels of performance higher than those they could attain by acting alone. The key notion here is that of *the zone of proximal development*. This defines the levels of performance that at any given point in children's development they may achieve when acting together with an adult or a peer, but not alone. Development is made possible by children participating in activities beyond their competence. Interacting with adults or more experienced peers and assisted by them, children are able to participate in activities that are beyond their capabilities when working independently. Through such social guidance, children gradually internalize the skills practised with adult support so that they can perform independently (for further discussion, see Vygotsky, 1978; also Wertsch, 1979; Cole, 1985; Bickhard, 1987, 1992a, 1992b; and Bickhard and Christopher, 1993).

There are two notions in contemporary cognitive developmental research sympathetic to the Vygotskian perspective which I would like to underline. The first is the notion of *intersubjectivity* encountered in the hermeneutical philosophy of Habermas (1970a) and Gadamer (1976) and further extended in frameworks of cognitive ontogenesis such as those of Rommetveit and his associates (Rommetveit, 1974, 1985; Rommetveit and Blakar, 1979) and Trevarthen and his associates (Trevarthen, 1980; Trevarthen and Logotheti, 1989). Intersubjectivity is manifested by human intentional acts and patterns of awareness being fundamentally inter-personal. This quality is the requisite for cognitive development. In other words, it is the fact that cognitive acts are inter-personal that makes learning and the acquisition of knowledge possible. As pointed out by Trevarthen (1979, 1982), it is an in-built inter-personal motivation, or even an instinct that sets the entire course of cognitive development into motion. Specifically, human beings have, since very early in life, a need to seek information and to receive it from other people. As further argued by Bråten (1987), in the early stages of life the child should be regarded not as an individual cognitive agent, but as a member of a child–parent dyad. It is only gradually that the child separates from this dyad and gains the ability to act more and more independently, and thus, to have an individual existence of his or her own. I shall return to this characterization of learning and development in Part II.

The contribution that the adult other offers is the theme of the second notion that I would like to underline – *scaffolding* (see Wood *et al.*, 1976). Essentially, scaffolding consists of the adult controlling those elements of the task to be performed that are beyond the child's initial capacity. This permits the latter to concentrate upon and complete only those elements that are within his or her range of competence. Eventually, the learner's competence will increase and he or she will master the task. Empirical observations indicate that, working with the child, adults adjust the degree of their involvement to the child's level of ability. Once the child is lured into some form of task-relevant activity, the adult constructs a supporting structure which holds in place whatever the child can achieve. This support connects the child's activity into the overall construction and provides a framework within which the child's action leads to and means something more general than he or she may have foreseen. As children master components of the task, they are freed to consider the wider context of what they can do, to take over more of the complementary activity, and the adult may 'de-scaffold' those parts which now stand firmly on their own. Thus, as suggested by Rogoff (1990), learning consists of a process of *guided participation*. In this process, the teacher provides a bridge between the familiar and the new, arranges the problem and structures it, and gradually transfers the responsibility of management to the child (see Rogoff and Gardner, 1984; Rogoff, 1989).

This scheme is not confined to child development. As pointed out by Rogoff (1990), all learning is achieved through a process of guided participation. Similarily, Lave (1988) suggests that apprentices learn by acting as legitimate, peripheral participants in activities performed by experts.

In fact, the other involved in one's cognitive development need not be an adult or a teacher. Several authors (Doise and Mugny, 1979; Mugny *et al.*, 1981; Glachan and Light, 1982) found that interaction with peers increases the level of children's performance – indeed, that the performance level of all participants is likely to increase. Specifically, even when two children do not know the answer to a problem, working together increases the chances of them coming up with it. Apparently, being confronted with alternative ways to approach a problem (even if these approaches are wrong) enables children not to be fixed in one approach. As a consequence, they ask new questions and view things differently; in this process, their level of cognitive performance increases. As indicated above, this is true not only of children but also of adults.

Lastly, let me return to an issue which I have considered from a conceptual point of view, namely, meaning. How do words gain their meaningfulness? In the first line of my critique I noted that meaning is couched in the pragmatics of word use; that is, in their early usages words are ingrained in the particular context of their employment. In Chapter 3 I referred to empirical research supporting this claim. Theoretical observations along this line were, however, made many years earlier by Mead. As noted, Mead observed that symbols gain their meaning through one's ability to take the perspective of the other and thereby relate to one's self as the other would. Prior to this, one is immersed in action. Indeed, it may be argued that had it not been for the presence of the other, words would not have gained their meaning. Specifically, words are meaningful to the other before they are to the one who actually produces them (see Kaye and Charney, 1980). Likewise, Vygotsky (1978) observed that the child's initial grasping movement acquires meaning and produces reactions in the inter-personal context long before it has any meaning for the child him- or herself.

Empirical observations corroborate this appraisal. In the early stages of language development the child merely utters sounds. These need not have meaning, or if they do, their meaning need not be fixed or well defined. For the hearer, however, some of the child's utterances may sound like actual words. Parents, especially, tend to hear words in the sounds their babies utter (see Snow, 1977; Kaye, 1982), and they direct their interaction with the child in a manner that is in line with the meaning they associate with these words. Repeated, such interaction results in the child's words gaining the meaning the parents – and the linguistic community at large – associate with them. Incidentally, the same holds for actions in general. As pointed out by Wertsch and Hickmann (1987), acting under the guidance of the adult, the child may execute actions before becoming aware of their functional significance. Becoming aware of these is one constituent of the transition from the joint activity with the adult to independent, individual performance.

Cultural evolution

Finally, many of the patterns noted above in the context of ontogenesis are also encountered in the evolution of culture. The similarity between the two domains is not accidental. After all, in their interaction with children adults also introduce the children into society and its culture (this has been emphasized by Vygotsky and other Marxist thinkers; for a general discussion, see Cole, 1985; Scribner, 1985). More important it seems that the cognitive processes in which cultural knowledge and skills are transferred are similar to those encountered in the teaching of the child. In both, guided participation and shared thinking are central. Evidently, much of cultural progress involves a long period of apprenticeship (John-Steiner, 1985). And as Newton is known to have said (and many before him; see Merton, 1965), even giants stand on the shoulders of other men. For further discussion of cultural evolution and its affinities to ontogenetic development, see the review by the team of the Laboratory of Comparative Human Cognition (1983).

Notes

1. Alternatively, one may say that the semantic interpretation relating the two pronouns is blocked, or that one cannot bind the two variables in the sentence. The details of the particular linguistic analysis should not bother us here.
2. In preparing this section I was assisted by Rachel Blass, whose scholarship in psychoanalytic theory I highly appreciate.

10 Non-cognitive psychological systems

> Among the most basic defects of traditional approaches to the study of psychology has been the isolation of the intellectual from the volitional and affective.
>
> *Vygotsky*

Last in this survey of functional relations of the cognitive system, I consider factors that do not pertain to the environment in which the mind is situated, but rather are part and parcel of psychology proper. I refer to what might (misleadingly, as I shall show) be referred to as the non-cognitive facets of the psyche – affect, volition and motivation, and those ill-defined structures usually labelled 'personality'. Unlike the others examined in this line of my critique – the body, the world, the social other – these cannot be regarded as factors existing in their own right that are, as far as the cognitive system is concerned, given. Yet, it seems to me that both structurally and functionally these non-cognitive facets of the psyche play a role quite analogous to that of the factors examined so far. For this reason, I include a discussion of them here. The discussion, note, is meant to examine not the non-cognitive psychological systems as such, but only their effects on the cognitive system and their involvement in cognitive performance. The converse effects – those that cognition exercises on the non-cognitive systems – are outside the scope of our discussion.

Affect

While affect is not usually classified as one of the higher mental functions, in recent years it has received increasing attention in cognitive circles, and if anything this trend seems to be intensifying. Cognitive models of affect have been offered by a number of cognitive scientists, especially Bower (1981), Oatley and Johnson-Laird (1987) and Ortony *et al.* (1988). In practically all cases the works are couched in RCVM. The paradigmatic account is that offered by Bower (1981). In it, moods and affective states are characterized in terms of semantic representational configurations with graded predicative modifications. For instance, being happy is characterized as a certain positive score on the scale of affect, being elated as a higher positive score, and being sad as a negativ' s"""""king that there is no principled reason why representational models should not be implemented in computers, some investigators have also argued that computers could indeed be endowed with emotions (Sloaman and Croucher, 1981; Frijda and Swagerman, 1987; but see Dennett, 1979c).

Conceptual considerations

The representational account of affect presents various conceptual problems. As will be evident, some of these are fully analogous to ones encountered in conjunction with words and their meaning. First, affective states, feelings and emotive reactions elude words. Second, affect seems to have a global, undifferentiated character that defies any anchoring in well-defined, specific terms. Third, it often brings together contradictory elements that cannot be captured by one single, verbal description.

That all these patterns have been indicated in the discussion of the problems of coding in Chapter 5 is not accidental. The two sets of problems are the manifestations of one and the same state of affairs. Both mark the non-separation of the cognitive and the affective; both mark the inability of representational accounts to capture fully the meaning of words. As noted in Chapter 5, it is for this reason that in describing emotions one frequently makes use of metaphoric language. Indeed, it has been suggested that affect should be one of the basic dimensions in the semantic analysis of words (see Osgood *et al.*, 1957).

Apparently it is for this reason that art is so important (and irreplaceable) in the expression of emotions and their communication. This is a vast topic which is well beyond the scope of this book (for a comprehensive discussion see Cassirer, 1944; Langer, 1967). Here let me just quote a comment from a letter by Felix Mendelssohn:

> People speak so much of music, but they say so little. In fact, I believe that words are not sufficient for this purpose, and had I found they were indeed sufficient, I would have certainly given up the composition of music. In general, people complain that music has too many meanings; no one knows for sure what he has to think when he listens to music, but it is easy for one to understand a verbal lecture. I myself feel just the opposite. Not only entire lectures are not clear to me, but even single words: so many are the meanings embodied in each word, to such a great extent is it given to misunderstanding – in comparison to fine music which fills your soul with a thousand things which are better than any parable. Music that I love does not tell me things which supposedly are not defined enough for them to be articulated in words. On the contrary, the things are clear to such an extent that verbal articulation will not succeed in expressing them at all. You will ask me what was in front of my eyes [during the act of composing] and I shall say – the song itself, as it is. Even if I matched these or other tones to a certain word or words, I could not convey this explicitly to anyone, for the meanings of words are not the same for all people. Only the song can express the identical content to one

person and to another, and evoke in both the same feeling. But this feeling cannot be defined in identical words. (My own free translation from a book on the history of music in Hebrew)

Perhaps the most serious problem of the representational account of affect is of the type referred to in Chapter 6 as 'missing qualities'. Specifically, the representational account disregards – and leaves unaccounted for – the basic quality of affects that differentiates them from pure cognitions, namely, their being felt and experienced in characteristic manners. Evidently, my knowing that a certain state of affairs is a happy one and my feeling it are two utterly distinct psychological states. Thus, consider the following pair of statements:

1. John's grandmother died.

2. My grandmother died.

By standard semantic representational accounts the two statements are, except for the particular specification of a variable, identical; but for me the difference between them is enormous. Whereas the first will probably leave me indifferent, the second will certainly agitate me and trigger an entire range of feelings and bodily reactions. John's reactions are likely to exhibit the converse pattern.

That semantic representational structures cannot capture emotions has been noted by one of the first critics of the representational view, William James (1884), who wrote:

> What kind of an emotion of fear would be left, if the feelings neither of quickened heart-beats nor of shallow breathing, neither of trembling lips nor of weakened limbs, neither of goose-flesh nor of visceral stirrings, were present, it is quite impossible to think. Can one fancy the state of rage and picture no ebullition of it in the chest, no flushing of the face, no dilatation of the nostrils, no clenching of the teeth, no impulse to vigorous action, but in their stead limp muscles, calm breathing, and a placid face? . . . The rage is as completely evaporated as the sensation of its so-called manifestations, and the only thing that can possibly be supposed to take its place is some cold-blooded and dispassionate judicial sentence, confined entirely to the intellectual realm. . . . A feelingless cognition that certain circumstances are deplorable, and nothing more. . . . The more closely I scrutinise my states, the more persuaded I become, that whatever moods, affections, and passions I have, are in very truth constituted by, and made up of, those bodily changes we ordinarily call their expression or consequence; and the more it seems to me that if I were to become corporeally anaesthetic, I should be excluded from the life of the affections, harsh and tender alike, and drag out an existence of merely cognitive or intellectual form. (pp. 193–4)[1]

Representationalists may, of course, counter that these somato-sensory differences are irrelevant. From a strict cognitive point of view, they may argue, statements such as (1) and (2) and the psychological states associated with them are on a par. They have similar (at times identical) informative content and as such they are coded in a similar representational manner. What these statements and states differ in is the ensuing reaction, which pertains to the domain of the body and as such is outside the province of cognition proper. Procedurally, the somatic reaction is post-representational: given the representationally specified content of a state and the meaning it has for the cognitive agent, different bodily reactions may be triggered.

The representational characterization involves two assumptions: first, that cognitive content and affective state can be separated from one another in a neat, modular fashion; second, that the former is primary. A host of empirical phenomena hold against this characterization, and the following survey of them suggests that both assumptions are unwarranted.

Empirical considerations

The classic critique is, of course, William James' which was referred to above and published in 1884. At about the same time Lange was working along similar lines; in 1885 the two published a book together, and the theory is thus known as the James–Lange theory (see James and Lange, 1885/1922). The following quotations are taken from James' original work (James, 1884); see also the chapter on the emotions in James (1890/1950):

> Our natural way of thinking about . . . emotions is that the mental perception of some fact excites the mental affection called the emotion, and that this latter state of mind gives rise to the bodily expression. My thesis on the contrary is that *the bodily changes follow directly the PERCEPTION of the exciting fact, and that our feeling of the same changes as they occur IS the emotion.* Common sense says, we lose our fortune, are sorry and weep; we meet a bear, are frightened and run; we are insulted by a rival, are angry and strike. The hypothesis here to be defended says that this order of sequence is incorrect, that the one mental state is not immediately induced by the other, that the bodily manifestations must first be interposed between, and that the more rational statement is that we feel sorry because we cry, anger because we strike, afraid because we tremble, and not that we cry, strike, or tremble, because we are sorry, angry, or fearful, as the case may be. Without the bodily states following on the perception, the latter would be purely cognitive in form, pale, colourless, destitute of emotional warmth. We might then see the bear, and judge it best to run, receive the insult and deem it right to strike, but we could not actually *feel* afraid or angry. (pp. 189–90; all emphases in the original)

The most forceful contemporary critique of the representational characterization of affect is that presented by Zajonc (1980, 1984; see also Zajonc *et al.*, 1982).

Zajonc argues that cognitive processing cannot be taken as the basis for the account of affect. Zajonc's critique addresses both assumptions indicated above. He marks that affect is both primary relative to cognition and non-dependent on it. Zajonc's critique has triggered agitated debates, especially to be noted is the counter-criticism marshalled by Lazarus (1982, 1984; for a comprehensive, conciliatory discussion, see Leventhal and Scherer, 1987).

The following survey is based largely on Zajonc's critique. However, the observations made here are not affected by Lazarus' criticism of Zajonc, mainly for underscoring the separation between cognition and affect. This Zajonc does in order to mark the non-dependence of affect on cognition. By contrast, what is of interest here is the converse relationship: the dependence of cognition on affect. Being primarily concerned with affect, Zajonc highlights the facet of independence; but from the perspective of cognition, the phenomena he surveys actually attest to the non-independence of cognition with respect to affect. This is further corroborated by Leventhal and Scherer's analysis of the Zajonc–Lazarus controversy. As they point out, there is much in the debate that involves semantic confusion and difference in underlying assumptions and perspective, not substantive disagreement on the empirical facts. In fact, as observed by Lazarus (1984), Zajonc's claim of the independence of affect and cognition is based in part on his identification of cognition with the domain of semantic representations, an identification to which I, of course, do not adhere. In sum, what is important here is not Zajonc's underlying assumptions, but the empirical facts he surveys. These support the claim made at the outset of this discussion: that cognition is not autonomous relative to affect, and that the latter is more basic than the former.

Affect is more basic in several respects. First, feeling is more pervasive than cognition: feeling, Zajonc observes, accompanies all cognition, but the converse is not the case. Second, feelings are inescapable and unavoidable, they are immediate and difficult to verbalize, and usually one can neither fake nor ignore them. Further, while one often forgets the details pertaining to a person's perceptual image or to information about him or her, one often retains the affective impression the person evokes. Remarkably, we are seldom wrong about what (or whom) we like or dislike. Indeed, as observed by Ittelson (1973), people's first level of response to the environment is affective. And as we all know, affective appraisals are quite resistant to subsequent cognitive information (see, for instance, Petty and Cacioppo, 1981). Finally, as will be noted below, affect is also primary in terms of both ontogenetic development and phylogenetic evolution.

A host of experimental findings, some quite surprising, support these phenomenological observations. Subjects exhibit differential attitudes towards stimuli even when no recognition is achieved (Wilson, 1975, 1979; Moreland and Zajonc, 1977; Kunst-Wilson and Zajonc, 1980). Particularly striking is the phenomenon of subception or subliminal perception. Stimuli that invoke anxiety or embarrassment are more difficult or take longer to be perceived. But for there to be such selective inattention there must be a mechanism for detecting these stimuli as distinct from neutral ones; this mechanism is likely to be affective, not cognitive-representational (see, for example, Ericksen, 1960; Blum and Barbour, 1979). Further, cognitive judgements and performance may be facilitated by affect. For instance, Hyde and Jenkins (1969) asked subjects to count the number of letters of words or to rate them for pleasantness: recall was best for the latter group regardless of whether subjects were told they would be tested for recall or not. Similarly, Patterson and Baddeley (1977) asked subjects to rate photographs of people either by facial features or by vague personality impressions. Recognition rate was higher in the second case.

These observations not only mark the primacy of affective appraisals and their non-dependence on strict cognitive processing, but also indicate that affect can accomplish tasks of cognitive (or cognitive-like) character. Specifically, affective responses serve identification and recognition, discrimination and classification, judgement and evaluation. This they do both reliably and fast, and independently of pure cognitive computation (see Naus and Halasz, 1979).

In addition to its implications for the relationships between cognition and affect, this state of affairs has more general implications. It indicates that cognitive accomplishments need not necessarily be achieved by what are usually taken to be paradigmatic cognitive means. If cognitive tasks can be achieved by the affective system, then perhaps what are regarded as paradigmatic cases of information processing are achieved by non-representational-computational means too.

Not only does affect manifest what may be regarded as cognitive accomplishment, it exerts an influence on cognitive function. Many empirical findings show that people's moods and affective states direct and bias various cognitive processes. First, emotion strongly influences the perceived meaning of verbal utterances (see Argyle, 1972; Ekman, 1979). Second, people seem to remember more easily material whose valences fits their current mood states; specifically, they tend to recall positively valued material when in positive moods and negatively valued material when in negative moods. It is also found that material is better retrieved when the mood context of the subject at the time of testing is congruent with that at the time of original learning, although the picture revealed by negative affect is not as clear as that revealed by positive affect (see Gilligan and Bower, 1983; Isen, 1984, 1987; Blaney, 1986; Singer and Salovey, 1988; Bower and Mayer, 1989; Urcos, 1989). And then, one's mood affects one's judgement: as everybody knows, when one is cheerful the world seems rosier (for reviews, see Isen, 1984, 1987; Mayer, 1986; Clark and Williamson, 1989). Indeed, one's style of decision making is affected by one's mood as well (see Isen, 1987; Fiedler, 1988). Similar effects are also noted in psychopathology: both elevation of mood and depression are associated with biases in memory, judgement and interpretation. The pertinent findings, however, are not always consistent or replicable; for a review, see MacLeod (1990). For comprehensive reviews of the role of affect in cognition and for criticial discussion, see Isen (1984) and Peeters and D'Ydewalle (1987).

Last but not least, there are indications that affect influences not only the content of cognitive material, but also the strategies of thought. Specifically, induced positive affects seem to have an effect on subjects' problem-solving strategies.

Furthermore, there are indications that affective (as well as motivational) states are conducive to creativity (see, for instance, Csikszentmihalyi, 1988).

Developmental considerations

Affect is also primary from a developmental point of view. As argued by Vygotsky (1987)[2], 'Thought . . . is not born of other thoughts. Thought has its origin in the motivating sphere of consciousness, a sphere that includes our inclinations and needs, our interests and impulses, and our affect and emotion. The affective and volitional tendency stands behind thought' (p. 282).

Both children's first actions and their first utterances are grounded in their needs, desires and wishes. As suggested by Sroufe (1979), 'The child grows not as a perceptive being, not as a cognitive being, but as a human being that experiences anxiety and anger, and that is connected to the world in an emotional way' (p. 462). As far as infants are concerned, the variety of stimulus conditions in the world differ only in how they make them feel. Thus, both the world and the meanings associated with it are in terms of the infant's affective life (see Stechler and Carpenter, 1967). Correspondingly, infants' subjective experiences consist of the experiential components of the affects that characterize their existence. Infants respond to their own bodily needs with emotion, and relate to objects and persons in their surroundings through affective expression (for a review, see Sroufe, 1979; also Piaget, 1952).

The same holds for language. As argued by Vygotsky (1986), the first functions of speech are emotional release (as well as social contact); only later does speech serve for communication. Further, affect is the basis for the first interactions of the child with the adult. Trevarthen (1983), argues that affect is the tie that brings together child and adult. On the one hand, infants' behaviour is governed by their affective needs; on the other hand, infants seem to posses rudimentary personal powers that affect their caretakers intimately so that within a short time after birth a subtle infant–caretaker relationship is established (see Trevarthen, 1979). Thus, affect is the basis for intersubjectivity, which as argued in Chapter 9 is indispensable for the child's cognitive development.

Likewise for consciousness. As suggested by Izard (1977, 1980, 1983), consciousness develops out of the emergence of discrete emotions and the development of relationships between affective experience on the one hand and sensory, perceptual and cognitive processes on the other. In its first stages consciousness is characterized primarily by sensory-affective processes. Awareness is essentially affective, and changes in it are a function of changes in the quality and intensity of affects. Affective responses occur mainly in relation to objects as global entities or as a class capable of eliciting a particular quality or intensity of affect. Later, consciousness consists primarily of affective-perceptual processes. The focus is on objects' unique perceptual features, and awareness can change as a function of changes in the intensity or duration of affective experience in relation to specific objects within a class. Later still, consciousness leads to a new level of awareness of self, of other persons, and of self–other interaction. This last development is invoked by socially induced affective states: fear, shame and shyness. Eventually, the increased variety of affects results in sensitivity to a wider range of objects, persons and situations, and the number of affect–percept and affect–concept relations increases rapidly. Sometime in the second half of the first year of life, affective experience achieves independence from direct sensory contact and may be evoked also when the object is symbolized or imagined.

Affect and the body

As pointed out by Zajonc (see the works cited above as well as Zajonc and Markus, 1983), the primacy of affect further manifests itself in the relationship between affect and the body. Zajonc points out that the intimate link between the two reveals not only mutual interaction, but a causal relationship that bodily states exert on affect. Since the data Zajonc presents also mark the primacy of the body relative to cognition, I will review them at some length.

In the literature, two versions of the view marking the causal relationship between body and affect are noted, one weak and one strong. The weak version is maintained by the *facial feedback theory* (Tomkins, 1962; Izard, 1977). According to this theory, the facial musculature provides the agent with feedback for the subjective experience of emotion. This version is weak in that it assumes that the emotion itself must have already been realized prior to the bodily change; the latter provides feedback but does not constitute a cause. Experimental procedures in support of the theory are typically conducted as follows. Unaware of the purpose of the manipulation and its relation to emotion expression, subjects are required to contract facial muscles so that they assume the expression of a positive or negative emotion while rating positive or negative emotion stimuli. Typically, subjects manipulated into a frown rate negative emotion stimuli more negatively and positive ones less positively than do subjects manipulated into a smile. Most experiments indicate that at least in terms of the broad classes of emotion feelings (positive or negative), the manipulation is effective; for a review, see Laird (1984).

The strong version was put forward at the beginning of the century by the French physician Israel Waynbaum (1907), who, after having been ignored for several decades, was discovered by Zajonc (1985), upon whose exposition my comments are based. According to Waynbaum the facial muscles act as ligatures on facial blood vessels and thus regulate cerebral blood flow; this, in turn, influences one's subjective feeling. Consequently, the changes in facial muscles as they take place in manifest expression determine the corresponding subjective states. Rather than serving as an underlying basis for the facial expressions, the internal, subjective states are thus products of the external changes in the body. For example, smiling – that is, the contraction of *zygomaticus major* – causes a momentary intra-cerebral hyperaemia which leads to a positive subjective feeling. Likewise, furrowing one's brow diverts blood circulation from the face to the brain, and hence facilitates mental concentration. Empirical data supporting this strong causal theory were furnished by Ekman *et al.* (1983), who asked subjects to manipulate their facial musculatures. As a result changes in heart rates were found that are usually associated with the various emotional states corresponding to the expressions produced. This was so even though the connections between the facial patterns and the emotions were not disclosed to the subjects. Similarly, Strack *et al.* (1988) found that subjects who were induced to smile rated cartoons as more funny than did those inhibited from smiling (see Laird, 1984).

Affect and the other

Affect is also intertwined with the social other. The primacy of affect thus highlights further aspects of the relationships between cognition and the social other. Interestingly, this was observed by James (1890/1950):

> [It is my consciousness of the attitude of my fellow-man towards me] that normally unlocks most of my shames and indignations and fears. The extraordinary sensitiveness of this consciousness is shown by the bodily modifications wrought in us by the awareness that our fellow-man is noticing us *at all*. No one can walk across the platform at a public meeting with just the same muscular innervation he uses to walk across his room at home. No one can give a message to such a meeting without organic excitement.

Modern developmental research presents corroborative evidence. As pointed out by Izard and her associates (Izard, 1977; Izard and Malatesta, 1987), the development of emotion is intricately tied to social development. It is through the socialization of emotion expressions that feelings are regulated. I will say more on the development of affect below.

Motivation and volition

Motivation is that driving force within which makes us agents of our own actions. We act because we want to act, because we want to accomplish goals and realize aims. Unlike affect and emotion, motivation and volition have not attracted much interest in the cognitive community.[3] Inasmuch as the cognitive literature deals with motivation, it does so in the same manner as that in which it deals with the contents of our knowledge. Goals (see, for instance, Schank and Abelson, 1977) are statements specified as such, in a declarative form, in people's systems of knowledge and belief. If, however, goals are what drives the cognitive system, a mere representational specification will not do.

Two possibilities may be envisioned. The first is that motivations, wishes, desires and the like are characterized in standard representational terms, just like regular semantic information. In this case, there is nothing special about the representations specifying motivations; they are just like any other representations in one's mind. But then, one is left with no account for exactly that which motivation is supposed to provide, namely, the driving force that results in the activation of certain representational structures and the application of certain computational manipulations to them. Indeed, if the representations specifying motivations cannot account for how the system operates, then the question still remains – what does? Whatever it is, it cannot be encoded in the standard representational manner, for then the problems noted in the first step of the analysis reappear.

Still pursuing the first possibility, one may suggest a tagging system. The tags will specify whether a representational structure encodes semantic knowledge or motivations, wishes and the like. Some interpeter, however, will have to read the tags. This interpreter will have to be of either the epistemic or the motivational type. If it is the former, one is faced with the classic problem of the homunculus. If it is the latter, then what drives the system is not the tagged representational structures of the first order, which, recall, were supposed to account for precisely this (i.e. to drive the system). If so, there is no sense in distinguishing these from other representational structures. However one plays with the division between representations of the two types, as long as motivation is accounted for in representational terms the same problems will present themselves.

The second possibility is that motivations are not encoded in representational terms. Whatever the pertinent structures and mechanisms are, they set the regular representations in the cognitive system in motion. The system could work, but the results would have a number of repercussions. First, the scope of the representational account would be significantly narrowed. Given that RCVM is posited as a general theory of psychology, this is not trivial. In fact, the problematic nature of such a limitation is not merely a question of scope. The motivational system accomplishes all sorts of task that are usually associated with the cognitive system proper: identification, classification, generalization, differential judgements and the like. Normally, such accomplishments are assumed to be achieved by means of the standard representational-computational machinery. The alternative here, however, rules this out. Thus, a non-standard machinery has to be postulated to account for tasks which are not categorically different from standard cognitive ones. If this machinery is successful then perhaps such non-standard mechanisms can account for the so-called standard cases as well. In other words, this state of affairs may suggest that there is no need for the postulation of representations even in the seemingly standard cases.[4]

Another repercussion of the second possibility pertains to the mechanisms relating the motivational structures and the standard representational ones. Surely, these mechanisms cannot be computations in the standard sense, for such computations apply only on standard semantic representations, whereas here some of the structures supposedly related by the computational operations are not of this type. However, if the computations are of a non-standard sort and yet apply on the standard representations, then one is confronted with a categorically new type of psychological system, in which some of the machinery applying on semantic representations is not computational in the standard sense. The door thus opens again to the possibility that non-standard operations apply in cases previously accounted for by standard ones. This might also be the case in domains of behaviour not pertaining to motivation at all – in which case the very foundations of RCVM would be shaken.

Still another problem presented by the representational account of motivation pertains to a more philosophical level. Who is it that wishes, desires, wants? As I will note below, RCVM attempts to characterize this self in standard semantic representational terms, specifying it as some marked cognitive module. But then, all the problems noted at the beginning of this discussion reappear. On the other hand, if the self is not specified in representational terms, then in addition to all the problems noted above, a new question arises: if there is – as practically everyone would assume – unity to the self, then this agent has to be the same one that is the reader and interpreter of representations. But I have shown that the postulation of a reader and interpreter is problematic for reasons that have nothing to do with motivation. Now the same problems reappear in conjunction with the motivationally defined self.

Finally, let me point out that many of the data regarding the development of affect also bear on motivation. In marking that the child is primarily an effective, not a cognitive being, one also marks that the child views the world in terms of desires and wants. Further, as noted above, motivational factors play a crucial role in problem solving and creativity (see Csikszentmihalyi, 1988). Motivational factors also constitute a key determinant of the enhanced cognitive performance manifested in group situations (see Sharan, 1990).

Personality

Extending motivation in the most general fashion and tying it to affect, we reach the domain of personality. Cognitive psychology assumes that one can study the so-called higher mental functions without considering the reasons that lead people to employ these functions, their conscious and unconscious interests, their motives and desires. A major school of psychology which has maintained an opposite point of view is psychoanalysis. Freudian psychoanalysis may very well be regarded as a cognitive theory. Indeed, Freud's famous chapter on representations in *The Interpretation of Dreams* (Freud, 1900/1954) is – from the perspective of cognitive research – amazingly modern. Basically, the psychoanalytic enterprise may be taken as presenting a thesis which diametrically opposes that of contemporary cognitive science: whereas RCVM assumes that cognition is autonomous, psychoanalysis assumes that it is not. In particular, the paradigmatic faculties of cognition – language, memory, reasoning and the like – cannot be divorced from motivational factors. Therefore, in attempting to understand how the cognitive faculties function one cannot ignore the so-called non-cognitive facets of the psyche.

To my knowledge, the only place in the cognitive literature proper in which problems pertaining to personality are noted is Haugeland (1985), who bases his argument on the following dialogue about chess:[5]

- Why did the [chess player] move its queen over here?
- To attack my rook and pawn, I assume.
- I see; but why is [he] attacking your rook and pawn?
- Well, they're the key to my whole defense; if [he] could get past them, [he] would have a clear path to my king.
- And what does [he] want that for?
- To win. Capturing the opposing king is how you win.
- Of course, of course; but why is [the player] trying to win?
  [at this point, Haugeland notes, one may get one of the following responses:]
- To earn public recognition and esteem and thereby validate or augment his own self-esteem.
- For the pride and personal satisfaction that come from accomplishing something difficult.
- To show off, strut his stuff, or prove his prowess. (pp. 238–9)

All these answers, Haugeland points out, involve the player's ego. They indicate that cognitive performance cannot be accounted for solely in cognitive terms. In order to account for goal-directed behaviour one has to make reference also to motivation, self-image, self-esteem and all sorts of factor usually subsumed under the vague umbrella of 'personality'. All these are usually ignored by cognitive scientists (and, as Haugeland further notes, are not applicable to computers).

Notes

1. The analogy between these comments and those made in conjunction with language is evident. Just as words are not the manifest expressions of underlying semantic states, so bodily states are not the expressions of underlying emotive states. Indeed, both lines of criticism are marshalled in Wittgenstein (1953).
2. This is a revised translation of Vygotsky (1986).
3. For interesting comments, see Norman (1980).
4. Note the similarity of this argument to that presented in conjunction with the problem of the homunculus.
5. In the dialogue a computer is playing chess, but later, Haugeland substitutes 'a lanky lad from Brooklyn'. For the sake of simplicity, I omit the names of the participants.

11 *Action and interaction*

In the beginning was the deed.
Goethe

In this last chapter of the second line of the critique, I consider three topics that complement the discussion in the preceding chapters. The first concerns an objection that may be raised against all that I have said in this line of the critique. The second pertains to bodily action in the world (as distinct from cognitive performance involving bodily movement and action in the world). The third has to do with the development of action.

Counter-arguments and responses

Against everything said throughout this second line of the present critique it can be argued that it is all beside the point. This counter-argument is fully analogous to the retort of the two-stage strategy discussed at length in the first line of the critique in conjunction with the argument from context. It would admit the problems marked in conjunction with the various non-cognitive factors, but would not deem them detrimental. In response to these problems a division of labour similar to the two-stage model of non-standard linguistic expressions would be proposed. In this proposal, the representational framework should only be concerned with behaviour which is paradigmatically cognitive. Patterns of behaviour involving non-cognitive factors would be relegated to theories (domains of investigation, investigators) outside cognition; for such responses see, for instance, Rey (1978), Chomsky (1980), Fodor (1980) and Pylyshyn (1984).

As in the two-stage models examined in Chapter 3, the division of labour suggested here is not workable. Three points will be marshalled against it. The first is a word of caution. Given the intricate relationships between the mind and the external world, the segregation between the cognitive and the non-cognitive might not be as well grounded as one might surmise at first glance. It may well be that the demarcation line between the two reflects not psychological reality as such, but rather the success of the representational paradigm of psychological investigation. This division is thus no more than the phrasing of a contingent state of affairs – outlining what the given framework can and cannot do – dressed in a theoretical, quasi-principled garb.

The second point pertains to *autonomy*. The counter-argument assumes that a line of demarcation between the cognitive and the non-cognitive can be drawn; in other words, that there is a relative autonomy between cognitive and non-cognitive behaviour. If this is not the case, however, the counter-argument is not valid. In a nutshell, a domain is autonomous with respect to another domain if all the phenomena in the first can be accounted for in terms pertaining to it and without considering phenomena or using terms pertaining to the second. The various patterns involving the world, the body, the social other and the other faculties of mind all suggest that the cognitive system is, in fact, not autonomous with respect to these domains. In Chapter 7 I noted how the body facilitates and even enables the performance of various cognitive acts. I observed that at times it is very difficult or even impossible to perform what might seem to be a purely cognitive task without activating the body in some fashion. Behaviours in which this pattern was observed included memory, expressing what one knows, perception, thinking, problem solving and creativity. Development and the acquisition of skills exhibited similar manifestations of non-autonomy. In Chapter 8 I noted that immersion in the external world is a similarly crucial facilitator of cognitive performance: immersed in the world one may achieve what one cannot otherwise. In Chapter 10 analogous patterns were marked with respect to the social world. The involvement of the social other is especially crucial in development. As I will show in Chapter 14, with respect to learning and cognitive development, adherence to autonomous cognition leads to a dead end. Together, all these patterns indicate that one cannot offer a complete account of cognitive phenomena without incorporating terms pertaining to what a pre-theoretical labelling would characterize as non-cognitive domains.

The third point has to do with *primacy*. For them to be relegated to a separate, second stage of analysis, the non-cognitive factors in psychology have to be functionally secondary to the cognitive. If this is not the case, and if the former are actually primary, then the counter-argument cannot be sustained. The phenomena surveyed in the previous chapters suggest that not only is the cognitive system not autonomous with respect to other, non-cognitive systems, it may even be dependent on them. Such dependence is detrimental to RCVM, and undermines the proposed division of labour. The primacy of the non-cognitive is exhibited in several dimensions. The first is the *phenomenological*: often, the involvement of the non-cognitive systems in cognitive tasks precedes that of the cognitive. The non-cognitive aspects of performance may also be faster than the cognitive. The second is the *procedural*: often, in order to perform cognitive tasks one has to involve one or more of the non-cognitive factors. The third is the *developmental*: in general, cognition seems to mark a progression from more to less dependence on non-cognitive factors. The fourth may be referred to as *systemic*: it appears that the basic principles governing the performance of the cognitive system are akin to skills associated with action in the external world – with moving about in the world, manipulating objects, and interacting with other human beings.

Action in the world

In the previous chapters I noted that human cognition cannot be modelled without taking into account seemingly extrinsic factors. I thus concluded that RCVM, being a framework that disregards them, cannot adequately account for various patterns of human cognitive behaviour. RCVM can, however, also be criticized from a complementary point of view, namely, that it cannot account for patterns of behaviour which are not paradigmatically cognitive – I refer to patterns that would standardly be subsumed under the label of motor action. Strictly speaking, such performance is outside the scope of present discussion. The subject matter with which I am concerned here is cognition, and my aim is to show that RCVM, because it ignores non-cognitive factors, cannot offer the basis for the modelling of mind. That RCVM cannot account for non-cognitive facets of behaviour is another, distinct topic. Yet, the discussion of non-cognitive performance may be pertinent none the less. First, RCVM purports to be a general framework for the analysis of human behaviour. There is nothing in its characterization that specifies that it be applied only to cognitive processes. The conceptual machinery adopted by this framework – symbolic representations and associated computational operations – is indeed cognitive, but the phenomena accounted for by it need not be confined to the cognitive domain. In fact, an inspection of the definition of RCVM (see (*) in the Prologue) reveals that there is nothing in it that limits the scope of the representational account to cognition. Indeed, RCVM's point of departure is that human behaviour – *all* behaviour – is grounded in knowledge; this subsumes both behaviour usually classified as cognitive and behaviour not usually so classified. Therefore, *a priori*, the specification of the knowledge employed by systems other than the purely cognitive should be in the realm of the representational framework.

Second, an offhand disregard of the non-cognitive patterns of behaviour may be too hasty. Even if these patterns are not in the main focus of the cognitive enterprise, important cognitive conclusions may still be drawn from their inspection. In particular, if behaviour usually characterized as non-cognitive reveals patterns similar to those exhibited by behaviour usually characterized as cognitive, and if the former are not accounted for in representational terms, then perhaps the latter should not be so accounted for either.

Third, if RCVM is not an adequate basis for the modelling of mind, others must be sought. As already hinted, the non-cognitive domain may offer at least some indications as to what such alternative bases might be. Therefore, the examination of non-cognitive patterns of behaviour may be of importance not only for the further limitations of RCVM that they mark, but also because they lay the grounds for the development of alternative, non-representational conceptual frameworks for psychology; such frameworks will be developed in Part II.

The following discussion focuses on four specific cases. These pertain to the three factors discussed in Chapters 7, 8 and 9 – the body, the world and the social other; affect and motivation are not discussed here because they do not pertain to the external world. (Note, however, that in Chapter 10 I examined not only the involvement of affect and motivation in cognition, but also how RCVM might account for these two non-cognitive systems.) This discussion is at best cursory; by no means is it intended to be comprehensive. The reader should bear in mind that in recent years the domain of motor performance and control has been a focus of much concentrated investigation, and has come to define an independent field of research. Only part of this involves cognition and cognitive modelling, and this book is not the place to discuss it. I will confine myself to pointing out some fundamental conceptual problems that the representationalist account of action presents.

Bodily movement

In conjunction with the body, two cases will be considered. The first pertains to bodily movement and is considered in this section, the second to motor performance and will be considered in the next section. While the second has received explicit attention in the cognitive literature, the first is, in itself, of minimal cognitive import. It is presented here mostly for future use related to the search for alternative theoretical frameworks for psychology.

   Bodily movement will be considered as it is manifested in swimming. According to RCVM, one behaves by virtue of possessing stored information in one's mind. However, as indicated earlier, not only is behaviour generally manifested without agents being able to spell out the information that supposedly underlies it, but the information agents do provide is often wrong, and at times may even be inconsistent with their actual (hence adequate) behaviour. These critical considerations have already been discussed in Chapter 7. Here, I would like to draw attention from the cognitive ramifications of movement to the characteristics of movement as such.

   Of specific interest is the modification of swimming with variations in the environment in which it takes place (assuming the same style of swimming in all cases). Thus, observe what happens to one's swimming when the water is more viscous (compare, for instance, swimming in a fresh-water lake, in the salty Mediterranean, and in the Dead Sea, which is highly saturated with oils and minerals). Observe it when the lake or sea is calm, and when it is agitated or stormy. Observe swimming under various conditions of handicap or impairment; for instance, when the swimmer carries something in one hand, or perhaps in two hands, or has his or her legs tied together. The observations will reveal that the actual patterns of the swimmer's bodily action vary with these differences. This may be expressed in changes in the angle at which the hands are inserted into the water, the tempo and rhythm of the stroke, the degree and force of the involvement of other parts of the body, etc. It makes no sense to assume that underlying all these changes are knowledge structures that the swimmer consults and manipulates as he or she swims. In addition to the general critical arguments pertaining to knowing-how discussed in Chapter 7, there are two specific arguments against the viability of the representational account. First, like the context variations in language, the variations in the body and the water environment are neither fixed in any predetermined fashion nor bounded. Second, they are unpredicted and present themselves to the swimmer in a rapid succession of on-going changes. Likewise, the swimmer's response to the variations is immediate. The immediacy is two-fold. First, there is practically no temporal delay; indeed, at times, even the slightest delay would be drastically deleterious. Second, and more importantly, the response progresses dynamically. Like the variation in the environment, the swimmer's response unfolds in an on-going manner. The immediate, continuous and ever-changing modification of swimming defies any characterization in terms of discrete, well-defined responses.

The dynamic nature of swimming suggests that rather than being defined in terms of a sequence of responses, it would be more accurately characterized as adaptation or, perhaps more accurately still, coordination. It is not that the swimmer considers the changes in the water and develops a corresponding change in his or her swimming. Rather, being in direct touch and in full tune with the aquatic environment, his or her body differentially positions itself at each and every moment. It is as if the body and the water constitute one single, unified system that maintains an on-going state of equilibrium. Knowing how to swim is being able to maintain a joint dynamic equilibrium with the water. This cannot be achieved by the execution of well-defined commands in a given plan of action. Rather, the equilibrium consists of an on-going, on-line coordination. The environment consists of a dynamics of changes, and likewise, behaviour is achieved through constant attunement to this dynamics.

Motor performance

The second case of behaviour pertaining to the body concerns motor performance. Whereas swimming may be dismissed as not pertaining to cognition, even in the broadest sense of the term, there are motor performances that cannot be so easily dismissed. The example I shall examine (one considered in the representationalist literature) is that of tying one's shoe. Unlike swimming, such a performance is distinctly human and, at least from the point of view of an external observer, may impress one as involving the following of some rules and the execution of a plan. What then is the psychological mechanism that enables one to tie one's shoes? The representational model would, I gather, describe this accomplishment as follows; the description is taken from Fodor (1981b):

> There is a little man who lives in one's head. The little man keeps a library. When one acts upon the intention to tie one's shoes, the little man fetches down a volume entitled *Tying One's Shoes*. The volume says such things as: 'Take the left free end of the shoelace in the left hand. Cross the left free end of the shoelace over the right free end of the shoelace . . .' etc.

When the little man reads the instruction 'take the left free end of the shoelace in the left hand', he pushes a button on a control panel. The button is marked 'take the left free end of a shoelace in the left hand'. When depressed, it activates a series of wheel cogs, levers and hydraulic mechanisms. As a causal consequence of the functioning of these mechanisms, one's left hand comes to seize the appropriate end of the shoelace. Similarly, *mutatis mutandis*, for the rest of the instructions.

The instructions end with the word 'end'. When the little man reads the word 'end', he returns the book of instructions to his library.

That is the way we tie our shoes. (pp. 63–4)

Indeed, this is how the representationalist will describe motor performance in general. Again, some of the problems the representational characterization presents are remarkably similar to those encountered in the case of the semantics of natural language in the first line of this critique. Thus, consider contextual variations.[1]. Usually I tie my shoes sitting, with my feet in the shoes and myself bending down to tie them. I could, however, tie the shoes while standing, or with my hands crossed, or with one hand tied, or under a mirror-like transformation (as when tying the shoes of a small child), or in a moving train, or on top of a slippery glacier, or in a boat in the middle of a gale, or in my own bedroom in the dark. All these variations definitely affect the way I tie my shoes: what I will be doing with my hands (and perhaps with other parts of my body as well) in the different situations of action will be very different.

All told, the situation of the representationalist's 'little man' is hopeless. The instructions this little man is to find in his volumes are bound to be inappropriate, insufficient or even utterly inapplicable. That the books could be amended with all requisite information is inconceivable. First, the variations are often idiosyncratic and there is no reason to believe that anyone could have thought of them before actually being confronted by them. Second, the variations are unbounded and cannot be fixed in any *a priori* fashion. Adding more and more instructions to the little man's books, or even adding more volumes to his library, will not do. No matter how detailed the specifications, there will always be situations of action that they do not cover. Third, the functions that relate variations in the environment to variations in performance are likewise ill-defined and not fixed. Fourth, there is a problem of composition. In the semantics of natural language, a standard procedure is to define basic primitives and rules of composition. As noted at the outset of this critique, this is essential for the representationalist account. Here, however, it is far from clear that any compositional function may work at all. Thus, consider tying one's shoes when standing in the dark. If one does not wish to have a separate book for this context, one might propose, in addition to the original 'tying one's shoes' book, consulting the book labelled 'standing' and that labelled 'darkness'. How, however, would one bring the information in all the books together? It is not unlikely that standing itself will be modified because of the lack of light. Hence, unforseen interactions between the parameters render well-defined compositionality practically impossible. Moreover, these parameters (think of variations in light and darkness) are likely to affect other behaviours as well. It would therefore be utterly non-parsimonious to specify their effects in a separate library whose topic is the tying of shoes, or any other particular behaviour, for that matter.

As in language, there are also medium variations. What if the laces are much longer than usual, or if – as often happens – they tear and are shortened? What if they are made of plastic or of wire? If they are soaked in water? Or in petrol? In all these cases the physical manipulation of the laces will be affected and their tying will differ from the standard. Yet, again, the representational account cannot handle these variations: instructions laid down in internal volumes could never specify what to do in all the various situations one may encounter.

Even if the variations of both context and medium could be specified in internal volumes (and let me emphasize again that this is not the case), how would they be manipulated? The manipulation of the volumes is complex: one has to evaluate the situation, decide which volume suits which situation, locate it, perhaps conjoin information specified in more than one volume. How will the little man accomplish all this? By RCVM, he will have to consult some second-order representations. There is no reason to expect these to be less complex than the representations of the first order. Indeed, as indicated in Chapter 2, the mappings between situation-specific plans and situations may themselves be context-dependent. As in the case of the semantics of natural language, the representationalist approach is bound to fail. If anything, here the situation is even more problematic. Tying shoes presents not only epistemic impasses but also the functionalist problems pertaining to both the body and the world which I surveyed in Chapters 7, 8 and 9.

So far I have considered the variations of context and medium precisely as such – variations that have to be accounted for. Yet, the role of these two factors is even more fundamental. In order to appreciate this, try to tie a shoe without there actually being a shoe to tie. In other words, try to imitate the action of tying a shoe. Apparently, the task is quite a difficult one, and it is not easy to carry on with it for an extended period of time. Clearly, this task is distinctly different from the standard tying of one's shoes. The moral of this pantomime is very important. For the task of tying one's shoe to be carried out there must be a context and a medium. The context and medium, then, are not mere factors that cognitive agents have to take into consideration and accommodate their performance to, they are necessary determinants without which action cannot exist nor be realized.

Finding one's way in the world

From the body let us turn to the world. As could be expected, the two cases are related. I shall consider an example mentioned in Chapter 8, namely, navigation. How does one move about in the world? How does one find one's way in it? Again, the representationalist answer is clear: there is a mental map which represents the world, and coupled to it is a plan of action. In order to find his or her way, the agent consults the map and the plan in his or her head. The plan specifies a target, the target is marked on the map, and an itinerary is traced. The route drawn on the map is then transformed into actual movement in the external world.

Again, straightforward though this account may seem at first glance, it is fraught with problems. Most of these should already be familiar from other domains of behaviour considered earlier. Nevertheless, and at the risk of being repetitious, I shall specify them here again, for encountering similar (or even identical) problems in very different domains is significant in its own right. The first problem is reminiscent of those noted in the epistemic part of this critique. The map can never specify all the information about the route in question. This is most eloquently articulated in a short story by Borges and Casares (1967) which recounts the case of an empire whose cartographers wanted to produce a perfect map of the land. Any map they came up with, however, was not satisfactory. Each, they found, was lacking: items found in the world were not specified in the map, the map blurred differences between things which in the world were distinct, it lumped things together. Eventually the cartographers realized that the only foolproof map would be a life-size model of the empire. But with this the map stopped being a map.

Even if a map could be complete, its usefulness would be questionable. In order to make use of the map one has to relate it to the world. But how can this be done? The problem is not only that of the gap discussed in Chapter 6. Gaps are encountered with the coupling of any internal representation and the external states of affairs to which it is said to refer. In the case of the internal map the problem is exacerbated by the fact that the world keeps changing. The change is twofold. First, there are changes in the physical landscape: trees grow, houses are built and destroyed, and so on; one's map could never be accurate. Second, there are changes induced by the cognitive agent. These relate to James Gibson's observations noted in Chapter 8. As one walks about in the world, what one sees changes due to one's own position in it. Just as perception is intertwined with the moving body, so the representation of space is intertwined with the world in which one moves. Since the movement is constant there is no sense in having a neutral, universal map. At least, the map should be amended with tags specifying the location of the agent, the perspective of his or her view, and the time of inspection. With this, however, the map one gets is very different from any standard map, and from any representational structure of the type usually specified in the psychological literature.

The contextual variation of the map and the putative tags by which it is to be amended bring back the manifold of problems noted in Chapter 4 in conjunction with the medium. The tags constitute an entire, very rich system. It is one thing to have a highly constrained number of tags serving as secondary, aiding devices; quite another to have an unbounded set of tags whose reading and interpretation is far from straightforward. Neither the mappings that relate the tags to the internal map nor those that relate them to the world are direct, nor is there any reason to suppose that they are well-defined or specified in any given mental repertory.

Moreover, since the world is ever-changing, the discrepancy between the map and the world is perennial. Thus, in order to interpret the map there is no way but to consult the world. With this, however, the map loses its very essence. If in order to know one's position on the map one has to know one's place in the world, if in order to know how to execute one's mental plan of navigation one must know how to find one's whereabouts in the world, then the map is much less useful than it seemed. It appears that in order to make use of the map one has to relate to the world by means of cognitive acts very similar, if not identical, to those one is supposed to apply on the hypothetical mental map. If so, however, perhaps one could do without the map altogether. The world, after all, is given anyway.

But is all this not how one actually navigates? At least if one is a member of modern Western civilization, does one not hold a map and direct oneself accordingly? The map will, indeed, suffer from all the limitations specified in the foregoing discussion, but this does not make it useless. The navigator does not follow the map blindly: reading the map the navigator constantly inspects the world in which he or she walks, marks discrepancies between the scenario in the world and what is indicated on the map, and when the situation so indicates he or she might even ignore the map and rely only on the information the world itself presents. All this is, of course, true, but this does not detract from the argument presented above. Our discussion was not about how one reads a map and navigates accordingly. Rather, its topic was how one walks about in the world and finds one's place and direction in it without a map. The representationalist answer to this question is that in one's head there is a map, and that the task is achieved by inspecting this map and following the trajectory marked on it. How does one read this mental map? What would one do when this map fails? When the concrete printed map fails, one may turn to one's cognitive system for assistance. When the mental map fails, it is the cognitive system itself that fails. The foregoing discussion was not meant to show that people cannot actually use maps. Rather, it attempted to show that mental representations in the form of maps cannot serve as the basis for people's locomotion and navigation. Even if locally such maps may seem to be of use, ultimately utterly different cognitive mechanisms will have to be employed. These, I have argued, are bound to make use of what people do anyway, namely, dynamically interact with the world, in the world.

Dancing

The last example I shall consider pertains to the social other, or more accurately, to the encounter between the body and the other. Just as the previous example involves an encounter between the body and the physical world, so this one involves an encounter between the body and the world of other people. Consider a couple dancing in a ballroom. Here are two people, moving fast and in perfect coordination. Yet, the dance is not planned beforehand; it is neither choreographed nor orchestrated. Nor is there any on-line communication or instruction between the two people. There are no verbal messages in which one person conveys to the other what steps he or she intends to make, nor are there any signs or clues with which to instruct the other what to do. Indeed, not only are messages and signs of this kind not passed, there is no way for them to be passed. The dancing is too fast, too spontaneous. Each dancer does not know what he himself or herself will be doing from one moment to the next. If in the midst of the dance a communication were to be made, the dancing would be hindered. Conscious reflection on what to do would result in similar hindrance. Indeed, the dancer cannot plan anything. Planning can take place only when a situation, or an array of situations, is given. Here, however, the environment changes all the time. Like the swimmer in the water, the dancer has to respond constantly to an environment which is in perpetual flux. Yet, the case of dancing is even more complex than that of swimming. In this case the very changes of the environment are, *inter alia*, caused by the action of the cognitive agent. Indeed, what constitutes the environment is another cognitive agent, another dancer. The two dancers are cognitive agents, and the two are environments, and together they are in a constant dynamics of change. With this, the distinction between agent and environment loses much of its sense.

There are, indeed, some forms of dancing in which the patterns noted reach a perfection which at times defies comprehension. One such is the Afro-Brazilian dance *capoeira*, an outgrowth of martial arts which consists of the very dynamic swinging of two people. The movements are quick and often violent. Each dancer has to be maximally attuned to his partner; any lack of alertness might result in an accident. Yet, there is no plan.

Similarly, consider the (Western) form of 'contact improvisation'. The following descriptions are by a prominent practitioner of this form of art (Paxton, 1982, 1988) and written on the basis of direct experience:

Each dance is a series of on-the-spot decisions. And they are on the spot. The soft skin is alert to the points of contact, signals telling the dancers where they are, orienting them to their partners and the floor. . . . The skin works most of the time on automatic pilot.

There are hazards. One of them is thinking ahead. What the body can do to survive is much faster than thought. . . . If thinking is too slow, is an open state of mind useful? Seems to be. . . . Memory cannot function consciously because at these speeds I can't think my way to safety. . . . One thing is clear. I have little memory, muscular or mental, of what I've danced. The specific movements my body executes when I improvise do not register consciously, and I can't reconstitute them. I feel transparent in the action.

Our reflexes move us, and this causes our partner to move. This cycle of movement responses is continuous and forms the basis of the dialogue. . . . The two bodies [are] acting as one within the domain of the physical forces. . . . Dancers ride and play these forces. Human touch unites the forces which act upon the body, with the sensations they provoke within the body. This interaction makes it possible to keep all the parts of both their bodies harmonizing.

It happens as a framework which considers the body in all its variety as the primary focus from which the mind can draw. With this, the dance is refinable to ever more precise relationships with the physical forces.

Understanding . . . with the mind is different than understanding with the body. . . . In a state of trust of the body and the earth, we believed we could learn to handle the forces involved in physical interactions between two people who permit each other the freedom to improvise.

These descriptions, by a person from an intellectual and professional background very different from that of either psychology or philosophy, include a number of elements which are by now familiar to us. First, the rapidity and immediacy of the dancing as well as its non-reflective character are noted. Second, the primacy of the body is singled out. The dancer attributes his knowledge to the body and describes himself as being carried by it. Third, the non-individual character of dancing is marked. The dance is achieved not by any planning by one dancer or another, but rather by the dynamic interaction between the two. Fourth, the arena in which the dancing, and the associated cognitive activity, takes place is characterized as being not within the province of each dancer alone, but in the point of contact of the two: a point in which bodies, world and other all meet and merge.

In addition to body, world and other, the dance involves yet another factor. As also indicated by the descriptions of contact improvisation, a crucial factor is time. Dancing involves not only the positioning of one's body and the execution of steps, but coordination in time. The temporal aspects present a whole array of problems that RCVM cannot handle. I shall turn to these in the next, third line of this critique.

A concluding illustration

In closing, let me point out that not only is the modelling of motor activities by means of representations not in line with observed facts, it also leads to sheer absurdities. If all behaviour is the expression of underlying representations, then representations should be found everywhere, even where they patently are not to be found. Not only should all speakers of natural language know their grammars and all listeners of music the theory of melodic contour and harmonic structure, but also all walkers the dynamics of locomotion. Eventually, children and animals would be attributed with the possession of knowledge that they surely do not have. A telling example of this result is given in a cartoon presented in Boden (1983) and shown in Figure 1.[2] The kingfisher's preying behaviour is in accordance with Snell's law, the physical law that specifies the course of light rays when they pass from an environment with one refraction coefficient to one with another. Would one say that Snell's law is mentally represented in the bird's mind?

The development of action

Body, world, social other and the non-cognitive faculties of mind are thus all non-cognitive factors that play a crucial role in the conduct of cognitive behaviour. Specifically, it appears that for action in the world to be executed, reliance on these factors is essential. This is most obvious in cognitive development. Further, both the non-autonomy of cognition and the primacy of factors other than the strict semantic, cognitive ones also manifest themselves most clearly in development. For this reason, I close this chapter with a second look at development. In the previous chapters it was considered with respect to each factor alone; here, it is considered as marking the global unity of the factors – their being the different facets of that basic human capability, action in the world.

   The primacy of the body and the world is evident. After all, the child is born by virtue of having a body, and on being born he or she is immersed in a world – both physical and social – which is already there. Furthermore, from the very first moment of life the child swims in the space defined by the biology of the body, by the needs for food, physical contact and warmth, by the social interactions imposed on him or her, by the constraints of the physical surroundings. It is in the context of all this that cognition evolves.

   In this process the non-cognitive precedes the cognitive. On the one hand, the non-cognitive factors have precedence over the cognitive ones, and the pragmatic over the semantic. This is manifested in the first activities of the child being tied to the various non-cognitive factors surveyed, and in knowing-how preceding knowing that. On the other hand, the world, and with it the manifold of meanings for the child, are first apprehended in terms of the child's interactions with non-cognitive factors. As pointed out by Dewey (1929), 'Things are objects to be treated, used, acted upon and with, enjoyed and endured, even more than things to be known. They are things *had* before they are things cognized' (p. 21).

Remarkably, the primacy of action is a key feature in the works of the two giants of modern developmental psychology, Piaget and Vygotsky. In the literature the developmental perspectives of the two are often contrasted (see, for instance, the discussion in Vygotsky, 1986), but actually their insights complement one another. Piaget underlines the primacy of action by noting that the early stages of development are rooted in sensory-motor activity, that is, in the child's bodily interaction with the physical world. Vygotsky underlines it by noting how it is couched in the child's interaction with the social world of other people. The following quotations from the works of these two scholars are paradigmatic. Here is what Piaget says: 'Psychologically, operations are actions which are internalizable . . . They are actions, since they are carried out on objects before being performed on symbols. They are internalizable, since they can also be carried out in thought without losing their original character of actions' (Piaget, 1957, p. 8). Piaget (1954) further argues that for the young child the identification of objects depends not so much on the nature of the objects encountered as on the actions evoked by them. Thus, for the child, the object is an extension of the action, not an independent entity that is perceived as such; for further discussion, see Piaget (1970).

Here are Vygotsky's remarks:

> At first the indicatory gesture is simply an unsuccessful grasping movement directed at an object and designating a forthcoming action. The child tries to grasp an object that is too far away. The child's hands, reaching toward the object, stop and hover in midair . . . Here we have a child's movement that does nothing more than objectively indicate an object. When the mother comes to the aid of the child and comprehends the movement as an indicator, the situation changes in an essential way. The indicatory gesture becomes a gesture for others. (Vygotsky, 1981, pp. 160–1)

These ideas were further developed by Vygotsky's disciples. The following observations are taken from Levina (1981):

> Initially, the child's behavior is syncretic. The motor and speech elements of this behavior are thoroughly intertwined. . . . Since adults are a constant part of the developing child's environment, speech, which first fulfilled the function of establishing social contact, gradually acquires an indicatory role with regard to the surrounding world. Initially it is through others' speech that the child becomes acquainted with the fact that speech allows us to

separate the environment into objects. Then s/he begins to use these same means himself/herself, at first in order to indicate objects for others and then for him/herself. (pp. 284–5)

The work of Werner and Kaplan (1963), with which I am extremely sympathetic, also deserves special mention. They write:

Before the child reaches a state at which he clearly uses bodily movements to depict events, he already executes bodily patterns of movement that seem to be mimetic-depictive, but are, in fact, only reactive or co-active; that is, the infant does not represent an event but responds to it by changes in bodily posture or limb movement. Thus, the young infant may respond to the mother or father rocking back and forth by rocking movements of his own, or he may react to rhythmic sound patterns by moving his body in a corresponding rhythmical pattern. Such a response pattern does not truly imitate the model event depictively but is only a motor resonance of it or, at the best, co-active with it; it is the kind of pattern manifested by adults when they 'unconsciously' tap their feet to music. (p. 86)

Modern empirical studies have corroborated these early observations, especially Bruner (1975a, 1975b, 1977, 1983), Karmiloff-Smith (1979), Bates (1987)[3] and, in particular, Eleanor Gibson and her associates (Gibson, 1969, 1982; Gibson and Spelke, 1983). Gibson's research programme focuses on the development of affordances and thus corroborates the ecological-psychological view mentioned throughout this line of the present critique. Experimental studies conducted by Gibson and her associates (see Gibson *et al.*, 1978, 1979; Gibson and Walker, 1984) examine patterns of habituation and dishabituation in the responses of very young children to stimuli differing on various dimensions. These studies reveal that in the first weeks and months of their life children detect invariances in terms of the activities they can produce. Such invariances are, for instance, rigidity and motion. The pertinent affordances are extracted in the course of action. With the progress of development, new actions become possible and thus new information for affordances is made available.

As revealed by the citations above, the contribution of the different non-cognitive factors is functionally the same. Further, they all work in concert, and in the execution of performance they are intertwined. Indeed, the joint interaction of the factors is so integrated that the separation between them is not always clear. Overall, the data indicate that early in the child's life, cognitive performance cannot be disentangled from the child's bodily activity and is ingrained in the child's bodily needs, affective states, desires and wants. In its early stages cognitive performance is also highly dependent on the availability of concrete entities in the external environment and on the aid of other people. With time, cognition gradually disentangles itself from these factors. I will say more on these developmental trends in the next line of this critique, and especially in Chapter 14.

Notes

1. Much of the following description of the complexities of tying shoes is based on observations by Amnon Levav.
2. I am very grateful to Prof. Margaret Boden for having allowed me to reproduce this cartoon.
3. Incidentally, Bates argues that referential gesturing is couched not in reaching and grasping, but in avoidance and boundary marking.

The third line of the critique

The first and second lines of the present critique were defined by reference to the rationales for the postulation of semantic representations presented in Chapter 1. The first line's point of reference was the epistemic rationale, that is, the postulation of representations as the repertory of the knowledge which presumably makes human behaviour possible. This line focused on the structural characteristics of the language of thought put forth by RCVM. It was pointed out that the unbounded variation of cognitive expression with context and its outstanding medium sensitivity defy any fixed, well-defined, well-formed, abstract, canonical code. The second line's point of reference was the functionalist rationale, that is, the postulation of representations as mediators governing the non-direct relationships between the mind and the world. This line focused on the various interactions between the cognitive system and other systems and domains. It was pointed out that cognition cannot be modelled as a closed autonomous system that disregards the external environment in which it is embedded. The third line of the critique to which I now turn is not based on any specific rationale for the postulation of representations. Rather, it is concerned with a dimension that encompasses all others, namely, time.

But, indeed, even though time as such was not presented as a rationale for the postulation of representations, it does feature in the rationales on which the first two lines of this critique are based. The knowledge assumed to be stored in one's mind extends and persists in time. This is what makes it possible for the same repertory of knowledge to serve as the basis for related or similar (and at times, identical) patterns of behaviour produced in different contexts and on different occasions. It also makes possible both the recognition of whatever one has already encountered and the recall of information about the past. In fact, since the flow of time is incessant, there is no use of knowledge that does not involve the mind's ability to extend, in one way or another, the scope of its application over time. Likewise, the activities allegedly performed through the mediation of representations are patterns that gain their realization in time. The interactions of the cognitive system with the world, the body and the social other come into being only as patterns that unfold in time.

The upshot of this third line of the present critique is that the representational perspective is fundamentally atemporal and hence seriously deficient. The deficiency is two-fold. On the one hand, in ignoring time, RCVM imposes a distorted view of the cognitive system and of psychological activity in general. On the other hand, since time is a crucial cognitive factor in its own right, its disregard is itself a deficiency.

This third line comprises three chapters. Chapter 12 is devoted to a basic, conceptual analysis: it contrasts the intrinsic temporality of cognition with the atemporality of RCVM. Chapter 13 examines action in time. Chapter 14 examines time as it pertains to the broader perspective of development and evolution, focusing on issues pertaining to the origins of knowledge and cognitive growth. It shows that the representational framework cannot account for the phenomenon of learning and that it entails unnatural, and even paradoxical, sequential orderings in psychology.

12 Time and temporality

Time is the man. The thinking man is he who measures, and he is at the same time the measure and the object being measured. Time is the only measurement which executes itself by itself, since thought is the only measure that measures itself.

Wilhelm Wundt

The atemporality of the representational framework

The representational framework is one in which time has no place. This characteristic is so fundamental that it is easily overlooked. RCVM's disregard of time is a general, principled one. The atemporality it assumes manifests itself in five respects. First, the definition of both semantic representations and associated computational operations is *non-temporal* in the sense that time or temporal specifications do not feature in it. Second, semantic representations are essentially *static*: they are instantiated as mental states, and attributed with existence regardless of whether they are being manipulated or whether anything is being done with them. Third, semantic representations are *inert*. Specifically, it is assumed that unless they are being operated upon they do not change. Thus, representations exhibit *permanence*: unless something happens to them, they have continuous existence in time. This is usually taken to be the characteristic of the cognitive system that accounts for people's having stable long-term knowledge and that makes the phenomenon of memory possible. Fourth, RCVM assumes a fundamental, twofold *segregation* between structures and processes. Conceptually, the definitions of representations and of the associated computational operations are *independent* of one another. Structurally, the representations and the computations are regarded as two *distinct* components of the cognitive machine.[1] Finally, the representational framework is *ahistorical* in that it assumes that one can study the present structure of the cognitive system and its mode of operation without looking at its past and the course of its development.

In arguing against the atemporal perspective imposed by RCVM, I will attempt to show the following: first, that the atemporality of RCVM is an inherent, principled characteristic; second, that human cognition is intrinsically temporal; third, that the temporal cannot be reduced to the atemporal. Together, these three lines of argument lead to the conclusion that RCVM cannot offer an account for some of the most important facets of human behaviour and that it is therefore fundamentally lacking.

The atemporal nature of semantic representations

Semantic representations are atemporal in terms both of their constituents and of the wholes they compose. The constituent elements of any representational system are defined in terms of a semantic or conceptual repertory. This repertory is atemporal: it neither depends on nor is affected by time. The rules governing the composition of symbols into large representational structures are not defined in temporal terms either. In essence, semantic representations are regarded as something like mental parchments, written documents lying in the mind. And like physical documents, the mental ones are taken to be endowed with an existence of their own. All in all, semantic representations are akin to the ideas postulated in Plato's philosophy. Of course, the representations of twentieth-century cognitive science are not attributed the same ontological status as Platonic ideas, yet in being atemporal both constructs are of the same type.[2]

The atemporal perspective imposed by RCVM extends to the computational operations associated with semantic representations. At first glance, this statement is likely to seem self-contradictory. Surely, computational operations proceed in time: on the one hand, each such operation takes time; on the other hand, it is by means of these operations that the cognitive system changes in time. Furthermore, the various operations differ in terms of the time needed for their application, and there are temporal constraints on their application in concert. Indeed, much of contemporary experimental cognitive psychology is based precisely on the fact that mental operations take time, that various such operations require different amounts of time, and that the time associated with their sequential application of these operations is a function of the times associated with the application of each one by itself. Had this not been the case, the most important method of experimental psychology – mental chronometry – would have been devoid of any sense or justification.

Admittedly, the operations as they are measured in the experimental situation do take time. This time, however, is not an intrinsic property of the representational system as such. The computational operations in question are structural ones. They are, in essence, Boolean-like operations similar to those encountered in logical calculi or transformational grammars. They move constituents, bring elements together and separate them, compute and assign values, and so forth. They are defined in an abstract, formal domain where time is not considered at all. As far as the representational theory is concerned, no temporal constraint is imposed on these operations. In other words, they could take any length of time – they could be faster or slower than they actually happen to be. There is nothing in the representational theory itself that either attributes temporality to the computational operations or assigns any specific temporal magnitude to them. That they do, in fact, take any (some) time is a technicality that the representational theory accepts as given but about which it has nothing to say. In sum, even though time is measured in psychological experiments and temporal variations are being recorded in them, time is not itself part of the representational theory.

Indeed, there is nothing in cognitive theory that could in any way constrain computational times. Representational models specify the course of information processing (i.e., the operations being applied and their sequential order) but not the particular times they should require. In this respect, note, these models contrast sharply with theories in physics, which specify not only processes and their relations but the corresponding temporal magnitudes. Representational models employ the measurement of (reaction) time as a major tool, but have nothing to say about absolute numerical magnitudes of time.

To my knowledge, the only place in the literature where the atemporality of cognitive computations has been explicitly pointed out is a short commentary by Pylyshyn (1979), later incorporated in Pylyshyn (1984). Pylyshyn claims that, being a physical dimension, time cannot be attributed to mental phenomena. In this respect time is no different from any other physical dimension. Clearly, no one would attribute length or mass to mental entities or processes. Pylyshyn thus argues against the validity of the method of reaction-time measurement in cognitive modelling. While I do not fully concur with his critique of mental chronometry, I do share his basic observation that time is not an intrinsic characteristic of computational operations.

Let me now turn to the more specific characteristics of semantic representations. I shall begin with the two structural characteristics listed in (**) in Chapter 1, namely, the inertness of representations and their static nature. Consideration of these two interrelated characteristics will lead to that of the segregation between structures and processes.

Inertness

As noted, by RCVM representations are assumed to lie in the storehouse of one's mind regardless of whether they are being manipulated or whether anything is being done with them. The representations remain unchanged unless, of course, they are being subjected to some processing. The following discussion aims to show that such a characterization cannot hold.

Let me take a closer look at the presumably inert representational system and inspect it at a moment when nothing happens and no computational work is being carried out. What does this mean? How can the representational structures 'lie' in the mind? At the very least, there must be some mechanism to sustain and maintain semantic representations. Indeed, there must be a mechanism that guarantees that whenever the representations are consulted they are the same ones. Perhaps there should be a control unit checking that this is the case and alerting one if it is not. All this requires work. Like a garden, representations cannot be left untended; they require cultivation and maintenance. For representations to exist and endure they must be embedded in a continuously active system. Representations, in other words, cannot be inert.

Indeed, the cognitive system is working incessantly, even at moments one would characterize as idle and in which we seem to do nothing. Throughout most of our waking life our eyes are open, our ears are attentive, information is passing through the sensory machinery all the time. And as the cognitive system is constantly presented with new input, any putative representational store should be constantly changing as well.[3]

Indeed, how else could it be? As Heraclitus noted, *panta chorei* – everything is in constant flux. And since, as I have shown in the second line of this critique, the mind is coupled with the world, this implies that the mind cannot be modelled as an inert system. As will be noted in Part II, at times the mind can locally dissociate itself from the world. It can, of course, delve into reminiscences of the past or fantasize about hypothetical futures. But to achieve this dissociation and maintain it for a while, the cognitive machinery must work full-time. Like any system exhibiting a degree of local closedness (think, for instance, of a refrigerator), the mind has to invest energy in order to dissociate itself from the world. Thus, whether it is busy or idle, whether it is immersed in the world or locally detached from it, the cognitive system is never inert.

Looked at from a biological point of view, the non-inertness of representations is quite evident. Being non-inert is, in fact, the key characteristic of the living. Superficially it may seem that living organisms and biological systems are well-defined entities of independent existence out there in the world. Yet, stop the biological activity of the body (I should perhaps say, that constitutes the body) and what you have is death. Soon the body will disintegrate and eventually the well-demarcated, solid, physical entity it seemed to be will disappear. The same holds for organs at all levels of biology. Take, for instance, the cell. The cell is an ever-active system. Its membrane is not an entity which is given; rather, it is created by the on-going, dynamic interaction between the two environments on its two sides. The membrane exists only as long as the physiological machinery is working. When it halts, the division between the internal and the external domains is obliterated, and so is the distinction between the living and the non-living. With this, life ceases. This is the key observation of Maturana's theory of autopoiesis (see, for instance, Maturana, 1978; Maturana and Varela, 1980, 1987). Autopoietic systems create their environment and are, in turn, created by it. Maturana and Varela show that this is true in neurophysiology, immunology, evolution and also cognition.

Similar observations were recently made by the advocates of connectionism. As pointed out by Rumelhart and McClelland (1986b):

There does not seem to be an appreciable decision phase during which a unit provides no output. Rather it seems that the state of a unit reflects its current input. To the degree that a unit represents a hypothesis and its activation level . . . represents the degree to which evidence favors that hypothesis, the activation level of the unit provides continuous information about the current evaluation of that hypothesis. (p. 133)

The authors note that this is in line with biological considerations of neural function and that they 'contrast starkly' with the picture presented by RCVM.

A pertinent point was made by Bergson (1944) in a somewhat different context. Bergson observed that human memory lacks some of the key characteristics of independent entities and therefore cannot be a faculty. In particular, Bergson noted that memory (i.e., the on-going recording of information) is not activated at will. Since semantic representations are taken to be the storehouse of memory, Bergson's observation readily applies to such representations as well.

This discussion has focused on the inertness of representations, but similar arguments may be made with respect to the computational operations associated with these representations. What happens to these operations when they are not being applied? Where are they held? How are they maintained? When working with physical tools we may pause and lay the tools aside; when not in use they will remain on the workbench or a shelf. For the cognitive system such options are, however, not available. By the logic of RCVM, all knowledge is constituted in semantic representations. The different computational operations are also part and parcel of one's knowledge. Hence, they too must be constituted in semantic representations. In sum, on the one hand representations have to be couched in a dynamic, ever-active system, and on the other hand computations have to be constituted in representations. Hence, by the logic of RCVM itself, neither the strict conceptual distinction nor the operational segregation between representations and processes can be maintained.

Not only are representations and computations intertwined, they actually consist of the same thing. For it to store information, the representational (in the weak sense) system has to be able to encode the world, make distinctions in it, identify and classify. All these constitute cognitive activities. In other words, it is by virtue of computational activity that the substrate of cognition serves its representational function. It is, thus, the very same system that represents knowledge, perceives, learns and processes information.

Structures v. processes and the dynamic nature of cognition

The foregoing discussion has focused on inertness, but in doing so it has already dealt with the other two characteristics of semantic representations: it has marked the primary dynamic nature of the cognitive system and argued against the segregation between structures and processes that RCVM assumes.

That the cognitive system is an ever-active, dynamic system in which there is no segregation between structures and processes is one of the key tenets of connectionism (Hinton and Anderson, 1981a; Zipser, 1986; Sejnowsky *et al.*, 1988; Amit, 1989; Churchland and Sejnowski, 1989; Feldman, 1989; and Smolensky, 1989). Here is how McClelland *et al.* (1986) put it:

In most models, knowledge is stored as a static copy of a pattern. Retrieval amounts to finding the pattern in long-term memory and copying it into a buffer or working memory. There is no real difference between the stored representation in long-term memory and the active representation in working memory. In PDP [parallel distributed processing] models, though, this is not the case. In these models, the patterns themselves are not stored. Rather, what is stored is the *connection strengths* between units that allow these patterns to be re-created. . . . The connections between [the] units in the system are such that activation of the unit will cause the pattern . . . to be reinstated. (p. 31)

Likewise: 'Using knowledge in processing is no longer a matter of finding the relevant information in memory and bringing it to bear; it is part and parcel of the processing itself' (p. 32). There are three highly interrelated points to note here. First, in the connectionist view, the representations of knowledge do not consist of given, stored data structures, but rather of patterns of activation. Second, given the foregoing characterization of representations, the affinity between structures and processes is marked; indeed, in essence, both are defined in the same manner – by patterns of connections. Third, the definitional affinity between structures and processes is coupled with a functional affinity: there is no clear-cut distinction between structures and processes; hence, the system is always in an active state – it is, in other words, intrinsically dynamic.

An important special case is that of learning. By RCVM, learning is a particular type of accomplishment of the cognitive system. It occurs on special occasions: when the system acquires new information. The procedures responsible for learning are applied to given semantic representations so that the new information is incorporated into the cognitive agent's repertory of knowledge. Connectionism views matters in a radically different way. As argued by Smolensky (1986): 'During learning, there need never be any decision that "now is the time to create and store a new schema". Or rather, if such a decision is made, it is by the modeler *observing* the evolving cognitive system and not by the system itself' (p. 261). In connectionist modelling, learning is the basic mode of operation. Given that the cognitive system is constantly exposed to input, it is always learning. Thus, in essence, learning accounts for all the changes manifested in the cognitive system. In effect, the dynamics of learning and the rules governing the workings of mind are one and the same.

Methodological considerations further support this view. The segregation between representations and computations presupposes two distinct cognitive components. By contrast, when a dynamic, on-going activation is assumed, the representational structures are a by-product of the activity of the system. In other words, for half the price, so to speak, one gets the same merchandise. This is surely what parsimony dictates. As Smolensky (1986) points out, the rationale underlying connectionist modelling is defined by 'the goal of establishing a subsymbolic computational environment where the mechanisms for *using* knowledge are simultaneously sufficiently powerful and analytically tractable to facilitate – rather than hinder – the study of learning' (p. 261). I shall return to this issue in Chapter 16.

Historicity

The last aspect of representations to be considered pertains to the history of the cognitive system. RCVM is inherently ahistorical. It assumes that the present state of the cognitive system can be studied without reference to its past, that knowledge can be studied without reference to how it was acquired, and that cognitive performance can be studied without reference to how its mastery was achieved. The question of the legitimacy of such an ahistorical view bears on issues that extend far beyond the scope of this book. This question has been a bone of contention not only in psychology but also in various other disciplines of the human and social sciences. Some thinkers have maintained that, indeed, one cannot understand the present states of systems without considering their past history. Further, it may be argued that once one knows the history of a system, one also knows much, if not all, of what is to be known about its present state. The prime protagonist of the historical view in philosophy is Hegel (1931). Hegel paved the road for Marxism, a world-view that, as we all know, had enormous effect on the whole spectrum of the human and social sciences. Vygotsky's psychology, to which much reference was made throughout the second line of this critique, clearly reflects this Marxist historical perspective (see, for instance, Vygotsky, 1978).

Curiously, the only other school of psychology in which the importance of past history is paramount is often considered to be at odds with Marxism. I refer to psychoanalysis, which, in a nutshell, maintains that to understand the present behaviour of the adult one has to gain access to the life of the child this person once was. In particular, it is assumed that people deal with other people in terms of patterns developed through the interaction with significant persons (notably their parents) early in life. As noted in Chapter 9, this view of inter-personal interaction is central to the psychoanalytic theory of object-relations.

Likewise, various continental philosophers have pointed out that people see the world in terms of their past experience. Here is how the German philosopher and social scientist Gadamer (1976) describes it:[4]

> It is not so much our judgements as it is our prejudices that constitute our being . . . the historicity of our existence entails that prejudices, in the literal sense of the word, constitute the initial directedness of our whole ability to experience. Prejudices are biases of our openness to the world. They are simply conditions whereby we experience something – whereby what we encounter says something to us. (p. 9)

Here I do not wish to deny the feasibility of non-historical cognitive research. I appreciate that even if the history of cognitive agents is a prime determinant of their present state of knowledge and behaviour, reference to this history is usually impractical. There is, however, an interesting complementarity between history and representation. Specifically, the more one ignores the history of a system, the greater is the need to refer to representational structures; and conversely, the more a cognizer's history is known, the smaller the need to refer to such structures.

The following demonstration is based on a line of reasoning presented by Shaw and Todd (1980) in the context of perception. Recall the functional relationship presented in Chapter 1, that specifying the behaviour of a cognitive agent in terms of the stimulation from the environment on the one hand and the state of the agent's cognitive system on the other hand. As noted, RCVM defines the second factor by the repertory of the system's representations. Bearing this in mind and following the logic of Shaw and Todd, the following functional relationship may be defined:

1. $R_n = f(R_{n-1}, E_n)$

In this formula, R_n is the cognitive system's present internal, hence representational, state. R_{n-1} is the system's state in the preceding point in time, and E_n is the present contribution of the environment. Similarly, by the same logic:

2. $R_{n-1} = f(R_{n-2}, E_{n-1})$

Hence, by substitution:

3. $R_n = f(R_{n-2}, E_{n-1}, E_n)$

And by repeated iteration:

4. $R_n = f(R_0, E_1, \ldots, E_n)$

The sequence $(E_1, \ldots, E_{n-1})$ defines all the environmental influences to which the organism was exposed up to the present point in time. Thus, equation (4) indicates that once the entire history of the organism is known there is no need to postulate any fixed, given representational state. Moreover, as (4) indicates there is a trade-off between representation and history: when the entire history of the agent is known, there is no need to postulate any representation; conversely, when there is a full specification of the system's present representational state, its history can be disregarded. Similarly for any intermediate characterization: inasmuch as the history of the system is not known a postulation of representational states is needed.

Correlative to the complementarity between representation and history is one between representation and learning. Usually, representational structures of knowledge are specified and both the history of their acquisition and their further change in time are ignored as separate, independent issues. However, as was suggested in the previous section and will be argued later, learning may be regarded as the basic phenomenon, and the seemingly static representations as abstract, idealized projections of the on-going cognitive flux in arrested moments of time. On such a view, cognition is to be modelled by specifying the dynamics of change, not in terms of underlying representations and the computational operations associated with them.

The temporality of human cognition

Against the atemporality of representations, the temporality of human existence and cognitive behaviour stands in glaring contrast. As pointed out by Kant (1781/1953), time is the most basic matrix (in his terminology, *a priori intuition*) in which all our mental life is couched. Our being in time is not merely a fundamental predicament of our existence in the world (for perhaps the grandest exposition of this, see Heidegger's classic *Being and Time*, 1962), it is also a non-trivial first principle of human psychology. As Merleau-Ponty (1962) states, temporality is the structure of all structures. In characterizing human psychology as couched in time I will underline a series of features.

The first is as fundamental as it is banal. Human beings live in time. Even the most stationary scene, one in which nothing seems to happen and nothing changes, extends in time and is so perceived. Likewise, all we do is being realized as we act in time. Our actions can be slow or fast, on-going or abrupt, but they can never escape time. As pointed out by Merleau-Ponty (1962, 1964), without time, being would become a pure platitude or motionless self-identity, and subjectivity would be inconceivable.

A second characteristic marking the fundamental temporality of cognition is its being – as described by Bergson – experienced as a continuous progress of the past which gnaws into the future and swells as it advances. Unlike abstract, physical time, psychological time, as we all know, is in constant motion. Bergson referred to this quality of human time as duration (see Bergson, 1944, 1950, 1983).

Third, both the input that the cognitive system registers and the output it produces gain their identity and their sense through being extended in time. As pointed out by Gibson (1960, 1966b), the stimulation provided by the world is not a set of punctate or momentary stimuli, but rather consists of sensory arrays in flux. This is most apparent in music. The following description, based on Husserl's (1964) phenomenological analysis, is from Dreyfus (1975):

> [I]f I am familiar with a melody the sound of each note depends on the surrounding notes. I do not hear a mere C sharp, for example, but a note with a quality which would be altered if it appeared in a different melody. In this way, the future and past of the melody are involved in the experience of any given note. (p. 155)

Fourth, cognitive acts take time. I am not referring to the mere fact that actions – actions of any kind – require a certain amount of time to be executed. This is, of course, true but it is trivial. Rather, I am signalling the fact that in their very essence cognitive performances are activities that unfold in time. An illustrative example is given by Merleau-Ponty (1962), who considers the task of evaluating the quality of silk. To check how smooth a fabric is one has to pass one's hand along the fibres. One cannot just touch the fabric and determine its texture: one has to travel along the fibre; and this, like all travelling, takes time. Let me emphasize again: the extension of the task in time is not due to the fact that one has to collect more and more information, and then integrate it. Rather, the checking is one, single act, and it is one that, in its very essence, has to extend in time.

Lastly, the human cognitive system is intrinsically temporal in that it is always active. I observed this in the previous section in arguing against the static nature of semantic representations. Other, most interesting (and, I gather, little-known) observations in this regard were made many years ago by the Polish psychologist Twardowsky; the following comments are based on Bobryk (1989).[5] According to Twardowsky (1912/1927), every human action leads to some outcome, result or product. The action of drawing results in a sketch, and that of dancing in a dance. As these examples indicate, the products of action are of two types: ones which endure after the termination of the action that produced them (like the drawing) and ones that exist only as long as the action producing them goes on (like the dance). Twardowsky's key point is that durable products of psychological actions do not exist. If so, and here I am returning to my own line of argumentation, then, indeed, psychological activity should take time. Specifically, if the products of psychological activity should have some duration (for instance, in order for them to have further effects), the activity should extend in time as well. Incidentally, as pointed out by Bobryk (1989), this indicates, once again, that the entities specified by representational models are not psychological.

Not only is human psychology intrinsically temporal, but human temporality is intrinsically psychological. As noted by many – notably William James (1950) and Bergson (1929, 1944) – psychological time is very different from physical time. First, as both James and Bergson point out, physical time is a mathematical construct which lacks that key characteristic of psychological time, *duration*. Second, human temporality is defined in terms not of an abstract measure but rather of the cognitive agent's being and acting in the world, and is thus laden with *meaning*. As pointed out by Fraisse (1964), human time is not a smooth, uniform continuum but rather is constructed in terms of structurally coherent, meaningful segments. We hear music, not sequences of individual tones, we walk rather than produce sequences of steps with our feet, we talk rather than utter one speech sound after another. Third, human time is *holistic*. The temporal is perceived and invested with meaning in terms of entire wholes. As noted by William James (1890/1950):

> It is only as parts of [a] *duration-block* that the relation of succession of one end to the other is perceived. We do not first feel one end and then feel the other after it, and from the perception of the succession infer an interval of time between, but we seem to feel the interval of time as a whole, with its two ends embedded in it. The experience is from the outset a synthetic datum, not a simple one; and to sensible perception its elements are inseparable, although attention looking back may easily decompose the experience, and distinguish its beginning from its end. (p. 610)

The above observations on melodic progression clearly show this to be the case.

Rhythm marks the holistic nature of human time most clearly: the very notion of rhythm has no sense except in terms of entire sequences that extend over time.

Extensive development of these insights into the temporality of human existence and human cognition are found in Gibson's theory of visual perception (Gibson, 1966a, 1979). Gibson points out that what one perceives are patterns of invariance. These, note, cannot be defined in terms of atomic units, but only in terms of entire structures. Furthermore, since the environment is ever-changing, it follows that the invariances themselves are often defined in terms that extend over time. From this Gibson concludes that higher-order structures, or events, are the basic units of perception (see Gibson, 1975).

The dynamic nature of the cognitive system implies that this system and the knowledge it manifests cannot be characterized in terms of static structures. The neural-like models of connectionism mentioned above are dynamic, and so are a few models of perception proposed in recent years by experimental psychologists, some of them followers of James Gibson. Of these, let me note Cutting and Puffitt (1981), who argue that the dynamic aspects of perception are primary, and Freyd (1989), who claims that the structures by which knowledge is mentally represented are dynamic and the coding of temporal information is essential. Freyd suggests that these structures are not only ever-changing, but also that they have a 'momentum', that is, they tend to perpetuate change in the direction of perceived motion even when the moving object is halted.

The representational account of time

RCVM is atemporal whereas human cognition and action are intrinsically temporal. But could the two not be reconciled? Can one not account for the temporality of cognition by means of atemporal semantic representations? I think not.

First and foremost, there is a problem of categorical difference: the atemporal cannot be made temporal. This, in fact, may be regarded as another manifestation of the problem of the missing qualities encountered in the second line of this critique. Just as it cannot account for the way constituents of formal, syntactically defined semantic representations are invested with meaning, gain intentionality and tie in with the world, so the representational framework cannot invest such constituents with semantic temporality. This appraisal is the cornerstone of Bergson's entire philosophy of time and evolution:

> I was very much struck to see how real time, which plays the leading part in any philosophy of evolution, eludes mathematical treatment. . . . Duration, which science eliminates, and which is so difficult to conceive and express, is what one feels and lives. (Bergson, 1983, pp. 12–13)

Throughout his writings, and especially in *Creative Evolution* (1944), Bergson points out that a system comprised of fixed, discrete, well-defined terms cannot characterize time. He is concerned with mathematics on the one hand and with that mode of cognition he refers to as the 'intellect' on the other hand. However, the system he criticizes exhibits precisely those structural properties by which semantic representations in the technical-psychological sense are defined (for an eloquent analysis of Bergson's critique of the intellect in the light of contemporary philosophy and cognition, see Lahav, 1990, to whose insights I am indebted). In particular, Bergson points out that the continuous cannot be reduced to the discrete, the ever-changing to the static, the wholistic to the elementary, the multi-valued to the uni-valued (the determinate); for similar contemporary observations, see Bickhard (1993).

To appreciate further the intrinsic temporality of human cognition and the failure of RCVM to account for it, let me turn to the consideration of the unit of time. This question has, of course, been much discussed in both philosophy and physics. In the psychological literature it is generally associated with the notion of the *psychological moment*.

In postulating this notion one assumes that there is a minimal unit of temporal extension that may serve for the measurement of psychological time. Operationally, such a unit may be defined by means of several measures: the shortest temporal extension that a stimulus must have in order to be perceived, the minimal temporal separation between two successive stimuli that allows for them to be perceived as distinct, or the minimal separation that allows the order of two stimuli to be determined. Various different values for these temporal extensions have been proposed. First, the values associated with the different operational measures differ. Second, they vary with the modality of the stimuli at hand, their physical characteristics, the task being performed and the level of practice of the subject making the judgement. Thus, values for the shortest perceivable stimuli are of the order of 120 milliseconds for light, and 10 to 50 milliseconds for sound (Durup and Fessard, 1930). Values for the minimal temporal separation between stimuli range from less than 10 to about 150 milliseconds, depending on the modality of the stimuli and their physical characteristics, as well as the level of practice of the subject making the judgement (Macar, 1985). The thresholds for order estimation are higher; their order of magnitude is 140–170 milliseconds (Michon, 1985). For reviews of the empirical findings, see Macar (1985) and Michon (1978).

The variability of estimates is telling. That the psychological moment cannot be evaluated without considering the particular setting casts doubt on the validity and utility of the postulation of such a notion. After all, if the identity of the psychological moment is fully dependent on the context of action, then there is not much benefit in postulating an absolute, universal, mathematical-like unit of psychological time.

This problem and my critical appraisal are completely analogous to those surveyed at the beginning of this critique, in the discussion of context. There the variations of meaning with context were taken to hold against postulating a context-free, semantic definition of meaning. Here analogous considerations mark the problematic nature of the postulation of an absolute, physical-like notion of psychological time.

From the basic terms by which time is defined, let me turn to temporality as a whole. The most salient characteristic of time is its *extensionality*. How can this be accounted for by the representational framework? The most natural representational strategy is, I gather, to treat extended time as a summation of individual moments each constituting a representational state. Each such state is a temporal slice. In themselves, these slices are atemporal; yet, given that each one is taken at a different moment in time, their summation results in an extended duration; hence a modelling of temporality is achieved. Straightforward though this account may seem, I do not think it is viable. Its pitfalls are neither specific to mental representations, nor even confined to the domain of psychology. The problem in question is, in fact, a very old one. As pointed out by Bergson (1983), it is that presented by Zeno's paradoxes, which purport to show that motion cannot be generated by a summation of discrete stationary states. Interestingly, this problem presents still another pattern of an unbridgeable gap. Even if the basic units of time are endowed with temporal extension, how is each one to be tied to the following one? The jump from each to the next, hence the continuity of time and its flow, are gaps that cannot be bridged.[6]

The compression of time

These arguments have pertained to the constructive perspective: they have pointed out that the temporal cannot be constructed out of the non-temporal, nor the dynamic out of the static. The viability of the representational account of time can also be criticized from the converse, reductive perspective. Temporal extension, it will be argued, cannot be reduced to non-temporal units.

In one sense, the reduction of the temporal to the non-temporal is just the rendering of the non-temporal into the temporal looked at from the other direction. In the particular domain of time, however, the problem of reduction has another, special manifestation. In this case, reduction is synonymous with squeezing, with making something shorter than it presently is. Can the duration of time be reduced? Can an action executed in time be compressed so as to be performed in a shorter period, or perhaps in a manner that does not depend on time at all? The question is not whether another action, of perhaps equivalent or even identical results, can be performed at a different speed. Surely, one may perform all sorts of action at different speeds. Can the same action, however, be temporally compressed?

For a concrete example, let me return to the domain of music. Can one hear a piece of music in a period of time shorter than the time that it takes to play the piece? Can one grasp music in such a time? Can one recall a melody and reproduce it in a shorter time? Music is essentially temporal and in order to perceive or apprehend it one has to follow its entire course in time. The sociologist Schutz (1964) has referred to this step-by-step temporal perception as 'polythetic', a term that contrasts with 'monothetic', which characterizes all-at-once processing. The musical content itself, he says, its very meaning, can be grasped only by reimmersing oneself in the on-going flux, by thus reproducing the articulated musical occurrence as it unfolds one step after another in time. Consequently, it will 'take as much time' to reconstitute the work in recollection as to experience it for the first time. In both cases the listener or rehearser has to re-establish the quasi-simultaneity of his or her stream of consciousness with that of the composer.

The units of time

How are the units of psychological time to be characterized? To address this question, let me turn from the experimental data to naturalistic, phenomenological observations. As will become apparent, these further reveal how different the unit of human time is from any mathematically or physically defined moment.

Let me start by considering the 'now', that stretch of time that presumably defines the present moment. I am now listening to music. What temporal extension does the indexical 'now' stand for? Is 'now' the minimal stretch of time that I perceive? Is it defined, for instance, by the *Re* that I am now hearing? This *Re*, however, could have been part of any piece of music. In itself it cannot define the music I am now listening to. What I am now listening to is a piano sonata by Schubert. I may be listening to the first movement of the sonata, perhaps even to its development section. I am not listening to a *Re*. What human beings perceive as the 'now' is thus distinct from what experimental psychologists characterize as the psychological moment.

I am now writing. To what does this last sentence refer? Does it refer to one single sentence? But which one? That which contains the word 'now' (the first sentence in this paragraph) or 'this sentence' (the second in the paragraph)? Apart from marking the fleeting nature of the now, these observations indicate that what I am now writing is not a sentence. Is it this paragraph? Is it this section? Is it my book, which I have been working on for so many years, which I am 'now writing'? Perhaps it is all of these? (For similar observations, see Gibson, 1966b.)

Incidentally, if it is the chapter or the book that I am 'now writing', this is quite a curious state of affairs (which does not mean that it is not the case): at this moment of my writing, the chapter is not finished yet, and nor is the book. Indeed, until this book goes to the printer the chapter of which our sentence is a part is still likely to undergo many changes. By the time the book is finished, 'that' sentence might not even be included in it.

These observations reveal a number of characteristics of the unit of psychological time; not accidentally, these echo the characteristics of human temporality noted in the first section of this chapter. First, the unit of human time is *thick* (see Huertas-Jourda, 1975): the atoms of human temporality are themselves endowed with duration. Unlike mathematical instances, the psychological moment still maintains something of the past and already embodies some of the future. Again, the clearest demonstration of this is provided by music. Here is how Husserl (1964), in a fine phenomenological observation, describes it: 'When a new note sounds, the one just preceding it does not disappear without a trace; otherwise, we should be incapable of observing the relations between the notes which follow one another' (p. 30). As pointed out by William James (1890/1950):

> The practically cognized present is no knife-edge, but a saddle-back, with a certain breadth of its own on which we sit perched, and from which we look in two directions into time. The unit of composition of our perception of time is a *duration*, with a bow and a stern, as it were – a rearward- and a forward-looking end. (p. 609)

Following E.R. Clay, James refers to the basic unit of our immediate experience as the *specious present*.

The second characteristic of units of psychological time is a corollary of the first: these units are higher-order structures constituting *wholes* or parts of wholes. Observations supporting this appraisal have already been presented. In particular, the tie between this assessment and Gibson's general view of cognition should be underscored. Gibson (1979) points out that one perceives not unitary snapshots of the world but rather structured wholes. Each view of the world, each sound we hear, each word, is being perceived as it makes itself present following an already perceived state of affairs and evolving into further perceptions. As already noted, according to Gibson, one perceives patterns of invariance. The invariance of sequential information can only be a pattern that extends in time.

Third, the unit of psychological time cannot be defined without the consideration of the *actions* that are being conducted during that period of time. Human temporality is inextricably intertwined with human action. Just as there is no action without time, so there is no time without action. Fraisse (1969) has instructive observations on this:

> Broadly speaking, the present is that which is contemporaneous with my activity. Obviously the changes to which it corresponds are determined by the scale on which I see them. The present is the century in which I live as much as the hour now passing. I can actually make an arbitrary division of the changes in relation to which I stand, by considering the past to date from a given moment. I can, for instance, contrast past centuries with the present century. This is the meaning of Janet's words: 'The duration of the present is the duration of a story'. . . .
> There also exists, however, a *perceived* present which can last only for the duration of the organization which we perceive as one unit. My present is one 'tick-tock' of the clock, the three beats of the rhythm of a waltz, the idea suggested to me, the chirp of a bird flying by . . . There is order in this present, there are intervals between its constituent elements, but there is also a form of simultaneity resulting from the very unity of my act of perception. Thus the perceived present is not the paradox which logical analysis would make it

seem by splitting time into atoms and reducing the present to the simple passage of time without psychological reality. Even to perceive this passage of time requires an act of apprehension which has an appreciable duration. (pp. 4, 84–5)

Taken together, all this indicates that the units of psychological time are *events*. Events are to be contrasted with the units of physics or the moments postulated in information-processing models of cognition. Whereas the former are absolute units defined in terms of neutral measures like those given by a watch, events are defined in terms which are couched in the organism's action in the world. This is tantamount to saying that human temporality (as well as its units) is defined in terms which are laden with meaning. In Chapter 8 I observed this was the case with respect to the world. In the light of the insights of James Gibson and his followers in the school of ecological psychology, I noted that the world in which organisms live is not the conglomeration of absolute, senseless, raw data, but rather consists of patterns imbued with meaning. These, in turn, are defined by the patterns of activity that the world affords the behaving agent in question. Here I note that the same applies to time (for related discussion, see McCabe, 1986).

By way of summary, let me consider a concrete case, that of the event called dancing. I am doing the tango. What constitutes this specific event? Is my dance composed of a concatenation of entities each of which is an elementary unit of dance? The single step cannot be considered a dance. Indeed, like the single musical note or an isolated word, it could occur as part of events which would not be called a tango and perhaps not even a dance. Is the unit of the dance the pattern of four steps by which the tango is defined? Apparently not, for the production of such a pattern – i.e., a sequence of four steps executed in the proper rhythm – does not constitute a dance. If it did, then the production of this pattern over and over again should be regarded as dancing over and over again. Evidently, it is not. And then, even though the basic pattern of the tango is fixed, the dance develops. What gives a particular dance its flavour, what makes a particular tango good is nothing that is confined to any single pattern of four steps. The dance, then, is an event that extends in time. It does not have any existence except as it unfolds in time. As will be argued at length in Part II, this is true of human action in general.

Lastly, let me note that the observations made throughout this discussion hold against a distinction which at first sight seems to be all but self-evident, that between memory and perception. This radical appraisal is, I find, one of Gibson's most interesting insights and I shall present it in his own words; as is immediately apparent, his analysis integrates many of the observations made throughout the foregoing discussion:

The seemingly innocent hypothesis that events are perceived has radical implications that are upsetting to orthodox psychology. Assuming that shorter events are nested within longer events, that nothing is instantaneous, and that sequences are apprehended, the usual distinction between perception and memory comes into question. For where is the borderline between perceiving and remembering? Does perceiving go backward in time? For seconds? For minutes? For hours? When do percepts stop and begin to be memories or, in another way of putting it, go into storage? . . . Equally embarrassing questions can be asked about expectation. (Gibson, 1975, p. 299)

And:

[The] . . . present time is certainly not a razor's edge . . . and no one can say when perception leaves off and memory begins. . . . Even at its simplest, a stimulus has some successive order as well as adjacent order . . . This means that natural stimulation consists of *successions* as truly as it consists of *adjacencies*. (Gibson, 1966a, p. 276)

Hence, Gibson (1966b) concludes that event perception implies a rejection of the division of the stream of awareness into a past, a present and a future, as well as the corresponding distinction between memory and perception (see also Gibson, 1979, pp. 253–4). Mark the similarity to much earlier observations by Bergson (1929): 'You cannot draw a line between the past and the present. . . . Our whole existence is something like this single sentence' (pp. 55–6). Interestingly, similar remarks were also made, on the basis of intuitive, phenomenological observations, by the contemporary artist David Hockney (1983):

[In pictures I made] I attempted to show the experience of walking, so that one might see the entire experience, in time. It means that you must look with your memory. Then it led me to believe that we're always looking with our memory, as memory is always present. Memory is part of vision – it's inescapable. I came to the conclusion that there is no such thing as objective vision. There can never be, because even the memory of the first instant of looking is then a part of the perception, and it adds up and it adds up. (pp. 28–9)

I shall return to Hockney and his work in the next chapter.

Notes

1. Thus, the following statement is paradigmatic: 'A long tradition has held that "contents" of the mind in some sense exist independently of the "processes" that create the contents, change them, and make use of them. Thus, in studying memory we are concerned with two questions: What the structures of memory is, and what processes operate upon it' (Tulving and Bower, 1974, p. 266).
2. For an illuminating discussion, see Katz (1981).

3. The term 'input' is, like so many other standard terms, misleading. It should not be taken as implying that sensory information is definable prior to and independently of the associated cognitive activity.
4. This quote is taken from Winograd and Flores (1986). I use this opportunity to acknowledge the influence of Winograd's writings on my thinking.
5. I thank Dr Jerzy Bobryk for drawing my attention to Twardowsky and his school.
6. For further, different arguments against the postulation of psychological quanta of time, see Vroon (1974).

13 *Action in time*

Time . . . was arranging the different periods of my life, thereby bringing me
to realize that in a book which aimed to recount a human life one would have
to use, in contrast to the 'plane' psychology ordinarily employed, a sort of
three-dimensional, 'solid' psychology.

Marcel Proust

The moral of the foregoing discussion is that action takes time. I emphasized that
this is not a mere technical limitation, but a manifestation of an intrinsic feature of
the cognitive system. I shall now examine this further. In this chapter three topics
will be considered. The first relates directly to the discussion in the previous
chapter: it concerns the unfolding of cognitive performance in time. The second is
action that involves timing; I will argue that such action, like action in the world
which I discussed in Chapter 11, cannot be accounted for in the framework of
RCVM. The third is the perception of change.

The unfolding of action in time

In Chapter 12 I marked the intrinsic temporality of human psychology. Let me now
turn specifically to cognition and show how this intrinsic temporality manifests
itself in various cognitive performances. The discussion will mark the principled
inadequacy of RCVM and at the same time lay the ground for an alternative view
of cognitive performance.

Perception

Let me start with a faculty that is usually not regarded as temporal, perception.
From the perspective of RCVM perception should, indeed, not take time. That is,
it should not take any time beyond that required for the sensory stimulation to be
registered, and for the information to be interpreted and incorporated in the system
of knowledge and belief. This time is 'technical': things take time just as things have
spatial dimensions or weight, but there is nothing intrinsically cognitive about these
processing times. In other words, they are required but do not affect the cognitive
activity as such.

Perhaps the only modern psychologist to have marked the intrinsic temporality of perception is, again, James Gibson. As noted in Chapters 8 and 12, Gibson (1966b, 1968, 1975, 1979) points out that perceiving is not the reception of a sensory snapshot in a given unit of time in the manner of a camera recording a scene (see also Johansson, 1975). Rather, organisms perceive as they move about in the world, explore it and interact with it. While it is true that upon opening one's eyes one is immersed in a visual scene that is complete, perceiving is not instantaneous (or accomplished in one unit of time). Whether one first perceives wholes and then detects details or whether one's gaze is first caught up in specifics and then one gradually appreciates the entire scene, seeing unfolds in time. Again, the point is not merely that the accomplishment that results in seeing requires a certain amount of time. Rather, it is that seeing is a dynamic process, one which is intrinsically temporal. Perception extends in time not because it involves the incorporation of more and more information, but because the organism actively interacts with the world in a way shaped not only by the layout of the environment but also by the identity of the organism, its past experience, its present concerns, its expectations of the future, and the repertory of modes of operation and patterns of behaviour at its disposal.

Let me give an example from my own experience. I am sitting at a station of the Parisian Metro and a curious advertisement draws my attention. I look at it, I read a word, I wonder what it means. I look at other elements in the advertisement, they make me see another pattern on the board, I look back at the picture, and now it makes sense. 'It is witty', I say to myself, 'interesting'. What did I characterize as interesting? Apparently, it was not the graphic or the linguistic material traced on the paper as such. Had I appreciated the meaning of the advertisement in less (or more) time, would it have been equally interesting? Would it have been interesting in the same way? I think not. What made the experience interesting was not only the material being perceived, but the entire process in which this experience evolved, the manner in which it unfolded. Hence, the only way to characterize this act of perception is as an entire episode, a little story if you wish, that unfolds in time.

As noted in Chapter 12, the painter David Hockney (1983, 1984) is very much interested in the dynamics of seeing and in its theoretical (including psychological) implications. Usually, it is said that, unlike music which progresses in time, paintings are static: they present themselves to the onlooker in one shot. Reflecting upon the process of looking at Chinese scrolls, Hockney came to appreciate that this is not so. The scrolls are too big for one to look at them all at once: to see the entire scroll one has to roll and unroll it. The painters of scrolls, Hockney observed, were keenly aware of this, and took this temporal factor into account when they painted. This insight led Hockney to incorporate time into his work. On the one hand, he created paintings which, like the Chinese scrolls or ancient Egyptian or Mesopotamian monumental art, direct the observer along a particular course of inspection. On the other hand, he started creating photographs in which the dynamic nature of looking-at was emphasized. These photographs are collages of many pictures of an object or a scene, taken from different angles and at slightly different times, and partially superimposed on one another. As claimed by the artist, and as ascertained by many people, they have a strong impact. Indeed, seeing them for the first time my impression was that these photographs are more real than any standard ones. One such photocollage is shown in Figure 2. It is titled 'a chair'.

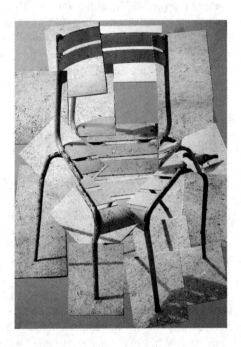

'Chair, Jardin de Luxembourg Paris, 10th August 1985'. © David Hockney

As Hockney points out, more than being about the things that they depict, his photocollages are about the act of looking. Indeed, what is an object for me is not confined to one snapshot. Rather, my percept of an object consists of different views of it. Seeing an object usually involves moving about in space around it, and often manipulating it. Indeed, my image of the object includes the face of it now in front of my eyes, but also those parts which are familiar to me but now hidden from my sight. Furthermore, it may include what I know about the object and my associations with it, affective and otherwise. This is, of course, in line with Gibson's observation, discussed in Chapter 12, that there is no clear-cut demarcation between the visual and the non-visual, between perception and memory.

The pictures a camera produces are categorically different. Indeed, the camera and the image it produces cannot serve as a good model for human perception. Just as the 'now' is not a unitary moment defined in absolute mathematical or physical terms independently of the actions people perform, so the 'views' we take of the world are not discrete, independent snapshots.

Remembering

At first glance it seems that there is nothing special in saying that remembering takes time. The psychological literature is replete with experiments that show that retrieval takes time, that scanning through memory takes time. But, again, the scanning and retrieval times indicated there are technical specifications. Figuratively, they may be likened to opening a drawer and picking out an item from it. The temporality of memory is different. The unfolding in time is part and parcel of the memory process itself.

Consider the following example. This report was presented by a friend of mine, A, when I asked him to recall the first time he met another friend, B; the two met in a gathering which took place in my home (contrary to what is said below, it was not my birthday, a later gathering where the two met again):

> I think it was when you invited people one day in the afternoon, a Friday afternoon. I sat on the balcony of your apartment, I sat in the left-hand corner of the balcony. It was quite crowded, I sat on the balustrade of the balcony. I think I was the person in the corner, maybe there was one more person. Then B entered, and all the people who were on the balcony rearranged themselves to free some place. I do not remember what I did, but I remember that I was active in making room. I think I moved to the corner, and then she sat a little bit to the right-hand side, in the direction of the room. When I saw her I understood that it was she. I started talking to her about printing.

And here is B's recollection of the same event:

> I met him at your place, at your birthday party. It was on your birthday when we were sitting on the balcony. It was the birthday and we were sitting on the balcony. He sat by the balustrade and I was sitting on the chair in front of him and C was sitting on his side. He told me about work he did, a project he did, an educational project, something political. They were distributing brochures. They did all sorts of educational activities, activities in schools, and he spoke also about the graphical aspects of this work.

These two reports are telling. Both reveal that remembering cannot be likened to the picking out of an object from a drawer, and both attest to the intrinsic temporality of remembering. A's recollection reveals that remembering consists in going along a path defined by a narrative. It takes time for A to arrive at the recounting of his meeting with B. His narration, like a story or a film, starts before the meeting. Apparently, in order to reach the memory of the meeting, A has to traverse a path similar to the one he traversed in real life before he actually met B. (For similar observations, see Casey, 1987.) While B begins with the meeting itself, her story presents other pertinent characteristics of remembering. Her story thickens and becomes more detailed as she goes along. It is the very act of remembering which fosters her memory. Over and over, she repeats what she has just said and with this adds another detail. Taken together, the two memorial narratives suggest that in remembering one does not retrieve pieces of information; rather, one relives an event. Remembering is itself an activity that evolves in time, hence an event.

Cognitive performance

Cognitive performance takes time too. Again, this is banal; again, what is important is that often activities have no meaning but as they unfold in time. Thus, consider verbal behaviour. People are talking and I press my way in, saying, 'I have to say something'. And I say it. It takes me two dozen sentences and so many minutes. But already at the moment in which I pressed my way into the conversation I knew all that I wanted to say. I did not know what exactly I would be saying. I did not construct a plan. There was nothing in my head that I could have pointed to as 'This is what I have to say'. Indeed, to specify that would probably have taken as much time as to actually say it. Thus, on the one hand saying takes time, and on the other hand, unless it unfolds in time, the act does not constitute saying.

These characteristics of the act of speaking generalize to all behaviour. Behaviour extends in time: what I have to say takes a couple of minutes to be said, the dance takes a quarter of an hour to be danced, the story of one's life takes so many years to unfold. Yet, the sentence, the idea, the dance, the melody are each one entity, one unit, one event. They are all events in time, ones that have no existence but as they extend and unfold in time.

This unfolding is especially marked in complex tasks that progress in stages. I have shown this in the second line of this critique in conjunction with the phenomenon of scaffolding. There I underlined the contribution of the world and the body in problem solving and creative work. Yet, this phenomenon also marks the unfolding of cognitive performance in time. As a rule, working step by step, people can achieve what, if attempted in one move, is absolutely beyond their reach. As noted, this is one of the key tenets of Vygotsky's developmental psychology (cf. his notion of the 'zone of proximal development'); for further discussion and references, see Chapter 9.

Learning

Perhaps the most evident case is that of learning. As we all know, learning takes time. Remarkably, this banal fact is not accounted for by RCVM. If learning is the incorporation of information presented to the cognitive system from the outside, why should it take time? Why should the acquisition of language take several years rather than one instant? (Indeed, as far as Chomsky is concerned language acquisition may be – and ideally, is – instantaneous. See Chomsky, 1975b, p. 15.) And if it is conceded that learning takes time, why does it take the time it does – why not less, why not more? I shall return to these questions at length in Chapter 14 and in Part II.

Performance in time

In the previous section (as well as in the entire discussion in Chapter 12) I have tried to show that in studying cognition, time cannot be disregarded. Given that RCVM is intrinsically atemporal, it is fundamentally inadequate for the modelling of cognition. In this section I consider the complementary question. I examine activities that manifestly involve time and try to show that RCVM cannot account for them. Two paradigmatic types of activity will be considered: performances involving serial action, and performances involving timing.

Serial action

Serial action will be considered through the examination of a series of tasks involving the recitation of a very familiar ordered list, the alphabet. These tasks are simple and the reader will be asked to perform them as he or she is following the text. As a first, preparatory task, recite the alphabet. This is a highly practised task and you should perform it with no difficulty. Now, recite the alphabet skipping every other letter. This will be somewhat more difficult. Apparently, many will recite the entire alphabet as it is, only avoid saying aloud every other letter. Check yourself for that. Reciting in this manner does not count as performing the required task. Whoever does this is actually reciting the entire alphabet, only suppressing the enunciation of every other letter. If, however, you did manage this task, try the following. Recite the series composed of the sequence of every third letter of the alphabet: A, D, G, etc. I would be surprised if this could ever be achieved without using the 'silent method'.

And if the tasks noted above did not cause you any trouble you might perhaps try reciting the alphabet backwards. Then recite it backwards skipping every other letter; or backwards saying one letter and skipping two. This is, I gather, practically impossible.

But, then, why are these tasks so difficult? *A priori* – from the perspective of RCVM – they should not be difficult at all. In this view, one has in one's head an ordered list of the names of all the letters in the alphabet. One goes over this list, finds the pertinent items, and says them aloud. Whether the items in question constitute the complete set of the letters of the alphabet or not should make no difference. In all cases, the list is there, represented in one's mind, and all one must do is read out specified information. Skipping operations should be among the most simple and elementary computational operations. Why can one not execute them, as (by RCVM) one presumably executes most elementary computational operations, without any manifest overt or semi-overt activity? Why is it necessary to go over the entire list? Why is the task so difficult?

Let me change domains. Pick a song with which you are very familiar. Perhaps you are even acquainted with its score. Sing the third bar of the song. Did you sing the first two bars as well? Now sing the third note of the first bar. Did you also sing the first two notes?

I could have set a much simpler task. Not everyone knows how to sing, but everyone can speak. Let me return, then, to a task considered in Chapter 7. What is the third syllable of the last name of the French emperor-dictator known as Napoleon the First? Could you utter this syllable without uttering the entire name, Bonaparte? In Chapter 7 a similar task was brought up as demonstrating the necessary involvement of the body in the specification of information which, by RCVM, is stored in one's mind. The task noted here marks the dependence of memory retrieval on the actual performance of an action in time.

One last task: tap on the table. Try tapping a complex pattern, the most complex pattern you can conceive of. How many times have you tapped the table with your hand? To answer this, I imagine, you are producing the pattern once again. You know it is the same sequence of taps. Now you start counting. You slow down and you count. The number is, I trust, more than seven, that magical psychological number (Miller, 1956). How did you know that it is, in fact, the same sequence of taps? It could not have been by means of counting: you have not yet determined the number of taps of which the pattern is composed. Something else must have happened: you felt it, you felt that it was right, that it was the same. The two sequences were deemed the same not by virtue of their having the same number of taps; rather, you knew that there was the same number of taps because it was the same rhythm and pattern.

Timed motor performance

The second type of activity to be considered is performance involving timing. I shall consider motor performance and in particular, an activity already considered in a different context in this book – piano playing. As noted, RCVM characterizes piano playing as the reading of a mental score represented in one's mind. This score – like the printed one musicians use in the outside world – specifies the notes that are to be played, their relative durations, the strength with which they should be generated and various other parameters of the player's mode of execution (e.g. phrasing, staccato, legato). Let me focus, however, on the most elementary constituents of the score, those that may be regarded as defining the content of the musical material: the identity of the notes and their durations. Are these sufficient as specifiers of the sequences of notes that the player is to produce on the piano? I think not. At best, the score specifies what the player should play, but it does not specify how this should be realized in time. In particular, the score is not sufficient for one to determine the tempo (i.e., the speed) at which the piece should be played. Admittedly, the score does often contain temporal indications such as 'largo', 'andante', 'presto' and the like. At times, there are also numerical indications specifying the duration of a unit note in terms of the metronome scale. And yet, it seems to me that even with these extra notations my critical claim still holds.

Consider the descriptive indications of tempo. How could these general, qualitative indications be translated into actual, specific time determinations? Calibration is needed, but this cannot be achieved by representational means alone. The representational specifications may offer semantic explications of the musical indications. For instance, they may consist of something like the following:

Largo – slow
Andante – moderate
Moderato – at medium speed
Presto – fast
Prestissimo – very fast

They may even offer numerical specifications such as these (the values indicated specify beats per minute):

Largo – 54
Andante – 96
Moderato – 116
Presto – 176
Prestissimo – 208

But how are these specifications to be realized? How is one to determine the extension in time of the notes? The representational musical code specifies relative durations, not absolute stretches of time. In order to map the former onto the latter one has to have an independent measure of time. Such a measure requires a clock, a mechanism which is not contained in the standard representational machinery.

Against possible retorts I will hasten to concede that the measuring device need not be representational. Our bodies may, of course, contain some physiological or even biochemical time-measuring device. Yet, whatever this device may be the problem remains: how is it to be incorporated in the representational account? The position advocated here is that it cannot. The problem is analogous to those of reference and interpretation discussed in the second line of this critique. It boils down to Wittgenstein's observation on the limits of language. Since the representational framework consists only of representations and computational operations defined upon them, its machinery cannot relate to entities and mechanisms outside itself. Therefore, the representational-computational machinery cannot account for the link between the representational specifications of time (whatever these may be) and any non-representational clock. One may refine the semantic representation of time, one may also perfect one's time-measuring device, but as long as one keeps to the representational framework one cannot link the two.

And then, how does one keep time, how does one play a piece and maintain the same tempo throughout? By RCVM, this would require the determination of the absolute measure of time for each unit played, and the performance of all units in line with this measure. In general, however, the determination of the absolute measure of time is more difficult than keeping the same time. I have shown this in conjunction with the production of rhythmic patterns as well as in the example of tapping. People repeat the same rhythm not by counting the beats, but by generating a pattern that feels the same, that their body deems the same. Having, on the basis of this sensory-motor feeling, produced the same rhythmic pattern, they may then observe the pattern they produced and measure it.

The perception of change and of motion

The third performance I shall consider is the perception of change. By RCVM, change is perceived through the comparison of two stimuli, one being an object or a state of affairs before the change, the other an object or a state of affairs after it.

Following James Gibson, Shaw and Pittenger (1978) have extensively criticized this modelling of the perception of change. Despite its seeming simplicity and straightforwardness, the model begs the question. In order to appreciate that the two stimuli are two occurrences of one object (or one state of affairs) that has undergone change, the cognitive system has to identify them as pertaining to the same equivalence class. In other words, even though the stimuli are distinct, they have to be classified as being the same. To do this, one has to detect the difference between the stimuli and abstract it. This difference, however, is, in effect, the very change that the system is supposed to perceive. This circularity, note, is the same as that marked in conjunction with features and similarity: the appraisal of similarity is a determinant of the very features on which standard models of similarity judgement are based.

As pointed out by Shaw and Pittenger, the model also involves an extremely implausible assumption regarding memory. It presupposes that the specific image of a pattern seen earlier can somehow be retrieved from amongst the multitude of other stored images, and be compared with the specific image of the pattern the system is currently attempting to recognize. This is an impossible feat. To accomplish it, either all of the myriad representations stored in memory must be randomly retrieved and compared, or there must be a procedure by which the identity relation can be established between the current image and that stored in memory. In other words, to recognize that a change in a given pattern has occurred, the perceptual system must first discover the identity of the pattern common to the images under comparison. This, however, is tantamount to the determination that the retrieved image is related to the new image by some specified transformation. But this transformation is nothing other than the change that is to be perceived. Hence, to perceive a change the system must already somehow know the change. However, to assume that the model knows the change is to assume exactly that which the model is supposed to explain.

But then, if the determination of change does not require a comparison between two given images, these images become dispensable. Perhaps what is being perceived to begin with is a progression over time, not a fixed image. This is, indeed, one of James Gibson's fundamental insights regarding perception. Gibson (1966b, 1976), recall, noted that what we perceive are not stimuli nor patterns or sequences thereof. Rather, perception is in essence the detection of invariances in arrays that are in constant flow. This is true both in time and in space. Just as one detects invariances that are co-temporal, so one detects invariances over time. In both cases, the determination of the invariant pattern precedes that of any of the entities that are assumed to constitute it.

In sum, just as the temporal cannot be reduced to the non-temporal, so the perception of motion cannot be reduced to the perception of given, static states of affairs, and the perception of change cannot be accounted for in terms of comparison between given states. But people do perceive motion, they do perceive change. This cannot be done by means of a system which is basically static, as RCVM assumes the cognitive system to be. Only a system that is intrinsically dynamic can achieve all this (for a similar assessment, see Bickhard, 1993; Bickhard and Christopher, 1993).

Against this one can bring the case of motion pictures. These consist of series of still pictures. Yet, since they succeed each other at a great speed, the result is a motion picture, that is, a picture in which movement is perceived. Is this not a very reasonable model for the perception of movement? Specifically, the suggestion is that the senses pick up snapshots of reality, which generate sequences of percepts that in turn are inspected by the mental eye. Since the percepts follow one another quickly, motion and change are perceived. Reasonable though it may appear, this account is, I think, not tenable.

First, unlike the shots taken by the camera, the putative perceptual snapshots are not independently defined. For the camera model of perception to be validated, the postulation of these snapshots has to be corroborated. As argued throughout Chapter 12, there are reasons to suspect that this postulation is not valid.

Second, as pointed out by Gibson (1968), motion is requisite for perception. Rather than deriving from the perception of static images, the perception of motion is a necessary condition for it. Indeed, when motion stops nothing is perceived. For perception to be accomplished, the sensory apparatus has to be in constant movement. In fact, as noted in Chapters 7, 8 and 11, perception is intertwined with the moving about of the entire body in the world.

Third, consider the putative mental eye, the mental component that scans the percepts and sees what appears to be motion. There are crucial differences between this and the physical eye of the spectator of a film. The mental eye is part and parcel of the perceptual-cognitive system, and as such, it has to be accounted for by means of one's psychological model. As far as the physical eye is concerned this need not be the case. However, if the physical eye is not part of the cognitive machinery, its account is not within the province of a psychological-representational model. In such a case, there is also bound to be the problem of how to tie the non-cognitive component of the perceptual vision to the cognitive one; in the light of the discussion in Chapter 6, this problem is likely to be insoluble. Alternatively, if the workings of the eye are to be accounted for in cognitive terms, one can refer to an interpretative module that receives the information from the eye and interprets the sequence of still pictures as movement. Accounting for the mental eye in this fashion, however, would lead to a postulation of a second-order eye, and so to an infinite regress. However this component is characterized, it is not clear that it could generate motion out of the series of still pictures that it receives. As I have shown in Chapter 12, motion cannot be generated out of what does not move – the temporal from the static. Indeed, here is another case of an unbridgeable gap and an associated homuncular problem.

14 Development

Some of the things we seem to be committed to strike me, frankly, as a little wild; I should be glad to know if there are ways of saving the psychology while avoiding those commitments.

Jerry Fodor

This chapter will focus on cognitive development. The discussion will centre on three arguments: that from origin, that from learning, and that from order. The first points out that RCVM cannot account for the origins of cognition and that consequently it drives one to a radical, implausible, nativist position. The second marks difficulties pertaining to the increase in knowledge – be it by way of learning or by creation. The argument examines the course of cognitive development and evolution; it points out that, viewed from the representational perspective, development and evolution manifest patterns which are unnatural and even paradoxical. Together, the three arguments lead to the conclusion that RCVM is at a loss in accounting for the developmental aspects of cognition.

The origin of knowledge

By RCVM, all mental activity is achieved through computational operations, which in turn are defined on given symbolic structures. Hence, for the operations to apply, semantic representations must already be present. This is true for all instances of cognitive performances, at all stages of development. So, from the very start, the cognitive system has to consist of some representational material. Without this, nothing cognitive can happen and, in particular, the process of development cannot even start.

In fact, the constraints RCVM imposes on the initial state of the cognitive system are even more specific. For anything to be processed by this system, it has to be represented. As pointed out in Chapter 5, this is tantamount to saying that all pertinent distinctions have to be already specified in the system. Thus, the set of distinctions, aspects and dimensions to which the cognitive system can relate – those it can recognize and process – have to be already specified before the system can do anything. RCVM, in other words, implies radical nativism.

This has been argued for most explicitly by Jerry Fodor in *The Language of Thought*

(1975). Fodor points out that computational operations manipulate symbols in given representations; they may organize these symbols and rearrange them, but they cannot create new distinctions in the representational system. Thus, in effect, cognitive activity consists of the selection of hypotheses from given represented structures. Consequently, the computational operations do not change the expressive power of the representational system. Again, this holds for all occurrences of processing, at all stages of cognitive development.

In sum, all representational models have to assume an already existing, non-empty representational core. How this core comes into being they cannot explain. As far as RCVM is concerned, the origin of knowledge cannot be accounted for.

But Fodor goes further. Both in *The Language of Thought* and elsewhere (Fodor *et al.*, 1980; Fodor, 1981a), he not only argues for the existence of an innate representational core, but propounds a radical stance by which practically everything that one knows is innate. Fodor's argumentation bears on the issue of learning, to which I now turn.

Learning

In the 1950s, before the cognitive revolution, learning was perhaps the most important topic of experimental psychological research. In particular, psychologists strove to discover regularities in the course of learning, to offer exact (often mathematical) formulations of its course, and to specify the mechanisms that govern it. With the advent of representationalism all this changed, and the study of learning was pushed aside and reduced to near non-existence. Basically, there were two reasons for this, one ideological and the other practical.

The ideological reason was often explicitly stated by representationalists. It was pointed out that psychologists of the previous era studied learning without specifying what it is that is actually being learnt. Before studying how the states of a system change, one must – so the representationalist line of reasoning went – study what these states actually are. By RCVM, those of the psychological system are states of knowledge. Hence, with the representational turn, the prime topic of cognition became the problem of representation. A shift was made from the study of learning to that of the definition of symbols and the larger structures they compose. The so-called problem of representation became the key issue of cognitive research (see Anderson and Bower, 1973; Kintsch, 1974; Bobrow, 1975; Minsky, 1975).

The practical reason was not usually stated. It is simply that RCVM cannot account for learning. One of the very few who was utterly explicit about this was, again, Jerry Fodor. Fodor, however, turns the practical limitation into a statement of principle. Following the line of reasoning traced in the previous section, Fodor concludes that learning is simply not possible. Therefore, by and large, all that one knows has to be already known at the onset of one's cognitive life. In other words, all knowledge is innate. As noted, the appraisal that learning is not possible runs throughout Fodor's *The Language of Thought* (for further discussion, see Fodor *et al.*, 1980; Fodor, 1981a).

The basis of Fodor's argument has already been noted. Representational-computational systems (which for Fodor are the only cognitive systems possible) cannot create new distinctions. Indeed, for information to be handled by such a system it has to be definable in terms of the set of distinctions already specified in this system. Information not definable in this fashion cannot be detected by the system, nor can it be amenable to processing. In other words, Fodor's view of mind allows for no qualitative change, and assumes that all cognitive change consists in the mapping of symbols onto other symbols. This also holds for the changes that underlie cognitive development. Hence, according to Fodor, in all stages of development the basic entities constituting the representational system are identical in type to those that constituted it in its first, initial state.

One might constrain the initial, innate core to a small, definable set. For instance, one could limit this set only to concepts and distinctions that are directly definable in sensory-motor terms. Fodor, however, argues even against this (see Fodor *et al.*, 1980; Fodor, 1981a). In essence, his argumentation follows the logic underlying the critique of semantic reductionism at the beginning of this book. In Chapter 2, I noted that the meaning of words cannot be defined in terms of a small set of so-called semantic primitives. Given the linguistic orientation of RCVM, this applies to concepts as well. In other words, whatever one knows cannot be defined in terms of a small set of concepts or distinctions. As pointed out by Fodor *et al.* (1980), this is tantamount to saying that concept learning, and with it practically all learning, is not possible.

Fodor himself characterizes his radical nativistic conclusion as 'blatantly preposterous', yet he finds it inevitable none the less. The conclusion is preposterous, indeed, for logically it need not stop at the ontogenetic scale but can be extended to the phylogenetic one. As Piaget comments, if taken seriously Fodor's nativistic line of argumentation leads to the conclusion

> that a baby at birth would already possess virtually everything that Galois, Cantor, Hilbert, Bourbaki, or MacLane[1] have since been able to realize. And since the child is himself a consequence, one would have to go back as far as protozoa and viruses to locate the seat of 'the set of all possibilities'. (Piaget, 1983, p. 26)

For further discussion, see Fodor (1986).

Fodor's denial of the feasibility of learning reflects, of course, that of Chomsky. In Chapter 9 I noted that a central tenet of Chomsky's meta-psychology is that the child does not acquire language by means of instruction, and that knowledge of language is innate (see Chomsky, 1972). In Chomsky's framework, the innate knowledge is that of the rules of language and, more specifically, the rules of syntax. In Fodor's theory of mind, nativism is all-encompassing: it pertains to the knowledge of semantic information and is not specific to any particular domain.

The nativism of Chomsky and Fodor has been extensively discussed in the contemporary philosophical literature (see, for instance, Stich, 1975). Fodor has even stated that, 'Everyone is a nativist in the long run' (Fodor, 1981a, p. 315). It seems to me that simple common sense suggests otherwise. Manifestly, people do extend the repertory of their knowledge. A psychological theory that cannot accommodate this banal fact is simply unacceptable.

But then, Fodor's argument may be turned upside-down. His line of deduction may be reversed and the radical conclusion to which it leads may be regarded as a demonstration by a *reductio ad absurdum* that representationalism is wrong. If the radical conclusion logically follows from a given set of first premises (as I admit it does), then one should conclude that something is wrong with that set. In other words, the moral of Fodor's critique of learning is that knowledge and cognitive activity cannot be defined in the manner assumed by RCVM (for further critiques of Fodor's nativistic argument, see Heil, 1981; Bogdan, 1983; Campbell and Bickhard, 1987).

Alternative, non-representational accounts of learning will be considered in Part II. Here, let me just state two preliminary conclusions which follow directly from the foregoing critical observations. First, since semantic representations do not afford a qualitative change and since radical nativism is simply absurd, the initial basis of the cognitive system cannot be representational. Second, since symbolic computational operations cannot create anything which is really novel, the mechanisms governing cognitive development cannot be computational in the standard sense of the term.

I opened this section with historical comments concerning psychological research of the pre-cognitive era, and I will end it with comments on what seems to herald the post-cognitive one – the new paradigm of connectionism. One of the main criticisms this paradigm marshals against representationalism is precisely that the latter cannot account for learning (see McClelland, *et al.*, 1986; Smolensky, 1986). With this, connectionism brings the study of learning and its modelling back into the forefront of cognitive research (see, for instance, Rumelhart and McClelland, 1986c; Sejnowsky and Rosenberg, 1987). Indeed, many regard the modelling of learning as one of the major accomplishments of connectionism. Representational-ists are aware of this, and some have counter-attacked by marking the limitations of the new models of learning (see, for instance, Lachter and Bever, 1988; Pinker and Prince, 1988). I do not wish to enter this debate here. As will be indicated in Chapter 20, my rejecting RCVM does not imply that I am a connectionist. In fact, I have found myself siding with some of the remarks raised by representationalists about connectionism, such as that connectionist models of learning presuppose some pre-represented distinctions. Many connectionist models, then, are not as radically different from representationalist ones as might at first appear. Unlike the representationalist, however, I regard this as holding against – not for – connectionism. I will return in Chapter 20 to further evaluation of connectionism (see also Shanon, 1992).

A broader perspective

In the previous section I noted that RCVM regards learning as a change in a cognitive system's states of knowledge. RCVM defines these states in terms of semantic representations. Yet, even the seemingly innocuous, more general characterization of learning as a change in knowledge states may be criticized. This characterization is not specific to RCVM, and is probably shared by many who might not label themselves as representationalists. It involves a series of assumptions regarding the nature of learning which are rarely stated explicitly.

First is the assumption that the representation of knowledge can be separated from its growth and expansion. This is the developmental manifestation of the more basic assumption regarding the separability of structures and processes examined in Chapter 13. Related to it is a presupposition of a basic asymmetry: for learning to be achieved, representations have to be there as a substrate. By contrast, representations are endowed with existence that does not depend on other factors, and in particular not on prior learning. It is this presupposition of asymmetry that has enabled the representationalist to focus on the problem of representation and almost totally disregard learning. As noted in Chapter 13, the contestation of the separation between representation and learning is one of the main tenets of connectionism.

Second is the assumption of autonomy. Specifically, this characterization assumes that learning is achieved – and correspondingly, that it may be studied – without reference to factors other than those defined by semantic representations and the computational processes associated with them. In particular, learning is conceived as taking place within the internal domain pertaining to the sphere of the individual who is acquiring new knowledge. Guided by such a conception, cognitive scientists take it for granted that when modelling learning they can disregard the physical world in which cognitive agents live and the other human beings with whom they interact. The discussion in Chapters 8 and 9 shows that this assumption is not warranted and that one's action in the world and interaction with others play a crucial role in the process of learning.

Third, in the representational characterizatioʻ oʻʻʻʻʻʻʻʻʻg, time has no place. RCVM's disregard of time has already been discussed at length in Chapter 13. In the case of learning, however, this disregard is especially curious: it is a basic and salient fact that learning takes time. Again, no one would deny this utterly banal statement. Yet, like computational operations in general, those responsible for learning are usually defined without reference to time. They are defined in terms of the symbolic structures they take as input and those they produce as output: such a structural definition says nothing about time. Theoretically, these operations could be achieved in no time, or they could take any amount of time. By RCVM, in other words, essentially learning should not take time.

By now, I have discussed all three assumptions – the first and third in Chapter 13, the second in Chapter 9. I will not repeat the criticism marshalled in those discussions. One further comment regarding the second assumption is, however, in place. Whereas the comments made in Chapter 9 focused in the main on empirical considerations, here I will highlight some conceptual problems.

As noted in Chapter 9, the psychological writings of Chomsky (1965, 1972, 1975b) are seminal to the representational critique of learning. Chomsky maintains that language is neither learnt nor taught. Just as children grow and reach biological maturation, so they develop language. In this process the role of other people is confined to triggering or to the supplying of superficial information (such as the particular couplings of the phonological forms and the semantics of words). In Chapter 9 I surveyed empirical data holding against this characterization of the role of others in the child's acquisition of learning language. Here, I would like to tie the discussion to the nativist stance.

Chomsky's argument is based, it seems, on the assessment that children's potential teachers – notably, their parents – themselves do not know what they are supposed to teach. After all, people much more knowledgeable in linguistic matters than the average person (hence the parents of the average child), and who have devoted a considerable part of their waking time to their study and definition, cannot provide a full characterization of the knowledge that should be passed to children if they are, in effect, being taught the language their adult companions speak. Those who have attempted to specify this knowledge are, of course, professional linguists. If they, who have invested so much effort in the enterprise, have not achieved a full specification of the knowledge of language, how could ordinary parents do it?

Chomsky's claim cannot be sustained. It would be valid only if teaching consisted of the passing of explicit information from one person, the teacher, to another, the learner. This conception of teaching is the complement of the representational conception of learning that is being criticized here. Just as learning is assumed to be the increment of well-defined knowledge in the representational system of one person, so teaching is assumed to be the transfer of such knowledge from one such system to another (see, for instance, Reddy, 1979). Admittedly, when children learn language (should I say, when parents teach language to their children) no such transfer takes place. But perhaps teaching (and learning) are achieved in a totally different manner?

In fact, the claim that parents cannot teach language to their children is couched in still another assumption, namely that in order to speak, parents (and people in general) must have a representation of the rules by which the grammar of their language is defined. At this point in the discussion it should be clear that this assumption is unwarranted. The moral of the first line of this critique was that regularities in behaviour need not be the manifestations of underlying represented knowledge. That of the second line was that knowing-how need not depend on knowing-that (even unconsciously so). Parents do, indeed, speak. This, however, does not imply that the grammar of the language has to be represented in their minds. Furthermore, for them to help children acquire language, parents need not (nor, indeed, do they) pass on the contents of stored semantic representations. Likewise, to acquire language children do not need to come into possession of such knowledge. But again, all this does not mean that the interaction between children and parents (or any other adult for that matter) does not play a role (even a crucial role) in children's acquisition of language. In sum: indeed, parents do not pass information represented in their minds to their children who, in turn, encode it into their mental repertories of knowledge. Yet, parents do instruct children who are acquiring language, and guide them in this process. To say that this does not constitute teaching not only implies a very simplistic view of teaching, but also closes the discussion before it begins.

In closing, let me note that RCVM's assumption of the autonomy of cognition and the doctrine of radical nativism are related. Specifically, when the former is relinquished one escapes the puzzle of learning, and with it the pitfalls of radical nativism. If children are viewed as lonely individuals who have to acquire language all by themselves, then one is stuck: learning language is, indeed, an impossible mission. However, as indicated in the second line of this critique, when the social other (in this case the parent) is taken to be an integral constituent of the cognitive system one studies (in this case, the child), the impasse is no longer there. In particular, as suggested in Chapter 9, the first steps into language should be viewed as a joint accomplishment of parent and child. In this conjunction, the dance examined in Chapter 11 is instructive. Rather than being viewed as a transmitter of information, the parent might be viewed as a leading dancer who guides his or her partner in a delicate *pas de deux*. More on teaching and learning will be said in Part II, in my presentation of an alternative non-representational view of mind.

The claims against the possibility of learning and the ensuing conclusion that knowledge is innate did not, of course, originate with Chomsky and Fodor. They have an old precursor in Plato and the classic section of 'Meno' (see Plato, 1937). In this dialogue, Socrates shows that geometrical knowledge is not learnt: it is recollected, with the instructor serving only as a trigger or a facilitator for the recollection of what the seemingly ignorant cognitive agent already knew beforehand. Plato's argument may be frowned upon as being outdated. Yet, in Shanon (1984a) I have shown that the cognitive view assumed by Plato, which leads him to his radical conclusion, is precisely that assumed by RCVM. Furthermore, the implicit assumptions – both methodological and substantive – associated with Fodor's argument on nativism are identical to those associated with Plato's (see also Shanon, 1991c). I shall return to some of these basic assumptions in Chapter 16.

Finally, let me consider a question introduced in Chapter 13: why does learning take time? As noted in Chapters 12 and 13, by RCVM this need not be the case. In this view, learning consists of the incorporation of information from a given source into one's system of knowledge and belief. From the standpoint of representationalism, this is tantamount to saying that another token (or several more tokens) of representations are added to one's semantic representational store. Representationalists admit, of course, that learning takes time, but this is regarded as a mere technicality (see Chomsky, 1975b). The following argument aims to show that this is not the case.

In the representational view just sketched, the mind is essentially a system of boxes, and learning is likened to the transfer of cognitive material from some external source and its storage in the boxes. At first glance this seems to be quite straightforward. However, what if the source starts moving? In this case, whoever is responsible for the transfer of cognitive material and its storage will have to be careful not to lose track of the source. If this agent is not sufficiently vigilant and agile, he or she may not manage to get the cognitive material that is presented. And what if the source moves constantly? Then, the only option is to follow it. Indeed, since it is not in a fixed, well-defined state, in order not to miss it, the system of boxes should be in continuous pursuit of it. In the long run, this is tantamount to saying that whoever is responsible for learning should be tied to the source and continuously change with it.

But, indeed, the source is moving all the time. As noted in Chapter 12, the world – both physical and biological – is in constant flux. This implies that the putative system of boxes should be in constant flux as well. With this, however, the characterization of the cognitive system in terms of boxes loses its utility. A system which is constantly changing lacks all that is characteristic of a box.

The foregoing argument suggests not only that learning should take time, but that it requires a constant interaction with the world. Specifically, what is suggested is that learning is achieved through an on-going, dynamic interaction with the world: as the source changes, so does the cognitive system which is coupled to it. In Hebrew, when one wants to say that one knows another person well, one often uses the expression, 'we have walked along a certain path together'. Indeed, one gets to know a friend, a spouse, an enemy not by reading out information about them but rather by following and interacting with them; in other words, by going some way together with them. Time passes and one realizes that one knows the other person. There is no well-specified moment in which it can be said that knowledge has been achieved. Likewise with learning in general: it consists in going some way together with the world. More on this will be said in Part II.

Ordering and sequencing

The argument from ordering and sequencing presents the following pattern of problems. The representational view, it appears, entails sequences that both developmentally and conceptually may be regarded as unnatural. Specifically, it imposes orders of complexity opposite to those marked as natural by independent considerations such as ontogenetic chronology and relative cognitive effort. Thus, patterns that representational accounts characterize as complex actually appear early in development (both ontogenetic and phylogenetic), whereas ones that are theoretically characterized as simple appear later. Similarly, patterns that these accounts characterize as complex turn out to require fewer resources than ones they characterize as simple. Unnatural orderings that RCVM imposes are encountered in a variety of phenomenological domains. The following survey presents a representative set of such domains; it need not, however, be exhaustive.

Language development

Language development has already been examined along with the sequential patterns it presents; here I will take a broader, integrative view and single out the moral of the various observations made. The discussion focuses on a series of trends revealed in language development, each associated with a relative ordering that RCVM defines; it will attempt to show that these orderings are countered by empirical data, entail an overall unnatural view of mind, and are internally incoherent.

The first ordering to be considered is the primacy RCVM ascribes to the semantic aspects of language relative to the pragmatic ones. Pertinent empirical data have been surveyed at various junctures in this critique. In particular, consider the involvement of context. By RCVM the semantic, context-free aspects of language are considered to be primary and the pragmatic and context-dependent ones secondary. Accommodation to context is supposed to be achieved through special, context-sensitive operations that apply to the semantic representations. Yet, what appears to be a main trend in language development is *de*contextualization. As noted, children's first steps into language are immersed in the context of their action in the world. It is only with further development that children gradually grow less and less dependent on the given context.

The ordering imposed by RCVM also counters the moral of the second line of this critique, where I marked the primacy of action relative to cognition. If anything, it is the pragmatic aspects of verbal behaviour, not the semantic ones, which are more related to action. Evidently, children act before they achieve command of language. Furthermore, whereas language is specific to human beings, action in the world is accomplished by all living organisms. It will be noted that the pragmatic aspects of verbal behaviour, not the semantic ones, are those closer to the non-verbal communication of other species, and in particular to that of the primates.

Apart from its countering the empirical data, the sequential ordering imposed by RCVM is also internally unnatural. Schematically, it can be described as follows:

> Non-verbal behaviour.
> > Semantic verbal behaviour.
> > Pragmatic verbal behaviour.

This ordering is suspect in that it places two types of behaviour that are phenomenologically related to one another (non-verbal and pragmatic verbal) at opposite ends of a scale. By contrast, the present critique suggests the following ordering:

Non-verbal behaviour.
Pragmatic verbal behaviour.
Semantic verbal behaviour.

Unlike that dictated by RCVM, this ordering is natural.

Second is the primacy of putative elementary, atomistic symbolic constituents relative to both larger structures and high-order relations. Conceptually, the primacy of well-defined elementary constituents leads to the nativistic impasse considered at the beginning of this chapter. Saying that such constituents are primary is tantamount to saying that they should be present at the onset of cognitive life. But where do they come from? Within the representational framework there is no way to account for the origin of these putative basic, elementary entities. One has to postulate either that they were always present, or an initial state which is cognitively empty and then a subsequent state in which the well-defined elementary entities are already present. The first option consists in the extreme nativistic position against which I have argued at the outset of this chapter; the second involves a move that cannot be accounted for and that presents yet another instance of an unbridgeable gap. Indeed, this situation is very similar to the gap presented by Zeno's paradoxes of motion, mentioned in another context in Chapter 12. The only way out is to regard the well-defined constituents as the products of cognitive activity, not the basis of it. The initial cognitive state would be ill-defined and undifferentiated, and development would consist in differentiation involving a qualitative change. The differentiated, well-defined articulated patterns would be the products of this process.

Varied empirical data suggest that this is, in fact, the case. In language development it is noted that children's early utterances are holophrases (the term 'holophrastic speech' is due to da Laguna, 1927), in which what seem to be single words express what an adult would express by an entire sentence. This is so because, for children, meaning is a global, unanalyzed whole.[2] The serial articulation by means of discrete lexical items is a later development (see, for instance, Bloom, 1973; Dore, 1975; Bates *et al.*, 1979, 1987). As I have shown in the first line of this critique, similar patterns are encountered in metaphor, in synaesthesia, in the appraisal of similarity (for a review, see also Kemler, 1983), and in gesture. In all these domains the early cognitive states manifest undifferentiated wholes that encompass what for the external adult observer seem to be different features, aspects or dimensions. For the cognitive agents themselves, however, the differentiation into discrete, well-defined constituents is a later development.

Related to the primacy of the global and undifferentiated is that of high-order relations. This assessment is central in James Gibson's psychology. As noted, according to Gibson we perceive not atomic sense data but patterns of invariance. Eleanor Gibson and her associates mark analogous patterns in the development of sensory perception (Gibson, 1969; Gibson and Spelke, 1983). As James Gibson emphasizes, the primacy of relations also has a temporal aspect. The representational perspective regards static elements as primary and movement, change and temporal dynamics as derivative. As argued in Chapter 13, the opposite seems to be the case (see also Johansson, 1973; and the discussion in Chapter 5).

Third and last is the relative ordering between structure and meaning. By RCVM, structures are assigned meaning by a process of interpretation: in other words, formal structures have primacy *vis-à-vis* interpreted ones. It is this view, I think, that leads to RCVM's pitiful account of reference and intentionality and to the associated problems of unbridgeable gaps and infinite regress. The only way out, I believe, is to reverse the order of things and to regard meaning, not formal structures, as primary. Specifically, if the representational account presents one with two entities that are manifestly tied to one another but which, in terms of this framework, cannot be bridged then perhaps the tie is elementary. In fact, such a view is very much in line with the appraisal above of the primacy of high-order relations.

Cultural evolution

As noted in Chapters 3 and 5, cultural evolution also marks the unnaturalness of the ordering implied by RCVM. It is not an accident that across cultures poetry is an earlier historical development than prose. By contrast, seemingly banal scientific and journalistic writing is a recent cultural phenomenon. Indeed, whereas poetry is encountered in practically every culture, writing of the latter kinds is encountered only in a small minority of civilizations. The sequential ordering implied by RCVM is, of course, just the opposite. According to it, scientific and journalistic writings are basic: in them, one writes exactly what one is assumed to have in one's mind, one's language is in general not loaded with a multitude of meanings, and no use of its medium is made. Again, the puzzle is resolved when the ordering is reversed and the figurative is regarded as more basic than the literal. With this reversal, poetry, the most metaphorical of all literary genres, is regarded as a direct reflection of the workings of the human psyche.[3] Poetry, not the expression of literal meaning, is a natural act. Indeed, precise, literal writing cannot be as simple as the representational view might lead one to believe. The evident intellectual effort involved in writing exactly what one wants to say, an effort familar to anyone who has engaged in this enterprise, is telling. If that which is in the mind were specified in a discursive fashion similar to that of natural language, such difficulty should not be encountered. This effort further indicates that writing is not the empty operation of transferring information from one place to another. This observation is in line with the comments on the act of writing made in Chapter 8 in which the physical aspects of creative writing were highlighted.

Psychoanalysis

The domain of psychoanalysis highlights cognitive phenomena not always dealt with by mainstream cognitive psychologists. Two topics will be mentioned here: the distinction between primary and secondary processes, and the phenomenon of dreaming.

The distinction between primary and secondary processes is one of the most fundamental in psychoanalytic theory (see Freud, 1900/1954). Primary processes govern primitive, irrational thinking, including the workings of the unconscious, whereas secondary processes govern rational, conscious thinking. Furthermore, the primary precede the secondary in development, and unlike secondary processes they are encountered in uncontrolled psychological states, of which dreaming is paradigmatic. Thus, both phenomenologically and from the theoretical perspective of psychoanalysis the primary processes are simpler than the secondary. But note: the former are metaphorical whereas the latter are not. A natural ordering would therefore be one that characterizes the primary processes as more basic than the secondary. Such an ordering is, of course, opposite to that dictated by RCVM.

Let me turn to dreaming. By the representational model the narrative progressions in the dream, like all meaningful expressions, are the products of the manipulation of underlying semantic representations. But then, a curious question arises: how is it possible that all of us can create intricate dramas while exercising minimal cognitive effort, whereas only very few can do so when awake, and with the investment of considerable skill and effort at that? The paradox disappears when it is realized that rather than being the product of transformations that apply to given semantic representations, the dream is the direct expression of the workings of the mind, which, as suggested towards the end of the first line of the present critique, are inherently metaphorical. For psychoanalytic analyses in line with this view, see Lacan (1977).

Regarding the dream as a direct reflection of the basic workings of the mind is also in line with the comments on action above. The dream is a narrative, and narratives are basically patterns of action in the world. When this is appreciated, the (very plausible) puzzle regarding the generation of dreams dissolves. Dreaming, the cognitive system does what it is primarily designed to do – act in the world. The fact that the action is confined to a world within only makes the action more free: acting in the theatre of their own minds, cognitive agents should not be bothered by risks, costs and concerns that in manifest acting in the world they must take into consideration (for further discussion, see Shanon, 1990c).[4]

Action in the world

The primacy of action in the world, the basic topic of the second line of the present critique, was underscored again and again throughout this discussion. Action involves a host of what may be referred to as non-cognitive factors – the body, the physical world, the social other, tools and artefacts, desires, wants and emotions. Their involvement in cognitive activity and cognitive development was discussed in Chapters 7–10. Here I would like to take a broader look, and consider the primacy of action in the world as accomplished by means of the joint interaction of all these factors.

By RCVM, action – like the pragmatic aspects of language – presupposes symbolic processing involving semantic representations. But, surely, just as pragmatics is more basic than semantics, so action in the world is more basic than processing.

Developmental data marking the primacy of action have been collected by investigators from different quarters. As noted in the second line of this critique, the primacy of action was underscored by both Piaget and Vygotsky (see references cited in Chapter 11). Studies conducted more recently by Eleanor Gibson and other researchers sympathetic to the ecological approach (Gibson *et al.*, 1979; Gibson, 1982; Gibson and Spelke, 1983; Gibson and Walker, 1984) further reveal that very young children detect invariances in terms of the activities they can produce. Young children cannot act adaptively without perceiving the affordances of their habitat, but they cannot perceive effectively without acting. The pertinent affordances are extracted in the course of action. With the progress of development, new actions become possible, and thus new information for affordances is made available and the range of feasible actions is extended further and further.

In addition to marking the primacy of action, these observations mark the interactive, dynamic nature of development and the intrinsic link between perception and action, and between organism and world. Furthermore, they highlight the intrinsic tie between action and meaning: meaning for organisms is defined by the totality of actions they can effect in the world.

Lastly, let me note that not only is RCVM's view of action and the ordering it imposes unnatural, it actually leads to paradox. An instructive example is the case of the kingfisher discussed in Chapter 11.

Cognitive breakdown

At the opposite side of development is the breakdown of cognitive function as it occurs in neuropathology. Numerous clinical observations suggest that aphasic patients often exhibit a higher level of linguistic performance when their language use is embedded in meaningful action. Patients may suffer from anomia and not be able to name objects presented to them; yet, in the midst of spontaneous action they may very well refer to those same objects by name (see Goldstein, 1948). Especially interesting are findings reported by Marcel (1988). Patients with problems in performing motor actions (e.g. picking up a vertical cylinder) may succeed in executing these same actions when embedded in natural acts, such as lifting a glass of water in order to drink; in naturalistic, non-test situations, as in the patients' own homes, the level of performance can be even higher. Following the general observation that more basic cognitive activities are more resistant to brain damage (for a general review, see Goldstein, 1948), these observations suggest once again that the pragmatic aspects of language are more basic than the semantic ones, and that the use of language in context is more basic than its use in isolation. Incidentally, these data also suggest that uttering a sentence may be easier (and thus, more basic) than uttering a single word in isolation.

A note on computers

Lastly, let me consider an order of complexity pertaining neither to human development nor to phylogenesis or cultural evolution. It is, I find, a very instructive one none the less. I refer to the relative achievements of computers and human beings. Strikingly, computers excel in many things that for people are very difficult. At the same time, there are many things that for people are very easy and that for the computer are downright impossible. As one goes down the ontogenetic scale, the difference becomes increasingly glaring. Apparently, it is precisely those things that little children can perform that computers cannot accomplish at all. Computers can solve integrals that no person can, but they cannot express emotions, they cannot interpret ill-formed messages, they cannot interact with other agents in a non-semantic fashion. In fact, they fail precisely with respect to all the factors and patterns that in this discussion have been marked as primary. For the computer, semantics is primary relative to pragmatics, context-free processing relative to context-dependent processing, the literal relative to the figurative. Computer processing dictates that the well-defined elementary constituents are basic and that larger symbolic structures are composed from them. Similarly, it assumes that constituents are primary relative to relations and formal structures relative to interpreted ones. The overall difference in relative orderings of complexity is telling. It provides sufficient reason to suspect that, whatever their seeming accomplishments, computers are categorically different from human beings. Even if computers produce behaviours that seem to be similar to those produced by people, the manner in which the two operate is very different. Thus, it is utterly wrong to take the computer as the basis for the modelling of mind. This is precisely what RCVM is doing (for further discussion, see Dreyfus, 1979; Haugeland, 1985).

Conclusion

Together, the different developmental sequences surveyed indicate that representations are not primary or basic from either a developmental, procedural or evolutionary point of view. If anything, representations and the processes associated with them appear in late stages of cognitive growth. Rather than being the basis for the workings of the mind, they are the products of it. Thus, instead of being characterized as the processor and manipulator of representations, the cognitive system should be characterized as their generator. Hence, representations cannot be taken as primordial psychological structures and cannot serve as the basis for cognitive modelling. Nor can computations. Computations are operations that map semantic representations onto other semantic representations. The processes governing the creation of representations cannot, therefore, be computational.

Notes

1. These are all famous mathematicians.
2. This whole may be regarded as an event in the Gibsonian sense noted in Chapter 12.
3. I am not referring here to advanced forms of poetry in which writers experiment with the limits of language and attempt to create new forms of expression.
4. This characterization of the dream is supported by other, independent research. Several investigators have recently proposed models which – in contradistinction to the orthodox Freudian analysis – do not regard the dream as the product of covert cognitive work, one guided by motivational factors and directed by intervening censorship. Rather, it is viewed as a natural, cognitive phenomenon resulting from the mind's being left free to run its own course. For a most interesting exposition of this view, see Foulkes (1985); see also Bergson (1925).

The fourth line of the critique

As noted at the outset, this is a psychological, not a philosophical, critique. Its topic is a particular theoretical framework in contemporary psychology: it is concerned with specific structures (representations in the technical-psychological sense), and it examines how suitable they are for modelling cognition. By contrast, philosophical critiques of representations are concerned with their status and role, regardless of their specific structural features. Such critiques ask not whether specifically defined representational structures are suitable for the modelling of mind, but whether such modelling necessitates the postulation of representations *tout court*. In the terminology introduced in Chapter 1, the subject of these critiques is representation in the naive and epistemic senses.

Yet, even though this critique is psychological, it bears on the philosophical questions as well. It appears that one can argue against the postulation of representations in the naive and epistemic senses not only on philosophical grounds, but also on psychological ones. With the completion of the three lines of the psychological critique, it seems that not only the profile of characteristics of semantic representations specified in (**) of Chapter 1 but also the very notion of mental entities sitting somewhere in the mind and serving for the representation of knowledge are not tenable. In this last chapter of the critical part of the book, I shall consider this notion. With this, I shall come full circle, for the problem of knowledge is most closely related to the epistemic issues with which I began this critique. As I shall show, the consideration relates to the other lines of the critique as well.

15 *Knowing*

Had the goat known it is a goat, its legs would have become entangled. Had the fish known it is a fish, it would have drowned to the depth of the river like lead. The goat, the fish, the mountain and the river know themselves in knowledge that does not know.

Chuang Tse

Preliminary observations

Let me begin with three simple, preliminary observations. The first has to do with the difficulty people have in reporting what the representations which supposedly serve as the basis for their manifest behaviour are. People use the words of language, but how many speakers can define these words? People recognize faces, yet they cannot specify what the features of those faces are. People enjoy music but, apart from musicologists, who can say what it is that makes music enjoyable, or sad, or Mozart-like? If knowledge is specified in semantic representations, and if behaviour consists of the execution of computational operations on these representations, then such difficulties should not occur. In fact, reporting the contents of the representations should be of the utmost simplicity for, on the face of it, this task involves the simplest possible operation that may be conducted on symbols, namely, articulating in natural language what is specified in the underlying language of thought. Curiously, people succeed in what, according to RCVM, are complex computational operations, but fail in this minimal, practically trivial, operation. This alone should be a good reason to suspect that the model is at fault in some fundamental respect.

Remarkably, not only is the articulation of the information that is presumably specified in semantic representations not possible, the comprehension of such articulated information is also very difficult. An illustrative example is presented in Fodor *et al.* (1980) in the following paraphrasing of a limerick:

There existed an adult male person who had lived a relatively short time, belonging or pertaining to St. Johns (a college of Cambridge University), who desired to commit sodomy with the large web-footed swimming birds of the genus *Cygnus* or subfamily *Cygninae* of the family *Anatidae*, characterized by a long and gracefully curved neck and a majestic motion when swimming. So

225

he moved into the presence of the person employed to carry burdens, who declared: 'Hold or possess as something at your disposal my female child! The large web-footed swimming birds of the genus *Cygninae* of the family *Anatidae*, characterized by a long and gracefully curved neck and a majestic motion when swimming, are set apart, specially retained for the Head, Fellows and Tutors of the College'. (p. 263)

To this one can retort by pointing out that there is nothing in the definition of representations that requires that they be open to conscious introspection. Admittedly, much of human mental life is unconscious. This is not only the basic tenet of psychoanalysis, but a fundamental conclusion of practically all modern cognitive psychological research. The central experimental paradigm in contemporary cognitive psychology, that employing reaction-time measurements, reveals that cognitive operations are usually of a temporal order of magnitude much smaller than that accessible to introspection (for the seminal study of the paradigm, see Sternberg, 1966). This, however, need not imply that people should not be able to report the contents of the representations that capture their knowledge of the world. As usually noted in the literature, the limitations of introspection pertain to people's not being conscious of mental operations, not to their being unable to report the contents of information assumed to be stored in their minds (see Nisbett and Wilson, 1977; as well as Shanon, 1984b). That the bulk of cognitive activity is unconscious, therefore, does not counter the observation presented here as a pretheoretical indication against the postulation of underlying semantic representations.

The second preliminary observation pertains to action. Usually, behaviour is not planned. When one engages in a conversation one does not recite what one has edited beforehand. Moreover, at times one has no prior knowledge of what exactly one is going to say. This is so even when conversations present some complicated and delicate manoeuvring. Indeed, frequently one may be anxious about what one will say at an expected encounter, and find it very difficult to make any decision on this. But when the encounter takes place, one just opens one's mouth and talks – and lo and behold: the conversation is managed according to one's best interests. Indeed, no rehearsed performance could be better. Here, for instance, is a report from Bertrand Russell (1967):

> I got back to Cambridge from Rome on New Year's Day 1914, and, thinking that the time had come when I really must get my lectures prepared, I arranged for a shorthand typist to come next day, though I had not the vaguest idea what I should say to her when she came. As she entered the room, my ideas fell into place, and I dictated in a completely orderly sequence from that moment until the work was finished. (p. 219)

The third observation concerns time. We all know that 'time passes' and that 'things take time', yet we do not sense time as such. We are cognizant of the flow of events, not of time. Merleau-Ponty (1962) noted that one does not observe time, but rather, one effects its passage.

These observations are all banal, but they are very revealing. Conceivably, representations could vary in their accessibility, but if no representation is accessible then there must be a reason. If under no circumstances is an entity detected, it is only reasonable to doubt that it exists at all. If usually we are not conscious of the knowledge that is supposedly stored in our minds, if such knowledge seems not to be necessary for us to act, then perhaps such knowledge simply does not exist.

Memory

Throughout this critique I have discussed the representation of knowledge and argued that semantic representations cannot specify the knowledge people have. But there is a more fundamental problem. Suppose that this knowledge could be representationally specified, how would it be consulted, how could it be utilized? This brings me to the consideration of memory.

At first glance, it would appear that memory presents the strongest case for RCVM. Indeed, memory is at the heart of the two main rationales for the postulation of representations introduced at the outset of this critique. Epistemically, what could the knowledge that is presumably represented in one's mind be, if not the totality of one's memories? Understanding, identification, classification, the appraisal of similarity, and practically any cognitive task you can name all involve the recognition of stored information in one's memory and its activation. Memory and representations are also related in terms of the functionalist rationale, in which representations are postulated as mediators between the cognitive agent's behaviour and the given state of affairs in the environment. The agent's present behaviour and past experience manifest an analogous relationship. Specifically, the representations may be regarded as the mediators that enable cognitive agents to relate in the present to their past.

Given the close tie between memory and representation, it seems that the most natural way to account for memory is to assume that the information one remembers is always there in one's mind. In recognition one consults these entities, in retrieval one activates them and, as it were, pulls them out. This view of memory is usually taken for granted not only by psychologists but also by neuroscientists and biologists; often, it is referred to as the *trace theory* (for a review, see Posner and Warren, 1972).

The representational characterization of memory seems self-evident and straightforward, yet when one begins to reflect on it one discovers that things are not so simple, and that it is fraught with problems. Consider recognition: I meet a person and recognize him as the one I met at the cinema two weeks ago. By the representational account, I am comparing the perceived image of the person to an image represented in my mental store. How do I ascertain that the two are images of the same person? To do this one should presumably compare the two images and judge their similarity. In Chapter 5, I noted that by the standard representational account the appraisal of similarity involves the comparison of features. But how are the features themselves judged as being the same? For this, another act of comparison has to be postulated. But then, in order to account for that comparison still another will have to be invoked. The seemingly straightforward representational account thus leads to an infinite regress. In fact, the problem indicated remains even when no recourse to features is made. However the comparison of the two images is achieved, it presupposes reference to a standard. The postulation of such a standard is tantamount to the postulation of representations of a second order. These in turn will require the postulation of representations of a third order. Here, again, is the infinite regress. The only way out, I presume, is to conclude that recognition is achieved in a totally different manner, one which does not involve mediating mental representations at all.

Retrieval presents further problems. How do I activate the representation that constitutes a memory? Do I not already have to know that there is in my representational store a memory pertaining to the stimulus at hand? To wish to remember something, do I not already have to know, hence remember, that very thing? And what about the process of activation itself? If it is to be accounted for by the regular representational-computational machinery, how is this machinery activated? Or perhaps the activation is achieved by processes other than the regular representational-computational ones; if so, then the representational account is not complete, as it was at first supposed to be.

Further still: suppose one has an image in front of one's mind's eye. How does one know that it constitutes a memory? Perhaps the image is something one perceives, or fantasizes, or thinks about? There is nothing in the represented image (or verbal-like information, for that matter) that distinguishes it as a memory of the past. The representational model cannot answer these questions (for further discussion along these lines, see Coulter, 1983).

The moral of this discussion is radical. It indicates that RCVM fails in what should have been its paradigmatic case. The recognition of stored represented information and its retrieval are at the basis of all representational cognitive activity. If the representational model fails in this task it cannot succeed in any other. This is so because from the representational perspective, all cognitive tasks always involve the identification and activation of stored representations.

An especially interesting argument against trace theory and the representational view of memory is presented by Bursen (1978). Since the argument is ingenious and I have never seen it elsewhere in the literature, I present it in the words of its author:

> [By trace theory, as by the standard representational view] when someone remembers a painting (when he 'sees it in the mind's eye'), it must be that a trace of the painting is being activated somewhere in the brain. . . . [This] trace . . . must be completely isomorphic to the painting, down to the smallest detail. . . . But now: Think . . . of how the Mona Lisa would look with a blue face. Many people are quite capable of visualizing this with no trouble. . . .

The trace theorist at first seems to have little trouble explaining this phenomenon . . . All he need say is that the visual trace of the Mona Lisa is being activated in a way slightly different from the usual one. Perhaps the trace is being activated and a colour generating mechanism simply changes the flesh tone to a blue tone. . . . [However,] consider: the trace theorist is saying that the brain is quite capable of producing an image of the Mona Lisa with a blue face, even though the original memory trace bears no indication of any such color in the face. . . . So even though there is no indication of blue color in the trace, nevertheless the (hypothetical) color generating mechanism steps in and puts in a blue color where the trace has an indication for flesh color. If this is possible, then . . . the very same sort of process could occur in the case where someone visualizes the Mona Lisa with a flesh colored face [:] the color generating mechanism steps in and puts in the flesh color rather than the green color indicated by the trace. And, [so with any image:] whenever I visualize something, the color generator simply puts in the proper colors. Maybe the color indicators of memory traces are in black-and-white. Or maybe just black. And that is to say that there might be no indication of color at all: the color generator just puts in the right colors, with no color indicators at all.

[But then,] various other optical features of the image can be varied at will. Not only can different colors be imagined for the Mona Lisa's face but (e.g.) different sizes for the head. I can easily produce an image of the Mona Lisa with a very small head. In this case, the trace theorist assumes that (say) a size-reducing mechanism acts on the normal head-size-indicator of the trace. But, of course, the same sort of process could go on when I visualize the Mona Lisa with a normal size head. That is, the size-reducing mechanism could act on an oversize-head-indicator, thus producing an image with a normal size head. . . . But this is tantamount to admitting that the trace need bear no indication of size at all. [Thus], any feature which can be changed in imagination is shown, by the same process of reasoning, to be inessential as part of the trace. We can (at least I can) easily visualize the Mona Lisa with a moustache, with an orange-sized head, or even with an orange for a head. Whatever mechanism generates these monstrosities is quite capable of generating the usual image of the Mona Lisa. So why . . . assume that there must be a trace . . . ? (pp. 43–7)

Empirical data corroborating these conceptual considerations were surveyed in the first line of this critique. As noted in Chapter 2, remembering is affected by all sorts of factor that the representational account would deem irrelevant: the particular context of action and its manner of articulation, and the cognizer's physical whereabouts, body, affective and motivational state, and interaction with other people. If remembering consists in the retrieval of information from a mental store of representations, this should not be the case. For further argumentation along this line, see Garner (1974), Bransford *et al.* (1977) and Jenkins (1977); for further arguments against the characterization of memory by means of mediating mental structures, see Coulter (1983) and Watkins (1990). Of direct relevance to psychology are also the philosophical critiques of Ryle (1949), Wittgenstein (1953), Malcolm (1963, 1971) and Ben-Ze'ev (1993).

If memory is not to be accounted for by means of mediating stored representations then it is bound to be *direct*. The construction of a full-fledged theory of direct memory is a complex matter that has yet to be achieved. Preliminary proposals for a non-representational theory of memory are dispersed throughout James Gibson's writings (see discussion in Chapter 12). Some further suggestions in this vein are presented in Earle (1956), Munsat (1966), Locke (1971), Wilcox and Katz (1981), Shanon (1991d) and Ben-Ze'ev (1993).

The representation of knowledge

The foregoing discussion focused on the retrieval of what cognitive psychologists refer to as episodic memory, that is, the repertory of past experiences of the individual cognitive agent. The critical arguments marshalled, however, apply just as well to semantic memory, that is, to the repertory of information which is not idiosyncratic. The study of semantic memory is one of the most important topics of contemporary cognitive psychological research. On the basis of experiments measuring patterns of response times, psychologists have defined various structures by which people's conceptual repertory and knowledge of the world is organized (for a review, see, for instance, Smith, 1978). Do these empirical findings not hold against the critical comments above? I think not. The experimental data present the differential times it takes to retrieve different types of information, and to retrieve specific pieces of information when other specific pieces are known. In no case is there a direct tapping of 'representations'. Rather, there are patterns in the activity of remembering and constraints on it. These patterns indicate that the course of remembering follows some 'paths' and is subject to constraints. From this it does not necessarily follow that representations are lying there in the mind. The only thing that does follow is that there is some cognitive activity that enables people to entertain, in the present, information or experiences pertaining to the past. The assumption that information has to be represented in the mind in an orderly fashion is a reiteration of the epistemic argument for the postulation of representations, not a direct corollary of the empirical findings.

John Anderson's observations on the indeterminacy of representational modelling are pertinent here. Anderson (1978) points out that since all our information regarding representations comes from measurements of computational operations, modelling actually consists of pairs of representational structures and associated computational operations. For any such pair, one can devise different pairings depending on how much responsibility one attributes to the representations and how much to the computational operations. While Anderson does not suggest this, at the limit one can have a pair in which the role of representations will be minimal, or even nonexistent.

A specific argument against the characterization of semantic memory and knowledge of the world by means of a fixed, determinate, organized repertory of semantic representations is presented by Bransford *et al.* (1977), who focus on the notion of semantic distance. Representational models of knowledge differ in details, but all assume that concepts related either semantically or episodically are stored more closely to one another than less related concepts. Arguing against this basic assumption, Bransford *et al.* (1977) consider the triad of concepts 'shirt', 'shoe' and 'rock'. The concepts 'shirt' and 'shoe' would seem to be 'closer together' than 'rock' and 'shoe'. But, argue Bransford *et al.*, in the context of looking for objects that could be used to pound a nail into a wall the relative distances change; now, 'shoe' and 'rock' seem to be 'closer together' than 'shoe' and 'shirt'. Hence, Bransford *et al.* conclude, knowledge of the world cannot be accounted for by fixed semantic representations.

Since knowledge and memory are the basis for all cognitive functioning, by implication this argument generalizes to practically all cognitive activity. A forceful critique of fixed structures being the basis for cognitive activity is put forward by Kolers and Roediger (1984). RCVM models cognitive activity in terms of computational operations applied to fixed representational structures. If, however, Kolers and Roediger argue, the patterns of cognitive performance vary with the context, there is no sense in postulating fixed structures that are invariant across situations. Once all the contingent variations are taken into consideration, the cognitive performance is accounted for and the need to recourse to an additional fixed structure vanishes.

Kolers and Roediger's argument invalidates one of the basic notions of information-processing psychology – the box. Generally, representationalists model cognitive activity in terms of structural components and of the chain of information processing from one to another; the components are usually characterized as boxes. But, Kolers and Roediger point out, these boxes say nothing more than that information is processed in a certain order. Once all the computational work has been specified, there is nothing to the boxes as such. 'The boxes contain only names' (p. 427). This argument holds not only against semantic representations having a particular profile of characteristics (as in (**) of Chapter 1), but against mental representations in general.

Lastly, let me return to the foundations of the representation of knowledge, the notion that representations stand for something else, that they, in other words, represent. With this, I move from the consideration of representation in the horizontal sense to that of representation in the vertical one. The most decisive critique of representation in this is that presented in the later writings of Wittgenstein (1953, 1958). As noted throughout this critique, the problems of reference and intentionality are also appreciated by the chief protagonist of RCVM, Jerry Fodor (see Fodor, 1980). In general, however, psychologists seldom address this problem. A rare, most notable exception is the critique by Bickhard (1993a,

1993b; for an up-to-date comprehensive discussion, see Bickhard and Terveen, 1993). Its focus is what Bickhard (1987) refers to as *encodingism*. Since the argument is crucial, and since it has not been made elsewhere in the literature, I present it in Bickhard's own eloquent words:

> Essentially encodings are representational stand-ins. To say that 'X' encodes 'Y' is, more precisely, to say that the encoding 'X' is to be taken as representing the same thing as the representation 'Y'. There is no 'X' with such a definition so long as the representation 'Y' is itself not well defined. If 'Y' is in turn an encoding, then it too must be defined in terms of some other represenation(s), and if these too are encodings, then they must be defined, and so on, until some base level of representations is reached in terms of which all encodings are defined. The issue is whether such basic, non-derivative representations can be encodings. (p. 39)

The moral of the argument (and of Bickhard's critique in general) is that encoding representations cannot be the basis for cognitive agents' knowledge of the world.

Evaluation and correspondence

For mental material to be judged as being a memory of the past, some evaluation has to take place. By RCVM, the evaluation consists of an appraisal of sameness: the mental material one now entertains in one's mind should have the same content as the representation which is there in one's long-term mental store. Similarly, for them to be invested with meaning, the words one now hears (or now produces) must have the same semantic representation as that of concepts in one's mental lexicon. In the same manner, for them to be identified and interpreted the percepts recorded by one's sensory system have to match represented semantic information. The measure of evaluation underlying all these cases is correspondence. By RCVM, for anything to be recognized, interpreted, comprehended or assigned meaning to, it has to correspond to stored semantic representations and match them. This is not surprising: RCVM is a primarily semantic theory, and correspondence is the standard measure of evaluation semantic theories of truth adopt (see Wittgenstein, 1922; Tarski, 1944). By this theory, propositions are true if they are in correspondence to states of affairs in the world. Likewise, in linguistic theories of semantics, words and sentences are meaningful by virtue of corresponding to concepts and compositions thereof.

Appraisals of sameness are at the heart of representational psychology. Indeed, there is perhaps no information-processing model that does not contain a matching stage as one of its basic components. How is this appraisal achieved? I have considered this issue several times by now. The paradigmatic representational model of similarity judgements (that proposed by Tversky and his associates; see Tversky, 1977) bases these judgements on the comparison of sets of features. But how are these features compared? How are they deemed to be the same? By the logic of RCVM, the only way for this to be achieved is by checking for correspondence. This requires a second-order judgement of similarity, and with this one is led to an infinite regress of the kind classically associated with the homunculus problem.

Faced with this unpalatable result one might say that the second-order judgement of similarity is not needed (see, for instance, Fodor, 1975). The features match because they fit, like hand and glove. Such a fit, however, cannot be achieved by representational-computational means (for then we are back to the problems encountered at step one). Rather, the determination of fit should be taken as an elementary operation that is not accounted for. But then, why not employ this procedure in the first stage too? Why turn to it only in the second?

These observations do not only apply to the comparison of features as conducted (*à la* RCVM) in the judgement of similarity. They apply across the board, in the comparison of concepts to concepts, and of percepts to concepts, of words to concepts, and of mental material entertained in the present to what was presumably entertained in the past. All this means that correspondence cannot be the mind's basic measure of evaluation. An alternative will be suggested in Chapter 22.

The varieties of knowing

The cognitive literature in general, and the representational literature in particular, assume that knowledge is tantamount to the knowledge of facts. This, however, is only one kind of knowledge, and perhaps the least typical. In Chapter 7 I mentioned knowing-how and noted that it cannot be reduced to the knowing of facts. Here the varieties of knowing will be further marked.

First – the case I shall discuss in the greatest detail – is that of knowing other people. Just as we know the world, so we also know the people that we meet in the course of our lives, and we understand them. Friends tell us their problems and we find what they say meaningful or senseless, we reflect upon it, we make a suggestion, we scold. But of course, people need not be our friends for us to understand what happens in the voyage of their lives. We hear of the lives of strangers, and form an opinion. We read diaries, biographies and works of literature, and we feel sympathy and compassion, envy and frustration, admiration and disgust. How do we do all this?

The knowledge involved cannot be the declarative knowledge on which representational models are usually based. First, our understanding of people often involves experiences that are new to us. Second, even if we had direct access to these experiences, it is not clear that we would thereby achieve the pertinent understanding that indeed we do. The move from data about people to understanding people is not trivial. Certainly, it is not achieved by means of any formal system of logical deduction. Nor is it likely that the inference is mediated by any other general system of rules. One's understanding of the other is based, it seems, on too many particulars. It involves an unbounded set of idiosyncratic information pertaining to the life history of the person and to the various contingencies of his or her present behaviour. On the one hand, such particulars defy any general system of inference. On the other hand, both their meaning and their significance depend on the entire history in which they are embedded. The same detail may be extremely significant in the context of one life, and utterly insignificant in that of another. Conversely, details that in general are not of much import may put the story of a life in a new light and radically affect one's interpretation of it.

Not only is the knowledge of the other not of the standard representational type, it is not an instance of knowing-how either. As pointed out by Berlin (1979), when we observe another human being or listen to him or her, when we try to understand the behaviour of our fellow men and women, we are not involved in action.

How the knowledge of the other is achieved is a topic for independent empirical investigation that has yet to be conducted. The option Berlin advocates is one he attributes to the eighteenth-century Italian philosopher Vico – knowledge by experience. According to Vico, we know and gain understanding of other people not by reference to what the modern student of cognition would call semantic representations, but rather through the lived interaction with others. And what do we do when such an interaction is technically not feasible? We put ourselves in the other's shoes, so to speak. This is in line with the mental models and the phenomenon of mental enactment considered in Chapter 8. Just as we construct models of physical objects and states of affairs in the external world, so we construct models of the lives of people and the social interactions between them. And just as we entertain everyday reasoning not by means of logical deduction but through the inspection and manipulation of hypothetical states of affairs whose viability and coherence we check, so we know and gain understanding of others by vicariously undergoing experiences and acting in the virtual theatre of our minds.

To my knowledge, the only contemporary cognitive scientist concerned with the issue of knowing the other is Haugeland (1985). Haugeland presents his case through an illustrative episode:

> A friend of mine tells a story about when she was in college and kept a white rat as a pet. It was tame enough to follow quietly at her heels, all around campus; but one day, startled by a dog, it took hasty refuge far up her pantleg. Unfortunately, it lodged itself so tightly that it couldn't back out; and, in the meantime, she didn't dare move, for fear of crushing it. So, after a moment's hesitation, she sheepishly let down her jeans, easing out a quivering rodent, and won a round of applause from delighted passersby.
>
> Most people find this anecdote amusing. Why? Much of it, surely, is that we identify with the young heroine and share vicariously in her obvious embarrassment, while at the same time feeling relieved that it didn't happen to us. Embarrassment (and the corresponding relief), however, can be

experienced only by a being that has some sense of itself – a sense that is important to it and that can be awkwardly compromised on occasion. If no personality or 'self-consciousness' were at stake, there would be nothing to be embarrassed (or relieved) on behalf of. The point is not merely that my friend's ego was involved in her original embarrassment, but that our egos are engaged as we hear the story, share in that embarrassment, and smile.

I suggest that such ego involvement may be integral to the process of understanding. This isn't just a variation on empiricism – that you can't know what 'embarrassing' means until you've experienced it yourself (as: you can't imagine licorice unless you've tasted some). Rather, the idea is more radical: that actual, current feelings (such as embarrassed twinges, vicarious excitement, and the like) may be essential factors in real-time understanding. People do get involved in what they hear, and their own reactions affect the listening – what they notice, how they conceptualize, what it reminds them of, and so on. Storytellers count on these responses, much as they count on common sense, taking advantage of them for efficiency, for disambiguation, for effect. (pp. 239–40)

From these observations Haugeland concludes that a system lacking any ego or personality would be incapable of understanding another person, either in real life or in stories being told.

[Such understanding] presupposes a kind of continuity and ongoing ownership. A single event cannot be shameful, embarrassing, or foolish in isolation, but only as an act in the biography of a responsible, historical individual – an enduring person. . . . With embarrassment, whether original or vicarious, it is essentially and necessarily the same me who then bumbled and now blushes. Only a being who cares about who it is as a continuing, selfsame individual can care about guilt or folly, self-respect or achievement, life or death. [Furthermore,] moral integrity, conscience, and the courage of one's convictions . . . are also integral to the structure of self. (p. 245)

As Haugeland also notes, vicarious understanding of the other is especially salient in the act of reading literature (for extensive discussion of this phenomenon, see Iser, 1978). Indeed, the narrative presents another basis for the knowledge and understanding of the other. In the narrative perspective (see Gergen and Gergen, 1983), understanding another person is tantamount to constructing a coherent story. This perspective is in line not only with the observations made above, but also with a host of independent observations in the clinical-psychological literature. As suggested by Bruner (1986), knowing how to construct a story and to make sense of one is a specific type of knowledge, one which contrasts with and complements knowledge gained through analysis and deduction.

Still other types of knowledge can be mentioned: that exhibited in the making of moral judgements and ethical decisions, and that pertaining to aesthetical evaluations and exhibited in the appreciation of the beautiful, the pleasant, the tasty. For reasons totally analogous to those indicated in conjunction with the knowledge of other people, in all these cases representational data structures and deductive processes coupled with them are of no avail. Rather, what suggests itself is some fundamental judgement of fit, of things suiting one another and going well together. This is indeed the kind of judgement one makes when appreciating a piece of music (for similar remarks, see Wittgenstein, 1980).

The plurality of types of knowledge noted here is reminiscent of proposals made in other contexts. First, let me mention Kant and his three critiques – the *Critique of Pure Reason*, the *Critique of Practical Reason* and the *Critique of Judgement*. In Kant's system the knowledge of truth, the knowledge of moral conduct and the knowledge of the beautiful each comprise an entire, full-fledged system. The true, the ethical and the aesthetical define three separate, non-reducible categories of knowledge. Second, there is the modern research of intelligence. As suggested by Gardner (1983), human intelligence is not one single faculty, but several distinct ones. Traditionally, intelligence has been equated with verbal and mathematical ability. There are, however, other types of intelligence; amongst these are manual intelligence, artistic intelligence and the delicate art of knowing how to interact with other people. Surely, there are people who are extremely intelligent as far as the manipulation of symbols is concerned, but utterly stupid in their day-to-day dealings with their fellow men and women. Third, there is contemporary philosophical literature. Many philosophical analyses claim that ethical and aesthetical judgements cannot be reduced to statements of fact (for discussions of this issue, see Hudson, 1969). Again, the cognitive psychologist may respond by arguing that cognition need not be concerned with ethics or aesthetics. A moment of reflection, however, will reveal that, if anything, a psychologist can ignore these domains even less than a philosopher can. It is totally legitimate for a philosopher to be interested in epistemology and the theory of truth, say, but not in ethics or aesthetics. By contrast, the cognitive psychologist is, by definition, concerned with the whole span of people's activities and accomplishments. Just as they perceive the world and gain comprehension of their surroundings, just as they understand language and determine what is true and what is false, so people make judgements as to what is right and wrong and what is beautiful, well-structured or harmonious (and one might add the sacred and the sublime).[1] All these are accomplishments of which practically each and every human being is capable. At least *a priori*, the student of cognition has no right to dismiss them as being outside the domain of his or her inquiry.

Lastly, let me mention human feats usually shunned by cognitive psychologists. Manifestly, people (and even more astonishingly – animals) accomplish various feats for which one has no explanation. These are usually encompassed under the terms 'intuition' and 'instinct'. Of course, failure to explain proves nothing. Yet, accounting for such feats in terms of representations and computational operations defies reason. As I have little to say about these phenomena, and since they border on the mysterious, I will make no further comment on them. I believe, however, that they are extremely important and deserve concentrated cognitive investigation (for further discussion, see Roszak, 1972).

Knowledge, cognition and behaviour

Here again, representationalists may say that theirs is a theory of knowledge, or rather of cognitive knowledge, and there is no sense in criticizing them for not being able to account for aspects of behaviour which are not based on knowledge, or for knowledge which is not cognitive.

This retort was encountered in conjunction with the second line of the critique and, as will be indicated below, is actually another manifestation of the two-stage strategy examined in the first line. In the context of knowledge it gains special significance. Essentially, it proposes a distinction between knowledge and behaviour. As defined at the outset of this book, RCVM sets itself to characterize all human behaviour in terms of knowledge. Much of what has been said throughout this critique aims to show that various aspects of human behaviour cannot be accounted for by RCVM. This retort is a reaction to this criticism. That RCVM cannot account for all human behaviour, representationalists will say, should not mean that it is of no value. As indicated in Chapter 11, representationalists can explain that their goal is the modelling of knowledge and its representation, not of behaviour in general. Those aspects of human behaviour which are based on knowledge can, they will claim, be modelled by RCVM, while those aspects which are not are outside its province; hence, representationalists will conclude, this framework cannot be criticized for not being able to account for them.

In the present context of a psychological (as contrasted with philosophical) critique, this retort has a special appeal. At the outset of this book, RCVM was defined by three tenets – (1), (2) and (3) of (*). By and large, this critique has centred on (2) and (3). I focused on representations in the technical-psychological sense, and I argued that such structures cannot serve to model the knowledge which is (according to (1)) the basis of human behaviour. Throughout the discussion, however, I assumed a link between knowledge and behaviour. What if this tie is dismissed? What, in other words, if the assertion that knowledge is the basis of human behaviour cannot be sustained? This is tantamount to the relinquishing of (1), the seemingly least significant of the three tenets of (*). *Prima facie*, this is a small price for RCVM to pay in order to be salvaged; for arguments along similar lines, see, for instance, Fodor (1980) and, in particular, his response to the commentary by Dreyfus.

For this retort to be valid, however, certain conditions must hold. First, the aspects of behaviour declared to be outside the realm of cognition must not be of much cognitive or psychological significance; otherwise theoretical commitments will narrow the scope of the theory so that too many phenomena pretheoretically deemed interesting will be left out. Second, there must be a clear-cut segregation between those aspects of behaviour that are based on knowledge and those that are not. Third, the former must be more basic than the latter and cannot depend on them.

Clearly, this is another manifestation of the two-stage strategy discussed, and dismissed, in Chapter 3. Indeed, as argued at length throughout all three lines of the present critique, not one of the said conditions is met. The aspects of behaviour at risk of being cast away include not only the odd varieties of knowledge mentioned in the previous section but also meaning and interpretation, perception and action, motivation and emotion, consciousness and self-hood. Getting rid of all these would result in a severely impoverished discipline. More significantly, as argued in Chapter 11, the knowledge-based aspects of behaviour are neither well demarcated nor primary. Last but not least, as indicated both throughout the first line of this critique and earlier in this chapter, the representational account suffers from serious shortcomings even as an account of knowledge and knowledge-based cognitive performance.

Thus, RCVM cannot be salvaged by drawing a line between knowledge-based behaviour and behaviour which is not based on knowledge, between the so-called cognitive proper and that which is not. Specifically, even when the commitment to tenet (1) of (*) is lessened, cognitive modelling along the lines defined by (2) and (3) is not feasible. But then, the representationalists' modification of their stance on (1) can be turned upon itself and directed against them. As argued in this chapter, not only can semantic representations in the technical-psychological sense not account for human behaviour, but it appears that knowledge cannot be the foundation on which behaviour – 'cognitive' or not – is based. As indicated by the second line of this critique, behaviour and cognition are intertwined with seemingly extraneous factors that together define action in the world. Not only can action in the world not be accounted for by knowledge, many aspects of cognitive performance cannot be accounted for by reference to knowledge alone, and their modelling requires reference to action in the world. In Part II I shall present a picture of mind in which action in the world, not knowledge, is the basis for both cognition and behaviour in general.

Knowing and cognizing

I end this chapter with a distinction bearing on many of the issues I have considered. It is between two kinds of knowing. In English they are referred to by the same verb, *know*, but in the lexicons of other languages the distinction is manifest: *la-da'at she* (know that; i.e., know with a sentential complement) and *la-da'at et* (know with a direct object) or *le-hakir* in Hebrew, *savoir* and *connaître* in French, *wissen* and *kennen* or *erkennen* in German. While the exact connotations associated with these terms may vary somewhat across these languages, it seems that in all of them the first member of the pair denotes knowledge as a repertory of information whereas the second denotes a relationship with that which is known.

By and large, contemporary cognitive science seems to be concerned with the former type of knowledge only. Thus, the problem often characterized as its central topic for investigation is that of the representation of knowledge, that is, of the information stored in the minds of people or in the data-bases of the computer. This knowledge may be about the world, but in all practical respects, in all aspects of its actual scientific study, the world has nothing to do with it. Thus knowledge is confined to a solipsistic realm of the kind Fodor (1980) talks about. The issue of real interest, however, is not the representation of knowledge but rather that of the world or whatever is known by the cognitive agent. By its essence, knowledge cannot be solipsistic: it involves a relationship, the crossing of boundaries. It is thus invested with a quality that representational systems as they are attributed to people or realized in computers utterly lack. This other kind of knowledge, that which bridges the gap between knower and known and which has an experiential quality, is better denoted by the second members of the lexical pairs above. Whereas contemporary cognitive science is concerned with the first type of knowledge only, psychology should shift the focus of its attention to the second.

Given that this distinction is of paramount importance, it is only natural to look for a lexical expression for it in English. In the title of this section I have presented the pair *know* and *cognize*. However, I cannot make up my mind which term to use for which sense. Should the use of the verb *know* be reserved for real knowledge, as distinct from the solipsistic knowledge imposed by the representational framework? In this case, the verb *cognize* would characterize that kind of knowledge with which contemporary cognitive science is concerned. Or perhaps, the etymological analogies should be followed and the verb *know* used to characterize the repertories of information currently studied by cognitive scientists, and the verb *cognize*, the cognate of the Latin *cogito*, to refer to the real knowledge, that which transcends the unbridgeable gaps between mind and world, between the organism and the environment? But, of course, the particular choice of terms is not critical. What is important is to appreciate that the English word *know* conflates two distinct senses, that RCVM focuses on one sense only, and that there are good reasons to direct cognitive science towards the study of the other. Everything else is, as they say, semantics.

The distinction between the two kinds of knowledge brings us back to the problems of reference and intentionality discussed in Chapter 6. The two types are respectively associated with content and aboutness, the two classical characteristics of intentionality. Thus, consider the *locus classicus*, Brentano's (1874/1973) definition of the intentional:

> Every mental phenomenon is characterized by . . . the reference to a content, the directness toward an object (which is not to be understood here as meaning a thing). . . . In the presentation something is presented, in the judgement something is affirmed or denied, in love loved, in hate hated, in desire desired, and so on. (p. 88)

In the literature it is generally assumed that the two characteristics go hand in hand.

This discussion indicates that this is not so. It suggests that cognitive science should shift its attention from the study of content and content structures to the study of aboutness. A psychologist who was fully aware of this is – again – James Gibson (1979):

> Perceiving is . . . not an appearance in the theater of [the individual's] consciousness. It is a keeping-in-touch with the world, an experience of things, rather than a having of experiences. It involves awareness-of instead of just awareness. It may be awareness of something in the environment or something in the observer or both at once, but there is no content of awareness independent of that of which one is aware. (pp. 239–40)

Thus, the most basic task of theories of perception, and of cognition in general, is to explain how organisms come into psychological contact with the world (see Gibson, 1975). This contact is the essence of intentionality, and intentionality is the counterpart of reference, which is the defining characteristic of representations. The moral of the discussion in Chapter 6 was that RCVM cannot handle reference and intentionality at all.

Let me end this chapter, and Part I, with a literary example. A poignant contrast between the two ways of knowing is presented in Tolstoy's 'The death of Ivan Ilych' (Tolstoy, 1960). The topic is death. As the following quotations show, it is one thing to know that all men are mortal, and quite another thing to know that one is oneself mortal:

> The syllogism he had learnt [in] logic: 'Caius is a man, men are mortal, therefore Caius is mortal' had always seemed to him correct as applied to Caius, but certainly not as applied to himself. That Caius – man in the abstract – was mortal, was perfectly correct, but he was not Caius, not an abstract man. . . .
>
> 'If I had to die like Caius I should have known it was so. An inner voice would have told me so, but there was nothing of the sort. . . . And now here it is!' he said to himself. . . .
>
> 'What is this? Can it be that it is Death?' And the inner voice answered: 'Yes, it is Death.' (pp. 131–2, 149)

Only on his death-bed did Ivan Ilych reach knowledge (cognition) of what he had cognized (known) since he was a child, namely, that all men are mortal.

Note

1. For a suggestion that the holy does, indeed, constitute a separate category of knowledge in the Kantian sense, see Otto (1967).

Intermezzo

16 *Why representationalism?*

> When you are criticising the philosophy of an epoch, do not chiefly direct
> your attention to those intellectual positions which its exponents feel it
> necessary explicitly to defend. There will be some fundamental assumptions
> which adherents of all the variant systems within the epoch unconsciously
> presuppose. Such assumptions appear so obvious that people do not know
> what they are assuming because no other way of putting things has ever
> occurred to them.
>
> *Alfred North Whitehead*

I have completed the critical part of this book and I am about to turn to the positive
part. Before doing so, however, let us pause and reflect. If in fact RCVM is so
inadequate, if indeed there are so many reasons not to adopt the representational-
computational perspective, why has it attained the dominant place that it holds? Why
is it endorsed by so many thinking, learned people, both in psychology and in other
disciplines? It seems to me that this is so because RCVM is founded on some basic
assumptions – ontological, epistemological, meta-theoretical and methodological.
These are not specific to psychology; they pertain to general outlooks both on the
order of things and on science. They are deeply ingrained in modern scientific
thinking and usually are simply taken for granted. Consideration of them places
RCVM in a broader intellectual perspective; with this, additional channels for its
evaluation and criticism open up.

In the following discussion the various basic assumptions are spelled out and their
inadequacy with respect to cognition and cognitive science is marked. Some of the
assumptions have already been noted throughout this critique. Here they will be
presented in an ordered, systematic fashion, their roots will be uncovered, and the
affinity between them will be marked.

The assumptions to be noted are of several types. The main distinction is between
substantive and *methodological* assumptions. The substantive reflect one's general
Weltanschauung: one's conception of the order of things, ontological and
epistemological perspectives, basic stance regarding the mind and its relationship
with the world. The methodological pertain to one's basic conception of the nature
of science, one's stance on the conduct of scientific investigation, and one's

conception of the nature of scientific theory. As I shall show, the substantive and methodological assumptions are not unrelated, and together cohere into one unified world-view.

The substantive assumptions

The assumption of place

I would like to begin with a basic *conceptual* assumption, one to which I refer as *the assumption of place*. This differs from all other assumptions to be surveyed in that it is directly linked to the notion of representation. Yet, while it is more specific than the others, it is also very general. The assumption is that, for things to exist, there must be some place in which they are located. In other words, being presupposes place. This is an old assumption. As observed by Aristotle: 'It is generally assumed that whatever exists exists "somewhere" (that is to say, "in some place")' (Aristotle, 1963, p. 277; Aristotle, incidentally, did not subscribe to this assumption).

While seldom stated explicitly, the assumption of place is at the heart of all representational psychology. Just as physical space is postulated as the place of all things, so mental representations are postulated as the underlying locus in which cognitive activity takes place. This is the essence of the most basic rationale for the postulation of representations, that to which I referred as naive in Chapter 1. The assumption carries over, however, to all the other rationales and to all the senses of representation surveyed.

The assumption of place is very common-sensical, but is it really necessary? It seems to me that it is not. To show this, let me turn to another domain of scientific inquiry. Both the assumption of place and the move to abandon it have an analogue in physics. It has to do with one of the most basic notions of classical physics, that of the ether. The ether is precisely this – the physical entity that affords place to all things (see Whittaker, 1960; Hesse, 1967). For centuries physicists strived to detect the ether, but in vain: no substantive physical qualities of it were ever found. Stripped of all properties that a physical body might have, the ether was left naked, and the only property that could be attributed to it was the role that *ex hypothesi* it was supposed to play, namely, being the place of things. Eventually, in one of the most important revolutionary moves of modern science, physicists discarded the assumption of place and concluded that the ether does not exist. This radical move was couched in both methodological considerations regarding theory construction and substantive considerations specific to physics. Methodologically, if an entity is postulated only in order to keep a pre-existing conception of the order of things but apart from that nothing can be attributed to it, parsimony dictates that it should be dispensed with. Substantively, the ether was postulated from a theoretical perspective according to which space is absolute and independent of matter. However, as shown by Einstein's general theory of relativity, this is not the case:

the geometry of space cannot be defined without reference to matter. Matter, by means of gravitation, determines the geometry of space so that the notion of an absolute, independent place no longer makes any sense. Instead of absolute space Einstein postulated a relational space, one defined by the totality of gravitational interactions in it.

The situation in cognition is analogous. The moral of the first line of this critique was that the human cognitive system is maximally sensitive to variations of both context and medium. The modelling of mind has, in other words, to take into consideration all the particulars of the situation in which cognitive performance is realized. But then, as pointed out by Kolers and Smythe (1984), the relevance of these particulars deprives the postulation of underlying mental representations of its usefulness. If cognitive processing is affected by all the particulars of its realization, if cognitive accounts have to make reference to all the particulars of the specific situation of action, then the postulation of an independent, abstract, universal substrate of mental representations becomes superfluous. Given that all variations are accounted for by the particulars of the situation, the ideological reasons are no longer sufficient to warrant the postulation of an additional, abstract, undetectable substrate – be it ether in the physical domain or mental representations in cognition. (For further discussion as well as for other analogies between modern physics and cognitive psychology, see Shanon, 1991e.)

Ontological assumptions

While RCVM is concerned with the mind, not with the world, it is not neutral with respect to the structure of things in the world. Indeed, RCVM is based on some very specific *ontological* assumptions:

1. *Naïve realism.* RCVM assumes that the world is out there, existing prior to and independently of the mind. I have shown this in the discussion of the relationships between mind and world in Chapter 8, where objections to this assumption were presented as well.
2. The *building blocks* of the world are assumed to be absolute, objective entities. They consist of facts, not of interpretations. As Wittgenstein said in his *Tractatus* (1922), 'The world is the totality of facts.' By contrast, meanings and interpretations are in the province of the mind: they are imposed by it upon the objective, meaning-free ontology of the world. As will be indicated below, this view is related to a formalistic approach regarding meaning and interpretation.
3. Related to the previous assumption is one on *atomism and compositionality.* RCVM assumes that the mind is built of elementary, atomic symbols which compose large representational structures. The interpretation of these large structures is a function of that of the atomic symbols out of which they are built. A notable manifestation of this assumption is encountered in semantic theory, where it is associated with the Fregean thesis of the compositionality of meaning

(Partee, 1984). While in itself the assumption pertains to cognition, it reflects an ontological stance according to which the world is built of atomic elements that combine into larger and larger structures (see, for instance, Carnap, 1967).

4. Hand in hand with the assumption of atomism and compositionality goes one on the *precedence of entities* relative to relations. Further, it is assumed that what are from a logical point of view relations of lower orders have precedence over relations of higher orders. The adherence to the strong definition of metaphor (that presupposing the existence of distinct, well-defined semantic domains prior to the metaphorical relationships between them) is a manifestation of this assumption.

Epistemological and meta-psychological assumptions

Even if they do not explicitly state this, cognitive theories are couched in *epistemological* views. This is also true of RCVM. As will be readily appreciated, the following assumptions are closely related to the ontological ones; in fact, these epistemological assumptions are, in many respects, the reflections in the internal domain of the ontological ones:

1. *A segregation between the mind and the world.* As repeatedly noted, this assumption manifests itself in a dichotomy both between the internal mental domain and the external physical one, and between the internal psychological domain and the sociological one.
2. *A segregation between the cognitive and non-cognitive levels.* This assumption is manifested with respect to the relationship both between the cognitive system and the so-called non-cognitive faculties of mind and between different components or systems within the cognitive domain. As will be noted below, it is rooted in Chomsky's meta-theoretical writings and, in particular, in his theory of levels (see Chosmky, 1975a). It is manifested in the separations between syntax and semantics and between semantics and pragmatics. These linguistic-theoretical separations reflect directly on psychology. We have encountered them in the separation between the context-free and the context-dependent, between the literal and the non-literal, between the so-called standard and non-standard expressions.
3. *The precedence of structure.* As in formal systems, it is assumed that systems are endowed with meaning through the projection of interpretation upon given structures. It is further assumed that the syntactically defined structures can exist independently in a non-interpreted manner.

Systems and their investigation

The epistemological and meta-psychological assumptions reflect some general assumptions on complex systems and their modelling:

1. *A dichotomy between structures and processes.* In the context of RCVM this assumption manifests itself in the principled segregation between representations and the computational operations associated with them. But, no doubt, the dichotomy is not specific to cognition. It is applicable to complex systems in general, and is reflected in the modelling of such systems in the various domains of both psychology and biology. As noted in Chapter 12, one of the most interesting contributions of the new paradigm of connectionism is its presenting a framework – both psychological and computational – in which this dichotomy is obliterated.

2. *A dichotomy between systems and their material realization.* In the context of RCVM, the prime manifestation of this is the disregard of the body. The dichotomy is assumed by both representational cognitive psychology and classical (non-connectionist) artificial intelligence. Some protagonists of connectionism (those not committed to the tie between neural networks and the brain) endorse it too. A direct corollary of this assumption is the accentuation of the affinity between human beings and computers. Indeed, with the disregard of material realization, these two are viewed as two instantiations of one species which George Miller (1983) has called 'informivores'. An explicit statement of this stance is the physical symbol hypothesis propounded by Newell (1980). As pointed out by Edelman (1987, 1991), similar assumptions are presupposed in various domains of biology.

3. *A segregation between systems and their history and development.* In RCVM, this is manifested in the assumption that one can study the present structure of the mind and its mode of operation without considering the cognitive agent's past history. Similarly, it is assumed that one can study adult cognition while leaving the study of ontogenetic development to an independent discipline, that of developmental cognitive psychology. Analogous assumptions are made about cultural evolution and phylogenesis. Again, similar ones are encountered in the life sciences: many biologists assume that one can study the morphology and physiology of organisms and biological systems separately from their development (see Edelman, 1987; Maturana and Varela, 1987). The critique of this assumption is central to the Marxist orientation in the social sciences (for psychological ramifications, see Vygotsky, 1978; as well as Wertsch, 1985b).

Meta-theoretical and methodological assumptions

The assumptions regarding systems bring us from the substantive to the methodological ones. As is already evident, the ontological and epistemological assumptions are coupled with ones on the nature of scientific theories and the methodology of scientific investigation. These include the following:

1. The *purity of terms*: the terms of one's cognitive theory should all be well-defined, fully specified terms pertaining to the cognitive domain. At no stage

of modelling is any vagueness or indeterminacy allowed. The reflection of this assumption (as well as those noted below) is specified in the definition of semantic representations in (**) of Chapter 1.

2. *Uniformity* and *completeness*: cognitive modelling has to be formulated fully and exclusively by means of one given set of terms. The coverage of the domain of interest by this set should be complete, and no noise is allowed. Furthermore, for any cognitive phenomenon only one characterization is allowed; the same type of characterization should cover all the phenomena in the domain of interest at all times. For instance, if a set of semantic primitives is defined, it should serve for the definition of all the words in the language. A corollary is the adoption of an all-or-none perspective, with no room for variation or gradation.

3. *Autonomy.* Autonomy is a technical term that deserves explicit definition and further critical analysis. These will be undertaken below and in Chapter 21. Here, let me say that on this assumption, cognition should be modelled solely by means of terms classified as cognitive. The affinity between this methodological assumption and the substantive ones on segregation is evident.

4. An important corollary of assumption (3) pertains to *time*. RCVM assumes that the modelling of cognition can be made without considering time. A ramification of the disregard of time is the adoption of a *structural*, not dynamic, perspective. As noted below, this assumption is to a great extent due to the Chomskian heritage in the study of mind; it also relates to the principled, idealized orientation indicated in (6) below.

5. In assuming autonomy, the student of mind also endorses a *compartmentalized research strategy*, in which one may study specific cognitive domains and components of the cognitive system while disregarding others. In addition to this division of labour, an order of investigation is assumed. For instance, structures may be studied without considering their dynamics and development, syntax without semantics, semantics without pragmatics, and the context-free without the context-dependent. A specific manifestation of this is the two-stage model of so-called non-standard expressions discussed in Chapter 3.

6. A *principled* orientation. The discussion centres on questions of existence and possibility, and matters are viewed in absolute, exhaustive terms. From such a principled orientation, states of affairs either hold or do not hold, and quantitative considerations are ignored. As in formal systems, if a case countering a generalization is met, it is concluded that the generalization does not hold. An important manifestation of this orientation is the frequent adoption of *idealizations*. Given that matters are regarded from a principled point of view, factors and considerations deemed non-principled are ignored. With this, contingent matters, situational variations, temporal fluctuations and inter-personal and other variations are dismissed. Further, matters are viewed in an all-or-none fashion, with no room for graded distinctions, fuzziness or indeterminacy. A corollary is there being no place for qualititative changes. Fodor's radical nativism is a clear manifestation of this.

7. An assumption regarding *formality*. This assumption encompasses all others. It is assumed that arguments and lines of reasoning entertained in formal disciplines such as logic and linguistics can readily be carried over to psychology. Furthermore, formal considerations, and in particular considerations of parsimony, coherence and internal consistency, are the measures by which cognitive theories are to be evaluated. A corollary is the disregard of time noted above.

8. Lastly, the purist, formalist approach implies the rejection of *noise* and any other factor or ingredient that, from a purist, formalist point of view, is deemed impure. A corollary is the adoption of the abstract perspective and the disregard of the medium, context variations and other idiosyncratic variations.

Synopsis

In this survey, I have taken a maximalistic track and distinguished between many assumptions. Yet, the different assumptions noted are not unrelated. Together, they combine into one coherent picture. Two fundamental principles seem to underly all of them, one substantive-metaphysical and the other theoretical-methodological. The substantive-metaphysical assumption is that of *dualism*; the theoretical-methodological one may be referred to as *theoretical-methodological purism*.

Dualism underlies all the assumptions regarding systems and their investigation, all the epistemological assumptions, as well as the pertinent ontological ones. Together, the various assumptions of segregation noted are, of course, the manifestations of a fundamental dualism, one that makes a sharp split between the internal and external domains. This segregation strictly confines psychology to the internal, mental world. In fact, in contemporary cognitive psychology the confinement is brought to an extreme. Unlike classical epistemology, modern cognitive psychology is concerned not with the status of knowledge, but only with the structures and mechanisms that make it possible. As indicated by Fodor's methodological solipsism, for all practical purposes, as far as RCVM is concerned the world does not exist (for further discussion along this line, see Sampson, 1981).

Theoretical-methodological purism (henceforth *purism*, for short) is the view according to which cognitive theories (and scientific theories in general) should be constructed by means of well-defined, pure terms in uniform, complete characterizations that follow formal reasoning and in which extrinsic factors are not relevant. Purism endorses a principled perspective, in which quantitative and other variations do not count and noise has no place. In such a perspective, theories and models are evaluated in terms of formal criteria, especially that of parsimony. A corollary is that, in essence, there is no difference between logic and linguistics on the one hand and psychology on the other hand. Hence, arguments and results in the former domain carry over, *mutatis mutandis*, to the latter. For instance, formal-logical or theoretical-linguistic demonstrations of properties of concepts, or constraints on their structure or concatenation, are taken as showing that corresponding properties or constraints apply to mental concepts and psychological structures. A paradigmatic example is Fodor's argument on the impossibility of concept learning, an argument based on the demonstration that a logical or semantic reduction of concepts is not possible (see Fodor *et al.*, 1980).

While distinct, dualism and purism are integrally related. Both involve the rejection of factors that scientists decide to disregard. Dualism rejects the various so-called non-cognitive factors surveyed throughout the present critique; purism rejects whatever does not square with neat formalism. Together, the two join to define what the cognitive scientists regard as the proper scope of cognition. Often, the considerations pertaining to dualism and purism are related. Specifically, the adoption of the former sets the ground for confining the domain of investigation in a manner that allows keeping to the exigencies of the latter.

In adopting the basic dualistic stance, representationalists not only impose a separation between the psychological and the physical, but also put the two on a par. They are taken to be the two facets of reality, two realms of equal status. Moreover, the parity is reflected in the intrinsic, more specific qualifications of the mental. By and large, it is assumed that the internal representational world is in some important respects a mirror image of the external one. This is in line with other tenets of RCVM. The first is the very definition of representation. In its most elementary sense, recall, representation is something that stands for something else. In particular, the knowledge represented in people's minds is taken to be knowledge of the world. Thus, it is only natural that representations reflect in some respects the characteristics of the world that they represent. Second, the equation between the internal and the external worlds reflects a basic positivistic view commonly held by scientists. As noted throughout the foregoing discussion, representational cognitive psychology is founded on various basic assumptions lying at the heart of classical natural science. I have shown this with respect to the assumption of place. The same holds for the entities that occupy place, the objects constituting the domain of investigation. Just as the classical Newtonian-positivistic world consists of elementary building blocks that combine into larger objects, so the representational internal world is built of basic units that combine together into large representational structures that eventually define everything one knows.

RCVM in perspective

There are indeed good reasons for embracing RCVM. It may be utterly misguided, but it has very deep and ancient roots – ontological, epistemological, theoretical and methodological. As mentioned in the Prologue, it was with an analysis of Plato's *Meno* that this entire critique started. The Socratic conclusions regarding nativism were, I thought, unacceptable, and I started to analyze the dialogue and uncover the assumptions, most of them implicit, that underly Socrates' argument. Doing so, I was startled to realize that I was actually specifying the premises of contemporary cognitive science. Consequently, I began to question the validity of what until that moment had seemed to me the self-evident foundations of the study of cognition (for details, see Shanon, 1991f).

That Plato may be a forefather of RCVM is not surprising. Platonism is the epitome of purism. A guiding principle in Platonic philosophy is the belief that the true, the good and the beautiful all converge into one. With this, ontological and epistemological idealism and formal purism coincide.

Descartes is the father of both analytic science and modern dualism. Chomsky (1966) is right: representational cognition is fundamentally Cartesian. Unlike Chomsky, however, I find Cartesianism detrimental. In fact, even Descartes was aware of the problems posed by the dichotomy between mind and body and was ill at ease with it. As a last recourse, he artificially connected the two by postulating a mysterious link between them in the pineal gland. It goes without saying that a modern student of mind cannot accept such a solution. (For other critiques of Cartesianism in modern cognition, see Shotter, 1975; Rorty, 1980; Sampson, 1981.)

In our century, many of the assumptions noted above have been associated with positivism. This is especially true of the formalistic methodological stance and of the assumptions of atomism and compositionality as they apply in language, epistemology and ontology. The positivistic perspective was advocated in the logical atomism of Russell (1956) and Wittgenstein (1922), and the works of the Vienna circle (e.g., Carnap, 1967).

And, of course, throughout the history of philosophy there have been those who have countered the Platonic–Cartesian tradition. The father of them all is Aristotle, who defied the Platonist separation between form and matter, between the ideal and the applied. It is no accident, I think, that unlike Plato, Aristotle was an observational-empirical scientist. Unfortunately, for historical reasons, in the annals of science Aristotle is often blamed for the dark ages of Western civilization. This is, however, the fault of the church that canonized him, not of Aristotle's teaching as such.

Quite a few philosophers parted from the Platonic–Cartesian tradition. Here let me just list names, many of them already mentioned throughout our discussion: Hegel, Marx, the existentialist-phenomenologist philosophers Heidegger, Merleau-Ponty and Sartre, as well as contemporary philosophers of the hermeneutic school (see, for instance, Habermas, 1970b, 1979; Gadamer, 1975). While these scholars lived and worked before the advent of modern cognitive science (and most even before the birth of modern psychology), there is a direct affinity between the issues with which they were concerned and the modern cognitive ones. Indeed, there are also direct historical links between the two: Vygotsky was a devout (albeit enlightened) Marxist, and Dreyfus' critique of artificial intelligence is a direct corollary of his work on existential philosophy. For contemporary treatises that mark this affinity, see Rorty (1980) and Dreyfus (1962).

In this discussion, I have focused on the ontological, epistemological, meta-theoretical and methodological roots of RCVM. Yet, it may be argued that RCVM is also rooted in assumptions pertaining to culture and ideology, society and politics.

Indeed, in recent years an increasing number of social scientists (although usually not cognitive psychologists) have argued that the scientific enterprise is not immune to ideological biases and socio-political influence. Specifically, some have argued that the individualistic orientation of RCVM may reflect the individualistic, socially alienating ideology of western capitalistic society. (For further discussion, see Sampson, 1977, 1981, 1983; Gergen, 1985, 1987; Gergen and Morawski, 1980; and Shotter, 1975.)

While I am not politically inclined at all, I do have a great interest in general cultural matters, on which see Romanyshyn (1989). In a brilliant analysis Romanyshyn presents the thesis that modern science and Western culture are rooted in the invention of representationalist (in the standard, not the cognitive-psychological, sense) perspective. In introducing it, European painters detached themselves from the world. Whereas medieval painters depicted the world from the point of view of people living and acting in it, Renaissance painters depicted it as an object out there, one they strived to represent as accurately as possible but with which they did not interact. Whereas the former maintained a participatory interaction with the objects of their painting, the latter subjugated these objects to an externally imposed, abstract, formal coordinate system. By extension, it may be argued that such detachment is the hallmark of Western European culture at large. I shall return to this in Chapter 18.

Given the deep-rooted intellectual background of RCVM, it is not surprising that it has analogues in other sciences. As noted throughout my critique, this is especially true of the life sciences. Various biological systems manifest regularities in behaviour and exhibit what may be regarded as knowledge. Usually, the brain is assumed to store all that the organism knows, and together with the entire neurophysiological system it is taken to be responsible for all psychological accomplishments. The genetic system carries information on the structure of organisms and passes it on from one generation to the next. The immune system recognizes molecules and classifies them so as to differentiate between what pertains to the self and what does not.

In all these domains, models like RCVM have been proposed. The organism is said to know and remember because the pertinent information is encoded in engrams stored in its brain. As noted in Chapter 5, the detectors and feature-analyzers usually specified in neurophysiological models of perception are very similar to those specified in representational-computational models in psychology. The genetic code is likened to a language with well-defined basic units that are very much like words (see Dobzhansky, 1962; Masters, 1970; Jakobson, 1971; for a critique, see Shanon, 1978). The molecules of the immune system are usually characterized in a similar fashion (see Jerne, 1974; Edelman, 1987).

Of course, there need not be complete parallelism between the models developed in biology and the representational ones developed in cognitive science. Still, the parallelism is substantial. In particular, the representational-like structures postulated in biology are not only representations in the weak naive, epistemic and functionalist senses, but often exhibit the characteristics of semantic representations in the strong technical-psychological sense. Specifically, in all the biological domains noted, coding systems have been defined. These are built of elementary, well-defined, semantic-like units that combine into large informational structures in accordance with rules of well-formedness. The codes – in particular the genetic code – are endowed with independent existence: their functioning is accounted for in terms of their structural, representational-like features, and they are largely autonomous from the bodily structures in which they are embedded. Furthermore, a segregation is assumed between the code and the computational processes associated with it, and a basic invariance across contexts is assumed.

Objections have been raised in all these domains. Maturana and Varela, whose work has been repeatedly cited throughout this book (Maturana, 1978; Maturana and Varela, 1980, 1987), have argued that living organisms and biological structures are autopoietic: they both create their environment and are created by it. The interaction between the two is dynamic, and defies modelling by means of fixed representational autonomous structures. More recently, Edelman (1987, 1989, 1991) has put forth a radical, comprehensive theoretical framework for biology which brings together immunology, neurophysiology, development and evolution, as well as cognition. He argues against the modelling of biological systems in terms of well-defined units, which do not leave room for noise, are primarily static, and impose a principled segregation between functional systems and their somatic realization. Similar arguments are also presented by Atlan (1979) and recently, in conjunction with the genetic code, by Lewontin (1992). Bursen (1978) notes explicitly that his critique of mental representations as memory engrams readily applies to brain codes as well.[1]

And surely, the representationalist perspective permeates the human and social sciences. It is so pervasive that there is not much sense in getting into it here. Psychoanalysis is founded on the belief that old memories are there, lying in the depths of one's mind, waiting to be uncovered as are the riches of the past by the archaeologist. Most students of personality and clinical psychologists maintain that people's 'personalities' are the reflections of some inner structures that lend regularity to their behaviour. Most contemporary scientific economics is based on the view that human beings are rational decision makers; this is also true of some of the more rigorous models in political science. Many of these models were directly influenced by ones developed within the psychological framework of RCVM, but not all. This is significant: it marks the deep roots of the representational view. Indeed, its great appeal in so many neighbouring disciplines – neuropsychology, social psychology, cultural anthropology and cultural studies – may be due precisely to representationalism being (mostly unawares) very deeply rooted in people's general view of the world. The investigation of the representational assumptions in all these disciplines, the examination of their validity, and the search for alternatives to them is, surely, a timely project. Further remarks on culture and its representationalist manifestations will be made in Chapter 18.

The Chomskian heritage

Of all scientific disciplines, Chomskian generative linguistics has had the greatest direct impact on representational cognitive psychology. First, Chomsky was one of the early and most important instigators of the cognitive revolution (see Chomsky, 1959). Second, the theoretical psychology of the most important protagonist of RCVM, Jerry Fodor, is a direct application of Chomsky's linguistic theory, methodological approach and basic view of mind. Let me, then, make a few specific comments on the Chomskian heritage in contemporary cognitive science. This cross-disciplinary relationship is a complex topic that has attracted extensive discussion, and by no means do I intend to cover it here. My only aim is to point out that many of the assumptions noted above are due to the Chomskian heritage, and that all told, their introduction into psychology was quite deleterious. For general discussions of the deleterious impact of Chomsky's thought on psychology see Robinson (1975) and Stabler (1983).

Chomsky's work is fraught with idealizations. As argued in the oft-quoted opening pages of *Aspects of the Theory of Syntax* (Chomsky, 1965):

> Linguistic theory is concerned primarily with an ideal speaker-listener, in a completely homogeneous speech-community, who knows its language perfectly and is unaffected by such grammatically irrelevant conditions as memory limitations, distractions, shifts of attention and interest, and errors (random or characteristic) in applying his knowledge of the language in actual performance. . . . To study actual linguistic performance, we must consider the interaction of a variety of factors, of which the underlying competence of the speaker-hearer is only one. In this respect, the study of language is no different from empirical investigation of other complex phenomena. (pp. 1–2)

The distinction between competence and performance marks a segregation between abstract knowledge of language and its processing in actual use. Chomsky repeatedly emphasizes that he is concerned with the former, not the latter. But the latter encompasses precisely what is of major interest to the psychologist: memory, perception, production, knowledge of the world, belief and judgement. This is tantamount to saying that all the issues of strict psychological concern are outside the domain of inquiry. A psychologist cannot, of course, subscribe to such a view.

As Chomsky rightly points out, all sciences involve idealizations. What is crucial, however, is to make sure that in making them one does not throw the baby out with the bath water, so to speak. This, I contend, is what happens when Chomsky's theoretical-linguistic, meta-scientific approach is incorporated into psychology. This is most salient in the case of learning. As already noted in several previous chapters, at the heart of Chomsky's theory of language learning is a radical disregard of time. As Chomsky says: '[We] assume that learning can be conceptualized as an instantaneous process' (Chomsky, 1975b, p. 15). But, of course, learning is not instantaneous. Indeed, its taking time is perhaps the most important fact about it.

Without time, learning is no longer learning, nor is atemporal psychology psychology.[2]

Chomsky's idealization also affects what one regards as the basic units of linguistic (and psycholinguistic) investigation. Only full-fledged, well-formed sentences are considered. Moreover, the investigation is based on only single, isolated sentences and the context in which verbal expressions are uttered (or heard) is ignored. This not only distorts the actual state of affairs encountered in verbal behaviour and development, but also leads to a theoretical impasse. That this is so is eloquently argued by Brown (1968):

> To many students of child speech . . . it seems that the linguistic data available to the child are so thin that we can only account for his knowledge by assuming that it is, in substantial degree, innate. It is possible, however, that the surface data seem as thin as they do because they are imagined in too static a form, as a set of still photos, unconnected model sentences. It may be as difficult to derive a grammar from unconnected sentences as it would be to derive the invariance of quantity and number from the simple look of liquids in containers and objects in space. The changes produced by pouring back and forth, by gathering together and spreading apart are the data that most strongly suggest the conservation of quantity and number. The changes produced in sentences as they move between persons in discourse may be the richest data for the discovery of grammar. (pp. 287–8)

Jerry Fodor extended Chomsky's position on the learning of language to learning in general. As noted, by a series of flawless deductive steps Fodor arrives at a ridiculous conclusion, namely, that all knowledge in innate. What went wrong? This is not the place for a complete, detailed exegesis of Fodor's argument. I will confine myself to saying that it all boils down to the substantive and methodological assumptions noted. Substantively, Fodor demands uniformity of processes; he allows for no noise, no impurity of terms, no gradation or incompleteness. Further, he demands that cognition be autonomous and allows for no intervention of what he deems external, non-cognitive factors. Methodologically, Fodor is an extreme purist and formalist. In fact, many of his arguments (notably in Fodor *et al.*, 1980) run as follows: he demonstrates that logically concepts cannot be reduced to semantic primitives, and then he concludes that psychologically concept learning is not possible. The argument would be valid only if psychology paralleled logic and linguistics. It does not – if only because the latter pertain to an idealized, atemporal domain and the former to real life.

Another issue in which Chomskian linguistics has had a crucial impact on RCVM is the scope of psychology. Since the most rigorous and extensive treatment of the problem of scope in the human sciences is found in theoretical linguistics, I will introduce this problem with a general sketch of its treatment there. As will become apparent, the demarcation of scope is entangled with the issue of autonomy mentioned earlier; the following discussion examines both issues in tandem.

Chomsky was concerned with the problem of scope throughout his entire career; the following statement with regard to semantics is paradigmatic:

> It seems that other cognitive systems – in particular, our system of beliefs concerning things in the world and their behavior – play an essential part in our judgements of meaning and reference, in an extremely intricate manner, and it is not at all clear that much will remain if we try to separate the purely linguistic components of what in informal usage or even in technical discussion we call 'the meaning of linguistic expression.' I doubt that one can separate semantic representation from beliefs and knowledge about the world. (Chomsky, 1977, p. 142)

With this, Chomsky concluded that semantics should be outside the realm of linguistic theory. The reasoning underlying this position is sound: it reflects the (fully understandable) fear that the consideration of semantics – let alone pragmatics – will lead to the opening of a Pandora's box whereby all sorts of extraneous factor – sociological, anthropological and cultural – will infiltrate linguistic theory. As a result, the linguistic domain will be contaminated and the formal rigour of linguistics compromised. Given that there is no clear demarcation between semantics and pragmatics, Chomsky decided to place both outside the realm of linguistics proper. In so doing, he confined the domain of linguistics but kept his theory as pure as possible.[3]

In time, even Chomsky could not ignore semantics. What he did, however, was relegate it to a separate, post-syntactic linguistic component. The syntactic component remained formally pure in that it did not contain semantic parameters, and the clear segregation between syntax and semantics was maintained. Yet, the problem of scope and the associated issues of theoretical purism and autonomy did not disappear from the linguistic stage. Indeed, they appeared at the centre of perhaps the most important and heated theoretical debate in generative linguistics since its inception, that in the 1970s between the proponents of autonomous syntax and those of so-called generative semantics. The former, led by Chomsky, held to the purity of syntax and its autonomy. In order to maintain these, they increasingly constricted the scope of syntax, pushing various phenomena either to pre-transformational structures or to post-transformational components of grammar. Eventually, the rich corpus of grammatical transformations which constituted the core of the standard transformational grammar shrank into one transformation. The generative semanticists, headed by Lakoff and McCawley, maintained that the seemingly impure semantic and pragmatic phenomena are of central importance and cannot be ignored. In incorporating semantic and pragmatic factors into the linguistic domain, they relinquished the autonomy of syntax and developed theories very different from the strict formalist ones of the earlier days of generative linguistics. (For a review of the debate on autonomy in generative linguistics, see Maclay, 1971; and Jackendoff, 1972.)[4]

This is not the place to go into details of the linguistic debate. The contention, though, involves more than specific issues in syntax and semantics, and cannot be settled by reference to purely linguistic data. At stake is the very nature of scientific theory and some basic decisions regarding how research in the human sciences should be conducted. The Chomskian position is purist: following the model of the formal disciplines of mathematics and logic, it wants to maintain as neat and formal a theory as possible. In fact, for Chomsky, this formal stance defines the domain of the scientific study of language: the linguistic domain is confined to that realm which can be subject to a rigorous formalistic treatment. The opposing camp was led by a different basic view of language. It maintained that the subject matter of linguistics is determined by the actual phenomenology of language, not by the scientist's *a priori* conception of what science should be. It might be tempting to opt for a maximally pure theory, but this cannot be done at the expense of the subject domain. One must study language as the human phenomenon that it is. If this implies that one's linguistic theory cannot be as pure as one could wish, then so be it. The consideration of semantic and pragmatic factors led generative semanticists to become more and more interested in general cognitive and psychological issues. This shift in interest resulted in a socio-professional shift that may be at least partially responsible for the fact that in the discipline of linguistics proper it was the opposite, autonomous camp that prevailed.[5]

Again the clearest case of the adoption of the Chomskian doctrine into psychology is found in the writings of Fodor. Thus, in the concluding discussion of *The Modularity of Mind* (Fodor, 1983), he proposes the following

> generalization, one which I fondly hope will some day come to be known as 'Fodor's first law of the Nonexistence of Cognitive Science': . . . The more global . . . a cognitive process is, the less anybody understands it. Very global processes, like analogical reasoning, aren't understood at all. (p. 107)

In line with this 'law' Fodor suggests that just as there is no serious philosophy of scientific confirmation, so there is no psychology of central processes.

The impoverished prospect for the study of cognition implied by Fodor's perspective appears even more severe when it is considered in conjunction with the moral of *The Language of Thought* (Fodor, 1975). There, Fodor notes that 'cognitive psychology is concerned with the transformation of representations', and contrasts it with 'psychophysics [which is concerned] with the assignment of representations to physical displays'. Yet, the transformations of representations, I take it, pertain to the central part of the mind, whereas psychophysics subsumes the study of the input systems. Thus, what constitutes (according to Fodor, 1975) the genuine subject matter of cognition is (according to Fodor, 1983) unstudiable, whereas those modular parts of mind (according to Fodor, 1983) that lend themselves to veritable scientific investigation are (according to Fodor, 1975) not at all cognitive and largely outside the scope of representational psychology.

The source of Fodor's pessimistic conclusion is, again, the assumptions surveyed earlier in this chapter. Methodologically, the conclusion is in line with the formalist perspective which assumes that for a theory to be scientific it has to abide by well-defined formal constraints. The modular parts of mind allow for that kind of theory, the non-modular parts seem not to. Substantively, the pessimistic conclusion follows from a structural perspective, according to which the study of cognition should be concerned only with those aspects of mind that are genuine manifestations of cognitive architecture, not ones that may be affected by a person's knowledge, beliefs, concerns or interest. Pylyshyn (1980) labelled this criterion *cognitive penetrability*. According to him, cognitive science should be concerned with those facets of behaviour that are cognitively *im*penetrable.[6] This emphasis on fixed structure is in line with Chomsky's characterization of cognition (and the study of language in particular) as the investigation of the organs of the mind (cf. Chomsky, 1980). As I shall show in the next section, it is also in line with the Ebbinghausian quest to find the quintessential rules of psychology.

Experimental ramifications

This discussion has focused on theory and meta-theory, but similar issues are encountered at the heart of mainstream experimental cognitive psychology. A perusal of the history of the discipline reveals a contrast between two traditions, epitomized by the contrast between two pioneers of memory research, Ebbinghaus (1885/1964) and Bartlett (1932).

Ebbinghaus, one of the founders of experimental psychology, strove to uncover the pure laws of learning and forgetting. Appreciating that these cognitive performances are affected by the particular items being tested, the specific situation of testing, what the subject knows and the like, Ebbinghaus maintained that the primary task of the scientific psychologist is to control for the effects of these 'noise' factors and eliminate them. For this, he perfected very rigid methods of research. In particular in his experiments he used items devoid of meaning – his famous nonsense syllables. Bartlett also appreciated that cognitive performance is affected by these various seemingly extraneous factors. However, he argued that rather than being extraneous to the meaning of information and subjects' knowledge, interests and beliefs are at the heart of cognitive processing. The cognitive system is not designed to process meaningless items, and cognitive processing cannot be separated from people's repertory of knowledge and belief. When these factors are stripped off nothing is left. There is, in other words, no pure system of memory, no pure law of learning. How learning and forgetting are affected by what Ebbinghaus regarded as noise factors is the very matter of cognition.

Ebbinghaus' and Bartlett's positions are paradigmatic, and have since appeared again and again in the history of psychology. The details change, but the basic contrast is the same. On the one hand, there are the purists who attempt to define a quintessential cognition. For this, they devise highly controlled settings and strict methodologies; often (as with Ebbinghaus) these are coupled with rigorous mathematical modelling. Psychologists of the other persuasion maintain that the clean experimental settings are utterly artificial, and that they eliminate the essence of cognition. The neat results obtained, they argue, are artefacts: they apply only under the very special, utterly artificial conditions that the experimenter creates.

Here, then, is a choice. One option is to try to construct a rigorous psychology, with parsimonious universal laws analogous to those of physics. This, however, can be achieved only at the price of having a psychology totally detached from real life, one dealing with only certain unrepresentative facets of human behaviour and presenting a very biased picture of the mind. The other option is to face psychological reality as it is. The price is giving up the beautiful theory one may understandably wish to have. Bluntly put, the choice is between truth and beauty. In physics (as well as in Platonic metaphysics and Chomskian linguistics), the two go hand in hand. In psychology (as, apparently, in all disciplines concerned with functioning systems, not with natural laws), this is not the case. Having to choose between truth and beauty, representationalists have veered towards the second. I opt for the first.

But then, as in the arts, there are different notions of beauty. When one accepts the fact that psychology is not a formal science, then one may find order, hence beauty, of a different type. While not formalizable in pure laws, what may at first seem to be a mess may exhibit regularities and inner structure none the less. I will expand on this in Chapter 22.

Conclusions

The moral of this discussion is that RCVM as a school of thought is not an isolated, distinctly modern phenomenon: it reflects a comprehensive, integrated world-view that has old roots in the tradition of the West. But as I have shown, it is wrong. In particular, none of the assumptions upon which it is based is warranted. These assumptions put cognition into a strait-jacket. Adopting them is tantamount to wishing to do psychology without being psychological. It is high time that the study of mind freed itself from the constraints of these old theories, which perhaps suited a different intellectual and scientific climate, but are no longer suitable. With this conclusion, let me turn to Part II, that concerned with the alternatives to RCVM.

Notes

1. Admittedly, the biological data and the models proposed to account for them are complex. The meta-theoretical view endorsed by biologists (and criticized in this discussion), however, does exhibit the characteristics noted here. If this were not the case, there would have been neither reason nor place for the criticism marshalled by the non-orthodox biologists referred to here.
2. As pointed out in Chapter 9, not only does Chomsky's account of learning assume unacceptable idealizations, it also involves an utter disregard of empirical data.

3. I find it remarkable how similar these observations by Chomsky are to those made in the first line of my critique. However, the conclusions drawn are diametrically opposite.
4. In fact, Chomsky could not maintain his original, purist position for long. While in the early days of generative grammar, linguistic theory and grammar (i.e., the theory of syntax) were taken as synonymous, with the change of the general *Zeitgeist* even he could not ignore semantic issues.
5. A call against Chomsky's position and for bringing pragmatics into the front line of research was made early in the history of generative linguistics by Bar-Hillel (see, for instance, Bar-Hillel, 1971). Arguing that language is infinitely pregnant with pragmatics, Bar-Hillel rebuked linguists and philosophers for being 'afraid of the pragmatic wastebasket'. Unfortunately, his call was not heeded; apparently, he was too much ahead of his time. The pragmatic turn in linguistics and psychology took place after his untimely death.
6. Pylyshyn employs his criterion in the context of mental imagery (see Pylyshyn, 1981). My empirical investigation of the phenomenology of mental imagery suggests that in following such a principled approach one is bound to miss some of the phenomenon's more interesting facets (see Shanon, 1989d).

Part II

Beyond representationalism – alternatives and ramifications

Introduction

Taken together, the different lines of the foregoing critique all lead to one and the same conclusion: RCVM is not as successful as might at first appear. Models based on semantic representations as defined at the outset of my discussion seem to face a host of fundamental problems. Indeed, it appears that these models are not even capable of accounting for those accomplishments of mind that are usually taken as reasons for the postulation of such representations. The first line of the critique indicated that semantic representations cannot account for the knowledge that presumably underlies people's behaviour. The second line indicated that semantic representations cannot account for the relationships between the cognitive system and other domains and systems. The third line indicated that the representational account is at a loss when attempting to confront time and the dynamic aspects of behaviour, learning and development. Conceptual problems pertaining to the notion of knowing marked in the fourth line further exacerbate an already problem-fraught situation.

In marking the shortcomings of RCVM and its limitations, the arguments in my critique undermine the validity of each and every one of the characteristics of semantic representations listed in (**) of Chapter 1. In marking the unbounded variation of cognitive expression with context and its similarly unbounded sensitivity to the medium, the first line of the critique indicates that the cognitive system cannot be characterized in terms of a well-defined and well-structured abstract code that is determinate and fixed. In marking the intimate involvement of cognition with domains and systems other than itself, the second line indicates that cognition cannot be characterized as an autonomous system defined solely in terms of symbolic structures and computational operations. In marking the various problems pertaining to time, the third line indicates that cognition cannot be characterized in a framework that is primarily static and ahistoric, and that the principled distinction and segregation between structure and process, basic to representational modelling, is untenable. The fourth line indicates that the tenet according to which behaviour is based on mentally represented knowledge is not as evident as it may seem at first. As further indicated, all the problems noted are couched in some basic, and apparently erroneous, assumptions regarding both the world and the mind. These problems are too fundamental to be amended by local accommodations such as limiting the scope of the representational account or coupling semantic representations with other structures and computational components.

All this implies that semantic representations cannot be the basis for either cognitive activity or the modelling of mind. In addition to their not defining the basic mode of cognitive behaviour, they are primary neither procedurally nor developmentally and they do not constitute what is generally the case. As has been suggested throughout Part I and will be further argued below, rather than cognitive activity being the product of the processing of representations, the converse is the case: if representations can at all be said to exist, they are the product of cognitive activity.

Part II considers the implications of the critique in Part I. The first two chapters of Part II present a sketch of a non-representational picture of mind: Chapter 17 details the overall structural characteristics of the mind as conceived in this picture and Chapter 18 describes its dynamics. Focusing on the phenomenon of consciousness, Chapter 19 probes the functional basis of this picture. The following chapters examine more general theoretical issues and lay the foundations for non-representational psychology. Chapter 20 surveys various alternative, non-representational frameworks for psychology, and Chapter 21 examines the nature of psychological explanation; methodological issues are considered as well. In the light of the theoretical considerations, Chapter 22 discusses further aspects of the picture of mind suggested in the first three chapters of Part II. The Epilogue presents an appraisal of the entire enterprise to which this book has been devoted.

17 A picture of mind

> Let human action be like water that quietly seeks out all the crevices of life, but does it silently and effortlessly. If resistance is met, it is best to rest passively until it is exhausted and then go on one's way. In other words, he who is completely identified with the course of nature flows effortlessly with it, never fighting or resisting such infinite power but utilizing its strength for one's own fulfillment. As water finds its way, gently, effortlessly, yet touching all points, so does the superior man conduct himself.
>
> *A Taoist text*

Part I was presented as a critique, that is, as a primarily negative discussion. Yet, in marking the inadequacies of RCVM and its limitations I also touched upon the positive. Specifically, I defined some of the basic characteristics of the cognitive system and laid the foundations for an alternative, non-representational picture of mind.

I use the term 'picture' advisedly. What is to be presented here is neither a model of the cognitive system nor a full-fledged theory. Rather, it is an overall picture. I have surveyed many and varied phenomena and shown that RCVM has great difficulty in accounting for them. In some cases, I concede, one could devise a representational solution to the problems raised. Likewise, in isolation some of the conceptual arguments made in the course of my critique might not be logically or philosophically conclusive, and one might come up with sophisticated ways to circumvent the problems they present. Yet, taken in their totality the phenomena surveyed and the conceptual observations made clearly indicate that something is fundamentally wrong with the cognitive perspective of RCVM. Together, they strongly suggest that a radical change of perspective should be made. With this, many cognitive phenomena are seen in a new light and a new, overall picture emerges.

The picture of mind to be drawn in this chapter consists of three main components, each corresponding to one of the three lines of critique marshalled in Part I. The three will be presented in three sections: the first examines *the substrate of cognition*, that putative locus of cognitive activity which, by the epistemic rationale for the postulation of representations, serves as the repertory of human knowledge and thus makes behaviour possible. The second focuses on what seems to be the basic functionalistic feature of the cognitive system, namely, *action in the world*. The third presents an overall scheme of the *development* of cognition in time. As I shall show, while primarily corresponding to one of the three lines of the critique, each of the three components also bears on the other two.

Before I begin to draw my non-representational picture of mind, however, let me take a closer look at its skeleton – the seven factors on which the critique in Part I focused.

The non-semantic factors

Although conceptually independent, the three main lines of my present critique are similar in that they all underline the significance – indeed, the primacy – of factors ignored by RCVM. Seven such factors were noted: the *context* of cognitive activity and the *medium* in which it is expressed, the *body*, the external physical *world* and the *social other*, the non-cognitive faculties of *affect and motivation*, and *time*. On the one hand, each of these factors is associated with a characteristic excluded by the definitions of semantic representations in (**) of Chapter 1. On the other hand, each presents patterns of human behaviour that are ignored by RCVM and cannot be accounted for by representational models. Henceforth, these seven factors will be referred to as the *non-semantic, non-representational factors*, or *non-SR* for short.

The definition of at least some of these factors calls for further clarification. Following the order of the discussion in Part I, I shall begin with *context*. Remarkably, while the appreciation of contextual effects is, nowadays, standard, the notion of context itself is universally taken to be self-evident. Indeed, a perusal of the literature reveals that in almost all cases, this notion is not defined (for notable exceptions see Clark and Carlson, 1981; Rogoff, 1982; Sperber and Wilson, 1986). But then, what is context? How should it be defined and so characterized as to be incorporated within one's modelling of mind? What does it mean to say that 'the meaning of a word varies with context'? The following discussion will show that these all but ignored definitional questions have some far-reaching ramifications.

The standard definitions of the term 'context' in English dictionaries (this is true for both the Oxford and the Webster Collegiate dictionaries) have a linguistic orientation. Context is defined in terms of the linguistic units in conjunction with which words appear. Yet, for psychology the characterization of context in terms of words is too narrow. Psychological contexts are not merely words that surround other words.

A second option is to define context in terms of states of affairs in the world. By this definition, context is constituted of the states of affairs in which entities are found (incidentally, both the Oxford and the Webster dictionaries choose this as their second definition). For psychology this second definition is problematic as well. Again, the problem is that of the appropriateness of the domain of discourse: psychology is not exhausted by states of affairs in the external physical world. Moreover, the characterization of context in terms of such states leaves unexplained the relationship between cognitive agents and the contexts in which they operate.

The inadequacy of the second option directs one inwards and brings forth a third possible option for the definition of context, the representational one. By it, mental representations specify both the knowledge of cognitive agents and the contexts in which they live and act. This is the option chosen by the rare representationally minded cognitive scientists who address themselves to the definition of context. For instance, Sperber and Wilson (1986) define context as 'the set of premises used in interpreting an utterance' (p. 15).

The representational characterization of context will not work either. With it, all the problems of contextual variation noted in Chapter 2 pop up again, introduced through the back door, so to speak. In adopting the representational option, one attempts to salvage the representational characterization of single semantic items only to confront the impossible task of offering a representational characterization of entire contexts. Students of human behaviour who failed to account for language in representational terms now take it upon themselves to account for the description of all of reality in such terms. Of course, there is no reason to expect the latter task to be any easier than the former. The representational option, then, presents a Pandora's box of which the student of cognition should beware.

In sum, context can be defined neither in linguistic terms, nor in representational ones, nor should it be pushed out to the external world. This presents an impasse: context can be accounted for neither in terms pertaining to the internal domain (for then, the epistemic problems are exacerbated), nor in terms pertaining to the external domain (for then, it becomes cognitively unaccountable). This suggests that context should be defined in a terminology which, by its nature, is neither internal nor external but interactionalist – pertaining to the interface between the internal and the external worlds. Terminologies of such kind have been suggested by several non-orthodox, non-representational theoretical frameworks (see Gibson, 1979; Maturana and Varela, 1980; and Bickhard and Terveen, 1993; I shall return to them in Chapters 20 and 21).

A moment's reflection reveals that the logic of this argumentation is quite remarkable. I introduced the problem of context in the first line of this critique. This is in line with standard practice in the literature: context is normally associated with the epistemic aspects of cognition. The foregoing analysis reveals, however, that context and the problems it presents also pertain to the second, functionalist line of the critique. Context undermines the representational enterprise in that it marks the limitation of RCVM not only in characterizing the knowledge people have and the semantics of natural language, but also in accounting for the relationship between the mind and the world. Thus, distinct as the two lines of critique are from a conceptual point of view, in substance they are intertwined. The epistemic study of knowledge and behaviour cannot dissociate itself from the functionalist consideration of the relation of cognition to whatever surrounds it.

Essentially, *medium* is the matrix of the contingent particulars by which cognitive expressions are articulated. In Chapter 4 I focused primarily on the phonological or graphological medium of the words of language. But, as noted, contentual domains and cultural frameworks may be regarded as media as well. And, of course, so are the different modalities of the arts. Medium, however, does not appertain solely to language and the products of culture. As shown in the discussion of tying shoes in Chapter 11, tools and instruments also have a medium. Each tool, each instrument has its own constitution, its build, its shape, its texture. These all impose a particular way of handling, a particular manner of operation. In the most general fashion, then, medium is what gives things their concreteness, what makes them real.

One should, however, not be misled by the way things are expressed in language. It is not that there are cognitive expressions or performances and there are the media in which they are realized. As noted in Chapter 4, content and medium are intertwined and there is no sense in regarding them as two separate components. Furthermore, there is no sense in talking of cognitive expressions and performances without specifying the medium in which they are articulated. Unarticulated thoughts, words and deeds simply do not exist. When thought, word or deed do exist, they are realized in a medium which is part and parcel of their identity, just as any aspect of their content is. In line with this are the claims made by Kolers and Smythe (1984) on what they term 'personal symbols' (see Chapter 2): 'Personal symbols are not written on any "mind stuff" that permits their being examined independently of their being experienced' (p. 290). Incidentally, there is an affinity between the point made here and ones in Chapter 16. The postulation of a 'mind stuff' for cognition to take place in is another facet of the assumption of place. And like the postulation of absolute space, that of independent medium is not needed. Just as (by the theory of realitivity) matter and space are intertwined, so are cognitive expressions and their medium (as well as their context).

Since neither context nor medium is an entity or constituent having independent existence, they are not usually acknowledged outside theoretical psychological discussions. It is only when one is engaged in the study of mind that one appreciates that cognitive performance is affected by variations of context and is sensitive to the contingencies of medium. One inspects behaviour and concludes that the cognitive system is context-dependent and medium-sensitive. Thus, rather than being given, independent factors, the two mark, in effect, properties that the cognitive system exhibits. Not so the factors presented in the second line of this critique. The body, the world and the social other have independent existence of their own, all people have direct acquaintance with them, and acknowledgement of their existence and significance is not confined to the theoretical psychological realm. While not manifestly present in the external world, motivation and affect are also acknowledged pretheoretically and are directly known by all. For this reason, unlike context and medium the four factors noted do not call for further definition.

I will, however, clarify two of the factors – the world and the so-called non-cognitive faculties of mind. The *world* with which psychology is concerned is not one that exists prior to and independently of the behaving agent. Psychologically speaking there is no world but that in which cognitive agents live and act. As far as the cognitive system is concerned, the world is the totality of what it senses and perceives, the totality of what affects it and what it, in turn, affects. As indicated in both the first and second lines of the critique, the world in which agents live and act is not an agglomerate of senseless entities. Rather, it is invested with meaning. Indeed, it is the totality of meanings that the agent invests in it. These, in turn, come into being in the manifold of actions that the agent realizes in the world, and which the world, on its part, enables the agent to realize. Again, the verbal labels are misleading. As I have shown throughout the second line of this critique, perception and action are intertwined. One perceives the world in terms of the totality of actions one exercises in it, one acts in the world that one perceives (for further discussion, see Neisser, 1976). In the ecological-psychological literature, as well as in my discussion of the world in Chapter 8, the co-definition of cognition and world was basically related to perception and action. Sensory perception, however, is not the only filter that defines our world. We all see the world in terms of our past experience, our vested and momentary interests, our desires, wishes and expectations. As noted, the world is not confined to the physical realm of the natural world. In addition to physical objects it includes tools and artefacts.

Similarly, *volition* is not an independent module driving the self into action. There is no sense in separating the cognitive agent's wishes, motives and desires from the overall matrix of one's knowledge and belief. These all develop throughout the course of a lifetime. On the one hand, they reflect the experience individuals have accumulated. On the other hand, they determine how individuals see the world and what they take to be the knowledge they possess. In fact, it may be said that a person is, in effect, the sum total of all his or her desires, wishes and interests as well as the beliefs that these have generated and the experiences to which they have led.

Being more complicated than the others, the factor *time* and its definition were discussed at length in Chapter 12. Let me just repeat that psychological time is distinct from physical time. Like the world, psychological time is not an abstract, independently defined dimension, and like the world, it is invested with meaning. Psychological time, in other words, is not a receptacle in which events take place. To view time in this manner is, again, a symptom of the assumption of place. Like context and medium, psychological time cannot be separated from cognitive expression and activity.

Bearing these comments in mind, let me present my non-representational picture of mind. I shall return to the seven factors at the end of the presentation.

The substrate of cognition

The first component of the picture of mind to be drawn here is what may be referred to as the substrate of cognition. Before I proceed, however, let me forewarn the reader that the notion of substrate is not as simple as one might surmise, and that the ontological and epistemological status of a substrate of cognition is far from being clear. For the time being, however, I shall hold the question of status in abeyance. The focus of my discussion will be the specification of the structural and functional properties that the substrate of cognition should have, whatever this substrate may be.

Keeping apart the question of properties and constraints and the question of existence and status is in line with the cognitive-psychological nature of this discussion. The first question pertains to the psychological critique of RCVM, whereas the second takes one from the psychological critique to the philosophical critique. In addition, the two-tier strategy has a number of advantages relating to exposition and to the construction of the argument. First, the question of properties and constraints is easier than that of status. Whereas the first question relates to issues usually discussed in the cognitive literature, the second opens the door for new issues and new, and rather speculative, views of mind. Second, in the cognitive literature the assumption that an underlying substrate does exist is standard. In particular, it is shared by RCVM and connectionism, the most salient contemporary non-representational framework in the cognitive sciences. Thus, when tracing the first sketch of a non-representational view of mind it is convenient to adhere to the assumption of the substrate's existence. I shall show that the putative substrate's properties are diametrically opposed to those specified by RCVM. This in itself is enough to invalidate the representational framework. The subsequent examination of the existence question will present still another blow to RCVM. A third consideration that favours the two-tier strategy pertains to the issue of realization. Even when the properties and constraints are fixed, the substrate may be realized in several distinct ways. Thus, one may accept the properties and constraints being specified, yet not agree with the status being imposed on the substrate. This affords on the one hand a common ground for different non-representational views, and on the other hand room for divergence between them. Lastly, the present strategy is in line with the modes of thought imposed by language: it is difficult to talk about the properties of something without assuming that it exists. Let me, then, turn to the properties.

All three main lines of my critique entail specifications and constraints for the putative substrate of cognition. Although the discussion in Part I is critical, the negative can readily be turned into the positive. The different limitations and inadequacies of the representational substrate are symptomatic of the properties of the alternative non-representational substrate and define the conditions it should meet.

The first line of the critique entails constraints that should be imposed on the substrate for it to serve as the repertory of the knowledge that is manifested by people's behaviour and that presumably serves as the basis for their action in the world. I have noted that, *contra* RCVM, the substrate cannot be characterized in terms of any fixed, determinate, well-defined, well-structured, abstract symbolic code. By contrast, the following should hold:

1. The substrate should be maximally sensitive to contextual variations.
2. It should maintain medium distinctions in their raw form.
3. The sensitivity to both context and medium should not be constrained *a priori*, nor should its degree of resolution be fixed.

4. The substrate should manifest non-differentiation. On the one hand, it should not differentiate between well-defined, given constituents. On the other hand, it should impose no fixed, predetermined differentiation between content and medium.

The second line of the critique entails constraints on the substrate as the basis for the cognitive agent's activity in the world. The crucial role of the four factors considered in that line – the body, the physical world, the social other and the non-cognitive faculties – indicates the following:

5. The substrate cannot be autonomous in the manner that semantic representations are. It cannot be modelled by means of entities that ignore the body and are confined to the internal domain of the single individual. Nor can it be divorced from the agent's interests, wishes, desires and affective states. By contrast, it should afford a direct tie with the body, the physical and social worlds and the non-cognitive faculties of the psyche.

The consideration of time in the third line of the critique further indicates the following:

6. The substrate can be neither primarily static and inert nor ahistorical. Rather, it should be dynamic and reflect both the agent's past history and the future as he or she envisions it.
7. There should not be a clear-cut segregation between the substrate and whatever operations apply to it.

The profile defined by (1)–(7) fully contrasts with that of semantic representations as defined in (**). It indicates that the putative substrate of cognition defies any characterization by means of an abstract, well-defined and well-formed canonical code which is primarily static, and which is defined independently of the procedures that apply to it and of the actual realization of cognition in the world. Hence, semantic representations cannot serve as the substrate of cognition. Such representations do not define the general cognitive case, and are primary neither procedurally nor developmentally nor in an evolutionary sense.

But is a substrate not, by its very definition, representational? As characterized above, the substrate may be referred to as representational only in the weak naive sense. By no means is it representational in the strong technical-psychological sense, which is the object of the present critique and the topic of this discussion. As will become apparent, it is not representational in the epistemic sense either.

Action in the world

The second component of my picture of mind has to do with the mind's mode of operation. The discussion of this component relates primarily – but not exclusively – to the second, functionalist line of this critique. What is the basic ability of the mind? What is the cognitive system essentially designed to do? By RCVM, this basic ability is the manipulation of symbols. Since these are constituents of semantic representations, with the demise of these representations, symbol manipulation can no longer be held to be the basic activity of the mind. My alternative picture of mind grounds cognition in action in the world.

The characterization of action in the world as the basic capability of mind is twofold: it marks the primacy of action relative to pure cognition, and underlines the situated nature of cognition. Empirical data supporting this twofold characterization were presented throughout the second line of the critique. As argued, the primacy of action manifests itself phenomenologically, procedurally, developmentally and systemically. Taken together, these various manifestations suggest that the principles of operation underlying paradigmatic cognitive activities – language, memory, perception, reasoning and problem solving – are akin to those met in executing action in the external world – in moving about in the world, in the manipulation of objects, and in interaction with other human beings. Even when confined to the internal domain, cognitive activity may be carried out through the simulation of action in the theatre of one's mind. Furthermore, as will be further argued below, the development of the cognitive system and its evolution in time could not have been possible had this system not been grounded in action. As noted in Chapter 14, grounding cognition in action also results in a coherent overall picture both ontogenetically and phylogenetically.

The characterization of action in the world as the cognitive system's basic capability entails shifting the locus of cognition. At first glance it seems trite to say that cognition, like psychological processes in general, takes place in one's head. By RCVM, cognition is achieved by the manipulation of symbols in semantic representations, and these are, of course, internal. However, once action replaces symbol manipulation as the cognitive system's basic ability, the locus of cognition is shifted. While symbol manipulation is defined with respect to a space of internal mental representations, action is defined in the domain of the real, external world. As employed here, the last epithet is to be contrasted with 'internal'; it may refer either to the external domain proper or to the interface between it and the internal one.

My characterization of cognition as external is threefold. First, it pertains to *principles of functioning*. As argued throughout this discussion, the basic principles of cognitive activity are of the type governing action in the external world. Even when it is conducted in the internal province of the mind, cognitive activity is achieved through operations akin to those people employ in manifest action in the physical and social worlds.

Second, the characterization pertains to *realization*. Cognitive performance manifests built-in reliance on the external world. For cognitive activity to take place, the world has to be there. Not only do the body, the physical world and the social other facilitate cognitive performance and enhance both its quality and its flow, they are necessary for cognitive activity to take place and be realized. In other words, the cognitive system is constructed in a manner that presupposes the existence and availability of the world. Cognitive operations are to be executed in the world, to make use of its on-going contributions. Without the world's availability, these operations are not defined, the conditions for their application are not met, and the momentum necessary for their continued execution is lacking. This requirement is ingrained; it is part and parcel of the way the cognitive system is structured. The requirement manifests itself both in the workings of the mature adult mind and in the development of the child: without there being an external world in all its manifestations, cognitive activity cannot proceed and cognitive development cannot start.

Third, there are *theoretical* considerations. The characterization indicates that cognitive scientists searching for regularities in their domain of interest (and this is, after all, the goal of all science) should not confine their quest to the internal domain. Rather, they should look at the coupling of the internal and the external. It is only there that meaningful regularities are to be found.

Thus, cognition is both situated and realized in the world. In order to appreciate this better, let me refer to a case discussed in Chapter 11 – swimming. As pointed out, one cannot swim without being in water. No matter how well-coordinated one's hand and leg movements are, without water they do not constitute swimming. Moreover, not only does the moving of one's limbs (and even torso) in the air not constitute swimming, but it is difficult to carry out such movements out of water.

What is the water's contribution to swimming? First, the on-going, flexible interaction with the world frees the cognitive system from the need to specify fully all the information pertaining to the performance in question. In this context, the term 'information' is meant to encompass both the knowledge associated with the task at hand and the plan for its execution. The swimmer does not have a complete plan specifying every move about to be made, nor is he or she in possession of all there is to know about the given water environment and about swimming in it. Rather, the swimmer is in tune with the water. As the water conditions change, the swimmer's body posture and movement change as well. Thus, swimming in the water may be likened to flying on automatic pilot. Before starting, the swimmer has to make a number of decisions: which particular body of water to enter, where to go, which style of swimming to adopt, what basic speed and energy level to opt for. Then much of what one does is set, one has only to keep one's eyes open and watch for the unsolicited, never-ending fluctuations of the water. Indeed, it is precisely because so much is already set by one's being situated in the water that the accommodation is manageable.

The reliance on the environment is not only practical in that it reduces memory load, it is vital. Even if one's memory capacity were unlimited, the pertinent information could not be specified in full. This is, after all, the moral of the first, epistemic line of this critique. Like the bird mentioned in Chapter 11, the swimmer traverses a trajectory defined by equations he or she cannot formalize, let alone solve. As indicated by students of the ecological school, moving along the trajectory is an on-going, dynamic process in which, through continuous adjustment to changes in the environment, the swimmer (and behaving organisms in general) maintains a stable flow. This flow, mark, is not given as such, but constituted by the very encounter of the moving agent and the world.

Second, the encounter with the water lends the particular act of swimming its specific identity. Out of water, there is no swimming, and in each body of water swimming receives different course and shape, hence different identity.

The third contribution of the water pertains to the extension of action in time. Being situated in the same body of water makes the sequence of one's actions one single, continuous activity. Like the representational slices of time dismissed in Chapter 12, the isolated operations specified in strict computational terms cannot connect into the one, smooth unity that manifests itself phenomenologically. Situated actions like the swimmer's, however, can. The water is there, in place, and it serves as a glue – as that which makes the successive movements of torso and limbs one integrated act of swimming. But just as there is no sense in postulating atomic slices of time, so there is none in postulating atomic segments of action. Therefore, the glue has to be all-encompassing. In other words, action has to be continuously immersed in the world.

Admittedly, swimming is not the cognitive behaviour *par excellence*. Yet, this activity is, I find, illustrative: it concretely manifests what is, in essence, true of cognition in general. In order to perform, the cognitive system has to have a world at its disposal. Cognitive activity, by its very nature, is to be carried out in the world and unfold in it. Without the world, no cognitive activity is possible.

Context, medium and action

The example of swimming also highlights the role of both context and medium. Specifically, it indicates that action has to be immersed in context, and that for it to be realized it has to be carried out in a medium. The following comments tie together context and medium on the one hand, and action on the other.

In Part I, context was presented primarily as a 'negative' factor (i.e., one inducing effects that RCVM cannot handle). Yet, as pointed out towards the end of the discussion in Chapter 2, context-dependence is highly advantageous. Given that it is impossible to specify all the information about all the possible scenarios in the world, it is crucial to make use of as much help as one can get from the world *in situ* at the time of the execution of action. As pointed out in Chapter 2, if this were not the case, language would not be possible. Language is salvaged by being incomplete and not fully differentiated. As noted, the words of language are inherently polysemous and metaphorical. Hence, used in context, the word gains specific, differentiated meaning, and in different contexts the same word will have different meanings. The word is like a tool that on different occasions may be used in different ways. And as in the case of tools, the manner of employment is not fully specified (or even known) before the actual execution of tasks. Like the swimmer who relies on the water, the speaker of language (as well as its hearer) relies on the context. The reliance is so ingrained that one is usually not even aware of it. (Manifestly, most people are not aware of the metaphoricity and pervasive polysemy of words.)

Thus, the cognitive system's sensitivity to context is a reflection of its basic mode of operation. The cognitive system is sensitive to context not because context is something that it must be constantly concerned with, but because only in context does it exist. For action to gain its identity and be individuated, context is necessary, because the cognitive system is built precisely for that – to act in the world, that is, in a given context.

This brings us full circle. Above, I noted that the definition of context brings one from the first line to the second; here is a converse pattern – the consideration of action brings one back to the context. On the one hand, for it to be definable context demands that there be an interaction between agent and environment. On the other hand, for action to be realized there must be a context in which it takes place.

What, however, is the context of action in which cognition takes place? By now, the answer is clear. It is the world; or rather, the complex defined by the non-SR factors considered in the second line of the critique. Specifically, cognition takes place as the embodied mind encounters the physical and social worlds.

What I am suggesting is that the relationship between meaning and context is a specific, albeit central, manifestation of that between action and the world as defined above. As suggested by Searle (1983), action is embedded in a background, that is, the totality of all that the cognitive agent (implicitly) knows. My suggestion is that the world serves as such a background. As argued by Heidegger (1962) and other continental philosophers (see Chapter 2), throwness in the world is a necessary condition for both being and action.

Just as it requires context, so action requires a medium. In Part I, I signalled the significance of the medium in which cognition is articulated; now I can show why this is the case. The reason should, by now, be evident: it is the actional character of cognition. As I observed, action realizes itself in the concrete, and has no existence otherwise. Medium lends action, and with it cognition, its concreteness.

In Chapter 4, medium was primarily presented as comprising the non-semantic aspects of language. The discussion here suggests a generalized notion of medium. Just as language attains concreteness and is realized in phonology and syntax, so cognitive performance attains concreteness and is realized in the space spanned by the non-SR factors of body, world and social other. In particular, discourse is realized in the on-going encounter with other people; memory is to a great extent realized when one engages in an interaction with objects, be they physical or ideational; thinking and problem solving are realized as the embodied self interacts with both physical objects and other persons or, in their absence, with mental models and virtual others that serve as substitutes for them.

But remember, language is misleading. It is not that there are things and there are realizations that correspond to them. Just as there cannot be a natural language without a particular phonology (have you not at times wondered how funny each language really sounds and whether it would not be more natural to have languages without such funniness?), just as there cannot be a soul without a body and a person without a face (indeed, an individual without a particular personality), so there cannot be action – hence, cognition – without a medium.

I will mention here a notion that ties in strongly with concreteness – resistance. In general, it may be argued that only when they encounter some impedance do things gain an identity of their own. For it to conduce an electric current, a conductor has to have a certain resistance. Bearing in mind this physical fact, Freud argued that it is a person's resistance, his or her inflexibility and limitations, that make him or her have a personality (for discussion, see Erikson, 1969, in particular pp. 65–6). The moral of the present discussion is that this is true of cognitive performance in general.

Context and medium are related. Critically, both mark the extreme sensitivity of human cognition to variations that cannot be fixed by a determinate coding system. Positively, they are the determinants that render cognition and cognitive activity real. Context defines the setting of cognitive activity; medium defines the manner in which this activity is articulated. Together, the two define the domain in which cognitive activity takes place.

So far in this book, context and medium have been presented as two distinct factors, but, as suggested in the first line of this critique, there is no clear-cut demarcation between the two. Hence, context and medium may be taken together and characterized as the two determinants of the space of *context–medium*. This space defines the domain of the cognitive. Just as physical phenomena take place in a space of time and place, so psychological phenomena take place in a space of context and medium.

Time

Time encompasses all the other non-SR factors. Indeed, as pointed out throughout the third line of this critique, it permeates cognition and all cognitive activity is impregnated with it. It is not that there is a cognitive system, and the factor time is added to it so as to account for how the system changes and develops. Rather, dynamic change over time (as contrasted with fixed structures coupled with a repertory of computational operations) defines the cognitive system and underlies its mode of operation and all its accomplishments. As pointed out in the existential and phenomenological philosophies of Bergson, Heidegger, Sartre and Merleau-Ponty, without time, being would become meaningless and self-hood and individual identity would be inconceivable.

Time and temporality pose conceptual problems that the other non-SR factors do not. Indeed, figuring out the nature of time and temporality is a challenge that has preoccupied philosophers and scientists throughout history. This book will not solve these problems. Here I confine myself to defining the place of time in the picture of mind drawn here and marking its specifically cognitive contribution.

Just as the cognitive system is designed to act in the world, so it is designed to act in time. Cognitive activity unfolds in time. In other words, in order for it to gain realization, cognitive activity has to extend in time. I have shown this in the discussion of temporality and the compression of time in Chapter 12, where I pointed out the notable case of music: music has no existence but as it unfolds in time – as it is conceived, composed, written down, read and, of course, played or sung. But, note, this is just like a painting having no existence except on the canvas. And in general, an action not executed (or enacted in the theatre of one's mind) is not action. These analogies suggest that time is a factor completely analogous to the other non-SR ones I have considered: an external factor in which cognitive activity is realized. And like all other so-called external factors, it is part and parcel of cognitive being and action: the two are mutually defined and have no independent existence.

Learning and cognitive development

The grounding of cognition in time and the functional commonality between time and the other non-SR factors is most apparent in learning and cognitive development. Autonomous representational cognition inevitably drives one to the conclusion that learning is not possible. If the child is viewed as an isolated individual who has to acquire the knowledge of both language and the world all by him- or herself one is stuck. On the one hand, the child does not have the ability to generate the requisite knowledge all by him- or herself; on the other hand, teaching in the sense of the passing of explicit information from other people to the child does not take place (and, as I have noted in Chapters 9 and 14, cannot take place). Put together, these observations imply that learning is a mission impossible. But learning does take place. There must be a way out!

When one relinquishes RCVM, and with it the assumption of autonomous cognition, that way is found. An autonomous, purely representational system cannot bootstrap itself and acquire knowledge; it also leaves room for only one kind of teaching, the explicit transfer of information that – in fact – does not exist. A non-autonomous, non-representational system frees one from these constraints. The key feature of such a system is its relying on and making use of the various non-SR factors. The following comments explain why this is the case and how learning and cognitive development are achieved.

First, there must be a mechanism to ensure that learning takes place. In itself the nascent cognitive system lacks not only the ability but also the desire to acquire knowledge. The human infant does not (cannot) appreciate the worth of knowledge. There is no reason why the infant should have any wish to acquire either knowledge or language. In order to drive the infant into learning, it should be sneaked up on him or her unawares. Specifically, the infant should be lured into learning without being cognizant of it. This is achieved by the tying of the cognitive system, and the process of learning with it, on to other systems, ones which are either available to the child or in which there is already an interest, such as those associated with the non-SR factors. Even before the child begins to care about cognition and language, he or she cares about the well-being of the body, physical comfort, and intake of food. Later, the infant cares about the relationship with the mother, and subsequently with other human beings. Hence, a way to lure the child into learning is to ground cognitive development in factors such as body, other and affect and gradually separate cognitive performance from them. Throughout the second line of this critique I have shown that this is indeed the case.

Second, for learning to begin, some material to be worked with should already be present. In other words, cognitive behaviour should be produced even before from a strict cognitive point of view there is reason or sense for it. That something is produced is ensured in two ways: the grounding of cognition in non-SR factors in the manner noted above, and the independent generation of material which in itself is neither meaningful nor functional but which may eventually be invested with meaning and become functional. As noted throughout the second line of the critique, the importance of these two ways is especially marked in the ontogenesis of meaning.

Third, to drive the child's primordial actions into language and cognition, external guidance is required. This is achieved through the involvement of another person, usually the child's caretaker who must meet several requirements. First, the caretaker should possess the information that will eventually be acquired, notably language. Second, in line with the comments in the first paragraph above, the child should be tied to this caretaker. Third, the caretaker should have interest in investing energy in and guiding the child into knowledge. Both the child's tie to the adult, and the adult's bond to the child are ensured by non-SR factors: bodily contact, physical comfort and a host of affective and motivational considerations.

Fourth, for the cognitive system to bootstrap itself the caretaker should direct the child's behaviour into meaningful action (action that the caretaker finds meaningful and deems important and good for the child to perform), even before the child finds the action so, or is aware of its use. Indeed, the caretaker often does this without being fully aware of what he or she is doing. As noted in Chapter 9, human parents have a propensity to see more in their children's behaviour than is actually there. In particular, I observed that parents find meaning in utterances which are merely random products of the child's articulatory apparatus. Believing that the utterances are meaningful, parents do two things: shape the utterances into well-formed articulations in the language they speak, and adjust the utterance to the context of its use. Phonology and semantics converge and the child's utterance is turned into words employed in accordance with the practice of the linguistic community of which the child is becoming a member. Jewish mothers are especially notorious for holding the belief that *their* children are geniuses, but apparently this is a basic human bias, one without which learning could never get off the ground.

Fifth, some contribution from the child is also needed. First and foremost, the child has to have a propensity to learn, i.e., to be guided by another person and eventually to imitate that person, follow what is being done and even seek knowledge. As argued by Trevarthen (1980), infants do have this propensity. This may seem trivial, but a moment's reflection reveals that it is not. People (all people, I presume) have a tendency to believe that *they* know better than anyone else. As manifested by all sorts of behaviours, this seems to be no less true of the little child. Often, the child wants his or her way and insists on it. Yet, at the same time, the child admits in effect that the one who really knows is the adult. If this were not the case, the child could not take part in the learning process.

Sixth, there should be a mechanism of teaching that does not consist in the explicit transfer of information from adult to child. This is where the phenomenon of scaffolding discussed in Chapter 9 manifests itself. Scaffolding consists in the adult's meeting the child in the latter's zone of proximal development. The situation is completely analogous to that of the bridging discussed in Chapter 8. There is a certain cognitive path to be taken, which is too long for the child to traverse alone. With assistance, however, the child is capable of traversing part of it. The adult accompanies the child in his or her voyage. Next time, the child may rely less on the adult's help, and eventually will be able to traverse the path alone. Step by step the distance the child can go will be increased: the child's zone of proximal development will be extended. Eventually, the child will have reached the end of the path, and will no longer be in need of the adult's assistance.

Seventh, as indicated by the above, cognitive growth requires a mechanism of coupling and decoupling. Specifically, the cognitive system attaches itself to another factor or system, goes along a certain path with it, and then dissociates itself from it and stations itself in a place which it would not have been able to reach otherwise. The process of coupling and decoupling is, I find, extremely important and I will expand on it further in Chapter 18, when the dynamics of mind is discussed.

Eighth, learning and cognitive growth take time. This is not trivial. By RCVM, there is no reason for it to be the case. At most, there may be a moment of maturation in which the cognitive system passes from a state in which it cannot perform to one in which it can (see Fodor, 1981a). What should be appreciated is that the very processes underlying learning and cognitive growth require time. Indeed, were it not for this, the other non-SR factors could not offer the contributions specified in the seven previous paragraphs. The luring by the social other, scaffolding, coupling and decoupling are all based on mechanisms that have to unfold in time. All assume step-by-step operation: what cognitive agents may not do in one step, they may be able to do piecemeal, with assistance that they will then relinquish.

Lastly, the patterns noted are not confined to ontogenesis, but are also encountered in adult learning and in the evolution of culture. As noted in Chapter 9, guided participation underlies all teaching, and scaffolding plays an essential role in thinking, problem solving and creativity, both scientific and artistic. Furthermore, similar patterns are met in the moment-to-moment execution of action. Given the intrinsic dynamic nature of the cognitive system, and the lack of clear-cut distinction between action and development, present and past, present and future, this is only to be expected. Just as we rely on the non-SR factors as we grow and develop, so we rely on them as our actions unfold in time. Many examples were given throughout Part I; here let me refer back to one concerning memory. Strictly speaking, as experimental cognitive psychologists have demonstrated again and again, the capacity of human memory is limited. Yet, functionally, with the help of mnemonics, notes and all sorts of recorded material, our ability to refer to things past is practically unconstrained.

As revealed by this discussion, the different non-SR factors all contribute to development in the same manner: they are all external factors without which cognition cannot exist, unfold and grow. Further, they all work in concert, and in the execution of performance they are very much intertwined. Indeed, the joint interaction of the factors is so integrated that the separation between them is not always clear.

Thus, learning and cognitive growth are grounded in the non-SR factors. Some of these impose themselves (as parents sometimes do); some we seek (as we seek parents and peers); some we encounter by sheer accident and hopefully know how to turn them to our profit (many developments in cultural history happen in this way); some we create for ourselves (as in enactment; see Chapter 19). The inherent reliance on the non-SR factors once again reveals that cognition is neither autonomous nor internal. Nor is it pure. The cognitive system is not the elegant, formal-like, perhaps even atemporal system that some cognitive scientists have wished it to be.

This picture of learning and cognitive growth indicates that for cognition to develop and grow, noise is necessary. Being formalist and purist, RCVM does not allow for noise. By contrast, in connectionist models noise is a cardinal factor. Indeed, it is the very factor that enables connectionist networks to achieve learning without explicit instruction (see Rumelhart, Hinton, McClelland, 1986; Rumelhart, Hinton and Williams, 1986; Amit, 1989); this, note, is one of the most significant accomplishments of the connectionist framework.

Highlighting the functional role of noise reflects a recent general development in different quarters – both in the informational and in the natural sciences. In particular, noise is central in the study of self-organizing systems (see, for instance, von Foerster, 1966), in the new paradigm of chaos research (see Mandelbrot, 1977; Gleick, 1988), and in various models in theoretical biology (see, for instance, Jerne, 1974; Edelman, 1987) and notably, in neurophysiological models of brain function (see, for instance, Skarda and Freeman, 1987; Goldberg *et al.*, 1990; Freeman, 1991). By way of example, let me refer to the biologist-philosopher Atlan and his book *Entre le Cristal et la Fumée* (1979; see also Atlan, 1987). As the title indicates, Atlan notes that life navigates between crystal and smoke. The former manifests maximal order, the latter minimal order – and both are dead. Life – and with it creative evolution – requires some, but not too much, noise and disorder. Noise is crucial for evolution, both biological and cognitive, but for it to be constructive its presence has to be limited: too much noise brings about destabilization and the system's behaviour gets out of control; too little noise does not allow the freedom that is essential for the novel and the unexpected. In the cognitive system noise is manifested in the non-uniformity of expressions, in lack of well-definedness and well-formedness, in the crucial contribution of randomness, in non-autonomy, and in the defiance of formal purism; more on this will be said in Chapter 19.

Further comments on the analogy between the cognitive picture drawn here and biological evolution are in place. The significance of random noise in the generation of new cognitive material and in pushing cognitive performance forwards is, of course, reminiscent of the Darwinian mechanism of mutation. Likewise, the guidance of behaviour by an external agent, its shaping and its investment with meaning are all reminiscent of the selection of mutations by the environment. When I was about to complete this chapter I stumbled by chance on an issue of *Scientific American* (Cairns-Smith, 1985) in which a model of the origin of living molecules was presented. What characterizes living molecules is their being joined together in a highly ordered structure. This structure is essential for them to have the qualities of life, and in particular replication. How, however, did such structure originate? Since the topic of analysis is the very first living molecules, this cannot be explained by any biological mechanism. Some non-biological factors must be introduced. Cairns-Smith suggests that the ordering of the molecules was a result of their sticking to another entity, one which is highly structured but not biological. He proposes that crystals of clay served this function. Remarkably, by way of clarifying his point Cairns-Smith refers to the notion of scaffolding which is so much used in the psychological literature and to which I have repeatedly referred here. He notes that one cannot construct an arch piecemeal: one cannot place one stone after the other – all have to be put up together. This is achieved by scaffolding: a curved wooden structure on which the stones are placed. Once they are there, the wooden structure is taken out, and because of the order between them, the stones remain in place as an arch.

The main topic of this discussion has been learning and the factors and patterns governing the process of cognitive growth. However, the discussion also marks the basic characteristics of the course of development. Specifically, taking a global, integrative perspective, we mark that development may be characterized in terms of two principal lines of progression. The first is that of *decontextualization and autonomy*. Development progresses from total immersion in the given context and dependence on it towards greater ability to divorce oneself from the context and gain relative freedom from it. One's behaviour gains more and more autonomy from non-cognitive factors: the body, the external world, the social other, motivation nd affect. At the early stages of development, the child is immersed in the world and his or her performance is tied to these non-cognitive factors and is dependent on them. As the child grows up he or she gradually depends less on these factors. Specifically, behaviour is less tied to sensory-motor activity, less dependent on assistance provided by other people, and more dissociated from bodily needs, desires and affective states. More on autonomy and dissociation will be said in Chapter 18.

The second main line of development is of *differentiation and solidification*: from that which is undifferentiated to that which is differentiated. This progression leads towards internal structuring: from that which is ill-defined to that which is articulated. It results in a fixation of meaning: from the multi-faceted, which is multi-determined and condenses different (yet undifferentiated) levels of meaning (including aspects of the medium) to the univocal and fixed.

These two lines of development cohere into one picture. They both indicate that the patterns of behaviour and cognitive accomplishments best characterized by representations and the computational operations associated with them are encountered in the later stages of ontogenesis. Representations, in other words, are not the basic cognitive state but rather the products of cognitive growth. The various sequential orders surveyed in Chapter 14 corroborate this.

Back to the substrate

Let me return to the substrate. I still have to consider the question of existence and status. Is a substrate needed at all, and if it is, in what sense? With this, I move from the psychological critique of RCVM as a theoretical framework in contemporary cognitive science to a philosophical critique of the notion of mental (as distinct from semantic) representation.

The question of existence hinges on two properties specifying the status of the putative substrate: that of being an *underlying* structure, and that of pertaining to the *internal*, properly cognitive, domain. The two are so fundamental that it is only too easy to take them for granted. *Prima facie*, it seems that it is practically a matter of definition to view the substrate of cognition as an underlying structure pertaining to a covert psychological level of which behaviour is a manifest, overt expression. This view is reflected not only in the strong cognitive-technical sense of representation, but also in the weaker senses associated with the naive and epistemic rationales. Indeed, it is shared by RCVM and connectionism. The two paradigms differ in the particular properties they attribute to the substrate: by RCVM, it has the properties specified in (**) of Chapter 1, whereas connectionism by and large attributes to it those presented in the characterization above. With respect to the two properties indicated here, however, there is no difference between the two paradigms: both postulate the substrate as the underlying level in which knowledge is stored and cognitive activity takes place.

But, in fact, the substrate of cognition manifests neither of the two properties just indicated. The following discussion defends this claim, and proposes an alternative notion of substrate. (The word 'substrate' is probably not the best with which to refer to the discussion's topic, but I use it for lack of any other.) By this alternative notion, the substrate is the set of conditions necessary for cognitive activity to take place. Defined as such, the substrate need not be an underlying structure nor an internal one; indeed, it does not have to be a well-defined structure at all.

What, then, does the substrate of cognition consist in? Being constituted by the meeting of the internal and the external, it encompasses cognitive agents' bodies, the physical and social environment in which they are situated and act, and all that may be regarded as constituting their personalities, knowledge and beliefs, desires and wants, past and future. The reader should not be misled by the reference to the constituents of the substrate as if they were separate, distinct entities. This reference reflects the structure and limitations of natural language. The substrate, however, is one. The different constituents that compose it are like the different coordinates of a space. Specifying the coordinates is necessary to define the space; yet, it is clear that the coordinates have no existence without the space.

This characterization suggests that the substrate is a sort of background like that proposed by Searle (1983) (see above). Searle is a philosopher, hence not much bothered by psychological specifications. Had he been pressed he would, I suspect, define his background in a manner that makes it quite like the substrate of connectionist models (see Searle, 1990a). I give Searle the benefit of the doubt, however, and leave the door open for his background to be regarded as a substrate albeit not an underlying structure. Yet, whatever the specifics of its psychological realization, the place of Searle's background is inside, in the head. The only item in the literature where I have actually encountered a similar notion of background is an unpublished doctoral thesis by Agre (1988). If I understand him correctly, Agre's background consists of the real world situation in which one acts. My notion of background may be regarded as bringing together Searle's notion and that of Agre (who does not mention the former in his work).

There is, however, another way to view the non-internal substrate. This is in line with the analogy between psychology and physics drawn in conjunction with the assumption of place in Chapter 16. In the classical Newtonian world-view, space was conceived as an absolute entity, independent of the bodies situated in it and their interactions. By contrast, Einstein's general theory of relativity proposes a relational view of space according to which space and objects are intertwined. Indeed, space is defined by the totality of objects and forces in it. Analogously, it may be suggested that the substrate of cognition is the totality of past and present interactions of the behaving organism and the environment. (For a development of this topic as well as a conceptual analysis of the nature of such cross-disciplinary analogies, see Shanon, 1991e.)

As for the second property of the substrate, its being internal, my stance is clear: that the substrate of cognition is not internal is a direct corollary of the claims made above in conjunction with the locus of cognition.

Lastly, it should be emphasized that the substrate is intrinsically dynamic. Life and the environment are in constant flux. Cognition, which brings the two together, cannot be otherwise. Indeed, both the external and the internal worlds change. The cognitive world is not confined to the present moment; it includes one's past (I do not even want to say memory of the past) and one's future (one's expectations, one's dreams). As I have shown in Chapter 12, there is no clear-cut distinction between memory and perception, and one's present behaviour cannot have sense without taking into consideration one's future. Hence, time, with the world, serves as a context: the environment of the now serves as a context in which the environment of the next moment takes place.

In closing the discussion of the substrate, let me consider it in the light of the different senses of representation introduced at the outset of this book. My present characterization of the substrate meets the requirements underlying the postulation of representations in both the epistemic and functionalist senses. This is, of course, without a commitment to representations in any stronger sense, and in particular, to semantic representations in the technical-psychological sense.

Consider the epistemic requirements. These dictate that the substrate of cognition should characterize the knowledge requisite for behaviour. Can this knowledge be external? Of course, it can. As noted throughout the foregoing presentation, the meaning of words is determined by the situation, not by a given, internal repertory of semantic knowledge; similar observations were made on knowledge of the world in general.

That the substrate as defined here meets the functionalist requirements is evident: action in the world and the interaction between mind and other systems are the basis upon which my entire picture of mind is built.

Back to the seven factors

As indicated at the beginning of this chapter, the seven non-SR factors comprise three clusters. First, there are context and medium, which define the structural characteristics of the cognitive system. These factors pertain to theory: they specify the basic characteristics the cognitive system exhibits. Next are three factors of which the world is constituted – body, world and other – as well as the so-called non-cognitive faculties. These define the milieu in which cognition is realized. Unlike context and medium, they are not theoretically defined: they are the constituents of the empirical reality in which the human cognitive system comes into being and operates. Last but not least, there is time.

The factors in each of the first two clusters are interrelated. That context and medium are related has been pointed out throughout this discussion. The two define the tangible reality in which cognition comes into being: context defines those aspects of it afforded by the environment in which the organism lives, medium those afforded by the available channels of expression. Paradigmatically, context has to do with the contents of expressions whereas medium pertains to their sensory-like aspects. There are, however, cases in which the distinction between the two is not clear-cut. I have shown this in Chapter 4 for content effects. Because these pertain to the particular mode in which information is presented or articulated, they are attributed to the medium. Yet, as indicated by their very name, they also pertain to content.

As repeatedly marked throughout Part I, body, world and social other are highly interrelated, and indeed, may be regarded as three facets of one unified whole. As in Part I, let me start with the body. That the body is tied to the world is evident: it is my having a material body that makes my existence one which is in the world. Without a body I could not relate to the world, nor could I act in or on it. As repeatedly argued by Merleau-Ponty (1962), the body presents a union of the subject and the world. It defines the milieu of one's habitation in the world and constitutes the measure of the world for one. As further pointed out by Merleau-Ponty, and in consonance with the insights of the adherents of ecological psychology, it is in the meeting of the body with the world that the latter gains its phenomenological existence, and it is by reference to the body that the world, despite all the changes and transpositions in it, maintains its constancy.

Relationships analogous to those between the body and the world hold between the body and the other. Through my body I know not only the physical world but also the social other. It is *qua* bodily entity that the other is presented to me, and it is by virtue of the other's having a body that I appreciate him or her as a subject. Furthermore, much of my interaction with the other is through the mutual engagements of our two bodies. Apparently, it is because of this that sex is so important in human life. In the sexual encounter body and other intertwine and practically converge into one.

Whereas the relationships between body and world and between body and other are ones of constitutive encounter, that between the world and the other is one of homology. The physical world and the social other are the two constituents of a totality that is the phenomenological world in which we live.

Together, body, world and other thus present one unified complex. What behaving agents have first and foremost is a body. It is by virtue of having a body that the self, as a psychological being, exists at all. The embodied self encounters a phenomenological world constituted by the physical and the social worlds. It is in this encounter that the self is defined. Furthermore, it is in the encounter of the embodied self with the physical and the social worlds that the arena of behaviour is formed. In essence, behaviour consists of acting in the world realized through the mutual encounter of body, world and other. Each particular instantiation of these encounters may be referred to as a *situation*, hence behaviour may be regarded – as has been suggested in other contemporary investigations (notably, Suchman, 1987; see Chapter 8) – as situated action, or more accurately as embodied situated action.

And what about the non-cognitive faculties? I have not referred to them because they are somewhat apart. Whereas body, world and other pertain to the external world in which one acts, affect and motivation pertain to the internal domain. Drawing to the end of the presentation, let me note that a relationship between the former and the latter none the less exists.

Admittedly, this relationship is speculative. I have spoken of embodied mind meeting the world outside; the body also meets the internal world. As noted in Chapter 10, affect and body are tightly linked; so are desires and the basic needs and interests of living beings. Above, I suggested that, *inter alia*, the self is constituted by the history of one's wishes and wants. Thus, I might speak of the self being constituted by the meeting of the internal and the external. The internal consists of the entire history that individuals carry along; the external is defined by the world – both physical and social – in which individuals find themselves. The two, the internal and the external, are realized by the body.

Turning to time, I underline the fact that cognition is intrinsically temporal. Everything one says about the cognitive has to include reference to time. This is especially true of all the factors I have considered. Throughout the foregoing discussion I have often talked about the various factors as if they were fixed entities. Again, this is due to the object-orientation imposed by natural language. One should always keep in mind that all the factors are in constant flux. As indicated in my analysis of swimming, cognitive agents actively contribute to this being the case: acting, they effect change, and with this the environment in which they live changes as well. I referred above to the situation as the basic frame of the context of action; it would be more accurate to characterize this frame as a situated *event*.

Not only are the non-SR factors not fixed, they are also not given. As noted at the beginning of this chapter, it is crucial to bear in mind that it is not that there are non-SR factors and there is a cognitive system that relies on them; rather, the non-SR factors are defined in terms of cognitive activity. I have shown this to be the case for each of the seven non-SR factors.

Since each of the three clusters has a distinct status of its own, they can be imposed upon each other. First, the complex defined by the factors of the second cluster is imposed upon the first so as to define the concrete realization of the system whose structural characteristics that first cluster specifies. Second, time envelops the two other clusters, thus marking the dynamic characters of all the factors. Everything I have said can be summarized in one sentence: human behaviour is rooted in *action* which is realized in a *medium* constituted in a *context* traced in the space of *time–world*.

18 *The representational and the presentational*

European man can't growl at Abo
Abo can't growl at the European
Because both might be good men
Both might be no good

Bill Nerdjie

The developmental patterns noted in Chapter 17 mark a contrast between two types of behavioural pattern, ones in which the relevance of the non-SR factors is marked and ones in which it is diminished. As I have shown, the main trend exhibited by cognitive development is a progression from the former to the latter. As further noted throughout Part I, and in particular in Chapter 14, the contrast between the two types of pattern is not confined to ontogenesis. It is encountered in different adult cognitive performances, contexts of performance, stages of the execution of cognitive tasks and aspects of cultural expression. In this chapter these two types will be characterized as two poles that define the phenomenology of human psychology and its dynamics.

I should emphasize that what is to be presented here is not a model specifying mental mechanisms and procedures. Rather, it is an overall sketch of the dynamics of mind specifying what the cognitive system described in Chapter 17 can actually do. This specification may be likened to those supplied with electrical appliances: these detail what a stereo system or a microwave oven can do and how one should operate it, not what their electronic structure is and how they work.

Crystallization

Before turning to the dynamics of mind I would like to single out a feature to which I shall refer as *crystallization*. This consists of the cognitive system's generation of concrete, articulated expressions. The term is meant to specify an operational feature, not a procedural sequence; it may also refer to the products of crystallization. The words I utter are an instance of such crystallization, and so is every concrete manifestation of behaviour that I perform. Articulated expressions need not, however, be publicly manifest in the external world. Thought sequences are non-overt crystallizations; the same applies to mental images, memories and dreams.

The notion of crystallization is reminiscent of ideas presented in connectionism, where the neural-like networks give rise to manifest expressions of behaviour. Yet, as noted in Chapter 17, in the connectionist picture of mind the substrate is an underlying structure. To appreciate that crystallization is possible without the generating substrate being thus, let me use an analogy. When rice is boiled and the water evaporates, ordered hexagonal holes are formed in the rice mass. Usually, the holes are identical in size and shape and their distribution across the surface is even. The rice is the substrate and the holes are the generated expressions: the rice is necessary for the holes to form, the holes can be generated only out of the rice, yet the rice is not an underlying structure.

An analogy which is perhaps even more pertinent is a state of affairs conceived by Stanislaw Lem, the science-fiction writer, in his novel *Solaris* (Lem, 1978). In this novel, a heavenly body which consists of a mass of heavy, viscous liquid is described. Occasionally (and in particular, in resonance to impinging stimulation), concrete entities (e.g. a house, a human being) are formed out of the liquid. This heavenly body is actually a cognitive agent, and the generated entities its thoughts.

For obvious reasons, crystallization may be thought of most readily with respect to an internal (most probably underlying) substrate. What is, however, remarkable is that it applies equally to the external world. Thus, consider perception. Immersed in the world, I see a scene. In itself, the scene is not made up of meaningful objects. It is in my act of seeing that the meaningful objects are generated. In other words, it may be said that it is in my act of seeing that the substrate constituted by the coupling of the mind and the world crystallizes into objects.

Likewise for the temporal dimension: as noted in Chapter 12, cognitive agents live and act in a background constituted of both their past and their future. The past is receding, the future is approaching. In between is the present, which has neither well-demarcated boundaries, nor any predetermined magnitude. The present is as much of time as I can crystallize. There are various such crystallizations. My present 'now' encompasses the sentence that I see emerging, amber on black, on the CRT screen. But, with the application of some extra psychological effort, it may extend to encompass everything I have written so far in this section, or perhaps in this chapter. When one is deeply involved in an issue, subject matter or task, the scope of one's present may be greatly extended. When about to deliver a lecture, I have the entire lecture in my grasp even though delivering it may take twenty or fifty minutes. Mozart is said to have been able to apprehend an entire symphony in what for him constituted one unit of time (see Einstein, 1946; Merleau-Ponty, 1964). Lastly, the past can be crystallized too. This is what happens when we remember, when we re-present past experiences in our minds.

Henceforth, expressions generated out of the substrate will be referred to as *presentations*. Like the patterns of behaviour mentioned at the beginning of this chapter, presentations, the cognitive expressions into which the substrate crystallizes, may be of two types. Some exhibit a profile of characteristics like that listed in (**) of Chapter 1. Specifically, they are composed of well-defined elements joined together in accordance with rules of well-formedness, the medium of their articulation may be of no relevance, and both their constituents and the dimensions upon which they are defined may be distinct and well differentiated. These expressions will be referred to as *representational*. Other expressions exhibit the opposite profile: they are not composed of well-defined elements, they blur the distinction between content and medium, they are not amenable to a clear-cut differentiation of dimensions. Following Langer (1942), I will refer to these as *presentational*.

The reader will have noticed the use of the adjectival forms 'representational' and 'presentational'. This choice of linguistic form is of paramount importance. In the literature the adjectival form completely corresponds, of course, to the nominal, and the two go hand in hand. 'Representations' are postulated as psychological entities characterized by a certain profile of properties. These properties, as well as any pattern that relates or pertains to representations, are referred to – with no more ado – as 'representational'. Here, a distinction between the nominal and the adjectival forms is proposed. The nominal form refers to entities – be they real or virtual, observable or hypothetical. By contrast, the adjectival form defines a cluster or a profile of properties. Naturally, the features of the entities called representations are those constituting the representational cluster. However, the entities (expressions, patterns) called presentations may have either a presentational or a representational profile (or, as I shall show below, an intermediate one). Thus, the term 'presentation' is employed here in two senses: as a generic term referring to the products of crystallization, and as one of two subsets of this term (that exhibiting 'presentational', as contrasted to 'representational', features). Linguistically, such usage is standard: as a rule, unmarked scalar terms refer both to the scale in its entirety and to its unmarked section. (Note: a young child may be asked how old he is, and even a short object has a certain length.)

Compared to the nominal terms, the adjectival have several advantages. First, unlike the nominal, they do not carry the implication of thing-hood or commit one to any view on underlying representations. Second, the attribution of these terms need not be confined to entities; it can also be applied to patterns of behaviour, processes, modes of interpretation. Third, the adjectival terms need not be confined to the internal domain. For instance, they can apply to entities pertaining to Popper's World Three – ideas and the products of culture (see Chapter 8). They can also be used to characterize different literary genres, modes of discourse, artistic styles and the like. Fourth, they may even apply to concrete entities in the world and their manner of use. This may be true both of tools and instruments and of artefacts and constructions. For instance, a mosaic may be regarded as more representational (in our sense) than a water colour (see Richards, 1936). Fifth, whereas the classification of entities as representations and non-representations is all or none, the attributions representational and non-representational are graded. This allows for a whole range of profiles: between the extreme representational and the extreme presentational, there may be an array of intermediate profiles exhibiting some representational characteristics (or some aspects or degrees thereof) and some presentational ones. Sixth, unlike the nominal classification, the adjectival attribution is not absolute but may be context-dependent. In particular, the same entity, expression or pattern may be regarded or addressed in one situation as representational and in another as presentational.

The dynamics of mind

Together, the representational and the presentational define two poles that span the universe of cognitive activity. Structurally, cognitive expressions are character-ized by different profiles along the representational–presentational continuum. At the two extremes are profiles exhibiting either all or none of the properties specified in (**). In between are profiles exhibiting some of these properties to different degrees. This variation is, of course, a source of great cognitive richness. Another is the fact that both the type of expression and the mode of interpretation can independently vary along the presentational–representational continuum. By way of marking the orthogonality of these variations, let me consider the four possible cases defined by the coupling of expression type and the way in which it is interpreted. These define paradigmatic extremes; between them a whole array of graded variations may be encountered.

The first case is that in which a representational expression is interpreted in a representational manner.[1] This case is encountered when one starts from well-structured expressions and subjects them to computational operations, thereby generating other well-structured expressions. Paradigmatic examples are logical deduction, syntactic operations, and the various types of formal reasoning employed in well-defined, well-circumscribed domains of discourse. Second is the represen-tational intepretation of presentational expressions, as in art criticism. The critic attempts to articulate, structure and differentiate what the artist has expressed in a presentational form. The third, converse case, in which representational expressions are interpreted in a presentational manner, is encountered in the practice of clinical psychologists who (with the so-called third ear, see Reik, 1948) attempt to listen not to the manifest content of what their clients say but to the meaning behind it. Rather than focus on the semantic aspects of utterances, clinicians pay attention to the meeting of content and medium and to the global, undifferentiated characteristics of the discourse. Finally, the presentational interpretation or elaboration of presentational material is encountered in the spontaneous, sequential development of mentation, expression and action. Such sequences are encountered in gestures and bodily movement, in improvised, unrehearsed singing, in dreams and fantasies, and in some aspects of narrative discourse and non-directed thinking. Given that this last, presentational-presentational case has not received much attention in the literature, I will consider some examples in further detail.

In addition to demonstrating the orthogonality of the presentational and the representational, the four cases also mark the broad scope of cognitive expression and processing. RCVM channels the focus of cognitive interest and confines it to the first, representational-representational type. This, however, defines a specific psychological profile, one out of many other possible ones. A psychological paradigm that from the start centres on only one profile certainly ignores much of cognitive phenomenology and thus misses much of the richness of human cognition. Directing cognitive scientists' attention to the other possible profiles is bound to expand and enrich the scope of psychological research.

These variations along the representational–presentational continuum are structural: they mark the plurality of types and pairings of cognitive expressions. Variation is also noted dynamically. Indeed, all human cognitive life may be regarded as an on-going interplay between the representational and the presentational. This interplay is observed on all temporal scales: ontogenetic development, the acquisition of skills, the moment-to-moment minutiae of performance, and the evolution of culture. Following are comments on the first two topics; the other two are discussed in separate sections below.

Child development

Observations on child development were made in Chapters 14 and 17. In the main, the data surveyed reveal that ontogenesis progresses from the presentational to the representational. Thus, consider language. As noted, the early phases of language are couched in the context of children's acting in the world. With the acquisition of verbal skills, children gain more and more autonomy from this context. Pragmatically, language use is decontextualized and the meaning of words and utterances gains fixedness. Semantically, children's use of words becomes more and more literal. Formally, their verbal output becomes increasingly rule-governed. Indeed, at times they overgeneralize the rules and apply them in all cases (Brown, 1973; Marcus *et al.*, 1992). Mature command of language requires further growth and development.

Expertise and skill

Adults learn and acquire new knowledge too. The progressions encountered in the development of expertise and the mastery of skills are especially illustrative. In the early stages one's performance depends on the particulars of the medium in which it is executed, and it is tied to specific contexts of use. With time, the performance crystallizes and solidifies so that one gains independence from the particularities of medium and context. Thus, consider a man learning how to drive a car. At the beginning he is at the complete mercy of the specific machine that is thrust upon him and any perturbation in the trajectory may lead him astray. With practice, things become familiar, the learner has a battery of rules at his disposal, and maintains control over the progression of the car. Similarly, the novice violin player may be able to produce a reasonable sound only with the one particular instrument she is familiar with; she will also be bound to the same string and fingering patterns. She might even be at ease playing only in one setting; say, in the privacy of her own room with the score placed on the stand in a particular manner. With time, these dependencies disappear and she may produce the same musical material in different settings, with different instruments and even in various manners and modes of interpretation. With the development of the skill, performers, be they drivers or players, thus gain autonomy *vis-à-vis* the context of activity and the particular medium of its execution. With this, the performance becomes less presentational and more representational.

But now, consider experts; for instance, the accomplished player of a musical instrument. What distinguishes such a player is the ability to be fully in tune with the medium and to exploit maximally the possibilities presented by the instrument. Eventually, the attunement is such that every single distinction counts. Indeed, an accomplished player gains such control over body and instrument that the two are fused into one. On the one hand, it may be said that the virtuoso plays not only with her hands, but with her torso and abdomen as well. On the other hand, the instrument may be seen as an extension of her body. Just as one's eye, face and hand manifest ones's entire personality, so does – in the hands of the virtuoso – the instrument (for pertinent data on the link between body and musical instrument, see Clynes, 1978).

Interesting observations consonant with this picture were made by the pianist Alfred Brendel (1976):

Those who look for contradictions will be amply satisfied. The profession of a performer is full of paradoxes, and he has to learn to live with them. He has to forget himself and control himself; he has to observe the composer's wishes to the letter and create the music on the spot; he has to be part of the music market and yet retain his integrity. . . .

[The pianist] should not have to struggle with the instrument, or impose his will tyrannically upon it, any more than the instrument should turn into a fetish, an object of idolization that dominates him. On the contrary, the player should make friends with the piano and assure himself of its services – especially when Pianism with a capital P is to be transcended. He should give the instrument its due by showing how capable it is of transforming itself. . . .

The characteristics of a concert hall – its greater or lesser resonance, brightness, clarity, and spaciousness of sound – are reflected in the player's technical approach and have an influence on his sense of well-being. . . . In the concert hall, each motionless listener is part of the performance. The concentration of the player charges the electric tension in the auditorium and returns to him magnified; thus the audience makes its contribution, helping the pianist to cope with his instrument. (pp. 129–39)

Sensitivity is noted not only to the body and to the instrument, but also to other non-SR factors – the physical setting and the presence of other people. Of utmost importance is the comment Brendel makes in the first paragraph cited here: masterful playing brings together what may seem to be opposites. As he notes, the virtuoso is on the one hand at one with the world, and on the other has full control over it. He plays everything that is specified by the score, yet transcends the score, in that in the playing any infinitesimal variation counts; therefore, the playing can be fixed by no score. The virtuoso is at the same time perfectly representational and fully presentational.

This characterization is by no means specific to music. Here, for instance, are observations made by another master, Suzuki, in his introduction to *Zen in the Art of Archery* by Herrigel (Suzuki, 1985); as befitting a Zen master, Suzuki's commentary extends beyond the specific domain of archery:

> If one really wishes to be master of an art, technical knowledge of it is not enough. One has to transcend technique so that the art becomes an 'artless art' growing out of the Unconscious. . . .
>
> In the case of archery, the hitter and the hit are no longer two opposing objects, but are one reality. The archer ceases to be conscious of himself as the one who is hitting the bull's-eye which confronts him. This state of unconsciousness is realized only when, completely empty and rid of the self, he becomes one with the perfecting of his technical skill. . . .
>
> Man is a thinking reed but his great works are done when he is not calculating and thinking. 'Childlikeness' has to be restored after long years of training in the art of self-forgetfulness. When this is attained, man thinks yet he does not think. He thinks like the showers coming down from the sky; he thinks like the waves rolling on the ocean; he thinks like the stars illuminating the nightly heavens; he thinks like the green foliage shooting forth in the relaxing spring breeze. (pp. 5–7)

And then, consider the domain with which I started the discussion of child development above – language. In a sense, linguistic development does not end with speakers gaining what is usually considered to be the normal level of verbal behaviour. Whereas adult speakers of language exhibit full mastery of language, writers proceed further. Not only do they play the instrument of language masterfully but at times they breach the linguistic frontiers and create new forms of expression. It is instructive to contrast creative writers with children. Children's verbal behaviour exhibits idiosyncrasies because they have not yet mastered the tool; creative writers exhibit personal signatures of style because they have the tool fully at their command. Normal adults are between the two: not as creative as writers, yet often more creative than they may suspect (for corroborative data, see Chapters 3 and 5).

General considerations

In sum, this discussion suggests a *spiral* progression. Learning usually consists of a progression from the presentational to the representational. Like the early stages in ontogenesis, those of performance are characterized by a presentational mode of operation. Acquisition of skill brings one to a stage in which one's behaviour may be described by a representational-like system. Mastered performance brings one back again from the representational to the presentational.

Yet, of course, the novice and the expert are not the same. The progression from the representational to the presentational does not bring one back to where one started. In the early presentational stage the context is external and domineering; in the late presentational stage the context has been internalized so that performers become one with their tool or instrument. Likewise, in the early stage the tie with the medium is one of dependence whereas in the later stage it is one of mastery.[2] For congruent empirical data and a modelling of the acquisition of skill, see Dreyfus and Dreyfus (1986).

Lastly, let me make a comment on teaching. This discussion has focused on the performing cognitive agent, who acquires a skill and gains expertise. Analogous patterns are observed, however, in good teaching, which presents a rich interplay between the presentational and the representational. For example, inspecting video recordings of master classes at the Jerusalem Music Center, I observed that two types of instruction were given. On the one hand, there were technical specifications: play rubato, save the bow, employ this kind of fingering. On the other hand, figurative language was employed: you play too beautifully, play red, or − 'pam, pam, rim, pam, pam', sing like a king. Remarkably, the instructions of the second type were the most effective. The master and the student had never met before the lesson; yet, when the latter was told to play red, he changed the manner of his playing, and the master was manifestly satisfied.

The basic capabilities of mind

Having drawn a non-representational picture of mind and having traced the basic courses of its dynamics, let me return to RCVM. How does the picture presented here compare with the representational one? To answer this question, let me examine what RCVM and my view take the basic cognitive capabilities to be. These define what might be regarded as the axioms of the two systems; they are introduced as (***') and (***''), respectively.

> (***') 1. The ability to refer by symbols.
> 2. The ability to manipulate these symbols by means of computational operations.

Even before turning to the alternative, I should note that as defined by (***'), RCVM is actually empty-handed. The moral of the critique in Part I was that the

representational framework is lacking with respect to both components of (***').
As indicated by the second line of the critique, the ability to refer is presupposed
in representational modelling, but it is left completely unaccounted for. Indeed, as
noted in Chapter 6, this basic capability is treated as nothing less than a miracle.
As for the second capability specified in (***'), the thrust of the present critique is
that symbol manipulation cannot offer a full, adequate account of the accomplishments of the cognitive system.

The discussion here and in Chapter 17 suggests the following alternative basic
capabilities of mind:

> (***") 1. The ability to act in the world.
> 2. The ability to crystallize cognitive activity into manifest
>   expressions.

The contrast between these two sets is critical in evaluating RCVM and the
alternative picture of mind I propose. The following comparison shows that the
system defined by (***") is advantageous. To appreciate this let me consider the
two capabilities specified in (***").

The first capability is more basic, and more general, than either of the two
specified in (***'). Whereas action cannot be accounted for in terms of the
representational model, the converse may be the case: both reference and symbol
manipulation may be couched in action (for a survey of empirical data showing how
this happens in ontogenesis, see Bates, 1987). Further, as noted in Part I,
conceptually, phenomenologically and developmentally action is more basic than
the manipulation of symbols. Even if it does not exist today, a theory of action is
bound to be an indispensable part of a general psychological theory. Such a theory
is needed anyway, even if the capabilities specified in (***') are taken as basic.
Hence, RCVM is manifestly non-parsimonious.

The key term of the second tenet of (***"), crystallization, marks the ability of
the substrate to concretize itself in tangible behavioural expressions. These include
the various manifestations of verbal discourse, thoughts one consciously entertains
in one's head, gestures of the face and the body, and motor performances in general.
As has been noted, some of the expressions generated from the cognitive substrate
may very well be of the representational type, and may exhibit – fully or partially –
the cluster of properties typically associated with semantic representations. The
important thing to notice is that once again system (***") affords more generality
than system (***'). The latter requires that all cognitive entities be of one type, the
representational; the former denies the basic role of representations, but leaves
room for both representational and non-representational expressions and modes
of behaviour.

A particularly noteworthy feature of (***") is that it allows for recursion.
Specifically, the first capability it specifies may be applied to the products of the
second so as to offer the basis for further cognitive activity. This is the case because
the generation of articulated, well-defined representational expressions is
tantamount to the creation of objects in the mind. With this, a context of action is

created in which one can act, just as one acts with objects in the world outside. I shall return to this in Chapter 19.

The characterization of both tenets of (***") in terms of object manipulation marks still another advantage of this system. This characterization ties the two capabilities of (***") together and presents them as the two manifestations of one and the same fundamental capability. On the one hand, the mind's basic ability is to act with objects, and on the other hand, the mind can itself create objects that may be the subject of further cognitive activity.

Functional considerations

Obviously, the two modes of behaviour, the presentational and the representational, have their own advantages. Each suits different sets of situations, interests and goals. The key feature that distinguishes the two is *autonomy*. The representational mode is used in situations in which autonomy is desired: in which cognitive agents wish to divorce themselves from the influences of the context, to be oblivious to the medium, to be shielded from past memories, concerns, and affective and other associations, and to distance themselves from the matrix of being and acting in the world. Deductive reasoning, hypothetical thinking, and some kinds of problem solving and planning are tasks favoured by such autonomy. Other tasks do not require autonomy and may even be hindered by it. In these, the tie to the body and the environment is important and one does not wish to ignore one's affective attitudes and responses. Such tasks call for the presentational mode of operation, which is employed in close inter-personal interaction, in situations in which affect is important, in the execution of skilled motor performances, and in conjunction with those ill-comprehended achievements generally attributed to instinct and intuition.

Two manifestations of autonomy should be highlighted. The first is that *vis-à-vis* other cognitive material. In principle, everything pertaining to the repertory of one's knowledge is connected to everything else. Marking this state of affairs, Fodor (1983) likens the mind to a (totally disorganized) Sears catalogue. This, incidentally, leads him to conclude that a scientific study of cognition is not feasible (see Chapter 16). Interconnectivity throughout the cognitive system is also assumed in connectionist models. Despite its principled interconnectivity, however, the cognitive system affords local dissociation. Cognitive connections may be severed and the free flow of cognitive activity blocked. With this are generated patterns of central modularity (Shanon, 1988c, 1993a), which shelter cognitive material from the bulk of what the cognitive agent knows and believes. This may be advantageous in problem solving, in considering hypothetical scenarios, and in conflicts of interests or values. Prejudice is another manifestation of central modularity.

The second manifestation of autonomy to be noted concerns time: cognitive agents are able to gain relative autonomy with respect to time. When tied to and dependent on the given context of action, one is totally submerged in the present.

When one gains relative autonomy from the given context, one can extend one's temporal reaches and engage in cognitive activity that is not confined to the boundaries of the immediate present. On the one hand, one can bring to mind memories of the past. On the other hand, one can speculate on states of affairs in the future as well as entertain scenarios which are utterly hypothetical.

These comments mark a contrast, but the optimal behaviour is of course an integrated one, in which both options – the representational and the presentational – are kept ever open. That this should be the case has been noted by many wise people. Aristotle recommended the middle way as the golden path, and the marriage of opposites runs as a main theme throughout the wisdom of the East. For instance:

> If you would have a thing shrink,
> You must first stretch it;
> If you would have a thing weakened,
> You must first strengthen it;
> If you would have a thing laid aside,
> You must first set it up;
> If you would take from a thing,
> You must first give to it. (Lao Tzu, 1963, p. 95)

The two cultures

The representational and the presentational are not only two modes of cognitive activity, they are also two modes of being in the world, viewing it, interacting with it, and attaining understanding of it. Thus, the representational and the presentational span not only the psychology of individual cognitive agents but also human culture and its various manifestations.

Our Western culture is fundamentally representational. First and foremost, it is to a great extent language-oriented. Specifically, it sees the world through the spectacles of natural language and regards formal logic as the paragon of analysis. Bergson (1944; see also Lahav, 1990) labelled representational-based thinking 'intellect' and contrasted it with 'intuition'. Dewey (1929) labelled it 'intellectualism':

> Intellectualism . . . is the theory that all experiencing is a mode of knowing, and that all subject-matter, all nature is, in principle, to be reduced and transformed till it is defined in terms identical with the characteristics presented to refined objects of science as such. (p. 21)

If the psychological hallmark of the representational is autonomy, its cultural hallmark is objectivity. As a world-view (not a paradigm in psychology), representationalism assumes that in order to understand one has to detach oneself from the world. The world is taken to be a totality of facts, that is, naked, objective data. These are amenable to analysis and understanding by anyone with the requisite knowledge and means. Explanation consists of the analysis of these data in terms of a fixed, determinate vocabulary of well-defined terms. If correct, the analysis has an absolute, universal validity that does not depend on the identity of the analyser or the context of the analysis.

The adoption of the representational world-view is not a mere theoretical matter; it also has important practical implications. One of the main reasons for which human beings strive to understand is to gain mastery of the world. The representational way to do this is to detach oneself from the world and to conquer it, as if it were a wild animal, a *terra incognita*. This enterprise has been, of course, a monumental success story. Western civilization and its technology have drastically reduced human beings' dependence on the physical environment and enabled them to live under various adverse conditions in which they could not have survived otherwise.

In general, art tends to be presentational. Yet, even works of art in Western culture manifest representational characteristics. In the visual arts this is noted in representational (in the standard sense) perspectival painting. As extentively argued by Romanyshyn (1989) (see Chapter 16), representational perspective induced an alienation between people and nature, and thereby opened the door for the development of science.

The presentational way is diametrically opposite. It regards the world not as a conglomerate of things out there, but as a matrix of meanings which cannot be separated from the beings who live in the world or from their interactions with it. To gain understanding, presentationalists strive to be at one with the world. Instead of adopting one fixed attitudinal mode in which to inspect and analyse the world, they strive to remain maximally free and flexible so as to increase their sensitivity and openness to the undifferentiated plurality of meanings in the world.

Like representationalists, presentationalists also strive to gain control of nature, but in a radically different way: becoming friends with it, becoming one with it; some might say – making love with it (see Roszak, 1972; Bird-David, 1992).[3] The traveller and writer Chatwin (1990) reports an explanation given to him by a North American Indian woman. She noted that in the old days navigators had a song for each journey: on the way out they would sing it from beginning to end, and on the way back they would sing it in reverse. A related contrast between two modes of navigation as they reflect two fundamentally different ways of interacting with the world was mentioned in Chapter 8. A contrast I find most instructive is that between modern architecture and folk architecture, the so-called 'architecture without architects' (Rudofsky, 1965). Compare a twentieth-century building of the international style to a traditional Mediterranean farm. The former could be placed anywhere, the latter is genuinely local; while the former resists the environment, the latter is part and parcel of it.

It is fashionable to contrast Western culture with Eastern, notably Chinese culture. But there are many other presentational cultures. My own first contact with them was in Australia. Although superficial, my exposure to aboriginal culture had great impact on me. In fact, it was one of the triggers of this entire critique of RCVM.

For the native Australian, places are not coordinates in a meaningless, abstract space, but rather the prints of events that took place in the dream-world, the golden era of days past. Aborigines find their way in the world not by means of an 'objective' map, but by retracing the stories of mountains, of rivers, of stones (see Isaacs, 1980; Chatwin, 1987). Especially remarkable are the Indians of the Amazonian rainforest, who have devised efficient medicinal preparations without knowledge of any 'scientific' chemistry. Their feats are, in fact, nothing less than extraordinary: on the one hand the multitude of plants in the forest is immense, on the other hand the combination of ingredients and the modes of their preparation are very specific. It is too simplistic to attribute these discoveries to mere trial and error. As noted by Davis (1991), trial and error may well account for certain steps in the discovery process, but essentially, 'it is but an euphemism distinguishing the fact that we actually have very little idea of how Indian people come up with their insights' (p. 352). I would say that the process has to be explained in non-representational terms. Instead of logical analysis, these discoveries involved cognitive capacities of the type that enables people to know and understand other people, to decipher the expressions of their faces and bodies, to feel empathy for them.

The contrast between the two lines of cultural expression is, of course, an extensive topic, one which cannot be developed further here. For pertinent discussions, see Shweder (1991) and Wagner (1986). Here let me just note that the contrast pertains to extreme poles. In reality, representational and presentational aspects are to be found, albeit in different dosages, in different cultures and in different expressions and products of the same culture. For instance, it may be argued that European art oscillates between classicism and romanticism, the former being more representational (in the technical sense specified here) than the latter (see Woelfflin, 1950; and the discussion in Shanon and Atlan, 1990).

Complementarity relations

Drawing to the end of the discussion, let me consider the relationship between the representational and the presentational from a broader, and admittedly speculative, perspective. The two poles of cognitive expression and activity seem to mark dualities and complementarity relationships of the kind encountered in physics and defined by Heisenberg's uncertainty principle. Heisenberg pointed out that one can study elementary particles only by using light. Light, however, interacts with the particles in question, affecting the physical state of affairs being measured. As a consequence, a limit is imposed on the accuracy of physical measurements. The more accurate is the measurement of one parameter (e.g. position), the less accurate will be the measurement of another, complementary parameter (e.g. momentum). It seems to me that the situation in cognition is similar: one can study the structures of mind only by subjecting them to activity which, in turn, affects them. Likewise, a series of cognitive complementarity relationships may be defined. Most of these have already been introduced in previous chapters; they are listed here again for the sake of completeness.

A word of caution before I proceed: drawing cross-disciplinary analogies is fraught with problems. In particular, one should be extremely careful not to draw unwarranted causal, ontological or metaphysical conclusions from such analogies. It should be pointed out, however, that regardless of the status and source of the analogies, the relationships to be noted are of genuine, intrinsic cognitive interest: they highlight both the state of affairs conducive to the postulation of representations and the considerations that make it dispensable. For further discussion, see Shanon (1991e).

First is the relationship between *representation and history*. As pointed out in Chapter 12, adopting a representational perspective limits one's appreciation of the historical dimension of cognition; conversely, the more a cognitive agent's history is known, the less need there is to specify representational structures and attribute them to this agent. In the extreme, when agents' full history is taken into account, all information about them is implied, hence no representational structure need be postulated (as noted, this argument is based on one presented by Shaw and Todd, 1980).

A related relationship is that between *knowledge and learning*. As noted in Chapter 14, the representational perspective regards knowledge, hence representation, as basic, and learning as secondary. There, a call for an alternative dynamic view was made in which learning, and dynamics in general, are taken as basic. In this view, which is endorsed by connectionism, cognition is regarded not as a succession of fixed, stationary representational states, but rather as a continuous dynamics in which learning is an on-going process governing cognitive activity. The more weight is given to learning, the less need there is to define knowledge in terms of representations; at the limit, the cognitive system may be defined solely in terms of the dynamics of learning. In this case, the seemingly static representations are viewed as abstract, idealized projections of the on-going flux in frozen moments of time.

The relationship between *representation and perception* was noted in conjunction with Gibson's theory of perception. In the representational framework, perception is characterized in terms of the fixation of input from the external world in mediating mental representations. By contrast, Gibson's ecological psychology places the information pertaining to perception out there in the world. In this theory, the objects of perception are not sense-data, but patterns invested with meanings defined in terms of the interaction of the perceiver with the environment. At the limit, perception is direct, without need for any mediating mental representation.

Analogous to the relationship between representation and perception is that between *representation and memory*. As noted in Chapter 12, the standard, representational view is to regard memory as the storehouse of representations, and recollection as the retrieval of cognitive material from this storehouse. An alternative view is to regard memory not as a representation of the past but as a re-presentation in the present. In this view, memory is not the retrieval of stored information, but rather the ability of the cognitive system to re-place itself in states it occupied in the past. Thus, the more dynamic one's account of memory, the less one has to resort to representational structures. Again, at the limit such structures need not be postulated at all, and one may talk of memory which is direct (for such proposals, see references cited in Chapter 15).

Notes

1. Remember, in this context, representational expressions are not underlying representations; rather, they are presentations with a representational profile.
2. This characterization is, of course, schematized. Real mastery requires a constant interplay between the representational and the presentational. Furthermore, the description was taken from the long-term, overall perspective; the finer details of execution reveal similar interactions between the presentational and the representational.
3. The analogy with the patterns noted above in conjunction with skills is evident; indeed, the two are manifestations of the same basic state of affairs.

19 Why (re)presentations?

How can I tell what I think until I hear myself speak?
C. S. Peirce

The sketch of the dynamics of mind drawn in Chapter 18 centred on the phenomenon of crystallization. Experientially, crystallization manifests itself in people's being conscious of cognitive material passing through their minds. Why is it so? Why, in other words, are there in our minds cognitive entities of which we are aware? This question is twofold: it examines the functional role of crystallization and of the presentations it produces, and it probes into the phenomenon of consciousness to explore its possible cognitive advantages. Following are several answers to this twofold question. These will lead to a more general discussion of the mind and its mode of operation.

Consciousness

Only when it is articulated in a particular medium can cognitive material be consciously experienced. Having a medium, the thoughts one entertains in one's mind become akin to objects in the real world, which are never abstract: a stone has this shape and not another, a hammer has a particular form and weight inducing a particular, optimal mode of handling and use. The same holds true of our bodies, of every expression of our behaviour, of the people we encounter in the course of our lives, and, in fact, of every actual situation in the world – they are all characterized by contingent particulars.

Since, in the picture of mind I advocate, the cognitive system's basic capability is to act in the world, the significance of cognitive material being akin to the concrete entities of the external world is obvious. The role of crystallization (and of the ensuing phenomenon of consciousness), I venture, is to create objects for interaction in the province of the cognitive agent's internal world. This is most advantageous, for such objects are not always available in the real world outside.

Having stated the basic reason for the crystallization of cognitive material, let me consider various manifestations of it. Three clusters of phenomena will be noted. The first pertains to features of the medium, the second to action in the world, and the third to flux and fixedness; as will be apparent, the three are interrelated.

The medium

For something to be amenable to consciousness, it has to be articulated in a particular medium. Lending medium to cognitive material is, I think, the key functional role of consciousness.

A priori, it should seem utterly reasonable for thought to be conducted without any medium. There are two states of affairs in which this could be the case. The first is that advocated by RCVM, in which thoughts are conducted in abstract, formally defined syntactic structures. I have argued at length against this. The second is one in which thoughts are conducted exclusively in terms of the contents being entertained. After all, is the function of thinking not to entertain contents? Indeed it is, yet, it appears that in the conduct of human thought not only content but also medium is pertinent. The inspection of empirical data (the corpus of thought sequences) reveals that this state of affairs has great functional advantage. Were thought conducted without a medium and governed only by considerations of content, cognitive agents could think only of what they wish to think of, and would be confined to their already established repertories of knowledge and belief. Following is a survey of patterns and phenomena in which this is manifested.

First, the articulation in a particular medium gives cognitive material *rawness*, namely, a richness of non-fixed, sensory-like characteristics which allows flexibility of use and of interpretation. With thing-hood, rawness is the hallmark of real objects in the world. As pointed out in Chapter 5, the objects we encounter in the world are not tagged with features; if they were, we could perceive them only in a fixed, universal manner. This is manifestly not the case: objects can be perceived and states of affairs interpreted in an unlimited number of ways. The articulation of thought in medium – hence, consciousness – ensures that mentation has this flexible openness as well.

This brings us to the second, and most important, contribution of medium - the generation of *novelty*. The articulation of thought in a specific medium and the introduction of aspects which, from the perspective of content, are irrelevant can introduce new elements that can lead one's train of thought in new directions. Thus, recall the sequences considered in Chapter 4:

1. 0. (reading) 'Let us begin with . . . '.
    1. begin is like Begin (the Israeli prime minister at the time).

2. 0. A girl calls a frisky dog 'Doni'.
    1. He is really frisky.
    2. She should have called him 'Shedoni'.
    3. Or for short, 'shed' (in Hebrew, devil).
    4. That has a meaning in English too, 'shed'.

In these sequences, thought progresses by virtue of a commonality in phonological or graphological form, which from a semantic or contentual point of view is meaningless. This commonality is, of course, accidental; yet, without it, the sequences could not have progressed in this manner, and the unplanned, unsolicited turns they introduce would not have taken place.

Evidently, the medium of language is usually semantically irrelevant. It becomes relevant by what may be regarded as a local coupling and decoupling of medium and content. Usually, medium and content are tied together; decoupling lends the medium local independence from content. When the medium is again coupled with content, cognizers may find themselves entertaining new contents.

Incidentally, the patterns noted also shed new light on the classic question regarding the dependence of thought on language. Does the language one speaks make one think in a particular fashion? Sapir and Whorf (Whorf, 1956) answered this question in the affirmative and advocated a linguistic relativism whereby language imposes a particular *Weltanschauung* on its speakers. Patterns like those surveyed above suggest an intermediate state of affairs for they indicate that the medium of language provides, in addition to content, other, non-semantic avenues that may be employed in the course of thinking. Rather than enslaving thought and moulding it in a specific, rigid fashion, language enriches human cognition. In this, polyglots may be likened to an orchestra with many different instruments: music may be played with only one instrument (the piano, say), but the orchestra enriches the performance and provides new possibilities.

As indicated in Chapter 4, medium is not confined to the domain of language. Analogous progressions and interplay between medium and content are also encountered in mental imagery, jokes and dreams. In another investigation (Shanon, 1989d), I have studied on-going sequences of mental images. Unlike the thought sequences discussed above, these were not spontaneous but triggered. Subjects were asked to close their eyes and picture in their mind a particular object or situation which the experimenter specified, then report the ensuing mental images as they progressed. The sequences reported revealed that the progression of images was directed not only by the subject matter being entertained but also by specific, contingent properties of the particular images pictured. For instance, the shape or colour of an image might bring to mind the image of an entity or event sharing that shape or colour, but pertaining to a totally unrelated subject domain.

The importance of the medium is paramount in the arts. As noted in Chapter 4, in the arts the distinction between content and medium is often blurred or even obliterated. In works of art there is no sense in distinguishing between the what and the how, between the content and the mode of presentation, between the representational and the presentational. In normal cognitive life every distinction may become relevant: it is a potentiality that is there in principle but does not always materialize. In works of art the potential is always an actualized reality: every distinction always counts. More on this will be said below.

Third, the medium effects noted above may be viewed as instantiations of a very general phenomenon, one not at all specific to cognition or psychology - the generation of novelty from redundancy and noise, and of order from disorder. As noted in Chapter 17, a system which is optimally ordered does not leave any room for movement, hence it affords no option for unplanned change. Redundancy and noise afford precisely this. In the case of verbal mentation, noise is instantiated by the medium. From a strict semantic point of view, the medium variations of language are not informative. Precisely for this reason, the medium affords new avenues for thought and eventually an arena for the creation of novelty. In other words, because it seems devoid of informational import the medium is not committing, and consequently it affords fluidity. Yet, recourse to the medium should be constrained, otherwise mentation risks getting out of control. This is what happens to the schizophrenic person (see Arieti, 1974).

In closing this section, let me note that medium-based patterns like those surveyed above are also encountered in artistic creation. Consider music. In music the analogue of content is melody, and that of progression by means of content is progression along the different harmonic degrees in the given key. However, at times musical progression is governed not by melody but rather by modulations, or modulated passages. Particularly relevant are enharmonic modulations, in which the melodic line shifts from one key to another by mediation of a chord that may receive one harmonic interpretation in one scale and a different one in another. Often, the move is made via several other chords close to that in question (i.e., differing from it in one semi-tone with respect to one of the notes of which the chord is composed); in this case the enharmonic modulation is coupled with a chromatic modulation. In both cases, the modulation may be characterized as a change in musical content produced by locally stripping one constituent of its interpretation and subsequently investing it with another. With this, novelty in the musical progression is achieved. In Western classical music, this type of move is especially prevalent in nineteenth-century romanticism.

Likewise in the visual arts: the study of painters mentioned in Chapter 8 revealed that on many occasions variations not pertaining to the content of the drawing were taken up by the artist and opened new avenues for the further progression of the drawing. Thus, analogous to the medium effects noted here are cases in which an unplanned variation in the manner of holding the drawing material or in the texture of the line generated a new distinction that was subsequently taken as a significant constituent of the drawing. Similarly, lines accidentally produced by a slip of the hand could be reinterpreted and incorporated within new graphic elements (hence, meaningful 'lexical items') in the drawing. For an especially interesting documentation of creative drawing, see the film *Le Mystère Picasso* by Clouzot, in which Picasso was filmed as he was engaged in unplanned, improvised painting. On many occasions the progression of Picasso's work was directed by the mediation of medium effects of the kind noted here.

Action in the world

The second cluster of patterns pertains to action in the world. Articulated, crystallized, conscious thought creates a world within a world. Phenomenologically, consciousness presents us with experiences akin to those we encounter in the external environment. Discursive thoughts that run through our minds are akin to the words we utter aloud, mental images and dreams are akin to the views we have around us when we walk about in the world, and at times, material entertained in the mind is akin to our interactions with other people (cf. example (2) in Chapter 8). Thus, consciousness consists in the creation of world-like scenarios in the theatre of one's mind.

The world within affords mental behaviour akin to activities we conduct both when manipulating objects and when interacting with other people. In the context of thought sequences, this is noted by the phenomenon of *enactment* introduced in Chapter 8. In enactment thought expressions are not taken as ideas that one entertains but rather are conferred with an assumed reality, thus defining an inner world that is locally endowed with a separate existence. As suggested in Chapter 8, the phenomenon of enactment may be viewed as the cognitive analogue of the linguistic performative. Traditionally, language is regarded as the expression of ideas one entertains in one's mind. This view was criticized by Wittgenstein (1953), who suggested that, rather than being the expression of ideas, meaning consists in the use of language as a tool. Subsequently, Austin (1962) suggested that language enables people 'to do things with words'. Linguistic expressions serving this function are referred to as 'performatives'. Analogously, in enactment one does not entertain ideas in one's mind; rather, one acts. Consciousness, then, allows one to do things with thoughts.

Another type of action in thought is *Gedankenexperimenten*, in which one creates entities in one's mind and manipulates them to examine hypothetical states of affairs. *Gedankenexperimenten* enable one to consider, in a pseudo-concrete fashion, various scenarios that might take place, though it is clear that they are not real. Such a manner of thinking is advantageous because it is on the one hand concrete, and on the other hand more readily realizable than the manipulation of real states of affairs. After all, the latter is not always possible and is usually more costly – and at times, risky – than the former.

Related to the patterns noted above is the phenomenon of *scaffolding* examined in the discussion of both the physical world and the social other. I noted there that objects, instruments and tools on the one hand, and other people on the other hand, serve as indispensable stepping-stones without which the cognitive agent may not be able to perform. As further noted in Chapter 14, this is crucial in development.

I also noted that people often generate their own scaffolding. As indicated in Chapter 8, when solving an arithmetical problem one traces on the paper numbers that enable one to proceed in the calculation. Similarly, when solving a geometrical problem one progresses through an on-going interaction with marks one jots down on the paper. It is only rarely that problems are solved in one go: usually, one's performance is piecemeal. One starts with something one knows, with a local move that is relatively simple and clear, and one traces a line on the paper. Having done so, the cognitive environment changes: the distance between oneself and the end state diminishes, even if only to a small extent. At this point, one may trace another line. The lines put on the paper successively create new cognitive environments, and eventually the problem whose solution was so far away at the outset will be solved. As indicated before, this process is especially important in creative work. In Chapter 8 pertinent examples were noted in both writing and painting.

I am suggesting here that consciousness offers self-scaffolding. The world within a world that consciousness creates presents the cognitive system with scaffolding even when the conditions for it are not present in the real world outside.[1]

Thing-hood

As pointed out in both the third line of this critique and Chapters 17 and 18, the basic cognitive state is one of dynamic flux. Yet, at times it is advantageous to hold the on-going motion, to stop time, so to speak. This is afforded by another ramification of crystallization and the articulation of mentation in a concrete medium, namely, thing-hood.

Thing-hood is advantageous in several respects, the first of which is its affording *control* over the progress of thought. Thought not amenable to conscious inspection runs the risk of running astray, losing purpose and direction. But is it not the case that much of human cognitive activity is carried out unconsciously? Is this not the main lesson of the most important paradigm of contemporary experimental cognitive psychology – that of reaction-time measurement? Theoretically, there are indeed functional advantages in agents' not being conscious of all the cognitive activities taking place in their cognitive systems. Agents may be viewed as masters, and the cognitive machinery as their servants: the masters are interested in getting things done, but do not wish to be bothered by the particulars of how they are accomplished. On this rationale, thinkers would be expected to be aware of the beginnings and ends of trains of thought, but not of their intermediate steps. Consequently, one would expect conscious thoughts to open with the definitions of problems, puzzles or concerns and terminate with solutions, resolutions, dissolutions, commands or dead ends. As detailed elsewhere (Shanon, 1989a), empirically this is not the case: people are conscious of cognitive material that has none of these functional roles. To appreciate the usefulness of cognitive material being (at least intermittently) amenable to consciousness, let me return to the allegory of the master and the servant: a totally uninvolved master, always aloof and not at all concerned with the way things are being executed, is surely not the best of administrators. Being conscious of intermediate stages in thinking affords feedback and allows one to monitor the progression of cognitive activity, to direct and perhaps redirect it. For specific examples, see Shanon (1989b).

Second, thing-hood lends thought material *distinctness* and relative *stability*. On the one hand, it shelters specific thought material from the general on-going activity of the cognitive system. On the other hand, it lends a degree of permanence to privileged cognitive material. This allows extended manipulation, as if it were placed on a workbench. Moreover, one can hold this material in abeyance: examine it, leave it, and come back to it.

The third functional advantage of thing-hood is *compartmentalization*. Articulated mentation is sequential: it runs along a single track, in a homogeneous fashion. In all likelihood unconscious thought processes are not conducted in such a manner. As suggested by connectionism, cognitive processing is achieved by means of the parallel activation of a large associative network. There are good reasons to believe that the brain operates in a similar fashion as well (for further, functional argumentation, see Baars, 1983). Parallel associative networks, however, raise problems of control. Given the size of the cognitive network and its speed of processing, the cognitive system may run on its own without much functional gain. However, between single-track, linear thought on the one hand, and unconstrained parallel processing on the other, an intermediate situation is possible, namely, local compartmentalization. Articulated in a medium and concretized, thought can be managed. It is no longer a neural-like activity running its own course, but rather an activity akin to the manipulation of objects in the real world. The image that comes to mind is that of a factory in which several production lines are employed: the manufactured products are placed on these lines and various tools are brought and applied to them there. The analogous cognitive pattern is channelling (Shanon, 1988b). Conducting thought along more than one channel allows the cognitive agent to consider more than one expression at the same time, to treat different cognitive expressions differentially, to focus on privileged information, and to move back and forth between different objects of mentation (for examples, see Shanon, 1993b). A particular case of compartmentalization is that between thought and meta-thought. The articulation of thoughts in words renders them into entities which one can inspect and scrutinize. The crystallization of thought in a medium, then, allows for *meta-observation* and *reflection*, a crucial feature of human cognition.

Fourth, objects may have properties that their constituents do not have. For instance, bricks are made of sand, but only with bricks, not heaps of sand, can one build; and only on pillars, not on scattered stones, can one place beams so as to construct bridges. Likewise in mentation: when solving a problem one does not wish to go back to first principles, but takes some cognitive material as given, and proceeds from that. The crystallization of thought in object-like entities is an important factor making this possible. (For independent discussions leading to similar conclusions, see Hofstadter, 1979; Kugler and Shaw, in press.)

At first glance, these comments on thing-hood seem to contradict the third line of the present critique, where the cognitive system was characterized as intrinsically dynamic. The contrast is only apparent. Indeed, the local thing-hood of mentation is important precisely because in general the cognitive system is in flux. In fact, flux and fixedness together define yet another complementary relationship to be added to those in Chapter 18. Mentation, it appears, oscillates between two modes – thing-hood and flux. Flux affords on-going contact with the external world, maximal sensitivity, and openness; thing-hood allows for focus, arresting the moment, limiting possibilities. In sum, one mode directs one towards the presentational, the other towards the representational. Each has its own advantages, and it is the concerted interaction between them that makes it possible for cognitive activity to proceed.

To argue for this point, let me present an episode which, I presume, is not idiosyncratic. I am at the top of a steep rocky slope. I have to descend it, but I am afraid. My solution is to run down as fast as I can. I jump from one stone to another, and by avoiding pausing on any one stone, I complete my descent. I cross the entire slope by never stopping on any of its constituent stones. The stones, in other words, are only positions that I touch because there is a limit to the distance I can cover in one step, not stations at which I ever stay. They are necessary, for without stepping on them the path could not be crossed, but there is no commitment to any given stone, and as soon as a stone is stepped upon it is already left behind.

It seems to me that this is a most fitting way of characterizing the progression of thoughts as they are articulated in language. The medium of language (and, concomitantly, being conscious of one's thoughts) serves the same function as the stones. The articulation of thoughts in language is needed, for without it thoughts would run uncontrolled in a manner that would risk being totally devoid of direction. Articulation endows expressions with specific properties, yet in themselves these properties are not committing. Thought progresses from one articulated expression to another, but the novelty in the progression lies in the fluidity of what seems to be concrete. The real dynamics of the progression of verbal-like thought is not in the moves between the seemingly fixed, phrase-like expressions, but in the constant oscillation of what at first glance seems to be stationary.

Lastly, let me note that this discussion also bears on connectionism. Remarkably, not only RCVM but also connectionism ignores both the relevance of the medium and the action-like nature of mentation. Connectionist networks are defined by semantic association and contextual contiguity. They lack the bi-dimensionality of content and medium. Further, the mode of operation in them is akin to neurophysiological firing, not to actions people conduct in the physical and the social worlds. And last but not least, in neural-like networks consciousness plays no role. Indeed, it does not feature in connectionist models, nor is it accounted for by them.

Manifest crystallization

This discussion has been concerned with crystallization as it manifests itself in the articulation of thought in words and images. This was only natural since the main topic of our concern was consciousness. Yet, crystallization is confined neither to thinking nor to the external world. After all, words are articulated cognitive expressions and they are manifest in the external world. The same is true of gestures, facial and bodily expressions, and, in fact, all motor performance and social interaction. That words be manifestly articulated is, of course, crucial for people to communicate with others. Here, let me underline some other functional advantages of such articulation, which are in line with the picture of mind I have drawn.

In the discussion of context in the first line of the critique, we noted that unlike formulae of a canonical semantic code, the words of natural language allow pragmatic flexibility and openness of meaning. Words, however, have another important feature: they are well-defined, concrete-like entities. The word, then, is an object on which one can focus and with which one can do things. Physical entities are the objects of manipulation, words the objects of interpretation. And just as physical entities may be manipulated in various manners, so words may be used and interpreted in different ways. Further, just as the tool, despite the various manners of its employment, is one and the same, so is the word, as noted in the discussion of polysemy in Chapter 2. There I observed that words, being distinct lexical items, allow for anaphoric relations between terms that actually have different meanings. Just as a screwdriver used to loosen a screw and to break a hole through a piece of paper is the same tool, so are words that are viewed and interpreted in different manners still the same.

These observations indicate that, rather than being the expressions of underlying meanings, words are cognitive articulations that can serve for inspection, interpretation and use. Thus, the interesting processes associated with words are to be found not at a covert level, but on the surface. The four paradigmatic types of interpretation presented in the previous chapter trace some possible lines for the study of such post-presentational processes.

What has been said above is, of course, not specific to words. A pertinent, by now classic, example was presented by Wittgenstein (1953): 'I see a picture; it represents an old man walking up a steep path leaning on a stick. How? Might it not have looked just the same if he had been sliding downhill in that position?' (p. 54). Likewise, when one smiles one does not express a state of one's mind or soul, when one moves one's body in a certain pattern one does not express inner personality traits or a certain covert frame of mind. The facial expression and the bodily movement are expressive not because they reflect underlying mental states, but because they are part and parcel of what one is. Indeed, as suggested by Werner and Kaplan (1963), all human behaviour is physiognomic. Behaviour, in other words, is the generation of presentations that, like metaphor, capture in a holistic unity what can then be defined as the composition of many elements.

Like words, facial expressions and bodily movement are subject to interpretation. Meaning, in line with Oscar Wilde's saying, is there on the surface; one only has to see it. In fact, we usually do this much better than our reflective mind thinks we do. More often than not this is how we really gain understanding of what is, after all, the object that our minds are designed to understand best – other people.

Art epitomizes all this. It is evocative not because it expresses, reflects or represents underlying meanings, but because it is authentic. Great masters are in tune with themselves and with the world around them, and have the talent to bring together what they know and what they sense, their mind and their eyes (or ears), what they are and what their hands (or fingers, or mouth) do; and above all, they are one with the particular instrument of their art – the brush, the chisel, the violin, the vocal chords – so that there is no longer a gap between who they are and what they do, between the content of their expression and the medium in which it is articulated. When created in this fashion, works of art lend themselves to an unbounded range of interpretations, and can retain their meaningfulness throughout generations.

Last but not least, let me note that through the articulation of cognitive activity, the self itself is crystallized. Like the holes created when rice is boiled, when action is invested the self is created out of the substrate constituted by the meeting of the cognitive agent and the world. Of course, much more can (and should) be said of the self. Doing so, however, extends beyond the scope of this book.

Let me close by noting that the discussion in this chapter sheds a new light on Wittgenstein's theory of meaning. Wittgenstein modelled meaning on the employment of tools and he highlighted the pragmatic, action-like aspects of language. However, like most philosophers, he was not concerned with the medium in which language is articulated. The foregoing discussion suggests that this attitude is ill advised. Specifically, it appears that the action-like aspects of language (and with them, those of conscious mentation) are intimately linked to the particular form in which language (and, *mutatis mutandis*, conscious mentation) is articulated. Indeed, it is by virtue of the concreteness with which medium endows language that the words which we utter, or which pass through our minds as we think, can serve as the vehicles of action.

Representations

The picture of mind drawn here and in Chapters 17 and 18 brings us back to the questions with which I started this book – the reasons for the postulation of representations and the different senses associated with this theoretical construct. Throughout the book I have examined the notion of underlying semantic representations and argued that such representations cannot serve as the basis for cognitive activity and, by implication, for a general theory of mind. Yet, this sense of representation was only one of the senses of the term presented at the outset of my discussion. Interestingly, the discussion here also places some of the other senses of the term in a new perspective. It is to these that I turn now.

In the picture of mind drawn in Chapters 17 and 18, several kinds of entity appear that in some sense (other than the technical-psychological) may be characterized as representational. One such entity is the substrate. As noted in Chapter 17, the substrate lacks any of the attributes by which semantic representations are defined, and it is not representational in the epistemic or functional senses either. Yet, it is representational in the sense termed here 'naive'. The postulation of representations in this sense, recall, is synonymous with one's stating that mental activity has taken place. Specifically, one notes the achievement of various cognitive tasks and concludes that some activity must have taken place for them to have come about; representations are postulated as the locus of this activity. As defined in the present picture of mind, the substrate exhibits these characteristics.

Second are the expressions into which the substrate crystallizes. These, as noted, comprise the cognitive expressions of which we are conscious. On the one hand, there are the manifest expressions of cognition such as the words and sentences of language, the movements of our bodies, our concrete actions in the world. On the other hand, there are the constituents of our conscious mentations: thought sequences, mental images, fantasies and dreams. The latter are all phenomenologically distinct entities which are internal. I have referred to them in the generic term 'presentations', and noted that at times they may exhibit representational profiles. Yet, in one sense – the experiential – these expressions are representations. Representations in this sense are precisely this – experientially distinct entities that exist in the mind.

And then, representations need not necessarily be mental. Given the external orientation I have advocated, since neither the substrate of cognition nor cognitive activity is confined to the internal domain, it is only natural that the representations that feature in our cognitive life be also not thus constrained. Like the various expressions of our behaviour, the objects to which our acting is tied can also serve as representations. Throughout this book I have underlined the central cognitive role of objects. The moral of the discussion in this chapter is that one important function of consciousness is to generate such objects in the theatre of our minds. Thus I arrive at representations in a sense mentioned at the very beginning of this book and then disregarded – the concrete, external sense.

These three instantiations of representation are telling. They are associated with the three weakest, seemingly trivial, senses of representation. Indeed, in Chapter 1, these senses were characterized as non-theoretical, and thus for all further purpose practically dismissed. It is curious to conclude, then, that if any senses of representation are salvaged by my critique, it is these weakest ones that precede any theoretical consideration, be it philosophical or psychological. Indeed, it is in anticipation of the conclusion specified here that these senses were actually incorporated in the introductory survey of Chapter 1.

In presenting my picture of mind, I also introduced senses of representation not specified in Chapter 1, namely, those associated with the adjectival – as contrasted with the nominal – reading, 'representational'. The epithet denotes a profile of characteristics by which cognitive expressions may be defined. As noted in Chapter 18, such adjectival use has many merits. Recall, the adjectival term and the nominal one need not converge. Representations in general, and representations in the experiential sense in particular, may exhibit either a representational or a presentational profile. In fact, in the terminology introduced in Chapter 18 these representations are actually *presentations*. As noted in Chapter 17, there is no contradiction here. 'Presentation' is a structural, generic term covering all cognitive expressions, be they presentational or representational. By contrast, representations are defined in terms of their status, namely, their being entities in the head. One might say that the moral of our story is that the experiential representations are actually presentations.

Note

1.   For other, totally independent, ideas on self-scaffolding, see Bickhard (1993).

20 Alternative non-representational frameworks

Let a thousand flowers bloom.

Mao Tse Tung

In this and the next chapter I turn to more general theoretical and methodological considerations. Here I consider the various possible non-representational theoretical frameworks for psychology. In Chapter 21 the nature of psychological explanation is discussed, and with it criteria for evaluating the frameworks are suggested.

The key word in the introductory paragraph is 'various'. The following discussion is guided by the appraisal that the alternatives to RCVM are many and diverse. Once representations are discarded there are various different avenues that the cognitive scientist can take. This is of special importance today, with the growing impact of connectionism. Connectionism presents the first serious challenge to RCVM. With its advent, the exclusive dominance of representationalism is, for the first time since the latter's appearance on the cognitive scene, being shaken. Yet, it is important to keep in mind that connectionism is not the only non-representational paradigm in the literature. Throughout the present critique, many references were made to other such paradigms. These are neither less interesting than connectionism nor of less potential value to the field. The lesser attention that they have received and the lesser impact that they have had are, it seems to me, to be attributed more than anything to sociological considerations (into which I will not enter, but which may be of interest in their own right). Once the existence of many non-representational frameworks is appreciated, two corollaries of practical import follow. The first is directed to those enthused by connectionism, the second to those who manifest scepticism. The first is that being a non-representationalist does not necessarily entail being a connectionist. The second is that neither the rejection of representationalism nor the adoption of connectionism necessarily bring one back to behaviourism.

The existence of a variety of alternatives presents questions of relative evaluation and a problem of choice. What are the relative merits of the different alternatives? What considerations should one entertain when making the choice between them? These are, I think, extremely important questions. A long struggle with them has led me to appreciate that whatever one chooses one has to accept not only the benefits but also the prices to be paid. I will develop this topic at length in Chapter 21.

Lastly, the existence of various theoretical frameworks may be telling in its own right. It may indicate both the substantive nature of the mind and the methodological strategies adopted in its investigation. The plurality of frameworks is, I think, not fortuitous. While the various alternatives in the literature have been developed independently, taken together they seem to define a coherent, structured typology. Indeed, they may be regarded as the different profiles in a space spanned by a small number of parameters. Towards the end of this chapter I will suggest that the different frameworks be viewed as the different responses to one common, fundamental problem that underlies psychological research.

Before presenting the typology of theoretical frameworks, let me note that those to be presented here differ in status. Some define well-established paradigms, others are non-orthodox schools constituting minority voices, still others are represented by the proposals of individual investigators. Some frameworks define unified schools, others delineate perspectives shared by various investigators who might differ with respect to more specific details. While such variations will be noted, in the present context they are not of substantive relevance. This discussion is typological, not topographic: rather than describe a given scientific state of affairs, my aim is to define a space of possibilities. The best way to span this space is, I think, to define paradigmatic profiles of clusters, underlining the differences between them while disregarding secondary differences within a cluster and graded variations between them. Even if it involves a measure of idealization, such an approach is the most suitable for drawing the dimensions spanning the space of possibilities in question. In favour of this approach, let me further note that whether lines of research are regarded as paradigms, schools of thought, specific models or speculative proposals may, to a great extent, reflect contingent sociological factors, rather than principled theoretical distinctions. Thus, even though the various alternative frameworks may differ in their established scientific status, theoretically it seems to me that they are, in fact, on a par. Each defines one possible line on which non-representational psychological research may be pursued; and together, they comprise what appears to be an integrated, coherent matrix (for further discussion, see Shanon, 1990d).

The parameters

The present typology is characterized as a space spanned by two parameters. The first one is *locus*: it specifies the assumed domain of psychological phenomenology. As repeatedly noted above, psychology is usually identified with the internal domain. This domain pertains to individual agents, it is covert and is not amenable to direct public observation. However, as suggested in Chapter 17, this need not be taken for granted. Psychological phenomenology need not be confined to the hidden inner beings of individual agents, but may pertain to the external domain of the observable environment (as well as the interface between agent and environment). In the typology to be presented here, these two loci will be referred to as *internal* and *external*. It should be pointed out that 'locus' need not specify a geometrically defined locale in which psychological activity takes place. Rather, it specifies a domain with particular structural and functional properties. Furthermore, as noted in Chapter 17, 'external' is used here in a weak sense: essentially, the term marks a contrast with the internal; it should thus be interpreted as 'non-internal'.

The second parameter specifies what, according to the given conceptual framework, are the *basic objects* of psychology. *Ipso facto*, this parameter also specifies the basic terms of the conceptual framework in question. Since the two perspectives – that of domain of reality and that of level of discourse – are intertwined, in the following discussion the expressions 'basic terms' and 'basic objects' will both be used. I shall return to the difference between the two and to their relationship in Chapter 21.

The following survey starts with the presentation of frameworks whose locus is internal. Of these, the first is representationalism. After representationalism, four alternatives to it are considered, which differ from it and each other in what they take the basic objects of psychology to be. Subsequently, corresponding external frameworks will be presented. The survey ends with the consideration of the paradigm that representationalism had originally come to replace, namely, behaviourism.

Internal theoretical frameworks

Representationalism

In terms of the parameters introduced above, representationalism is a framework whose locus is internal and whose basic terms or objects are symbolic representations. It will be noted that for the cognitive revolution, both parameters were crucial. On the one hand, the cognitive approach advocates the modelling of psychological processes by means of symbolic representations and computational operations that apply on them. On the other hand, this approach stipulates that between the phenomenological level of folk psychology and that of the underlying neurophysiological substrate there is another, distinct autonomous level – the cognitive. What characterizes this level is that it is both internal and mental. (As indicated in Chapter 1, paradigmatic representational models are those presented in Newell and Simon, 1972; Schank, 1972, 1975; Anderson and Bower, 1973; Newell, 1980; and for further theoretical discussion, see Chomsky, 1959; Fodor, 1968b, 1975; Pylyshyn, 1984).

Weakly computational models

We now turn to the non-representational theoretical frameworks. The first one to be mentioned does not assume the existence of underlying semantic representations in the strong sense, but does assume some kind of underlying, internal substrate. Since this substrate is not representational in the strong sense, models of this type will be referred to – for lack of a better term – as *weakly representational*. Actually, since the models vary in how committed they are even to representations in the weak sense, it might be more suitable to refer to them as *weakly computational*. On the one hand, this last term marks the centrality of computation in these models; on the other hand, it marks a contrast with classical symbolic computation. The weakly computational paradigm *par excellence* is *connectionism* (see Hinton and Anderson, 1981b, McClelland and Rumelhart, 1986a; Rumelhart and McClelland, 1986a). Connectionism is not representational in that it does not stipulate the existence of underlying symbolic representations. Instead, it assumes that the substrate of cognitive activity is a large, neural-like associative network. Likewise, the operations employed in connectionist models are not ones of symbol manipulation, but rather parallel, distributed patterns of activation in the network.

Against this characterization it may be argued that connectionist models are nevertheless representational; in fact, some of their proponents characterize their own models as such (e.g. McClelland, 1988; Smolensky, 1988; see also Fodor and Pylyshyn, 1988a). As explained in Chapter 1, what we have here is a confusion between the weak and strong senses of the term 'representational'. Connectionist models are representational only in the weak sense, not in the strong one which is the focus of discussion here; the same applies to their being computational.

Actional models

The term 'actional' denotes a quite heterogeneous class of models independently proposed in different quarters and for different reasons. Common to them all is the appraisal that cognition is rooted in action, so that mental activity should be characterized in terms akin to those employed in analyzing performance in the world. The actional perspective characterizes cognition not as the manipulation of the symbols of the language of thought, but rather in terms of object manipulation, activities or skills. Perhaps the most famous action-based model is Johnson-Laird's (1983) theory of mental models, discussed in Chapter 8. A general framework for action-based cognitive science is also presented by the non-standard programme for artificial intelligence suggested by Winograd and Flores (1986). Other pertinent suggestions were made by Kolers and his associates (Kolers and Roediger, 1984; Kolers and Smythe, 1984) as well as in my own study of thought sequences (see Shanon, 1989a).

Intensional models

Before presenting the next non-representational framework, let me draw some terminological distinctions. The reader will notice that the term in the subheading above is spelled with an 's'. This spelling is intentional. The consideration of the terms 'intention' and 'intension' (and the corresponding terms 'intentionality' and 'intentional', 'intensionality' and 'intensional') and of the difference between them merits a separate discussion. Here only basic clarifications will be made; these are couched in a distinction between the contexts in which these terms are used. In the context of everyday language, *intention* is that which specifies the reason for the deliberate activities of a free agent. In the classical philosophical context, by contrast, the term *intentionality* is central; it denotes the property of relating to something other and outside, i.e., the property of aboutness. The first to single out this property as the key characteristic of mental states was Brentano (1874/1973). In the technical semantic context, the term *intension* is introduced, defined by contrast to the term 'extension' (see Carnap, 1947). Whereas extension defines the meaning of a term or an expression by specifying the entities or states of affairs to which it applies, intension is a semantic object not so defined. Intensional is the adjective pertaining to such entities. In this context, as well as in the linguistic one, certain specific features of intensional statements and sentences have been marked, especially the so-called opacity of intensional contexts which results in the non-substitutivity of co-referential terms (see Quine, 1960).

And then, what about the cognitive-psychological context? It seems that in this context two senses (or clusters of senses) are intended, and that the distinction between them is seldom, if ever, made. On the one hand, there is a general sense in which intentionality specifies goal-directed behaviour (see Boden, 1975; Johnson-Laird, 1983). On the other hand, there is a more theoretical sense in which intention and intentionality characterize that which pertains to meaning. In order to distinguish between these two senses and in the light of the precedent in logic and linguistics, I shall keep the term 'intention' (with a 't') and its derivatives to the first sense, and the term 'intension' (with an 's') and its derivatives to the second.

Let me return to the survey of theoretical frameworks. At the heart of the intensional perspective is the appraisal that the basic terms of psychology are – to use a phrase coined by Heidegger – invested with meaning, not contentless formal structures. In essence, the appraisal is that psychology should be concerned with meanings, the forms in which they are expressed, their development and progress, their function and their use. The following statement by Searle (1984) summarizes this position: 'What we want from the social sciences and what we get from the social sciences at their best are theories of pure and applied intentionality' (p. 85). Clearly, what is referred to here is not goal-directed behaviour (although, surely, there can very well be an overlap between meaningfulness and goal-directedness). Being totally in agreement with the basic position stated in this sentence, I would have, however, replaced the last word in it with 'intensionality'.

At first glance, the marking of the intensional perspective as an alternative theoretical framework for psychology may strike one as curious. Is meaning not, in any view, the key facet of cognition? After all, contemporary cognitive science of all persuasions is primarily concerned with semantic phenomena, semantic processing, and structures and operations associated with them. While factually this is the case, in an essential sense cognitive scientists shy away from meaning. As noted, contemporary cognitive scientists study how meaning is represented, how it is processed, but not the matrix of meaning itself. As pointed out by Searle (1980b), meaning is universally taken for granted, but not accounted for. As argued at length in Chapter 6, RCVM cannot account for reference, a notion that from its own perspective is perhaps the most basic of all. Representational psychology also avoids meaning in being fundamentally syntactic. Specifically, it assumes that the processing of information is conducted by virtue of the formal-structural properties of the information, not its content. Correspondingly, representational models are defined in terms of formal structures and formal operations, not of contents.

The paradigmatic intensional models, as this perspective is defined here, are some of the major works of phenomenological philosophy. The appraisal that psychological investigation cannot divorce itself from meaning and that psychological terms are laden with meaning is fundamental in the philosophies of Heidegger (1962), Merleau-Ponty (1962) and Sartre (1957). According to this appraisal, the world that human beings perceive and in which they live and act is constituted not of naked sense-data or objectively defined things, but rather of things and situations invested with meaning.

Perhaps the clearest case of intensional models in psychology is presented by explanations based on narration (see Bruner, 1986). Narrative explanation accounts for phenomena by means of incorporating them into well-structured stories. While not usually labelled as such, psychoanalytic explanations are usually of this kind. Indeed, it is not an accident that psychoanalysts are often interested in myth and have offered theories not only of individual personality and behaviour but also of culture. The classic examples are the later works of Freud (e.g. Freud, 1983) and those of Jung and his followers (see Jung, 1964). More recently, a call for narrative explanation has been made in social psychology (see Gergen and Gergen, 1983; Sarbin, 1986). Other intensional models are encountered in the paradigm of ethnomethodology in sociology (Garfinkel, 1967), in the interpretative study of culture (as in Geertz, 1973)[1] and in the cognitive anthropology of Wagner (1986).

Phenomenological research

While in the philosophical literature the term 'phenomenological' is usually associated with investigations of the type here called intensional, my present use of the term is stricter and more radical. The approach here labelled phenomenological focuses not on the underlying substrate of behaviour and the procedures of its generation but on the manifest expressions of behaviour. This usage is consistent with the following definition presented in the *Encyclopaedia Britannica*:

'Phenomenology' is, in the 20th century, mainly the name for a philosophical movement whose primary objective is the direct investigation and description of phenomena as consciously experienced, without theories about their causal explanation and as free as possible from unexamined preconceptions and presuppositions. (Spiegelberg, 1975, p. 3)

In focusing on the manifest expressions of behaviour, the phenomenological approach relinquishes the goal of specifying underlying structures and associated procedural mechanisms. At first sight, this might seem to counter the very essence of scientific quest. I think not. It entails, however, a need for the definition of entirely new questions for psychological research as well as a new methodological basis for psychological investigation and theory construction. These questions will be taken up in Chapter 21.

External theoretical frameworks

Since symbols, by definition, presuppose the internal domain, there are no external symbol-based frameworks. By contrast, there are external counterparts to all four non-representational frameworks mentioned above.

Weakly computational models

The external weakly computational type is exemplified in the school of ecological psychology founded by Gibson (1966a, 1979; see also Turvey and Shaw, 1979; Turvey *et al.*, 1981). Before I proceed, let me make an important clarification. It seems to me that in Gibson's writings there are two lines of thought which actually define two variants of ecological psychology. While in the literature the two are presented together and no explicit distinction between them is made, to my mind, they present two very different theoretical perspectives (for a recent, independent discussion that can be read as sharing the same appraisal, see Costall and Still, 1989; Heft, 1989). In the present typology the two occupy markedly different slots – the present one of weakly computational models and that of external intensional ones discussed below. The variant constituting the external weakly computational type is that trying to define visual perception as the detection of invariants in the optical array. In this variant modelling is highly mathematical: the environment is defined in terms of gradients of flow, and the behaviour of the organism is analogous to that of moving bodies as characterized in fluid dynamics (cf. Carello *et al.*, 1984). Like connectionist ones, models of this kind are on the one hand not symbolic (the substrate to which they apply are not symbols) but on the other hand they are computational (in the weak non-representational sense). Like connectionist models, these models employ tools that for the standard psychologist are not common, and their terminology and means of analysis are often not psychological.

The models are external because they stipulate that the locus of perception is not in the mind within but in the world outside. All relevant information is assumed to be out there, and the organism has to pick it up, not to detect it and then process and interpret it.

Actional models

External actional models stipulate on the one hand that cognition is rooted in action and on the other hand that its locus is the external environment, be it biological or social-cultural. Paradigmatic of this type is the work of Vygotsky (1978, 1986) and his followers in the Soviet school of activity theory (Leontiev, 1978; Wertsch, 1981; Kozulin, 1986). In the English-speaking world this approach may be traced to the work of George Herbert Mead (1938). Contemporary adherents of this approach are social psychologists of the interactional and constructionist bent (Berger and Luckman, 1967; Blummer, 1969; Forgas, 1982). Unlike cognitive social psychologists who try to extend the information-processing paradigm from the realm of individual, mental behaviour to that of inter-personal, social behaviour, these investigators take the converse perspective and regard cognition as an extension of one's behaviour in the public, social domain (see, for instance, Forgas, 1983; and Chapter 9).

There are also developmental models that follow the external actional perspective. In them, cognitive development is rooted in children's activity in the world and their interactions with other people (see, for instance, Bruner, 1977). Applied to language acquisition, this approach characterizes development as a progression from the pragmatic to the semantic, one which is achieved by a process of decontextualization (Bates, 1976, 1979; see also Bickhard, 1987, 1992b).

Intensional models

Intensional models of the external type are encountered in the second variant of Gibsonian psychology. This variant centres on the notion of affordance, i.e., the patterns of activity that an environment enables the agent to perform (in addition to the references cited above, see Gibson, 1979; Shaw and Bransford, 1977; Shaw and McIntyre, 1974; Shaw *et al.*, 1981). Affordances such as 'edible', 'tranversable', 'flyable' are properties neither of the behaving agent nor of the environment alone; rather, they are properties of the couplings of agent and environment (for a review, see Michaels and Carello, 1981). It is in this sense that they are here called external. The characterization of behaviour by reference to affordances is labelled intensional because its basic terms are patterns bestowed with meaning.

As indicated by the examples above, affordances couch meaning in action: the organism perceives and conceives the environment in terms of the activities it can potentially accomplish in it. This actional aspect of affordances is neither accidental nor particular. External intensional models are prone to couch the basic meaningfulness of psychological terms in the organism's interaction with the world, so these models are action-based as well. On the other hand, actional models – internal or external – need not be intensional. Similarly, internal intensional models need not be actional. There are also philosophical models of semantics which may be characterized as external and intensional; these include the works of Putnam (1975a, 1988), situational semantics as developed by Barwise and Perry (1983), and hermeneutical investigations such as those of Gadamer (1976). An extension of the intensional approach to the non-psychological domain is presented in Maturana and Varela's paradigm of autopoiesis (Maturana, 1978; Maturana and Varela, 1980; Varela, 1979).

Phenomenological research

In the phenomenological perspective, the difference between the internal and external domains is not of much substantive import. Since analyses pertaining to this perspective focus on the surface, whether the expressions under investigation are internal or external does not make a crucial difference. Thought sequences are internal, and so are dreams. External expressions that may be investigated in the same manner include sequences of verbal discourse, spontaneous singing, and artistic creations in word, visual form and sound.

Behaviourism

Strictly speaking, behaviourism is not one of the currently entertained alternatives to representationalism; yet, it defines a distinct slot in the typological space of theoretical frameworks for psychology. Behaviourism is an external non-representational framework with a rather special stance on the choice of the basic objects of psychology: its goal is the construction of a psychological theory whose basic entities are not psychological. This goal is grounded in the appraisal that, to be scientific, psychology has to be fully incorporated into the unified family of sciences. For this, behaviourism attempts to analyze behaviour in terms of entities that are directly observed in the external world (cf. Keller and Schoenfeld, 1950).

The goal behaviourism set itself was laudable: behaviourism tried to do psychology by means of the theoretical machinery already available in the natural sciences – in other words, without any extra cost. If this were possible, it would be a real accomplishment. The problem is that the enterprise is not feasible. As pointed out in Chapter 1, this was one of the reasons for the postulation of representationalism. As indicated throughout the second line of this critique, I agree with the representational critique of behaviourism: one cannot do psychology solely in terms pertaining to the physical world.[2]

From the point of view of the typology here, behaviourism is special: it breaks the symmetry. All non-representational frameworks considered so far have come in pairs: for each given choice of basic objects (or basic terms), two frameworks have been presented – one internal and one external. Behaviourism, by contrast, has no internal counterpart. And yet, a symmetry, or rather an anti-symmetry, may be defined. Just as behaviourism is an external perspective without an internal counterpart, so the representational framework is an essentially internal framework without an external counterpart. Whereas behaviourism tries to model behaviour without postulating any specific psychological terms, RCVM stipulates that in order to explain behaviour one has to postulate a level of analysis (and with it, a level of reality) which is psychological proper. Indeed, in arguing against behaviourism, RCVM did more than call for another, representational basis for psychological analysis and explanation. In postulating the representational basis, it also stipulated that between the neurophysiological level and that of folk psychology, there is still another autonomous level – that of the mental. Thus, just as behaviourism is essentially non-psychological, so representationalism is essentially psychological. In terms of this typology, it is a framework that stipulates that the locus of psychology is strictly internal and its basic object are symbols. In sum, with the breaking of symmetry there is yet another symmetry. Behaviourism and representationalism are both frameworks that apply to one locus only, so they complement each other as the two extremes of the space of psychological frameworks. All other frameworks surveyed may be regarded as interim cases between them.

The psychological predicament

Having completed the survey of the various alternative theoretical frameworks in psychology, let me take a broader, somewhat speculative perspective. The internal structure of the above typology suggests that the variety of theoretical frameworks is perhaps not accidental. The following discussion suggests that the different frameworks constitute different answers to one problem, a problem that functions as a fundamental driving force for all psychological research. This problem is the outcome of coupling the two basic facets of scientific psychology. On the one hand, psychology is supposed to be concerned with the internal domain; on the other hand, psychological phenomena are marked by being imbued with meaning. The pursuit of a scientific enterprise that brings these two facets together is highly problematic. On the one hand, the internal domain is not publicly observable; on the other hand, the study of meaning presents a host of issues usually associated with speculative philosophical investigation. Thus, a psychological predicament presents itself: a psychology which is genuinely psychological incurs the danger of not being scientific. The various theoretical frameworks surveyed may be seen as different ways in which psychologists have (by and large unbeknownst to them) confronted this predicament. Given that the problem it poses is generated by the coupling of the internal and the intensional, any solution to it requires a compromise with respect to one of these two parameters. The following discussion characterizes the various frameworks from this point of view.

Let us begin with representationalism. This is the internal framework *par excellence*. The internal domain is maintained, however, at a heavy price, namely, the abandonment of intensionality. As noted throughout this critique, even though RCVM assumes that symbols and representations are the carriers of meaning, it does not account for their meaningfulness. Almost all the other frameworks I have considered compromise with respect to the other parameter, that pertaining to the internal nature of psychology.

The compromise may be achieved along three lines, all of which involve some sort of *externalization*. The first involves the externalization of *locus*; it is opted for by all the models characterized here as external. The second keeps the locus of psychology within but models the mind in terms akin to those met in the external *world*; it is encountered in the various actional models. The third restricts the psychological domain and confines it to the *surface* only; it is adopted by the phenomenological approach.

The three lines of externalization cover all the frameworks I have considered except one, connectionism. For this, and in the light of the special impact this paradigm nowadays has on cognitive science, this framework deserves special consideration.

Connectionism: further considerations

As noted, of all the non-representational frameworks connectionism is the first that has seriously challenged RCVM and resulted in a veritable change in the cognitive sciences. Apart from this general import, the consideration of connectionism is also of special importance to me personally. As noted in the Prologue, my own critique of RCVM developed independently of, and to a great extent prior to, the advent of connectionism. Becoming aware of this new paradigm and of its accelerating impact on psychology, I found myself bothered and perplexed. On the one hand, I fully shared (and still do) connectionism's critique of RCVM. I was also very sympathetic to its ideas and proposals for the modelling of mind. For a while, I felt that, indeed, connectionism presented the answer, and stopped working on my own project. Yet, deep down, I felt I was not a connectionist. My intellectual roots were different and I have neither the training nor the ability to invent mathematical and physical models like those advanced in connectionism. I was thus tormented with a question: if one is not a representationalist, does one have to be a connectionist? Is there a difference between the connectionist and myself? Intuitively I felt that there is, yet it took me much reflection to spell it out.

In what then do I differ from connectionists? The substantive differences between their view of cognition and mine will be detailed in Chapter 21; here let me consider only differences of principle. These pertain to the nature of theory in psychology, the goals it sets itself, its basic terms and objects, and the kind of explanation it adopts. The bottom line of the following evaluation is that connectionism is not a psychological theory, nor, in fact, a cognitive one.

The appraisal that connectionism is not cognitive or psychological was put forward by Fodor and Pylyshyn (1988a). As I have pointed out at length elsewhere (Shanon, 1992), they equate being cognitive with being representational in their classical sense. Hence, their verdict that connectionism is not cognitive does no more than beg the question. In the following lines, I will also argue that connectionist models are not cognitive, but on different grounds; for a full exposition of this case, see Shanon (1992).

In principle, there are two ways in which one might demarcate a field's proper boundaries. The first is *extrinsic*: it involves sociological considerations pertaining to the standards and practices of a scientific community at a particular time. The second is *intrinsic*: it attempts to define the demarcation in terms of some basic characteristics. Given that it is this second vein which will concern me most in this discussion, let me begin by commenting briefly on the first.

Extrinsically, a model is deemed to pertain to a particular scientific discipline if it is couched in a theoretical framework with which the members of that scientific community are familiar, with which they feel relatively comfortable, or which they do not regard as being too far afield. Such a definition may have very little theoretical substance and, of course, it is bound to change with the times and as the demography of the scientific community and the relative prominence and influence of its members change. Yet, it seems to me that – whether explicitly or implicitly – scientists do hold sociological considerations of such a kind, and that the particular issue of what is 'cognitive' is not immune to them. The new paradigm of connectionism presents more orthodox, classically trained cognitive psychologists with a theoretical and methodological machinery which is, at least to some, foreign, pertaining to specialized domains in mathematics and physics with which many psychologists are not familiar and do not feel at home. Such lack of familiarity is, of course, not a reason for not adopting these concepts and procedures in cognitive psychological modelling. After all, the importation of theories and techniques from other, at times seemingly distant, fields has been germane in the development of all sciences – and cognitive psychology is no exception (viz. the impact of linguistics on the one hand and computer science on the other). This, however, does not detract from the difficulties and the sense of uneasiness that the encounter with new theoretical frameworks and methodological practices is likely to generate. The new paradigm may thus be frowned on as foreign. Admittedly, these considerations are ill defined, and perhaps even unjustified, but they seem to reflect a sociological reality none the less. Given these qualifications, currently so-called classical representationalism seems to be cognitive while connectionism does not.

The intrinsic considerations pertain to one's definition of the domain of psychology and one's view of what psychological explanation is. I will discuss these topics in Chapters 21 and 22. Here let me just state my position, which is that the domain of the psychological is defined by meaning. The psychological realm is, in other words, circumscribed by the domain to which meaning can be ascribed. Thus, a phenomenon is psychological only inasmuch as it pertains to meaningful behaviour. Correspondingly, conceptual frameworks will be deemed psychological if they pertain or are related in some intrinsic manner to meaning. A model will be deemed psychological (or cognitive) if its basic terms are psychological in this sense. Specifically, genuine psychological terms are ones which are *laden with meaning*, which are intrinsically meaningful. Just as patterns of overt behaviour or the words of natural language are meaningful, so the basic terms of cognitive theory are expected to be.

How does connectionism stand with regard to all this? Again, full consideration of this bears on the discussion in Chapter 21. Yet, it is evident that the basic terms of connectionist models are not specifically psychological. The neural-like networks of these models could have been part of physical, neurophysiological, immuno-logical or abstract mathematical models. Further, it is clear that these networks are not imbued with meaning. This does not mean that connectionist models cannot in principle account for the phenomenon of meaning. Indeed, it might be a remarkable emerging property of the dynamics of such networks. The resulting account, however, would not be genuinely psychological. It would offer an explanation of psychological phenomena by non-psychological means. Whether the account is feasible is, of course, a question that empirical research must eventually settle.

Before I go on with the evaluation of connectionism, let me pause and check how representationalism fares with respect to these considerations. As noted, one of the key facets of the cognitive revolution brought by RCVM was the definition of an independent, autonomous psychological level, distinct from both the neurophysio-logical level of biology and the physical level of the environment. By RCVM, this specifically psychological level is constituted by semantic representations. *Prima facie*, these are genuinely psychological both ontologically, as the basic objects of a domain, and theoretically, as the basic terms of a theory. After all, representations are distinct in both respects from the objects and terms one encounters in the natural sciences, in particular from those of neurophysiology, physical science, ecology and, let us not forget, of behaviourism, the school of psychology that RCVM challenged. Yet, semantic representations, despite their name, do not meet the requirement set here. They are not laden with meaning. As repeatedly noted throughout this book, even though representations are assumed to be the carriers of meaning, they cannot account for either meaningfulness or intensionality.

Remarkably, these comments bring us back to behaviourism. RCVM takes meaning for granted, behaviourism denies it. Thus, different as these frameworks are, in one fundamental respect they are alike – both avoid meaning. This adds another, and most important, dimension to the anti-symmetry between the two I have noted above.

Let me take stock: this discussion reveals that the basic terms of neither representationalism nor connectionism are genuinely psychological. Furthermore, the two theoretical frameworks are similar in that they are internal. Thus, then, we arrive at a rather unexpected conclusion: of all the non-representational frameworks considered, the closest to representationalism is connectionism. Surely, the two are radically different – they define different basic terms and propose very different models; yet, they share some fundamental assumptions on both the mind and the nature of psychological explanation. Specifically, both assume that the locus of psychology is internal and regard psychological explanation as the modelling of underlying processes (and not incidentally, both have generated models in artificial intelligence).[3]

In sum, not only is connectionism not the only alternative to RCVM, in many respects it is not even the one I would recommend. On the one hand, connectionism is not genuinely psychological; on the other hand, it might not be radical enough. I turn in Chapter 21 to the consideration of genuine psychological explanation and the new avenues for theory and research it opens.

Notes

1. The following appraisal by Geertz (1973) is telling: 'The analysis of [culture] is to be . . . not an experimental science in search of laws but an interpretative one in search of meaning'.
2. This characterization of behaviourism is, I am aware, somewhat simplistic. Behaviourism is not a monolithic school, and neo-behaviourism, especially as developed since the cognitive revolution, is remarkably sophisticated and has mentalist components (for a review, see Zuriff, 1985). The present characterization is, however, in line with characterizations of behaviourism as it is usually perceived in contemporary cognitive science. For better or for worse, these are taken from the perspective of the dominant representational view. Given this (conceptually unjustified) sociological state of affairs and since the representational perspective is the starting point of this discussion, the perhaps stereotyped characterization of behaviourism is maintained here. Even if the actual situation in the terrain is more varied and more subtle, this stereotyped profile has an essential place in the space of possibilities which is the subject matter of the present discussion. Let me also point out that while there are behaviouristic models incorporating seemingly internal mechanisms (e.g. mediating stimuli and responses), the difference between these models and the more radical behaviouristic ones is not critical. As indicated by Fodor (1965), essentially the former converge to the latter.
3. It is curious that while the proponents of representationalism regard semantic representations as genuine cognitive psychological terms, they also attribute them to the computer.

21 *Psychological explanation*

> Don't look for anything behind the phenomena; they themselves are the theory.
>
> *Goethe*

In this chapter I will examine a variety of issues pertaining to psychological explanation, to theory construction in cognition, and to the methodology of cognitive research. On the one hand, this will serve to evaluate the different theoretical frameworks presented in Chapter 20. On the other hand, it will lay the foundations – both theoretical and experimental – for alternative non-representational cognitive psychology. Taking a more abstract perspective, the discussion will also present some fundamental choices that any student of cognition should make, and the patterns of considerations, prices and costs they involve.

Preliminary distinctions

As noted, in choosing a framework for their work, *ipso facto* scientists make both *ontological* and *theoretical* decisions. The two kinds of decision are reciprocally coupled and may be regarded as the two sides of one coin. Ontologically, a particular *domain of reality* is chosen as constituting what is, according to the specific scientist's view, the world. This entails a choice of what are taken to be the *basic elements* of the scientist's ontology. Corresponding to these ontological choices are the theoretical ones of *level of discourse* and *basic terms*. The level of discourse specifies the theoretical perspective of the explanation, and the basic terms specify the basic constituents of the theory.

Many will, of course, maintain that ultimately all phenomena in the world pertain to one single, universal ontological domain – the physical. Correspondingly, they will claim that all explanations should be phrased in terms of the vocabulary of physical theory. Whether this is indeed the proper approach to take (i.e., whether this approach is the one to capture the absolute truth, that which is methodologically preferable, pragmatically more useful, or affords more understanding) is one of the central questions in the philosophy of science, and this is not the place to examine it in any depth. What should be clear, however, is that the universal, materialistic option leaves no room for any discussion specific to psychology. Following this option is tantamount to adopting the view that psychological theories should be reduced to neurophysiological (or even biochemical) theories, and hence that there is no place for psychological explanation proper. If this is the case, then – in the present context – there is nothing more to be said. I continue none the less, led by the appraisal that there is a genuine psychological domain and, correspondingly, room for genuinely psychological scientific explanation.

Assuming, then, that there is more than one domain of reality, and more than one level of scientific discourse, let me specify three such domains and levels. These differ with respect to their choice of what the modern scientist will, I assume, dismiss as metaphysical in the utterly pejorative sense - the basic *essence* of things. My use of the term, however, is rather weak: I refer not to any reified entity, but to the fundamental property defining one's ontology. The term and associated distinctions thus pertain more to the scientist's view of the world than to the description of any ultimate reality.

The first essence to be noted is *matter*, which defines the physical domain of reality. In the materialistic view, the world is constituted of physical entities. The basic elements of one's ontology are thus taken to be the elementary building blocks of matter. Correspondingly, adopting the materialistic level of discourse implies that the basic terms of one's theory are what the physicist specifies. Unless one believes in the existence of all sorts of non-physical entities (deities, spirits and souls, the living force), the materialistically defined physical domain is comprehensive. Likewise, the materialistic level of discourse is universal; it applies to all phenomena. In particular, one can have materialistic explanations of physical, biological and also psychological phenomena.

The second essence is *organization*. The corresponding domain is that of functional systems. The basic elements are their constituents. The level of discourse is that specifying the functional roles of the constituents and the relationships between them. Likewise, the basic terms of one's theory are functionally defined. The organizational domain is not as comprehensive as the materialistic one. Yet, it is still broad and varied: it subsumes biological and psychological phenomena, as well as ones pertaining to sociology and the study of artificial systems. (For a programmatic proposal for organizational explanation, see von Bertalanfy, 1968.)

The essences (or whatever term one wishes to use to refer to them) of matter and organization are common in scientific parlance. As noted, they both apply in various domains and may also be applied to psychology. Thus, psychological explanation may proceed along either materialistic or organizational lines. The question is whether there is room also for psychological explanation which is genuinely psychological. This discussion is guided by the belief that there is. Coupled with this is the appraisal that, in addition to those of matter and organization, there is an essence that is specifically psychological. This essence is *meaning*. This is tantamount to saying that, just as the world may be viewed as realizations of matter or as organized systems, so it may be viewed in terms of meanings and their configurations. As noted both in Part I and in the picture of mind drawn here, it seems to me that psychologically the world is precisely this: configurations of meanings.

A last distinction pertains to the resolution of the basic terms of one's theory and to the relationship between them and the phenomena being accounted for. At stake is not just a question of order of magnitude but one having to do with the basic qualities of the basic terms. The distinction to be noted here is that between *elements* and *units*, and it is based on the insights of the great Soviet psychologist, Vygotsky (see Vygotsky, 1986; as well as Wertsch, 1985b; Zinchenko, 1985). Explanation in science, Vygotsky notes, usually involves a reduction to elements, that is, the constituents of which an entity is composed. In general, elements do not exhibit the properties of the entities they compose. By contrast, units do exhibit the characteristics of the total entity; they are the smallest entities that do so. For instance, whereas biological elements include subcellular organelles and structures, the real unit of biological analysis, Vygotsky maintains, is the cell.

Genuinely psychological terms

If the psychological domain is that of meaning, genuinely psychological terms are terms that are laden with meaning. So far, only a general characterization of such terms has been given. Here I shall consider several possible instantiations. More precisely, the following types may be regarded as defining criteria (not necessarily mutually exclusive or comprehensive) by which terms may be judged as being genuinely psychological.

The first characteristic of genuine psychological terms is exhibiting *intensionality*. This is in line with recurrent suggestions that intensionality is the marking quality of the psychological (see Brentano, 1984/1973; Dennett, 1979b; Searle, 1983; Putnam, 1988). As repeatedly noted, not being capable of accounting for intensionality has been advanced as a major criticism of RCVM (see, for instance, Searle, 1980a); for further discussion, see Boden (1975), Double (1986) and Vollmer (1986).

The second characteristic is being subject to *interpretation*. This criterion is substantially weaker than the previous one. Whereas intensionality requires that genuine psychological terms exhibit intrinsic semantic properties, this criterion demands only that terms be amenable to a mapping onto a domain that is semantic. The stipulation is not specific to the psychological domain: formal logical systems are subject to interpretation in this sense. Interpretation, however, presupposes a system of interpretation. If this system is outside the domain deemed psychological, the range of psychological phenomena the model can account for is substantially reduced, and so is the usefulness of the criterion.

Third, the genuinely psychological may be defined as that which pertains to people. As argued by Secord (1990, p. 77), 'If we are to understand the behavior of *persons*, then we have no choice but to deal with the attributes that *persons* have'. Neither symbol manipulation of the representational type nor associative activation of the connectionist type is an attribute of this kind. For suggestions along this line, see Bechtel (1987) and Margolis (1990).

Fourth, the genuinely psychological may be characterized as that which exhibits the characteristic features of *human behaviour in toto*. This is proposed in the spirit of Vygotsky's suggestion that psychological explanation should be based not on a reduction to elements but rather on an analysis by units. As noted above, unlike elements, units exhibit the characteristics of the wholes they compose. Following the example of the cell in biology, Vygotsky advocated that psychology should define units as the basis for any explanation it offers. Such units should exhibit internal structure, be readily integrated with the organism's real action in the world, tie together different faculties of mental function, and manifest distinct patterns of development. According to Vygotsky, linguistic signs meet these requirements; his followers in the Soviet school of activity theory defined the basic units in terms of concrete action in the world as manifested in the use of tools (for discussion, see Wertsch, 1985b; Zinchenko, 1985). For another, quite radical, proposal that psychology should be concerned with the human person as a whole, see Shotter (1975).

Fifth, the genuinely psychological may be identified with that which pertains to the *conscious* or to that which is potentially conscious. From the perspective of contemporary cognitive science, this suggestion may seem preposterous. After all, one of the most salient findings of modern cognitive research is that most human cognitive life is not accessible to consciousness. Yet, the conscious does define a domain which is uniquely psychological; a proposal demarcating psychology in similar terms is presented in a recent paper by Searle (1990a).

Types of explanation

Explanations differ with respect not only to the level on which they are conducted and the basic terms they use, but also to the type of account they offer. Following is a survey of such types; as will become apparent, some are more amenable to one or more particular levels of explanation:

1. *Componential* explanations characterize phenomena in terms of their components. Paradigmatically, materialistic explanations are of this type.
2. *Mechanistic or procedural* explanations characterize phenomena by specifying the processes that bring them about. Usually, mechanistic or procedural explanations are coupled with materialistic ones. Standard explanations in the natural sciences specify the material constituents of things on the one hand, and describe the interactions between these and the forces that apply to them on the other. The dominant line of explanation in contemporary cognitive psychology is also of this type. Specifically, cognitive accounts usually consist of computational models of the procedures of mind.
3. *Functionalistic-organizational* explanations address the phenomena to be

explained as constituting organized wholes, and define the roles different components play, their interactions and the way they achieve their function or generate their products.

4. *Historical* explanations, like mechanistic-procedural ones, attempt to characterize how given states of affairs came about. Developmental-psychological accounts are of this type, marking overall trends in the course of development and specifying constraints on it. This need not involve reference to underlying, covert processes.

5. *Teleological* explanations analyze given states of affairs in reference to general goals and in comparison to optimal states of affairs. The analysis may also involve functionalist-organizational considerations.

6. *Interpretative or narrative* explanations attempt to impose structure on phenomena by viewing them in terms of a story. When a set of phenomena is tied into one coherent narrative, explanation is said to have been achieved.

7. *Formal-structural* explanations define structures and associated constraints. Their key characteristic is that they are not temporal. A paradigmatic case is that of generative-transformational grammar, which specifies what, from a formal point of view, the entity human language consists in. Even when the theory specifies operations (e.g. grammatical transformations), these should not be interpreted as procedures in time. For a general exposition, see Chomsky (1965, 1975b, 1980); for a summary and evaluation of the pertinent psycholinguistic data, see Fodor *et al.* (1974); and for a most interesting (although not often referred to) position, see Katz (1981).

As is clear from this survey, the natural sciences usually employ componential and mechanistic explanations. By and large, the natural sciences are concerned with the material composition of things and its change in time. Correspondingly, scientific theories define the mechanisms that generate these compositions and the procedures that govern the dynamics of their change. In attempting to attain the status of a full-fledged science, psychology in general and cognition in particular have followed suit. In analogy to the specification of material composition, cognitive models specify the underlying structures of mind; likewise, in analogy to the specification of material mechanisms, cognitive models specify the computational operations that apply to these structures. Thus, most explanations in contemporary scientific psychology are procedural. This is true both of RCVM and of connectionism, which regard explanation as the specification of the chains of processing that result in the generation of manifest performance. Moreover, in both, processing is tied to an underlying, covert level whose overt expression is cognitive performance. In RCVM the underlying level is representational in the strong technical-psychological sense; in connectionism it is representational only in the weaker naive and epistemic senses.

In the light of the present critique of RCVM, and given the comments on connectionism in Chapter 20, however, I confront an uneasy situation. On the one hand, I concluded that semantic representational accounts are not adequate for explaining psychological phenomenology. Furthermore, my picture of mind is in many respects in line with that drawn by connectionism. Yet, as noted in Chapter 20, connectionist accounts are not genuinely psychological.

It is fundamental to this discussion that, like all the alternative options surveyed, the enterprise of genuine psychological research involves a price. If the underlying procedures that generate behaviour are non-psychological, and if a genuine psychological perspective is to be maintained, then perhaps procedural explanation in psychology should be abandoned. This option is radical. With it, psychology departs from the standard tradition of modern science.

Non-procedural explanation

Many will object, saying that non-procedural explanation is not at all explanatory (see, for instance, Allport, 1984). Let me respond.

First, the objection may be rooted in an inability (or unwillingness) to relinquish RCVM. Specifically, it may be argued that the only way to explain the mind's activity is in terms of procedural models, and these have to be representational-computational. But there is no reason to equate psychological explanation with explanation using representational-computational terms. Further, the identification of scientific explanation with the specification of underlying mechanisms is not necessary either. Modelling by means of mechanisms is a means, not a goal. What one tries to achieve in psychological research is an understanding of the mind. For this end modelling mechanisms may be very helpful, but as indicated by the foregoing survey of types of explanation, it is only one way to realize this goal. Thus, in evaluating a cognitive psychological framework, the specification of mechanisms should not be an absolute criterion. Rather, one should examine whether the framework offers a unified terminology for the characterization of a large variety of phenomena, whether it reveals general principles that recur in different domains, whether it offers a sound functional account, whether it defines constraints on the domain of investigation, and whether it allows for the definition not only of what actually is the case, but also of what potentially could or could not have been.

Second, procedural explanation in psychology is far from being the success story that it might appear at first sight. Ideally, one might perhaps opt for procedural explanation, but as I have shown over and over again in this critique, it delivers much less than meets the eye. First, there is much that representational-computational modelling cannot account for. Second, the phenomena it does account for may pertain only to very particular types of behaviour. Specifically, representational-computational models may be successful only when dealing with well-circumscribed aspects of psychological phenomenology, examining local phenomena and disregarding a host of crucial factors and considerations. Third, as noted in Chapter 6, one should always bear in mind that despite its robust appearance, RCVM rests on very shaky foundations.

That the success of representational-computational models is deceptive was noted by Wittgenstein years before the advent of RCVM. He pointed out that, 'In psychology there are experimental methods and conceptual confusions. The existence of experimental methods makes us think that we have the means of solving the problem which troubles us; though problems and method pass one another by' (Wittgenstein, 1953). This appraisal is not the mere whim of a philosopher detached from empirical research, one who lived almost half a century ago. Here we have an appraisal that recently appeared in one of the main journals of mainstream academic psychology:

> Memory theorizing appears to be progressing nicely. Indeed, judging from the sheer number of pages it consumes in the literature, it appears to be progressing as never before. But the appearance is deceptive, for something is wrong. Very wrong. (Watkins, 1990, p. 328)[1]

Admittedly, adopting the non-procedural perspective involves drastic changes in the conduct of psychological research. First and foremost, non-procedural psychological research changes the direction in which attention is focused. Whereas procedural psychology studies the underlying mechanisms of mind, non-procedural psychology is concerned with what there is on the surface. With this, the goals of psychological analysis change as well: instead of specifying procedures of generation and mechanisms of processing, psychological investigation will be concerned with the structural constraints on cognitive expressions, the dynamics of their progression in time, the functions they serve, the contextual dependencies associated with them, the course of their ontogenesis and the history of their evolution in cultures and societies. These changes in the object of study entail changes in the scope of the phenomena being investigated. When searching for underlying mechanisms one can, and would choose to, focus on local, circumscribed phenomena. By contrast, when attempting to define constraints and general patterns one has to broaden the scope of inspection. There are various ways to do this: analyze large cognitive structures (e.g. texts instead of words, entire chains of behaviour instead of local tasks), examine large bodies of data, inspect the contexts in which performance is carried out, follow performances longitudinally and inspect both their past history and their progression. All this implies that new questions have to be defined, new methods of investigation developed, new types of analysis and explanation devised, new types of theory constructed. My estimate is that rather than being impoverished, psychology may be very much enriched by such a change of perspective.

To present concrete examples for non-procedural cognitive research, four lines of investigation will be suggested. The first follows Wittgenstein's recommendation (1953, p. 66) in his critique of featural analyses of the meaning of words: 'look and see'. In this approach, students of cognition are to collect many phenomenological observations and examine them in the light of the theoretical questions with which they are concerned. This type of research is dialectic: one's theoretical considerations guide one in one's observations, and the empirical observations lead one to elaborate further one's theoretical stance. Experimental cognitive psychologists are likely to dismiss this line of investigation as being reactionary and primitive: does it not draw psychology back to its pre-scientific era? Not necessarily. Contemporary cognitive psychology has perfected methodologies of experimental research, but in so doing it has at times neglected basic theoretical considerations on the one hand, and ignored the observation of naturalistic behaviour on the other. The call made here is to direct the investigator's resources to these relatively neglected areas.

The second line of investigation directs the cognitive scientist to the study of large bodies of behaviour. Its goal is to subject them to a formal analysis in a manner analogous to that employed by the structural linguist. The linguist constructs a theory of a language, of its structures and its constraints, not a procedural model for the production or comprehension of language. In the same manner, inspecting large bodies of cognitive expressions allows comprehensive typologies of the cognitive domain under investigation to be drawn and constraints on the space of its instantiations to be specified.

This line of investigation may be criticized as being merely descriptive. While, admittedly, it is grounded in description and classification, it can give rise to a theoretical account that extends beyond this level even though it is concerned with phenomena that lie on the surface. To defend this claim, let me refer to my own research on thought sequences (Shanon, 1984b; 1989a). Given a large body of such sequences, I have examined the types of relationships by which two consecutive expressions in a sequence may be coupled. It appears that all these types may be ordered in a multi-dimensional typology whose significance is twofold. First, in defining the dimensions by which types of relation are ordered, one shifts from the mere description of actual relations to the consideration of the totality of possible relations as a system. In this respect, the typology may be likened to a cognitive Mendeleyev table. With the consideration of the types as a system, one may gain insight into principles underlying the domain under investigation and appreciate the logic which defines it. Second, the typology allows one to turn from the study of the actual to that of the potential as well as the non-potential. It defines a multidimensional space, which in turn indicates possibilities that may not be actualized. The non-actualized points present non-possible types of thought relation. Thus, the typology allows one to answer a question that has often been considered unanswerable, namely, what are thoughts that are not thinkable? Surely, this is far from mere description of given facts (see Shanon, 1989a).

Third, one may investigate the on-going dynamics of cognitive performance. The investigation will consist in a detailed, minute-by-minute inspection of tasks and the course of their execution. Particular issues of interest will include the adoption of a representational or a presentational strategy, the contexts associated with each, the manner in which one moves from the one to the other, the involvement with the various non-SR factors, the patterns of immersion in context and distancing, coupling and decoupling, autonomy and differentiation. As a result, the cognitive dynamics of the task will be traced. Careful protocols of performance have indeed been taken by investigators from different theoretical orientations. When one 'looks and sees', one realizes that things are very different from what representational-computational modelling would have us believe (see, for instance, Coulter, 1983; Middelton and Edwards, 1990; as well as my own investigations of the phenomenology of consciousness and creativity described in Chapter 19).

The fourth line of investigation is to take a diachronic perspective, studying the temporal aspects of behaviour. Specifically, patterns of development are to be investigated and the regularities in their progressions are to be defined. This line too may be criticized as being merely descriptive, hence non-theoretical. Again, I do not subscribe to this verdict. A biological analogy may be helpful: consider classical embryology, that practised before the advent of molecular biology. The classical embryologist described sequences of development, but not the molecular mechanisms by which morphological changes come about. Were the descriptions devoid of any theoretical import? I do not think so. The purpose of scientific theory is to define constraints on domains of phenomenology, and this the classical embryological models do. Examples of such constraints are: the specification of stages that always occur before others; the specification of the limitations on further development that given stages impose; the contexts in which stages of development are realized. All these issues can be readily applied to cognition as well (for discussion along similar lines, see Bickhard, 1992b).

The lines of investigation suggested may have one of two main orientations. The first is dynamic. It follows the progression of cognitive activity in time, attempts to trace the dynamics of cognitive activity and its development and to define its regularities and the constraints it is subject to. In terms of the distinctions made in Chapter 20, the investigations pertaining to this orientation are phenomenological. The explanations they offer are of the functional-organizational, historical, interpretative and narrative types. The other orientation is atemporal and adopts formal-structural explanation. As noted above, the one domain of cognition in which such investigation is paradigmatic is linguistics. A formal-structural investigation in psychology would attempt to define constraints on cognitive structures without probing into the processing associated with these structures. My work on thought sequences described above is an attempt to develop such a formal-structural framework of study and analysis in cognition.

These lines of investigation may be summarized in terms of the questions they define. In particular, three basic questions are noted: what is the *geography* of mind? What is its *dynamics*? What are its *development and evolution*? The first question is concerned with the systematic delineation of behaviour and the various patterns of its expression, the second with the progression of cognitive activity and the manner of its realization, and the third with the long-term aspects of cognition – ontogenetic as well as cultural. In focusing on these questions, the non-procedural approach abandons the question which is the prime focus of contemporary cognitive science – both representational and connectionist – namely: what is the underlying *mechanics* of mind? At first glance, it would seem that once this last question is abandoned, nothing much is left for cognitive research. I hope this discussion indicates that this is far from being the case.

Lastly, two cardinal advantages of the questions associated with the non-procedural approach will be noted. First, they have conceptual precedence. Before one investigates what the mechanisms that underlie cognitive activity are, before one investigates how such activity is realized either neurophysiologically or computationally, one should clarify what these activities consist in. For instance, before one studies the underlying mechanisms of memory one should define what memory, and in particular human memory (as distinct, for instance, from computer memory), actually is. In their haste to focus on the question of mechanics, cognitive scientists often overlook this. However, the phenomenological questions remain even if and when one succeeds in specifying the putative underlying machinery of mind. The validity of this statement is not affected by the specific nature of the machinery – it remains true whether this machinery is symbolic-representational, connectionist or neurophysiological. The second advantage is a corollary of the first. Since they are concerned with the definition and characterization of psychological phenomenology, the questions noted here pertain to what may be regarded as genuinely psychological. By contrast, the question of underlying mechanisms pertains to implementation, and so may be outside the genuine psychological domain. The definition of this domain is the topic of the discussion both in the next section and in Chapter 22.

The scope of cognition

The critique of RCVM and the ensuing opening of new lines of cognitive investigation call not only for a change in the type of explanation in psychology but also for a redefinition of the scope of the field.

I have alluded to the issue of scope at various points throughout Part I. In particular, I noted that, confronted with arguments marking the inability of representationalism to account for some aspects of psychological phenomenology, cognitive scientists often dismiss these as pertaining to a domain outside the scope of cognition. Likewise, when certain seemingly non-cognitive factors are marked as pertinent, the representationalist often responds by confining the scope of cognition so as not to include them (see Fodor, 1980, 1983). Nowadays, such moves often appear in representationalist responses to connectionism (see Fodor and Pylyshyn, 1988a; Lachter and Bever, 1988; Pinker and Prince, 1988; Prince and Pinker, 1988; for a discussion, see Shanon, 1992).

As argued throughout Part I, the representationalist redefinition of the scope of psychology cannot be sustained. First, in essence, it blatantly begs the question. By RCVM, cognition is the domain of semantic representations and the computational operations associated with them. Faced with data that cannot be accommodated within this characterization, representationalists declare that the phenomena at hand do not count, and dismiss them as non-cognitive. Unless it is taken before the empirical investigation commences, unless it is independently justified and theoretically motivated, such a move is simply not acceptable.

Second, the redefinition of the scope of psychology results in a mismatch between the theory's characterization of the cognitive or psychological domain and its scope, and the corresponding pretheoretical characterization. Specifically, some phenomena that pretheoretically would be classified as cognitive or psychological are dismissed and ignored. This is a serious price that one should carefully consider when defining the scope of psychology and of cognition.

Third, the dismissal of phenomena can be theoretically beneficial only if there is a clear-cut line between what is within the domain of inquiry and what is outside. If there is no such line, no matter how narrow the scope of the domain, it is quite likely that one will never be able to get rid of what one deems extrinsic factors. Alternatively, one may be pushed to narrow one's domain more and more, only to be left with one that is artificially defined, leaves much of what is of interest out, and views the phenomena of interest with bias. Indeed, if the role of the seemingly extrinsic factors is central, this narrowing of scope will result in an utterly distorted view and a fundamental misunderstanding of the phenomena. To my mind, this is what has happened in representational cognition. As I have shown throughout the second line of this critique, there is no clear-cut line between the so-called cognitive proper and the so-called non-cognitive. Performances which are cognitive *par excellence* involve factors that the purist may regard as non-cognitive. Factoring the latter out will also take out phenomena that all would regard as paradigmatically cognitive. Thus, in order to keep the domain of investigation cognitively pure, representationalists are bound to be pushed to confine the domain artificially into a very narrow scope, one countering all pretheoretical notions of what is cognitive. In fact, it is very likely that such an absolutely pure domain does not exist at all. In other words, either representationalists are to shrink the cognitive domain to nonexistence (or at most, to a ridiculously narrow scope) or they have to compromise on its purity. If, however, the latter course is taken, and if compromise is made anyway, then why not stick to the natural, broader definition of the domain?

Fourth, leaving the so-called non-cognitive out results in a skewed, and most probably wrong, view of cognition. As I have shown, these factors play an essential role in cognitive functioning. The cognitive system's very mode of operation assumes their prior existence and on-line availability. This is true both in ontogenesis and in normal mature functioning. Accounts confined to situations in which the non-cognitive factors are not relevant may be formally aesthetic and may well fit the data, but they are categorically misleading. Such models will define only very special conditions in which the cognitive system may be placed. By no means can such conditions reflect the system's general, prevalent or natural mode of operation.

Lastly, the exclusion of non-palatable phenomena can result in an extremely impoverished psychology. Phenomenologically, human psychology is rich. It would be a shame to narrow its scope just because the phenomena do not square with one's theoretical framework.

Let me take stock. Faced with phenomena their model cannot account for, psychologists have two options: to dismiss the phenomena, thereby keeping the original flavour of the model, or to address the phenomena but change the model. Each of these options involves costs. The costs of the representational option were enumerated throughout this critique. The choice is clear. If psychological phenomenology does not square with a certain type of theory, perhaps the theory is wrong, and perhaps one's general view of mind and behaviour should change.[2]

The cognitive problematics

As I have shown throughout this discussion, the theoretical problems noted are not specific to any single domain of cognition. Similar problems, similar patterns of argumentation, similar strategies for confronting problems, and similar solutions recur in practically all cognitive domains. This is one of the most important insights I have gained from this enterprise: varied though it is, the cognitive field is one. Adopting a global, somewhat abstract perspective, one realizes that this domain presents a unified and coherent cluster of patterns, one that may be referred to as the 'cognitive problematics' (as noted in the Introduction to Part I, the French often speak of *la problematique*). To conclude the consideration of psychological theory and psychological explanation, I shall present a summary sketch of the patterns of problems that together constitute the cognitive problematics, and of the strategies that may be adopted in response to them.

Taking a global, somewhat abstract perspective, the various problems noted in this critique of RCVM fall into one of a small number of types:

1. Problems of *incompleteness*. These are of two subtypes. First, there are problems of *non-exhaustion*: being fixed and determinate, representational models are constrained and cannot specify all the distinctions and variations that are or may be cognitively relevant. Such problems were encountered in the discussion of context, medium, body, affect and time. Second, there are problems of *confinement*: representational models cannot account for the tie between the cognitive system and other systems, and detailed as these models may be, there remain residues unaccounted for. Problems of this type are encountered in the various patterns of unbridgeable gaps, in the various cases of missing qualities, and in conjunction with temporality.
2. *Impasse.* Because they disregard what they deem to be external factors and do not allow for impurities and noise, representational models cannot account for many accomplishments of the cognitive system, and reach an impasse when attempting to account for development and evolution.
3. *Higher orders.* Representational accounts often require recourse to a second level of processing. The paradigmatic case is that of the homunculus; similar patterns were encountered in conjunction with pragmatic issues, various aspects of knowledge, memory and the perception of change, and all sorts of

judgement and evaluation (e.g. the classification of contexts, the appraisal of similarity, the determination of adequacy).
4. Problems of *petitio principii* (begging the question). Often, for computational operations to apply, some prior evaluation is needed. For this to be achieved, however, processing of the same kind that the representational model sets itself to explain has to be invoked. Such problems were met in conjunction with the two-stage strategy, the appraisal of similarity, the dynamic aspects of cognition and memory.
5. *Paradoxes*. Representational accounts often lead to attributions of knowledge and ability that simply defy reason; they also result in counter-natural orderings of phenomena. Problems of this kind were met in the accounts of non-declarative modes of knowing, in learning and in development.

The ways in which RCVM responds to these problems can also be grouped in a small number of patterns:

1. *Patching up*. Confronted with problems, RCVM may add up cases, distinctions and components. I have shown this with both context and medium, where additional features and tags were introduced in the hope that they could accomplish what an original set of features and tags could not. The recourse to higher-order structures and components is similar.
2. *Compartmentalization and division of labour*. A standard response from RCVM is to compartmentalize the cognitive domain and define ordered modules for investigation. A division of labour is declared: cognitive investigation is directed towards certain problems, while subdomains or levels and issues not within their scope are relegated to later stages of research or to other disciplines.
3. *Passing the buck*. When a problem is met, it may be put aside and relegated to a higher order of analysis. The paradigmatic case is the problem of interpretation: since interpretation cannot be accounted for in representational-computational terms, it is relegated to a second-order interpretative module. However, since the second-order module cannot be accounted for within the model either, the problem is bound to be passed on to modules of still higher orders or else be left unaccountable.
4. *Adjustment of scope*. A more extreme response is to declare the bothersome problems altogether outside the realm of relevance. With this, the boundaries of the cognitive realm are redefined, the scope of the psychological domain is adjusted, and an autonomous stance is adopted.
5. *Methodological purism*. Similarly, representationalists may react by perfecting their methodology of research – cutting out bothersome factors, controlling for more and more variations, clearing up any detectable noise or impurity. Likewise, they may increase the formal rigour of their theories and constrain them with more background conditions and principled idealizations.
6. *Deus ex machina*. At times it is simply impossible to say that the bothersome is irrelevant. In such cases one can ascribe it to the province of (theoretical)

foundations. This is most salient in the cases of reference and intentionality and the representationalist response of methodological solipsism.

As I have shown, these responses are of little utility:

1. The patching up will never be complete. Some local problems may be addressed, some specific cases may be accounted for, but on the whole, the basic problems are not addressed and are bound to keep reappearing. As indicated in the discussion of the meaning of words, this state of affairs may be likened to that of Ptolomaic cosmology. Its fate can only be the same.
2. No clear lines of demarcation may be drawn between the issues one would like to be concerned with and those one would like to disregard or relegate to a later stage of analysis or investigation.
3. Once one does turn to the later stages of analysis, one often realizes that there is no longer any need for the accomplishments of putative earlier stages. Likewise, in the later stages of investigation, researchers may find that problems investigated in the earlier stages receive simpler and more elegant accounts, or merely dissolve.
4. The issues one decides to disregard, set aside or defer may be the more basic and general ones. Indeed, they may be the more interesting and important ones. Not confronting them may result in a radically biased view of mind and in confining one's theory to an artificially limited domain. Eventually, the theory may reflect not any cognitive reality but only the contrived state of affairs – either theoretical or experimental – that the representationalists themselves have created.
5. Principled idealizations and strategies labelled as merely methodological intertwine with issues of substance. As I have repeatedly pointed out, by not confronting the problems of reference and intentionality, the entire representationalist enterprise finds itself resting on utterly shaky foundations.
6. Last but not least, in the process, one gains less and less understanding of what really matters.

The alternative proposals made here also exhibit some basic recurrent patterns:

1. The problems due to the fixedness, well-definedness, well-formedness and determinacy of basic terms may be responded to by dispensing with all these properties. In the picture of mind proposed here, the basic terms of cognitive theory are neither pure nor well-formed, neither complete nor uniform. Similarly, the constituents of mind are neither fixed nor differentiated.
2. The problems of confinement and impasse may be responded to by having as basic terms ones that are already tied to that which cognition must be connected with, and that already have properties which, by RCVM, should be imposed at a later stage. On the one hand, these terms should be defined by the coupling of mind with the various so-called external factors; on the other hand, they should be laden with meaning and be inherently dynamic.

3. The problems of higher order and the subsequent patching up and ordered compartmentalization should be responded to in the same manner. In its desire to maintain the purity and neatness of its account, RCVM often pushes what it deems to be problematic to later stages of analysis or attributes it to separate modules or systems. If the problems are bound to reappear in these other stages or components, one might as well dispense with the artificial purity and neatness of the first stage altogether. With this, the need for separation between stages vanishes.

4. The failures of a strictly demarcated autonomous cognition can be responded to by expanding the scope of the field, so that it also encompasses the so-called non-cognitive factors. In particular, seemingly external factors and domains are incorporated into the psychological realm, and boundaries between psychological systems and mental modules are obliterated.

5. Purist formalism and methodologies of empirical research are given up. As noted both in Chapter 16 and above, basically, the choice is between purism and truth. This characterization is, I admit, extreme, but it does capture the real state of affairs in cognitive science.

Methodological ramifications

The topics of this chapter are theories and explanations, yet having mentioned lines for future investigation, let me comment on the methodology of research.

Cognitive psychology, aspiring to be scientific, is primarily an experimental enterprise. The laboratory setting, however, is not neutral, but affects cognitive agents and their behaviour. It places subjects in a situation which demands autonomy. In it there is separation. Furthermore, in verbal research one usually studies material which is not meaningful to the subjects – not only non-words and nonsense syllables, but also decontextualized words, sentences or even small paragraphs of text. All these mean nothing to the subjects in their real lives. They are all meaningful only within the context of the experiment. This context, then, is not neutral. Indeed, the sterile laboratory setting is precisely that which induces the representational mode of behaviour.

But what about experimental data? These, I maintain, pertain only to a very particular mode of cognitive activity, that corresponding to the artificial laboratory setting. Thus, the data indicate precisely that – subjects' behaviour under laboratory conditions. They should not be taken as facts about human cognitive behaviour in general.

In fact, the move from empirical data to theoretical accounts is usually less direct than one might think. It is guided by one's theoretical view. This is true of all science, but is especially striking in cognitive psychology. When studying the representation of knowledge in the mind, one never taps representations in any direct manner. One inspects computational operations, and measures the times associated with their application. Usually, one takes differential computational times and on the basis of these one construct maps of the geography of the mind: in other words, what one has are computation times, and what one constructs are representational topographies. The move is based on the assumption that in order to have the computations working, one has to have representations. But this is nothing more than the naive rationale for the postulation of representation. In effect, all one can say is that, indeed, computational operations take differential times to apply and that there are all sorts of constraints and interdependencies to which their application is subject – nothing more. How could it be possible without representations? This is already a conceptual (and perhaps philosophical) question, one that cannot be decided on the basis of empirical data alone.

The move from data to modelling is also affected by the particular paradigm in which one works. Nowadays, the cognitive psychological literature is replete with experiments whose data are modelled in connectionist terms. Most notable are experiments in the study of lexical decisions and conceptual structure. Technically, there is nothing new about these experiments. They could have been carried out (and many actually were) a decade ago, before the advent of connectionism. In those days, the results were interpreted and modelled in representational terms. It would be most interesting to survey the entire cognitive literature and see how the move from experimental results to theories is made – in particular, how the move to either a representational or a connectionist interpretation is made. I would venture to say that much of the move is not dictated by the experimental results themselves. The project is extensive, and this is, of course, not the place to comment further on it.

Notes

1. Indeed, Watkins attributes the pitiful state of the art to what he refers to as mediationism, that is, 'the doctrine that memory is mediated by some sort of memory trace'. He claims that 'the rejection of mediationism would serve both to replace mechanistic theories with laws or other models of explanation and to focus research on the actual experience of memory and on the context in which it occurs'. (p. 328).
2. See the discussion of the Chomskian heritage in Chapter 16, especially note 2 there.

22 Extensions and ramifications

Nothing is of greater consolation to the author of a novel than the discovery of readings he had not conceived but which are then prompted by his readers.

Umberto Eco

Bearing in mind the foregoing methodological comments on psychological theory and psychological explanation, let me return to my picture of mind and consider various extensions and ramifications of it. In the course of the discussion, I shall also show that some problems raised throughout Part I are now seen in a new light or dissolve.

The psychological domain

A significant part of Chapter 21 was devoted to methodological issues delineating the scope of psychological theory. Let me now turn from the general meta-theoretical and methodological considerations to the particular picture of mind proposed here and ask what, in this picture, the scope of the psychological domain actually is. Two criteria for its definition will be proposed. The first is that specified at the beginning of Chapter 21, namely, meaning; the second relates to the discussion in Chapter 19 and pertains to consciousness.

The definition of the psychological domain in terms of the meaningful is twofold. On the one hand, the cognitive system is designed to entertain meanings. Unlike the computer (and unlike the cognitive models stipulated by both RCVM and connectionism), it does not operate upon meaningless structures, be they well-formed (as in representationalism) or not (as in connectionism). Whatever the cognitive system operates upon is imbued with meaning. On the other hand, the world is perceived only inasmuch as it is meaningful. As pointed out in Chapters 5 and 8, psychologically speaking the world does not consist of conglomerates of naked, raw data. As far as cognitive agents are concerned, the world is the manifold of meanings, be they constituted in physical objects and other living organisms or generated by the agents themselves.

Turning to the second criterion, let me restate some of the conclusions from Chapter 19. There, I argued that genuine psychological explanation is not to be concerned with covert, underlying structures and processes. I also highlighted the significance of activities taking place out there, on the surface, so to speak. Together, these two claims suggest that the subject matter of psychology more or less coincides with the domain of the conscious. Specifically, the suggestion is that psychology be circumscribed by that which is amenable to consciousness, be it actually or potentially so.

This delineation of the psychological in terms of the conscious should be understood in tandem with the characterization of the locus of psychology as external. In the view advocated here, recall, the domain of the conscious is not confined to the internal world, but encompasses overt behaviour in the external world too. What the psychological excludes is the realm of internal, underlying processes. Instead of this covert realm, psychological research should focus on the domain of the overt – that manifested in actual behaviour in the world, and that pertaining to activities conducted in the world within. Consciousness encompasses both.

The move suggested here is, interestingly, analogous to one made by Freud. The demarcation between the conscious and the unconscious is, of course, central to Freud's psychological theory. In defining it, however, Freud faced a problem: consciousness can be defined by two criteria, and the extensions of the two do not coincide. On the one hand, there is the pretheoretical, experiential criterion: the conscious is that which is experienced as such. On the other hand, there is the theoretical, psychodynamic criterion. According to psychoanalytic theory, unconscious psychological material is characterized by certain energetical qualities; typically, it is libidinal and is kept unconscious so as not to menace the ego. Now, there are psychological materials that experientially are not conscious yet lack these psychodynamic qualities. Appreciating this, Freud introduced the notion of the preconscious, comprising psychological material that by the experiential criterion is not conscious yet does not pertain to the unconscious as defined by the theoretical criterion; it is, in other words, material that happens not to be conscious, but is capable of becoming so (see Freud, 1933). Similarly, in suggesting that the psychological be circumscribed by the conscious, I am not suggesting that the scope of psychology be determined solely in terms of given phenomenological experience. I am saying, however, that material that in principle cannot be amenable to consciousness is outside the scope of psychology. Much of the subject matter of contemporary cognitive psychology is of this nature (for independent discussion leading to similar conclusions, see Searle, 1990a).

In defining the psychological domain in terms of the conscious, I find myself answering the question of why certain information is not amenable to consciousness. In Chapter 15 I pointed out that people cannot specify the semantic definitions of words, often act without conscious planning, and are not conscious of time in the abstract. Now, all this becomes clear: underlying definitions of words do not exist, actions need not be the products of predefined plans, and, psychologically speaking, there is no such thing as time divorced from being and action in the world. Further observations on this will be made below.

The basic terms: a reprise

These considerations of scope bring me back to the question of basic terms with which I opened the discussion in Chapter 21. As noted throughout Part I, the basic terms of RCVM, the symbols of which semantic representations are composed, cannot account for meaning nor for the relationships between the mind and the world. (This is tantamount to saying that they fail to meet both the epistemic and the functionalistic rationales for the postulation of representations.) The only way out is that suggested in the discussion of unbridgeable gaps in Chapter 6 – to posit both meaning and the tie with the non-cognitive from the very start. In other words, the basic terms of psychology should already be imbued with meaning and should tie together the cognitive and the non-cognitive – mind and body, mind and world, mind and social other, cognition and the non-cognitive faculties of mind.

In one way or another, the basic terms of all the theoretical frameworks I have characterized as intensional, as well as many of the action-based ones, meet this requirement. Especially to be noted are Gibson's affordances: in ecological psychology, meaning is constituted by the patterns of interactions between the organism and the environment. Similarly, the units of analysis in Vygotsky's psychology, and more notably in the school of activity theory developed by his followers, bring together the individual and the social other and define meaning in terms of their interaction. Analogously, in the biologically oriented theory of autopoiesis of Maturana and Varela (1980), the basic terms bring together organism and world.

My own suggestion is to define the basic terms of psychological theory in terms of the non-SR factors on which the present picture of mind is based. Specifically, my suggestion is the following:

> (****) The basic terms of psychology are septuples defined by the conjunction of the seven non-SR factors.

An important feature of the terms defined in (****) is that they are units in the Vygotskian sense. As indicated in Chapter 21, Vygotsky suggested that the unit of psychology is the word, because it brings together internal thought and manifest articulation. Vygotsky's followers found various faults with this suggestion and proposed that the unit of psychology is the action (see Wertsch, 1985b). The proposal made here follows the spirit of both Vygotsky and his followers in that it brings together several seemingly independent factors.

The characterization specified in (****) highlights comments made at the end of the presentation of the picture of mind in Chapter 17: it is not that there is a cognitive system on the one hand, and various factors on the other hand. Rather, the cognitive system and the non-SR factors are co-defined. Here I have defined the basic terms of cognition by means of the non-SR factors. At the same time, as emphasized throughout the discussion, the non-SR factors are themselves defined in terms of cognitive activity. The mutual co-dependence is also manifested functionally. On the one hand, the non-SR factors are required for the cognitive to come into being and to develop and for cognitive activity to take place. On the other hand, these factors themselves are defined in terms of the spectacles of the cognitive system.

The locus of cognition: a reprise

In the typology of theoretical frameworks drawn in Chapter 20, one dimension was defined by the basic terms and the other by the locus of cognition. Bearing in mind the foregoing comments on the cognitive domain and its extension, let me make a few additional comments on this second dimension.

I have argued that the locus of cognition is external. In Chapter 17, I specified three senses of this characterization, pertaining to principles of functioning, to realization and development, and to theoretical regularity. Here, I would like to emphasize that the characterization is not merely a matter of abstract considerations pertaining to theories and their construction; it has direct implications for how specific faculties of mind and patterns of cognitive performance are to be conceived.

Thus, consider memory. This faculty is of cardinal importance because, as indicated in Chapter 15, in essence it defines the core of the cognitive system. As noted, this is especially true of the way cognition is modelled in both the representationalist and the alternative connectionist frameworks. Given this centrality, the characterization of memory as external gains special significance. It consists of more than the assessment that in order to remember it is beneficial for people to rely on various tools and artefacts as memory aids. That the pen and the paper, the book and the computer are helpful, even indispensable, for the recording of information and its retrieval is incontestable. Appreciating this, one can, however, still maintain that memory, and cognition in general, are internal. Specifically, the various memory aids can be deemed as secondary mechanisms that serve precisely as aids that enhance the cognitive system's ability to retain information, extend the scope of its data-base, and facilitate memory access to it. These are needed when the tasks the cognitive system has to accomplish are difficult, and when the system risks losing control of things.

I hope that (now that he or she is cognizant of the cognitive problematics) the reader sees that this characterization of the cognitive state of affairs is just another manifestation of the two-stage strategy encountered so many times throughout this book (being so deep-rooted, it is extremely obstinate). Specifically, the characterization amounts to a claim that basically memory is internal: remembering consists in the retrieval of information from mentally stored semantic representations; the tools and artefacts are employed when the load on the internally defined memory system is extensive. Again, I object. To view them as mere aids would be to miss the whole point of the external view of cognition advocated here.

These tools and artefacts (as well as settings in the physical world and other people) are employed not just because memory is in need of external assistance, but because the very capacity governing memory behaviour is the ability to manipulate objects in the world (as well as the propensity to interact with other human beings). This is so both in the case of the developing child and as far as adult cognitive performance is concerned. The ability to remember without relying on the external world is a derivative, acquired ability (as is the ability to use language in a semantically detached, decontextualized manner). As Vygotsky (1978, 1981) claimed, the internalization of cognitive activity is the end product of ontogenetic development, not the primary, basic mode of cognitive operation. Memory (as well as perception and action, language and thinking) is situated in the world. All these cognitive faculties are designed, first and foremost, as activities in the world. It is in this sense that they are external.

In sum, human memory's reliance on the physical world is not due to limitations of the cognitive system (as RCVM would have it), but reflects the functional principles on which this system is designed.[1] Thus, what is remarkable (in other words, what is complex, what is to be regarded as exceptional, what is to be set as a question for inquiry) is not the fact that we rely on external, physical and ideational entities in order to remember, but rather the fact that we can remember (and think, and reflect) when these entities are not immediately present. As noted in Chapter 19, to a great extent we are able to do so because we can create similar, virtual entities in the theatre of our mind.

This foregoing characterization of memory has one noteworthy corollary that I shall highlight: computers do not remember. In the literature, much discussion is devoted to the question of whether computers are intelligent, whether they can be creative, whether they can have emotions (for references, see the discussion in Chapter 6). Yet, to my knowledge, the ability of computers to remember has never been questioned. Of course, computers can serve for the retrieval of stored information. They may actually be very helpful in this, and they may be better at it than people. But they do not engage in the act of remembering. On the one hand, they handle information precisely in the manner that, by the foregoing analysis, people do not; on the other hand, they manifest none of the crucial characteristics of human memory that I have surveyed. In particular, their remembering does not consist of action in the world, and does not exhibit the intrinsic temporality noted in the discussion of memory in Chapter 15.

Let me conclude with a comment on another key cognitive faculty – language. Language is the hallmark of representationalist, hence internal, cognitive science. But, again, look and see, and mark the obvious: Language is not internal! Contemporary theoretical linguistics has led us to identify language with syntax and semantics, and has driven the phonological articulation of language aside as if it were a contingent necessity devoid of any theoretical significance (many grammarians and all philosophers of language totally ignore phonology and morphophonemics). But there is no language without articulation, and articulation is, of course, in the public domain. In fact, language may be regarded as the linking chain that brings together the basic cognitive ability of acting in the external world and the derivative achievement of being able to engage in thinking without the world. On the one hand, language is concrete – it has no realization without the emitting of sound. On the other hand, unlike physical objects (but like our physical body), it could not exist in the world without there being cognitive agents to produce it. As argued in Chapter 19, it is this twofold character that makes language so important in our ability to engage in thought, reasoning and reflection. In Chapter 19, I underscored the fact that people think in words. However, as I commented there, and in the light of the observations above, let me note that, in effect, what we human beings do is think *with* words, just as we think with objects, with tools and instruments, with other people, and at times with symbols, that is, entities we create in our minds. As Mallarmé observed: 'The poet does not write with thoughts but with words'.

Extensions of the cognitive domain

In the picture of mind advocated here, the world in which cognition takes place is constituted by the meeting of the embodied self with, on the one hand, the physical world and, on the other hand, the social world of other human beings. Interestingly, in these encounters, the domain of the cognitive is extended in two ways, which correspond to the two worlds that the embodied cognitive agent meets. The meeting of the body and the world results in tools and artefacts; that of the body and the social other results in language and various inter-personal interactions. When these two extensions are joined together, the cognitive domain spans the entire manifold of society, civilization and culture.

Let me begin the discussion of the encounter of the body and the world and the extensions it generates with the consideration of tools. These may be regarded as direct extensions of the body. This is how Popper (1972) describes it:

> Man, instead of growing better eyes and ears, grows spectacles, microscopes, telescopes, telephones and hearing aids. And instead of growing swifter and swifter legs, he grows swifter and swifter motor cars . . . Instead of growing better memories and brains, he grows paper, pens, pencils, typewriters, dictaphones, the printing press, and libraries. (pp. 238–9)

And of course, had these lines been written just a couple of years later, the computer would have been added to the list and would even have crowned it.

This equivalence between organs of the body and tools is based on an evolutionary parallelism and on general functional considerations, but in fact, the tie is even more intimate than such an analogy implies. On the one hand, we use tools as if they were parts of our bodies, especially in skilled behaviour, where body and tool fuse into one functional whole. On the other hand, the manner in which we use our bodies is governed by principles of the same kind as those employed in our use of tools. In the words of Merleau-Ponty (1962):

The thing is correlative to my body and, in more general terms, to my existence, of which my body is merely the stabilized structure. It [the thing] is constituted in the hold which my body takes upon it . . . Its articulations are those of our very existence. (p. 320)

Here I shall venture to go one step further and – in line with observations made in Chapter 19 – suggest that what Merleau-Ponty claims of the body is true of the mind as well.

A famous example of a tool's being an extension of the body is that of the blind man and the guiding stick presented by Polanyi (1962). The blind man holds in his hand the proximal end of the stick; he senses, however, what is touched by the other, distal end. It is as if the stick extended the length of the man's fingers: instead of touching the pavement with the tips of his fingers, he is touching it with the end of his stick. But the one who touches both the stick and the pavement, who perceives the itinerary, interprets what he perceives and acts upon it, is the blind person. Whatever he does is accomplished by his cognitive system. As far as this system is concerned, the tips of the person's fingers are no less distant from the pavement than is the stick (for further discussion, see Shanon, 1991d).

The case of the blind man and the stick presents, then, what may be referred to as the *principle of distal action*. Both in the use of the body and in the use of tools, action takes place distally, at the point where the body (or the tool that extends it) meets the external world. With this, another principle manifests itself, the *principle of mechanistic ignorance*. Just as we are not cognizant of the physiology that makes our limbs work, so we are – at least most of us, in most cases – totally ignorant of the mechanisms underpinning the various instruments we use. I, for one, have no idea how a television set works, which does not in the least hinder me in the use of this appliance. It is all very simple: in order to turn the television on I press the red button on the right-hand side; in order to turn it off I press that button again. The same state of affairs is encountered when we lift things: we move our hands, grasp what we wish to lift, raise our hands and, lo and behold, whatever is held in the hand is lifted along with it. Of course, we all know this, but this does not make the observation less telling.

So far I have focused on human-made objects as extensions of the body; now let me focus on them from the perspective of the other constituent at hand, namely, the world. Rather than focusing on human-made objects *qua* tools I shall focus on them *qua* artefacts.

The artefacts human beings produce populate the world and alter the environment in which we live. Most of the readers of this book (and of course, its author) would, I imagine, find themselves totally at a loss if plunged back into the environment to which our biological bodies adapted when *homo sapiens* evolved. The ecosystem in which we live consists, in other words, not only of the natural – physical and biological – environment of the world, but also of the manifold of human-made objects. Consequently, the affordances presented to us by the world pertain not only to the natural environment, but also to our modifications of its landscape and to the artefacts we have placed in it (see Gibson, 1979; and for further extensions, Heft, 1989; Shanon, 1991b).

The entities human beings create are not confined to physical, concrete objects. In addition to hammers, television sets and computers, humankind has created not only books, paintings and software, but also numbers and mathematical structures, philosophical distinctions and theories, gods and notions of justice and benevolence. These, too, populate the world in which people live. Indeed, they define the habitat of cultures no less than do the physical, material entities. And just as different species inhabit different physical worlds, so different cultures reside in different cultural worlds. Indeed, it seems to me that the notion of affordance discussed at various junctures throughout this book is readily extendable to the cultural domain (for further discussion, see Chapter 8 and references noted there).

The encounter of the embodied cognitive agent with the social other is no less important than his or her encounter with the world. In particular, it will be noted that the body is what makes language articulated, hence public; the social other is what makes language meaningful. As noted in Chapter 9, even when one speaks to oneself one is addressing an other. The body also affords all sorts of inter-personal interactions. An ultimate meeting (perhaps even fusion) of body and social other is achieved in sexual intercourse.

The two extensions corresponding to the two homologous encounters I have examined are themselves homologous. The similarity between verbal behaviour and the manipulation of tools has often been made in the literature (notably by Wittgenstein, 1958; see also Gibson, 1979, p. 134); here, I would like to draw attention to two facets of this similarity that, to my knowledge, have not been previously noted. These correspond to the two principles of action marked in conjunction with the use of tools – that of distal action and that of mechanistic disregard.

In conjunction with the first, let me draw attention to the phenomenon of labelling discussed in Chapter 2. When I see the name 'Prof. Cohen' posted on a door I do not conclude that Prof. Cohen is a door or that the door is named after her, but rather that the office which one enters through the door on which the sign is posted belongs to, or is usually occupied by, Prof. Cohen. This is a linguistic manifestation of the principle of distal action. In the linguistic context, patterns that manifest this are usually referred to as metonyms, that is, figures of speech in which the name of one thing is used in order to refer to another, associated or connected thing. For instance, the phrase, 'lands belonging to the Crown' denotes lands which belong to the person who has a crown on his or her head. They might even belong not to that man or woman personally but to the institution associated with him or her. Unlike metaphor, which has received focal attention not only in linguistics but in the cognitive sciences in general, metonym has not been much dealt with. One of the leading general reference books in semantics suggests, for instance, subsuming the latter under the former (Lyons, 1977; vol. 2, p. 548).

As for the principle of mechanistic ignorance, recall the observation made in Chapter 15 and discussed earlier in this chapter: people are usually unable to articulate either the definitions of the meanings of words or the rules that govern human behaviour, and do not consciously plan or rehearse their actions before executing them. By RCVM, these patterns are accidental, the result of the fact that much of our mental life is not amenable to conscious inspection. In the present view, they are all manifestations of one, very basic principle of human action.

Meaning and interpretation

Throughout this discussion I have underlined the central role that meaning plays in psychology in general and in cognition in particular. What is meaning? By now, my stance on this matter should be clear. As far as cognitive agents are concerned, meaning is the manifold of actions and interactions that the world affords them. Since, in the picture of mind I advocate, action is defined by the unfolding of a path that the embodied self traces in the space of time–world spanned by the seven non-SR factors, meaning is to be defined in similar terms. Furthermore, in line with the identification of the psychological with the meaningful, I propose that the basic units of meaning be defined, like the basic terms of psychological theory, by (****).

An important clarification is in place. Above, and throughout this book, I have emphasized that cognition is grounded in meaning. The reader should beware not to give this statement a representationalist reading. The patterns of meaning that serve as the basis of cognition are not conceptual structures or representational schemata. In saying that both the basic terms of cognition and meaning are defined in terms of the non-SR factors, I am defining meaning in terms of action in the world. We view (or rather, encounter) the world not through mental categories but through our being and acting in it. Cognition is indeed intrinsically imbued with meaning, but meaning is inherently action-based.

Meaning may also be related to the second criterion by which the psychological domain is defined, consciousness. In line with the characterization of the psychological as the domain of the conscious, I propose that consciousness be defined in similar terms. This deserves further investigation. Here, let me just note that this makes readily explicable a common observation in the literature, namely, that people are conscious of the content of cognitive activity, not of the (putative) mental operations involved in the generation and processing of these contents (see Nisbett and Wilson, 1977). In the psychological literature, this is attributed to the time order of mental operations and to constraints on introspection. From the perspective of my picture of mind, this state of affairs is only natural. First, I postulate no underlying operations (for further discussion along this line, see Malcolm, 1971). Second, this pattern is just another manifestation of the principle of distal action. Third, if psychological phenomenology in general is defined in terms of content, it is only natural that the phenomenology of consciousness be defined in the same manner. After all, as noted in Chapter 19, consciousness consists in the construction in the mind of a world similar to the external one. Corroborating this view is the fact that conscious material is always experienced in terms of narratives (see Jaynes, 1977). Indeed, the same holds for dreams (see Shanon, 1990c).

Characterizing meaning in terms of action puts several issues considered in Part I in a new light. First, consider polysemy. The characterization at hand dispenses with the need to postulate different representations for the multifarious senses of words. My knowledge of how to use a tool does not consist of a repertory of representations of the various uses I can make of it: no such repertory could ever cover all the different modes of action associated with the tool. A screwdriver can be used not only for fixing screws but also for cutting, hammering, piercing, stretching, bending, and so on. Furthermore, there is no limit to the positions and manners in which a screwdriver may be held and used, even for actions having the same verbal label. Knowledge of tool use does not consist of reading out stored instructions, but of knowing how to handle the tool in that place in the world where the tool is situated. It seems to me that the same holds for words.

These comments resolve a seeming contradiction that the reader may have detected. Throughout this book I have underlined the polyvalence of meaning and at the same time marked the particular significance that words have in context. Rather than running contrary to each other, these two aspects of the meaning of words are two facets of the same basic state of affairs: both manifest the inherent context-dependence of language. Potentially, the range of interpretations that words can have is unbounded; once they are used in context, however, words are usually univocal. Since meaning is determined by both word and context, the word itself need not be semantically fixed, hence its undeterminateness and polyvalence. For the same reason, once the word is embedded in context, its meaning is determined and fixed.

Once again, let me emphasize that it is not that there is a plurality of meanings and that context selects between them. Just as cognitive activity has no realization outside the world, so meaning has no realization out of context. The unbounded plurality of meaning is a potentiality that determines the nature of cognitive theory and constrains cognitive modelling. In actuality, when language is immersed in the matrix of action in the world, it has one interpretation.

But once uttered, the words can again be subject to many interpretations. For the cognitive agent who produces them, the meaning of words, like the sense of the actions he or she performs, is determinate. However, for the person who hears (or reads) them, the words are presentations that may be inspected and interpreted in many ways, some not even foreseeable by the person who produced them. As Eco (1984) notes, this does not at all detract from the genuineness of these interpretations. As noted in Chapter 19, if anything, the opposite is the case: this attests to the authenticity of the act of their creation.[2]

The last remarks bear on another seeming contradiction in the discussion of meaning throughout the book. On the one hand, I have underscored the convergence of meaning and action; on the other hand, I have claimed that meaning is 'out there, on the surface'. In the framework of representationalist psychology adopting the modelling of underlying procedures as its canon of explanation, these two characterizations are contradictory. In the framework of the picture of mind drawn here and the non-procedural explanation I advocated, they are not. From the perspective of the cognitive agent, meaning and action are, indeed, one. However, the products of both expression and action are in the public domain, and as such are endowed with independent existence. Indeed, once produced, cognitive expressions can become the raw entities I talked about in Chapter 19. Like objects in the world, these can be a source of further interpretations, and they enrich the world (i.e., the manifold of meanings) with yet more meaning. They can also guide their own producers to lines of action, as was argued in the discussion of self-generated scaffolding. In Chapter 19, I observed that this is also true of thoughts one produces in the theatre of one's own mind.

Recipients can interact with the cognitive expressions they hear, read or observe either presentationally or representationally. In the presentational mode, recipients may resonate to these expressions, be emotionally affected by them, or take them as triggers for associations, conscious or not. In the representational mode, recipients will attempt comprehension by analysis. For instance, they will define features and attributes, specify the aspects of meaning and its constituents, and decompose the metaphorical into distinct semantic components. Different people and different contexts may induce the one mode or the other (or some combination of the two).

This characterization of the representational mode of interpretation puts the clarification comments made at the end of Chapter 3 in place. Meaning is not constituted in underlying semantic representations, neither perceptual stimuli nor words are made up of features, and metaphorical expressions are not generated by mapping one semantic domain onto another. However, in the representational mode, observers may see features in the things they perceive, decompose the meaning of words into semantic primitives, and analyze metaphors as mappings across domains. All these semantic distinctions do not pertain to a fixed, underlying representational level; rather, they are generated through processes that may be referred to as post-presentational.

These two modes of interpretation are completely analogous to the two modes of performance marked in conjunction with the mastery of skills. The analogy is not accidental. The cognitive expressions produced by our fellow human beings are like the instruments which musicians play. Like the accomplished musician, wise people, that is, people with sound intuitions and developed sensibilities, may fully rely on the presentational mode. Usually, comprehension is achieved through an on-going use of both the presentational and the representational modes. Often, one gains unconscious or semi-conscious understanding presentationally, only to go on and examine things representationally before one has the feeling that one has, indeed, achieved full understanding. RCVM strives to account for comprehension exclusively in representational terms. This, I maintain, involves a biased and sadly impoverished view of cognition.

Throughout this discussion I have characterized meaning in terms of the immersion of cognitive expression in the context of action in the world. As noted, meaning is generated (or rather, unfolds) in the meeting of words and context. Once again, however, it should be emphasized that words and context are not separate, unconnected constituents. The words one utters are part and parcel of the context of action, and they too are determinants of the space of meaning. Just as they gain meaning in context, so they do through being juxtaposed with other words. As Maupassant claimed, such a juxtaposition is one of the most important means by which meaning is created: 'Words have a soul. Most readers, and even writers, demand only that they should have a sense. One has to find that soul, which appears in the contact of words with other words' (de Maupassant); for an extended discussion along this line, see Barfield (1977). This is most apparent in metaphor, where words are usually juxtaposed with words with which they are not often paired. Other than that, however, there is no principled difference between such expressions and the so-called more standard linguistic ones. That the creation of meaning through the juxtaposition of words with other words is indeed a very basic and pervasive phenomenon is indicated by the phrasal compositions examined in Chapter 3. There we also encountered generation of meaning as it is manifested in the juxtaposition of words with objects (recall the discussion of labelling). What we now appreciate is that in essence, there is no difference between all these cases. In the light of the picture of mind I have drawn and my characterization of action with objects as the basic cognitive skill, this is a natural conclusion.

The last remarks bring us back to the phenomenon of polysemy discussed at the beginning of this section. Above (and throughout the first line of the critique), I argued that polysemy could not be accounted for if meaning were the overt expression of underlying representations. By contrast, juxtaposition of the type just noted renders the polyvalence of meaning utterly natural. After all, there need not be any limitation on the number of things with which a word may be juxtaposed or to which it may be tied.

Considering juxtaposition highlights the fact that words and the basic terms of cognition gain their meaningfulness in being embedded in a larger space of other words and other terms. This is in line with another observation made at various junctures in this book, namely, that higher-order relations have cognitive primacy over the constituents of which they are composed. This ties interestingly with the key observation of the foregoing discussion – that words and the basic terms of cognition are laden with meaning. The ingrained meaningfulness of cognitive expressions and the primacy of larger structures and of higher-order relations are both the corollaries of the same fundamental feature – namely, that the basic terms of cognition are units (in Vygotsky's sense). As such, and unlike the elements of atomistic models, they are of substance: being laden with meaning, they are not naked, and being part and parcel of a large matrix, they are not of minimal magnitude. The contrast with the picture endorsed by RCVM is glaring. By RCVM, the basic terms of cognition are naked atomic constituents and meaning is derived through their composition into larger structures, which, in turn, are subject to interpretation imposed onto them. The two seemingly distinct basic features of cognitive expressions noted here (ingrained meaningfulness and the primacy of larger structures and of higher-order relations) join in defining the negation of the representational characterization of meaning that I reject.

The basic cognitive terms of RCVM are not only atomistic and naked, but also static and inert. By contrast, in the picture of mind advocated here, cognition is intrinsically dynamic. As argued in the third line of this critique, cognition and cognitive activity are defined in terms not of entities but of events. This is true of meaning as well. Again, this fits nicely with the picture sketched in this chapter. On the one hand, events are higher-level structures. On the other hand, the creation of meaning through the juxtaposition of words with other words is itself an on-going, dynamic process. As indicated throughout this discussion, meaning is not merely generated (and likewise, cognitive expression and activity are not merely produced), it (and likewise, they) unfolds.

Lastly, consider reference and the problem of the unbridgeable gap it presents. If reference is to be accounted for in semantic-representational terms, then how human beings learn to use words in order to refer is a mystery that cannot be accounted for. However, once an action-based, pragmatic perspective is taken, the problem is dissolved. It is not that children possess symbols which they have to tie to the world, nor that there are given objects in the world and children have to invent mental representations that will stand in a referential relationship to them. Neither the separate objects nor the reference relationship are basic. What is basic and primary is the very tie that RCVM cannot account for. This tie is part and parcel of children's initial state of being, that is, acting in the world.

Pertinent observations in this regard were made by Werner and Kaplan (1963), even before the representational revolution in cognitive psychology took place. They pointed out that reference is an outgrowth of motor-gestural behaviour. Reaching evolves into pointing, and calling-for into denoting. This evolution takes place in the context of the pragmatic situation of action. Interestingly, Werner and Kaplan note that it is in the course of being shared with other people that symbols gain their denotative function. More recently, Anglin (1979) showed that the order in which terms of reference are acquired by children is associated with the actions that the children can perform with the objects named. Children are not left alone: from the first year of life, they look to adults to interpret situations in a process of social referencing (Feinman, 1982; Gunnar and Stone, 1984). This is facilitated by children's obtaining information from the direction in which caregivers point and gaze. Indeed, it appears that even very young infants adjust their gaze when adult partners change the direction in which they are looking (Scaife and Bruner, 1975; Bruner, 1987; Butterworth, 1987).

In sum, the unbridgeable gap of reference and the problem of interpretation haunting RCVM dissipate when one appreciates that reference is not merely a relationship between concepts in the mind and objects in the world and that interpretation is not imposed on meaningless symbolic structures. Rather, both reference and meaning are part and parcel of one's action in the world. They are there from the very start. Inasmuch as the child acts, he or she finds meaning in the world; and inasmuch as the child finds things meaningful, he or she can act on and with them. As the child grows older, reference relations and meanings are differentiated and refined through the on-going interaction between the child and the environment; in this process all factors considered in the second line of this critique are involved.

Ontology and adequacy

Related to meaning are two topics that extend beyond the domain of psychology proper. The first is ontology, the second the criterion of adequacy.

Although this book is concerned with psychology, more than once in my discussion I have alluded to ontology. This is no accident. First, psychology – especially in the view advocated here – is not divorced from the world. Second, as noted in Chapter 16, psychological theories are couched in some basic notions regarding the order of things. Both psychological and ontological theories may reflect these notions. Specifically, RCVM is symptomatic of a world-view assuming the existence of basic elementary entities which combine together to form larger entities. In this view, elements have precedence over both larger entities and relations, structures over interpretations, the static over the dynamic, and there is a principled segregation between structures and processes and between structures and interpretations. This critique argued against each and every component of this world-view as it manifests itself in cognition. At the same time, however, a change in the ontological world-view is implied. After all, it would be highly unnatural to have one's cognition and world manifest categorically distinct orders of things. The alternative ontology exhibits at least the following characteristics. First, it ties together mind and world, organism and environment. Second, its basic terms are already invested with meaning. Third, it does not assume compositionality. Fourth, it gives precedence to wholes and so-called higher-level relations. Fifth, its basic state is the dynamic. Ontological proposals highlighting this include the cosmology drawn by Whitehead (1929) and the dynamic models proposed by Prigogine (1980). The new theories of chaos may also provide new frameworks for both ontology and cognition (see, for instance, Skarda and Freeman, 1987; Shanon, 1993c).

Let me turn to the criterion of adequacy. Representational theories assume as this criterion a measure of truth: representations stand for things and states of affairs in the world, they might even be said to be reflections or copies of the world. As noted in Chapter 15, in the framework of RCVM the recourse to a correspondence criterion of adequacy is universal – it underlies any use one makes of concepts and is thus the basis for memory and recognition, identification and classification, comprehension and interpretation. With the demise of representations, one can no longer refer to correspondence as a measure of adequacy. What is the alternative?

It is a sense of fit: instead of corresponding to underlying representations, things have to fit, to get along together, to click. By way of example, let me consider, again, the domain of music. How does one apprehend music? How does one appreciate that it is appealing? Or interesting, or gay, or sad, or dramatic? How can one tell that it is Schubert or Debussy, or eighteenth-century baroque? As noted in Chapter 15, to assume that this is all achieved by means of one's consulting stored representations defies reason. The way out is that suggested to me by my friend Georges Amar, a painter and a non-academic (hence, not tied to established dogma) philosopher. How does one determine that a painting is well composed, that it sits well? By dancing it, Georges says. (The reader will appreciate that all this applies to music just as well – in fact, even more obviously.) Two aspects of this solution should be noted. First, it relegates the act of judgement to a so-called non-cognitive performance – bodily posture and movement. Second, in lieu of correspondence it adopts fit as its basic criterion.

Representationalists are likely to retort by asking how the fit is determined. For this, they will say, one must refer to some representation, one has to apply some computational processes. But I have already been through all this, and shown that it leads only to a dead end. The thing to do is to abandon the representational-computational account. It is not by means of reference to representations and the computational processing thereof that the fit is determined. Rather, one relies on non-cognitive factors like those discussed in the second line of this critique. The body knows whether things are balanced or not, whether they are in equilibrium or not, whether they fit or not. Agents moving about in the world know how to find their way in it. Social agents appreciate whether the other is kind, or honest, or boring, or attractive. Likewise, affectively one knows that things are good or bad (for the given agent), pleasant or not so. And ethically, one appreciates that things are right or wrong, fair or despicable. In all these cases what is being determined is whether or not things fit, click, or feel right.

I have shown this in several cases throughout this book. I know that I am replicating the same sequence of taps because that is what it feels like. The tapping in both cases gives the same feeling. This is achieved not by means of a correspondence to a representation, not by an internal count, but by some sort of fit (for independent discussion of this notion, see Shepard, 1984). This fit, note, is temporal. It is not an appraisal of the sameness of two given entities. The same number of taps is produced not because in both cases the same number of items is specified in some mental store. Rather, the two are the same because they have the same music, or rather – because they constitute the same dance.

Years after Georges shared his insightful observations with me, I found the same idea in Wittgenstein:

> Understanding a sentence is much more akin to understanding a theme in music than one may think. What I mean is that understanding a theme in music lies nearer than one thinks to what is ordinarily called understanding a musical theme. Why is just *this* the pattern of variation in loudness and tempo? One would like to say 'Because I know what it's all about.' But what is it all about? I should not be able to say. In order to 'explain' I could only compare it with something else which has the same rhythm (I mean the same pattern). (One says 'Don't you see, this is as if a conclusion were being drawn' or 'This is as it were a parenthesis', etc. How does one justify such comparisons? – There are very different kinds of justifications here.) (Wittgenstein, 1953, part 1, no. 527)

While any word – one would like to say – may have a different character in different contexts, all the same there is *one* character – a face – that it always has. It looks at us. – For one might actually think that each word was a little face; the written sign might be a face. And one might also imagine that the whole proposition was a kind of group-picture, so that the gaze of the faces all together produced a relationship among them and so the whole made a *significant group*. But what constitutes the experience of a group's being significant? (Wittgenstein, 1980, vol. 1, no. 322)

The affinity between these observations and the discussion in the previous section is evident. They are also in line with my characterization of sensory-motor, kinaesthetic and rhythmic sensation as basic determining factors in the identification of things and the appraisal of sameness.

Interestingly, these observations mark yet another pattern in which different considerations entertained throughout this book tie in. The discussion of adequacy brings together what, at the beginning of the book, were referred to as the horizontal and vertical perspectives in the study of semantics. Usually, compositionality and well-formedness pertain to the horizontal dimension. Here observations on compositionality and well-formedness have been made in conjunction with the determination of adequacy, an issue usually associated with the vertical dimension. That the two dimensions meet is consonant with my rejection of meaning as the reflection of a more basic, underlying level. In fact, the two key features of the picture of meaning drawn in the previous section – ingrained meaningfulness and the primacy of large structures – also seem to be associated with the two different perspectives – the vertical and the horizontal, respectively. Yet, as noted in the previous section, with the rejection of RCVM the two cohere into one unified whole.

Let me close with marking another affinity between what Wittgenstein says above and the picture of mind advocated in this book. Wittgenstein likens the understanding of language to the understanding of music. Being in full agreement with Wittgenstein, I would proceed further and extend the musical characterization to cognitive activity in general. By RCVM, piano playing is modelled by means of internal representations and computational operations applied to them. The moral of the present critique is that not only is such a modelling of piano playing fundamentally wrong (recall the discussion in Chapters 11 and 13), but representations and computations are not suitable even for the modelling of what representationalists consider to be the paradigmatic manifestations of human cognition. The more appropriate way to account for cognition is to characterize it in terms of an activity such as piano playing.

Time

Throughout the previous chapters I have repeatedly underlined the intrinsic temporality of cognition. I have also noted that time is one of the various non-SR factors, and I have marked that one ability of the cognitive system is to gain autonomy from these. Further, I have noted that in being able to recollect past memories and speculate about the future, human beings gain some autonomy with respect to time. But of course, we always depend on time. As noted by Proust in *Remembrance of Things Past* (and especially in the concluding volume, *Time Regained*), people cannot escape time. Yet, to a certain degree we all do. In line with my analysis of the 'now' in Chapter 12, I may say that the psychological present is that stretch of time that one manages to hold in one's grasp. Since the 'now' is defined in terms of events, that is, in terms of wholes that are meaningful to one, the more meaningful experiences are to one, the greater will the extension of the 'now' be, hence the longer one's specious present. With this, one's ability to overcome the domination of time will be enhanced and one will be able to achieve a higher degree of autonomy relative to it. To a certain extent, we are all familiar with this: we have all internalized the meaningful histories of our existence – not as internal representations, but as part and parcel of who we are, who we take ourselves to be. Some people, in conjunction with particular cognitive performances, have achieved exceptional mastery over the bounds of time. As noted in Chapter 18, Mozart is said to have been able to grasp a symphony instantaneously as one whole, as if it were a picture. Mystics and people experiencing some of the so-called altered states of consciousness have reported being out of time (as well as being off the ground, outside their bodies, and outside the given physical environment). Others have mastered time intellectually: Plato and Spinoza did so in their philosophical systems. These take a perspective that is beyond time, *sub specie aeternitate*. Such idealized states of affairs are, of course, outside the frame of standard psychology. Or more accurately, they may be viewed as the (unattainable, in the mathematical sense) limit of human cognition. Ironically, RCVM, and in particular the metapsychology of Chomsky and Fodor, attempt to construe cognitive science on the foundations of this limit. In God's eyes, this might be cognition; in human practice it is definitely not.

An example

Let me conclude with an example from my own experience. This example illustrates some of the ideas presented in this chapter, and has to do with this very project. In the spring of 1981, while at a conference on auto-organization which took place in Normandy, I was asked, at a day's notice, to deliver a lecture. I knew what the topic of this lecture would be: a series of arguments marking the inadequacy of the representationalist view of language and cognition. I sat down and jotted down a list of such arguments on paper. This took about a quarter of an hour. To deliver the lecture took me an hour. Then, on returning to Israel, I wrote a paper based on the lecture. It took me several weeks to write this paper. Three years later I began working on this book. It extended over a period of about six years. Yet, this book is a presentation of those very same basic ideas that I had in mind in France more than ten years ago. Does this mean that all the long time that has passed since was dispensable? Absolutely not. For it to be realized, this entire project had to unfold in time – to be put down on paper, shaped, inspected, reshaped and eventually gain its own independent realization in the form of a book.

Above, I have used the phrase, 'I had in mind'. Like so many other linguistic expressions, this one too is misleading. It is, of course, not the case that I had an idea in my mind and had to put it down on paper. I should perhaps have used an expression such as, 'I sensed that something was the case' or, 'I intuited'. The subsequent long process of reflection and writing was a process of crystallization whereby the insights and intuitions differentiated and gained shape and form. Thus they were invested with real existence, and as such served as scaffolding for the further writing of the book. As the writing progressed, it was more and more like working on a painting on canvas. More than expressing ideas, I was manipulating objects out there in the world – the words on the computer screen. Once this book is complete, when it is printed on paper and bound, its existence will no longer depend on me. When read, the text will then serve as the basis for further interpretation.

Notes

1. By way of further corroboration, let me mention a study now in progress, conducted with my student, Dan Lassri. In this, subjects are presented with simple household objects (e.g. scissors, a pencil, a ball) and asked whether they have any childhood memories associated with these. Usually, the subjects take the object and manipulate it. It is through this manipulation that memory unfolds.
2. Let me draw attention to the insightful comment made by Merleau-Ponty (1962): 'Authentic language is a "paradoxical operation" because it uses given meanings to capture an intention that transcends them, while at the same time it "fixes" these sedimented structures and "recasts them all" by using them in a new context' (p. 445).

Epilogue

Understanding

Let the mind be enlarged according to its capacity, to the grandeur of the mysteries; and not the mysteries contracted to the narrowness of the mind.
Francis Bacon

I have gone a long way. I have examined RCVM and criticized it, sketched a non-representational picture of mind, presented an entire array of alternative theoretical frameworks for psychology, and proposed guidelines for alternative psychological explanation and research. However, I have presented no models, no procedures, no formal structures, no mappings or transformations. Does this mean that nothing has been achieved, that nothing has been gained? This is a question I have repeatedly asked myself while working on this project. In saying this, I mean that I do feel that I have learnt something, that I have, if you wish, gained some understanding. Understanding pertains to the question, 'What is it all about?'. Having conducted so many experiments in the laboratory, having completed so many field studies, having analyzed the data and having specified the models, the question still remains – 'What does it all mean?'. This last chapter presents some thoughts and reflections on this question.

The question of basics

Whether it is explicit about it or not, every cognitive theory takes a stance on what it deems the basics of cognition to be. No matter what, one must always start with something, and there is always bound to be something that one ends up leaving unexplained. The choice of basics has various manifestations, both substantive and methodological; as is noted below, all have far-reaching ramifications.

Substantive issues

Substantively, the question of basics manifests itself in an issue already discussed at length, namely, the specification of the basic capabilities of mind. As noted, the specification of these is perhaps the key ingredient of any picture of mind. In specifying the basic capabilities of mind the cognitive scientists make their statement as to what makes the cognitive system tick. RCVM's stance is clear: what the cognitive system does, what the mind is designed to do, is manipulate symbols. Once this stance is adopted, the nature of cognitive modelling and cognitive explanation is to a great extent determined. Of course, the details of specific models remain to be added, but their general character is fixed.

Specifying the basic capabilities of mind has several further ramifications. It entails answers to questions such as, 'What does it mean to be a cognitive agent?', 'What does it mean to be an intelligent creature?', 'What does it mean to be a person?', and 'What is the nature of mind?'. One may try to dismiss these questions as metaphysical, but they cannot be avoided. Whether one realizes it or not, whether one admits it or not, one always adopts some stance *vis-à-vis* them.

One particular ramification will be singled out. As noted throughout this book, in stating that the basic capability of mind is symbol manipulation, RCVM stipulates that in essence there is no difference between human beings and computers. This demands further reflection. Even before one examines the problems – both conceptual and empirical – that RCVM may confront in accounting for the phenomenology of behaviour, even before, in other words, one engages in a project like the one undertaken in this book, one might wish to pause and ask oneself whether one would indeed like to adopt a world-view that places human beings and computers on a par.

I appreciate that it is only natural for scientific theories to be influenced by the technological advancements of their time. This is true of all sciences, and it has certainly been so of the science of mind. Over the years the mind has been modelled in terms of Newtonian mechanics, hydraulics, electronics and telephone communication. The current modelling of the mind in the image of the computer is but another manifestation of this recourse to technology. Heuristically, such a move can indeed be very productive: it can lead the scientist to new ways of thinking, define new questions for research and present totally novel theoretical possibilities. Yet, one should be extremely careful. Taking the recourse to technology too seriously may eventually result not in the opening of possibilities but in tying one to a particular frame of thinking, in constraining one's imagination, and hence in the closing of options. This is certainly true of contemporary cognitive science. Undoubtedly, the cognitive revolution of the past thirty years would not have occurred had it not been for the contemporary computer revolution and the wide exposure of psychologists to the new sciences of information. Yet, at the same time the study of mind has paid an enormous price. The computer metaphor imposes the representational view of mind, hence all the problems discussed in this book. Perhaps the recourse to computer terminology and models was essential for cognition to become a true science, but with it the field has, in effect, gone astray.

Methodological issues

In specifying the basic capabilities of mind, cognitive scientists determine what in effect are the axioms of their theory. They have, however, choice in this regard, and the different choices can have significantly different ramifications. In deciding what constitutes the foundations of one's theory, one should exercise good judgement. As noted in earlier chapters, examining the foundations of a theory may drastically affect one's evaluation of a scientific paradigm. The paradigm may generate a plethora of empirical findings, substantiate them with statistical analyses and mathematical formulations, construct models and build theories, and may look like one big success story. But then, one might look at the foundations only to discover how fragile it all is. Either the foundations defy common sense, or they are shrouded in mystery, or they involve a price that is too heavy to be paid, or they do not tie in with some other general principles. As argued, in the case of RCVM much of this seems to be the case.

Second, specifying the basic capabilities of mind also entails a position on what is simple and what is complex. The ordering of the complexity of phenomena has important implications. It involves an appraisal of what is interesting, it dictates the goals of one's research programme and affects the course of investigation one conducts, and it defines criteria for the evaluation of the outcome of one's work. In this regard, RCVM resembles, I think, the man in the famous Sufi tale who looks for his key not where he has dropped it but where there is more light. In directing its attention to what can be modelled in terms of representations and computational operations, cognitive science has distanced itself from the very essence of cognition. It may have come up with well-defined models, but in so doing it has endorsed a view that utterly misses what it is that makes the mind tick, all that is genuinely cognitive-psychological.

Third, in specifying the basics one states not only what one takes for granted, but also what one decides to leave unexplained. The admission that one's theory cannot be all-encompassing, that some things have to be left unexplained, need not be regarded only in a negative way. In deciding what one leaves unexplained, one is making a statement on what one finds most awesome, most wondrous. It is, in other words, a definition of what one takes to be the mysterious. I know that the mere mention of such a word in a scientific context may be seen by many as sufficient reason for utter rebuff, dismissal and ridicule. Yet, in the end, does it not all have to do with mystery, and is it not the sense of mystery that makes the entire scientific pursuit so exciting? I was delighted when, in an article in the *New York Review of Books* (Gombrich, 1989), I found the following quotation from the writings of James Gibson: 'Psychology, or at least American psychology, is a second rate discipline. The main reason is that it does not stand in awe of its subject matter. Psychologists have too little respect for psychology.' (Reed, 1982). I suspect that psychologists adopt this stance because they are so anxious to be 'scientific'. Yet, mystery is admitted by many respected scientists in other, established disciplines. Physicists admit it when confronting the creation of the universe and the beginning of time, biologists when discovering over and over again how complex and efficient the structure of living organisms and their functioning are. Many names could be cited in this conjunction. My particular choices are Weisskopf, who opened his *Knowledge and Wonder* (Weisskopf, 1962) with Francis Bacon's adage, 'Wonder [is] the seed of knowledge'; Schrödinger, who opened his *My View of the World* (Schrödinger, 1964) with a motto underscoring the point that riddle is the generator of truth; McClintock, whose life was characterized as a quest guided by 'a feeling for the organism' (see Keller, 1983); and last but not least, Albert Einstein. Einstein regarded the feeling of wonder as the basis for creative thinking and he rooted his entire intellectual history in it (see Einstein, 1949); for further discussion of Einstein's feeling of awe, see Frank (1949).

My first teacher of linguistics, the grammarian Robert Lees, once said something that has reverberated in my mind many times since: that a scientific discipline is mature when it has its own paradox. (He made this statement while introducing the Peters–Bach paradox.) If it is to mature, cognitive science has to face its own mysteries boldly. Surely its subject matter, the mind, presents a mystery well deserving the company of both that of the cosmos and that of the phenomenon of life.

The mysterious, however, is too precious to be chosen without care. One should not waste one's mysteries, so to speak. What one labels as mysterious should be a truly baffling puzzle worthy of this characterization. Furthermore, its negative character notwithstanding, the choice should be illuminating. To appreciate what is to be taken as mysterious, what is to be left unexplained, is a significant achievement in its own right.

Lastly, let me underscore a point already made in Chapters 20 and 21: choices need not be either absolute or universal, they may also reflect considerations of suitability in a situation. Understanding a domain requires an ability to appreciate the benefits that are important for one and the costs one is ready to pay (and costs there always are), and an ability to gauge the benefits against the costs so as to arrive at a decision fully cognizant of its broader implications. The issues examined above – the picture of mind, the basic capabilities, the mysterious – are all considerations of which one should not be oblivious.

Questions for further research

The choice of basics not only determines what are to be deemed the important topics for investigation but also defines the specific questions for research, both empirical and theoretical. Changing one's stance on the question of basics may result in the dissolution of heretofore puzzling questions and the appearance of new ones on the cognitive scene. The shift from a representational to a non-representational psychology involves a whole array of such reversals:

1. *Decontextualization.* Instead of asking how the pragmatic aspects of language are tied, added to or imposed on the semantic ones, one should ask how language dissociates itself from its pragmatic aspects and becomes fixed and semantically well defined. Specifically, since meaning is dependent on context,

the question now arises as to how literal meaning, which is independent (or relatively independent) of context, is created.

2. *Differentiation.* Rather than asking how words and actions are invested with different meanings, one should ask how the basic, multi-faceted, undifferentiated meaning crystallizes to become fixed and univocal. Further, given that metaphorical meaning is primary, how is literal meaning created?

3. *Abstraction.* Given that the basic structures of modes of operation of cognition are not abstract, how is it that the system can dissociate itself from the medium so that the latter becomes irrelevant?

4. *Autonomy.* Given that cognition consists basically of acting in the world, how do cognitive agents dissociate themselves from the dynamic dependence on their bodies, the world, the social other, affect and motivation, and the immediacy of the present?

5. *Stabilization and fixation.* Since the cognitive system is basically in constant flux, how is it that the existence of fixed, stable entities is experienced? Given that the different faculties of the mind are all interconnected, how is compartmentalization made possible? And since psychology and ontology are not unrelated, one may also ask how is it that there are objects in the world?

Each of these questions defines cognitive functions to be studied and corresponding components to be incorporated into cognitive theory. The functions may be grouped in two clusters. On the one hand, there are negative functions. These include functions of inhibition and disregard: decontextualization, abstraction and uncoupling, autonomy and dissociation. On the other hand, there are the positive functions of differentiation and stabilization; these manifest themselves in crystallization and the generation of particular, fixed, well-defined cognitive expressions. The two types of function are, of course, related; in fact, they may be regarded as the two sides of one coin: it is only in reducing its sensitivity to external stimulation, in breaking its primordial tie with the environment, in keeping away from the incessant flux of life, that the cognitive system can attain its own, distinct existence and have an impact on the world.

One qualification: I have referred to the questions and their redefinition as reversed. But, of course, this attribution is only relative. If anything is upside-down it is RCVM and the questions it poses. This view characterizes cognition, and psychology in general, in a biased, lop-sided manner. The questions listed above come by way of rectifying this state of affairs.

The cognitive problematics

Last but not least, we have gained an understanding of what I have referred to as the 'cognitive problematics'. The cognitive problematics may be regarded as the ultimate moral of this entire enterprise – what remains when all is said and done. In Chapter 21, when presenting the general sketch of the cognitive problematics,

I focused on issues of theory construction and methodology. But as attested throughout this book, these issues and those pertaining to the substance of cognition are intertwined. The cognitive problematics is at the same time that of cognition and of cognitive science. In particular, to the similarities between the different arguments marshalled against RCVM there correspond affinities between the different factors associated with those arguments. Likewise, to the patterns that recur in my critical argumentation and in the various possible responses to it there correspond general principles governing the workings of mind. As shown throughout this book, the many different behaviours in which cognitive agents engage are the manifestations of some very basic capabilities. In other words, the cognitive performances are various, but the cognitive system is fundamentally one. Indeed, it is due to its internal coherence and the affinities and interrelations between its constituents that my alternative picture of mind becomes meaningful and gains its veracity.

An appreciation of the cognitive problematics is, I believe, of paramount importance. It can save cognitive scientists a great deal of trouble – it can help them avoid pitfalls and escape dead ends. Embarking upon new scientific inquiries, it is most beneficial to appreciate the mistakes of the past. Thus, gaining understanding of the cognitive problematics drawn here is of extreme potential constructive value for any future cognitive research.

A last remark

Still, one may persist and ask: but how does it all happen? You have specified no underlying mechanisms or flow chart of processing. Indeed, I have not. What I have done is tell a story – the story of cognition. I hope that having heard this story you understand the mind somewhat better and have a better feel of what it is all about. I hope that you appreciate better what is interesting about cognition, what makes it special, what its accomplishments are and what it finds difficult, how it develops, what makes it run. It is like understanding a person. Understanding a person does not consist in specifying the structures of the neurophysiological activity in the person's brain, nor in the specification of the software of his or her mind and the flow charts of the processes that presumably take place in it. As Fodor and Pylyshyn (1988a) say (about connectionism), it is all implementation (by 'it' I refer to neurophysiological accounts, connectionist networks *and* classical representational-computational models), and as such it is outside the scope of psychology proper. Think of the stories that novels relate. They do not consist of the specifications of any underlying processes, be they biological, virtual-neurological, computational or symbolic. One reads the story of the life (or a period or a day in the life of) a person. One follows the story, one travels for a while together with that individual, and eventually one gains understanding of him or her. When understanding has been achieved one discovers that one can tell a story. The moral of my discussion is that the same holds for the mind. Instead of modelling cognitive tasks, we should strive to understand them. In other words, we should appreciate the factors involved in the execution of these tasks, the conditions which affect them, the dynamics of their execution and the course of their acquisition.[1] In a nutshell, we should be able to tell a story, a comprehensible narrative of these tasks. If this narrative is adequate, it is bound to fit well with the narratives of other tasks. Eventually, the narratives will all tie together into the epic of the mind.

This, then, is what I have done in this book: I have followed the paths of the mind and told its story. And as in the case of people, there is much more to be told. One can go on and inspect the mind as it acts in different contexts, as it accomplishes different feats. More details can be added to the stories, and the narrative can be extended in time. One can inspect specific episodes in the history of the mind, examine the minutiae of particular behaviours, trace the long chain of cognitive development and evolution. As Zuccaro counsels, if the observation is careful, if the recounting is sincere, then one is bound to tell a genuine and meaningful story, one which will further readers' understanding and make them appreciate something they did not before. Some readers may then go on and add their own contributions to the story.

Note

1. A similar, although not identical, call is made by Shotter (1975), who argues that psychology should be concerned not with the discovery of principles of behaviour but with understanding how human beings can be responsible for their lives. Rather than probe deeply into the inner workings of things and discovering their rock-bottom, ultimate causes, psychologists should study people's options as to how to live.

References

Abeles, M. (1982). *Local Cortical Circuits: An Electrophysiological Study*. Berlin: Springer Verlag.

Adams, A.K. and Bullock, D. (1986). Apprenticeship in word use: social convergence processes in learning categorically related nouns. In S.A. Kuczaj and M.D. Barrett (eds), *The Development of Word Meaning: Progress in Cognitive Development Research* (pp. 155–97). New York: Springer Verlag.

Agassi, Y. (1973). Methodological individualism. In J. O'Neill (ed.) *Modes of Individualism and Collectivism* (pp. 185–212). London: Heinemann.

Agmon, E. (1990). Music theory as cognitive science: some conceptual and methodological issues. *Music Perception*, **7**, 285–308.

Agre, P.E. (1988). *The Dynamic Structure of Everyday Life*. Technical Report 1085, MIT Artificial Intelligence Laboratory.

Alba, J.W. and Hasher, L. (1983). Is memory schematic? *Psychological Bulletin*, **93**, 203–31.

Alberti, L.B. (1435/1966). *On Painting*. New Haven: Yale University Press.

Allport, A. (1984). Alternatives to the computational view of mind: the body or the bathwater? *Journal of Verbal Learning and Verbal Behavior*, **23**, 315–24.

Allport, G.W. (1937). *Personality: A Psychological Interpretation*. New York: Holt.

Amit, D.J. (1989). *Modelling Construction*. Cambridge: Cambridge University Press.

Anderson, J.R. (1978). Arguments concerning representations from mental imagery. *Psychological Review*, **85**, 249–77.

Anderson, J.R. and Bower, G.H. (1973). *Human Associative Memory*. Washington, DC: Winston.

Anderson, J.R. and Ortony, A. (1975). On putting apples into bottles – a problem of polysemy. *Cognitive Psychology*, **7**, 167–80.

d'Andrade, R.G. (1981). The cultural part of cognition. *Cognitive Science*, **5**, 179–95.

d'Andrade, R.G. (1989). Culturally based reasoning. In A. Gellatly, D. Rogers and J.A. Sloboda (eds), *Cognition and Social Worlds* (pp. 132–43). Oxford: Clarendon Press.

Anglin, J.M. (1979). The child's first terms of reference. In N.R. Smith and M.B. Franklin (eds), *Symbolic Functioning in Childhood* (pp. 167–84), Hillsdale, NJ: Lawrence Erlbaum.

Argyle, M. (1972). Non-verbal communication in human social interaction. In R.A. Hinde (ed), *Non-Verbal Communication* (pp. 243–69). New York: Cambridge University Press.

Arieti, S. (1974). *Interpretation of Schizophrenia*. New York: Basic Books.

Aristotle (1963). *The Physics*. London: Heinemann.

Armstrong, S.L., Gleitman, L.R. and Gleitman, H. (1983). What some concepts might not be. *Cognition*, **13**, 263–308.

Asch, S. and Nerlove, H. (1960). The development of double function terms in children: an exploration study. In B. Kaplan and S. Wapner (eds), *Perspectives in Psychological Theory* (pp. 47–60). New York: International Universities Press.

Asmolov, A.G. (1986). Basic principles of a psychological analysis in the theory of activity. *Soviet Psychology*, **2**, 78–102.

Atlan, H. (1979). *Entre le Cristal et la Fumée*. Paris: Seuil.
Atlan, H. (1986). *A Tort et à Raison: Intercritique de la Science et du Mythe*. Paris: Seuil.
Atlan, H. (1987). Self creation of meaning. *Physical Scripta*, **36**, 563–76.
Austin, J.L. (1962). *How to Do Things with Words*. Oxford: Clarendon Press.
Baars, B.J. (1980). *A Cognitive Theory of Consciousness*. Cambridge: Cambridge University Press.
Baars, B.J. (1983). Conscious contents provide the nervous system with coherent, global information. In R.J. Davidson, G.E. Schwartz and D. Shapiro (eds), *Consciousness and Self-Regulation*, Vol. 3 (pp. 41–79). New York: Plenum Press.
Baddeley, A.D., Eldridge, M. and Lewis, V. (1981). The role of subvocalisation in reading. *Quarterly Journal of Experimental Psychology*, **33A**, 439–54.
Bakhurst, D. (1990). Social memory in Soviet thought. In D. Middelton and D. Edwards (eds), *Collective Remembering* (pp. 203–27). London: Sage.
Bar-Hillel, Y. (1954). Indexical expressions. *Mind*, **63**, 359–79.
Bar-Hillel, Y. (1971). Out of the pragmatic wastebasket. *Linguistic Inquiry*, **2**, 401–7.
Barfield, O. (1977). *The Rediscovery of Meaning and Other Essays*. Middletown, OH: Wesleyan University Press.
Barlow, H.B. (1980). Nature's joke: a conjecture on the biological role of consciousness. In B.D. Josephson and V.S. Ramachandran (eds), *Consciousness and the Physical World* (pp. 79–92). London: Pergamon.
Bartlett, F.C. (1932). *Remembering: A Study in Experimental Social Psychology*. Cambridge: Cambridge University Press.
Barwise, J. and Perry, J. (1983). *Situations and Attitudes*. Cambridge, MA: Harvard University Press.
Bates, E. (1976). *Language and Context: The Acquisition of Pragmatics*. New York: Academic Press.
Bates, E. (1979). *The Emergence of Symbols*. New York: Academic Press.
Bates, E. (1987). Temperament in infancy. In J.D. Osofsky (ed.), *Handbook of Infant Development* (pp. 1101–49). New York: John Wiley.
Bates, E., Camaioni, L. and Volterra, V. (1979). The acquisition of performatives prior to speech. In E. Ochs and B. Schiefflin (eds), *Development Pragmatics* (pp. 111–29). New York: Academic Press.
Bates, E., Kintch, W.W. and Masling, M. (1978). Recognition memory for aspects of dialogue. *Journal of Experimental Psychology: Learning and Memory*, **4**, 187–97.
Bates, E., O'Connel, B. and Shore, C. (1987). Language and communication in infancy. In J.D. Osofsky (ed.), *Handbook of Infant Development* (pp. 149–203). New York: John Wiley.
Bateson, G. (1972). *Steps Towards an Ecology of Mind*. New York: Ballantine Books.
Baudelaire, C. (1961). Correspondances. In *Oeuvres Complètes*. Vol. 1 (p. 11). Paris: Gallimard.
Bechtel, W. (1987). Connectionism and the philosophy of mind: an overview. *The Southern Journal of Philosophy* (Supplement), 17–41.
Bekerian, D.A. and Bowers, J.M. (1983). Eyewitness testimony: were we misled? *Journal of Experimental Psychology: Learning, Memory, and Cognition*, **9**, 139–45.
Ben-Ze'ev, A. (1981). J.J. Gibson and the ecological approach to perception. *Studies in History and Philosophy of Science*, **12**, 107–39.
Ben-Ze'ev, A. (1983). Towards a different approach to perception. *International Philosophical Quarterly*, **23**, 45–64.
Ben-Ze'ev, A. (1993). *The Perceptual System: A Philosophical and Psychological Perspective*. New York: Peter Lang.
Berger, P. and Luckman, T. (1967). *The Social Construction of Reality*. London: Allen Lane.
Bergson, H. (1911/1982). Le rêve. In H. Bergson, *L'Energie Spirituell: Essais et Conferences* (pp. 85–109). Paris: Presses Universitaires de France.

Bergson, H. (1925). Le souvenir du présent et la fausse reconnaissance. In H. Bergson, *L'Energie Spirituelle: Essais et Conferences* (pp. 117–61). Paris: Librairie Felix Alcan.

Bergson, H.L. (1929). *Matter and Memory*. New York: Macmillan.

Bergson, H.L. (1944). *Creative Evolution*. New York: Modern Library.

Bergson, H.L. (1950). *Time and Free Will*. New York: Macmillan.

Bergson, H.L. (1983). *An Introduction to Metaphysics: The Creative Mind*. Totawa, NJ: Rowman and Allanheld.

Berkowitz, L. (1988). *Advances in Experimental Social Psychology*. New York: Academic Press.

Berlin, I. (1979). *Against the Current*. London: Hogarth Press.

Bernstein, L.E. (1981). Language as a product of dialogue. *Discourse Processes*, **4**, 117–47.

Berreman, G. (1966). Anemic and emetic analyses in social anthropology. *American Anthropologist*, **68**, 346–54.

Berry, D.S. and Zebrovitz McArthur, L. (1986). Perceiving character in faces: the impact of age-related cranofacial changes on social perception. *Psychological Bulletin*, **100**, 3–19.

von Bertalanfy, L. (1968). *General System Theory*. New York: George Braziller.

Bickhard, M.H. (1987). The social nature of the functional nature of language. In M. Hickman (ed.), *Social and Functional Approaches to Languages and Thought* (pp. 39–65). New York: Academic Press.

Bickhard, M.H. (1992a). How does the environment affect the person? In L.T. Winegar and J. Valsiner (eds), *Children's Development within Social Contexts: Metatheory and Theory* (pp. 63–92). Hillsdale, NJ: Lawrence Erlbaum.

Bickhard, M.H. (1992b). Scaffolding and self scaffolding: central aspects of development. In L.T. Winegar and J. Valsiner (eds), *Children's Development within Social Contexts: Research and Methodology* (pp. 33–52). Hillsdale, NJ: Lawrence Erlbaum.

Bickhard, M.H. (1993a). How does the environment affect the person? In L.T. Winegar and J. Valsiner (eds), *Children's Development within Social Contexts: Metatheory and Theory* (pp. 63–92). Hillsdale, NJ: Lawrence Erlbaum.

Bickhard, M.H. (1993b). Representational content in humans and machines. *Journal of Experimental and Theoretical Artificial Intelligence*, in press.

Bickhard, M.H. and Christopher, J.C. (1993). The influence of early experience on personality development. *New Ideas in Psychology*, in press.

Bickhard, M.H. and Richie, D.M. (1983). *On the Nature of Representation: A Case Study of James Gibson's Theory of Perception*. New York: Praeger.

Bickhard, M.H. and Terveen, L. (1993). *The Impasse of Artificial Intelligence and Cognitive Science and its Solution*, in press.

Bird-David, N. (1992). Beyond 'the original affluent society': a culturalist reformulation. *Current Anthropology*, **33**, 25–47.

Birenbaum, M. and Talsuoka, K.K. (1981). Effects of different instructional methods on error types and the underlying dimensionality of the test (Part 1). Research report 81-3 CATM, Computer Based Education Research Laboratory. Urbana, IL: University of Illinois.

Black, M. (1962). *Models and Metaphors*. Ithaca, NY: Cornell University Press.

Black, M. (1979). More about metaphor. In A. Ortony (ed.), *Metaphor and Thought* (pp. 19–43). Cambridge: Cambridge University Press.

Blaney, P.H. (1986). Affect and memory: a review. *Psychological Bulletin*, **99**, 229–46.

Block, N. (1980a). Troubles with functionalism. In N. Block (ed.), *Readings in Philosophy of Psychology*, Vol. 1 (pp. 268–307). Cambridge, MA: Harvard University Press.

Block, N. (1980b). Are absent qualia possible? *Philosophical Reveiw*, **89**, 257–74.

Bloom, L. (1973). *One Word at a Time*. The Hague: Mouton.

Blum, G.S. and Barbour, J.S. (1979). Selective inattention to anxiety-linked stimuli. *Journal of Experimental Psychology: General*, **108**, 182–224.

Blumer, H. (1969). *Symbolic Interactionism: Perspective and Method*. Englewood Cliffs, NJ: Prentice Hall.

Bobrow, D.G. (1975). Dimensions of representation. In D.G. Bobrow and A. Collins (eds), *Representation and Understanding: Studies in Cognitive Science* (pp. 1–34). New York: Academic Press.

Bobryk, J. (1989). Cognitive science: the science of artifacts. *Polish Psychological Bulletin*, **3**, 1–12.

Boden, M.A. (1975). Intentionality and physical systems. *Philosophy of Science*, **37**, 200–14.

Boden, M.A. (1983). Artificial intelligence and animal psychology. *New Ideas in Psychology*, **1**, 11–33.

Bogdan, R.J. (1983). Critical discussion: Fodor's representations. *Cognition and Brain Theory*, **6**, 237–50.

Borges, J.L. (1970). Pierre Menard, author of the Quixote. In J.L. Borges, *Labyrinths* (pp. 62–71). London: Penguin.

Borges, J.L. and Casares, A.B. (1967). Naturalismo al dia. In J.L. Borges and A.B. Casares (eds), *Cronica de Bustos Domecq* (pp. 35–43). Buenos Aires: Editorial Losada, S.A.

Bower, G.H. (1981). Mood and memory. *American Psychologist*, **36**, 129–48.

Bower, G.H. and Mayer, J.D. (1989). In search of mood-dependent retrieval. *Journal of Social Behavior and Personality*, **4**, 121–56.

Bransford, J.D. and Franks, J.J. (1971). The abstraction of linguistic ideas. *Cognitive Psychology*, **2**, 331–50.

Bransford, J.D., McCarrell, N.S., Franks, J.J. and Nitsch, K.E. (1977). Toward unexplaining memory. In R. Shaw and J. Bransford (eds), *Perceiving, Acting and Knowing: Toward an Ecological Psychology* (pp. 431–66). Hillsdale, NJ: Lawrence Erlbaum.

Bråten, S. (1987). Dialogic mind: the infant and the adult in protoconversation. In M. Carvallo (ed.) *Natura, Cognition and System*, Vol. 1 (pp. 187–207). Dordrecht: D. Reidel.

Brendel, A. (1976). *Musical Thoughts and After Thoughts*. Princeton, NJ: Princeton University Press.

Brentano, F. (1874/1973). *Psychology from an Empirical Standpoint*. London: Routledge and Kegan Paul.

Brewer, M.B. (1988). A dual process model of impression formation. In T.K. Srull and R.S. Wyer (eds), *Advances in Social Cognition*, Vol. 1 (pp. 1–36). Hillsdale, NJ: Lawrence Erlbaum.

Brown, J.S. and Burton, R.B. (1978). Diagnostic models for procedural bugs in basic mathematical skills. *Cognitive Science*, **2**, 155–92.

Brown, R. (1968). The development of WH questions in child speech. *Journal of Verbal Learning and Verbal Behaviour*, **7**, 279–90.

Brown, R. (1973). *A First Language: The Early Stages*. Cambridge, MA: Harvard University Press.

Brownell, H.H., Potter, H., Michelow, D. and Gardner, H. (1984). Sensitivity to lexical denotation and connotation in brain-damaged patients: a double dissociation? *Brain and Language*, **22**, 253–65.

Brownell, H.H., Simpson, T.C., Bihrle, A.M., Porter, H.H. and Gardner, H. (1991). Appreciation of metaphoric alternative word meaning by left and right hemisphere damaged patients. *Neuropsychologia*, **28**, 375–83.

Bruner, J.S. (1975a). From communication to language – a psychological perspective. *Cognition*, **10**, 255–87.

Bruner, J.S. (1975b). The ontogenesis of speech acts. *Journal of Child Language*, **2**, 1–19.

Bruner, J.S. (1977). Early social interaction and language acquisition. In H.R. Schaffer (ed.), *Studies in Mother–Infant Interaction* (pp. 271–89). New York: Academic Press.

Bruner, J.S. (1983). *Child's Talk: Learning to Use Language*. New York: Norton.

Bruner, J.S. (1986). *Actual Minds, Possible Worlds*. Cambridge, MA: Harvard University Press.

Bruner, J.S. (1987). The transactional self. In J. Bruner and H. Haste (eds), *Making Sense: The Child's Construction of the World* (pp. 81–96). London: Methuen.

Buber, M. (1923/1958). *I and Thou* (second edition). New York: Charles Scribner's Sons.

Bursen, H.A. (1978). *Dismantling the Memory Machine*. Dordrecht: D. Reidel.

Butterworth, G. (1987). Some benefits of egocentrism. In J. Bruner and H. Haste (eds), *Making Sense: The Child's Construction of the World* (pp. 62–80). London: Methuen.

Cairns-Smith, A.G. (1985). The first organisms. *Scientific American*, **252**, 74–83.

Campbell, R.L. and Bickhard, M.H. (1987). A deconstruction of Fodor's anticonstructivism. *Human Development*, **30**, 48–59.

Caramelli, N. (1993). Bartlett's concept of 'schema' and cognitive psychology. *New Ideas in Psychology*, in press.

Carello, C., Turvey, M.T., Kugler, P.N. and Shaw, R.E. (1984). Inadequacies of the computer metaphor. In P. Gazzaniga (ed.), *Handbook of Cognitive Neuroscience* (pp. 229–48). New York: Plenum Press.

Carnap, R. (1947). *Meaning and Necessity*. Chicago: University of Chicago Press.

Carnap, R. (1967). *The Logical Structure of the World*. London: Routledge and Kegan Paul.

Carroll, J.S. and Payne, J.W. (1976) (eds). *Cognition and Social Behavior*. Hillsdale, NJ: Lawrence Erlbaum.

Carter, A.L. (1975). The transformation of sensorimotor morphemes into words: a case study of the development of 'more' and 'mine'. *Journal of Child Language*, **2**, 233–50.

Casey, E.S. (1987). *Remembering: A Phenomenological Study*. Bloomington: Indiana University Press.

Cassirer, E. (1944). *An Essay on Man*. New Haven: Yale University Press.

Cattell, R.B. (1957). *Personality and Motivation Structure and Measurement*. Yonkers-on-Hudson: World Books.

Charney, R. (1979). The development of *here* and *there*. *Journal of Child Language*, **6**, 69–80.

Chatwin, B. (1987). *The Songlines*. New York: Viking.

Chatwin, B. (1990). *What am I Doing Here?* London: Picador.

Chertok, L. and Michaux, D. (1977). Dynamics of hypnotic analgesia: some new data. *Journal of Nervous and Mental Disease*, **164**, 88–96.

Chomsky, N. (1959). A review of B.F. Skinner's Verbal Behavior. *Language*, **35**, 26–58.

Chomsky, N. (1965). *Aspects of the Theory of Syntax*. Cambridge, MA: MIT Press.

Chomsky, N. (1966). *Cartesian Linguistics*. New York: Harper and Row.

Chomsky, N. (1972). *Language and Mind* (revised edition). New York: Harcourt Brace Jovanovich.

Chomsky, N. (1975a). *The Logical Structure of Linguistic Theory*. New York: Plenum Press.

Chomsky, N. (1975b). *Reflections on Language*. New York: Pantheon Books.

Chomsky, N. (1977). *Language and Responsibility*. New York: Pantheon Books.

Chomsky, N. (1980). *Rules and Representations*. New York: Columbia University Press.

Churchland, P.M. and Churchland, P.S. (1990). Could a machine think? *Scientific American*, **262**, 32–7.

Churchland, P.S. Sejnowski, T.J. (1989). Neural representation and neural computation. In L. Nadel, L.A. Cooper, P. Culicover and R.M. Harnish (eds), *Neural Connections, Mental Computation* (pp. 1–15). Cambridge, MA: MIT Press.

Clark, E.V. (1983). Meanings and concepts. In J.H. Flavell and E.M. Markman (eds), *Handbook of Child Psychology*, Vol. 3 (pp. 787–840). New York: John Wiley.

Clark, E.V. and Clark, H.H. (1979). When nouns surface as verbs. *Language*, **85**, 797–811.

Clark, H.H. (1979). Responding to indirect speech acts. *Cognitive Psychology*, **4**, 430–77.

Clark, H.H. (1983). Making sense of nonsense. In G.B. Flores D'Arcais and R.J. Jarvella (eds), *The Process of Language Understanding*. Chichester: John Wiley.

Clark, H.H. and Carlson, T.B. (1981). Content for comprehension. In J. Long and A. Baddeley (eds), *Attention and Performance IX* (pp. 313–30). Hillsdale, NJ: Lawrence Erlbaum.

Clark, H.H. and Gerrig, R.J. (1983). Understanding old words with new meanings. *Journal of Verbal Learning and Verbal Behavior*, **22**, 591–608.

Clark, H.H. and Lucy, P. (1975). Understanding what is meant from what is said: a study in conversationally conveyed requests. *Journal of Verbal Learning and Verbal Behavior*, **14**, 56–72.

Clark, H.H. and Marshall, C.R. (1981). Definite reference and mutual knowledge. In A.Y. Joshi, B.L. Webber and I.A Sag (eds), *Elements of Discourse Understanding* (pp. 10–63). Cambridge: Cambridge University Press.

Clark, M.S. and Williamson, G.M. (1989). Moods and social judgments. In H.L. Wagner and A.S.R. Manstead (eds), *Handbook of Psychophysiology: Emotion and Social Behavior* (pp. 347–70). Chichester: John Wiley.

Clynes, M. (1978). *Sentics: The Touch of Emotions*. Garden City: Anchor Books.

Cohen, B.H. (1986). The motor theory of voluntary thinking. In R.J. Davidson, G.E. Schwartz and D. Shapiro (eds), *Consciousness and Self-Regulation: Advances in Research and Theory*, Vol. 4 (pp. 19–54). New York: Plenum Press.

Cole, M. (1985). The zone of proximal development: where culture and cognition create each other. In J.V. Wertsch (ed.), *Culture, Communication and Cognition: Vygotskian Perspectives* (pp. 146–61). Cambridge: Cambridge University Press.

Cole, M. and Gay, J. (1972). Culture and memory. *American Anthropologist*, **74**, 1066–84.

Cole, M., Gay, J., Glick, J.A. and Sharp, D.W. (1971). *The Cultural Context of Learning and Thinking*. New York: Basic Books.

Cometa, M.S. and Eson, M.E. (1978) Logical operations and metaphor comprehension: a Piagetian model. *Child Development*, **48**, 649–59.

Cooper, L.A. and Shepard, R.N. (1973). Chronometric studies of the rotation of mental images. In W.G. Chase (ed.), *Visual Information Processing* (pp. 75–176). New York: Academic Press.

Costall, A. (1991). Frederic Bartlett and the rise of prehistoric psychology. In A. Still and A. Costall (eds), *Against Cognitivism: Alternative Foundations for Cognitive Psychology* (pp. 39–54). Hemel Hempstead: Harvester Wheatsheaf.

Costall, A. and Still, A. (1989). Gibson's theory of direct perception and the problem of cultural relativism. *Journal for the Theory of Social Behavior*, **19**, 433–41.

Coulter, J. (1983). *Rethinking Social Theory*. London: Macmillan.

Craik, F.M. and Kirsner, K. (1974). The effect of speaker's voice on word recognition. *Quarterly Journal of Experimental Psychology*, **26**, 274–84.

Cross, T.G. (1978). Mother's speech and its association with rate of linguistic development in young children. In N. Waterson and C.E. Snow (eds), *The Development of Communication* (pp. 199–216). Chichester: John Wiley.

Csikszentmihalyi, M. (1988). Motivation and creativity: toward a synthesis of structural and energistic approaches to cognition. *New Ideas in Psychology*, **6**, 159–76.

Cutting, J.E. and Puffitt, D.R. (1981). Gait perception as an example of how we may perceive events. In R.D. Walk and H.L. Pick (eds), *Intersensory Perception and Sensory Integration* (pp. 249–73). New York: Plenum Press.

Dascal, M. (1981). Strategies of understanding. In H. Parret and J. Bouveresse (eds), *Meaning and Understanding* (pp. 327–52). Berlin: Walter de Gruyter.

Dascal, V. (1991). Walking the tight rope: the psychotherapeutic potential of enacting a movement metaphor. *Assaph – Studies in the Theatre*, **7**, 103–12.

Dascal, V. (1992). Movement metaphors: linking theory and therapeutic practice. In M. Stamenov (ed.), *Current Advances in Semantic Theory* (pp. 151–7). Amsterdam: John Benjamins.

Davidson, D. (1978). What metaphors mean. In S. Sacks (ed.), *On Metaphor* (pp. 29–45). Chicago: Chicago University Press.

Davis, W. (1991). Towards a new synthesis in ethnobotany. In M. Rios and H. Borgtoft Pedersen (eds), *Las Plantas y el Hombre* (pp. 339–57). Quito: Ediciones ABYA-YALA.

Dement, W.C. (1976). *Some Must Watch While Some Must Sleep*. New York: Norton.

Dennett, D.C. (1979a). *Brainstorms*. Hemel Hempstead: Harvester Wheatsheaf.

Dennett, D.C. (1979b). Intentional systems. In D. Dennett (ed.), *Brainstorms* (pp. 3–22). Hemel Hempstead: Harvester Wheatsheaf.

Dennett, D.C. (1979c). Why you can't make a computer that feels pain. In D. Dennett (ed.), *Brainstorms* (pp. 190–229). Hemel Hempstead: Harvester Wheatsheaf.

Dennett, D.C. (1988). Quining qualia. In A.J. Marcel and E. Bisiach (eds), *Consciousness in Contemporary Science* (pp. 42–77). Oxford: Clarendon Press.

Derrida, J. (1976). *Of Grammatology*. Baltimore: Johns Hopkins University Press.

Descartes, R. (1911). *The Philosophical Works of Descartes*. Vol. 1. Cambridge: Cambridge University Press.

Dewey, J. (1929). *Experience and Nature*. London: Allen and Unwin.

Dobzhansky, T. (1962). *Mankind Evolving*. New Haven: Yale University Press.

Doise, W. and Mugny, G. (1979). Individual and collective conflicts of centrations in cognitive development. *European Journal of Social Psychology*, **9**, 105–9.

Dore, J. (1975). Holophrases, speech acts and language universals. *Journals of Child Language*, **2**, 21–40.

Double, R. (1986). On the very idea of eliminating the intentional. *Journal for the Theory of Social Theory*, **16**, 210–16.

Downing, P. (1977). On the creation and use of English compound nouns. *Language*, **53**, 810–42.

Dreyfus, H.C. (1962) (ed.). *Husserl, Intentionality and Cognitive Science*. Cambridge, MA: MIT Press.

Dreyfus, H.L. (1975). Human temporality. In J.T. Fraser and N. Lawrence (eds), *The Study of Time II* (pp. 150–63). New York: Springer Verlag.

Dreyfus, H.L. (1979). *What Computers Can't Do: A Critique of Artificial Reason* (second revised edition). New York: Harper and Row.

Dreyfus, H.L. (1981). From micro-worlds to knowledge representation: AI at an impasse. In J. Haugeland (ed.), *Mind Design* (pp. 161–204). Cambridge, MA: MIT Press.

Dreyfus, H.L. and Dreyfus, S.E. (with Athanasiou, T.). (1986). *Mind Over Machine*. New York: Free Press.

Duncan, S.D. and Fiske, D.W. (1977). *Face-to-face Interaction: Research, Methods and Theory*. Hillsdale, NJ: Lawrence Erlbaum.

Durup, G. and Fessard, A. (1930). Le seuil de perception de la durée dans l'excitation visuelle. *Année Psychologique*, **31**, 52–62.

Earle, W. (1956). Memory. *The Review of Metaphysics*, **10**, 3–27.

Ebbinghaus, H. (1885/1964). *Memory*. New York: Dover.

Eco, U. (1984). Postscript, *The Name of the Rose*. New York: Harper Brace Jovanovich.

Edelman, G.M. (1987). *Neural Darwinism*. New York: Basic Books.

Edelman, G.M. (1989). *The Remembered Present*. New York: Basic Books.

Edelman, G.M. (1991). *Bright Air, Brilliant Fire: On the Matter of the Mind*. New York: Basic Books.

Edwards, D. and Middelton, D. (1986). Joint remembering: constructing an account of shared experience through conversational discourse. *Discourse Processes*, **9**, 423–59.

Edwards, D. and Middelton, D. (1987). Conversation and remembering: Bartlett revisited. *Applied Cognitive Psychology*. **1**, 77–92.

Einstein, A. (1946). *Mozart: His Character, his Work*. London: Cassell.

Einstein, A. (1949). Autobiographical notes. In P.A. Schlipp (ed.), *Albert Einstein: Philosopher-scientist* (pp. 2–95). Evanston, IL: The Library of Living Philosophers.

Ekman, P. (1979). About brows: emotional and conversational signals. In M. Von Cranach, K. Foppa, W. Lepenies and D. Ploog (eds), *Human Ethology* (pp. 169–202). London: Cambridge University Press.

Ekman, P., Friesen, W.V. and Ellsworth, P. (1972). *Emotion in the Human Face*. New York: Pergamon.

Ekman, P., Levenson, R.W. and Friesen, W.V. (1983). Autonomic nervous activity distinguishes among emotions, *Science*, **221**, 1208–10.

Empson, W. (1947). *Seven Types of Ambiguity*. New York: New Directions.

Ericksen, C.V. (1960). Discrimination and learning without awareness: a methodological survey and evaluation. *Psychological Review*, **67**, 279–300.

Erikson, E.H. (1969). *Gandhi's Truth: On the Origins of Militant Nonviolence*. New York: Norton.

Evans, J.St.B.T. (1982). *The Psychology of Deductive Reasoning*. London: Routledge and Kegan Paul.

Fainsilber, L. and Ortony, A. (1987). Metaphorical uses of language in the expression. *Metaphor and Symbolic Activity*, **2**, 239–50.

Farr, R. (1982). The social origins of the human mind: a historical note. In J.P. Forgas, (ed.), *Social Cognition* (pp. 247–58). London: Academic Press and European Association of Experimental Psychology.

Fauconnier, G. (1985). *Mental Spaces*. Cambridge, MA: MIT Press.

Feinman, S. (1982). Social referencing in infancy. *Merril-Palmer Quarterly*, **28**, 445–70.

Feldman, J.A. (1989). Neural representation of conceptual knowledge. In L. Nadel, L.A. Cooper, P. Culicover and R.M. Harnish (eds), *Neural Connections, Mental Computation* (pp. 69–104). Cambridge, MA: MIT Press.

Ferrier, L. (1978). Word, context and imitation. In A. Lock (ed.), *Action, Gesture and Symbol: The Emergence of Language* (pp. 471–83). London: Academic Press.

Fiedler, K. (1988). Emotional mood, cognitive style, and behavior regulation. In K. Fiedler and J.P. Forgas (eds), *Affect, Cognition and Social Behavior* (pp. 100–19). Toronto: Hogrefe.

Fish, S. (1980). *Is There a Text in this Class?* Cambridge, MA: Harvard University Press.

Fisher, R.P. and Cuervo, A. (1974). Memory for physical features of discourse as a function of their relevance. *Journal of Experimental Psychology: Learning, Memory and Cognition*, **9**, 130–8.

Flavell, J. and Draguns, J. (1957). A microgenetic approach to perception and thought. *Psychological Bulletin*, **54**, 197–217.

Fodor, J.A. (1965). Could meaning be an R$_m$? *Journal of Verbal Learning and Verbal Behavior*, **4**, 73–81.

Fodor, J.A. (1968a). *Psychological Explanation: An Introduction to the Philosophy of Psychology*. London: Random House.

Fodor, J.A. (1968b). The appeal to tacit knowledge in psychological explanations. *Journal of Philosophy*, **65**, 627–40.

Fodor, J.A. (1975). *The Language of Thought*. New York: Thomas Y. Crowell.

Fodor, J.A. (1980). Methodological solipsism considered as a research strategy in cognitive psychology. *The Behavioral and Brain Sciences*, **3**, 63–110.

Fodor, J.A. (1981a). The present status of the innateness controversy. In J.A. Fodor, *Representations* (pp. 257–316). Cambridge, MA: MIT Press.

Fodor, J.A. (1981b). *Representations*. Cambridge, MA: MIT Press.

Fodor, J.A. (1983). *The Modularity of Mind*. Cambridge, MA: MIT Press.

Fodor, J.A. (1986). Why paramecia don't have mental representations. *Midwest Studies in Philosophy*, **10**, 3–25.

Fodor, J.A. (1987). *Psychosemantics*. Cambridge, MA: MIT Press.

Fodor, J.A. (1990). *A Theory of Content and Other Essays*. Cambridge, MA: MIT Press.

Fodor, J.A. and Pylyshyn, Z.W. (1988a). Connectionism and cognitive architecture: a critical analysis. *Cognition*, **28**, 3–71.

Fodor, J.A. and Pylyshyn, Z.W. (1988b). How direct is visual perception? Some reflections on Gibson's ecological approach. *Cognition*, **9**, 139–96.

Fodor, J.A., Bever, T.G. and Garrett, M.F. (1974). *The Psychology of Language*. New York: McGraw-Hill.

Fodor, J.A., Garrett, M.F., Walker, E.C.T. and Parkes, C.H. (1980). Against definitions. *Cognition*, **8**, 263–368.

von Foerster, H. (1966). On self-organizing systems and their environments. In M. Yovits and S. Cameron (eds), *Self-organizing Systems*. London: Pergamon.

Forgas, J.P. (1982) (ed.). *Social Cognition*. London: Academic Press and European Association of Experimental Psychology.

Forgas, J.P. (1983). What is social about social cognition? *British Journal of Social Psychology*, **22**, 129–44.

Foulkes, W.D. (1985). *Dreaming: A Cognitive Psychological Analysis*. Hillsdale, NJ: Lawrence Erlbaum.

Fraisse, P. (1964). *The Psychology of Time*. London: Eyre & Spottiswoode.

Frank, P.G. (1949). Einstein, Mach, logical positivism. In P.A. Schlipp (ed.), *Albert Einstein: Philosopher-scientist* (pp. 271–86). Evanston, IL: The Library of Living Philosophers.

Freedman, N. (1989). Two principles of communicative functioning. In R.R. Riber (ed.), *The Individual, Communication, and Society: Essays in Memory of Gregory Bateson* (pp. 279–300). Cambridge: Cambridge University Press.

Freeman, W.J. (1991). The physiology of perception. *Scientific American*, **264**, 78–85.

Freud, S. (1895/1950). Project for a scientific psychology. In *Standard Edition*, Vol. 1 (pp. 283–343). London: Hogarth Press.

Freud, S. (1900/1954). *The Interpretation of Dreams*. London: Allen and Unwin.

Freud, S. (1914/1955). From the history of an infantile neurosis. In *Standard Edition*, Vol. 17 (pp. 3–124). London: Hogarth Press.

Freud, S. (1923). The Ego and the Id. In *Standard Edition*, Vol. 19 (pp. 3–66). London: Hogarth Press.

Freud, S. (1933). *New Introductory Lectures on Psycho-analysis*. New York: Norton.

Freud, S. (1940). A note upon the 'mystic writing-pad'. *International Journal of Psycho-Analyses*, **21**, 469–74.

Freud, S. (1950). *Totem and Taboo*. London: Routledge and Kegan Paul.

Freud, S. (1983). *The Penguin Freud Library. Vol. 13: The Origins of Religion*. London: Penguin.

Freyd, J. (1989). Dynamic mental representations. *Psychological Review*, **94**, 427–38.

Frijda, N. and Swagerman, J. (1987). Can computers feel? Theory and design of an emotional system. *Cognition and Emotion*, **1**, 235–57.

Fryer, D.H. (1941). Articulation in automatic metal work. *American Journal of Psychology*, **54**, 504–17.

Furrow, D., Nelson, K.E. and Benedict, H. (1979). Mother's speech to children and syntactic development: some simple relationships. *Journal of Child Language*, **6**, 423–42.

Gadamer, H.G. (1975). *Truth and Method*. New York: Seabury Press.

Gadamer, H.G. (1976). *Philosophical Hermeneutics*. Berkeley: University of California Press.

Galton, F. (1883). *Inquiries into Human Faculty and its Development*. London: Macmillan.

Gardner, H. (1983). *Frames of Mind: The Theory of Multiple Intelligences*. New York: Basic Books.

Gardner, H. and Winner, E. (1978). The development of metaphorical competence: implications for humanistic disciplines. In S. Sacks (ed.), *On Metaphor* (pp. 121–40). Chicago: University of Chicago Press.

Gardner, H., Brownell, H.H., Wapner, W. and Michelow, D. (1983). Missing the point: the role of the right hemisphere in the processing of complex linguistic materials. In E. Perecman (ed.), *Cognitive Processing in the Right Hemisphere*. New York: Academic Press.

Gardner, H., King, P., Flamm, L. and Silverman, J. (1975). Comprehension and appreciation of humorous material following brain damage. *Brain*, **98**, 399–412.

Gardner, H., Kirchner, M., Winner, E. and Perkins, D. (1975). Children's metaphoric productions and preferences. *Journal of Child Language*, **2**, 125–41.

Garfinkel, H. (1967). *Studies in Ethnomethodology*. Englewood Cliffs, NJ: Prentice Hall.

Garner, W.R. (1974). *The Processing of Information and Structure.* Hillsdale, NJ: Lawrence Erlbaum.

Gati, I. and Tversky, A. (1982). Representations of qualitative and quantitative dimensions. *Journal of Experimental Psychology*, **8**, 325–40.

Gati, I. and Tversky, A. (1984). Weighting common and distinctive features in perceptual and conceptual judgements. *Cognitive Psychology*, **16**, 341–70.

Geertz, C. (1973). *The Interpretation of Cultures.* New York: Basic Books.

Geiselman, R.E. (1979). Inhibition of the automatic storage of speaker's voice. *Memory and Cognition*, **7**, 201–4.

Geiselman, R.E. and Belezza, F.S. (1976). Long-term memory for speaker's voice and source location. *Memory and Cognition*, **4**, 483–5.

Geiselman, R.E. and Belezza, F.S. (1977). Incidental retention of speaker's voice. *Memory and Cognition*, **5**, 658–66.

Geiselman, R.E. and Craweley, J.M. (1983). Incidental processing of speaker characteristics: voice as connotative information. *Journal of Verbal Learning and Verbal Behavior*, **22**, 15–23.

Gelman, R. and Shatz, M. (1978). Appropriate speech adjustments: the operation of conversational constraints on talk to two-year-olds. In M. Lewis and L. Rosenblum (eds), *Interaction, Conversation and the Development of Language* (pp. 27–61). New York: John Wiley.

Gergen, K.J. (1985). The social constructionist movement in modern psychology. *American Psychologist*, **210**, 266–75.

Gergen, K.J. (1987). The language of psychological understanding. In H.J. Stam, T.B. Rogers and K.J. Gergen (eds), *The Analysis of Psychological Theory* (pp. 115–55). Washington, DC: Hemisphere.

Gergen, K.J. (1989). Social psychology and the wrong revolution. *European Journal of Social Psychology*, **19**, 463–84.

Gergen, K.J. and Gergen, M.M. (1983). Narratives of the self. In T.R. Sarbin and K.E. Scheibe (eds), *Studies in Social Identity* (pp. 254–73). New York: Praeger.

Gergen, K.J. and Morawski, J. (1980). An alternative metatheory for social psychology. In L. Wheeler (ed.), *Review of Personality and Social Psychology* (pp. 326–52). Beverly Hills: Sage.

Gerrig, R.J. and Gibbs, R.W. (1988). Beyond the lexicon: creativity in language production. *Metaphor and Symbolic Activity*, **3**, 1–19.

Gibbs, R.W. (1979). Contextual effects in understanding indirect requests. *Discourse Processes*, **2**, 2–10.

Gibbs, R.W. (1983). Do people always process the literal meaning of indirect requests? *Journal of Experimental Psychology: Learning, Memory and Cognition*, **9**, 524–33.

Gibbs, R.W. (1984). Literal meaning and psychological theory. *Cognitive Science*, **8**, 275–304.

Gibson, E.J. (1969). *Principles of Perceptual Learning and Development.* New York: Appleton-Century-Crofts.

Gibson, E.J. (1982). The concept of affordances in development: the renascence of functionalism. In W.A. Collins (ed.), *The Concept of Development: The Minnesota Symposia on Child Psychology*, Vol. 15 (pp. 55–82). Hillsdale, NJ: Lawrence Erlbaum.

Gibson, E.J. and Spelke, E.S. (1983). The development of perception. In P.H. Mussen (ed.), *Handbook of Child Psychology. Vol. 3: Cognitive Development* (pp. 1–76). New York: John Wiley.

Gibson, E.J. and Walker, A. (1984). Development of visual-tactual affordances of substance. *Child Development*, **55**, 453–60.

Gibson, E.J., Owsley, C.J. and Johnston, J. (1978). Perception of invariants by five-month-old infants: differentiation of two types of motion. *Developmental Psychology*, **14**, 407–15.

Gibson, E.J., Owsley, C.J., Walker, A. and Megaw-Nice, J. (1979). Development of the perception of invariants: substance and shape. *Perception*, **8**, 609–20.

Gibson, J.J. (1960). The concept of the stimulus in psychology. *American Psychologist*, **16**, 694–703.

Gibson, J.J. (1966a). *The Senses Considered as a Perceptual System*. Boston: Houghton-Mifflin.

Gibson, J.J. (1966b). The problem of temporal order in stimulation and perception. *Journal of Psychology*, **62**, 141–9.

Gibson, J.J. (1968). What gives rise to the perception of motion? *Psychological Review*, **75**, 335–46.

Gibson, J.J. (1975). Events are perceivable but time is not. In J.T. Fraser and N. Lawrence (eds), *The Study of Time II* (pp. 295–301). New York: Springer Verlag.

Gibson, J.J. (1976). The myth of passive perception: a reply to Richards. *Philosophy and Phenomenological Research*, **37**, 234–8.

Gibson, J.J. (1977). The theory of affordances. In R. Shaw and J. Bransford (eds), *Perceiving, Acting and Knowing* (pp. 67–82). Hillsdale, NJ: Lawrence Erlbaum.

Gibson, J.J. (1979). *The Ecological Approach to Visual Perception*. Boston: Houghton-Mifflin.

Gilligan, S.G. and Bower, G.H. (1983). Reminding and mood-congruent memory. *Bulletin of the Psychonomic Society*, **21**, 431–4.

Glachan, N.M. and Light, P.H. (1982). Peer interaction and learning. In G.E. Butterworth and P.H. Light (eds), *Social Cognition: Studies of the Development of Understanding* (pp. 238–62). Hemel Hempstead: Harvester Wheatsheaf.

Gladwin, T. (1964). East is a Big Bird: Navigation and Logic on Pultowat Atoll. Cambridge, MA: Harvard University Press.

Gleick, J. (1988). *Chaos: Making a New Science*. Harmondsworth: Penguin.

Glucksberg, S., Gildea, P. and Bookin, H.B. (1982). On understanding non-literal speech acts: can people ignore metaphors? *Journal of Verbal Learning and Verbal Behavior*, **21**, 85–98.

Gödel, K. (1964). What is Cantor's continuum problem? In P. Benaceraff and H. Putnam (eds), *Philosophy of Mathematics* (pp. 258–73). Englewood Cliffs, NJ: Prentice Hall.

Goldberg, A.L., Rigney, D.R. and West, B.J. (1990). Chaos and fractals in human physiology. *Scientific American*, **262**, 34–49.

Goldblum, N. (1990). A psycholinguistic study of the distinctiveness of metaphor. Unpublished doctoral dissertation. Jerusalem: The Hebrew University.

Goldstein, K. (1948). *Language and Language Disturbances*. New York: Grune & Stratton.

Gombrich, E.H. (1989). Distinguished dissident. *The New York Review of Books*, 19 January.

Gonzalez, E.G. and Kolers, P.A. (1982). Mental manipulation of arithmetic symbols. *Journal of Experimental Psychology: Learning, Memory and Cognition*, **8**, 308–19.

Goodall, J. (1971). *In the Shadow of Man*. Boston: Houghton-Mifflin.

Goodman, N. (1976). *Languages of Art*. Indianapolis: Hackett.

Gordon, D. and Lakoff, C. (1971). Conversational postulates. *Papers from the 7th Regional Meeting of the Chicago Linguistic Society* (pp. 63–84). Chicago: Chicago Linguistic Society.

Greenfield, P. and Smith, J. (1976). *The Structure of Communication in Early Development*. New York: Academic Press.

Grice, H.P. (1975). Logic and conversation. In P. Cole and J.L. Morgan (eds), *Syntax and Semantics, Vol. 3: Speech Acts*. New York: Academic Press.

Gunnar, M.R. and Stone, C. (1984). The effects of positive maternal affect on infant responses to pleasant, ambiguous, and fear-provoking toys. *Child Development*, **55**, 1231–6.

Gur, R.E., Gur, R.C. and Harris, L.J. (1975). Cerebral activation, as measured by subjects' lateral eye movement, is influenced by experimenter location. *Neuropsychologia*, **13**, 35–44.

Haber, R.N. (1979). Twenty years of haunting eidetic imagery: where's the ghost? *The Behavioral and Brain Sciences*, **2**, 583–629.

Habermas, J. (1970a). Introductory remarks to a theory of communicative competence. In H.P. Dreitzel (ed.), *Recent Sociology*, Vol. 2 (pp. 115–48). London: Macmillan.

Habermas, J. (1970b). *Knowledge and Human Interests*. Boston: Beacon Press.

Habermas, J. (1979). *Communication and the Evolution of Society.* Boston: Beacon Press.

Halle, M. and Stevens, K.N. (1964). Speech recognition: a model and a program for research. In J.A. Fodor and J.J. Katz (eds), *The Structure of Language* (pp. 604–12). Englewood-Cliffs, NJ: Prentice Hall.

Halliday, M.A.K. (1975). *Learning to Mean: Explorations in the Development of Language.* London: Edward Arnold.

Hardyck, C.D. and Petrinovich, L.F. (1970). Subvocal speech and comprehension level as function of the difficulty of reading material. *Journal of Verbal Learning and Verbal Behavior*, **9**, 647–52.

Harré, R. (1987). Enlarging the paradigm. *New Ideas in Psychology*, **5**, 3–12.

Harré, R., Clark, D. and De Carlo, N. (1985). *Motives and Mechanisms: An Introduction to a Psychology of Action.* London: Methuen.

Harris, R.J. (1976). Comprehension of metaphors: a test of the two-stage processing model. *Bulletin of the Psychonomic Society*, **8**, 312–14.

Harris, R.J., Lahey, M. and Marsalek, F. (1980). Metaphors and images: rating, reporting and remembering. In R. Honeck and R. Hoffman (eds), *Cognition and Figurative Language* (pp. 163–81). Hillsdale, NJ: Lawrence Erlbaum.

Haskell, R.E. (1987a). Giambattista Vico and the discovery of metaphoric cognition. In R.E. Haskell (ed.), *Cognition and Symbolic Structures: The Psychology of Metaphoric Transformation* (pp. 67–82). Norwood, NJ: Ablex.

Haskell, R.E. (1987b). Cognitive psychology and the problem of symbolic cognition. In R.E Haskell (ed.), *Cognitive Psychology and the Problem of Symbolic Structures: The Psychology of Metaphoric Transformation* (pp. 85–102). Norwood, NJ: Ablex.

Hastie, R., Ostrom, T.M., Ebbesen, E.B., Wyer, R.S., Hamilton, D.L. and Carlston D.M. (1980) (eds). *Person Memory: The Cognitive Basis of Social Perception.* Hillsdale, NJ: Lawrence Erlbaum.

Haugeland, J. (1978). The nature and plausibility of cognitivism. *The Behavioral and Brain Sciences*, **1**, 215–60.

Haugeland, J. (1985). *Artificial Intelligence: The Very Idea.* Cambridge, MA: MIT Press.

Hausman, C.R. (1984). *A Discourse on Novelty and Creation.* Albany: State University of New York Press.

Heft, H. (1989). Affordances and the body: an intentional analysis of Gibson's ecological approach to visual perception. *Journal for the Theory of Social Behavior*, **19**, 1–30.

Hegel, G.W.F. (1931). *The Phenomenology of Mind.* London: Allen and Unwin.

Heidegger, M. (1962). *Being and Time.* New York: Harper and Row.

Heil, J. (1981). Does cognitive psychology rest on mistake? *Mind*, **90**, 321–42.

Held, R. and Freeman, S.J. (1963). Plasticity in human sensorimotor control. *Science*, **142**, 455–62.

Held, R. and Hein, A. (1963). Movement-produced stimulation in the development of visually guided behavior. *Journal of Comparative and Psychological Psychology*, **56**, 872–6.

Henle, P. (1958). Metaphor. In P. Henle (ed.), *Language, Thought and Culture* (pp. 173–95). Michigan: University of Michigan Press.

Hess, E.H. (1965). Attitude and pupil size. *Scientific American*, **212**, 46–54.

Hesse, M. (1967). Ether. In P. Edwards (ed.), *The Encyclopaedia of Philosophy*, Vol. 3 (pp. 66–9). New York: Macmillan.

Hinton, G.E. and Anderson, J.A. (1981a). Models of information processing in the brain. In G.E. Hinton and J.A. Anderson (eds), *Parallel Models of Associative Memory* (pp. 9–44). Hillsdale, NJ: Lawrence Erlbaum.

Hinton, G.E. and Anderson, J.A. (1981b). *Parallel Models of Associative Memory.* Hillsdale, NJ: Lawrence Erlbaum.

Hjelmquist, E. (1984). Memory for conversations. *Discourse Processes*, **7**, 321–36.

Hockney, D. (1983). *On Photography.* New York and Zurich: Andre Emmerich Gallery.

Hockney, D. (1984). *Camerawalks*. London: Thames and Hudson.

Hofstadter, D.R. (1979). *Gödel, Escher, Bach: An Eternal Golden Braid*. New York: Basic Books.

Hubel, D.H. and Wiesel, T.N. (1979). Brain mechanisms of vision. *Scientific American*, **241**, 150–62.

Hudson, W.D. (1969). *The Is/Ought Question*. London: Macmillan.

Huertas-Jourda, J. (1975). Structures of the 'living present': Husserl and Proust. In J.T. Fraser and N. Lawrence (eds), *The Study of Time II* (pp. 163–96). New York: Springer Verlag.

Husserl, E. (1964). *The Phenomenology of Internal Time-consciousness*. Bloomington: Indiana University Press.

Hyde, T.W. and Jenkins, J.J. (1969). The differential effects of incidental tasks on the organization of recall of highly associated words. *Journal of Experimental Psychology*, **82**, 472–81.

Inhoff, A., Lima, S. and Carroll, P. (1984). Contextual effects on metaphor comprehension and reading. *Memory and Cognition*, **12**, 558–67.

Issacs, J. (1980). *Australian Dreaming: 40,000 Years of Aboriginal History*. Sydney: Landsdowne Press.

Isen, A. (1984). Toward understanding the role of affect in cognition. In R.S. Wyer, Jr., and T.K. Srull (eds), *Handbook of Social Psychology*. Vol. 3 (pp. 179–236). Hillsdale, NJ: Lawrence Erlbaum.

Isen, A. (1987). Positive affect, cognitive processes, and social behavior. In L. Berkovitz (ed.), *Advances in Experimental Social Psychology*, Vol. 20 (pp. 203–53). New York: Academic Press.

Iser, W. (1978). *The Act of Reading: A Theory of Aesthetic Response*. Baltimore: Johns Hopkins University Press.

Istomina, Z.M. (1975). The development of voluntary memory in preschool-age children. *Soviet Psychology*, **13**, 5–64.

Ittelson, W.H. (1973). Environment perception and contemporary perceptual theory. In W.H. Ittelson (ed.), *Environment and Cognition* (pp. 1–19). New York: Seminar Press.

Izard, C.E. (1977). *Human Emotions*. New York: Plenum Press.

Izard, C.E (1980). The emergence of emotions and development of conciousness in infancy. In J.M. Davidson and R.J. Davidson (eds), *The Psychobiology of Consciousness* (pp. 193–216). New York: Plenum Press.

Izard, C.E. (1983). Emotion–cognition relationships and human development. In C.E. Izard, G. Kagan and R.B. Zajonc (eds), *Emotions, Cognition and Behavior* (pp. 17–37). Cambridge: Cambridge University Press.

Izard, C.E. and Malaesta, C.Z. (1987). Differential emotions theory of early emotional development. In J.D. Osofsky (ed.), *Handbook of Infant Development* (pp. 494–554). New York: John Wiley.

Jackendoff, R. (1972). *Semantic Interpretation in Generative Grammar*. Cambridge, MA: MIT Press.

Jackendoff, R. (1976). Towards an explanatory semetic representation. *Linguistic Inquiry*, **7**, 89–150.

Jackendoff, R. (1987). *Consciousness and the Computational Mind*. Cambridge, MA: MIT Press.

Jackson, F. (1982). Epiphenomenal qualia. *Philosophical Quarterly*, **32**, 127–36.

Jacobson, E. (1964). *The Self and the Object World*. New York: International University Press.

Jakobson, R. (1971). Linguistics and the other sciences. In R. Jakobson (ed.), *Selected Writings*, *Vol. 2* (pp. 655–96). The Hague: Mouton.

James, W. (1884). What is an emotion? *Mind*, **2**, 188–204.

James, W. (1950). *The Principles of Psychology*, Vol. 1. New York: Dover.

James, W. and Lange, C. (1885/1922). *The Emotions*. Baltimore: Williams and Wilkins.

Jarvella, R.J. and Collas J.G. (1974). Memory for the intention of sentences. *Memory and Cognition*, **2**, 185–8

Jaynes, J. (1976). *The Origin of Consciousness in the Breakdown of the Bicameral Mind.* Boston: Houghton-Mifflin.

Jenkins, J.J. (1977). Remember that old theory of memory? Well, forget it! In R. Shaw and J. Bransford (eds), *Perceiving, Acting and Knowing* (pp. 413–31). Hillsdale, NJ: Lawrence Erlbaum.

Jerne, N.K. (1974). Towards a network theory of the immune system. *Annual Immunology* (Institut Pasteur), **125**, 373–89.

Johansson, G. (1973). Visual perception of biological motion and a model for its analysis. *Perception and Psychophysics*, **14**, 201–11.

Johansson, G. (1975). Visual motion perception. *Scientific American*, **232**, 76–88.

John-Steiner, V. (1985). *Notebooks of the Mind: Explorations of Thinking.* Albuquerque: University of New Mexico Press.

Johnson, D.W. and Johnson, R.T. (1975). *Learning Together and Alone: Cooperation, Competition, and individualization.* Englewood Clifs, NJ: Prentice Hall.

Johnson, M.G. (1980). A philosophical perspective on the problems of metaphor. In R.C. Honeck and R.R. Hoffman (eds), *Cognition and Figurative Language* (pp. 47–80). Hillsdale, NJ: Lawrence Erlbaum.

Johnson, M.G. (1987). *The Body in the Mind: The Bodily Basis Of Reason and Imagination.* Chicago: University of Chicago Press.

Johnson-Laird, P.N. (1982). Thinking as a skill. *Quarterly Journal of Experimental Psychology*, **34A**, 1–29.

Johnson-Laird, P.N. (1983). *Mental Models.* Cambridge MA: Harvard University Press.

Johnson-Laird, P.N. (1988). A computational analysis of consciousness. In A.J. Marcel and E. Bisiach (eds), *Consciousness in Contemporary Science* (pp. 357–68). Oxford: Oxford University Press.

Johnson-Laird, P.N., Legrenzi, P. and Legrenzi, M.S. (1972). Reasoning and the sense of reality. *British Journal of Psychology*, **63**, 395–400.

Jouvet, M. (1980). Paradoxical sleep and the nature–nurture controversy. *Progress in Brain Research*, **53**, 331–46.

Jung, C.G. (1964). *Man and his Symbols.* London: Aldus Books.

Kandinsky, W. (1963). *Concerning the Spiritual in Art.* New York: G. Wittenloorn.

Kant, I. (1781/1953). *Critique of Pure Reason*, trans. N.K. Smith. New York: Macmillan.

Karmiloff-Smith, A (1979). *A Functional Approach to Child Language.* Cambridge: Cambridge University Press.

Katz, J.J. (1972). *Semantic Theory.* New York: Harper and Row.

Katz, J.J. (1981). *Language and Other Abstract Objects.* Totowa, NJ: Rowman and Littlefield.

Katz, J.J. and Fodor, J.A. (1963). The structure of a semantic theory. *Language*, **39**, 170–210.

Katz, S. (1987). Is Gibson a relativist? In A. Costall and A. Still (eds), *Cognitive Psychology in Question* (pp. 115–27). Hemel Hempstead: Harvester Wheatsheaf.

Kaye, K. (1979). Thickening thin data: the maternal role in developing communication and language. In M. Bullowa (ed.), *Before Speech* (pp. 191–206). Cambridge: Cambridge University Press.

Kaye, K. (1982). Organism, apprentice and person. In E.Z. Tronick (ed.), *Social Interchange in Infancy.* Baltimore: University Park Press.

Kaye, K. and Charney, R. (1980). How mothers maintain 'dialogue' with two-year-olds. In D.R. Olson (ed.), *The Social Foundations of Language and Thought* (pp. 211–30). New York: Norton.

Keenan, J.M., MacWhinney, B. and Mayhew, D. (1977). Pragmatics in memory: a study in natural conversation. *Journal of Verbal Learning and Verbal Behavior*, **16**, 545–60.

Keller, E.F. (1983). *A Feeling for the Organism: The Life and Work of Barbara McClintock.* San Francisco: Freeman.

Keller, F.S. and Schoenfeld, W.N. (1950). *Principles of Psychology.* New York: Appleton-Century-Crofts.

Kemler, D.G. (1983). Holistic and analytic modes in perceptual and cognitive development. In T.J. Tighe and B.E. Shepp (eds), *Perception, Cognition, and Development: Interactional Analysis* (pp. 77–102). Hillsdale, NJ: Lawrence Erlbaum.

Kemler, D.G. (1989). The nature and occurrence of holistic processing. In B. Shepp and S. Ballesteros (eds), *Object Perception: Structure and Process* (pp. 357–86). Hillsdale, NJ: Lawrence Erlbaum.

Kemler, D.G. and Smith, L.B. (1978). Is there a development trend from integrity to separability in perception? *Journal of Experimental Child Psychology*, **26**, 498–507.

Kemler, D.G. and Smith, L.B. (1979). Assessing similarity and dimensional relations: the affects of integrality and separability on the discovery of complex concepts. *Journal of Experimental Psychology: General*, **108**, 133–50.

Kemper, S. (1981). Comprehension and the interpretation of proverbs. *Journal of Psycholinguistic Research*, **10**, 179–83.

Kendon, A. (1972). Some relationships between body motion and speech. In A. Siegman and B. Pope (eds), *Studies in Dyadic Communication* (pp. 177–210). New York: Pergamon.

Kendon, A. (1975). Gesticulation, speech and the gesture theory of language origins. *Sign Language Studies*, **9**, 349–73.

Kendon, A. (1984). Some uses of gestures. In D. Tannen and M. Saville-Troike (eds), *Perspectives on Silence* (pp. 215–34). Norwood, NJ: Ablex.

Kennedy-Hewitt, E. (1979). The muse on your right: the explanation of opaque metaphor. *Language and Style*, **12**, 131–45.

Keysar, B. (1989). On the functional equivalence of literal and metaphorical interpretations in discourse. *Journal of Memory and Language*, **28**, 375–85.

Kintsch, W. (1974). *The Representation of Meaning in Memory*. Hillsdale, NJ: Lawrence Erlbaum.

Kintsch, W. and Bates, E. (1977). Recognition memory for statements from a classroom lecture. *Journal of Experimental Psychology: Human Learning and Memory*, **3**, 150–8.

Kirsner, K. (1973). An analysis of the visual component in recognition memory for verbal stimuli. *Memory and Cognition*, **1**, 449–53.

Kohut, H. (1971). *The Analysis of the Self*. New York: International University Press.

Kohut, H. (1977). *The Restoration of the Self*. New York: International University Press.

Kolers, P.A. (1976). Reading a year later. *Journal of Experimental Psychology: Human Learning and Memory*, **5**, 554–65.

Kolers, P.A. and Gonzales, E. (1980). Memory for words, synonyms and translations. *Journals of Experimental Psychology: Human Learning and Memory*, **6**, 53–65.

Kolers, P.A. and Ostry, D.J. (1974). Time course of loss of information regarding pattern analyzing operations. *Journal of Verbal Learning and Verbal Behavior*, **13**, 599–612.

Kolers, P.A. and Roediger, H.L. (1984). Procedures of mind. *Journal of Verbal Learning and Verbal Behavior*, **23**, 425–49.

Kolers, P.A. and Smythe, W.E. (1984). Symbol manipulation: alternatives to the computational view of mind. *Journal of Verbal Learning and Verbal Behavior*, **23**, 289–314.

Kosslyn, S.M. (1980). *Image and Mind*. Cambridge, MA: Harvard University Press.

Kosslyn, S.M. and Schwartz, S.P. (1977). A data driven simulation of visual imagery. *Cognitive Science*, **1**, 265–96.

Kozulin, A. (1986). The concept of activity in Soviet psychology. *American Psychologist*, **41**, 264–74.

Kripke, S.A. (1980). *Naming and Necessity*. Cambridge, MA: Harvard University Press.

Kugler, P.N. and Shaw, R. (in press). Symmetry and symmetry-breaking in thermodynamic and epistemic engines: a coupling of first and second laws. In H. Haken (ed.), *Synergetics of Cognition*. Heidelberg: Springer Verlag.

Kunst-Wilson, W.R. and Zajonc, R.B. (1980). Affective discrimination of stimuli that cannot be recognized. *Science*, **207**, 556–8.

Laboratory of Comparative Human Cognition (1983). Cultural and cognitive development. In W. Kussen (ed.), *Handbook of Child Psychology, Vol. 1: History, Theory and Methods* (pp. 294–356). New York: John Wiley.

Lacan, J. (1977). *Ecrits: A Selection*. London: Tavistock.

Lachter, J. and Bever, T.G. (1988). The relation between linguistic structure and associative theories of language learning: a constructive critique of some connectionist models. *Cognition,* **28,** 195–247.

da Laguna, G. (1927). *Speech: Its Function and Development*. New Haven: Yale University Press.

Lahav, R. (1989). Against compositionality: the case of adjectives. *Philosophical Studies,* **57,** 261–79.

Lahav, R. (1990). Bergson and the hegemony of language. *The Southern Journal of Philosophy,* **28,** 329–42.

Laird, J.D. (1984). The real role of facial response in the experience of emotion: a reply to Tourangeau and Ellsworth, and others. *Journal of Personality and Social Psychology,* **47,** 909–17.

Lakoff, G. (1987a). Cognitive models and prototype theory. In U. Neisser (ed.), *Concepts and Conceptual Development* (pp. 43–100). Cambridge: Cambridge University Press.

Lakoff, G. (1987b). *Women, Fire and Dangerous Things: What Categories Reveal about the Mind*. Chicago: University of Chicago Press.

Lakoff, G. and Johnson, M. (1980a). The metaphorical structure of the human conceptual system. *Cognitive Science,* **4,** 195–208.

Lakoff, G. and Johnson, M. (1980b). *Metaphors We Live By*. Chicago: University of Chicago Press.

Lakoff, G. and Turner, M. (1989). *More than Cool Reason: A Field Guide to Poetic Metaphor*. Chicago: University of Chicago Press.

Langer, S. (1942). *Philosophy from a New Key*. Cambridge, MA: Harvard University Press.

Langer, S. (1967). *Mind: An Essay on Human Feelings*. Baltimore: Johns Hopkins University Press.

Lao Tzu (1963). *Tao Te Ching*. Baltimore: Penguin.

Lave, J. (1988). *Cognition in Practice*. Cambridge: Cambridge University Press.

Lave, J., Murtaugh, M. and de la Rocha, O. (1984). The dialectic of arithmetic in grocery shopping. In B. Rogoff and J. Lave (eds), *Everyday Cognition* (pp. 67–94). Cambridge, MA: Harvard University Press.

Lazarus, R.S. (1982). Thoughts on the relations between emotion and cognition. *American Psychologist,* **37,** 1019–24.

Lazarus, R.S. (1984). On the primary of emotion. *American Psychologist,* **39,** 124–9.

Lehman, H.E. (1980). Schizophrenia: clinical features. In H.I. Kaplan, A.F. Freedman and B.J. Sadock (eds), *Comprehensive Text Book of Psychiatry*, Vol. 2 (pp. 1153–91). Baltimore: Williams and Wilkins.

Leibniz, G.W. (1985). *The Monadology and Other Philosophical Writings*. New York: Garland.

Lem, S. (1978). *Solaris*. New York: Berkeley Publishing.

Leontiev, A.N. (1978). *Activity, Consciousness and Personality*. Englewood Cliffs, NJ: Prentice Hall.

Lettvin, J.Y., Maturana, H.R., Pitts, W.H. and McCulloch, W.S. (1961). Two remarks on the visual system of the frog. In W.A. Rosenblit (ed.), *Sensory Communication* (pp. 757–76). New York: John Wiley.

Leventhal, H. and Scherer, K. (1987). The relationship of emotion to cognition: a functional approach to a semantic controversy. *Cognition and Emotion,* **1,** 3–28.

Levina, R.E. (1981). L.S. Vygotsky's ideas about the planning function of speech in children. In J. Wertsch (ed.), *The Concept of Activity in Soviet Psychology* (pp. 279–99). Armonk, NY: Sharpe.

Lewkowicz, D.J. and Turkewitz, G. (1980). Cross-model equivalence in early infancy: auditory visual–intensity matching. *Developmental Psychology*, **16**, 597–607.

Lewontin, R. (1992). The dream of the human genome project. *The New York Review of Books*, **39**, 31–40.

Lishman, J.R. and Lee, D.N. (1973). The autonomy of visual kinesthesis. *Perception*, **2**, 287–94.

Lock, A. (1978). The emergence of language. In A. Lock (ed.), *Action, Gesture and Symbol: The Emergence of Language* (pp. 3–18). London: Academic Press.

Locke, D. (1971). *Memory*. London: Macmillan.

Lowenberg, I. (1975). Identifying metaphors. *Foundations of Language*, **12**, 315–38.

Lyons, J. (1977). *Semantics*. Cambridge: Cambridge University Press.

Macar, F. (1985). Time psychophysics and related models. In J.A. Michon and J. Jackson (eds), *Time, Mind and Behavior* (pp. 112–30). Berlin: Springer Verlag.

Maclay, H. (1971). Overview. In D.D. Steinberg and L.A. Jakobovits (eds), *Semantics* (pp. 157–82). Cambridge: Cambridge University Press.

MacLeod, C. (1990). Mood disorders and cognition. In M.W. Eysenck (ed.), *Cognitive Psychology: An International Review* (pp. 9–56). Chichester: John Wiley.

MacNamara, J. (1977). From sign to language. In J. McNamara (ed.), *Language Learning and Thought*. New York: Academic Press.

Malcolm, N. (1963). Three lectures on memory. In N. Malcolm (ed.), *Knowledge and Certainty* (pp. 185–240). Englewood Cliffs, NJ: Prentice Hall.

Malcolm, N. (1971). The myth of cognitive processes and structures. In T. Mischel (ed.), *Cognitive Development and Epistemology* (pp. 385–92). New York: Academic Press.

Malinowsky, B. (1948). *Magic, Science and Religion and Other Essays*. Boston: Beacon Press.

Mandelbrot, B.B. (1977). *Fractals: Form, Chance and Dimension*. San Francisco: Freeman.

Marcel, A. (1983a). Conscious and unconscious perception: experiments on visual masking and word recognition. *Cognitive Psychology*, **15**, 197–237.

Marcel, A. (1983b). Conscious and unconscious perception: an approach to the relations between phenomenal experience and perceptual processes. *Cognitive Psychology*, **15**, 238–300.

Marcel, A.J. (1988). Phenomenal experience and functionalism. In A.J. Marcel and E. Bisiach (eds), *Consciousness in Contemporary Science* (pp. 121–58). Oxford: Clarendon Press.

Marcus, G.F., Pinker, S., Ullman, M., Hollander, M., Rosen, T.J. and Fei Xu (1992). Overgeneralization in language acquisition. *Monographs of the Society for Research in Child Development*. **57** (serial no. 228).

Margolis, J. (1990). Explicating action. In D.N. Robinson and I.P. Mos (eds), *Annals of Theoretical Psychology*, Vol. 6 (pp. 39–74). New York: Plenum Press.

Marks, L.E. (1975). On colored-hearing synesthesia: cross-modal translations of sensory dimensions. *Psychological Bulletin*, **82**, 303–31.

Marks, L.E. (1978). *The Unity of the Senses: Interrelations among the Modalities*. New York: Academic Press.

Marks, L.E. (1982). Synesthetic perception and poetic metaphor. *Journal of Experimental Psychology: Human Perception and Performance*, **8**, 15–23.

Marks, L.E. (1990). Synaesthesia: perception and metaphor. In F. Burwick and W. Pape (eds), *Aesthetic Illusion: Theoretical and Historical Approaches* (pp. 28–40). Berlin: Walter de Gruyter.

Marks, L.E. and Bornstein, M.H. (1987). Sensory similarities: classes, characteristics, and cognitive consequences. In R.E. Haskell (ed.), *Cognition and Symbolic Structures: The Psychology of Metaphoric Transformation* (pp. 49–66). Norwood, NJ: Ablex.

Marks, L.E., Hummeal, R.J. and Bornstein, M.H. (1987). Perceiving similarity and comprehending metaphor. *Monograph of the Society for Research in Child Development*, **52** (serial no. 215).

Masson, M.E.J. (1984). Memory of the surface structure of sentences: remembering with and without awareness. *Journal of Verbal Learning and Verbal Behavior*, **10**, 608–13.

Masters, R.D. (1970). Genes, language and evolution. *Semiotica*, **2**, 295–320.

Matthews, R.J. (1971). Concerning a 'linguistic theory' of metaphor. *Foundations of Language*, **7**, 413–25.

Maturana, H.R. (1978). Biology of language: the epistemology of reality. In G.A. Miller and E. Lennberg (eds), *Psychology and Biology of Language and Thought* (pp. 27–63). New York: Academic Press.

Maturana, H.R. and Varela, F.J. (1980). *Autopoiesis and Cognition*. Dordrecht: D. Reidel.

Maturana, H.R. and Varela, F.J. (1987). *The Tree of Knowledge: The Biological Roots of Human Understanding*. New York: Shambhala.

Mayer, J.D. (1986). How mood influences cognition. In N.E. Sharkey (ed.), *Advances in Cognitive Science* (pp. 290–314). Chichester: Ellis Horwood.

McCabe, V. (1986). Introduction: event cognition and the conditions of existence. In V. McCabe and G.J. Balzano (eds), *Event Cognition: An Ecological Perspective* (pp. 3–23). Hillsdale, NJ: Lawrence Erlbaum.

McClelland, J.L. (1988). Connectionist models and psychological evidence. *Journal of Memory and Language*, **27**, 107–23.

McClelland, J.L. and Rumelhart, D.E. (1986a). *Parallel Distributed Processing: Explorations in the Microstructure of Cognition. Vol. 2: Psychological and Biological Models*. Cambridge, MA: MIT Press.

McClelland, J.L. and Rumelhart, D.E. (1986b). A distributed model of human learning and memory. In J.L. McClelland and D.E. Rumelhart (eds), *Parellel Distributed Processing: Exploration in the Microstructure of Cognition. Vol. 2: Psychological and Biological Models* (pp. 170–215). Cambridge, MA: MIT Press.

McClelland, J.L., Rumelhart, D.E. and Hinton, G.E. (1986). The appeal of parallel distributed processing. In D.E. Rumelhart and J.L. McClelland (eds), *Parallel Distributed Processing*. Vol. 1 (pp. 3–45). Cambridge, MA: MIT Press.

McCloskey, M. (1983). Naive theories of motion. In D. Gentner and A.L. Stevens (eds), *Mental Models* (pp. 299–324). Hillsdale, NJ: Lawrence Erlbaum.

McGeoch, J.A. and Iriow, A.L. (1952). *The Psychology of Human Learning*. New York: Longman.

McGuigan, F.J. and Rodier, W.I. (1968). Effects of auditory stimulation on covert oral behavior during silent reading. *Journal of Experimental Psychology*, **76**, 649–55.

McNeill, D. (1975). So you think gestures are nonverbal? *Psychological Review*, **92**, 350–71.

McNeill, D. and Levy, E. (1982). Conceptual representations in language activity and gesture. In R. Jarvella and W. Klein (eds), *In Speech, Place, and Action: Studies in Deixis and Related Topics* (pp. 271–95). Chichester: John Wiley.

Mead, G.H. (1922). A behavioristic account of the significant symbol. *Journal of Philosophy*, **19**, 157–63.

Mead, G.H. (1934). *Mind, Self and Society*. Chicago: University of Chicago Press.

Mead, G.H. (1938). *The Philosophy of the Act*. Chicago: University of Chicago Press.

Medin, D.L. and Schaffer, M.M. (1978). A context theory of classification learning. *Psychological Review*. **85**, 207–38.

Melkman, R. (1988). *The Construction of Objectivity: A New Look at the First Three Months of Life*. Basel: Karger.

Meltzoff, A.N. and Moore, K.M. (1977). Imitation of facial and manual gestures by human neonates. *Science*, **198**, 75–98.

Merleau-Ponty, M. (1962). *The Phenomenology of Perception*. London: Routledge and Kegan Paul.

Merleau-Ponty, M. (1964). *Le Visible et L'Invisible: Suivi de Notes de Travail*. Paris: Gallimard.

Merleau-Ponty, M. (1973). *The Prose of the World*. Evanston, IL: Northwestern University Press.

Merton, R.K. (1965). *On the Shoulders of Giants*. New York: Free Press.

Michaels, C.F. and Carello, C. (1981). *Direct Perception*. Englewood Cliffs, NJ: Prentice Hall.

Michon, J.A. (1978). The making of the present: a tutorial review. In J. Requin (ed.), *Attention and Performance*, Vol. 7 (pp. 89–111). Hillsdale, NJ: Lawrence Erlbaum.

Michon, J.A. (1985). The compleat time experiencer. In J.A. Michon and J. Jackson (eds), *Time, Mind and Behavior* (pp. 20–52). Berlin: Springer Verlag.

Middelton, D. and Edwards, D. (1990). *Collective Remembering*. London: Sage.

Miller, G.A. (1983). The study of information. In F. Machlup and U. Mansfield (eds), *The Study of Information* (pp. 111–13). New York: John Wiley.

Miller, G.A. (1956). The magical number seven plus or minus two: some limits on our capacity for processing information. *Psychological Review*, **63**, 81–97.

Minsky, M. (1968). Matter, mind and models. In M. Minsky (ed.), *Semantic Information Processing* (pp. 425–32). Cambridge, MA: MIT Press.

Minsky, M. (1975). A framework for representing knowledge. In P.H. Winston (ed.), *The Psychology of Computer Vision* (pp. 211–77). New York: McGraw-Hill.

Mischel, W. (1968). *Personality and Assessment*. New York: John Wiley.

Mischel, W. (1973). Towards a cognitive social learning reconceptualization of personality. *Psychological Review*, **80**, 252–83.

Morehead, D.M. and Morehead, A.E. (1974). From signal to sign: a Piagetian view of thought and language during the first two years. In R. Schiefelbusch and F.L. Lloyd (eds), *Language Perspectives: Acquisition, Retardation and Intervention*. Baltimore: University Park Press.

Moreland, R.L. and Zajonc, R.B. (1977). Is stimulus recognition a necessary condition for the occurrence of exposure effects? *Journal of Personality and Social Psychology*, **35**, 191–9.

Morris, C.W. (1938). Foundations of the theory of signs. In O. Neurath, R. Carnap and C.W. Morris (eds), *International Encyclopedia of Unified Science* (pp. 79–137). Chicago: University of Chicago Press.

Morris, M. (1991). Why there are no mental representations? *Minds and Machines*, **1**, 1–30.

Mugny, G., Perret-Clermont, A.-N. and Doise, W. (1981). Interpersonal coordinations and social differences in the construction of the intellect. In G.M. Stephenson and J.M. Davis (eds), *Progress in Applied Social Psychology*, Vol. 1 (pp. 315–43). New York: John Wiley.

Munsat, S. (1966). *The Concept of Memory*. New York: Random House.

Murray, D.J. (1966). Vocalisation-at-presentation and immediate recall, with varying recall methods. *Quarterly Journal of Experimental Psychology*, **18**, 9–18.

Myers, P.S. (1986). Right hemisphere communication impairment. In R. Chapey (ed.), *Language Intervention Strategies in Adult Aphasia* (pp. 444–61). Baltimore: Williams and Wilkins.

Nabokov, V. (1974). *Strong Opinions*. London: Weidenfeld & Nicolson.

Nagel, T. (1974). What is it like to be a bat? *Philosophical Review*, **83**, 435–50.

Nagal, T. (1986). *The View from Nowhere*. Oxford: Oxford University Press.

Naus, M.J. and Halasz, F.G. (1979). Developmental perspectives on cognition processing and semantic memory structure. In L. Cermak and F. Craik (eds), *Levels of Processing in Human Memory* (pp. 259–88). Hillsdale, NJ: Lawrence Erlbaum.

Navon, D. (1977). Forest before trees: the precedence of global features in visual perception. *Cognitive Psychology*, **9**, 353–83.

Neisser, U. (1976). *Cognition and Reality*. San Francisco: Freeman.

Neisser, U. (1982). *Memory Observed*. San Francisco: Freeman.

Nelson, K.E., Carskaddon, G. and Bonvillian, J.D. (1973). Syntax acquisition: impact of experimental variation in adult verbal interaction with the child. *Child Development*, **44**, 497–504.

Newell, A. (1980). Physical symbol systems. *Cognitive Science*, **10**, 135–83.

Newell, A. and Simon, H.A. (1972). *Human Problem Solving*. Englewood Cliffs, N.J.: Prentice Hall.

Newport, E.L., Gleitman, H. Gleitman, L.R. (1977). Mother, I'd rather do it myself: some effects and non-effects of maternal speech style. In C.E. Snow and C.A. Ferguson (eds), *Talking to Children: Language Input and Acquisition* (pp. 109–50). Cambridge: Cambridge University Press.

Nietzsche, F.W. (1956). *The Birth of Tragedy and the Genealogy of Morals*. Garden City, NY: Doubleday.

Nisbett, R.E. and Wilson, T.D. (1977). Telling more than we can know: verbal reports on mental processes. *Psychological Review*, **84**, 231–59.

Norman, D.A. (1980). Twelve issues for cognitive science. *Cognitive Science*, **4**, 1–32.

Norman, D.A. and Rumelhart, D.E. (1975). *Explorations in Cognition*. San Francisco: Freeman.

Norman, W.T. (1963). Toward an adequate taxonomy of personality attributes: replicated factor structure in peer nomination personality ratings. *Journal of Abnormal and Social Psychology*, **66**, 452–8.

Nunberg, G. (1979). The non-uniqueness of semantic solutions: polysemy. *Linguistics and Philosophy*, **3**, 143–84.

Oatley, K. and Johnson-Laird, P.N. (1987). Towards a cognitive theory of emotions. *Cognition and Emotion*, **1**, 29–50.

Ochs, E. (1979). Introduction: what child language can contribute to pragmatics. In E. Ochs and A.B. Shieffelin (eds), *Developmental Pragmatics* (pp. 1–17). New York: Academic Press.

Olson, D. (1976). Culture, technology and intellect. In L.D. Resnick (ed.), *The Nature of Intelligence* (pp.189–202). Hillsdale, NJ: Lawrence Erlbaum.

Olson, D.R. (1980) (ed.). *The Social Foundations of Language and Thought*. New York: Norton.

Ortony, A. (1975). Why metaphors are necessary and not just nice. *Educational Theory*, **25**, 45–53.

Ortony, A. (1980). Some psycholinguistic aspects of metaphor. In R.P. Honeck and R.R. Hoffman (eds), *Cognitive and Figurative Language* (pp. 69–83). Hillsdale, NJ: Lawrence Erlbaum.

Ortony, A. Clore, G.L. and Collins, A. (1988). *The Cognitive Structure of Emotions*. Cambridge: Cambridge University Press.

Ortony, A., Schallert, D.L., Reynolds, R.E. and Antos, S.J. (1978). Interpreting metaphors and idioms: some effects of context on comprehension. *Journal of Verbal Learning and Verbal Behavior*, **17**, 465–77.

Osgood, C.E. (1980). The cognitive dynamics of synesthesia and metaphor. In R.P. Honeck and R.R. Hoffman (eds), *Cognitive and Figurative Language* (pp. 203–38). Hillsdale, NJ: Lawrence Erlbaum.

Osgood, C.E., Suci, G.J. and Tannenbaum, P.M. (1957). *The Measurement of Meaning*. Urbana, IL: University of Illinois Press.

Osherson, D.N. and Smith, E.E. (1981). On the adequacy of prototype theory as a theory of concepts. *Cognition*, **9**, 35–58.

Otto, R. (1967). *The Idea of the Holy*. Harmondworth: Penguin.

Paivio, A. (1971). *Imagery and Verbal Processes*. Toronto: Holt, Rinehart.

Palmer, S.E. (1978). Fundamental aspects of cognitive representation. In E. Rosch and B.B. Lloyd (eds), *Cognitive and Categorization* (pp. 262–303). Hillsdale, NJ: Lawrence Erlbaum.

Palmer, S.E. and Kimichi, R. (1986). The information processing approach to cognition. In T.J. Knapp and L.C. Robertson (eds), *Approaches to Cognition: Contrasts and Controversies* (pp. 37–77). Hillsdale, NJ: Lawrence Erlbaum.

Papert, S. (1980). *Mindstorms: Children, Computers and Powerful Ideas*. New York: Basic Books.

Partee, B.H. (1984). Compositionality. In F. Landman and F. Veldman (eds), *Varieties of Formal Semantics* (pp. 281–314). Dorchester: Foris.

Patterson, K.E. and Baddeley, A.D. (1977). When face recognition fails. *Journal of Experimental Psychology: Human Learning and Memory*, **3**, 406–17.

Paxton, S. (1982). Chute transcript. *Contact Quarterly*, Spring/Summer, 16–17.

Paxton, S. (1988). Fall after Newton. *Contact Quarterly*, Fall, 38–9.

Pea, R. (1980). The development of negation in early child language. In D.R. Olson (ed.), *The Social Foundations of Language and Thought* (pp. 156–86). New York: Norton.

Peeters, R. and D'Ydewalle, G. (1987). Influences of emotional states upon memory: the state of the art. *Communication and Cognition*, **20**, 171–90.

Penfield, W. (1951). Memory mechanisms. *Transactions of the American Neurological Association*, **76**, 15–31.

Penfield, W. (1959). The interpretative cortex. *Science*, **129**, 1719–25.

Pepper, S. (1942). *World Hypothesis*. Berkeley: University of California Press.

Petty, R.E. and Cacioppo, J.T. (1981). *Attitudes and Persuasion: Classic and Contemporary Approaches*. Dubuque, IA: Brown.

Piaget, J. (1952). *The Origins of Intelligence in Children*. London: Routledge and Kegan Paul.

Piaget, J. (1954). *The Construction of Reality by the Child*. New York: Basic Books.

Piaget, J. (1957). *Logic and Psychology*. New York: Basic Books.

Piaget, J. (1962). *Play, Dreams and Imitation in Children*. New York: Norton.

Piaget, J. (1983). Piaget's theory. In P.H. Mussen (ed.), *Carmichael's Manual of Child Psychology* (third edition) pp. 703–32. New York: John Wiley.

Piaget, J. (1988). The psychogenesis of knowledge and its epistemological significance. In M. Piatelli-Palmerini (ed.), *Language and Learning: The Debate between Jean Piaget and Noam Chomsky* (pp. 23–34). Cambridge, MA: Harvard University Press.

Piatelli-Palmerini, M. (1980). *Language and Learning: The Debate between Jean Piaget and Noam Chomsky*. Cambridge MA: Harvard University Press.

Pinker, S. and Prince, A. (1988). On language and connectionism: analysis of a parallel distributed processing model of language acquisition. *Cognition*, **28**, 73–193.

Pittenger, J.B. and Shaw, R.E. (1975). Perception of relative and absolute age in facial photographs. *Perception and Psychophysics*, **18**, 137–43.

Plato (1937). *The Dialogues*. London: Random House.

Poincaré, H. (1958). Mathematical creation. In B. Ghiselin (ed.), *The Creative Process* (pp. 33–42). New York: Mentor Books.

Polanyi, M. (1962). *Personal Knowledge*. Chicago: University of Chicago Press.

Polanyi, M. (1966). *The Tacit Dimension*. Garden City: Anchor Books.

Polge, J. (1988). Parfums: l'empire d'essences. *Le Point*, **804**, 75–9.

Pollio, H.R. and Pickens, J.D. (1980). The development structure of figurative competence. In R.P. Honeck and R.R. Hoffman (ed.), *Cognition and Figurative Language* (pp. 311–40). Hillsdale, NJ: Lawrence Erlbaum.

Pollio, H.R., Fabrizi, M.S., Sills, A. and Smith, M.K. (1984). Need metaphoric comprehension take longer than literal comprehension? *Journal of Psycholinguistic Research*, **13**, 195–214.

Popper, K.R. (1957). *The Poverty of Historicism*. London: Routledge and Kegan Paul.

Popper, K.R. (1972). *Objective Knowledge*. Oxford: Clarendon Press.

Posner, M.I. and Warren, R.E. (1972). Traces, concepts and conscious constructions. In A.W. Melton and E. Martin (eds), *Coding Processes in Human Memory* (pp. 25–44). Washington, DC: Winston.

Preston, J.H. (1963). A conversation with Gertrude Stein. In B. Ghiselin (ed.), *The Creative Process* (pp. 157–68). New York: Mentor Books.

Prigogine, I. (1980). *From Being to Becoming*. San Francisco: Freeman.

Prince, A. and Pinker, S. (1988). Subsymbols aren't much good outside a symbol-processing architecture. *Behavioral and Brain Sciences*, **11**, 46–7.

Proust, M. (1983). *Remembrance of Things Past*, Vol. 2. New York: Penguin.

Putman, H. (1973). Reductionism and the nature of psychology. *Cognition*, **8**, 263–368.

Putman, H. (1975a). *Mind Language and Reality: Philosophical Papers*, Vol. 2. Cambridge: Cambridge University Press.

Putman, H. (1975b). The meaning of meaning. In H. Putman, *Mind Language and Reality: Philosophical Papers*, Vol. 2. (pp. 215–71). Cambridge: Cambridge University Press.

Putman, H. (1981). *Reason, Truth and History*. Cambridge: Cambridge University Press.

Putman, H. (1988). *Representation and Reality*. Cambridge, MA: MIT Press.

Pylyshyn, Z.W. (1979). Do mental events have durations? *The Behavioral and Brain Sciences*, **2**, 277–8.

Pylyshyn, Z.W. (1980). Cognition and computation: issues in the foundation of cognitive science. *The Behavioral and Brain Sciences*, **3**, 111–69.

Pylyshyn, Z.W. (1981). The imagery debate: analog media versus tacit knowledge. *Psychological Review*, **87**, 16–45.

Pylyshyn, Z.W. (1984). *Computation and Cognition*. Cambridge, MA: MIT Press.

Quine, W.V.O. (1960). *Word and Object*. Cambridge, MA: MIT Press.

Radley, A. (1990). Artefacts, memory and a sense of the past. In D. Middelton and D. Edwards (eds), *Collective Remembering* (pp. 46–60). London: Sage.

Reddy, M.J. (1979). The conduit metaphor – a case of frame conflict in our language about language. In A. Ortony (ed.), *Metaphor and Thought* (pp. 284–325). New York: Cambridge University Press.

Reed, E.S. (1982). *James Gibson and the Psychology of Perception*. New Haven: Yale University Press.

Reik, T. (1948). *Listening with the Third Ear*. New York: Farrar, Straus.

Rey, G. (1978). Worries about Haugeland's worries. *The Behavioral and Brain Sciences*, **1**, 246–8.

Rey, G. (1983). A reason for doubting the existence of consciousness. In R.J. Davidson, G.E. Schwartz and D. Shapiro (eds), *Consciousness and Self Regulation*, Vol. 3 (pp. 1–36). New York: Plenum Press.

Richards, I.A. (1936). *The Philosophy of Rhetoric*. London: Oxford University Press.

Ricoeur, P. (1979). The metaphorical process as cognition, imagination and feeling. In S. Sacks (ed.), *On Metaphor* (pp. 141–57). Chicago: University of Chicago Press.

Rimbaud, A. (1937). *Oeuvres de Arthur Rimbaud*. Paris: Mercure de France.

Robinson, I. (1975). *The New Grammarians' Funeral*. Cambridge: Cambridge University Press.

Roediger, H. (1980). Memory metaphors in cognitive psychology. *Memory and Cognition*, **8**, 231–46.

Rogoff, B. (1982). Integrating context and cognitive development. In M.E. Lamb and A.L. Brown (eds), *Advances in Developmental Psychology*, Vol. 2. Hillsdale, NJ: Lawrence Erlbaum.

Rogoff, B. (1989). The joint socialization of development by young children and adults. In A. Gellatly, D. Rogers and J.A. Sloboda (eds), *Cognition and Social Worlds* (pp. 57–82). Oxford: Clarendon Press.

Rogoff, B. (1990). *Apprenticeship in Thinking: Cognitive Development in Social Context*. New York: Oxford University Press.

Rogoff, B. and Gardner, W. (1984). Adult guidance of cognitive development. In B. Rogoff and J. Lave (eds), *Everyday Cognition: Its Development in Social Context* (pp. 95–116). Cambridge, MA: Harvard University Press.

Romanyshyn, R.D. (1982). *Psychological Life: From Science to Metaphor*. Austin: University of Texas Press.

Romanyshyn, R.D. (1989). *Technology as Symptom and Dream*. London: Routledge.

Rommetveit, R. (1974). *On Message Structure: A Framework for the Study of Language and Communication*. New York: John Wiley.

Rommetveit, R. (1985). Language acquisition as increasing linguistic structuring of experience and symbolic behavior control. In J.V. Wertsch (ed.), *Culture, Communication and Cognition: Vygotskian Perspectives* (pp. 205–34). Cambridge: Cambridge University Press.

Rommetveit, R. and Blakar, R.M. (1979) (eds). *Studies of Language, Thought and Verbal Communication*. London: Academic Press.

Rorty, R. (1980). *Philosophy and the Mirror of Nature*. Oxford: Blackwell.

Rosch, E. (1978). Principles of categorization. In E. Rosch and B.L. Lloyd (eds), *Cognition and Categorization* (pp. 28–48). Hillsdale, NJ: Lawrence Erlbaum.

Ross, E.D. (1983). Right-hemisphere lesions in disorders of affective language. In E. Kertesz (ed.), *Lateralization in Neuropsychology* (pp. 493–508). New York: Academic Press.

Ross, J.R. (1970). On declarative sentences. In R. Jacobs and P.S. Rosenbaum (eds), *Readings in English Transformational Grammar* (pp. 222–72). Boston: Ginn.

Roszak, T. (1972). *Where the Wasteland Ends*. New York: Doubleday.

Rothkopf, E.Z. (1971). Incidental memory for location of information in text. *Journal of Verbal Learning and Verbal Behavior*, **10**, 608–13.

Rousseau, J.J. (1966). On the origin of language. In J.H. Moran and A. Gode (eds), *Two Essays of J.J. Rousseau and J.G. Herder*. New York: Frederick Ungar.

Rowe, M.H. and Stone, J. (1980). Parametric and feature extraction analyses of the receptive fields of visual neurons. *Brain, Behavior and Evolution*, **17**, 103–22.

Rudofsky, B. (1965). *Architecture without Architects*. Garden City, NY: Doubleday.

Rumelhart, D.E. (1979). Some problems with the notion of literal meaning. In A. Ortony (ed.), *Metaphor and Thought* (pp. 78–90). Cambridge: Cambridge University Press.

Rumelhart, D.E. and McClelland, J.L. (1986a). *Parallel Distributed Processing: Explorations in the Microstructure of Cognition. Vol. 1: Foundations*. Cambridge, MA: MIT Press.

Rumelhart, D.E. and McClelland, J.L. (1986b). PDP models and general issues in cognitive science. In D.E. Rumelhart and J.L. McClelland (eds), *Parallel Distributed Processing: Explorations in the Microstructure of Cognition. Vol. 1: Foundations* (pp. 110–46). Cambridge, MA: MIT Press.

Rumelhart, D.E. and McClelland, J.L. (1986c). On learning the past tenses of English verbs. In J.L. McClelland and D.E. Rumelhart (eds), *Parallel Distributed Processing. Vol. 2: Pyschological and Biological Models* (pp. 216–72). Cambridge, MA: MIT Press.

Rumelhart, D.E. and Norman, D.A. (1988). Representation in memory. In R.C. Atkinson, R.J. Hernstein, G. Lindzey and R. Duncan Lace (eds), *Steven's Handbook of Experimental Psychology* (second edition) (pp. 511–87). San Francisco: Freeman.

Rumelhart, D.E., Hinton, G.E. and McClelland, J.L. (1986). A general framework for parallel distributed processing. In D.E. Rumelhart and J.L. McClelland (eds), *Parallel Distributed Processing: Explorations in the Microstructure of Cognition. Vol. 1: Foundations* (pp. 45–76). Cambridge, MA: MIT Press.

Rumelhart, D.E., Hinton, G.E. and Williams, R.J. (1986). Learning internal representations by error propagation. In D.E. Rumelhart and J.L. McClelland (eds), *Parallel Distributed Processing: Explorations in the Microstructure of Cognition. Vol. 1: Foundations* (pp. 318–64). Cambridge, MA: MIT Press.

Russell, B. (1956). *Logic and Knowledge*. London: Allen and Unwin.

Russell, B. (1967). *Autobiography*. London: Allen and Unwin.

Ryle, G. (1949). *The Concept of Mind*. Cambridge: Hutchinson.

Sachs, J.D.S. (1967). Recognition memory for syntactic and semantic aspects of connected discourse. *Perception and Psychophysics*, **2**, 437–42.

Sampson, E.E. (1977). Psychology and the American ideal. *Journal of Personality and Social Psychology*, **35**, 767–82.

Sampson, E.E. (1981). Cognitive psychology as ideology. *American Psychologist*, **39**, 730–4.

Sampson, E.E. (1983). Deconstructing psychology's subject. *Journal of Mind and Behavior*, **4**, 135–64.

Sampson, E.E. (1988). The debate on individualism. *American Psychologist*, **43**, 730–43.

Sarbin, T.R. (1986) (ed.). *Narrative Psychology: The Storied Nature of Human Conduct*. New York: Praeger.

Sartre, J.-P. (1957). *Being and Nothingness*. London: Methuen.

de Saussure, F. (1916/1966). *Course in General Linguistics*. New York: McGraw-Hill.

Scaife, M. and Bruner, J. (1975). The capacity for joint visual attention in the infant. *Nature*, **253**, 265–6.

Schank, R. (1972). Conceptual dependency: a theory of natural language understanding. *Cognitive Psychology*, **3**, 552–631.

Schank, R.C. (1973). Identification of conceptualizations underlying natural language. In R.C. Schank and K.M. Colby (eds), *Computer Models of Thought and Language* (pp. 187–247). San Francisco: Freeman.

Schank, R.C. (1975). The role of memory in language processing. In C.N. Cofer (ed.), *The Structure of Human Memory* (pp. 162–89). San Francisco: Freeman.

Schank, R.C. and Abelson, R.P. (1977). *Scripts, Plans, Goals and Understanding*. Hillsdale, NJ: Lawrence Erlbaum.

Schlesinger, I.M. (1986). *Do We Really Think in Words?* Working Paper no. 18. Jerusalem: The Hebrew University.

Schrödinger, E. (1964). *My View of the World*. Cambridge: Cambridge University Press.

Schutz, A. (1964). Making music together: a study in social relationship. In A. Broderson (ed.), *Alfred Schutz: Collected Papers. Vol 2: Studies in Social Theory* (pp. 159–78). The Hague: Martinus Nijhoff.

Schutz, A. (1967). *The Phenomenology of the Social World*. Chicago: Northwestern University Press.

Scribner, S. (1977). Modes of thinking and ways of speaking: culture and logic reconsidered. In P.N. Johnson-Laird and P.C. Wason (eds), *Thinking: Readings in Cognitive Science* (pp. 483–500). Cambridge: Cambridge University Press.

Scribner, S. (1984). Studying working intelligence. In B. Rogoff and J. Lave (eds), *Everyday Cognition* (pp. 9–40). Cambridge, MA: Harvard University Press.

Scribner, S. (1985). Vygotsky's uses of history. In J.V. Wertsch (ed.), *Culture, Communication and Cognition: Vygotskian Perspectives* (pp. 119–45). Cambridge: Cambridge University Press.

Scribner, S. (1986). Thinking in action: some characteristics of practical thought. In R.J. Sternberg and R.K. Wagner (eds), *Practical Intelligence* (pp. 13–30). Cambridge: Cambridge University Press.

Scribner, S. and Cole, M. (1981). *The Psychology of Literacy*. Cambridge, MA: Harvard University Press.

Searle, J.R. (1975). Indirect speech acts. In P. Cole and J.L. Morgan (eds), *Syntax and Semantics, Vol.3: Speech Acts* (pp. 59–82). New York: Academic Press.

Searle, J.R. (1979). Metaphor. In A. Ortony (ed.), *Metaphor and Thought* (pp. 92–123). Cambridge: Cambridge University Press.

Searle, J.R. (1980a). Minds, brains and programs. *The Behavioral and Brain Sciences*, **3**, 417–57.

Searle, J.R. (1980b). The background of meaning. In J.R. Searle and M. Bierwisch (eds), *Speech Act Theory and Pragmatics* (pp. 221–32). Dordrecht: D. Reidel.

Searle, J.R. (1983). *Intentionality: An Essay in the Philosophy of Mind*. Cambridge: Cambridge University Press.

Searle, J.R. (1984). *Minds, Brains and Science*. Cambridge, MA: Harvard University Press.

Searle, J.R. (1990a). Consciousness, explanatory inversion, and cognitive science. *The Behavioral and Brain Sciences*, **13**, 585–642.

Searle, J.R. (1990b). Is the brain's mind a computer program? *Scientific American*, **262**, 20–5.

Secord, P.F. (1990). The need for a radically new human. *Science Annals*, **90**, 75–87.

Sejnowsky, T.J. and Rosenberg, C.R. (1987). Parallel networks that learn to pronounce English text. *Complex Systems*, **1**, 145–68.

Sejnowsky, T.J., Koch, C. and Churchland, P.S. (1988). Computational neuroscience. *Science*, **241**, 1299–306.

Serafine, M.L. (1988). *Music as Cognition: The Development of Thought in Sound*. New York: Columbia University Press.

diSessa, A.A. (1982). Unlearning Aristotelian physics: a study of knowledge-based learning. *Cognitive Science*, **6**, 37–75.

Shanon, B. (1974). A study of human long-term memory in natural and artificial conditions. Unpublished doctoral dissertation. Stanford University.

Shanon, B. (1976). Aristotelianism, Newtonianism and the physics of the layman. *Perception*, **5**, 241–3.

Shanon, B. (1978). The genetic code and human language. *Synthese*, **39**, 401–15.

Shanon, B. (1980). Labeling. *Journal of Pragmatics*, **4**, 43–9.

Shanon, B. (1982a). *The Myth of the Box and the Package*. Working Paper No. 3. The Rotman Center for Cognitive Science. Jerusalem: The Hebrew University.

Shanon, B. (1982b). Colour associates to semantic linear orders. *Psychological Research*, **44**, 75–83.

Shanon, B. (1982c). Identification and classification of words and drawings in two languages. *Quarterly Journal of Experimental Psychology*, **34A**, 135–52.

Shanon, B. (1983a). Que disent les oiseaux? Reflexion sur une theorie de la communication. In J.P. Dupuy and P. Dumouchel (eds), *Auto-organization* (pp. 407–11). Paris: Seuil.

Shanon, B. (1983b). Descartes' puzzle: an organismic approach. *Cognition and Brain Theory*, **6**, 185–95.

Shanon, B. (1984a). Meno – a cognitive psychological view. *The British Journal for the Philosophy of Science*, **35**, 129–47.

Shanon, B. (1984b). The case for introspection. *Cognition and Brain Theory*, **7**, 167–80.

Shanon, B. (1987a). Cooperativeness and implicature – a reversed perspective. *New Ideas in Psychology*, **5**, 289–93.

Shanon, B. (1987b). The non-abstractness of mental representations. *New Ideas in Psychology*, **5**, 117–26.

Shanon, B. (1988a). The similarity of features. *New Ideas in Psychology*, **6**, 307–21.

Shanon, B. (1988b). The channels of thought. *Discourse Processes*, **11**, 221–42

Shanon, B. (1988c). Remarks on the modularity of mind. *British Journal for the Philosophy of Science*, **39**, 331–52.

Shanon, B. (1989a). Thought sequences. *The European Journal of Cognitive Psychology*, **1**, 129–59.

Shanon, B. (1989b). Why do we (sometimes) think in words? In K.J. Gilhooly, M. Keane, R. Logie and G. Erdos (eds), *Lines of Thinking: Reflections on the Psychology of Thinking* (pp. 5–14). Chichester: John Wiley.

Shanon, B. (1989c). A simple comment regarding the Turing Test. *Journal for the Theory of Social Behavior*, **19**, 249–56.

Shanon, B. (1989d). *Mental Images – A Phenomenological Investigation*. Working Paper No. 28. The Rotman Center for Cognitive Science. Jerusalem: The Hebrew University.

Shanon, B. (1990a). The knot in the handkerchief. *Metaphor and Symbolic Activity*, **5**, 109–14.

Shanon, B. (1990b). Consciousness. *Journal of Mind and Behavior*, **11**, 137–52.

Shanon, B. (1990c). Why are dreams cinematographic? *Metaphor and Symbolic Activity*, **5**, 235–48.

Shanon, B. (1990d). Non-representational frameworks for psychology: a typology. *The European Journal of Cognitive Psychology*, **2**, 1–22.

Shanon, B. (1991a). Chauvinism misdirected: a reply to Henley. *Journal for the Theory of Social Behavior*, **21**, 363–71.

Shanon, B. (1991b). *Cultural Affordances*. Working Paper No. 30. The Rotman Center for Cognitive Science. Jerusalem: The Hebrew University.

Shanon, B. (1991c). Post-scriptum: treize ans plus tard. In M. Canto-Sperber (ed.), *Les Paradoxes de la Connaissance* (pp. 355–9). Paris: Editions Odile Jacob.

Shanon, B. (1991d). Memory as a tool: an analogy with the guiding stick. *New Ideas in Psychology*, **9**, 89–93.

Shanon, B. (1991e). Cognitive psychology and modern physics: some analogies. *European Journal of Cognitive Psychology*, **3**, 201–34.

Shanon, B. (1991f). Le Ménon: une conception de psychologie cognitive. In M. Canto-Sperber (ed.), *Les Paradoxes de la Connaissance* (pp. 336–53). Paris: Editions Odile Jacob.

Shanon, B. (1992). Are connectionist models cognitive? *Philosophical Psychology*, **5**, 235–55.

Shanon, B. (1993a). Central modularity. *Scientific Contributions to General Psychology*, in press.

Shanon, B. (1993b). Why are we (sometimes) conscious of our thoughts? *Pragmatics and Cognition*, **1**, 25–50.

Shanon, B. (1993c). Fractal patterns in language. *New Ideas in Psychology*, **11**, 105–9.

Shanon, B. and Atlan, H. (1990). Von Foerster's Theorem on connectedness and organization: semantic applications. *New Ideas in Psychology*, **8**, 81–90.

Sharan, S. (1990). Cooperative learning: a perspective on research and practice. In S. Sharan (ed.), *Cooperative Learning: Theory and Research* (pp. 285–300). New York: Praeger.

Shatz, M. (1978). Children's comprehension of their mother's question-directives. *Journal of Child Language*, **5**, 39–46.

Shaw, R.E. and Bransford, J. (1977). Introduction: psychological approaches to the problem of knowledge. In R.E. Shaw and J. Bransford (eds), *Perceiving, Acting, and Knowing: Toward an Ecological Psychology* (pp. 1–39). Hillsdale, NJ: Lawrence Erlbaum.

Shaw, R.E. and McIntyre, M. (1974). Algoristic foundations to cognitive psychology. In W. Weimer and D. Palermo (eds), *Cognition and the Symbolic Processes* (pp. 305–62). Hillsdale, NJ: Lawrence Erlbaum.

Shaw, R. and Pittenger, J. (1978). Perceiving change. In R.L. Pick and E. Saltzman (eds), *Models of Perceiving and Processing Information* (pp. 87–204). Hillsdale, NJ: Lawrence Erlbaum.

Shaw, R.E. and Todd, J. (1980). Abstract machine theory and direct perception. *The Behavioral and Brain Sciences*. **3**, 400–1.

Shaw, R.E., Turvey, M.T. and Mace, W. (1981). Ecological psychology: the consequence of a commitment to realism. In W.B. Weimer and D. Palermo (eds), *Cognition and the Symbolic Processes II* (pp. 159–226). Hillsdale, NJ: Lawrence Erlbaum.

Shepard, R.N. (1984). Ecological constraints on internal representation: resonant kinematics of perceiving, imagining, thinking and dreaming. *Psychological Review*, **91**, 417–47.

Shepard, R.N. and Metzler, J. (1971). Mental rotation of three dimensional objects. *Science*, **171**, 701–3.

Shepp, B.E. (1978). From perceived similarity to dimensional structure: a new hypothesis about perceptual development. In E. Rosch and B.B. Lloyd (eds), *Cognition and Categorization* (pp. 135–67). Hillsdale, NJ: Lawrence Erlbaum.

Shoemaker, S. (1980). Functionalism and qualia. In N. Block (ed.), *Readings in Philosophy of Psychology*, Vol. 1 (pp. 251–67). Cambridge, MA: Harvard University Press.

Shotter, J. (1975). *Images of Man in Psychological Research*. London: Methuen.

Shotter, J. (1984). *Social Accountability and Selfhood*. Oxford: Blackwell.

Shotter, J. (1990). The social construction of remembering and forgetting. In D. Middelton and D. Edwards (eds), *Collective Remembering*. London: Sage.

Shweder, R.A. (1991). *Thinking Through Cultures: Expeditions in Cultural Psychology*. Cambridge, MA: Harvard University Press.

Siegel, R.K. and West, L.J. (1975). *Hallucinations: Behavior, Experience and Theory*. New York: John Wiley.

Simon, H.A. (1976). Discussion: cognition and social behavior. In J.S. Carrol and J.W. Payne (eds), *Cognition and Social Behavior* (pp. 253–67). Hillsdale, NJ: Lawrence Erlbaum.

Singer, J.A. and Salovey, P. (1988). Mood and memory: evaluating the network theory of affect. *Clinical Psychology Review*, 8, 211–51.

Skarda, C.A. and Freeman, W.J. (1987). How brains make chaos in order to make sense of the world. *The Behavioral and Brain Sciences*, 10, 161–95.

Sloaman, A. and Croucher, M. (1981). Why robots will have emotions. *Proceedings of the Seventh International Joint Conference on Artificial Intelligence* (pp. 197–202). Vancouver.

Smith, E.E. (1978). Theories of semantic memory. In W.K. Estes (ed.), *Handbook of Learning and Cognitive Processes*, Vol. 6 (pp. 1–56). Hillsdale, NJ: Lawrence Erlbaum.

Smith, L.B. and Kemler, D.G. (1977). Developmental trends in free classification: evidence for a new conceptualization of perceptual development. *Journal of Experimental Child Psychology*, 24, 279–98.

Smith, L.B. and Kemler Nelson, D.G. (1984). Overall similarity in adults classification: the child in all of us. *Journal of Experimental Psychology: General*, 113, 137–59.

Smith, S.M. (1982). Enhancement of recall using multiple environmental contexts during learning. *Memory and Cognition*, 10, 405–12.

Smolensky, P. (1986). Information processing in dynamical systems: foundations of harmony theory. In D.E. Rumelhart and J.L. McClelland (eds), *Parallel Distributed Processing. Vol. 1: Foundations* (pp. 194–281). Cambridge, MA: MIT Press.

Smolensky, P. (1988). On the proper treatment of connectionism. *The Behavioral and Brain Sciences*, 11, 1–74.

Smolensky, P. (1989). Connectionist modeling: neural computation/mental connections. In L. Nadel, L.A. Cooper, P. Culicover and R.M. Harnish (eds), *Neural Connections, Mental Computation* (pp. 49–69). Cambridge, MA: MIT Press.

Snow, C.E. (1977). The development of conversation between mothers and babies. *Journal of Child Language*, 4, 1–22.

Snow, C.E., de Blauw, A. and van Roosmalen, G. (1979). Talking and playing with babies: the role of ideologies of child-rearing. In M. Bullowa (ed.), *Before Speech* (pp. 269–88). Cambridge: Cambridge University Press.

Snyder, L.S., Bates, E. and Bretherton, I. (1981). Content and context in early lexical development. *Journal of Child Language*, 8, 565–82.

Sperber, D. and Wilson, D. (1986). *Relevance: Communication and Cognition*. Oxford: Blackwell.

Spiegelberg, H. (1975). *Doing Phenomenology: Essays on and in Phenomenology*. The Hague: Martinus Nijhoff.

Sroufe, A.L. (1979). Socioemotional development. In J.D. Osofsky (ed.), *Handbook of Infant Development* (pp. 462–516). New York: John Wiley.

Stabler, E.P., Jr. (1983). How are grammars represented? *The Behavioral and Brain Sciences*, 6, 381–421.

Staudenmayer, H. (1975). Understanding conditional memorizing with meaningful propositions. In R.J. Falmagne (ed.), *Reasoning: Representations and Process in Children and Adults*. Hillsdale, NJ: Lawrence Erlbaum.

Stechler, G. and Carpenter, G.A. (1967). A viewpoint on early affective development. In J. Hellmuth (ed.), *The Exceptional Infant*, Vol. 1 (pp. 163–89). Seattle: Special Child Publications.

Steiner, G. (1975). *After Babel: Aspects of Language and Translation*. London: Oxford University Press.

Sternberg, S. (1966). High speed scanning in human memory. *Science*, 153, 652–4.

Stich, S.P. (1975). *Innate Ideas*. Berkeley: University of California Press.

Stich, S.P. (1983). *From Folk Psychology to Cognitive Science: The Case Against Belief*. Cambridge, MA: MIT Press.

Stigler, J.W. (1984). 'Mental abacus': the effect of abacus training on Chinese children's mental calculation. *Cognitive Psychology*, 16, 145–76.

Strack, F., Martin, L.L. and Stepper, S. (1988). Inhibiting and facilitating conditions of the human smile: a non-obtrusive test of the facial feedback hypothesis. *Journal of Personality and Social Psychology*, **54**, 768–77.

Suchman, L.A. (1987). *Plans and Situated Actions*. Cambridge: Cambridge University Press.

Sudnow, D. (1980). *Talk's Body: A Meditation between Two Keyboards*. Harmondsworth: Penguin.

Suzuki, D.T. (1985). Introduction to Eugen Herrigel. *Zen in the Art of Archery*. London: Arkana.

Swindale, N.V. (1990). Is the cerebral cortex modular? *Trends in Neuroscience*, **13**, 487–92.

Tarski, A. (1944). The semantic conception of truth and the foundation of semantics. *Philosophy and Phenomenological Research*, **4**, 341–76.

Tolstoy, L. (1960). *The Death of Ivan Ilych and Other Stories*. New York: Signer.

Tomkins, S. (1962). *Affect, Imagery, Consciousness*, Vol. 1. New York: Springer Verlag.

Towe, A.L. (1975). Notes on the hypothesis of columnar organization in somatosensory cerebral cortex. *Brain, Behavior and Evolution*, **11**, 16–47.

Trevarthen, C. (1979). Instincts for human understanding and for cultural cooperation: their development in infancy. In M. von Cranach, K. Foppa, W. Lepenies and D. Ploog (eds), *Human Ethology*, (pp. 530–71). Cambridge: Cambridge University Press.

Trevarthen, C. (1980). The foundations of intersubjectivity: development of interpersonal and cooperative understanding in infants. In D.R. Olson (ed.), *The Social Foundations of Language and Thought* (pp. 316–42). New York: Norton.

Trevarthen, C. (1982). The primary motives for cooperative understanding. In G.E. Butterworth and P.H. Light (eds), *Social Cognition: Studies of the Development of Understanding* (pp. 77–109). Hemel Hempstead: Harvester Wheatsheaf.

Trevarthen, C. (1983). Emotions in infancy: regulators of contacts and relationships between persons. In K. Scherer and P. Ekman (eds), *Approaches to Emotion* (pp. 129–57). Hillsdale, NJ: Lawrence Erlbaum.

Trevarthen, C. and Logotheti, K. (1989). Child and culture: genesis of co-operative knowing. In A. Gellatly, D. Rogers and J.A. Sloboda (eds), *Cognition and Social Worlds* (pp. 37–56). Oxford: Clarendon Press.

Tulving, E. and Bower, G.H. (1974). The logic of memory representations. In G.H. Bower (ed.), *The Psychology of Learning and Motivation*, Vol. 8 (pp. 265–301). New York: Academic Press.

Tulving, E. and Thompson, D.M. (1971). Retrieval processes in recognition memory: effects of associative context. *Journal of Experimental Psychology*, **87**, 116–24.

Tulving, E. and Thompson, D.M. (1973). Encoding specificity and retrieval processes in episodic memory. *Psychological Review*, **80**, 352–73.

Turing, A.M. (1950). Computing machines and intelligence. *Mind*, **59**, 433–60.

Turvey, M.T. and Shaw, R. (1979). The primacy of perceiving: an ecological reformulation of perception for understanding memory. In L.G. Nillson (ed.), *Perspectives on Memory Research: Essays in Honor of Uppsala University's 500th Anniversary* (pp. 167–222). Hillsdale, NJ: Lawrence Erlbaum.

Turvey, M.T., Shaw, R.E., Reed, E.S. and Mace, W.M. (1981). Ecological laws of perceiving and acting: in reply to Fodor and Pylyshyn. *Cognition*, **3**, 237–304.

Tversky, A. (1977). Features of similarity. *Psychological Review*, **84**, 327–52.

Tversky, A. and Gati, I. (1978). Studies of similarity. In E. Rosch and B.B. Lloyd (eds), *Cognition and Categorization* (pp. 81–98). Hillsdale, NJ: Lawrence Erlbaum.

Tversky, A. and Gati, I. (1982). Similarity, separability and the triangle inequality. *Psychological Review*, **89**, 123–54.

Twardowsky, K. (1912/1927). Actions and products. Comments on the border area of psychology, grammar and logic. In J. Pelc (ed.), *Semiotics in Poland 1984–1969*. Warsaw and Boston: Reidel.

Ullman, S. (1980). Against direct perception. *The Behavioral and Brain Sciences*, **3**, 325–33.

Urcos, C.G. (1989). Mood state-dependent memory: a meta-analysis. *Cognition and Emotion*, **3**, 139–69.

Varela, F.J. (1979). *Principles of Biological Autonomy*. New York: North Holland.

Verbrugge, R.R. (1979). The primacy of metaphor in development. *New Directions for Child Development*, **6**, 77–84.

Vico, G. (1948). *The New Science*. Ithaca, NY: Cornell University Press.

Vollmer, F. (1986). Intentional explanation and its place in psychology. *Journal for the Theory of Social Behavior*, **16**, 285–98.

Vosniadou, S. (1989). Context and the development of metaphor comprehension. *Metaphor and Symbolic Activity*, **4**, 159–71.

Vosniadou, S. and Ortony, A. (1983). The emergence of the literal–metaphorical–anomalous distinction in young children. *Child Development*, **54**, 154–61.

Vosniadou, S., Ortony, A. and Reynolds, R. (1984). Sources of difficulty in children's understanding of metaphorical language. *Child Development*, **52**, 728–31.

Vroon, P.A. (1974). Is there a time quantum in duration experience? *American Journal of Psychology*, **87**, 237–45.

Vygotsky, L.S. (1978). *Mind in Society*. Cambridge, MA: Harvard University Press.

Vygotsky, L.S. (1979). Consciousness as a problem in the psychology of behavior. *Soviet Psychology*, **17**, 3–35.

Vygotsky, L.S. (1981). The genesis of higher mental functions. In Wertsch, J.V. (ed.), *The Concept of Activity in Soviet Psychology* (pp. 144–85). Armonk, NY: Sharpe.

Vygotsky, L.S. (1986). *Thought and Language*. Cambridge, MA: MIT Press.

Vygotsky, L.S. (1987). Thinking and speech. In R.W. Rieber and A.S. Carton (eds), *The Collected Works of L.S. Vygotsky* (pp. 375–86). New York: Plenum Press.

Wagner, R. (1986). *Symbols that Stand for Themselves*. Chicago: University of Chicago Press.

Wagner, S., Winner, E., Chicchetti, D. and Gardner, H. (1981). Metaphorical mappings in human infants. *Child Development*, **52**, 728–31.

Wapner, W., Hamby S. and Gardner, H. (1981). The role of the right hemisphere in the apprehension of complex linguistic materials. *Brain Language*, **14**, 15–33.

Warren, W.H. (1984). Perceiving, affordances: visual guidance of stair climbing. *Journal of Experimental Psychology: Human Perception and Performance*, **5**, 683–703.

Warren, W.H. and Whang, S. (1987). Visual guidance of walking through apertures: body-scaled information for affordances. *Journal of Experimental Psychology: Human Perception and Performance*, **13**, 371–83.

Wason, P.C. and Johnson-Laird, P.N. (1972). *Psychology of Reasoning: Structure and Content*. London: Batsford.

Wason, P.C. and Shapiro, D. (1971). Natural and contrived experience in a reasoning problem. *Quarterly Journal of Experimental Psychology*, **23**, 63–71.

Watkins, M.J. (1990). Mediationism and the obfuscation of memory. *American Psychologist*, **45**, 328–35.

Waynbaum, I. (1907). *La Physionomie Humaine: Son Mécanisme et son Rôle Social.* Paris: Alcan.

Weisskopf, V.F. (1962). *Knowledge and Wonder*. New York: Doubleday.

Weisstein, N. (1969). What the frog's eye tells the frog's brain: single-cell analyzers in the human visual system. *Psychological Bulletin*, **72**, 157–76.

Wells, G.L. and Petty, R.E. (1980). The effects of overt head movement on persuasion: compatability and incompatability of responses. *Basic and Applied Social Psychology*, **1**, 219–30.

Werner, H. (1948). *Comparative Psychology of Mental Development*. Chicago: Follett.

Werner, H. and Kaplan, B. (1963). *Symbol Formation: An Organismic Developmental Approach to Language and the Expression of Thought*. New York: John Wiley.

Wertsch, J.V. (1979). From social interaction to higher psychological processes. *Human Development*, **22**, 1–22.

Wertsch, J.V. (1981). *The Concept of Activity in Soviet Psychology*. Armonk, NY: Sharpe.

Wertsch, J.V. (1985a). *Culture, Communication and Cognition: Vygotskian Perspectives.* Cambridge: Cambridge University Press.

Wertsch. J.V. (1985b). *Vygotsky and the Social Formation of Mind.* Cambridge, MA: Harvard University Press.

Wertsch. J.V. and Hickmann, M. (1987). Problem solving in social interaction: a microgenetic analysis. In M. Hickmann (ed.), *Social and Functional Approaches to Language and Thought.* San Diego: Academic Press.

Wheelwright, P. (1962). *Metaphor and Reality.* Bloomington: Indiana University Press.

Whitehead, A.N. (1929). *Process and Reality.* Cambridge: Cambridge University Press.

Whittaker, E. (1960). *A History of the Theories of Ether and Electricity.* New York: Harper and Row.

Whorf, B.L. (1956). *Language, Thought and Reality.* Cambridge, MA: MIT Press.

Wilcox, S. and Katz, S. (1981). A direct realistic alternative to the traditional conception of memory. *Behaviorism*, **9**, 227–39.

Wilkins, M.C. (1928). The effect of changed material on the ability to do formal syllogistic reasoning. *Archives of Psychology*, **4**, 209–41.

Wilson, W.R. (1975). Unobtrusive induction of positive attitudes. Unpublished doctoral dissertation. University of Michigan.

Wilson, W.R. (1979). Feeling more than we can know: exposure effects without learning. *Journal of Personality and Social Psychology.* **37**, 811–21.

Winner, E. (1979). New names for old things: the emergence of metaphoric language. *Journal of Child Language*, **6**, 469–91.

Winner, E. and Gardner, H. (1977). The comprehension of metaphor in brain-damaged patients. *Brain*, **100**, 719–27.

Winner, E. and Gardner, H. (1979). Sensitivity to metaphor in organic patients. *Brain*, **102**, 209–41.

Winner, E. and Gardner, H. (1986). Attitudes and attributes: children's understanding of metaphor sarcasm. In M. Perlmutter (ed.), *Perspectives on Intellectual Development: Minnesota symposium on child psychology*, Vol. 19 (pp.131–52). Hillsdale, NJ: Lawrence Erlbaum.

Winner, E., McCarthy, M. and Gardner, H. (1980). The ontogenesis of metaphor. In R.P. Honeck and R.R. Hoffman (eds), *Cognitive and Figurative Language* (pp. 341–61). Hillsdale, NJ: Lawrence Erlbaum.

Winner, E., Rosensteil, A.K. and Gardner, H. (1976). The development of metaphoric understanding. *Developmental Psychology*, **12**, 289–97.

Winner, E., Wapner, W., Cicone, M. and Gardner, H. (1979). Measures of metaphor. *New Directions for Child Development*, **6**, 67–75.

Winnicott, D.W. (1964). Further thoughts on babies as persons. In *The Child, the Family and the Outside World* (pp. 85–92). Harmondsworth: Penguin.

Winograd, T. (1976). Towards a procedural understanding of semantics. *Revue Internationale de Philosophie*, **26**, 260–303.

Winograd, T. (1978). On primitive prototypes, and other semantic anomalies. In D. Waltz (ed.), *TINLAP-2: Theoretical Issues in Natural Language Understanding* (pp. 25–32). Urbana, IL: University of Illinois.

Winograd, T. (1980). What does it mean to understand language? *Cognitive Science*, **30**, 209–41.

Winograd, T. and Flores, C.F. (1986). *Understanding Computers and Cognition: A New Foundation for Design.* Norwood, NJ: Ablex.

Wittgenstein, L. (1922). *Tractatus Logico Philosophicus.* London: Routledge and Kegan Paul.

Wittgenstein, L. (1953). *Philosophical Investigations.* Oxford: Blackwell.

Wittgenstein, L. (1958). *The Blue and Brown Books.* Oxford: Blackwell.

Wittgenstein, L. (1980). *Remarks on the Philosophy of Psychology*, Vol.1. Oxford: Blackwell.

Woelfflin, H. (1950). *Principles of Art History.* New York: Dover.

Wood, D.J. (1980). Teaching the young child: some relationships between social interaction, language, and thought. In D.R. Olson (ed.), *The Social Foundations of Language and Thought* (pp. 280–96). New York: Norton.

Wood, D.J., Bruner, J.S. and Ross, G. (1976). The rule of tutoring in problem solving. *Journal of Child Psychology and Psychiatry*, **17**, 89–100.

Wyer, R.S., Jr and Srull, T.K. (1984) (eds). *Handbook of Social Cognition*, Vols. 1. and 2. Hillsdale, NJ: Lawrence Erlbaum.

Wyer, R.S., Jr and Srull, T.K. (1986). Human cognition in its social context. *Psychological Review*, **93**, 322–59.

Wyer, R.S., Jr and Srull, T.K. (1989). *Memory and Cognition in its Social Context*. Hillsdale, NJ: Lawrence Erlbaum.

Zajonc, R.B. (1965). Social facilitation. *Science*, **149**, 269–74.

Zajonc, R.B. (1980). Feeling and thinking: preferences need no inferences. *American Psychologist*, **35**, 151–75.

Zajonc, R.B. (1984). On the primacy of affect. *American Psychologist*, **39**, 117–23.

Zajonc, R.B. (1985). Emotional and facial efference: a theory reclaimed. *Science*, **228**, 15–21.

Zajonc, R.B. and Markus, H. (1983). Affection and cognition: the hard interface. In C.E. Izard, G. Kagan and R.B. Zajonc (eds), *Emotions, Cognition and Behavior* (pp. 73–102). Cambridge: Cambridge University Press.

Zajonc, R.B. and Sales, M.S. (1966). Social facilitation of dominant and subordinate responses. *Journal of Experimental Social Psychology*, **2**, 160–8.

Zajonc, R.B., Pietromonaco, P. and Bargh, J. (1982). Independence and interaction of affect and cognition. In M.S. Clark and S.T. Fiske (eds), *Affect and Cognition: The Seventeenth Annual Carnegie Symposium on Cognition* (pp. 211–27). Hillsdale, NJ: Lawrence Erlbaum.

Zinchenko, V.P. (1985). Vygotsky's ideas about units for the analysis of the mind. In J.V. Wertsch (ed.), *Culture, Communication and Cognitition* (pp. 94–118). Cambridge: Cambridge University Press.

Zisper, D. (1986). Biologically plausible models of place recognition and goal location. In J.L. McClelland and D.E. Rumelhart (eds), *Parallel Distributed Processing: Explorations in the Microstructure of Cognition. Vol. 2: Psychological and Biological Models* (pp. 432–70). Cambridge, MA: MIT Press.

Zubek, J.P. (1969) (ed.). *Sensory Deprivation: Fifteen Years of Research*. New York: Appleton-Century-Crofts.

Zuccaro, F. (1607/1961). *Idea de Pittoria, Scultori et Architetti del Federigo Zuccaro*. Turin: A. Disserolio.

Zuriff, G.E. (1985). *Behaviorism: A Conceptual Reconstruction*. New York: Columbia University Press.

Subject index

Reference index